lonely planet

Estonia, Latvia & Lithuania

John Noble
Nicola Williams
Robin Gauldie

D0033985

Estonia, Latvia & Lithuania

1st edition

Published by
Lonely Planet Publications
Head Office: PO Box 617, Hawthorn, Vic 3122, Australia
Branches: 155 Filbert St, Suite 251, Oakland, CA 94607, USA
               10 Barley Mow Passage, Chiswick, London W4 4PH, UK
               71 bis rue du Cardinal Lemoine, 75005 Paris, France

Printed by
Pac-Rim Kwartanusa Printing
Printed in Indonesia

Photographs by

Miervaldis Balodis	Livijus Grigaliunas	Sulev Kalamae
John Noble	Colin Richardson	Jonathan Smith
Eduards Voitkuns	Gabrielius Žemkalnis	

Front cover: Street scene on Toompea, Tallinn, Estonia (Jonathan Smith)

Published
September 1997

Although the authors and publisher have tried to make the information as accurate as possible, they accept no responsibility for any loss, injury or inconvenience sustained by any person using this book.

National Library of Australia Cataloguing in Publication Data

Noble, John, 1951 – .
Estonia, Latvia and Lithuania.

Includes index.
ISBN 0 86442 416 7.

1. Baltic States – Guidebooks. I. Gauldie, Robin.
II. Williams, Nicola, 1971 – . III. Title.

914.790486

John Noble

John comes from the valley of the River Ribble in northern England. Increasing interruptions to a mainstream journalism career, for travel to various bits of the globe, eventually saw him abandon Fleet Street for a Lonely Planet trail which has taken him to four continents and more than a dozen LP books, from *Sri Lanka* and *Indonesia* to *Spain* and *Mexico*. With John King he wrote the 1991 *USSR* guide and was then involved as author or co-author in all three of that book's successors after the break-up of the USSR: *Russia, Ukraine & Belarus*, *Central Asia* and *Baltic States & Kaliningrad*, which was the predecessor of this book. He is now based in southern Spain.

Nicola Williams

Nicola caught the travel bug in 1990 while crossing Indonesia as an impoverished student. After three months bussing and boating it from Jakarta to East Timor, and back, she returned to the UK to study a Master's degree at London's School of Oriental & African Studies. Following a two-year stint as a journalist with the *North Wales Weekly News*, Nicola moved to Latvia to bus it round the Baltics as features editor for the English-language newspaper *The Baltic Observer*. Having travelled the length and breadth of the Baltic region as editor-in-chief of the Lithuanian-based *In Your Pocket* Baltic and Russian city guide series, Nicola is now in France bugging her Baltic mates through email.

Robin Gauldie

Born in Dundee, Scotland, Robin first hit the road as an independent traveller, then as a reporter for *Travel Trade Gazette Europa* and since 1988 as a freelance travel writer, editor and photographer. He has written guides to Greece, Germany, Amsterdam, Goa and Dublin for a variety of publishers and edits *Destination ASEAN*, a quarterly magazine for independent travellers and holidaymakers visiting South East Asia. He was among the first wave of travel writers to visit the Baltic republics after independence from the USSR.

From the Authors

Nicola Williams Big thanks and smiles to Reine d'Hanens, Nomeda Navickaitė and Anja Coppieters for their unrelenting heroics; to baltomaniac Matthias Lüfkens for being my hero; and to M & D, Michelle, Neil I & II. Smiling thankyous too, to Juozas Aleksiejūnas from the KGB Museum in Vilnius, Doug Balchin, Philip Birzulis, James Carrol, Tricia Cornell, Steven Dewar,

Andrius Dundzila, Arne Kaasik and Anne Kurepalu from the Lahemaa National Park, Ellen & Sharad Ladva, Christa & Karl Otto Lüfkens; to Jane Fitzpatrick and Craig MacKenzie at LP Australia, Marina at LP France, Diccon at LP UK and Sasha at LP US; Neil McGowan of the Russa Experience, Vilnius' Ortiz trio, Christopher Rikken, Irina Rapanovich, Vikis Satkevičius and Narimantas Šerkšnys, Alfred Schlosser from the Yantarny Amber Mine, Maureen Sharpe, Ance Steinboks, Robert Strauss of Compass Publications, Ed Stoddard, Michael Tarm, Neil Taylor of Regent Holidays, Oleg Temple, Tiina & Aarne Vaik for their room with a view, Douglas Wells from the Estonian Tourist Board, Alex Whitney, and Vera Zimogliadova.

Robin Gauldie Neil Taylor, of Regent Holidays, provided an inexhaustible fund of information, opinion and advice. I'd also like to thank traveller and photographer David Mace, who persuaded me to go with him to the Baltics just after independence and who helped me trawl the World Wide Web for up-to-the-minute information on the fast-changing political and cultural scene.

This Book
The book is based upon Lonely Planet's *Baltic States & Kaliningrad – travel survival kit*, written by John Noble. Nicola Williams updated all but the Facts about the Region and Facts about Estonia/Latvia/Lithuania chapters which were updated by Robin Gauldie.

From the Publisher
The coordinating editor of this book was Craig MacKenzie. He was assisted by Darren Elder, Liz Filleul, Steve Womersley and Adrienne Costanzo. Lyndell Taylor coordinated the mapping and design of the book, with mapping assistance from Louise Klep, Mark Griffiths, Tamsin Wilson, Andrew Tudor, Anthony Phelan and Matt King. Illustrations were drawn by Michelle. Lewis, Lyndell Taylor & Rachel Black, who was also responsible for the colour wraps.

Thanks
Many thanks to the travellers who used *Baltic States & Kaliningrad – travel survival kit*, and wrote to us with helpful hints, useful advice and interesting anecdotes:

Heino Anderson, Mark Andress, A Ashmore, Alena Blochova, Cathy Bowden, Amanda Brace, Francesco Brizzi, Abe Brouwer, Gertrude Buckman, Carol Burrett, Tomiasz Calikowski, Rowland Cobbold, Catherine Crimmens, Antonija Dodds, Henry Elsner, B Fischer, Keith Fountain, Simon Gooch, Roland Grosse, Anelle Hensoul, Mike Hirshorn, Nora Horgan, Tony & Ruth Housden, Adam Johnson, Lasse Kemilainen, Wally & Barbara Labrom, Jill Landry, Richard H Lockhart, Martin Lovgreen, Christine March, Sarah Marrs, Gavin McEwan, Peter Merry, J Mussche, James Potter, Linda Riley, U Roll, Paul Spevacek, Dries van der Haegen, Maurice Walshe, Stephanie West, Richard Wilkinson, Frank Wilson, RC Wolters, Judith Young

Warning & Request
Things change – prices go up, schedules change, good places go bad and bad places go bankrupt – nothing stays the same. So, if you find things better or worse, recently opened or long since closed, please tell us and help make the next edition even more accurate and useful.

We value all of the feedback we receive from travellers. Julie Young coordinates a small team who read and ackowledge every letter, postcard and email, and ensure that every morsel of information finds its way to the appropriate authors, editors and publishers.

Everyone who writes to us will find their name in the next edition of the appropriate guide and will also receive a free subscription to our quarterly newsletter, *Planet Talk*. The very best contributions will be rewarded with a free Lonely Planet guide.

Excerpts from your correspondence may appear in updates (which we add to the end pages of reprints); new editions of this guide; in our newsletter *Planet Talk*; or in the Postcards section of our web site – so please let us know if you don't want your letter published or your name acknowledged.

Contents

<u>LATVIA</u>

Boxed Asides

A Day on Mars................. 367	Canoe & Cycle Trips 275	National Characteristics 32
Air Travel Glossary........... 80	Day of the Setus 182	Online Changes................. 54
Amber Trail....................... 433	Flower Power..................... 353	Paganism vs
Beginning with B 340	Flying Heroes.................... 375	Christianity....................... 330
Baltic Calendar................. 63	From Russia with Love...... 291	Swedish Influence 185
Baltic Sea 198	Getting the Last Laugh...... 350	Where is Prussia? 413
Black Magic...................... 239	Ignalina 362	

Map Legend

BOUNDARIES

International Boundary

Regional Boundary

ROUTES

Freeway

Highway

Major Road

Unsealed Road or Track

City Road

City Street

Railway

Underground Railway

Tram

Walking Track

Walking Tour

Ferry Route

Cable Car or Chairlift

AREA FEATURES

Parks

Built-Up Area

Pedestrian Mall

Market

Cemetery

Reef

Beach or Desert

Rocks

HYDROGRAPHIC FEATURES

Coastline

River, Creek

Intermittent River or Creek

Rapids, Waterfalls

Lake, Intermittent Lake

Canal

Swamp

SYMBOLS

✪ CAPITAL		National Capital
◉ Capital		Regional Capital
◌ CITY		Major City
● City		City
● Town		Town
● Village		Village
■	▼	Place to Stay, Place to Eat
☎	▓	Cafe, Pub or Bar
✉	☎	Post Office, Telephone
❶	❺	Tourist Information, Bank
◕	℗	Transport, Parking
⛫	⌂	Museum, Youth Hostel
⌂	Å	Caravan Park, Camping Ground
✛	✚	Church, Cathedral
☪	✡	Mosque, Synagogue
☸	☷	Buddhist Temple, Hindu Temple
✛	★	Hospital, Police Station

◔	⛽	Embassy, Petrol Station
✈	✝	Airport, Airfield
▭	❀	Swimming Pool, Gardens
❖	🐘	Shopping Centre, Zoo
❦	⛺	Winery or Vineyard, Picnic Site
←	A25	One Way Street, Route Number
⛫	▲	Stately Home, Monument
⛩	◙	Castle, Tomb
⌒	⌂	Cave, Hut or Chalet
▲	☀	Mountain or Hill, Lookout
⛯	⚓	Lighthouse, Harbour
)(	◎	Pass, Spring
⚲	⚴	Beach, Surf Beach
	∴	Archaeological Site or Ruins
		Ancient or City Wall
		Cliff or Escarpment, Tunnel
		Railway Station

Note: not all symbols displayed above appear in this book

Regional Map Index

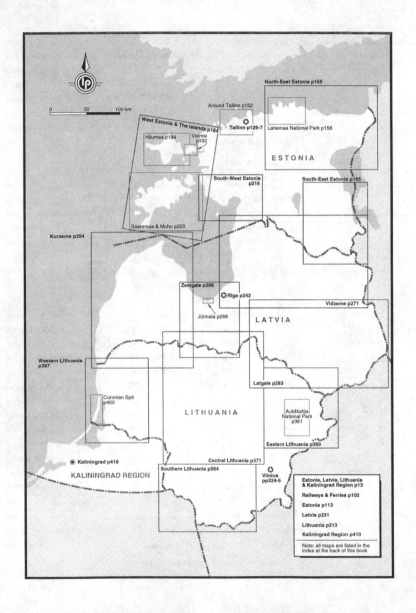

0   50   100 km

North-East Estonia p155

Around Tallinn p152

West Estonia & The Islands p184

Tallinn p126-7   Lahemaa National Park p156

Hiiumaa p194   Vormsi p192

ESTONIA

South-West Estonia p216

South-East Estonia p165

Kurzeme p294

Saaremaa & Muhu p203

Zemgale p289   Riga p242

Vidzeme p271

Jūrmala p268   LATVIA

Western Lithuania p387

Latgale p283

LITHUANIA

Aukštaitija National Park p361

Curonian Spit p400

Eastern Lithuania p360

Kaliningrad p418

Central Lithuania p371

KALININGRAD REGION

Southern Lithuania p364

Vilnius pp324-5

Note: all maps are listed in the index at the back of this book

Introduction

Since the three Baltic states – Estonia, Latvia and Lithuania – regained their independence in 1991, they have raced along the road towards a free market economy at lightning speed.

They burst onto the world scene almost from nowhere in the late 1980s as leading players in the break-up of the Soviet Union of which, the world learned, they had been unwilling members since the 1940s. Previously they had been, in the awareness of much of the world, almost semi-mythical places that might have existed in an old atlas or a grandparent's stamp collection.

The ration coupons, bread queues, fuel shortages and hyper-inflation of the early independence period are now nothing more than a bitter memory for the Balts today, who enjoy a lifestyle slowly approaching western norms. The ranks of the privileged few who drive big fast cars, display flash mobile phones and sport the latest chic fashions on the streets are growing as every day passes.

These three tiny countries are now desperately doing everything they can to attract visitors. And while the tourist infrastructure is far from complete, growing numbers of travellers are taking the opportunity to see for themselves what these confetti states on the fringe of Europe are really like. What we find measures up, in a degree, to the fairy-tale image – castles everywhere, quaint folk costumes which still come out at festival times, unspoilt countryside, forests and lakes inhabited by legends and myths, and rural villages where you can still be welcomed as one of the first western travellers to unearth

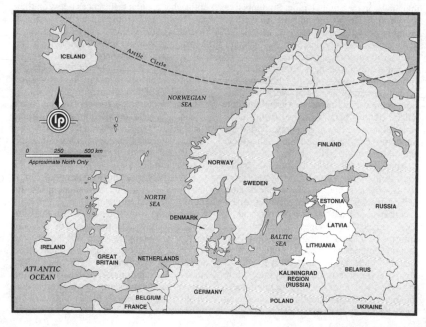

such parts. Even the trams that rattle round city streets seem relics of an earlier age.

Sadly, it is impossible, however, not to notice the damage done to the appearance of city and country by drab Soviet apartment blocks and dirty factories and to social harmony by divisive, initiative-sapping methods of political control and heavy immigration from Russia.

Life for visitors is getting better and better. In contrast to the privations of the Soviet era and early independence years, it is now a joy to find a fast-growing supply of quality places to stay and eat that don't always cost the earth, friendly smiling people in service industries, shops filled with imported goods as well as fine local produce, an increasingly lively entertainment scene, and media and museums that no longer have to bend the truth.

Part of the fascination of visiting the Baltic states today is witnessing their rapid change. Although independence has brought new opportunities for some with talent, initiative and energy, life for many is even tougher than it was in the Soviet Union. Students live on less than US$30 a month and the average monthly pension is no more than US$60, while prices are now practically at western levels. But surprisingly no one has revolted against economic changes brought about by an independent government. Unlike before, people now have hope. Impoverished pensioners know that life for their grandchildren will be 10 times better than the life they have endured, and for that reason they cherish the freedom – despite the hardships – that they, and others, fought so dearly for.

Apart, perhaps, from Lithuania's medieval golden age, the Baltic states have always been something of a backwater, tucked away in a remote corner of Europe – except of course to their own peoples and, in recent times, their hundreds of thousands of émigrés scattered round the world. For several centuries a succession of dominating foreign rulers pushed the native peoples almost entirely into the countryside, while the towns and cities – whose architecture is the region's main tourist magnet today – were created by incomers.

Today, Estonian, Latvian and Lithuanian roots still lie very much in the countryside. Here are whole nations with their own languages, customs, and a wealth of colourful, musical festivals to discover, and whole sweeps of history, little known outside the immediate region, to explore.

The Baltic landscape surprises, too. While rarely spectacular, it has a gentle, rolling beauty that gradually grows on you in summer (though in the dull days of winter it can seem bleak and dreary).

One aspect of travelling in the Baltic states that disconcerts some visitors is the rather glum, pessimistic outward bearing of many people – a product of perennial economic hardship and the dispiriting effect of Soviet rule. But once you break through this surface, you'll generally find people are surprisingly happy to be able to help western visitors.

Though the outside world tends to view the three Baltic states as a single entity, they are three very different countries with separate languages, histories and traditions and noticeable general differences between their native peoples. Estonians are stereotypically reserved, efficient and polite; Lithuanians are more gregarious and less organised; and Latvians are somewhere between the two extremes. Discovering the contrasts between the three countries is part of the fascination of travel in the Baltic states.

In the south-western corner of the region lies a place that's in strong contrast to all three Baltic states. The Kaliningrad Region is a slice of Russian territory wedged between Lithuania, Poland and the Baltic Sea, disconnected from the rest of Russia.

Until 1945, when the Red Army took it, it had been German for seven centuries. Its main city, Kaliningrad (then known as Königsberg), was a focus of the Prussian state, which was at the heart of German history for so long. Since WWII the city and region of Kaliningrad have been repeopled and rebuilt predominantly by Russians. The surviving traces of its German past, amid the Soviet-created present, are haunting evidence of the power of politics and war over ordinary people's lives.

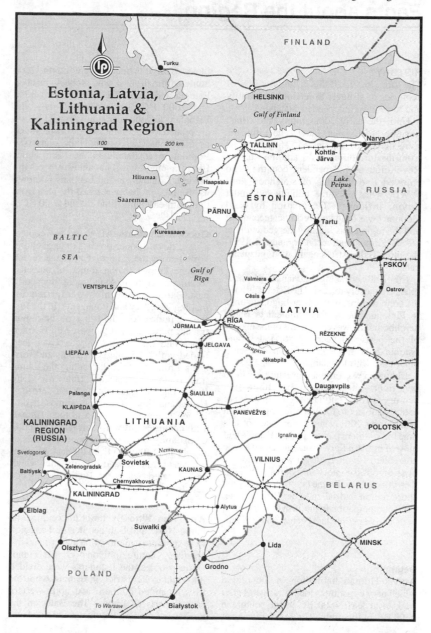

Facts about the Region

HISTORY

The story of the Baltic nations is one of centuries of struggle to retain their identity and to achieve independent statehood.

Until the early 20th century, the ethnic identities of Estonia, Latvia and Lithuania were denied or suppressed. They emerged from the turmoil of WWI and the Russian Revolution as independent countries and enjoyed two decades of statehood until WWII, when all three initially fell under Soviet influence. Occupation by Nazi Germany was followed by Soviet reconquest and the region was forcibly merged with the USSR. Almost half a century later, in 1991, the three Baltic states again won independence.

Ethnically speaking, Latvians and Lithuanians are closely related. The Estonians have different origins, with closer linguistic links to Finland than to their immediate Baltic neighbours. However, in terms of the history of the past 800 years or so, Latvia and Estonia have more in common with each other than with Lithuania.

Lithuania was once a powerful state in its own right – at its peak in the 14th to 16th century – but Latvia and Estonia were entirely subject to foreign rule from the 13th to the early 20th century. For much of this time the southern part of modern Estonia and most of modern Latvia were governed as one unit called Livonia. Latvia was not thought of as a political entity in its own right until the 19th century. By the late 18th century the entire region had fallen under Russian rule. Until emancipation in the 19th century, most of its native people had been serfs for centuries.

Beginnings

Arrival Human habitation in the region which now constitutes the Baltic states goes back to at least 9000 BC in the south and 7500 BC in the north. The first forebears of the present inhabitants were Finno-Ugric hunters from the east, who probably reached Estonia and parts of Latvia between 3000 and 2000 BC. Their descendants – the Estonians and the now almost extinct Livs – are related to other Finno-Ugric peoples such as the Finns, Lapps and Hungarians (see Population & People in the Facts about Estonia chapter). The ancestors of the modern Lithuanians and Latvians – known as 'Balts' – probably reached the area from the south-east some time around 2000 BC.

Outside Contacts All these newcomers settled down sooner or later to agriculture. Well before the time of Christ the region became known as the source of amber – fossilised tree resin found along the south-east Baltic coast which was prized for making jewellery and ornaments. In the first few centuries AD, the tribes of the region traded, particularly in amber, with German tribes and the Roman empire. Later they traded with (and fought) Vikings and Russians. From the 8th or 9th century the Viking trade route to Russia and Ukraine was along the Daugava river through modern-day Latvia and Belarus. Russian armies tried to invade Estonia and Latvia in the 11th and 12th centuries but were defeated. Orthodox Christianity, however, did penetrate parts of Latvia and Lithuania from the east. Many of the castle mounds and hill-fort sites which are scattered across the Baltic countryside date from this era.

Who Was Who By the 12th century the Finno-Ugric and Balt peoples in the region were split into a number of tribal groups – all practising nature religions. Of the Finno-Ugric peoples, the Estonians were divided into eight to 12 districts in Estonia, while the Livs inhabited northern and north-western coastal parts of Latvia. The Balts on the territory of modern Latvia were divided into

12th Century Tribes

ESTONIA
ESTONIANS
Lake Peipus
LIVS
BALTIC SEA
LATVIA
LATGALS
ZEMGALS
SELONIANS
COURS
SAMOGITIANS
LITHUANIA
Nemunas
AUKŠTAITIAI
PRUSSIANS
BELARUS
KALININGRAD REGION (RUSSIA)
YOTVINGIANS
POLAND
Vistula
Daugava

Approximate Distribution of pre-German Tribal Groups, 12th Century AD

the Latgals or Letts in the east, who were grouped into at least four principalities; the Cours or Couronians in the west, with five to seven principalities sometimes united under one king; the Zemgals or Semigallians in the centre, again, sometimes united; and the Selonians in the eastern centre, south of the Daugava. The Cours, Zemgals and Selonians were on the fringes of what is now modern-day Lithuania.

Lithuania had two main groups of its own: the Samogitians (or Žemaičiai) in the west and the Aukštaitiai in the east and south-east. In what is now south-west Lithuania and neighbouring parts of Poland were the Yotvingians or Sūduviai – also a Balt people – later to be assimilated by the Lithuanians and Poles. A little further west, between the Nemunas and Vistula rivers, were the Prussians, the westernmost Balt people. (Other Balts to the east, in eastern Belarus and neighbouring parts of Russia, were already in the process of being assimilated by Slavs.)

Germanic Conquest & Rule
Latvia & Estonia – the Knights of the Sword The region was dragged into written history by the *Drang nach Osten* (urge to the east) of Germanic princes, colonists, traders, missionaries and crusading knights. Having overrun Slavic lands in modern-day eastern Germany and western Poland in the 12th century, the Germanic expansionists turned their attention to the eastern Baltic. Traders visited the mouth of the Daugava river, near Rīga, in the mid-century.

Following papal calls for a crusade against the northern heathen, Germanic missionaries arrived in the area but achieved little until Albert von Buxhoevden was appointed Bishop of Rīga in 1201. Bishop Albert built the first Germanic fort in the Baltics at Rīga, which became the region's leading city, and in 1202 established the Knights of the Sword – an order of crusading knights whose white cloaks were emblazoned with blood-red swords and crosses – to convert the region by conquest. The invaders gave the name Livonia (after the Liv people) to the area around the Gulf of Rīga and the territories inland from it.

Despite strong resistance, this unwholesome brood had subjugated and converted all of Estonia and Latvia within a quarter of a century – except for the Zemgals and Cours in western Latvia. Southern Estonia fell to the knights in 1217 with the defeat of the Estonian leader, Lembitu. Denmark, an ally of Bishop Albert, conquered northern Estonia about 1219, landing on the site of modern-day Tallinn. The knights took control of all of Estonia in 1227, having also subdued the Estonian islands in that year. The Livs had been conquered by 1207 and most of the Latgals by 1214.

Prussia – the Teutonic Order In the 1220s another band of Germanic crusaders, the Teutonic Order, was invited into Mazovia (in modern-day central-northern Poland), to protect it against raids by the Prussians. Founded in Palestine in 1190 as a charitable organisation, the Teutonic Order had developed a military character and begun crusading in Europe. Its method of 'protecting' Mazovia was essentially to

Knight of the Teutonic Order

exterminate the Prussians and to bring in settlers from the German states. The Prussians resisted until 1283, by which time all their lands were in the hands of the Teutonic Order. Among the forts the order founded on the conquered Prussian territory were Memel (which is now Klaipėda in Lithuania) in 1252, Königsberg (now Kaliningrad) in 1255, and Marienburg (now Malbork in Poland) where the order set up its headquarters in 1306. The few Prussians left were eventually assimilated by their conquerors; they ceased to exist as a separate people by the end of the 17th century. (For more on the history of Prussia see the Where is Prussia? aside in the Kaliningrad Region chapter).

Final Subjugation of Estonia & Latvia The Knights of the Sword, meanwhile, had received a couple of setbacks. First they earned a ticking-off from the pope for their brutality, then, returning laden with booty from a raid into Samogitia in 1236, they were attacked and defeated by Zemgals and Samogitians at Saule (probably modern Šiauliai in Lithuania).

The next year they were compelled to reorganise as a branch of the Teutonic Order and became known as the Livonian Order. Northern Estonia was returned to Danish rule in 1238. In 1242 the Russian prince Alexandr Nevsky of Novgorod decisively defeated the Livonian knights on (frozen) Lake Peipus, in eastern Estonia, curbing their eastward expansion. In the 1260s the knights subjugated Courland, undeterred by the Cours' strategy of making a separate peace with the pope. In 1290 they completed the conquest of Latvian territory by defeating the Zemgals. Eventually the Livonian Order settled its headquarters at Wenden (now Cēsis in Latvia). All the native tribes in the area now known as Latvia, with the exception of a few Livs, were assimilated into one group – the Latgals or Letts – by the 16th century.

The peoples of Estonia, meanwhile, continued to rise up in intermittent revolt, the last and biggest of which was the Jüriöö (St George's Night) Uprising of 1343-46. Denmark, unsettled by this, sold northern Estonia to the Livonian Order in 1346. This meant that Germanic nobles were in control of the Baltic seaboard from west of Danzig (modern Gdańsk in Poland) all the way to Narva in north-east Estonia. In addition they controlled territory up to 250 km inland and the Estonian islands. The major gap in their Baltic domain was Lithuania. Protected by forests, the Lithuanians were able to restrict the invaders to a thin coastal strip despite repeated attacks in the 14th century.

Germanic Rule The Germanic rulers divided the region into a number of fiefdoms headed variously by the Prussian-based Teutonic Order, the Livonian Order and their vassals – the archbishop of Rīga; the bishops of Courland (Kurzeme), Dorpat (Tartu) and

Ösel-Wiek (west Estonia) who owed allegiance to the archbishop; the bishop of Reval (Tallinn), who didn't – and the sometimes-free city of Rīga.

The Hanseatic League of traders, which controlled commerce in the Baltic and the North Sea, brought prosperity to German-dominated Hanseatic towns like Rīga, Reval, Dorpat, Pernau (Pärnu), Windau (Ventspils), Wenden (Cēsis) and Königsberg (Kaliningrad), all on the trade routes between Russia and the west. But the local Finno-Ugric and Balt inhabitants of Estonia and Latvia were reduced to feudal serfs. The indigenous

nobility had been wiped out and the new German nobility dominated Estonia and Latvia till the 20th century.

Medieval Lithuania

Mindaugas & Gediminas In the mid-13th century Mindaugas, the leader of the Aukštaitiai, managed to unify the Lithuanian tribes for the first time. He also accepted Catholicism in a bid to defuse the threat from the Teutonic Order. Lithuania's first Christian buildings were constructed at this time. Neither the conversion nor the unity lasted, however. Mindaugas was assassinated, most

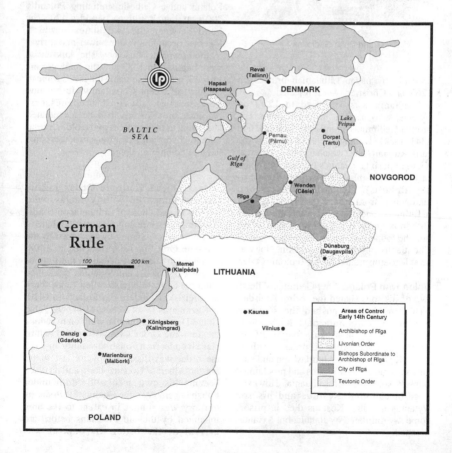

Grand Duke Gediminas

probably by pagan Lithuanian princes, in 1263, and Christianity was rejected.

Lithuania was reunified in 1290 by Vytenis, who became its grand duke. His brother Gediminas, grand duke from 1316 to 1341, took advantage of the decline of the early Russian state (which had been based at Kiev) to push Lithuania's borders south and east into Slav-inhabited territory (modern-day Belarus). He invited traders and landowners from around the Baltic to settle in Lithuania and protected both Catholic and Orthodox clergy. But, like Mindaugas before him, he found his own willingness to accept Christianity opposed by pagan kin. Nor was he able to stop attacks by the Teutonic Order.

Union with Poland After Gediminas' death two of his sons shared the realm. Algirdas, based in Vilnius, pushed the southern borders of Lithuania past Kiev while Kęstutis, based at Trakai, fought off the Teutonic Order. After Algirdas' death in 1377, Kęstutis drove Algirdas' son and successor, Jogaila, from Vilnius and proclaimed himself sole ruler of Lithuania. However, Jogaila captured Kęstutis and his son Vytautas in 1382. Kęstutis died in prison, some say murdered by Jogaila, but Vytautas escaped.

Jogaila faced conflicting advice from his princes on how to respond to the growing threat from the Teutonic Order. The Orthodox among them advised alliance with Moscow, the rising Russian power in the east, and conversion to Orthodoxy, while the pagan princes suggested conversion to Catholicism and alliance with neighbouring Poland. Jogaila's decision to take the latter path was a watershed in east European history. In 1386 he married Jadwiga, crown princess of Poland, forging a Lithuanian-Polish alliance against the German knights. Jogaila became Władysław II Jagiełło of Poland and a Catholic, initiating Poland's 200 year Jagiełłon dynasty and a 400 year bond between the two states – which together became a major power and a rival to the emergent Muscovy. The Aukštaitiai were baptised in 1387 and the Samogitians in 1413, making Lithuania the last European country to accept Christianity. Just a few years earlier, Jogaila's predecessors, Algirdas and Kęstutis, had been cremated according to the practices of the old religion: burnt on pyres with their treasures, weapons, horses and hunting dogs.

Defeat of the Teutonic Order Jogaila patched things up with Vytautas, who became Grand Duke of Lithuania on condition that he and Jogaila would share a common policy. Samogitia (occupied by the Teutonic Order in 1398) rebelled in 1408, which led to a decisive defeat for the Teutonic Order by Jogaila and Vytautas' combined armies at Grünwald (also called Tannenberg or Žalgiris), in modern-day Poland, in 1410.

Kazimieras IV of Poland (1447-92), also Grand Duke of Lithuania, went on to reduce the Teutonic Order's Prussian realm and to place it under firm Polish suzerainty. In 1525 the order was dissolved by its last grand master, Albert of Hohenzollern, and its lands became his own secular fiefdom under Polish hegemony – the Duchy of Prussia. Its territory was similar in extent to the area inhabited by the old Prussians before the arrival of the order. Its capital was

Königsberg, where the Teutonic Order's headquarters had been transferred in 1457.

Lithuanian Expansion Vytautas (known as 'the Great') extended Lithuanian control further to the south and east. At the time of his death in 1430 Lithuania stretched beyond Kursk in the east and almost to the Black Sea in the south – the greatest extent it was to reach. Lacking a big population to colonise its acquisitions or the military might to rule by force, Lithuania maintained its territories through diplomacy, allowing conquered lands to keep their autonomy and Orthodox religion.

Polonisation Lithuania sank into a junior role in its partnership with Poland, especially after the formal union of the two states (instead of just their crowns) at the Treaty of Lublin in 1569 during the Livonian War with Muscovy, and the end of the Jagiełłon line in 1572. Lithuanian gentry adopted Polish culture and language; Lithuanian peasants became serfs. The joint state became known as the Rzeczpospolita (Commonwealth). The 16th century religious Reformation sent a wave of Protestantism across the Commonwealth, but in the 1570s this was reversed by the Counter-Reformation. Lithuania and Poland remain predominantly Catholic today.

Swedish, Polish & Russian Rule

Livonian War The confederation of Catholic, Livonian Order and semi-independent towns through which Germans controlled Latvia and Estonia became fatally weakened by the mid-16th century: the Hanseatic League was losing its hold over Baltic commerce; the Reformation threatened the Catholic ecclesiastical states from the 1520s onwards; the Livonian Order lost its military strength after the death of its last capable master, Walter von Plettenberg, in 1535; and peasant discontent was growing.

Poland and Lithuania began to cast interested eyes over Livonia and Estonia, but so did other growing regional powers – Muscovy, under Ivan the Terrible, and Sweden. It was Ivan, looking for access to the Baltic Sea, who invaded first. And so, in

1558, began the Livonian War – a 25 year spell of bloodshed, misery and devastation in which Ivan seemingly ravaged, occupied or besieged nearly every town in mainland Estonia and the eastern half of Latvia. Estonia lost nearly two-thirds of its population during this and subsequent wars which lasted until 1629.

The Livonian Order, unable to resist the Russian invasion, disbanded. Its territories either sought the protection of neighbouring powers or were battled over by them. Poland-Lithuania fought Russia for Livonia proper (eastern Latvia and southern Estonia), eventually triumphing in 1582 – but not before Ivan had taken, then been expelled from, areas of Lithuania itself. Sweden took 20 or so years to finally expel the Russians from northern Estonia, also acquiring west mainland Estonia and the island Hiiumaa in 1582. The last master of the Livonian Order made Courland (western Latvia) and Zemgale (central Latvia) his own personal duchy, owing allegiance to Poland. Even Denmark joined in, taking possession of some ex-church lands in Courland

Ivan the Terrible

and west Estonia for a while; it held on longest to the island Saaremaa which was finally transferred to Sweden in 1645. Rīga was independent from 1561 to 1582 then autonomous under Polish rule.

Swedish Dominance The Russian menace dealt with for the time being, Protestant Sweden and Catholic Poland-Lithuania settled down in 1592 to fight each other in the Baltic lands. By 1629 Poland had been forced to hand over Rīga and most of Livonia (eastern Latvia and southern Estonia) to Sweden. The only piece of Livonia that stayed in Polish-Lithuanian hands was Latgale, the south-east, which is why Latgale is the stronghold of Catholicism in Latvia today. Sweden successfully defended its gains against Russia and Poland in a couple more wars in the 1650s.

Swedish rule, which consolidated Lutheran Protestantism in Estonia and most of Latvia, is looked back on fondly as it was a relatively enlightened episode in the two countries' long history of foreign oppression. The 17th century Swedish kings, Gustaf II Adolf (Gustavus Adolphus) and Carl (Charles) XI, tried to raise Estonian and Latvian peasants from serfdom and introduced universal elementary education, translated the Bible into Estonian and Latvian, and founded Dorpat (Tartu) University – but their efforts were severely hampered by frequent wars, plagues and famines.

Russian Wars Meanwhile, conflict between Poland-Lithuania and Muscovy continued. Rzeczpospolita forces briefly took Moscow in 1610 and besieged it again in 1617; but in 1654 it was Russia's turn to invade the Rzeczpospolita and take significant territory from it.

Russia finally succeeded in reaching the Baltic shores under its westward-looking tsar, Peter the Great, in the Great Northern War (1700-1721), which destroyed Sweden as a regional power. Sweden surrendered its Baltic possessions – Estonia and central and north-east Latvia – to Russia at the Treaty of Nystad in 1721. The war was another period of devastation for Estonia and Latvia. At the end of it, according to one Russian general, neither bark of dog nor crow of cock could be heard anywhere from Narva to Rīga.

Prussian Revival In 1618 Prussia was joined through royal marriage to the powerful north German state of Brandenburg, centred on Berlin. In 1660 Brandenburg purchased suzerainty over Prussia from Poland, and in 1701 the elector of Brandenburg was crowned as the first Prussian king at Königsberg. In the 18th century the Prussia-Brandenburg axis became a major European power, with a military and bureaucratic bent, under Frederick the Great; and cracks appeared in the Polish-Lithuanian Rzeczpospolita, where various factions called in Russian help from time to time.

Partitions of Poland Finally the Rzeczpospolita was so weakened that Russia, Austria and Prussia (as the Prussia-Brandenburg state was called) simply carved it up in the Partitions of Poland (1772, 1793 and 1795-96). Most of Lithuania, along with the Polish-Lithuanian possessions Latgale

SWEDEN
Revel (Tallinn)
Stockholm
ESTONIA
RUSSIA
Areas of Control Mid-17th Century
■ Polish
□ Swedish
LIVONIA
Rīga
BALTIC SEA
COURLAND
Königsberg (Kaliningrad)
LITHUANIA (RZECZPOSPOLITA)
PRUSSIA
Swedish & Polish Control
0   150   300 km
Warsaw ●
POLAND (RZECZPOSPOLITA)

and Courland, went to Russia. A small chunk of western Lithuania went to Prussia, which now stretched uninterruptedly across northern Poland from its original core around Königsberg to its Brandenburg territories.

The 19th Century
National Revivals Russian rule brought privileges for the Baltic-German ruling class in Estonia and Latvia but greater exploitation for the peasants. Finally the Estonian and Latvian peasants were freed, between 1811 and 1819, and permitted to move freely and own land from the mid-19th century. In Lithuania, which got involved in the Polish rebellion against Russian rule in 1830-31, the peasants were not freed till 1861, the same year as the rest of Russia. Lithuania was also involved in a second Polish rebellion against Russia in 1863. Later, thousands of Lithuanians, and fewer Latvians and Estonians, migrated to the Americas.

The liberation of the serfs enabled the Baltic national revivals of the second half of the 19th century and early 20th century by allowing the native peoples to move into trades, professions, commerce and intellectual circles. In the north the revivals focused particularly around educated Estonians and Latvians at Dorpat (Tartu) University; Vilnius University had been shut down in 1832. Slowly the three native Baltic peoples crawled out from under the doormat of history. They began to express their cultures and senses of nationality; to teach, learn and publish in their own languages; to hold their own song festivals and stage their own plays. Railways were built from Russia to the Baltic ports. By 1914 Rīga had a population of 500,000 and had become an important international port. It also grew, like Tallinn and Narva, into an industrial centre. In Estonia and Latvia there was almost total literacy by 1900.

Russification The national movements were strengthened, if anything, by the unpopular policy of Russification which was followed by the Russian authorities, especially towards the end of the century.

Estonia, Livonia and Courland were governed as separate provinces, but Lithuania, after the rebellions, was treated as part of Russia itself. Russian law was imposed on the region (as early as 1840 in Lithuania) and the Russian language was used for teaching. Catholicism was persecuted in Latvia and Lithuania. From 1864 books could only be published in Lithuanian if they used the Russian alphabet, while books, newspapers and periodicals in Polish (which was spoken by the Lithuanian gentry) were banned altogether. Lithuanian publishing continued among Lithuanians living in eastern Prussia (including the first newspaper in Lithuanian) and was smuggled into Lithuania.

Meanwhile in Prussia By the late 19th century the Prussian state formed the basis of a united Germany which stretched, uninterrupted, from the border of France to that of the Russian empire. The Prussian king Wilhelm I, crowned in Königsberg in 1861, was proclaimed the first kaiser (emperor) of this new empire, in Versailles in 1871 – thanks to his aggressive chancellor (prime minister) Otto von Bismarck.

Independence
Effects of Russian Revolutions Ideas of Baltic national autonomy and independence were first seriously voiced during the 1905 Russian revolution. When Estonian and Latvian revolutionaries started burning manor houses, there were harsh reprisals with about 1000 people being shot.

During WWI, Germany occupied Lithuania and western Latvia in 1915 but didn't reach Rīga, eastern Latvia or Estonia until late 1917 or early 1918. Baltic nationalists initially hoped the war would bring their nations some kind of improved status within Russia; only with Russia's February Revolution in 1917, which overthrew the tsar, did the idea of full independence really take off. But there were wars and some complicated comings and goings to negotiate first.

In March 1917, Russia passed a bill for Estonian self-government and the first Estonian parliament, the Diet Maapäev, met in July in Toompea Castle, Tallinn. Following the October Revolution in Russia, a communist administration was set up for Estonia, but when the German forces reached mainland Estonia in February 1918, the communists fled. On 24 February the Diet Maapäev declared Estonian independence. Next day, however, the Germans occupied Tallinn. In Lithuania, under German occupation, a Lithuanian national council, the Taryba, had declared independence on 16 February.

In March 1918, Russia's new communist government, desperate to get out of the war, abandoned the Baltic region to Germany in the Treaty of Brest-Litovsk.

Baltic Independence Wars On 11 November, 1918, Germany surrendered to the western allies. The same day, a Lithuanian republican government was set up. In Latvia, peasant, middle class and socialist groups declared independence on 18 November and the leader of the Farmers' Party, Kārlis Ulmanis, formed a government. The Estonian independence declaration of February was repeated in November. Soviet Russia now launched a military and political campaign to win back the Baltic states, but this was eventually defeated by both local opposition and outside military intervention – in Estonia's case it constituted a fleet of British ships and volunteer fighters from Scandinavia and Finland. Estonia's prime minister, Konstantin Päts, was able to declare Estonia free of enemies in February 1919.

In Latvia, fighting continued until 1920 between nationalists, Bolsheviks, and lingering German occupation forces and Baltic Germans (under the anticommunist General von der Goltz, who still hoped to bring the Baltic region back under German sway). The Ulmanis government had a communist rival in Valmiera headed by Pēteris Stučka. The Red Army took Rīga in January 1919, and the Ulmanis government moved to Liepāja, where it received British naval protection. In May, von der Goltz drove the Red Army from Rīga but he was then defeated at Cēsis by Estonian and Latvian troops, who drove

the Red Army from most of the rest of Latvia. Ulmanis returned to Rīga only to have another army attack the city in November 1919, this time of anticommunist Russians and Germans organised by von der Goltz and led by an obscure adventurer called Pavel Bermondt-Avalov. The Latvians, however, defeated it, and in December the last German troops left Latvia. The last communist-held area, Latgale, also fell to Latvia.

In Lithuania, things were complicated by the re-emergence of an independent Poland which wanted Lithuania either to reunite with it or to cede it the Vilnius area, which had a heavily Polish or Polonised population. The Red Army installed a communist government in Vilnius in January 1919, but was driven out of Lithuania by August. But it was Polish troops who took Vilnius, and Poland retained Vilnius – apart from three months in 1920 – right through till 1939. The 'Vilnius issue' therefore was a constant source of Lithuanian-Polish tension. Independent Lithuania's capital was Kaunas. German forces finally left Lithuania in December 1919.

In 1920 Soviet Russia signed peace treaties with the parliamentary republics of Estonia, Latvia and Lithuania recognising their independence in perpetuity.

The Independence Years Despite a promising start, the three Baltic republics – caught between the ascendant Soviet Union and, by the early 1930s, an openly expansionist Nazism which glorified the historic German eastward urge – soon lapsed from democracy into authoritarianism. All three republics came to be ruled by regimes which feared the Soviet Union more than the Third Reich. In Estonia the anticommunist, antiparliamentary 'vaps' movement won a constitutional referendum in 1933 but was outflanked in a bloodless coup by prime minister Päts, who took over as dictator. In Latvia from 1934, Ulmanis headed a nonparliamentary government of unity which tried to steer between the strong Nazi extreme and the left. Lithuania suffered a military coup in 1926, and from 1929 was ruled by Antanas Smetona along similar lines to Mussolini's Italy.

Meanwhile in Prussia (Again) After WWI, Danzig (Gdańsk) became a free state. Poland gained a narrow corridor of land through to the coast between Gdańsk and Germany. East Prussia – as the original Prussian lands focused on Königsberg were now known – was cut off from the rest of Germany, though remaining German territory. Memel (Klaipėda), an 'international territory' after WWI, was seized by Lithuania in 1923, then in 1939 by Germany in Hitler's last land grab before WWII.

WWII & Soviet Rule
Soviet Occupation On 23 August, 1939, Nazi Germany and the USSR signed the Molotov-Ribbentrop non-aggression pact, which also secretly divided eastern Europe into German and Soviet spheres of influence. Estonia and Latvia were put in the Soviet sphere and Lithuania in the Nazi one. When Lithuania refused to join the Nazi attack on Poland in September 1939, it was transferred to the Soviet sphere. The USSR insisted on 'mutual-assistance pacts' with the Baltic states, gaining the right to station troops on their territory. Lithuania's pact regained it Vilnius in October 1939 (the Red Army had taken the city in its invasion of eastern Poland at the same time as Germany had invaded western Poland).

Those Baltic Germans who hadn't left for Germany during the 1920s land reforms departed in 1939 or 1940 in response to Hitler's *Heim ins Reich* (Home to the Reich) summons. By August 1940 Estonia, Latvia and Lithuania had been placed under Soviet military occupation, communists had won 'elections', and the three states had been 'accepted' as republics of the USSR.

The Soviet authorities began nationalisation and purges. Within a year or so of their takeover, according to various estimates, somewhere between 11,000 and 60,000 Estonians were killed, deported or fled; 45,000 Lithuanians suffered the same fate; and in Latvia the figure was about 35,000.

Many of the deportees were children or elderly. Many went in mass deportations to Siberia, beginning on 14 June, 1941.

Nazi Occupation When Hitler invaded the USSR and occupied the Baltic states in 1941, many in the Baltics initially saw the Germans as liberators. The Nazi-occupied Baltic states were governed together with Belarus as a territory called Ostland. Some local people collaborated to varying degrees with the Nazi occupation. Some joined in the slaughter of the Jews, gaining a reputation for cruelty at least as bad as that of their German masters. Nearly all Lithuania's Jewish population – between 135,000 and 300,000 people according to varying estimates – were killed in camps or ghettos. Latvia's Jewish population of perhaps 90,000 was virtually wiped out. An estimated 5000 Jews were killed in Estonia. Thousands of other local people, and Jews and other peoples brought from elsewhere, were killed in the Baltic states by the Nazis and their collaborators.

An estimated 140,000 Latvians, 45,000 Lithuanians and 50,000 Estonians were enlisted in German military units – some voluntarily, some conscripted. Other people were conscripted for forced labour. There was also nationalist and communist guerrilla resistance against the Nazis. Somewhere between 65,000 and 120,000 Latvians, plus about 70,000 Estonians and 80,000 Lithuanians, succeeded in escaping to the west in 1944 and 1945 to avoid the Red Army's reconquest of the Baltic states. Many others were captured on the way and sent to Siberia. Altogether, Estonia lost something like 200,000 people during the war. Latvia lost 450,000 and Lithuania 475,000.

Soviet Reoccupation The Red Army reconquered the Baltic states, except Courland (which was still in German hands when Germany surrendered in May 1945), by the end of 1944. Many cities were badly damaged in fighting between the advancing Soviet forces and the Nazi occupiers. The battle for East Prussia in 1944-45 was one of the fiercest of WWII, with hundreds of thousands of casualties on both sides. Königsberg was nearly flattened by British air raids in 1944 and by the Red Army's final assault from 6 to 9 April, 1945. Many of the surviving Germans were sent to Siberia; the last 25,000 were deported to Germany in 1947 and 1948. Königsberg was renamed Kaliningrad, after a sidekick of Stalin's, and rebuilt and repeopled mostly by Russians. Since WWII, the northern half of East Prussia has formed Russia's Kaliningrad Region and the southern half has been in Poland.

Soviet Rule Between 1944 and 1952, with Stalin's Soviet rule firmly established in the Baltic states, agriculture was collectivised. As many as 60,000 Estonians, 175,000 Latvians and 250,000 Lithuanians were killed or deported between 1945 and 1949, many of them in March 1949 during the collectivisation. Thousands of people – known as 'forest brothers' – took to the woods rather than live under Soviet rule. A few offered armed resistance. They were effectively crushed by 1952 or 1953, but the last, an Estonian called August Sabe, was not cornered by the KGB until 1978. He drowned swimming across a lake trying to escape.

With post-war industrialisation, the Baltic republics received such an influx of migrant workers, mainly from nearby regions of Russia, Belarus and Ukraine, that the native Estonians and Latvians feared they would become minorities in their own countries. This further increased the Baltic dislike of Soviet rule. Resentment also grew over issues like the allocation of housing and the top jobs. Industrialisation shifted the population balance from the countryside, on which the Baltic economies had been based before WWII, to the towns. It helped bring the Baltic states high living standards, in Soviet terms, but also brought environmental problems. Religion was repressed and tourism restricted, though Tallinn enjoyed a steady flow of visitors, trade and investment from nearby Finland, a neutral state with a peculiarly close relationship with the USSR. This gained Estonia a reputation as the most westernised of the Baltic states, both during Soviet rule and in its aftermath.

Towards New Independence
First Steps Through the decades of Soviet rule, the Baltic peoples still hoped for freedom. In the late 1980s, Soviet leader Mikhail Gorbachev began to encourage *glasnost* (openness) and *perestroika* (restructuring) in the USSR. Pent-up Baltic bitterness came into the open and national feelings surged into mass demands for self-rule.

The Singing Revolution The Baltic peoples seriously began to believe in the possibility of independence in 1988. In March some Latvian government members joined a public meeting to commemorate one of the Stalin deportations. Several big rallies on environmental and national issues were held in Latvia, with 45,000 people joining hands along the coast in one anti-pollution protest. And in Estonia, huge numbers of people gathered to sing previously banned national songs and give voice to their longing for freedom in what became known as the Singing Revolution. An estimated 300,000 – about one in three of all Estonians – attended one song gathering in Tallinn. Some 250,000 people gathered in Vilnius to protest on the anniversary (23 August) of the Molotov-Ribbentrop Pact.

Political Steps Popular fronts, formed in each republic to press for democratic reform, won huge followings. The local communist parties joined them in virtual alliance. Estonia's Popular Front, claiming 300,000 members, called for Estonian autonomy, democracy, and cuts in Russian immigration at its first congress in October 1988. All three republics paid lip service to perestroika while actually dismantling Soviet institutions. In November 1988, Estonia's supreme soviet passed a declaration of sovereignty, announcing that USSR laws would apply in Estonia only if it approved them.

Lithuania came to lead the Baltic push for independence after its popular front, Sajūdis (The Movement), won 30 of the 42 Lithuanian seats in the March 1989 elections for the USSR Congress of People's Deputies.

On 23 August, 1989, the 50th anniversary of the Molotov-Ribbentrop Pact, some two million people formed a human chain stretching from Tallinn to Vilnius, many of them calling for secession. In November, Moscow granted the Baltic republics economic autonomy and in December the Lithuanian Communist Party left the Communist Party of the Soviet Union – a pioneering act which was a landmark in the break-up of the USSR. Equally daringly, Lithuania became the first Soviet republic to legalise non-communist parties. Estonia and Latvia soon followed.

Lithuania Declares Independence Vast pro-independence crowds met Gorbachev when he visited Vilnius in January 1990. Sajūdis won a majority in the elections to Lithuania's supreme soviet in February, and on 11 March this assembly declared Lithuania an independent republic. In response, Moscow carried out weeks of intimidatory troop manoeuvres around Vilnius, then clamped an economic blockade on Lithuania, cutting off fuel supplies. The pressure was finally removed after 2½ months, when Sajūdis leader Vytautas Landsbergis agreed to a 100 day moratorium on the independence declaration in exchange for independence talks between the respective Lithuanian and USSR governments. No foreign country had yet recognised Lithuanian independence.

Estonia and Latvia followed similar paths, but more cautiously. In spring 1990 nationalists were elected to big majorities in their supreme soviets (or parliaments) and re-instated their pre-WWII constitutions, but declared 'transition periods' for full independence to be negotiated. Estonia led the way towards a market economy by abolishing subsidies on some important everyday goods.

The Events of 1991 Soviet hardliners gained the ascendancy in Moscow in winter 1990-91, and in January 1991 Soviet troops and paramilitary police occupied and stormed strategic buildings in Vilnius and Rīga. Thirteen people were killed in the storming of the Vilnius TV tower and TV centre, five in the storming of the Interior Ministry in Rīga, and hundreds were hurt. The parliaments in both cities were barricaded; the people stayed calm; the violence drew western condemnation of Moscow and the immediate threat subsided.

In referendums in February and March 1991, big majorities in all three states voted in favour of secession from the USSR. However, the west, not wanting to weaken Gorbachev further, gave only lukewarm support to the Baltic independence movements.

Everything changed with the 19 August, 1991, coup attempt against Gorbachev in Moscow. Estonia declared full independence on 20 August and Latvia on 21 August (Lithuania had done so back in March 1990). The western world recognised their independence and so, finally, did the USSR on 6 September, 1991.

On 17 September, 1991, the three Baltic states joined the United Nations and began taking steps to consolidate their new-found nationhood, such as issuing their own postage stamps and currencies. In 1992 they competed independently in the Olympic Games for the first time since before WWII. The pope visited all three states in September 1993 but, such landmarks apart, the Baltics dropped out of the world's headlines.

Since independence, the three new states have in many ways grown apart, rather than together. There have been differences over economics and border controls, and the three states found themselves competing for the same foreign investment and aid. Baltic émigré communities in the west were an important source of investment for all three states, and influenced politics too. Germany became a big investor, but since German reunification much investment which might have come to the Baltics has been diverted into the former German Democratic Republic. Estonia's close ethnic, economic and transport links with Finland encouraged a flood of Finnish investment as well as Swedish interest. Latvia looked to Sweden and Denmark. Lithuania took up its old quarrel with Poland where it had left off in 1939, and tried (harder than Estonia and Latvia) to build relationships with the CIS, while also looking west. Trade and other forms of cooperation between the three Baltic states, however, have remained relatively minor. Each has its own army and police force, but because of the Baltics' leaky borders and location between east and west, smuggling and organised crime dominated by the 'mafias' of the CIS remain a problem.

Nervous of Russian sabre rattling and hungry for economic stability, all three republics would like to join NATO and the European Union, but western reluctance to annoy Russia, and the EU's own problems, mean neither organisation is likely to let them in soon. The 1996 Russo-US agreement, which removed NATO objections to the stationing of 600 Russian tanks and other forces near Baltic borders, is especially resented.

And in Kaliningrad Kaliningrad remained a closed military enclave until 1991, when 50,000 German visitors flooded in during its first 'open' year. The region remains part of Russia. After the break-up of the USSR it was declared a free-trade zone, a move finally ratified in January 1997. Foreign trade, especially with Poland and Lithuania, boomed and a trickle of investment began, though plagued by a cumbersome bureaucracy. South Korean car maker KIA Motors signed a US$1 billion deal to build 50,000 cars a year in Kaliningrad, creating up to 50,000 jobs in its factories and supplier industries. The deal is a make or break chance for Kaliningrad – if all goes well, other big companies will follow; if not, they will shy away.

GEOGRAPHY

It's tempting to sum up the geography of the Baltic states in two words: 'small' and 'flat'. From the northernmost point of Estonia to the southern tip of Lithuania is only 650 km. As for altitude, the land rarely rises much above 300m, and in parts of Latvia it's even below sea level. However, the Baltic peoples do make quite a lot of their 'uplands'.

The coastal regions are generally the lowest lying. The whole of west Estonia, most of the Zemgale region of central Latvia, and most of the Kaliningrad Region are below 50m. Lithuania has a wide central lowland belt, running from north to south and up to 80 km across. The low lying regions are generally the most fertile. However, there's more of geographical interest than these basic facts suggest. The coasts vary from cliff to dune to low lying marshy margins. The inland landscape is gently rolling as a result of deposits left behind on the bedrock of the North European Plain by the glaciers which covered the region before about 12,000 BC. And the region is crossed by many rivers, some of which have cut surprisingly deep valleys, and is dotted with thousands of lakes and a range of vegetation.

The Baltic states and the Kaliningrad Region between them have about 5000 km of coastline, the majority of it (3794 km) being around the indented fringes of Estonia's mainland and islands. Some stretches of coast are low lying, reedy and wet – the kind of place where it's hard to tell where land ends and sea begins. There are also lengths of cliff or steep bank, over 50m high in parts, and long stretches of dunes often fronted by sweeping, sandy beaches and covered with pine woods. These create a really refreshing fragrance in combination with the salty sea air.

Little of this coast faces the open Baltic Sea, as much of it fronts the gulfs of Finland and Rīga or is protected from the open sea by islands. The most extraordinary feature of the coastline is the Curonian Spit (Lithuanian: Neringa; Russian: Kurshskaya kosa) – a sandbar 98 km long and up to 66m high, but nowhere more than four km wide.

One thing the Baltic states don't lack is lakes. There are around 9000 of them according to some counts, though the distinction between a lake and a pond must be hard to make in some cases! Most of the lakes are small and shallow, and Latvia and Lithuania have the greatest numbers, especially in their south-east and north-east uplands respectively. Estonia has the biggest lakes: Lake Peipus and Võrtsjärv.

Lots of rivers wind their way across the land. The two biggest, both flowing in from Belarus, are the Daugava, which crosses Latvia from the south-east to enter the sea near Rīga, and the Nemunas, which crosses south-west Lithuania then forms the Lithuania-Kaliningrad border for its final 100 km or so to the Curonian Lagoon. Other major rivers include the Narva, flowing north from Lake Peipus to the Gulf of Finland and forming the Estonia-Russia border; the Gauja, looping 440 km entirely within eastern Latvia; the 350 km Venta, rising in Lithuania and entering the sea in western Latvia; and the Pregolya which collects most of the waters of the Kaliningrad Region and enters the Kaliningrad Lagoon just west of Kaliningrad city.

Not surprisingly in such a low lying region, there are a lot of bogs, swamps, fens and marshes. These occupy as much as one-fifth of Estonia and one-tenth of Latvia, though you see little of them as you travel those countries' roads. They're a useful resource, especially for their peat.

GEOLOGY

Amber (fossilised tree resin, millions of years old) has been a source of Baltic prosperity since the earliest times. Five centuries before the birth of Christ it was valued by the ancient Greeks for its medicinal and semi-magical properties, and it commands high prices still. Mined from deposits in Estonian and Latvian peat bogs, it remains fairly plentiful. Other geological 'assets' have proved a mixed blessing. Both Estonia and Latvia have large deposits of oil shale, a sedimentary rock rich in hydrocarbons. Opencast shale mining scars the landscape in several places, and its use as a power plant fuel causes severe air pollution. Meanwhile, off-shore oil deposits recently detected close to the Latvian and Lithuanian coasts have become a source of friction between the two countries, causing disagreement over coastal borders and undersea mineral rights.

CLIMATE

The Baltic states' climate is temperate, but on the cool and damp side. It verges on the continental as you move towards the inland extremities where, in winter, it's typically 2°C to 4°C colder than on the coasts but in summer may be a degree or two warmer. From May to September, the best time to visit (see When to Go under Planning in the Facts for the Visitor chapter), daytime highs throughout the region are normally between 14°C and 22°C. It's unusually warm if the temperature reaches the high 20s. July and August, the warmest months, are also wet, with days of persistent showers. May, June and September are more comfortable, while late June can be thundery. At these northern latitudes days are long in summer, with a full 19 hours of daylight at midsummer in Estonia. April and October have cold, sharp, wintry days as well as mild springlike or autumnal ones.

In winter – November to March – temperatures rarely rise above 4°C and in parts of the region may stay below freezing almost permanently from mid-December to late February. Winter hours of daylight are short, and sometimes it never seems to get properly light at all. The first snows usually come in November, and there's normally permanent snow cover from January to March in coastal regions – but up to an extra month either side in the inland east. In some coastal areas, some recent winters have been much milder, with no lasting snow cover. Slush under foot is something you have to cope with in autumn, when snow is falling then melting, and spring, when the winter snow cover is thawing.

Annual precipitation ranges from 500 to 600 mm in lowland areas to 700 to 900 mm

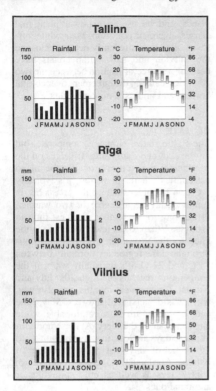

Tallinn

Rainfall / Temperature

Rīga

Rainfall / Temperature

Vilnius

Rainfall / Temperature

in the uplands. About 75% of it usually falls as rain, 25% as snow. Winters can be foggy.

Coastal waters average 16°C to 21°C in summer – July and August are the warmest months. The gulfs of Finland and Rīga freeze occasionally, and the straits between Estonia's islands and the mainland usually freeze for three months from mid-January. The open Baltic Sea coast almost never freezes.

ECOLOGY & ENVIRONMENT

Pollution dating from the Soviet period is gradually being curbed, but upgrading or replacing sources of pollution – especially sources of power – remains a problem. Estonia has stopped mining its large phosphorite reserves, but the continued mining of oil shale in its north-east and its use as a fuel for thermal power plants in Narva still causes pollution. Estonia's Gulf of Finland coast is also polluted in places by wastes at the Sillamäe Soviet military nuclear plant.

Life expectancy in the Baltic states is lower – and infant mortality higher – than European norms. Though the Baltic Sea as a whole is gradually getting cleaner, virtually all the Baltic states' coastal waters are polluted – partly by chemical pollution washing out from rivers and partly by untreated sewage pumped straight into rivers or the sea. The biggest city in the region, Rīga, lacked any kind of modern sewerage system until 1991. Today Rīga has a treatment plant but it can only handle less than half the city's sewage. Tap water in many parts of the Baltic states – including Rīga – is still reportedly tainted by chemical as well as organic pollutants. Many rivers and ground waters are polluted by industrial wastes, fertilisers and pesticides.

FLORA & FAUNA
Flora

Large portions of the region are still forested – about 40% of Estonia and Latvia, over a quarter of Lithuania, and 20% of the Kaliningrad Region. In some areas forest cover increased during the Soviet period because of the abandonment of farmland during collectivisation. Pine forests account for up to half the forest cover and tend to be concentrated nearer the coasts, while inland forests are more often mixed. Birch is the most common deciduous tree. Juniper shrubland is characteristic of parts of Estonia, especially the islands and western mainland. Northern Kurzeme and northern Vidzeme are the most forested parts of Latvia. In Lithuania, the south – particularly the southwest – is the most densely forested area.

A favourite forest recreation of the local people is gathering the many edible mushrooms and berries that grow there in late summer and autumn. You'll see people laden with them returning from the countryside on weekend buses and trains and selling them in markets and on street corners.

Western coastal regions tend to have the greatest range of wild flowers because of their milder climate.

Fauna

The Baltic states have more large wild mammals than anywhere else in Europe but seeing them in the wild requires patience, determination and, ideally, the services of an expert local guide.

Estonia has about 800 brown bear and Latvia a few. Elk, deer, wild boar, wolves and lynx inhabit the forests of all three countries in varying numbers, though you're not likely to bump into any in the wild without some guidance. In Estonia and Latvia there are beavers on inland waters and seals along the coasts, and all three Baltic states have large

otter populations – 4000 in Latvia, 3000 in Estonia and 1500-2000 in Lithuania.

Estonia's animal populations include 40,000 deer (of which 10,000 are shot by hunters annually), 400 wolves (also culled), 900 lynx (more than in the whole of western Europe), 2600 beavers, 10,000 wild boar (5000 shot a year) and several thousand elk.

Some of Estonia's islands and coastal wetlands and Lake Žuvintas in southern Lithuania are important breeding grounds and migration halts for water birds. Latvia harbours 6500 pairs of white stork (six times as many as in the whole of western Europe).

One species you're likely to encounter anywhere in summer is the mosquito.

Cruelty to Animals

Limited hunting of species including the brown bear, wolf and lynx is, sadly, permitted and could pose a threat to their future, especially if not strictly regulated.

National Parks & Reserves

Each of the three Baltic states has one national park established in the 1970s, and Lithuania has four others designated more recently. There are also many nature reserves of varying degrees of control.

The national parks protect areas of natural, historical, architectural and archaeological importance. Some parts of them are strict reserves, off limits to everyone except a few specialists, but recreation is encouraged in other sectors. All are partly inhabited and can be reached by public transport. They have accommodation possibilities either within their territory or on their fringes. The nature reserves tend to be more remote and harder to reach, but still worth getting to if you're interested. Some have organised visitor facilities. There's detailed information on individual national parks and nature reserves in the Facts about Estonia/Latvia/Lithuania chapters, and in the regional chapters.

GOVERNMENT & POLITICS

The Baltic states are maturing independent republics. As the post-Soviet era dawned, Estonia was the first to hold elections (in

A deer's antlers are covered with velvet while they are still growing.

1992) under its own system. It was followed later that year by Lithuania and by Latvia in June 1993. Since then, the political situation has remained fluid (as it has in most post-Soviet states in eastern Europe), with a plethora of nationalist parties, social democrats, reformed post-communist parties, (now avowing commitment to democracy and the free market) and a host of splinter groups appealing for votes in each country. None has been able to win a convincing electoral mandate and overall parliamentary majority (though Lithuania's conservatives came within a whisker of doing so in late 1996), and coalition governments seem likely to dominate Baltic politics for the foreseeable future.

There is more information on the government and citizenship requirements of each of the Baltic states in the Facts about Estonia/Latvia/Lithuania chapters.

ECONOMY

As part of the USSR, the Baltic states enjoyed high living standards compared with other Soviet republics. Hopes for a rapid transition after independence from Soviet-style prosperity to western standards of living were dashed by the collapse of the Soviet rouble (wiping out most people's meagre savings), runaway inflation, and a harsh introduction to the downside of consumer capitalism – soaring unemployment, plummeting purchasing power, and an end to the rudimentary but universal Soviet social welfare system. In the aftermath of independence, inflation topped 1000%, far outstripping earnings. But the painful post-independence years are paying off, with inflation down to around 20 to 35% and the currencies of the Baltic republics have proved remarkably stable.

During the Soviet era the Baltic states were manufacturing centres, but their industries were woefully inefficient in free-market terms and few weathered exposure to the capitalist world well. The last few years have seen sweeping changes in employment patterns, with many more people employed in sectors such as food and clothing production, while heavier industry has lagged behind.

All three states have followed broadly similar paths of economic restructuring – gradual privatisation of state-owned businesses, property and land; removal of state subsidies to industry, agriculture and consumers; and agreements on economic austerity with the International Monetary Fund and other world financial bodies to attract vital foreign loans and investment. All three countries need to exploit overseas markets, but each has developed its own foreign trade policy. Estonia's approach to foreign trade has been the most liberal, while Lithuania and Latvia have taken a more protectionist line.

A general free trade agreement between the Baltic republics was signed in 1993, and an agricultural free trade agreement which removed all export and import tariffs and quotas on agricultural produce was signed in June 1996. Also in 1996, Estonia and Latvia reached a provisional agreement on their maritime border and fishing rights.

The Baltic states are short on natural resources, except for timber. Estonia and Latvia have useful reserves of peat in their bogs, and Estonia has its oil shale. Lithuania has an oil refinery and some oil reserves, but virtually all oil and gas has to be imported. The recent discovery of oil deposits off the coasts of Lithuania and Latvia has caused bickering between the two.

More facts about the post-independence economic development of each Baltic country will be found under the individual country sections.

POPULATION & PEOPLE

According to the 1989 Soviet census, Estonia has 1.56 million people, Latvia 2.7 million and Lithuania 3.68 million. These figures have since dropped a little owing mainly to emigration of Russians to Russia. The Kaliningrad Region has about 900,000 people.

Ethnic identity is a continuing sore point, especially in Latvia and Estonia, where ethnic Estonians and Latvians are barely in the majority. Lithuanians greatly outnumber the Polish and Russian minorities in their own country. For more on what 'Estonian', 'Latvian' and 'Lithuanian' mean, see Population & People in the Facts about Estonia/Latvia/Lithuania chapters. Other ethnic groups present in smaller numbers include Jews, Gypsies, Tatars, and Germans (in Lithuania), as well as nationalities of the former Soviet Union. The population of the Kaliningrad Region is predominantly Russian.

Though there were quite a few Russians in the Baltic states before WWII (about 8% in Estonia, 10% in Latvia and 3% or 4% in Lithuania) their current numbers are chiefly a result of immigration during the Soviet period, when many came to work in the new industries that were being set up in the Baltics. Before WWII two-thirds to three-quarters of the population of the Baltic states lived in the countryside; today it's only a quarter to one-third.

The presence of some two million ethnic Russians presents a social problem. Their relations with the native Baltic peoples are strained – with the possible exception of Rīga where Russians have been established since the early 19th century.

The Baltic peoples tend to see their Russian residents as colonists from an unwelcome imperial power, who rarely tried to integrate into local society or learn the local languages.

Hard-line Baltic nationalists would no doubt like to see most of the Russians 'go home', even though many of them have lived all their lives in the Baltic states. There are also fears that their presence could provide hard-line Russian nationalists with a pretext for a renewed attempt to reincorporate the Baltics into the CIS (though this possibility seems increasingly remote). What's actually happening is that most non-native residents in Estonia and Latvia are being required to learn the local language before they can become citizens of these states. Lithuanians, with a smaller Russian minority in their midst, do not have the understandable fear of being swamped that Estonians and Latvians feel, and Lithuania's citizenship policy is more relaxed.

The Russians are typically working class and are mostly congregated in the main cities. They form about half the population of Tallinn, over half that of Rīga and one-fifth of that of Vilnius. The industrial towns of north-east Estonia are overwhelmingly Russian-populated. Latvians are a minority in all seven of Latvia's biggest cities.

Lost People

The history of the Baltic states in the 20th century is studded with groups of people who have disappeared. Emigration for straight economic reasons apart, war, Nazi and Soviet terror, and Soviet deportations have all caused horrifying drops in the countries' populations at various times. Estonia's population fell from 1.14 million in 1939 to 854,000 in 1945; Latvia's from 2.5 million in 1914 to 1.6 million in 1920; and Lithuania's from 3.1 million in 1940 to about 2.5 million in the mid-1950s.

In WWII the Nazis exterminated virtually all the Jews in the three states. Estimates vary, but they average around 200,000 to 300,000 Jews killed in Lithuania, 100,000 or so in Latvia, and fewer in Estonia.

The Baltic Germans, the upper class who had dominated Estonia and Latvia for centuries, left for Germany in the mid-1920s when they lost most of their lands in agrarian reforms and in 1939-40 when they were summoned 'home' by Hitler. They had numbered a few tens of thousands. Estonia lost virtually its whole Swedish population of about 8000 when they left for Sweden in 1943-44 under an agreement with the German occupiers.

Some 220,000 Poles, including most of the educated ones, left or were deported from Lithuania to Poland in 1945-58. Those 'Poles' who stayed in Lithuania were mostly Belarusian speakers living in rural areas with Polish Catholic churches – nearly all in the two south-eastern districts of Vilnius and Šalčininkai. They became the focus of controversy when their regional councils were accused of supporting the August 1991 coup

National Characteristics

It is always dangerous to generalise about 'national characters' but there are some clear general differences between Estonians, Latvians and Lithuanians.

Estonians and Lithuanians usually seem to be at the extremes, with Latvians somewhere in between. The stereotypical Estonian is reserved, efficient, short on praise, and polite. Lithuanians are stereotypically more gregarious, welcoming, and emotional – placing greater emphasis on contacts and favours than method and calculation.

The independence campaign of the late 1980s and early 90s puts the contrast in a nutshell. In Lithuania this was romantic, daring, cliff-hanging and risky, with at least 20 deaths. In Estonia it was cool, gradual, calculated and bloodless, leading to the unkind saying that 'Estonians would die for their freedom – to the last Lithuanian'. Latvia's path to independence lay, as usual, somewhere between the two extremes.

The three countries' introduction of new currencies to replace the Russian rouble after they gained independence likewise varied enormously. Estonia brought in its *kroon* cleanly, efficiently and with minimum fuss over a single weekend in mid-1992. Not only that, the Estonian government was then smart enough to secretly (and illegally) sell the 70 tons of Russian rouble banknotes it withdrew from circulation, reportedly to Chechnya for US$1.9 million! Latvia introduced its *lats* gradually in 1993 after an intermediate phase with a transitional currency called the Latvian rouble. Lithuania had to undergo two sets of transitional banknotes, a succession of postponements, and the sacking of the head of the national bank, before its *litas* finally appeared in June 1993. Then the notes had to be reprinted all over again because they were too easy to forge!

But with a much smaller Russian minority in their midst than Latvia or Estonia and a grander history behind them, Lithuanians seem to have a greater confidence in their national identity – and are all the more fun for it! Of the three Baltic states, it is the only country where its toppled Lenin can still be seen, even if he is on the scrap-heap in the backyard of a factory! In contrast, authorities in Latvia and Estonia keep the communist's whereabouts a closely guarded secret. Likewise, the unveiling of a memorial statue to the American rock singer Frank Zappa, legendary for his anti-establishment songs, is something that only the Lithuanians would dare do.

Bureaucracy certainly seems its most Byzantine in Latvia where armed Guards of Honour still stand, as rigid as stone, in front of the freedom monument in Rīga from sunrise to sunset come rain, hail or 10 foot of snow! Following the example set by the enterprising, predominantly Russian population in Rīga at least, Latvians have perhaps the best developed entrepreneurial sense of the three peoples. Given the ethnic tensions that run equally high between Latvians and Russians, however, it is fair to say that Latvians are also the least at ease with foreigners.

Some people find the Estonian reserve frustrating. An invitation to an Estonian's home – unless you're a relative – is a rare treat. But such an attitude can also be seen as an admirable form of self-reliance. Certainly the Estonian modesty and embarrassment about advertising is a joy to anyone who likes to make up their own mind about where to stay, eat and so on. You'll hardly ever find anyone trying to pressure you into some particular choice.

There are some traits which all three peoples share. One, which many visitors find disconcerting, is the outwardly glum, pessimistic, sometimes brusque bearing of many people. This can be put down to at least three things. One is that life has never been easy for the majority of people in this part of the world. Another is the weather: long, dark, cold winters never make anybody very happy (there's a marked brightening of everybody's mood in spring and summer). A third factor is the legacy of the Soviet era, when trust in strangers could be risky.

But in happy contrast to all this – and all the more pleasing because of it – you'll find that once you break the ice, people are often only too pleased to do what they can to help a western visitor.

Another trait the Baltic peoples share is a very strong feeling for their land; even those who live in cities frequently abandon them to visit family, friends, or their own cottages in the country. The universal custom of taking flowers when visiting someone's home is one reflection of this love of nature. Flower stalls and markets for such a purpose are to be found in every town, often open ridiculously late at night, and travellers can be seen nurturing bunches of blossoms for hours on crowded buses in order to present them to their host upon arrival.

Attachment to local roots is, perhaps, also a cause of the Baltic peoples' surprisingly sparse contact with each other. Though the outside world tends to think of the three Baltic states as one group, each is actually very much its own little world.

There are obviously neighbourly connections between the three states, but it is a good deal less common than you might expect for Estonians, Latvians and Lithuanians to speak each other's languages; do business with each other; or visit, have friends in – or even know much about – each other's countries. ∎

attempt in Moscow and collaborating with the KGB. The Lithuanian parliament imposed direct rule on the two districts in September 1991, dissolving the two regional councils, which caused tensions in Lithuania's relations with Poland. New councils were elected to office in 1993.

The Kaliningrad Region has seen the biggest ethnic change of the whole region. During and after WWII, virtually its entire German population disappeared: some fled, some were sent to Germany, some were deported to Siberia, and some were shot. They were replaced with people from the USSR – mainly Russia. In the last few years some ethnic Germans from Russia (mainly the Volga region) have made their way to Kaliningrad.

ARTS & CULTURE
Folk Culture
Native folklore survived centuries of foreign dominance, thanks largely to a rich oral tradition of songs, verses and chants on subjects like the seasonal cycle, farming and the land, family life, love and myths. It's widely thought that women composed most of these. The Latvian and Lithuanian verses, known as *dainas*, are often short and poetic and have been compared to the Japanese *haiku*. The oldest Estonian song type, going back to the first millennium BC, is the runic chant, based on lines of eight syllables with a theme gradually developing from line to line. Runic verses are still sung at weddings on the island of Kihnu.

In the 19th century, great collections of folk lyrics and tunes were made by people like Krišjānis Barons in Latvia and Jakob Hurt in Estonia; over 1.4 million folk lyrics and 30,000 tunes have been written down in Latvia alone. There's much interest in folk rhymes and music today with numerous societies and groups devoted to them, but they're also a living tradition with regional variations. Particularly unusual are the chants of the Setumaa region in south-east Estonia and those known as *sutartinės* in north-east Lithuania.

More immediately impressive, and evi-

dence of the age-old power of song in the Baltic cultures – though centred more on 19th and 20th century songs than the oldest traditions – are the huge national song festivals (held every five years), which played a great part in awakening national feelings in the 19th century and keeping them alive in the Soviet period. The late 1980s independence fervour was christened the Singing Revolution in Estonia because of its song festivals (held in 1988). One of them was attended by an estimated 300,000 people (around one in three of all Estonians), who sang previously banned songs and rekindled their national spark.

There are also quite a few folk festivals in the Baltics each year and these, particularly the annual Baltika festival, are probably your best bets for catching folk songs, music and dance as well as the colourful traditional costumes which are one of the few instantly recognisable trademarks of the Baltic states.

Lithuanian folk costume

The costumes vary from region to region (in some places from parish to parish), but you can rely on the women to sport long and colourful skirts, embroidered blouses, jackets or shawls, and an amazing variety of headgear from neat pillboxes to vast, winged, fairy-tale creations. Male gear tends to be plainer and more obviously a product of peasant existence. The women's styles have been influenced by German and other fashions from the towns. See Public Holidays & Special Events in the Facts for the Visitor chapter for more on song and folk festivals.

Folk music and dance performances are also regularly given at Rocca al Mare in Tallinn, the Open-Air Ethnography Museum in Rīga, and the Lithuanian Country Life Museum at Rumšiškės near Kaunas.

Many traditional musical instruments may accompany folk songs. Each of the three states has its own version of the zither – the *kannel* in Estonia, the *kokle* in Latvia and the *kanklės* in Lithuania. Bells, pipes, flutes and fiddles also feature. In Lithuania you may see the *birbynė*, a pipe with an animal horn attached, or the long wooden trumpet called the *daudytė* or the *skudučiai* from the northeast, which is like a set of pan pipes with each note produced by a different player, playing a different pipe.

Arts

Few Baltic artistic figures or works, past or present, are internationally known. Until the 19th century, Estonian, Latvian and Lithuanian culture were largely foreign dominated, and when they did emerge in their own right in the 19th and 20th centuries, they remained, with some exceptions, isolated by geographical, linguistic or political barriers or by their chiefly local relevance.

Literature Literature in the Baltic states draws heavily on the rich folklore heritage of each of the native peoples. Modern Estonian and Latvian literature got going with the writing of national epic poems in the mid-19th century – *Kalevipoeg* (Son of Kalev) in Estonia and *Lāčplēsis* (The Bear Slayer) in Latvia. These epics were based on legends and folk tales which had been part of the oral tradition over preceding centuries. The giants of 20th century literature in these countries are the Estonian novelist Anton Hansen Tammsaare and the Latvian poet and playwright Jānis Rainis, who spent much of his life in exile in Siberia and Switzerland for his trenchant criticisms of tsarist social and political oppression. He has been compared with Shakespeare and Goethe. More recently the Estonians Jan Kross, a novelist, and Jaan Kaplinski, a poet, have received international acclaim.

The first major fiction in Lithuanian was the poem *Metai* (The Seasons) describing the life of serfs in the 18th century. Jonas Mačiulis, known as Maironis, is regarded as the founder of modern Lithuanian literature for his poetry written around the turn of this century. Lithuania also shares the credit for some major Polish writers who grew up in Lithuania, including contemporary Nobel laureate Czesław Miłosz.

In the Soviet years many leading writers and artists went into voluntary or forced exile and most other talent was stifled. In the post-Soviet era, the cultural scene has changed so fast and there has been such a flood of outside influences that writers, artists and musicians in all three countries seem to have been somewhat stunned, with many still struggling to assimilate their new freedoms.

The literature of each of the Baltic states is discussed in more detail in the Facts about Estonia/Latvia/Lithuania chapters.

Visual Arts The art scene is pretty active in the Baltic states and there are lots of galleries and museums in the capital cities displaying past and present art, but few Baltic artists have managed to cause much of a stir internationally. The overall story of the regional art scene can best be described as emergent. There was a flowering of many national artists around the turn of the 19th century, under western influences like impressionism, which was followed by decades of experimentation and uncertainty in the early

20th century and forced conformity in the Soviet era. Like some other art forms, the visual arts seem to be struggling to find new directions now that the Soviet straitjacket, which shaped their approach for so long even in rebellion, has been removed. Some good modern work is in the field of applied art and handicrafts, often influenced by folk art.

Music Rock thrives, particularly in Estonia and Latvia where there are big annual festivals (see Public Holidays & Special Events in the Facts for the Visitor chapter). Jazz is particularly popular in Lithuania.

Rock, pop music and the disco and nightclub scene have boomed since independence, arguably at the expense of the classical performing scene, which was state-funded but has been strapped for cash in the new era – see Entertainment in the capital city sections. The region's best known composer is the Estonian Arvo Pärt, who writes mainly choral works.

All three capitals have opera and ballet companies and several theatres. Drama played a part in the 19th century national revivals, and Rīga was the pre-eminent performing arts centre before WWI and between the world wars. Its ballet, which produced Mikhail Baryshnikov, among others, goes back to the 1920s and was one of the best in the Soviet Union. Since independence there have been problems of funding and dwindling audiences for some companies.

For more information on the arts and culture of each of the Baltic states see the Facts about Estonia/Latvia/Lithuania chapters.

SOCIETY & CONDUCT

The post-independence Baltic states are young societies in every sense of the word. Large chunks of all three economies are in the hands of pushy young men (mostly, as this is still a very male-dominated society) with mobile phones and smart German cars. A few of the older generation even look back with a certain nostalgia to the Soviet era when a certain equality of poverty prevailed.

Some business visitors find these young dynamos obnoxiously cocky, but there's no doubt that youth lends the new Baltics a certain energy. That said, most people are quite formal – it takes a while to get onto first-name terms. Don't expect big smiles all round – but don't mistake a reserved attitude for indifference or hostility. Estonians are especially poker-faced – one national motto goes: 'May your face be as ice'. At the other extreme, Lithuanians are seen by other Balts as hot-headed, romantic and unpredictable, while Latvians are reported to be warmer than Estonians but more cool-headed than Lithuanians.

Dos & Don'ts

Although the road to westernisation has been pretty well trodden in the Baltic states, you will still encounter some Soviet-style bureaucracy. Be patient when things do not work as smoothly or as quickly as you would like – a short temper or adopting a patronising tone will only hinder things further.

Baltic people do not greet each other with a hug or kiss. Men always shake each other's hands. Flowers are a universal greeting, but only give odd-numbered bouquets as even-numbered offerings (including a dozen red roses!) are for mournful occasions. If you are invited to a private home, take flowers or a bottle – but never money – as a gift for your host. Take your shoes off when you enter and do not shake hands across the threshold. Do not whistle inside either. Both actions bring bad luck and will be severely frowned upon.

Muttering just a few words in the local language will raise instant smiles. In Latvia and Lithuania, speaking Russian as a foreigner is acceptable in most cases. In Estonia, however, try every other language you know first – be it English, German or Finnish – as speaking Russian is often met with a hostile response, or no response at all.

Prostitution is rife in the capitals. Incidents do occur where western clients are drugged, robbed and left lying in the gutter – literally. For your personal safety and for the sake of the young girls at hand, often forced by their parents to work the streets, it is better not to engage in this activity.

Women should refrain from wearing revealing clothing as this can attract undue attention.

If you go market shopping, take your own plastic bag with you as the only ones sold, if sold at all, feature nude women on both sides. If you're buying eggs, take a box with you unless you want them scrambled.

Don't get drunk in public or you could be arrested. Don't walk on the grass in Rīga or you could likewise be arrested. And don't try to bribe police officers – it no longer works.

RELIGION

After decades of persecution and discouragement under Soviet rule, religion – which chiefly means Christianity – enjoys full freedom again and is experiencing a revival. It was an important element in the national independence movements of the 1980s and 90s.

The leading faith among Estonians is Lutheranism but they are a rather irreligious people – only 23% of them reckoned to have religious convictions in an opinion poll held in 1991-92. Lutheranism is also the leading faith among Latvians but there's a significant Roman Catholic community too, especially in Latgale, the south-eastern region. Lithuanians are mostly Roman Catholics and more enthusiastic about their creed than the Lutherans to their north. The Catholic Church is a conservative force in Lithuanian society. Its head is the Archbishop of Kaunas, Cardinal Vincentas Sladkevičius. Russian Orthodoxy is the faith of most Russian believers throughout the region, which makes it important in places with big Russian populations such as Tallinn, north-east Estonia, Rīga and the Kaliningrad Region. There are also, particularly in Lithuania, some Old Believers – a schismatic sect of the Russian Orthodox church which has come in for intermittent persecution since it rejected a number of church reforms back in the 17th century.

Many customs and beliefs connected with the land and the seasons survive – perhaps most notably the 23 June midsummer celebrations. See Public Holidays & Special Events in the Facts for the Visitor chapter for information on the midsummer events.

Orthodoxy made some inroads into the region from the Slav regions to the east before Catholicism took over from the west in the 13th and 14th centuries (after desultory efforts since the 10th century). The brutal conversion of Estonia and Latvia by German crusaders, as well as the atheist influences of the Soviet period when even Christmas celebrations were banned for a long time, make it hardly surprising that support in those countries for the Lutheran church, to which the German ruling class turned with the Reformation in the 1520s, is still lukewarm. Lithuania fought off the German knights but its leaders eventually accepted Catholicism as part of the deal with Poland which led to the knights' long-term defeat. Still, as late as 1377 and 1382, the Lithuanian princes Algirdas and Kęstutis were cremated in rituals of the old religion – dressed in silver and gold and burnt on pyres together with their treasures, weapons, horses and hunting dogs.

The Reformation which swept across Europe in the 16th century triumphed in Estonia and most of Latvia, where Lutheranism became established under German or Swedish rule. But Catholicism survived in Lithuania and Latgale, controlled by Poland. The local churches – Lutheran and Catholic – endured oppression under Russian rule in the 19th century as well as in the Soviet periods.

LANGUAGE

Basic English is now widely spoken in hotels and shops, but in general only the best educated and those at higher levels in tourism have conversational English.

German and (in Estonia) Finnish are also useful. Getting to know a few words and phrases in the local languages will help you find your way around and will please any locals you utter them to. Things are complicated by the fact that there are four local languages – Estonian, Latvian, Lithuanian and Russian – and if you're travelling quickly between the different countries they tend to merge into a confused morass. In the Kaliningrad Region, German is probably more useful than English but local knowledge of both is poorer than in the Baltic states and some words of Russian are extremely useful.

The one language that nearly everyone understands throughout the region is Russian. But Estonians, Latvians and Lithuanians have little fondness for the tongue of their former imperial rulers and can be touchy about being addressed in Russian. If you do know some Russian it's advisable to make the attempt to communicate in some other language first – try English, and if that doesn't work then say you don't speak Estonian/Latvian/Lithuanian and ask if the other person understands Russian. The Russian minorities in the Baltic states, and of course people in the Kaliningrad Region, are only too happy to be addressed in Russian. Most signs in the Kaliningrad Region are in Russian only – so it certainly helps to get on top of the Cyrillic alphabet used for Russian.

See the Language Guide at the back of the book for more information on the Baltic languages and Russian (including the Cyrillic alphabet), and for useful words and phrases.

Facts for the Visitor

PLANNING

When to Go

Summer and spring are far and away the best times of year to travel in the Baltics. There is better weather, longer daylight and more fresh food. People are happier, cottage gardens blossom with flowers, and there's more happening in the way of festivals and outdoor events. Summer starts some time in May and ends some time in September. July and August, the warmest months (temperatures up to 30°C), are also among the wettest and there can be days of persistent showers, particularly in July. May, June and September, while a bit cooler, are often more comfortable.

July and August are also the months which bring the majority of foreign tourists, when low-budget hotels and hostels in the capitals can get fully booked. Some ferries to the Baltic states may also be full. Spring – April and May – has a real magic to it, it's when the land and the people really open up after the long, dark and dreary winter. June is the month of midsummer celebrations and festivities which bring home the Baltic peoples' close ties to nature and remind us of their pagan past.

Winter is very much a second best season. Though there'll usually be a picturesque sprinkling (or more) of snow on the ground and in the trees, there may also be only a few hours of semi-daylight every 24 hours. If you dress warmly there's no reason why you can't spend a reasonable length of time out of doors in winter. Locals enjoy ice-fishing and skating on the frozen lakes, tobogganing (wherever they can find a slope), and skiing. Theatre and concert-going is at its peak in winter.

The time in-between seasons is, well, in between. April and October have cold, sharp, wintry days as well as mild, spring-like or autumnal ones. There's often a lot of slush underfoot, particularly during the late March and April thaw.

Maps

Thankfully the age of deliberately distorted Soviet maps is over. Good, accurate town and regional maps are sold cheaply and are widely available in bookshops, news kiosks, petrol stations and hotels in the Baltic states. Some of them are available in the west too, but at higher prices. The only map you really need to buy in advance is one of the region as a whole.

City & Town Maps Good cheap accurate street plans – often highlighting hotels, restaurants and places of visitor interest – are widely available in practically every Baltic city and town. Avoid street maps published before 1990 which are likely to contain Soviet 'mistakes'. A good half of street names listed will also be out of date, now that the Baltic states have jettisoned communist names.

The Baltics' leading map publisher, Jāņa Sēta in Rīga (see Rīga – Maps), publishes a wide range of top quality 1:15,000 or 1:7000 scale maps covering most cities and towns in Latvia, Lithuania and Estonia. These cost US$1.40 and are distributed in all three Baltic states. If you're planning to visit the major towns and cities in all three Baltic states, it is worth picking up a copy of its excellent pocket-size, spiral-bound *Baltic States Road Atlas* (1:500,000), published in 1996 and costing US$4.50. It contains 56 city and town maps as well as road maps covering the entire Baltic region. Jāņa Sēta also sells topographic maps from the former Soviet army general staff.

The Vilnius-based Briedis map publishers (see Vilnius – Maps) produce maps of most towns in Lithuania and some in Latvia, as well as a 1:40,000 scale map of Kaliningrad, which is only readily available in Vilnius. The German publisher Verlag Gerhard Rautenberg (see Books) put out an *Aktueller Stadtplan* (City Map) in 1993. The scale is 1:10,000. The map is not easily available in Kaliningrad either but you can order it by post from the publisher – who also publishes a 1938 map of the city, showing its pre-WWII layout with Nazi street names, and other Kaliningrad Region maps, atlases and guide books.

Country Maps The excellent 1996 *Eesti Maanteede Atlas* (Estonian Road Atlas) in paperback, covering the whole of Estonia at 1:200,000 scale, is invaluable to anybody spending any time beyond Tallinn. It's fairly widely available in Estonian bookshops, hotels and kiosks for up to 95 EEK.

For Lithuania there is the *Atlasas '95-96* published by Briedis publishers and sold for around 16.80 litų. It is the most widely available atlas of its kind in Lithuania, covers the whole of Lithuania in useful detail, and can be picked up at practically every petrol station as well as bookshops.

The best country maps of Latvia are produced by Jāņa Sēta (see City & Town Maps). Its wide selection includes a road map of Latvia in 1:400,000 scale for around 2.40 lati; a road map of Latvia (1:650,000; 0.50 lati), which includes general information in English about the country and a detailed A4-size map of Rīga; and an administrative map of Latvia (1:400,000; 1.20 lati) with the regional divisions marked.

Jāņa Sēta publishes road maps of Lithuania and Estonia too. The *Lithuania Road Map* (1:500,000; 15 litų) includes city maps of Vilnius, Kaunas, Klaipėda, Šiauliai and Panevežys, while the *Estonia Road Map* (1:500,000; 46 EEK) has city maps of Tallinn, Tartu and Pärnu.

In Kaliningrad you can pick up the locally produced 1995 *Kaliningrad Oblast* map of the Kaliningrad Region, in Russian, cheaply and readily. It's at 1:200,000 scale and seems accurate. Verlag Gerhard Rautenberg (see the City Maps section) has published *Das nördliche Ostpreussen* (Northern East Prussia), a map of the Kaliningrad Region with old German place names given beside the new Russian ones.

Regional Maps A good map of the whole Baltic states is useful for planning and needs

to be bought in advance. *Lithuania Estonia Latvia* (Cartographia, Budapest), *Estonia, Latvia, Lithuania* (Bartholomew, Edinburgh) and *Baltische Staaten* (Ravenstein Verlag, Bad Soden am Taunas, Germany) are very similar 1:850,000 scale maps of the three countries plus most of the Kaliningrad Region, which will be adequate for most travellers.

In-country, Briedis' 1:1,000,000 scale motoring map, *Via Baltica – Baltic States Road Map*, with coverage from Helsinki to Warsaw, is worth picking up. It is sold for around US$2 in most bookshops.

What to Bring

Don't bring too much! If you only plan to stay in the larger towns and cities, you can buy anything or everything when you arrive. If you're going to be doing much travelling around, a backpack is the easiest receptacle to carry your things in. A light day-pack is also useful. Unless you plan to camp or sleep out, a sleeping bag is not necessary. A towel and soap will be useful if you're staying in cheap hotels, which don't always provide them. A universal sink plug is very useful – as is an adapter plug for electrical appliances and a good wad of tissues or toilet paper (to be carried with you at all times!).

In summer, bring a light waterproof garment or an umbrella to protect you from the odd rainshower. In spring and autumn there may be cold snaps, so take some warm headgear, gloves, a coat (or at least a warm leather or padded jacket) and either thermal underwear or some very warm trousers. In winter, there is snow (lots of it!) so bring some good waterproof boots (also handy for when the thaw sets in). Your clothing should be able to cope with permanent subzero temperatures, and thermal underwear is essential if you're sensitive to the cold. Whether it rains, hails or shines, an indestructible pair of shoes or boots tough enough to combat the most invincible of cobblestones and icy sidewalks is a definite must.

Bring spare tapes for your camcorder, contact lens solutions and any special medicines you might need. Western toiletries are readily available, although you might want to bring condoms (locally produced condoms are available; quality not guaranteed). A small torch (flashlight) and an alarm clock might also come in handy. In summer bring mosquito repellent or coils. An electric water-heating element will enable you to purify suspect tap water by boiling it and to make your own hot drinks. A Swiss army knife never goes amiss. If you like your food spicy, bring your own Tabasco sauce.

SUGGESTED ITINERARIES

Here are some suggested itineraries ranging from a week long stay in the Baltics to a six month stint:

One week
a whistlestop capital-tour of Vilnius, Rīga and Tallinn
Two weeks
a whistlestop regional-tour taking in the three capitals and Kaliningrad with a couple of day trips to the Lithuanian, Latvian or Estonian coast; to the Gauja National Park in Latvia, the Estonian islands or the Lahemaa National Park
One month
Vilnius to Kaliningrad, travelling up the Curonian Spit to Nida, Klaipēda and Šiauliai taking in the Hill of Crosses; up to Rīga, with day trips to Jūrmala and the Gauja National Park; to Pärnu, Haapsalu and across to the Estonian islands; up to Tallinn, with a day trip to Paldiski through the Lahemaa National Park to Narva, and back down the eastern realm through Tartu and Daugavpils to Vilnius
Two months
an extension of the one month tour with day trips from Vilnius to Kaunas and Trakai; an exploration of the east of the Kaliningrad Region en route to Kaliningrad; stop-overs in Liepāja, Ventspils and the Kurzeme region on your way to Rīga; several days in south-eastern Estonia and a bicycle or canoeing trip
Six months
Enough time to rewrite this book!

HIGHLIGHTS

Savouring the long white nights Estonia shares with St Petersburg; scouring the Baltic coastline for amber; scaling the sand dunes of Nida; or sampling the local cuisine, including Lithuania's infamous Zeppelin and Latvia's disgusting black Balzams, are just some of the joys to be found in the Baltic states and Kaliningrad Region.

Vilnius has the largest Old Town in eastern Europe, and a statue of Frank Zappa. The Kaliningrad Region is home to the world's only opencast amber mine and the ugliest Soviet building of all time. Rīga has what must be the cheapest (drinkable) champagne in the world, and Estonia has some great islands and bogs to explore.

And finally, in all three Baltic states, while their Soviet past has been well and truly dumped, quirky reminders of the former Soviet days are making something of a comeback – a legless Lenin, deserted army barracks, and nostalgic nightclubs touting cabaret acts dressed in Red Army uniforms or paratroopers' undershirts are all part of the act. It's a Baltic show that should not be missed!

VISAS & DOCUMENTS
Passport

Your number one document is your passport. Make sure its validity extends to at least two months after the end of your Baltic travels as this may be a requirement for some visas.

Visas for the Baltic States

The three Baltic states all issue their own visas. All three states have lengthening lists of nationalities that don't need visas. Since 1992 all three have adhered to 'common visa space', meaning that for most western nationalities, if you have a visa for any one of the three Baltic states, it is good (for the term of its validity) for the other two as well. Even if you don't need a visa for the country or countries you're visiting, you still need to carry your passport.

Estonia, however, has backtracked on this to a certain extent. Since March 1993, it has only recognised Latvian and Lithuanian visas for the passport holders of some 32 countries. And in 1997, Estonia recognised reciprocal visa-free travel with Norway and Finland while drafting a preliminary agreement with Sweden. Citizens of other countries – mainly those in Africa, South America, Asia and the former USSR – need a separate Estonian visa even if they have a Latvian or Lithuanian one. Canadians and Australians should also note that even though they do not need a visa for Estonia and Lithuania, they *do* need a visa to enter Latvia.

Visas are cheaper if obtained in advance at an Estonian, Latvian or Lithuanian embassy or consulate than at the border or airport when you arrive.

To enter the Kaliningrad Region, you need a Russian visa (see Russian Visas section below).

Who Needs Visas? In early 1997, all three Baltic states require visas from all nationalities *except* the following:

Estonia
Andorra, Australia, Bulgaria, Canada, Czech Republic, Denmark, Finland, Hungary, Ireland, Japan, Latvia, Liechtenstein, Lithuania, Monaco, New Zealand, Norway, Poland, San Marino, Slovakia, UK, USA and the Vatican City
Latvia
Czech Republic, Estonia, Denmark, Hungary, Ireland, Lithuania, Poland, Slovakia, UK and the USA
Lithuania
Australia, Bulgaria, Canada, Cyprus, Czech Republic, Denmark, Estonia, Hungary, Iceland, Ireland, Italy, Japan, Korea, Latvia, Liechtenstein, Malta, Norway, Poland, Slovakia, Slovenia, Switzerland, UK, USA, Vatican City and Venezuela

Types of Visa Each Baltic state issues three main types of visa: transit, single entry, and multiple entry. The fees you have to pay for them vary enormously. The costs given here give a general idea of what you can expect to pay.

Lithuanian visas are free to Austrian and Swedish citizens.

Transit These are non-extendible visas valid for 48 or 72 hours. Single entry transit visas cost from US$10, the cheapest being Estonian and Latvian visas issued at embassies or consulates. Single entry transit visas issued on arrival at the border usually cost twice as much. Note that Lithuania does not issue

transit visas at its borders (only single entry – see below). Estonia and Latvia issue double entry or multiple entry transit visas too, but these are dearer and are only available from embassies and consulates, not on arrival.

Single Entry Embassies and consulates issue these visas for periods up to a usual maximum of six months for Estonia and 90 days for Latvia or Lithuania. Single entry visas obtained on arrival are only available for 10 days. They can be extended. From embassies or consulates, single entry visas cost between US$10 and US$25. On arrival in Latvia they cost around US$12; on arrival in Lithuania around US$40; and on arrival in Estonia, US$35.

Because of the Baltic states common visa space, a single entry visa for any of the three countries allows you to travel back and forth across the Estonian-Latvian and Latvian-Lithuanian borders as many times as you like within its term of validity, provided you don't leave the Baltics during that time. Not all border officials seem to understand this detail; insist on your rights.

Multiple Entry These are issued for various periods up to 12 months, but are only available from embassies and consulates – not on arrival. Latvian multiple entry visas are valid for a stay of up to three months within one calendar year. They cost between US$50 and US$120.

Applying for Visas You can get visas in advance at Estonian, Latvian and Lithuanian embassies and consulates in most countries. On arrival in Latvia, you will only be issued a 10 day single entry visa at the port or airport, and a 48 hour transit visa at land borders. Note that visas are no longer issued at the Russian-Latvian border. On arrival in Lithuania, only citizens of countries belonging to the European Union or people arriving from a country where there is not a Lithuanian Consulate will be issued with a 10 day single entry visa. Estonia issues a 72 hour transit visa or a 10 day single entry visa at borders to passport holders of the following countries:

Austria, Belgium, France, Germany, Israel, Italy, Korea, Luxembourg, Malta, Netherlands, Portugal, South Africa, Spain, Sweden, Switzerland

Embassies and consulates usually process visa applications in a few days at most, although some do offer a substantially more expensive 'fast lane' visa which usually takes no more than 24 hours.

When applying at an embassy or consulate you normally need to supply your passport, a completed application form, and one photo. For a transit visa you may have to show a visa for the country you're going on to. Invitations are *not* required for single entry and transit visas. Applications for a multiple entry visa, however, have to be accompanied by an official invitation from an officially registered organisation in the country to which you are applying for a visa.

Visa Extensions Once in the Baltics you can extend a single entry visa. In Estonia go to the National Immigration Board (☎ 2-664 442) at Lai 38/40, Tallinn. In Latvia go to the visa office (☎ 7219 119, 7219 834) in the Department of Immigration and Citizenship at Raiņa bulvāris 5, Rīga. You must apply at least three days before the expiry of your existing visa. Single entry visas can also be upgraded to multiple entry here. In Lithuania go to the immigration department (☎ 22-725 864, 22-725 853) at Saltoniškių 19 or the immigration office (☎ 22-756 453) at Verkių 3, Vilnius.

Russian Visas
You need a Russian visa to go to the Kaliningrad Region as it is part of Russia. You also need a Russian visa if you are travelling through mainland Russia on the way to or from the Baltic states. A Russian visa is a separate document, not stamped in or attached to your passport, listing the cities you have been granted permission to stay in and the dates of your stay in the country. It

is an exit permit too – so don't lose it or you'll have a tough time actually leaving the country. A listing of Russian embassies can be found in the Kaliningrad Region chapter.

Note that if you intend to continue on to St Petersburg for example after completing your Kaliningrad and Baltic stint, you must be in possession of a double or multiple entry Russian visa. Any trip to other parts of Russia from the Kaliningrad Region involves crossing foreign territory before re-entering Russia.

Types of Russian Visa There are six types of Russian visas available to foreign visitors, all of which are non-extendible: tourist, private, business, transit, student and 'on-the-spot' visas.

A tourist visa is intended primarily for tourism but can also cover business and some other trips. One of the things you're supposed to produce when applying for it is confirmation of already booked accommodation, which can be complicated and expensive to get. Private visas need to be supported by a personal invitation. Business visas require a letter of invitation from a Russian company guaranteeing to put you up for your stay. A transit visa, valid for 48 hours, is for 'passing through' and does not require proof of accommodation. Student visas are flexible, extendible and require proof of enrolment at an accredited Russian school or university. And 'on-the-spot' are basically fast-track business visas issued at airports by InTourist. To get one of these you have to be met at the airport by a representative of a Russian company who will 'invite' you to Russia. This is the only type of visa which can be obtained at borders.

Applying for a Russian Visa At some Russian embassies and consulates, getting any kind of visa can be a time consuming, frustrating experience even once you have got all the paperwork together. The Russian embassies in the three Baltic capitals are notoriously bureaucratic. At embassies and consulates in other major capitals the process is less taxing though usually quite slow. If there's any kind of travel agency involved in planning your trip then it's easiest to let them handle your visa application, although it will cost more. Some specialist agents have their own short cuts and arrangements which will greatly simplify things.

To apply yourself, you need a passport (valid at least a month beyond your return), three photos, a completed application form including entry/exit dates, a handling fee (typically US$30 or so), and the relevant invitation or proof of accommodation depending on the type of visa you are applying for. This last item means, for a tourist visa, confirmation of hotel bookings – officially, but in practice not necessarily, for your whole stay; for a transit visa, a ticket or ticket voucher with confirmed times and dates; and for an ordinary visa, an invitation from an organisation or private person. Once your documents have been handed over you should receive your visa within 10 days. Most embassies also offer a 'quick visa', issued within three of four days for at least twice the price.

Obtaining the necessary invitation or proof of confirmed accommodation from establishments in the Kaliningrad Region can be particularly tough. There are a couple of agencies in Kaliningrad who provide visa support (see Kaliningrad Region – Facts for the Visitor) but they are not very 'western' in their customer-relations skills and attempting to get a response from them, let alone the vital documentation, can be tiresome.

One way around this is to plan a trip that includes St Petersburg or another destination in Russia, which requires applying for a multiple entry visa. The visa can usually be issued on the strength of a St Petersburg booking – but remember when you fill in your application form to mention Kaliningrad as a destination. If the destination on your visa reads only St Petersburg then you will not be permitted entry to the Kaliningrad Region.

Even if you do not actually intend visiting St Petersburg you may in fact find that contacting the St Petersburg International Hostel (☎ 812-329 8018; fax 812-329 8019; email ryh@ryh.spb.su; http://www.spb.su/ryh) at 3rd Sovetskaya Ulitsa 28, St Petersburg, is the easiest, quickest and least painful way of obtaining that required 'invitation' or 'proof of booking'. It is registered with the Russian Ministry of Foreign Affairs, meaning that it can issue invitations in support of visa applications, recognised by all Russian consulates. The hostel charges US$25/50 for visa support for a single/double entry tourist visa and it also requires that you pay a non-refundable deposit of one night's accommodation in the hostel (even if you do not intend staying there). Visa support bookings can also be made via fax or email; the necessary visa support invitation is then faxed back to you. The hostel's mailing address (via Finnish post) is St Petersburg International Hostel, PO Box 8, SF-53501, Lappeenranta, Finland. For visa support and advice you can also contact Russian Youth Hostels & Tourism (☎ 310-379 4316; fax 310-379 8420; email 71573.2010@compuserve.com), 409 N Pacific Coast Hwy, 106/390, Redondo Beach, CA 90277, USA.

Once in Russia (be it Kaliningrad or St Petersburg!), *all* Russian visas have to be registered with OVIR (Otdel Viz I Registratsii), the Visa and Registration Department, within three days of your arrival in the country. If you're staying in a hotel, you will be asked to surrender your passport and visa when you check in so that the hotel administration can do this for you. Officially, the company or organisation who invited you to Russia is responsible for your registration. If you register your visa after 72 hours you have to pay a fine of around US$10. If you leave Russia with your visa not registered at all, the Russian customs officials can fine you.

HIV/AIDS Testing You do *not* need an AIDS test to apply for a Russian visa. An AIDS test is only required for foreigners staying in Russia for longer than three months. In the Baltic states, you only require an AIDS test if you intend applying for a residence permit, which you need if you stay longer than three months.

Belarus Visas

All western visitors need a visa to enter Belarus. Trains between Poland and Lithuania, unless they take the direct Suwałki-Šeštokai route, pass across about 60 km of Belarusian territory en route. If you're taking one of these trains you need a Belarusian visa. Belarusian border guards will gladly march you off the train to the immigration office to make you buy a transit visa for around US$30 to US$50. Visas are *not* issued at road borders.

There are Belarusian embassies in all three Baltic capitals, each of which issues visas. To apply for a visa you need your passport, a completed application form, two passport photographs and an invitation. Invitations in support of visa applications are sold for around US$4 from the Viliota Travel Agency (☎ 22-652 238) at Basanavičiaus 15, Vilnius, which issues them on the spot. You can then trudge to the Belarusian embassy and line up to submit your application. The embassy issues tourist visas, valid for one month from the date you stipulate on your application form, for around US$20. It usually takes three days but it does more costly 'fast-track' visas too.

Other Visas

Don't forget that you may need visas for other countries on your trip – such as Poland, where (at the time of writing) citizens of some western nations still need visas – and make arrangements to get them in good time.

Photocopies

It is strongly advisable to make photocopies of all vital documents, including your passport, airline tickets, driving licence and other important travel documents, and keep them in a separate place to the originals. Jot down the serial numbers of your travellers' cheques and your credit card details too. Leave a copy of all these things with someone at home.

Travel Insurance

A fully comprehensive travel insurance policy to cover theft, loss and medical problems is a good idea, especially if you intend to do a lot of travelling. A policy which covers the costs of being flown out of the country for treatment is a definite bonus, given the still limited in-country facilities.

Driving Licence & Permits

If you are planning to drive to or in the region, an International Driving Permit (IDP) will be useful, although, if you don't have one, your own national licence (if from a European country) should suffice – see the Getting There & Away and Getting Around chapters. It's obtainable, usually cheaply, from your local automobile association such as the AA or RAC in Britain. However, British driving licence holders should note that licences not bearing a photograph of the holder have been known to upset traffic police so try to get an IDP before you arrive. You will also need your vehicle's registration document. In Estonia and Latvia accident insurance is compulsory.

Hostel Card

An International Hostel Federation (IHF) card brings discounts of up to 20% in most hostels in the three Baltic states. Hostelling organisations in each of the Baltic capitals are affiliated to the IHF and the number of hostels under their control is expected to increase as the hostel scene develops. Don't expect any discounts in the Kaliningrad Region; hostels need to make their way there first.

Student & Youth Cards

The two main cards pretty flash around the Baltic states these days are the International Student Identity Card (ISIC) and the Euro<26 card, the International Youth Card of the Federation of International Youth Travel Organisation (FIYTO), available to people who are 26 or under but not a student. Both are accepted in dozens of establishments in larger towns and cities, entitling card holders to discounts of up to 50% on theatre and cinema tickets, museum entrance fees and nightclubs. Some hotels also offer discounts to card holders. Both cards are issued at special Student and Youth travel agencies; you'll need your passport and two passport photos. They can also issue you with a list of places in the Baltics where your card will 'talk'.

Both cards are completely useless in the Kaliningrad Region.

Senior Cards
There are few discounts available to older people; a handful of museums in Tallinn will give you a discount off the entrance fee but that is about it.

EMBASSIES
Since 1991 the Baltic states have opened numerous new diplomatic missions overseas, most of which are open during regular office hours. Many countries have also set up their own embassies or missions in the Baltic capitals. Details of diplomatic missions for each of the Baltic states can be found under Embassies & Consulates in the relevant Facts for the Visitor chapters later in the book.

CUSTOMS
All three Baltic states ban the import or export of firearms, ammunition, explosives, drugs or narcotics without special permission. Latvia and Lithuania also prohibit the import and export of pornography. Beyond that the customs rules vary and are subject to change. Baltic embassies and consulates should be able to tell you the latest if there's anything you're concerned about.

Customs forms are available at border points if you're bringing into the Baltic states anything you think might be queried when you take it out again – such as hordes of money, works of art, furs or jewellery. If you think that a painting or other cultural object you want to buy in the Baltic states may attract customs duty or require special permission to export, check with the shop or seller before you buy.

Further details on customs restrictions for each of the Baltic states are given in the relevant Facts for the Visitor chapters later in the book. Customs restrictions for the Kaliningrad Region can be found in the Kaliningrad Region chapter.

MONEY
Baltic travel will also improve your mental arithmetic, because, if you travel through all three states and the Kaliningrad Region, you'll end up using four different currencies.

Until 1992, when the three Baltic states started introducing their own currencies, the whole region used the Russian rouble. The Kaliningrad Region still does, given it is part of Russia.

Prices in the Estonian, Latvian and Lithuanian chapters of this book are given in local currency – Estonian *krooni* (EEK), Latvian *lati* and Lithuanian *litų* – whose values have remained completely settled ever since they were introduced. Prices in the Kaliningrad Region chapter are given in US$ as the value of the Russian rouble is subject to fluctuation. Currency information specific to each of the Baltic states can be found in the relevant Facts for the Visitor chapters later in the book. The Russian rouble is discussed in the Kaliningrad Region chapter.

The best currencies to bring into the Baltics are US dollars or Deutschmarks, although most western currencies are perfectly acceptable and can easily be exchanged (especially Finnish marks and Swedish krona in Estonia). Get rid of Polish złoty, Russian roubles, Ukrainian currency and other east European money before you enter the Baltic states. Exchange rates for them are poor. Within the Baltic states it is easy to change one Baltic currency into another, although rates are not always as favourable as with other currencies eg US dollars.

Costs
Despite their status as ex-Soviet republics there are few bargains to be had in the Baltic states. Latvia is generally the most expensive, with prices comparable to those of Scandinavia. Accommodation is pricey and will be your biggest cost, especially in Estonia. Goods in the shops vary from Helsinki-priced (which means some of the

most expensive in western Europe) to cheap, but then that usually applies to the quality too. Eating out in Lithuania is still ridiculously cheap and by far the cheapest of the Baltics. Overland travel in all three is still very affordable.

Accommodation On a middle-range budget you can get comfortable homestays for about US$25 per person a night or hotel rooms for US$60 to US$80 a double. You can go a lot cheaper too – at cheap hotels, hostels or camping grounds you'll rarely pay more than US$8 or US$10 and often a lot less. Some hotels have rooms for US$5 or US$8. Then again you can go up to more than US$200 a double at the very top hotels – though US$100 to US$160 is nearer the normal top-end mark.

Food The cost of eating is on the rise, although if you avoid the establishments aimed solely at western business customers or more affluent tourists, you should end up paying no more than US$10 for an evening meal (without drinks). In Vilnius and the more provincial towns of all three Baltic states though, you'll rarely pay more than US$4 for the same. Everywhere, you can cut costs to the bone – US$1 or less – by eating at the cheap canteens or cafeterias, some of which serve perfectly adequate food, and by buying some of your own food at markets and shops. If you do patronise the top-end places, a meal will typically be in the US$20 to US$30 range – or more.

Transport This is getting more expensive but is still cheap by western standards. Fares vary a bit from country to country but, very roughly, US$3 will take you 150 km by bus or 200 km by train. A bus or train from Tallinn to Vilnius – the length of the region – is about US$17 at the time of writing. Things get more expensive if you take to the air or use a lot of taxis or guided tours, but you probably won't need these much unless you're in a big hurry.

Petrol prices are fairly constant; that is,

constantly rising. In early 1997, western-grade petrol was around US$0.50 a litre.

Two-Tier Prices Gone are the days when westerners had to line up at a separate 'foreigners' desk to buy air tickets, or expect, as a matter of course, to pay twice as much as a local would for the same hotel room. There is one desk and one price for all now in every hotel, restaurant and travel bureau in the cities and larger towns. A two or even three-tier pricing system is still intact, however, in some 'Soviet-block' hotels in more provincial or predominantly Russian-populated areas. Here, CIS citizens from outside the Baltics pay about a third more than Baltic residents for the same generally grotty room, while foreigners pay a third more again.

Carrying Money
Don't be deceived by the Oliver Twist-style street kids – particularly prevalent in Rīga – that look so sweet and pitiful. Pickpockets are rife in the Baltic capitals and larger cities, and as a westerner you automatically attract attention. A money belt worn inside your clothing is a good idea. Always divide your money up and carry it in several different places on your person and in your baggage. Leaving a secret stash in your hotel room is *only* a good idea if you're staying in a more expensive hotel.

Cash
Make sure whatever currency you bring is in pristine condition. Marked, torn, or simply very used notes will be refused. US one dollar notes issued before 1990 are not generally accepted either.

Get rid of smaller denomination notes and coins as they cannot be exchanged in other countries. Baltic currencies cannot be exchanged in the Kaliningrad Region, but Russian roubles can be exchanged in the Baltic states. If you are travelling to other parts of Russia after Kaliningrad it is worth changing extra money as the exchange rate is generally more favourable in the Kaliningrad Region.

Travellers Cheques

A limited amount of travellers' cheques are useful because of the protection they offer against theft. It is difficult to find places to exchange them though once you are out of the cities. American Express and Thomas Cook have a couple of offices in the Baltic states where you can get replacement cheques. Eurocheques can be cashed in most banks. Forget cheques full stop in the Kaliningrad Region.

ATMs

Automatic teller machines (ATMs) accepting Visa and MasterCard/Eurocard are equally widespread in the cities and larger towns (except the Kaliningrad Region). Some are inside banks and post offices but the majority are on the streets, enabling you to get cash 24 hours a day. Most ATMs are multi-lingual, using the five main European languages.

Credit Cards

Credit cards are widely accepted in hotels, restaurants and shops, especially at the upper end of the market. Visa, MasterCard/Eurocard, Diners Club and American Express all crop up. One thing they are essential for is renting a car. You can get cash advances on Visa and MasterCard/Eurocard in the cities and larger towns although once in the provinces, cards become less useful. Banks will generally tack a 2 to 5% commission on to the amount of a cash advance. They will also want to see your passport before agreeing to make the advance. Major hotels often give cash advance on credit cards too.

International Transfers

Direct bank-to-bank wire transfer is possible at most major banks (see relevant city sections) although you may need to open a bank account to do so. Usually a commission of up to 5% is charged on the amount you want to transfer; the service takes about five days.

Currency Exchange

Every town will have somewhere you can change cash. Usually it's either a bank, or a special exchange office or kiosk doing nothing but currency exchange. The latter crop up in all sorts of places but particularly transport terminals – airports, bus stations and train stations. Exchange rates do vary from one outlet to another. The posted rates usually take account of commission. For opening hours see Business Hours below.

Black Market

In Kaliningrad there's a so-called black market. Individuals with money to change hang around stations, banks, markets, hotels and so on. You might get a slightly better rate from such people, but you might also get ripped off – and it is illegal.

Tipping & Bargaining

It's fairly common, though not compulsory, to tip waiters 5 or 10% by rounding up the bill. A few waiters may try to tip themselves by 'not having' any change.

Some bargaining (but not a lot) goes on at flea markets. Savings are not likely to be more than 10 or 20% of the initial asking price.

POST & COMMUNICATIONS
Post

Mail service in and out of the three Baltic states is up to western European standards – if that is anything to go by!

Sending Mail Letters and postcards take about two to four days to western Europe and seven to 10 days to North America. Occasionally a letter or parcel might go astray for a couple of weeks but generally everything arrives; if you come up against any problems remind yourself that until a few years ago all mail and telephone calls had to be routed through Moscow and took far longer (if they got through at all).

If you are travelling to one of the Baltic states after Kaliningrad, it is better to save your mail to post there. From Kaliningrad, the post is still quite erratic. Mail takes up to seven days to reach European countries and up to two weeks to more distant destinations.

Comparative Postal Rates from the Baltic States

	Domestic	To CIS	To Europe	To USA
Estonia	2.50 EEK (US$0.19)	3.50 EEK (US$0.27)	4 EEK (US$0.31)	7 EEK (US$0.55)
Latvia	0.08 lati (US$0.16)	0.12 lati (US$0.24)	0.16 lati (US$0.32)	0.24 lati (US$0.48)
Lithuania	0.40 litų (US$0.10)	1.20 litų (US$0.30)	1.20 litų (US$0.30)	1.20 litų (US$0.30)

Postcards will generally not arrive at all unless you stick them in an envelope.

Buy your stamps at a post office (Estonian: *postkontor*; Latvian: *pasts*; Lithuanian: *paštas*; Russian: *pochta*), and post your mail there too. The table above shows the cost of sending a postcard or a letter up to 20 grams in early 1997.

A one kg air-mail parcel costs about US$10 to anywhere in the world from Lithuania, US$12 to US$16 from Estonia, and US$8 to US$12 from Latvia. Expensive international express-mail services for letters and parcels are available in the capital cities.

Receiving Mail Delivery times for mail sent to the Baltic states from other countries are generally similar to those for outward mail. The way in which addresses are written conform to western norms:

Kazimiera Jones
Veidenbauma iela 35-17
LV-5432 Ventspils
Latvia

Veidenbauma iela 35-17 means Veidenbaum Street, building No 35, flat No 17. Postcodes in Estonia are the letters EE plus four digits, in Latvia LV plus four digits, and in Lithuania LT plus four digits.

In the Kaliningrad Region, addresses are written in the same way as they are throughout Russia, ie in reverse order:

Russia
654321 g. Kaliningrad
ulitsa Gorbachova
d. 85 kv. 91
Ivanov, Alexey Vladimirovich

The 654321 is the postcode, g stands for *gorod* (city or town), d for *dom* (house) and kv for *kvartira* (flat).

For people wanting to receive mail while on the move, there are poste-restante mail services in the central post office in Tallinn and at the post office next to the train station at Stacijas laukums 1 in Rīga. Letters should be addressed with the full name of the recipient followed by one of the formats below:

Poste Restante   Poste Restante
Rīga 50   Central Post Office
LV-1050   Narva maantee 1
Latvia   EE-0001 Tallinn
                           Estonia

Poste restante is kept for one month at both post offices.

Telephone

Telephone services in the three Baltic states have been completely overhauled since the demise of the Soviet Union, with new exchanges, allowing direct digital connections to the west replacing the slow and decrepit, analogue Soviet system routed through Moscow. International calls can be made from practically every private phone you'll come across, as well as all the new public cardphones in the streets.

Until the restructuring is complete (estimated to be around 2003) little quirks and idiosyncrasies within each of the three systems will remain. Even then, making local and international calls from each Baltic country will differ slightly.

The region does have some things in common! Any calls can be made from the phone in your hotel room (markedly more expensive and best avoided) and from public cardphones, found on the street and at strategic locations in towns such as bus and train stations, post offices and hotel lobbies.

In some rural areas and in the entire Kaliningrad Region, you will encounter old token-operated phone booths. These Soviet monstrosities – which *only allow local calls* – are hotly pursued worldwide by phonebox collectors who have been known to install the entire Doctor Who set-up in their homes.

Throughout this book, city codes are listed in brackets under the relevant town heading. International country codes are Estonia 372, Latvia 371, Lithuania 370, Russia 7.

Estonia Public cardphones accept chip cards, worth 30, 50 or 100 EEK, which are widely available at post offices, hotels and most kiosks.

Most telephone numbers in Tallinn are digital and have seven digits, compared to the old six digit analogue numbers. On the islands and in some remote areas, five digit analogue numbers are still used.

Local Calls Simply dial the number of the subscriber. In Tallinn, you need to dial 2 before the subscriber's number if you are dialling an analogue six digit Tallinn number from a digital number.

National Calls To call other cities in Estonia dial 8, followed by the city code and telephone number. If you are dialling an analogue six digit number in Tallinn, dial 2 before the city code.

International Calls The access code for international calls is 8-00, followed by the country code, city code and telephone number. If you are calling from an analogue phone, you need to wait for a dial tone after dialling 8. To call AT&T dial 8-00 8001 001.

Calling Estonia from Abroad Dial the country code (372) followed by the city code, dropping the first 2 of the city code (ie, no city code for Tallinn, Tartu 7, and so on). However, if you are calling a six digit

number in Tallinn, you still need to dial 2 before dialling the subscriber's number.

Latvia Public card phones accept *telekartes*, worth one, five or 10 lati, which can be bought from kiosks, shops and post offices. New coin-operated phones, accepting everything from one santīmi to 2 lati coins, can be found at some bus and train stations and in hospitals. In more remote areas and some cities such as Daugavpils, the old token-operated phones from which only local calls can be made are still quite common. These accept 'žetons' (0.4 santīmi), which are available from kiosks and post offices.

Most telephone numbers in Rīga, Cēsis and Ventspils are digital and have seven digits, compared to the old five or six digit analogue numbers. Within a few years, however, Latvia's telephone system will be the first of the three Baltic states to be completely digitalised, meaning that all numbers will have seven digits. Until this happens though, numbers are changing every month. If you find that a number listed in this book is no longer valid, call the English-speaking Lattelekom helpline (☎ 079, 7282 222).

Local Calls To call another digital number from a digital phone, simply dial the subscriber's number. To call a digital number from a five or six digit analogue phone dial 1, wait for dial tone, followed by the subscriber's number. If you are calling an analogue telephone number from a digital phone, dial 2 followed by the subscriber's number.

National Calls From a digital phone, you do not need a city code when calling another seven digit digital number in Latvia; simply dial the subscriber's number. If you are calling a five or six digit analogue number though from a digital phone, you need to dial the city code.

Calling from an analogue phone to another analogue phone, you need to dial 8, wait for the dial tone, dial 2, followed by the city code. If you are calling a digital number from an analogue phone, you do not need the city code; simply dial 8, wait for the tone, then 2, followed by the subscriber's number.

International Calls From digital phones, the international access code is 00, followed by the country code, city code and subscriber's number.

You cannot make direct international calls from an analogue phone. If you want to you can book a call through an operator (☎ 1-116) which can take anything from 10 minutes to an hour to get through. It is probably easier though to use a cardphone on the street, from which a direct international call can easily be made.

Calling Latvia from Abroad If you are calling a seven digit digital number, simply dial the country code (371) followed by the subscriber's number. You do not need a city code.

If the number you are calling has five or six digits, you need a city code; dial the country code, city code and subscriber's number.

Lithuania & Kaliningrad Region The process of switching from analogue to digital lines has not yet started in Lithuania or the Kaliningrad Region. However, international calls can still be made from all private phones and public card phones.

Public cardphones in Lithuania accept magnetic strip cards (tear the perforated corner off to use), sold for 3.45 to 28.32 litų from news kiosks and post offices. In Kaunas, some Vilnius suburbs and rural areas, you will still find the old Soviet phones from which only local calls can be made. These phones used to accept tokens which are no longer sold, meaning you can just pick up the hand-set and dial!

Public cardphones are not so common in the Kaliningrad Region. There are many old token-operated phones from which only local calls can be made. Tokens for these are still sold in most kiosks and post offices for US$0.10.

Local Calls Completely straightforward – just dial the subscriber's number!

National Calls To call other cities in Lithuania, dial 8, wait for the tone, then dial the city code and telephone number. The same applies for calls to other cities within the Kaliningrad Region.

International Calls To make an international call from Lithuania or the Kaliningrad Region, dial 8, wait for the tone, then dial 10, followed by the country code, city code and telephone number.

Calling Lithuania or Kaliningrad Region from Abroad To call Lithuania, dial the country code (370) followed by the city code, dropping the first 2 of the city code (ie Vilnius 2, Kaunas 7, and so on). To call the Kaliningrad Region dial the country code for Russia (7), followed by the regional code (011), then the city code, dropping the first 2 (ie Kaliningrad 7-0112, Svetlogorsk 7-011533, and so on).

Former USSR Regional Codes If you are calling from an analogue phone in Estonia or Latvia, or any phone in Lithuania and the Kaliningrad Region, the former USSR regional codes for the Baltics and other former Soviet republics still work. This means that calls between the Baltic states or Russia in effect become national calls (as opposed to international calls), ie dial 8, wait for the tone, followed by the regional code and city code.

Former USSR regional codes include Estonia 014, Latvia 013, Lithuania 012, St Petersburg 812, Moscow 095, Kaliningrad 011, Minsk 017, Kiev 044.

Costs Most hotels add a 5 to 10% service charge to calls made from your room. In Estonia, a one minute long distance call costs 1.5 EEK (US$0.11) within Estonia; 5 EEK (US$0.40) to Latvia, Lithuania and Russia. All telephone calls are 25% cheaper between 10 pm to 7 am.

In Latvia it's 0.08 lati (US$0.16) per

minute within Latvia; 0.20 lati (US$0.40) to Estonia or Lithuania; and 0.58 lati (US$1.16) to Russia. Calls are 30% cheaper at weekends, and on weekdays between 8 pm and 7 am. Local calls between two analogue phones are free.

In Lithuania local calls are still free although this is expected to change. Intercity calls in Lithuania are 0.20 litų (US$0.05) within Lithuania; 1.65 litų (US$0.41) to Latvia or Estonia; and 3.57 litų (US$0.89) to Russia.

In the Kaliningrad Region calls made within a 200 km radius are US$0.24, within 600 km US$0.35 and up to 3000 km US$0.60 a minute. Calls to the Baltic states are US$0.87 a minute and to European Russia US$1.23 a minute (41 times more expensive than when the first edition of this book was researched).

The table below shows the cost, at the time of writing, of a one-minute call to various parts of the world.

Fax, Telegraph & Email

Practically every hotel and organisation in the Baltic states is contactable by fax. There are reasonably priced public fax services, both outgoing and incoming, in the main cities throughout the region, mainly at post offices and in all major hotels.

Telegrams cost US$0.39 a word to send from Estonia, for instance, to western Europe. They can be sent from any post or telegraph office and reach most European countries well within 48 hours; an 'urgent' telegram is US$0.78 a word. Telegraph is *telegraaf* in Estonian, *telegrāfs* in Latvian, *telegrafas* in Lithuanian, and *telegraf* in Russian.

An increasing number of hotels and travel agents have email accounts, many of whom take bookings in this way too. There are cybercafés in Rīga and Vilnius from where you can send and receive your email messages. There are local access telephone numbers for Sprint in Tallinn, Rīga, Vilnius, Kaunas and Klaipėda (check out the Post & Communication sections in the relevant chapters).

BOOKS

The Baltic states have many bookshops and foreign books can be found. Some of the following books will crop up but it's better to try to get the ones you want before you go. In any case the more you read in advance, the better you'll be prepared. Local language phrasebooks and dictionaries are widely available.

Most books are published in different editions by different publishers in different countries. As a result, a book might be a hardcover rarity in one country while it's readily available in paperback in another. Fortunately, bookshops and libraries search by title or author, so your local bookshop or library is best placed to provide detailed information on the availability of the following recommendations.

International Telephone Call Charges (per minute)

	To Finland or Sweden	To Poland	To Elsewhere in Europe	To North America	To Australia
Estonia	5 EEK or 7.50 EEK (US$0.39 or US$0.59)	7.50 EEK (US$0.59)	11 EEK (US$0.87)	20 EEK (US$1.59)	33 EEK (US$2.60)
Latvia	0.71 lati (US$1.42)	0.68 lati (US$1.36)	0.98 lati (US$1.96)	1.18 lati (US$2.36)	1.30 lati (US$2.60)
Lithuania	5.80 litų (US$1.45)	3.57 litų (US$0.89)	5.80 litų (US$1.45)	10.50 litų (US$2.62)	12.39 litų (US$3.09)
Kaliningrad	US$2.45	US$2.45	US$2.45	US$3.20	US$3.20

Lonely Planet

If you're travelling to Kaliningrad and other parts of Russia, *Russia, Ukraine & Belarus – travel survival kit* is useful – 1192 pages of practical and invaluable information, and over 80 maps. If you're following the 'Scandinavian route' via the Baltics, *Scandinavian & Baltic Europe on a shoestring* is highly recommended. Lonely Planet's *Estonian Phrasebook*, *Latvian Phrasebook*, *Lithuanian Phrasebook* and *Russian Phrasebook* by James Jenkin are all handy and portable.

Guidebooks

There is a colourful variety of locally produced guides, some more useful than others. *Come to Lithuania – A Tourism and Business Guide*, published by the Lithuanian Information Institute in 1996 serves best as a reference book with lots of listings, including some hotels and travel agencies. Along similar lines is *Rīga – For Business and Tourism*, published in 1996 by the map publishers Jāņa Sēta. Useful for museum buffs is *Latvijas Muzeji – Museums of Latvia*, produced by the Latvian Museum Association in 1996. It has a brief review with opening hours and entrance fee details of every museum in Latvia. Latvian Encyclopaedia Publishers publishes small guides to *Kurzeme*, *Kuldīga* and *Ventspils*, each of which contains maps and sightseeing routes in English and Latvian. Two quality photoguides worth picking up in Estonia are *Altja* and *Saaremaa 55 Years Later*. Both contain excellent photographs shot by Estonian photographer Peeter Tooming in 1994. *Lithuania by Car* by A Semaška describes various driving routes through the country.

Worth pocketing are the city guides *Rīga, Vilnius, Kaunas, Klaipėda & Kaliningrad In Your Pocket*. The Vilnius-based publishers say a *Tallinn In Your Pocket* is coming soon. Other city guides include *Rīga This Week*, *Tallinn This Week* and *City Paper* (see Newspapers & Magazines later in this chapter).

Travel

Among the Russians by Colin Thubron, an Englishman's account of driving every-where he could in the pre-*glasnost* Soviet Union, takes in Tallinn and Rīga, and captures the gloomy, resigned mood of the time.

If you can manage to track it down, *Russia* by J G Kohl includes a quite lengthy section on the Baltic states among its German author's account of his travels in the tsarist empire in the 1840s.

Letters from Latvia written by Lucy Addison and edited by Rhona Chave is an impelling read. It is the journal of 79 year old Lucy Addison who, at the outbreak of WWII, refused to leave Latvia, but instead stayed in her country of birth to endure the Soviet, German, then Soviet again, occupations. She wrote the journal in the form of letters which could never be sent to her grandchildren in England.

Laurens Van Der Post's *Journey into Russia*, which is an account of the author's travels through Soviet Russia in the 1960s, also relates his visits to Rīga, Vilnius and Tallinn at that time.

History & Politics

The classic works in English on Baltic history are two weighty tomes – *The Baltic States: The Years of Independence 1917-40* by Georg von Rauch and *The Baltic States: Years of Dependence 1940-1980* by Romualdas Misiunas and Rein Taagepera, covering the Soviet era. These books have lengthy bibliographies if you're interested in following things up.

The Baltic States and Europe by two British scholars, John Hiden and Patrick Salmon, focuses on Baltic diplomatic history but also gives accounts of the Soviet era and of the reform movement which saw it out. *Northern Europe in the Early Modern Period* by David G Kirby also covers the Baltic states. Focusing just on one state is S C Rowell's *Lithuania Ascending: A Pagan Empire within East-Central Europe 1295-1345*.

Published in 1996 in hardback, by the Historical Institute of Latvia in association with the US Memorial Museum, is *The Holocaust in Latvia 1941-1944: The Missing Center* by Andrew Ezergailis. Its 465 pages provide a most comprehensive, insightful and balanced account of this provocative subject, addressing among other things the sensitive issue of Latvian participation in the holocaust.

General

Until recently there was a dearth of modern non-specialist books in English on the Baltic states. But the gap has been well and truly filled by *The Baltic Revolution* by Anatol Lieven. The author, who is half Irish and half Baltic German (of a family which traces its lineage back to Germanised Liv chieftains), grew up in London but spent the early 1990s as the Baltic states correspondent for the London *Times*. His book entertainingly and thoroughly surveys both the past and present of the region, and is full of unique insights and startling information (such as the phrase 'going to Rīga' is a Lithuanian colloquialism meaning 'to vomit').

The Singing Revolution by Clare traces the Baltic states' path towards their new independence through an account of travels there in 1989 and 1990. It also provides background on the Soviet and earlier periods of outside rule.

The 1980 winner of the Nobel prize for literature, Czesław Miłosz, who grew up in Vilnius in a part-Polish, part-Lithuanian family, occupies a leading position in modern Polish literature. The last chapter of his *The Captive Mind*, written in 1951-52, deals with the Soviet occupation of the Baltic states.

Forest of the Gods by Lithuanian dramatist Balys Sruoga is locally published and available in Vilnius. It is a powerful account of the author's time spent in the Stutthof Nazi concentration camp in the early 1940s. The book was censored for many years and only published in 1957, 10 years after Sruoga's death. It has since been translated in five languages.

Hell in Ice, also available locally, is the first-hand account of Lithuanian Onutė Garbštienė, who was deported to Siberia in 1941 along with her two small children who she fought to raise and keep alive.

Picture books worth a weighty glance include *Latvian National Costumes*, published by Rīga's Jāņa Sēta in 1995, and *Senoji Lietuvių Skulptūra* (The Old Lithuanian Sculpture), which presents the development of Lithuania's treasured roadside shrines and crosses through the ages (R Paknio Leidykla, 1995).

Fiction

Like many writers living under repressive governments, Estonia's most celebrated novelist, Jaan Kross, who was exiled to Siberia for eight years under Stalin, has used historical tales to address contemporary themes. *The Czar's Madman*, first published in 1978, was among the first Baltic writing to become available in English when published by Harvill in 1992. One strand of the work is woven around the true story of Timotheus von Bock, an Estonian German noble whose honesty compelled him to write to Tsar Alexander I suggesting changes in the way Russia (of which Estonia was then part) was governed. Von Bock was locked away for his pains.

The Good Republic by William Palmer tells the story of a young man in a Baltic country who, more by accident than design, gets involved in a minor way in the Nazi bureaucracy during WWII then escapes to exile in London but returns 'home' decades later to suffer unexpected nightmarish consequences from his past. The book conjures up well the atmosphere of the pre-WWII Baltics, the Soviet and Nazi occupations, and the feel of émigré life. It also lays bare the moral dilemmas facing the occupied peoples in the war years.

Bohin Manor by Tadeusz Konwicki, a leading modern Polish writer who was born in Lithuania, is set in Lithuania in the aftermath of the 1863 uprising. Using the past to comment on more contemporary events (like Jaan Kross), Konwicki evokes the tensions between locals, their Russian rulers and a Jewish outsider, as well as the foreboding and mysterious nature of the Lithuanian backwoods.

For a sense of the atmosphere of 1930s

Latvia and Estonia, track down *Venusburg*, one of Anthony Powell's early novels. Published in 1932, it tells the amusing tale of an English journalist trying unsuccessfully to make his name as a foreign correspondent amid the exiled Russian aristocrats, Baltic German intellectuals, and earnest local patriots of the era.

Foreign-Language Books

There's an enormous amount published on the Baltic states and Kaliningrad in German. *Königsberg Kaliningrad* by Henning Sietz (1992, Edition Temmen) is particularly recommended. Any decent bookshop in Germany should have a selection but enthusiasts could try writing for catalogues to Baltic-specialist booksellers and publishers such as Edition Temmen, Hohenlohestrasse 21, D-28209 Bremen; Harro von Hirschheydt, Hagebuttengang 1, D-30900 Wedemark; Mare Balticum, Helker Pflug, Rubensstrasse 7, D-50676 Köln; Neuthor-Verlag, Postfach 3402, Neuthorstrasse 3, D-64702 Michelstadt; and Verlag Gerhard Rautenberg, Blinke 8, Postfach 1909, 2950 Leer.

ONLINE SERVICES

The use of the Internet and electronic mail has taken off at a lightning pace in the last two years. Email account holders can subscribe for free to the Baltic discussion group *Balt-L* (listserv@listserv.rl.ac.uk); to *Omri-L* (listserv@listserv.acsu.buffalo.edu), which mails out daily news reports on eastern Europe and Russia, including the

---

Online Changes

The email and web site addresses published in this book were correct at the time of research but they are particularly prone to change in this region, so don't be surprised if that proves to be the case. Readers are directed to Lonely Planet's World Wide Web site (http://www.lonelyplanet.com) for up to the minute travel information. ∎

Baltic states and Kaliningrad Region; *Estonia Today* (mailserver@ace.vm.ee), a weekly review of Estonian news; and *News File Lithuania* (is@urm.ktl.mii.lt), a weekly review of Lithuanian news. Hot Web sites include:

http://www.inyourpocket.com
> hotel, restaurant, bar, nightclubs, theatre listings; calendar of events; what to see; plane, train and bus schedules; plus everything else included in *Rīga, Vilnius, Kaunas, Klaipėda & Kaliningrad In Your Pocket* except the maps in their paper versions

http://www.ciesin.ee/NEWS/index.html
> *News about the Baltics, Central & Eastern Europe* has links to English-language media sources on the Net including the Baltics On-line; local newsagencies ETA (Estonia), LETA (Latvia) and ELTA (Lithuania); Baltic News Service (BNS) with daily news in English

http://www.tdd.lt/links/indexe.html
> the *Lithuania Home Page* has more than 400 links to other Lithuanian sites: updated info on visas, customs, hotels, restaurants, media, culture, world-wide Lithuanian organisations, music, sports etc

http://www.online.lt/
> *Lithuania On-Line*, the final link to access every known Lithuanian site

http://www.ciesin.ee/ESTCG
> the *Estonia Country Guide*

http://www.ee/etb/home.htm
> regularly updated home page of the *Estonian Tourist Board* with lots of hot links including to the Ministry of Foreign Affairs (updated visa & embassy info etc) homepage

NEWSPAPERS & MAGAZINES

There is a small but select choice of English-language publications published in the Baltic states, most of which are a useful information source for the increasing number of English-speaking locals as well as the active ex-pat community.

The weekly *Baltic Times* (email times@baltictimes.riga.lv; http://www.lvnet.lv/BalticTimes), the offspring of a merger in 1996 between the ailing Rīga-based *Baltic Observer* and the equally ailing Tallinn-based *Baltic Independent*, is published in Rīga every Thursday and enjoys moderate success as the only English-language newspaper to cover the three Baltic states. It has a fair balance of news and business stories, features, entertainment listings and some useful classifieds. The bimonthly Tallinn-based *City Paper* (email cityp@pb.uninet.ee) – a news magazine and Baltic city guide rolled into one – contains some fine analytical pieces on Baltic politics written by contributing journalists overseas, and runs hotel, restaurant and bar listings for the three capitals. Both have an overseas subscriptions system and are sold locally in news kiosks and hotels for around US$1; the *City Paper* can be difficult to find in Latvia and Lithuania.

Also available overseas is *Lithuanian Papers* (email a.tuskunas@educ.utas.edu.au), an annual journal published by the Lithuanian Studies Society at the University of Tasmania, Australia (PO Box 777, Sandy Bay, Tas 7005, Australia); and *Bridges*, a Lithuanian-American news journal published 10 times a year (email vidutis@paltech.com; Suite 217, 2060 North 14th Street, Arlington, VA 22201, USA). You can subscribe to both.

The Baltic Review (email tbr@zzz.ee; http://www.zzz.ee/tbr) is a quarterly English-language journal, containing in-depth features and political analysis on affairs in the three Baltic states. It is sold locally in most bookshops.

For a more practical orientation around town there is a clutch of city guides: *Rīga This Week* and *Tallinn This Week*, published by different companies, are both distributed for free in some hotels and travel agencies. Both come out roughly every two months, containing somewhat outdated, but still useful information about the two capitals. Despite the cult following it seems to have gained since launching itself in the grey days of 1992, *In Your Pocket*'s feet remain as firmly on the ground as ever. The guides *Rīga, Vilnius, Kaunas, Klaipėda, Minsk & Kaliningrad In Your Pocket*, contain everything you need to know to eat, sleep, go out, see and travel in the cities they pocket.

Imported English-language newspapers and magazines are slightly harder to get in Vilnius than in Rīga or Tallinn where you can easily pick up a copy of the London *Guardian*, *Times* or the *International Herald Tribune* on the day of publication or the next day. The same story goes for *Time*, *Newsweek* and *The Economist*. Typically one of these newspapers/magazines will cost US$3/6. German papers are available in Rīga and Vilnius, while Finnish ones are available in Tallinn.

Details of local-language publications available in each of the Baltic states are given in the country-specific Facts for the Visitor chapters later in the book.

RADIO & TV

All middle and top-end hotel rooms, and some bottom-end ones too, have a TV. Only those in top-end hotels – and some western-style bars and restaurants – receive CNN, BBC, Eurosport, MTV and other western satellite stations. Further details are given in the relevant Facts for the Visitor chapters later in the book.

VIDEO SYSTEMS

PAL and SECAM are the two main systems used in the region. However, that things are changing all the time and it is best to check on arrival which is the 'in' system. PAL is not compatible with SECAM.

PHOTOGRAPHY & VIDEO

Sunlight can be a rarity in the Baltic states. Some fast film, ASA 400 or more, is useful if you want to try taking photos in dim light. Carry spare camera batteries, especially in winter when the cold can make them sluggish.

Kodak, Agfa and Fuji film and basic accessories like batteries are widely available in towns and cities from hotels, and specialist outlets noted in the city and town sections of this book. There are also plenty of quick print-processing outlets. Not all places sell slide or black/white film so you might want to bring your own to save running out at that vital moment.

TIME

Estonian, Latvian, Lithuanian and Kaliningrad time is GMT/UTC plus two hours. When it's noon in the Baltic states it's 1 pm in Moscow, noon in Helsinki, 11 am in Warsaw, 10 am in London, 8 pm in Sydney, and 5 am in New York. When daylight saving is in force, it is GMT/UTC plus three hours.

In 1996 Estonia, Lithuania and the Kaliningrad Region – along with the rest of Europe – put their clocks back a month later than usual, meaning daylight saving was in force from the last Sunday in March to the last Sunday of October. Latvia, however, stunned everyone by sticking to the old system of changing the clocks in September. This meant that for exactly one month Latvia was an hour behind its Baltic neighbours, causing absolute havoc to inter-Baltic plane, train and bus schedules. It is assumed that Latvia will keep in line with the rest of Europe in future!

The 24 hour clock is used for train, bus and flight timetables. Kaliningrad has dropped the old Soviet practice of using Moscow time *(Moskovskoe vremya)* for schedules. Flight, bus, train and ferry timetables are now listed in local time *(mestnoe vremya)*.

All three Baltic states and the Kaliningrad Region follow the American way of listing dates: the month is listed first, followed by the day and then the year, ie 02/03/97 refers to 3 February, 1997, as opposed to 2 March, 1997.

ELECTRICITY
The Baltic states and the Kaliningrad Region run on 220V, 50Hz AC. Most appliances that are set up for 240V will handle this happily. Sockets require a European plug with two round pins. Some sockets are only compatible with the thinner pin Russian plugs, in which case you have to shop for an adapter locally. Large supermarkets sometimes sell them.

WEIGHTS & MEASURES
Estonia, Latvia, Lithuania and Russia all use the metric system, sometimes to amusing excess in some Soviet-style restaurants where menus still spell out the weight of bread, meat and fish per 10g (a 100g hot dog

in a 50g bun doused with 10g of ketchup is written on the menu as 100/50/10). More common is the practice of serving drinks by weight – a standard shot of spirits is 50g and a glass of wine 200g.

LAUNDRY
There's laundry service in the better hotels. It normally takes two days. There are laundromats in all the major cities.

HEALTH
The Baltic states are, on the whole, pretty healthy places to travel around. Though medical care is not entirely up to western standards your chances of needing any are low.

Predeparture Preparations
Bring with you all medicines and pharmaceuticals you think you'll need on the trip – including condoms or other contraceptives. These are available (chiefly in the main cities) but you cannot rely on getting any particular thing where and when you need it. Take plenty of mosquito repellent in summer.

Health Preparations Make sure you're healthy before you start travelling. If you are embarking on a long trip make sure your teeth are OK; there are lots of places where a visit to the dentist would be the last thing you'd want.

If you wear glasses take a spare pair and your prescription. Losing your glasses can be a real problem, although in many places you can get new spectacles made up quickly, cheaply and competently. Contact lenses are impossible to replace.

If you require a particular medication take an adequate supply, as it may not be available locally. Take the prescription or, better still, part of the packaging showing the generic rather than the brand name (which may not be locally available), as it will make getting replacements easier. It's wise to have a legible prescription or a letter from your doctor with you to show that you legally use the medication. It's surprising how often over-the-counter drugs from one place are illegal without a prescription or even banned in another.

Insurance A travel insurance policy covering theft, loss and medical problems is a very good idea. Travel agents, including student travel agencies, can help you arrange one. Read the conditions before buying insurance and check to see if it covers ambulances or a flight home. If it's a policy on which you have to pay for your treatment first, then reclaim the money later, make sure you keep all relevant documentation.

Medical Kit A small, basic medical kit is a wise thing to carry, particularly if you are going off the beaten track. Consider aspirin or paracetamol for pain or fever; an antiseptic for cuts; bandages and Band-aids; antihistamines – which are useful for allergies, as decongestants for colds, to ease itching from bites or stings, and to help prevent motion sickness; something for diarrhoea like Imodium or Lomotil; scissors; insect repellent; a broad-spectrum antibiotic; and, to avoid possible contamination through dirty needles if you have to have an injection, a sterile pack of disposable syringes, available from medical supply shops. If you use the antibiotics, follow the prescribed dosage and intervals exactly.

Immunisations No immunisations are required for any of the Kaliningrad Region or the three Baltic states, except in Latvia where it is advisable to get a vaccine against tick-borne encephalitis if you intend to spend a lot of time in forested areas. All along the coastline in Jūrmala, there are large 'tick' signs warning you where ticks are rife. You might consider vaccination against hepatitis A. Make sure your tetanus, polio and diphtheria vaccinations are up to date. In all three Baltic states you must have an AIDS test before you can be issued a residence permit, which you need if you plan to stay longer than three months.

Basic Rules
Everyday Health Normal body temperature is 37°C or 98.6°F; more than 2°C (4°F) higher indicates a high fever. The normal adult pulse rate is 60 to 100 per minute (children 80 to 100, babies 100 to 140). You should know how to take a temperature and a pulse rate. As a general rule the pulse increases about 20 beats per minute for each °C (2°F) rise in fever.

Respiration (breathing) rate is also an indicator of illness. Count the number of breaths per minute – between 12 and 20 is normal for adults and older children (up to 30 for younger children, 40 for babies). People with a high fever or serious respiratory illness (such as pneumonia) breathe more quickly than normal. More than 40 shallow breaths a minute may indicate pneumonia.

You can avoid insect bites by covering bare skin when insects are around, by screening windows or beds and by using insect repellents.

Water Take care with water – both the tap and sea varieties. Tap water in several places *is* unclean. Definitely in Rīga, and probably in Vilnius, it needs to be boiled before you drink it. In other places check with locals whether the tap water is safe to drink or not. If in any doubt boil it or drink something else (mineral water is a cheap, widely available substitute). To purify water thoroughly you should boil it for 10 minutes. Alternatively, you can do it chemically. Chlorine tablets kill many but not all pathogens. Iodine is very effective and is available in tablet form (such as Potable Aqua) but follow the directions carefully as too much iodine can be harmful.

Sea water is similarly dodgy because of pollution, which is chiefly untreated sewage although there's chemical pollution as well. Every so often, various environmental groups issue warnings not to swim in the sea. It is fair to say, however, while the sea could do with a massive clean-up, beachgoers still venture into the water. In 1993, the local authorities at Estonia's main coastal resort, Pärnu, declared that the waters there were now harmless. Many of the inland lakes in all three Baltic states are cleaner than the sea waters, but you should take local advice anywhere.

Food & Nutrition Food is generally OK but if in any doubt – for instance if you're suspicious about the piece of meat hidden under the sauce on your plate – leave it. Wash fruit and other things from markets, but make sure you dry off any unboiled tap water. The basic guide is your own good sense – if you're dubious about something then don't eat it. Ice cream from street vendors is sometimes a potential hazard, but there really are few cases of travellers contracting stomach problems in the Baltic states. More of a potential problem is the possibility of getting run-down through poor nutrition if you're eating irregularly and poorly. Try not to go hungry, and eat as much and as varied vegetable matter as you can. This isn't always as easy as it sounds because the Baltic diet is fairly stodgy and meat-based. Get fresh fruit from markets. Especially in winter it's a good idea to take along vitamin pills.

Medical Problems
Hepatitis A This is a very common disease worldwide. The symptoms are fever, chills, headache, fatigue, feelings of weakness and aches and pains, followed by loss of appetite, nausea, vomiting, abdominal pain, dark urine, light-coloured faeces, jaundiced skin and the whites of the eyes may turn yellow. In some cases you may feel unwell, tired, have no appetite, experience aches and pains and be jaundiced. You should seek medical advice, but in general there is not much you can do apart from resting, drinking lots of fluids, eating lightly and avoiding fatty foods. People who have had hepatitis must forego alcohol for six months after the illness, as hepatitis attacks the liver and it needs that amount of time to recover.

The routes of transmission are via contaminated water, shellfish contaminated by sewerage, or foodstuffs sold by food handlers with poor standards of hygiene.

Taking care with what you eat and drink can go a long way towards preventing this disease. This is a very infectious virus and either a shot of gamma globulin or the Havrix 1440 vaccination is recommended. Gamma globulin is an injection where you are given the antibodies for hepatitis A, which provide immunity for a limited time. Havrix 1440 is a vaccine, where you develop your own antibodies, which gives lasting immunity.

Hepatitis B This is also a very common disease, with almost 300 million chronic carriers in the world. Hepatitis B is spread through contact with infected blood, blood products or bodily fluids, for example through sexual contact, unsterilised needles and blood transfusions, or via small breaks in the skin. Other risk situations include having a shave or tattoo in a local shop, or having your body pierced. The symptoms of type B are much the same as type A except that they are more severe and may lead to long term problems. Persons who should receive a hepatitis B vaccination include anyone who anticipates contact with blood or other bodily secretions, either as a health-care worker or through sexual contact with the local population, particularly those who intend to stay in the country for a long period of time.

Sexually Transmitted Diseases Gonorrhoea, herpes and syphilis are among these diseases; sores, blisters or rashes around the genitals, discharges or pain when urinating are common symptoms. In some STDs, such as wart virus or chlamydia, symptoms may be less marked or not observed at all in women. Syphilis symptoms eventually disappear completely but the disease continues and can cause severe problems in later years. The treatment of gonorrhoea and syphilis is with antibiotics.

There are numerous other sexually transmitted diseases, for most of which effective treatment is available. However, there is no cure for herpes and there is also currently no cure for AIDS.

HIV/AIDS HIV, the Human Immunodeficiency Virus, may develop into AIDS, Acquired Immune Deficiency Syndrome. Any exposure to blood, blood products or bodily fluids may put the individual at risk. The disease is often transmitted through sexual contact or dirty needles.

HIV/AIDS can also be spread through infected blood transfusions; some developing countries cannot afford to screen blood for transfusions. Vaccinations, acupuncture, tattooing and ear or nose piercing can be potentially as dangerous as intravenous drug use if the equipment is not clean. If you do need an injection, ask to see the syringe unwrapped in front of you, or better still, take a needle and syringe pack with you overseas. It is a cheap insurance package against infection with HIV.

Fear of HIV infection should never preclude treatment for serious medical conditions. Although there may be a risk of infection, it is very small indeed.

Encephalitis From May to September there is a risk of tick-borne encephalitis in forested areas in Latvia. Encephalitis is inflammation of the brain tissue. Symptoms include fever, headache, vomiting, neck stiffness, pain in the eyes when looking at light, alteration in consciousness, seizures and paralysis or muscle weakness. Correct diagnosis and treatment require hospitalisation. Ticks may be found on the edge of forests and in clearings, long grass and hedgerows. A vaccine is available (see Immunisations earlier in this section).

Ticks You should always check your body if you have been walking through a potentially tick-infested area as ticks can cause skin infections and other more serious diseases. If a tick is found attached, press down around the tick's head with tweezers, grab the head and gently pull upwards. Avoid pulling the rear of the body as this may squeeze the tick's gut contents through the attached mouth parts into the skin, increasing the risk of infection and disease. Smearing chemicals on the tick will not make it let go and is not recommended.

Motion Sickness Eating lightly before and during a trip will reduce the chances of motion sickness. If you are prone to motion sickness try to find a place that minimises disturbance near the wing on aircraft, close to midships on boats, near the centre on buses. Fresh air usually helps; reading and cigarette smoke don't. Commercial motion-sickness preparations, which can cause drowsiness, have to be taken before the trip commences; when you're feeling sick it's too late. Ginger (available in capsule form) and peppermint (including mint-flavoured sweets) are natural preventatives.

Medical Treatment
Ordinary pharmacies may contain more local traditional remedies – herbal and so on – than medical preparations of the type the west is used to. However, there are now quite a few pharmacies in the capitals and other towns stocking imported western medicines – see the town and city sections.

There are few alternatives to the dismal local medical system, which is short on both facilities and training, if you do need serious attention. There are some private clinics offering western-standard medical care but they are expensive. In an emergency seek your hotel's help first (if you're in one) – the bigger hotels may have doctors on call. Emergency care is free in all three states. Secondly, your embassy or consulate may be able to recommend a doctor or hospital, but if things are serious be prepared to go straight home or to Scandinavia.

TOILETS
Public toilets in Tallinn are well signposted, clean and a sheer pleasure to use compared to the vile, stinking black holes you will generally encounter elsewhere in the Baltics. Regardless of their lack of cleanliness, you are obliged to pay a small fee on entry in exchange for a few sheets of exceedingly rough toilet paper or squares of newspaper. Many Baltic sewerage systems can't cope

with toilet paper. If a bin or basket is placed in the cubicle, put toilet paper in there. Bring your own toilet paper and be prepared to squat.

Smelly public toilets can be found at every bus and train station in the Baltics. As a westerner, you can quite easily stroll into any large hotel in the major cities and use their toilets without upsetting the staff too much. Alternatively, do what everyone else does and pop into the nearest McDonald's.

The letter **M** marks a men's toilet in Estonian or Russian, **V** in Latvian or Lithuanian. **N** indicates a women's toilet in Estonian, **S** in Latvian, **M** in Lithuanian and **Ж** in Russian. Some toilets sport the triangle system instead: **▼** for men and **▲** for women.

WOMEN TRAVELLERS

The Baltic peoples have some fairly traditional ideas about gender roles, but on the other hand they're pretty reserved and rarely impose themselves upon other people in an annoying way. If anything, western women are likely to find less aggravation from men in the Baltics than at home although unaccompanied women may want to avoid a few of the sleazier bars and beer cellars. Many local and western women travel on overnight buses and trains alone without coming to any harm or experiencing tremendous hassle. If you're travelling on a train at night, play safe and use the hefty metal lock on the inside of the carriage door.

In the large cities in Latvia particularly, a lot of Russian women walk around with skirts so short you can practically see their bottoms – much to the delight of many male travellers who come to the Baltics mistakenly assuming that *all* young Baltic and Russian women are desperate for their attention. Unfortunately, western women travellers who follow suit in this scanty attire, risk being treated as prostitutes. In some tourist hotels prostitution is a fact of life, and a woman sitting alone in a lobby, corridor or café might be also propositioned.

Organisations

The small womens' group within the Latvian Centre for Human Rights and Ethnic Studies (☎ 211 097; fax 7820 113; email enukab@stoat.riga.lv) at Vecpilsētas 13/15, 4th floor, Rīga, Latvia, can provide women travellers with practical advice. It publishes some excellent papers on womens' issues in Latvia and can put you in contact with other womens' groups. For matters relating to contraceptives and sexual issues contact Papardes Zieds (☎ 7287 321, 7821 227), Skolas 3, Rīga, Latvia.

GAY & LESBIAN TRAVELLERS

There is a fairly active gay and lesbian scene in the three Baltic capitals although it is still in its infancy. Latvia was the first eastern European country to host a lesbian wedding, in 1995, but same-sex marriages remain unrecognised in all three states. Rīga is the most gay-friendly capital but public expressions of affection are treated with contempt by some. Lithuania is the least tolerant of the three Baltic states and 'gay-bashing' incidents have been known to occur.

Organisations

For information on gay and lesbian parties and events contact the Estonian Lesbian Union (email elvell@saturn.zzz.ee).

The Latvian Association for Sexual Equality (☎ 7223 293; email lasv@com.latnet.lv), at Puškina 1a, publishes *The Gay Guide to Rīga*, listing gay bars, beaches, clubs and cruising parks, which can also be accessed on the Internet (http://dspace.dial.pipex.com/town/parade/gf96).

The Lithuanian Gay League (☎ 22-239 282, 22-655 940, 22-651 638; email forter@cs.ektaco.ee; http://www.cs.ektaco.ee/forter) in Vilnius arranges accommodation for gay and lesbian travellers, runs the Gay Centre which has a book and video library, screens films every Wednesday evening and organises Saturday night parties at an unpublicised location. Its mailing address is PO Box 2862, LT-2000 Vilnius. The Lithuanian Movement for Sexual Equality (LMSE) has support groups in Vilnius (☎ 22-655 640), PO Box 720, Vilnius LT-2038; and Kaunas (☎ 27-791 293), PO Box 973, Kaunas LT-3026. Both organise parties, as does the Lithuanian Lesbian League (SAPHO), at PO Box 2204, Vilnius LT-2049.

DISABLED TRAVELLERS

With their cobbled streets, rickety pavements and old buildings the Baltic region is completely nonuser-friendly for disabled travellers. In Estonia contact the Baltic Association of Rehabilitation of Disabled Persons at the University Department of Special Education (☎ 27-270 071; fax 27-935 041), Tiigi 78, EE-2484 Tartu. In Latvia contact its sister association at the Vaivari Children's Rehabilitation Centre (☎ 7-66 211; fax 7-66 124), Asaru 61, Jūrmala LV-2008. If you plan to visit Lithuania, get in touch with the Disability Information and Consultation Bureau (☎ & fax 22-731 425), at Vytauto 15, Vilnius. All three have a registry of services available for the disabled visiting the countries.

TRAVEL WITH CHILDREN

If you intend travelling across the region by public transport with young children, take every opportunity to break up the journey. Bus and train journeys between regional cities and the different Baltic states can be long and arduous with little to make the journey pass quickly. Take sufficient food and drink supplies as once you're on the bus from Vilnius to Rīga, you're stuck on it! Despite some drivers' nasty glares, if you smile sweetly they will generally stop by the roadside for a quick loo break. Many of the larger hotels have family rooms or will put an extra bed in the room for you. And remember, Rīga has the only permanent circus in the Baltics! See Lonely Planet's *Travel with Children* by Maureen Wheeler for more information.

DANGERS & ANNOYANCES
Crime

Crime in the Baltic states has increased markedly since independence, but that's starting from a pretty low level. You should certainly guard against theft from hotel rooms, particularly in cheap or slackly run hotels lacking much supervision, by keeping valuables with you or in a hotel safe. Carrying your own padlock can be a help. You should also be careful when walking along poorly lit city streets at night. Some of the prostitutes working in tourist hotels rob their customers.

Car theft is rife in all three Baltic states, particularly if you're driving a western car. Don't leave anything valuable in your car when it is parked. Stripping the inside bare of its stereo and all personal belongings is still not sufficient to deter some thieves who are into stealing car batteries, door locks, tyres and even windscreen wipers. Car emblems also appear to be hotly pursued.

You're sure to hear about the 'mafia' while you're in the Baltic states. These are not Sicilians but the ex-USSR's own version of organised crime. They're not one organisation but many different gangs, stereotypically hailing from the former southern areas of the Soviet Union – Georgia, Azerbaijan, Armenia and the Russian parts of the Caucasus – but in reality from anywhere in the ex-USSR including the Baltic states. The mafia is into any sort of third-rate activity that will turn a few bucks including arms dealing, drugs, metals smuggling, prostitution, buying up state businesses on the cheap by frightening off other potential buyers, and extortion from any profitable business they can get their claws into.

The mafia should not hold any terrors for the average visitor. You're most likely to come across it as a slob-like presence – a small knot of thick-set men sporting five o'clock shadows and cheap leather jackets – at a taxi rank or in a restaurant or café that it frequents.

Service

Most of the surly, rude, obstructive goblins employed in service industries in the Soviet era have miraculously changed character now that pleasing the customer has become worthwhile, but there are still one or two hangovers from the bad old days. When you encounter them, all you can do is grit your teeth and quietly persist until you've got what you need.

Rip-Offs

Taxi drivers may cheat foreigners the world over and those in the Baltic states, especially at airports and outside the main tourist hotels, are no exception. A few tips on avoiding rip-offs are given in the city sections.

Drunks

Drunks on the streets and in hotels can be a nuisance in the evenings, especially at weekends. In Tallinn they're as likely to be foreign tourists as locals. Steer clear and don't get involved!

Border Guards

Baltic border guards are not out to rip you off. They are just suckers for stamps – and for the old Soviet way of doing things, which means service without a smile. At road borders these stamp-obsessed, snail-paced creatures are at their meanest – the longer the line, the colder they are. All you can do is smile sweetly, make sure you have your paperwork at the ready and be glad that *you* don't have to be a borderguard.

Smoking

Smoking is not appreciated in some restaurants, although few places ban it. Many public places such as waiting rooms, bars and lobbies are wreathed in tobacco smoke, and some cheaper hotel rooms retain a semipermanent aroma of it.

Ethnic Relations

A number of Estonians, Latvians and Lithuanians have what can only be called racist attitudes towards Russians and other ex-Soviet nationalities in their midst. While it's easy to understand the resentment the Baltic nationalities feel towards Russia, and even towards Russian people, with whom they have some clear cultural differences, it's not clear what possible good could come from some people's send 'em home mentality. You may find these sort of ideas a barrier to communication with some people. On the other hand, when it comes

to action rather than words, the Baltic governments have been pretty careful to avoid provoking any serious trouble with their legislation in these fields.

LEGAL MATTERS

Note that in Rīga, you have to stick to the public footpaths in city parks. If the police catch you walking on the grass, you can be fined 5 lati. In Vilnius, you are allowed to sit/lie/sunbathe on the grass in city parks but you are not allowed to sleep. Police patrol on horseback to make sure your eyes are not shut.

If you are unfortunate enough to be arrested in the Baltics you have the same basic legal rights as in the west. You have the right to be informed of the reason for your arrest (before being carted off to the police station) and you have the right to inform a family member of your misfortune (once you have been carted off). You cannot be detained for more than 72 hours without being charged with an offence, and you have the right to have your lawyer present during questioning.

BUSINESS HOURS

Shops open weekdays from 8, 9 or 10 am to 6, 7 or 8 pm; and Saturday from 8, 9 or 10 am to some time between 1 and 5 pm. Some close for lunch, or on Mondays. Cafés open from about 9 am to 8 pm; restaurants, from noon to around midnight. Museums often close on Monday and Tuesday.

PUBLIC HOLIDAYS & SPECIAL EVENTS

National holidays vary from country to country (see the relevant Facts for the Visitor chapters later in the book). Each of the Baltic states also celebrate a number of commemorative days when shops, apartment blocks and offices are obliged by law to fly their national flag (in Latvia, you can be fined if you don't).

All three Baltic states have fat festival calendars encompassing religion, music, song, art, folk culture, handicrafts, film, drama and more. Summer is the busiest time of year. Some festivals are annual, others one-off – see Facts for the Visitor in the

The Baltic Calendar

Shrove Tuesday Traditionally Shrove Tuesday, falling seven weeks before Easter, has always been celebrated in the Baltic states. It marked the end of a harsh Baltic winter and was a day for baking pancakes and barley bread in preparation for the strict Lenten fast to follow. Cattle, after being penned up all winter, would be let loose to run free in the fields. In Estonia, the remains of the Christmas *kringel* bread would be fed to the cows to fortify them for the coming season. In all three states, children would go on long sled rides; the longer their journey the taller the flax would grow that year. In Lithuania, doing the washing or dragging a block of wood on a rope also contributed to a better harvest.

Today in Estonia and Latvia the traditional food is still shared at the table, although in Estonia cream-filled buns seem to have usurped the more meagre flour and eggs diet. In Lithuania, the much loved tradition of parading through the streets in a masked disguise in return for sweets and small gifts is still very much alive. Accompanying the masked revellers in the carnival is the traditional *Moré*, an effigy dressed in women's clothes and dragged along, fixed to a cartwheel. In Vilnius, the *Moré*, symbolising winter, is still taken to the top of Taurus Hill and set alight.

Spring Equinox In Lithuania, this pagan feast *(lygiadienis)* is still celebrated, marking the day when spring bursts into flower. Amid a carnival of song and dance, the church bells ring and a new flame is lit. In Vilnius, within the walls of Gediminas Castle, wizards – symbolising earth, water, fire and grass – converge to light the new flame and burn it for all to see from the top of Gediminas Hill.

Easter Easter is very much an 'egg holiday' for all three Baltic states, although if you're hoping for a commercially wrapped chocolate egg in a flash cardboard box, forget it. The old-age tradition of hard-boiling eggs and then painting or dying them a rainbow of colours is an integral part of the Balts' Easter celebrations. Friends, families and work colleagues exchange painted eggs with great enthusiasm. Various egg games are always played, ranging from the smash and run variety to playing boules with them down a hill.

In Estonia and Latvia, the Easter Bunny has hopped his way into town since the 16th century. In Lithuania, the Easter Granny arrives on her horse made from wax, pulling a cart filled with eggs, which she hides in the trees. By sunrise she has gone (her horse would melt otherwise).

Midsummer In pagan times it was a night of magic and sorcery when witches would run naked and wild, bewitching flowers and ferns, people and animals. In the agricultural calendar, it marked the end of the spring sowing and the start of the summer harvest. In Soviet times, it became a political celebration. A torch of independence was lit in each capital and its flame used to light bonfires throughout the country.

Today Midsummer, Summer Solstice or St John's Day, falling on the 24 June, is the Balts' biggest party of the year. In Estonia it is known as Jaanipäev, in Latvia as Jāni or Jānu Diena, and in Lithuania as Joninés or Rasos (the old Pagan name).

Celebrations start on 23 June, particularly in Latvia where the festival is generally met with the most gusto. Traditionally, people flock to the countryside to celebrate this special night amid a land of lakes and pine forests. Special beers, cheese and pies are prepared and wreaths strung from grasses while flowers and herbs are hung around the home to bring good luck and keep families safe from evil spirits. Men adorn themselves with crowns made from oak leaves, and women with crowns of flowers.

Come the night preceding 24 June, bonfires are lit and the music and drinking begins. No one is allowed to sleep until the sun has sunk and risen again – anyone who does will be riddled with bad luck for the coming year. Traditional folksongs are sung, dances danced and those special beers, cheese and pies eaten! To ensure good luck, you have to leap back and forth over the bonfire. In Lithuania, clearing a burning wheel of fire as it is rolled down the nearest hill brings you even better fortune. In Estonia, revellers swing on special double-sided Jaanipäev swings, strung from trees in forest clearings or in village squares.

Midsummer's night is a night for lovers. In Estonia the mythical Koit (dawn) and Hämarik (dusk) meet but once a year for an embrace lasting as long as the shortest night of the year. Throughout the Baltic region, lovers seek the mythical fern flower, which only blooms on this night. The dew coating flowers and ferns on this night is held to be a purifying force, a magical healer, and a much sought-after cure for wrinkles! Bathe your face in it and you will instantly become more beautiful, more youthful. However, beware the witches of Jaanipäev/Jāni/Joninés, who are known to use it for less enchanting means.

Continued next page

Christmas The most important day of the year in the Baltic calendar is 24 December. Traditionally it is a day when the family stays at home; celebrations with friends and neighbours are only enjoyed on 25 December. In Estonia, Latvia and Lithuania, the family table is covered with straw, and the culinary feast is served upon it. Places are also laid for any deceased relatives. In Lithuania, the feast comprises 12 vegetarian dishes. Meat is only eaten on the 25th. In Estonia, pepper biscuits and a German-style knotted bread with nuts known as *kringel* are the order of the day. Blood sausages, traditionally containing a small gift inside, are also served. Various fortune-telling games are played throughout the region.

Today, the red-cheeked, white-bearded Santa Claus is a celebrated figure. The gifts he bears are traditionally opened on Christmas Eve. During the Soviet era, he did not exist, however. Children had to go to school on Christmas Eve and Christmas Day, and Santa Claus was replaced by the soulless Father Frost who dropped gifts down chimneys on New Year's Eve instead. ■

---

country-specific chapters for details. Public holidays for each country are also listed here.

Three regular events stand out: the Baltic song festivals, the midsummer celebrations, and the Baltika folk festival.

Song Festivals

The national song festivals held every five years in each of the Baltic states are the most emotive events on the calendar. So strong is the power of song, particularly in Estonia and to a slightly lesser degree in Latvia, that the campaign for independence from the USSR became known as the 'Singing Revolution'. The first Estonian song festival was held in Tartu in 1869, during the Estonian national awakening, and helped to show that Estonians could emulate their German overlords. The first Latvian song festival followed in 1873 but Lithuania didn't begin till 1924.

The song festivals climax with giant choirs of 10,000, 20,000 or 30,000 people, from several hundred choirs, singing in huge open-air amphitheatres in the national capitals to vast audiences of 100,000 or more. Often they're accompanied by simultaneous dance festivals, with thousands of dancers in traditional dress creating huge, intricate patterns. The next song festival will be held in Tallinn in 1999 and Vilnius in 2000. The last song festival was in Rīga in 1995.

Midsummer

In a part of the world with such a short summer and long, dark winters it's only natural that midsummer, when night barely falls at all, should be an important festival time. The night of 23 June, preceding what's known as Jaanipäev in Estonia, Jāni or Jānu Diena in Latvia, and Rasos or Joninės in Lithuania (all meaning St John's Day, 24 June), is the climax of events. It's considered a night with magical powers, and the traditional way of celebrating it is to head out into the countryside to dance, sing and make merry round bonfires and to seek the mythical fern flower which, it's said, only blooms this night and brings luck to any who find it (see The Baltic Calendar aside for more details). Celebrations are always the biggest and best in Latvia.

Baltika Folklore Festival

The Baltika annual international folklore festival, which has taken place in each Baltic capital in turn since 1987, is a week (usually in mid-July) of music, dance, exhibitions and parades focusing on Baltic and other folk traditions. In 1997 the Baltika will be held in Latvia; in 1998 it's due in Estonia, and in 1999 in Lithuania.

ACTIVITIES

The Baltics have been getting far more organised in recent years. A colourful variety of activities are now accessible to those wanting to pursue a special interest with organised clubs and hire outlets set up in many cases. While still lagging behind the west, there is no doubt that taking advantage of what's on offer will still enable you to discover some of the wilder, more beautiful parts of the region.

Cycling

Cycling is a pretty cool way of traversing the Baltic region given it's so damn flat. Plenty of places rent bicycles and there are some fun cycling tours on the market. See the Bicycle section in the Getting Around chapter.

Winter Sports

Skiing (mainly cross-country), ice skating and tobogganing are all popular. Otepää in south-east Estonia is the main skiing centre – there are downhill runs, a ski jump and hire outlets where you can get all the gear. In Latvia the Gauja valley is a winter sports centre: there's a bobsleigh run at Sigulda and a ski jump at Valmiera. Again, you can hire equipment once you arrive. There is also an outdoor ice skating rink in Rīga, open when it is below -3˚C. In Lithuania, the north-eastern Aukštaitija National Park attracts cross-country skiers.

Bird-Watching

The Estonian islands, parts of Latvia and the west coast of Lithuania attract large numbers of bird-watchers. In Latvia, Eastbird (☎ & fax 331 920) at Noras 3, about 20 km south of Rīga in Baldone, offers guiding for bird-watchers. In Estonia, contact the bird ringing centre in the Matsalu Nature Reserve (☎ & fax 247-78 413) which arranges day hikes and guiding in the reserve. The Estonian Ecotourism Association (☎ 2-6316 809; fax 244-43 779; email ecotourism@www.ee; http://www.ee/ecotourism) arranges a four day bird-watching tour of Matsalu. Its mailing address is PO Box 84, EE-3600 Pärnu, Estonia. Bookings can be made through Haapsalu Travel Service or Mere Farmstead Tourism (see Accommodation – Farmstays in this chapter). *Bird-watching Localities in Estonia* (Eesti Loodusfoto, Tartu, 1996) is sold for 45 EEK from most tourism information centres in Estonia.

Canoeing

Canoeing is a popular activity locally. In Latvia the Gauja, Salaca and Abava rivers and the Latgale lakes region all offer uninterrupted routes over several days. Organisations offering trips for small groups include the Tourist Club of Latvia (☎ 7221 731, 7221 113; fax 7227 680) at Škārņu iela 22, LV-1350 Rīga; and Makars tourism agency (☎ 973 724; fax 972 006) at Peldu 1, Sigulda (see the Vidzeme and Latgale chapters for more on its programmes). Both can rent you all the necessary equipment including waterproof clothing and tents to sleep in at night.

In Lithuania the north-eastern Aukštaitija National Park is a good canoeing area with another big network of interconnected lakes. The park's tourism and recreation centre organises trips and rents equipment (see Eastern & Southern Lithuania chapter for details). The Estonian Ecotourism Association arranges weekend and five-day caneoing trips round the wild bogs of Soomaa National Park in south-west Estonia.

Fishing

In the depths of the Baltic winter there is no finer experience than dabbling in a touch of ice-fishing along with the local, vodka-warmed fishers on the frozen Curonian Lagoon, off the west coast of Lithuania. The Fisherman's Club (☎ 22-618 301) at Stiklių 6 in Vilnius provides advice on all types of fishing and arranges fishing trips in Lithuania. In north-east Estonia, contact the Lahemaa National Park Visitors' Centre (☎ 232-34 196; fax 232-44 575; email teet@lklm.envir.ee), Lääne-Virumaa, EE-2128 Viitna. Elsewhere along the Estonian coastline you need a fishing permit to fish – contact the National Estonian Board of Fisheries (☎ 2-6411 016; fax 2-441 958), Lai 39/41, EE-0001 Tallinn.

Flying & Gliding

In Latvia, the Cēsis Flying Club (☎ 41-22 639, 9-353 309), Cēsis, arranges flying and gliding lessons and trips over the Gauja National Park. In Vilnius there is also a flying club (see Activities in the Vilnius chapter for details). If you want to fly in a hot-air balloon and bungee jump from it contact the Bungee Jumping Club of Latvia (see Sigulda in the Vidzeme chapter for details).

Horse Riding

Most tourist farms in Estonia have horses and arrange treks. Contact any of the regional tourist information centres for details. The Tallinn Riding Centre (☎ 2-559 670), Paldiski 135, EE-0035 Tallinn, can also help. Particularly idyllic is horse trekking round the tiny island of Abruka off Saaremaa's south coast (see West Estonia & the Islands chapter for details). In Latvia, Turaidas muiža (☎ 974 584), Turaidas 10, Sigulda, organises various horse-riding activities in the Gauja National Park.

Sauna

Most hotels have saunas, and there are also some public bath-houses with saunas. The basic sauna is a wooden room with benches and a hot stove, usually surrounded by bricks or stones, on which you toss water to produce clouds of steam. A sauna is relaxing, cleansing, said to be good for the lungs and on occasion is said to come close to a religious experience. An invitation to share a sauna is a hospitable gesture. Lightly switching the body with a bunch of birch twigs increases perspiration and tingles the nerve ends.

LANGUAGE COURSES

Vilnius University runs Lithuanian language courses although they are quite pricey. In early 1997, an intensive one/two-week summer course cost US$320/500. A two-month course (22 hours a week) is US$2000. Courses have to be booked in advance. For information write to the Praktinės lietuvių kalbos katedra (Practical Lithuanian Language Department) at Vilniaus Universitetas, Universiteto 3, LT-2734 Vilnius, Lithuania.

WORK

The Baltic states have enough difficulties keeping their own people employed so there's not much temporary work for visitors. Most westerners working here have been posted here by companies back home. However, these *are* times of change and opportunity, and there is some scope for people who want to stay a while and carve themselves a new niche – though, in western terms, you couldn't expect to get rich doing so. The English language is certainly in demand, and you might be able to earn your keep (or part of it) teaching it in one of the main cities. It's better still if you speak Estonian, Latvian or Lithuanian (or even German, Russian, or a Scandinavian language). Very occasionally jobs for English speakers are advertised in the local English language press.

ACCOMMODATION

There's a wide range of accommodation in the Baltic states and you'll probably get most out of your trip by trying a variety of types. A few nights in private homes will bring you closer to the people and their way of life than a couple of weeks in hotels.

Reservations

Book ahead wherever you plan to stay as vacancies, particularly during summer, can be scarce. Agents in other countries as well as in the Baltic states itself can make bookings for you but they work mainly with the more expensive hotels and may charge a commission.

Camping

In the Baltic states or Kaliningrad Region, a campsite (Estonian: *kämpingud*; Latvian: *kempings*; Lithuanian: *kempingas*; Russian: *kemping*) is not normally what we understand by a campsite in the west. While there are a few tent-only sites, most campsites consist of permanent wooden cabins or, occasionally, brick bungalows, with a few spaces to pitch tents too. Most of them are in quite pretty, remote spots, often overlooking a lake or river but often hard to reach unless you have a private vehicle. Cabins vary in shape and size but are usually small one-room affairs with three or four beds. Showers and toilets are nearly always communal and vary dramatically in cleanliness. Many sites have a bar and/or cafeteria, and sauna.

Campsites are usually open only in summer, from some time in May or June to the end of August or mid-September. Estonia is quite well provided with campsites (perhaps 40 or 50 are dotted around the country) but there are fewer in the other states, especially Latvia. A night in a campsite cabin typically costs US$8 to US$10 per person but there are a few superior new places which charge up to US$25.

University Accommodation

Universities in Tartu, Rīga and Vilnius have rooms available in student hostels and the like for typically US$12 to US$15 per person per night. Most of the rooms are quite clean, have two or three beds, and share showers and toilets with two or three other rooms. Booking ahead is advisable in all three cities. See city sections for details.

Hostels

The hostel network has developed in leaps and bounds in the past couple of years, although there is still room for development. Rooms get massively booked up in summer and if you don't book in advance, it can be impossible to get a bed for the night. Estonia has the most advanced network, followed by Lithuania, while Latvia has very few and Kaliningrad, none at all! All three are affiliated to the International Hostelling Federation.

Estonia The Estonian Hostels Association (Balti Puhkemajad) has 11 hostels in Estonia: three in Tallinn, one in Maardu, three in Pärnu, one in Kuressaare on the island of Saaremaa, one in Käina on the island of Hiiumaa, one in Põlva (south Estonia), and one in Harju country (northwest). Information is available from the hostel headquarters (☎ 2-6461 457, 2-6461 455; fax 2-6461 595; email puhkemajad@online.ee) at Tartari 39-310, EE-0001 Tallinn (see Tallinn chapter for more details).

Prices in the Estonian hostels range from US$3.50 to US$19; the average rate in most is US$8. No card or membership is currently needed but HI members are given 10% discount in some hostels. Accommodation ranges from suburban nine-storey Soviet tower blocks to private homes, to wooden cottages in a pine forest. Most rooms hold three or four people, with bedding provided. Showers and toilets are generally shared and there are cooking facilities in most. Some supply meals, have saunas and a laundry; others arrange watersports and skiing.

Advance bookings are strongly recommended for all the hostels. Bookings can be made via the association's Web page (http://www.planet-nc.com/eyh) or through Helsinki or St Petersburg hostels with whom it co-operates. Contact the Finnish Youth Hostel Association (SRM) of Yrjönkatu 38B, SF-00100 Helsinki (☎ 09-694 0377, fax 09-693 1349); the Eurohostel at Linnankatu 9, SF-00160 Helsinki (☎ 09-66 4452, fax 09-65 5044); or the St Petersburg International Hostel at 3rd Sovetskaya Ulitsa 28, St Petersburg (☎ 812-329 8018; fax 812-329 8019; email ryh@ryh.spb.su; http://www.spb.su/ryh; mailing address: St Petersburg International Hostel, PO Box 8, SF-53501, Lappeenranta, Finland).

Latvia So far, the Latvian Hostels Association (LaJTMA; Latvija Jaunatnes tūrisma mītņu asociācija) at K Barona 32-11, Rīga (☎ 7217 544), has only made strides in Rīga where it runs four hostels. Rooms have three to 10 beds costing around US$12 a night and facilities are shared.

Lithuania Lithuanian Hostels (Lietuvos Nakvynės Namai) at Filaretų 17, Vilnius LT-2001 (☎ 22-696 627; fax 22-220 149; email root@jnakv.vno.soros.lt) runs five hostels in Lithuania: one each in Vilnius, Kaunas, Ignalina, Šiauliai and Palanga. A bed in a shared room is US$2.50 to US$10 a night which includes breakfast and linen in most. HI members get 25% discount in some hostels.

Hotels

There are hotels to suit every budget in the

Baltics. Hotel accommodation, especially in the mid and upper ranges, however, is extremely scarce in Estonia and Lithuania and must be booked in advance for the summer months. In Latvia, mid-range and expensive rooms are readily available year-round, however, there is a distinct shortage of low-budget accommodation.

Bottom End Cheap hotels are still getting used to the idea of westerners, who in the Soviet era were steered very clear of these less than shining examples of the communist way of life. These hotels are typically ageing, gloomy places whose stereotypical customer is a man in a vest, lying on his bed quaffing vodka, chain-smoking and watching TV. Rooms tout among the most disgusting colour schemes you are ever likely to encounter, while toilet and wash facilities can be equally grim. Every middle-sized town has at least one of these old Soviet relics. Some (just to ensure those fading memories of the joys of the Soviet era don't die out completely!) still adhere to the former double or triple pricing scheme dependent on your country of origin. Face control is another method of pricing in some.

However, some cheap hotels are much better kept than others and the better ones can be quite a bargain. You may get a spacious and clean (if not exactly jovial) room with TV and private bathroom for as little as US$10 a double.

Middle-Range & Expensive These are basically the hotels that westerners were lodged in during the Soviet era, plus the new breed of comfortable or luxury hotel that has emerged, often with western money and management, in the 1990s. At the very top of the range – places like the Palace in Tallinn, the Hotel de Rome in Rīga or the Stikliai in Vilnius – a double room is more than US$200. At the other end of the scale there are some pleasant, clean and modern little establishments in the US$35 to US$55 range. In between there's a whole range of prices and types of hotel.

Homestays

Paying to stay in a private home is one of the most interesting types of accommodation, providing western visitors with a unique opportunity to get a behind the scenes shot of local life. Sharing your breakfast table with your host family each morning will give you more of an idea of what local life is really like than any number of nights in a hotel ever could. Sampling traditional home cooking is another joy, hard to find elsewhere. You will probably be expected to pay extra for it though.

In a few mainly rural places, old traditions of hospitality linger and if you're asking around for a room you may be offered one for nothing. In such cases a parting gift (flowers, sweets etc), offered in some other way to avoid giving offence, can be a good way of saying thank you. In many homes everybody takes their shoes off once inside the door to keep the floors clean. You'll be offered a pair of slippers to wear indoors.

Throughout the Baltics and the west, there are a number of agencies who arrange accommodation in private homes in the Baltics in advance. Information on agencies dealing only with the cities where they are located is given in the relevant city/town sections. The following all cover a number of different cities and towns:

American-International Homestays, PO Box 1754, Nederland, CO 80466, USA (☎ 303-642 3088 or toll-free 800-876 2048; fax 303-642 3365; email ash@igc.apc.org; http://www.spectravel.com/homes) – bed and breakfast with a local family in Baltic cities and Russia starting at US$49 per person a night; full homestay accommodation including dinner, transportation and English-speaking guide/interpreter is US$99/179 for a single/double; a two week pre-planned Baltic trip is $2500 including airfare from New York

CDS Reisid, Raekoja plats 17, EE-0001 Tallinn, Estonia (☎ 2-445 262; fax 2-6313 666; email cds@zen.estpak.ee) – B&B featuring English-speaking families throughout Estonia, also Vilnius and Rīga, 25/35 EEK a single/double; full board with city tours and host always available US$55/90

Family Hotel Service, Mere 6, Tallinn, Estonia (☎ & fax 2-441 187) – rooms in flats throughout Estonia including the islands, and St Petersburg;

mostly US$15 to US$36 per person per night; also a few unoccupied flats

Bed & Breakfast Rasastra Ltd, Sadama 11, EE-0001, Tallinn, Estonia (☎ & fax 2-602 091) – B&B in family homes and separate apartments throughout Estonia, Latvia, Lithuania and St Petersburg from US$15 per person a night

Gateway Travel, 48 The Boulevarde, Strathfield, NSW 2135, Australia (☎ 02-9745 3333, fax 02-9745 3237) – Baltic homestays from around US$200 a week including some meals

IBV Bed and Breakfast Systems, 13113 Ideal Drive, Silver Spring, MD 20906, USA (☎ 301-942 3770, fax 301-933 0024) – B&B in Baltic capitals, US$85/95 a single/double a night

Litinterp, Bernardinų 7-2, LT-2000 Vilnius, Lithuania (☎ 22-223 850; fax 22-223 559; email litinterp@post.omnitel.net; http://www.omnitel.net/litinterp) – B&B with local families throughout Lithuania for US$15/25 a single/double a night; arranges car and bicycle rental too

Patricia, Elizabetes 22-6, LV-1011 Rīga, Latvia (☎ 7284 868; fax 7286 650) – rooms in private flats throughout Latvia between US$15 and US$20 per person

Schenker-Rhenus Reisen, Hohe Brücke 1, D-20459 Hamburg, Germany (☎ 040-36 135 448, fax 040-36 135 434) – bookings for Estonian Ecotourism Association

Tourist Club of Latvia (Rīga Tourist Information Bureau), Skārņu 22, LV-1350 Rīga, Latvia (☎ 7221 731, 7217 377, fax 7227 680) – rooms in homes in a few Latvian and Lithuanian towns, about US$15 per person

Farmstays

Ecotourism is a growing phenomenon in the Baltics, particularly in Estonia and Latvia where organisations specialising in country holidays have been set up. Accommodation consists of a private room in a farmhouse, manor or cottage in a rural or coastal area. Host families provide home-cooked meals, and arrange various activities such as fishing, boating, horse-riding, mushroom and berry-picking in the forest etc. Bookings can be made in advance through agencies in the Baltics or overseas. They include:

Country Traveller Association (Lauku Ceļotājs), Kuģu 11, LV-1048 Rīga, Latvia (☎ 7617 600, 7617 024; fax 7830 041) – arranges B&B accommodation in a variety of rural settings all over Latvia for US$30 to US$40 a night; also lets whole farmhouses and cottages and takes

advance bookings for campsites, hotels and motels in Latvia

Deutsche Landwirtschafts-Gesellschaft, Eschborner Landstrasse 122, D-60489 Frankfurt (☎ 069-247 880; fax 069-247 88110) – takes bookings for the Country Traveller Association

Estonian Farmers Union (ETKL), Liivalaia 12, EE-0106 Tallinn, Estonia (☎ 2-683 410; fax 2-6311 045) – runs a network of B&B accommodation based around 28 farms in rural and not-so-rural Estonia, starting at around US$23 a night

Fédération Nationale des Gîtes de France, 56, rue Saint Lazare, F-75009 Paris (☎ 01 49 70 75 75; fax 01 49 70 75 80) – takes bookings for the Country Traveller Association

Haapsalu Travel Service, Karja 7, EE3170 Haapsalu, Estonia (☎ 247-45 037, fax 247-45 335) – handles bookings for the Estonian Ecotourism Association which offers rooms in farmhouse and country accommodation for around US$20 to US$30 per person per night (including continental breakfast). Many of the properties are in idyllic locations in south-east and west Estonia including the islands; bookings can also be made through one of the appointed agents overseas; also arranges camping and takes bookings for Ecotours

Mere Farmstead Tourism, Pikk 60, EE3300 Kuressaare (☎ & fax 251-54 461; email lii@evk.oesel.ee; http://www.ee/ecotourism) – handles bookings for the Estonian Ecotourism Association

Lomarengas Finnish Country Holidays, Malminkaari 23, SF-00700, Helsinki, Finland (☎ 09-351 61 321; fax 09-351 61 370) – takes bookings for the Estonian Ecotourism Association

Holiday Homes & Sanatoriums

Many of the holiday homes that in Soviet times were reserved for members of particular organisations are now open to general trade, and while some are tatty and institutional, others are as good as decent hotels. The better ones give an idea of the rewards that awaited those who succeeded in the communist system. Prices in such places range widely but often include full board. A holiday home is likely to be called a *puhkebaas, puhkekodu, puhkemaja,* or *pansion* in Estonia; a *pansionāts* in Latvia; a *poilsio namai* in Lithuania; and a *pansionat* in Kaliningrad and elsewhere in Russia. In some places you will find old Soviet sanatoriums, now functioning in part as middle-range straight hotels.

FOOD

Things have changed rapidly on the Baltic eating scene since the late 1980s when getting a half-decent meal involved a great deal of planning and patience. Thanks to just a couple of western-style places hitting each of the capitals in the mid-1990s, the entire eating scene has been revolutionised, so much so that today in the major cities it can – sadly – be quite tough to track down traditional national cooking.

The onslaught of brightly lit bistros, funky bars, fast-paced burger bars and sophisticated restaurants, has yet to spread to provincial Latvia, Lithuania and Estonia where one can still indulge in a simple but fine home-cooked meal typical of that region.

The Language Guide at the back of the book includes words and phrases you will find useful when ordering food and drink.

Types of Eateries

The stereotypical Soviet-style restaurant, with its surly door attendant, invisible waiters, ear-splitting pop group and parties of drunken revellers, practically belongs to another age now – although such establishments can still be found in some places. The days of speaking English very loudly to get service are also long gone; today attempt even a few words in the local language and you will be greeted with a near joyous response!

Eating is still relatively cheap, though improved standards have brought higher prices, notably in Estonia and Latvia where you easily pay western prices in the cities and larger towns. There are numerous restaurants with food and service of western quality as well as menus in English where you get a three-course meal for no less than US$10 – and indeed a lot more in some places. At the other end of the scale are canteens and cafeterias, where you can fill up for around US$1. These places, incidentally, rarely have menus in English but this is no problem given what's on offer is on display and you can just point at what you want. Their food is no gourmet's delight but it's usually quite palatable and filling.

Fast food is rife in the region with McDonald's running sit-down restaurants and numerous drive-ins in each of the capitals and some larger towns. There is also a wide variety of locally run chains which offer cheap feeding for around US$3.

The three capitals in particular have excellent café scenes with a variety of fun, off-beat and more traditional places serving up good coffee, fresh and very delicious breads and pastries, as well as alcoholic drinks and light hot meals.

Ordering

Most restaurants and cafés have clear, multilingual menus which accurately describe what they've got for you to eat – in English.

In some pre-independence establishments, the menu is only written – by hand – in the local language, complete with the exact weight in grams of each dish, the price (which is always some silly amount, never rounded up), and the signature of the director and accountant! Your best bet here is to simply ask the waiter what he recommends, given that most dishes listed will probably not be available anyway.

In these places you'll also find the Russian custom of consuming large helpings of *zakuski* (hors d'oeuvres) such as tomato, beetroot or cucumber salads, smoked fish, or cold meats, alive and well. Forget ordering just one 'main' dish unless you want to leave hungry; order three or four hors d'oeuvres too.

What You Get

It's simple really – in the cities and larger town you can get almost anything you fancy, be it Chinese, Indian, Mexican or Hungarian. Restaurants and cafés specialising in cuisines from all over the world are springing up left, right and centre, so much so that you might find yourself getting extremely frustrated that you are not sampling anything different to that at home. In fact, because many food products still have to be imported, coupled with the fact that the Baltic diet as a whole is not particularly hot on spices, you might well find that what you end up eating is simply a tasteless, poorer quality version of the same ethnic dish you'd be served in the west.

Once out of the major population centres though, you should have a chance to sample some local dishes. A typical main course in a provincial restaurant usually consists of a piece of grilled or fried meat or fish, along with chips and small amounts of a couple of boiled vegetables.

However, this is only a pallid reflection of real local diets, and you won't truly experience what Baltic people eat unless you're lucky enough to enjoy some home cooking. If you do, the care with which it's prepared and the variety of tastes and textures which can be extracted from some pretty ordinary ingredients will be a pleasant surprise. Notes on some local specialities are given in the Estonia, Latvia and Lithuania Facts for the Visitor chapters.

Common food items throughout the region include pancakes, which come with different fillings – fruit, meat, curd, cheese, jam, sour cream etc – and in a variety of sizes; sausage, usually cold and sliced; and dairy products – milk is turned to curd, sour cream and cottage cheese as well as plain old butter, cream and cheese. Four common ways of cooking meat of almost any kin are as a shashlik (kebab), carbonade (officially a chop but in practice it could be almost any piece of grilled meat), 'beefsteak' (any piece of fried meat), and stroganoff (cubes of meat in sauce or gravy).

Vegetarians in the Baltics will suffer. Despite so many western-style restaurants opening, few seem to realise that there is more to vegetarian cooking than simply slapping out a vegetable side dish as a main course. Estonian and Russian at least have words for 'vegetarian' (Estonian: *taimetoitlane*; Russian: *vegetarianets* – male, *vegetarianka* – female). And given the rate with which the eating scene has developed so far, vegetarians should be able to look forward to a nut roast in the Baltics pretty soon.

Self-Catering

Most towns have a market, open every day, with a surprising range of fruit and vegetables sold at good prices (though they may be beyond the pockets of many locals). Bread is easy to get from bakeries at under US$0.60 a loaf. Food shops may not have a great variety but they'll have something worth buying. A kg of cheese from a shop or market will normally be in the US$2 to US$4 range. There are western-style supermarkets and 24 hour shops selling a vast range of western imports in all three Baltic states – but not Kaliningrad.

DRINKS
Nonalcoholic Drinks

Tap water can be dodgy – see the Health section. A good cheap substitute (a few US cents a bottle) is mineral water, of which there are numerous brands. Be wary of some locally produced ones though (usually the ones in beer-size glass bottles) which are so salty it is comparable to drinking sea water. Tea, coffee and fruit juices are easy to get throughout the region. Coke, Fanta etc are sold everywhere.

Alcoholic Drinks

Good beer is brewed in the Baltic states and is available in most restaurants and cafés, alongside more expensive imported German and Scandinavian beers (and even Guinness in some bars) which generally cost about US$1 more. Local beer is also sold in shops, kiosks, bars and western-style pubs. It normally comes in half-litre bottles in shops and kiosks which cost about US$1, and on-tap in most bars which costs US$2 to US$3. You can also buy the mostly inferior draught ale with which people fill cans at kiosks, some shops, and breweries.

Most Baltic beer is light, fairly flat, and of medium strength. Utenos alus and Kalnapilis are Lithuania's best brews; the light Saku beer and the heavier Saare beer from the island of Saaremaa are Estonia's prime choices; Aldaris is Latvia's most popular. Here and there you can get good strong stout – known in Latvia as *tumšais* and in Lithuania as *porteris*. Vodka, brandy and champagne, all from various areas of the ex-USSR and the west, are served everywhere too.

Some Estonian cafés and bars serve tasty, warming *hõõgvein* (mulled wine). Latvia's speciality is Rīga Black Balsam (Rīgas Melnais Balzāms), a thick, dark, bitter and potent liquid with supposedly medicinal properties. In Lithuania you may find mead *(midus)* or jolly little fruit liqueurs called *likeriai* – about US$0.25 for 50 grams in a café or bar.

ENTERTAINMENT

The three Baltic capitals are becoming increasingly happening places with every month that passes; while the university cities of Kaunas and Tartu, and the summer resorts of Pärnu, Jūrmala and Palanga, are more than active enough to satisfy the western traveller. The nightlife has developed so much in recent years that nostalgic theme bars and clubs recapturing the Soviet experience of just seven years ago are beginning to sprout in the major cities.

There are regular live-music venues and one-off concerts of rock, pop, folk, jazz and blues – by visiting foreign stars as well as local artists. Rīga is considered the Baltic's clubbing (and casino) capital, Tallinn is the place to drink (thanks to the Finns' wild enthusiasm), whereas it is in Vilnius that the heart of fun theme bars and low-key dance parties is said to lie.

Classical music, opera and ballet feature strongly in all three cities with festivals of music, dance and theatre being an integral part of the entertainment and arts calendar. See the individual capital city chapters for more details.

THINGS TO BUY

The Baltic states may not be among the world's shopping meccas, but what is available is often pretty good value. If you're considering buying anything of much monetary, artistic or historic value ask about the rules on exporting things of that kind as there are some restrictions.

Amber

Amber – pine resin fossilised 40 to 55 million years ago – is one of the most distinctive souvenirs of the region. It washes up on beaches and is brought up in fishing nets – especially in the southern half of the region – and alluvial deposits from rivers are mined in the Kaliningrad Region. This translucent, surprisingly light material has been made into jewellery in the region for thousands of years (see The Amber Trail aside in the Kaliningrad Region chapter for more).

Modern amber jewellery is widely available today in Lithuania (especially), Latvia and the Kaliningrad Region, in shops, markets and on street stalls. The cheapest necklaces, made with small pieces of poor colour, cost little over US$4 while the best in city shops go for over US$50, sometimes up to US$100.

Amber pieces come in a variety of shades and sizes and some are a result of a heat and compression treatment which combines small pieces into bigger ones. More old fashioned ways of treating it include boiling in honey to make it darker, or in vegetable oil to make it lighter. Pieces with 'imperfections' such as grains of dirt, or vegetation inside are more likely to be original and may be more valuable. The most sought after pieces are those containing *Jurassic Park*-style insects!

Handicrafts

Excellent and original pottery, ceramics and stained-glass panels are made in the Baltic states and are sold in most art and craft shops at a reasonable price. Easier to get home in one piece are woodcarvings and leatherwork. Small pottery bells of all shapes and sizes, beautifully woven wicker baskets and painted eggs are popular in Lithuania. Quite unique are the various figures and animals sculpted from straw that you'll discover in Estonia.

A couple of shops sell Baltic national costumes – not cheap though. More practical are the snow-flake patterned, hand-knitted woollen garments from Estonia. Woven sashes, table cloths and runners are good buys to be had in all three states. Rīga stages a big crafts fair, the Gadatirgus, with much of Latvia's best produce on sale, on the first weekend in June (get there at 6 am for the quality buys). Vilnius has a similar event, the Kaziukas Fair, around St Casimir's Day, 4 March.

Art

Paintings and prints galore are on offer at galleries, shops and open-air art markets throughout the region, ranging from quite attractive little city views or landscapes to the latest in local avant-garde outpourings. Prices and tackiness levels range widely.

Getting There & Away

The fact that you can travel direct to the Baltic states and on to their western and eastern neighbours, with minimal fuss, is the ultimate proof that Soviet writ no longer rules here. There are now so many ways of travelling into the Baltics that the choice is almost mind boggling. And there is certainly no need to stick with the same form of transport all the way to the Baltics. It's perfectly feasible to fly or take a bus to Warsaw and then enter Lithuania by train, or fly to Helsinki and sail from there to Estonia, for example. Once in the Baltic states, distances are relatively small.

Information in this chapter is particularly vulnerable to change – prices for international travel are volatile, routes are introduced and cancelled, schedules change, special deals come and go, and rules and visa requirements are amended. Airlines and governments seem to take a perverse pleasure in making price structures and regulations as complicated as possible. You should check directly with the airline or a travel agent to make sure you understand how a fare (and ticket you may buy) works. In addition, the travel industry is highly competitive and there are many lurks and perks. Get opinions, quotes and advice from as many airlines and travel agents as possible before you part with your hard earned cash. The details given in this chapter should be regarded as pointers and are not a substitute for your own careful, up-to-date research. Fares in this chapter have been converted to US$ for ease of comparison.

Travel Agencies

Here's a sampler of places to start asking about transport to or from the Baltic states and neighbouring countries. Some are travel agencies specialising in the region (who may have some of the cheapest air tickets), others are general budget, student or youth travel agencies. Also look at the ads in the travel pages of newspapers and 'what's on' magazines. You could try the *Independent*, the *Observer*, the *Sunday Times*, *Time Out*, or *TNT* in Britain; Berlin's *Zitty*; the *New York Times*, *LA Times*, *Chicago Tribune*, or *San Francisco Chronicle Examiner* in the USA; Toronto's *Globe & Mail* in Canada; the Melbourne *Age* or the *Sydney Morning Herald* in Australia; or the *South China Morning Post* in Hong Kong. *Travel Unlimited* newsletter (PO Box 1058, Allston, MA 02134, USA) publishes details of cheap airfares and courier opportunities to worldwide destinations from the USA, Britain, western Europe and elsewhere.

Estonian, Latvian, and Lithuanian embassies, consulates, tourist offices overseas and émigré organisations may be able to help with information on charter flights or other economical ways of getting to the Baltic states (look in capital or major city phone books).

Information on travel ticket outlets within the Baltic states is given in the relevant city and town sections of this book.

Australia

Contal Travel, 84 Wentworth Ave, Surrey Hills, NSW 2010 (☎ 02-9212 5077) – Polish-run travel agency with fares to the Baltics; also has a Brisbane office

Eastern Europe Travel Bureau, 5th floor, 75 King St, Sydney, NSW 2000 (☎ 02-9262 1144, fax 02-9262 4479); 343 Little Collins St, Melbourne, Vic 3000 (☎ 03-9600 0299, fax 03-9670 1793) – Russia, eastern Europe, Trans-Siberia specialist; offices in other state capitals

Gateway Travel, 48 The Boulevarde, Strathfield, NSW 2135 (☎ 02-9745 3333, fax 02-9745 3237) – Baltics, ex-USSR and Trans-Siberia specialist

Red Bear Tours, 1st level, Kings Cross Plaza, 471 St Kilda Rd, Melbourne, Vic 3004 (☎ 03-9867 3888, fax 03-9867 1755) – Russian budget travel specialist; cheap Trans-Siberia packages

STA – student/youth/discount travel specialist with offices in major Australian and world cities

Well Connected Travel, 89 Ferguson St, Forestville NSW 2087 (☎ 02-9975 2355, 0414-451301; fax 02-9451 6446) – specialists in Baltic connections including Baltic tours and sea cruises

Austria

ÖKISTA, 9 Garnisongasse 7, Vienna (☎ 0222-401 480) – student travel agency which is also open to non-students

Belgium

Acotra, Rue de la Madeleine 51, Brussels (☎ 02-5128607) – student travel

Connections Travel Shop, Rue du Marché-au-Charbon 13, Brussels (☎ 02-550 01 00) – useful ticket agent

Canada

FB On Board Courier Services, offices in Montreal (☎ 514-631 7925); Vancouver (☎ 604-278 1266), and Toronto (☎ 905-612 8095) – courier flights

Finncharter, 20 York Mills Rd, Suite 402, North York, ON M2P 2C2 (☎ 416-222 0740; fax 416-222 5004) – Baltic tours including Estonia

Travel CUTS, 187 College St, Toronto (☎ 416-2406) – student/youth/discount travel agency with branches in major cities

Denmark

FremadRejser, Vesterbrogade 43, 1, DK-1620 Copenhagen V (☎ 31 22 04 04, fax 31 22 22 77) – hotel and travel bookings and tours to the Baltic states and Kaliningrad

Kilroy Travels, Skindergade 28, DK-1159 Copenhagen K (☎ 33 11 00 44, fax 33 32 32 69) – budget travel agency; especially useful for tickets if you're a 'young' (under 26) or a student under 35; offices in other cities

Transalpino, Skougade 6, Copenhagen (☎ 33 14 46 33) – student, youth, discount specialist

Finland

Kilroy Travels, Kaivokatu 10d 5, 00100 Helsinki (☎ 09-680 7811) – budget travel agency; useful for tickets if you're a 'youth' (under 26) or a student under 35; offices in other cities

France

Council Travel, 31 Rue Saint Augustine, Paris 75002 (toll-free 0800 1481 48; ☎ 01 44 55 55 44; fax 01 44 55 55 46) – branch of USA's biggest student and budget travel agency

Selectour Voyages, 29 Rue la Huchette, Paris 75005 (☎ 01 43 29 64 00) – discount air tickets

Voyages et Découvertes, 21 Rue Cambon, Paris 75001 (☎ 01 42 61 00 01) – cheap tickets

Germany

Alternativ Tours, Wilmersdorfer Strasse 94, D-10629 Berlin (☎ 030-8 81 20 89) – discount flights

Baltisches Reisebüro, Bayerstrasse 37/1, D-80335 Munich (☎ 089-59 36 53 or 089-59 36 94; fax 089-52 59 13) – big range of tours to all three Baltic states and Kaliningrad Region

Bavaria Studentenreisebüro, Augustusplatz 9, D-04109 Leipzig (☎ 0341-211 4220) – youth and student tickets

Deutsches Reisebüro, Emil-von-Behring-Strasse 6, D-60439 Frankfurt am Main (☎ 069-95 88 00;

fax 069-95 88 10 10) – tours to Baltic states and other parts of ex-USSR

Greif Reisen A Manthey, Universitätsstrasse 2, D-58455 Witten-Heven (☎ 02302-2 40 44; fax 02302-2 50 50) – tour company specialising in Kaliningrad Region, Neringa and Klaipéda; also covers other Baltic states and Poland

Ost-Reise Service, Artur Ladebeck Strasse 139, D-33647 Bielefeld (☎ 0521-14 21 67; fax 0521-15 25 55) – Baltics, Kaliningrad & eastern Europe specialist

Reisebüro Alainis, Revalweg 4, D-87700 Memmingen (☎ 08331-35 82) – tours and individual bookings to Baltic states and Kaliningrad Region

Schnieder Reisen, Harkortstrasse 121, D-22765 Hamburg (☎ 040-380 20 60) – big range of tours and individual bookings to Baltic states and Kaliningrad Region

STA Travel, Berger Strasse 118, D-63016 Frankfurt am Main (☎ 069-43 01 91) – cheap tickets

Ireland

USIT Travel Office, 19 Aston Quay, Dublin (☎ 01-679 8833) – specialising in youth and student travel

Italy

CTS, Via Genova 16, off Via Nazionale, Rome (☎ 06-46 791) – discount and student/youth travel agency; offices throughout Italy

Netherlands

ILC Reizen, NZ Voorburgwal 256, Amsterdam (☎ 020-620 51 51 for flights; 020-622 43 42 for other) – flights, trains, buses

Malibu Travel, Damrak 30, RG-1012 Amsterdam (☎ 020-623 68 14) – long established cheap flight specialist

NBBS, Rokin 38, Amsterdam (☎ 020-624 0989) – Dutch nationwide student travel agency

New Zealand

Sun Travel, 407 Great South Rd, Penrose, Auckland (☎ 09-525 3074, fax 09-525 3065) – offers Trans-Siberian packages; individual travel bookings

Norway

Kilroy Travels, Cortablersgt 30, 0254 Oslo (☎ 22 45 32 00; fax 22 45 32 05) – budget travel agency; especially good if you're a 'youth' (under 26) or a student under 35

Poland

Biuro Turystyki Lauer, ulica Piwna 24, Gdańsk (☎ 0-58-31 16 19)

Spain

TIVE, Calle José Ortega y Gaset 71, Madrid (☎ 091-401 1300) – student/youth travel

Sweden

Kilroy Travels, Kungsgatan 4, Box 7144, S-10387 Stockholm (☎ 08-23 45 15; fax 08-10 16 93) – budget travel agency; especially worth trying for tickets if you're a 'youth' (under 26) or a student under 35

Nordisk Reseservice, Engelbrektsgatan 18, S-10041 Stockholm (☎ 08-791 50 55; fax 08-791 40 90) – travel and tour agency knowledgeable on Baltics

Switzerland

GIB, Eigerplatz 5, CH-3007 Bern (☎ 031-371 81 51) – tours to the Baltic states and Kaliningrad

SSR, Leonhardstrasse 10, CH-8001 Zürich (☎ 01-261 29 56) – budget travel specialist; branches in other cities

UK

ACE, Babraham, Cambridge, CB2 4AP (☎ 01223-835 055; fax 01223-837 394) – art, architecture-oriented tours etc

Campus Travel, YHA Adventure Shop, 174 Kensington High St, London W8 7RG (☎ 0171-938 2188) – student and youth travel specialist with about 30 branches in university towns

Council Travel, 28A Poland St, London W1 (☎ 0171-437 7767) – branch of USA's biggest student and budget travel agency

Finlandia Travel, 227 Regent St, London W1R 7DB (☎ 0171-409 7334) – cheap flights to the Baltics

Martin Randall, 10 Barley Mow Passage, Chiswick, London W4 4PH (☎ 0181-742 3355; fax 0181-742 1066) – tours focusing on art, architecture etc

Progressive Tours, 12 Porchester Place, London W2 2BS (☎ 0171-262 1676; fax 0171-724 6941) – tours and individual bookings, some cheap flights

Regent Holidays, 15 John St, Bristol, BS1 2HR (☎ 0117-921 1711; fax 0117-925 4866; email 106041.1470@compuserve.com; http://www.regent-holidays.co.uk) – leading British Baltic specialist; tours, individual bookings, cheap flights

Scantours, 21-24 Cockspur St, 4th floor, London SW1Y 5BN (☎ 0171-839 2927; fax 0171-839 5891) – flights to Scandinavia; Baltics and Scandinavian tours

STA Travel, 74 Old Brompton Rd, London SW7 (☎ 0171-937 9962; 0171-361 6161) – branch of worldwide student/budget travel agency; branches in major British and European cities

Trailfinders, 215 Kensington High St, London W8 (☎ 0171-937 5400) – discount tickets, travel bookshop, visa service; also offices in Birmingham, Bristol, Glasgow and Manchester

USA

Airhitch, 214 Broadway, 3rd floor, New York, NY 10025 (☎ 212-864 2000; email airhitch@netcom.com) – New York-based specialist in cheap single airfares to Europe

American-International Homestays, PO Box 1754, Nederland, CO 80466 (☎ toll-free 0800-876 2048; ☎ 303-642 3088; fax 303-642 3365) – homestay tours or customised homestays in the Baltic states and ex-USSR

Baltic-American Holidays, 501 Fifth Ave, Suite 1605, New York, NY 10017 (☎ 212-972 0200; fax 212-972 0208) – specialist in group and individual trips to the Baltics

Baltic Tours, 77 Oak St, Suite 4, Newton, MA 02164 (☎ 617-965 8080; fax 617-332 7781) – flights, individual and group tours

Council Travel – student/youth/discount travel agency with offices in many cities including New York (☎ 212-661 1450) and Los Angeles (☎ 310-208 3551)

EuroCruises, 303 West 13th St, New York, NY 10014 (☎ 800-668 3876 (reservations), 800-661 1119 (brochures), 212-691 2099; fax 212-366 4747)

GT International, 9525 South 79th Ave, Hickory Hills, Il 60457-2259 (☎ 708-430 7272; fax 708-430 5783) – Baltic specialists; tours and individual bookings

IBV Bed and Breakfast Systems, 13113 Ideal Drive, Silver Spring, MD 20906 (☎ 301-942 3770; fax 301-933 0024) – Baltic homestays with or without flights

Intourist, 630 Fifth Ave, Suite 868, New York, NY 10111 (☎ 212-757 3884; fax 212-459 0031)

Orbit Travel (☎ 213-466 7248) – information on courier flights in Los Angeles

STA Travel, 3730 Walnut St, Philadelphia, PA 19104 (☎ toll-free 0800-777 0112; ☎ 215-382 2928; fax 215-382 4716) – student/youth/discount travel agency with offices in many cities

Union Tours, 245 Fifth Ave, Suite 1101, New York, NY 10016 (☎ toll-free 0800-451 9511; ☎ 212-683 9500; fax 212-683 9511; telex 425304 UNTO) – group and individual flights and packages to the Baltics

Worldwide Visas, Washington DC (☎ 800-692 0203; email visas@imssys.imssys.com)

Air

Until 1989 there were no scheduled international flights into the Baltic states. Now you can fly direct from a dozen or so western countries, and with a single change of plane from a great many more. Finnair, Lufthansa (Germany), SAS (Scandinavia), Lot (Poland), and Austrian Airlines are among the airlines flying into the Baltics that have worldwide connections to their home countries.

As well as scheduled flights there are also charter flights from some countries. Another option is to fly to a nearby country (Finland,

Comparative Apex Return Fares from Western & Central Europe

From:		Finland	Sweden	Denmark	Poland	Germany	UK
To:	Tallinn	US$110	US$250	US$364	US$275	US$465	US$390
	Rīga	US$250	US$250	US$464	US$218	US$390	US$310
	Vilnius	US$350	US$460	US$400	US$110	US$418	US$315

Poland and Sweden are the most convenient) and do the last leg by sea or overland. This may work out both cheaper and more interesting. Flights to Warsaw on Lot, the Polish airline, are often sold at big discounts all over the world. New routes are also opening all the time.

Buying Tickets

Travel agents, as well as the airlines themselves, should be able to sell you tickets for any of the scheduled flights. SAS, Lufthansa and Finnair are among airlines offering cheap 'youth' fares for under-26s on some routes. Like other cheaper fares these may only able to be booked a week or two before departure. Many airlines also have 'general sales agents' appointed to sell discounted tickets for certain routes. In the case of the Baltics, these are often travel agents who specialise in the region. See the preceding Travel Agencies section for details of some of these. Also get quotes from student, youth, and general discount ticket agents.

Single flights at regular fares are sometimes as expensive as returns, but open-jaw tickets (on which you fly into one city and out of another) are quite widely available for the Baltic capitals and St Petersburg. On SAS, single youth fares between Scandinavia and the Baltic capitals can be combined to form the equivalent of open-jaws. The budget conscious should bear in mind when planning their departure that Tallinn has no airport tax.

Travellers with Special Needs

If you have special needs of any sort – you're a vegetarian, require a special diet, are travelling in a wheelchair or with a baby – alert the airline you are flying with as soon as possible. Remind it when you reconfirm your flight (at least 72 hours before departure) and again when you check in. If you intend flying with any of the Baltic state carriers or with a smaller, private airline, check before you book your ticket that they can meet your needs adequately. Some airlines, ie the aircraft they use, are better suited to cope with special requests than others.

The Baltic Airlines

Since 1992 each Baltic state has had its own state airline carved out of the old Soviet Aeroflot monopoly. These are Estonian Air, Air Baltic, and LAL (Lithuanian Airlines, or Lietuvos Avialinijos). The Latvian airline, Air Baltic, is in partnership with SAS.

In addition, there are the independent Latvian airlines, Rīga Airlines; Air Lithuania (Aviakompanija Lietuva), an independent Lithuanian enterprise that mainly flies in and out of Kaunas; and ELK Airways and Baltic Aeroservis, two independent Estonian airlines that essentially operate domestic flights.

Despite initial teething problems – poor Soviet-style service, primitive customer information and advertising, and Soviet-made planes which weren't popular with some passengers – the state airlines are now as efficient and reliable as their western rivals. The fares they offer have dropped in recent years to compete with other airlines sharing the same route. However, they do not offer special student or youth fares, meaning if you're a student or under 26 it is often cheaper to fly with a western airline, such as

SAS or Finnair, which offers discounted fares.

Ticket Offices You don't always go to an airline itself for the cheapest fares on its flights; many travel agents offer negotiated fares with the airlines. The Baltic airlines all have their own ticket offices or general sales agents in other countries which is useful to know. Estonian Air has the following offices:

Denmark
    Nyhavn 63a, Copenhagen K (☎ 33 32 00 23; fax 33 32 15 99); c/o Maersk Air, Vester Farimagsgade 7, 2nd floor, DK-1606, Copenhagen V (☎ 32 31 45 40; fax 32 31 45 90)
Finland
    PO Box 1, SF-01531, Vaantaa, Helsinki (☎ 09-821 381; fax 09-870 1708); Lentoasemantie 1, International Terminal, SF-01530, Vaantaa, Helskini (☎ 09-61 51 39 00; fax 09-61 51 39 01)
Germany
    Walter-Kolb Strasse 9-11, D-60594, Frankfurt am Main (☎ 069-628 029; fax 069-610 637)
Netherlands
    Kruizweg 635, 2132 NB, Hoofddorp, PO Box 75569, ZP-1118 Schiphol (☎ 020-65 311 34; fax 020-65 311 30)
Russia
    K-340 Airport, Sheremetyevo 1, R-103340 Moscow (☎ 0578-2190, 0578-4685; fax 0578-2743)
Sweden
    Drottninggatan 65, S-11136 Stockholm (☎ 08-233 666; fax 08-233 669)
    Gustav Adams Torg 47, PO Box 4026, S-20311 Malmö (☎ 040-122 560; fax 040-79 730)
    Södra Hamngatan 37-41, Box 11214, S-40425 Göteborg (☎ 031-800 130; fax 031-800 137)
Ukraine
    Ploshchad Peremogi 2, 252135 Kiev (☎ & fax 044-555 7271)

Air Baltic tickets are sold at most SAS offices worldwide. Its other offices include:

Belarus
    Smok Travel Agency, 43 Skoriny Ave, Minsk 220005 (☎ 017-2204 202; fax 017-2200 614)
Finland
    Keskatu 7a, 4th floor, FI-00100 Helsinki (☎ 09-228 021; fax 09-179 730)
Poland
    International Express, 19/21 ks, J Popieluszki, Warsaw (☎ & fax 022-337 136)

Sweden
    Frösundaviks allé 1, Solna, SE-195 87, Stockholm (☎ 08-797 1685; fax 08-797 1865)
UK
    Chapman Freeborn Travel, 7 Buckingham Gate, London SW1E 6JP (☎ 0171-828 4223; fax 0171-630 8302)
USA
    1990 Post Blvd, Suite 1630, Houston, TX 770-3813 (☎ 713-9611 270; fax 713-9619 298)

LAL's international sales offices include:

Australia
    Suite 17, 37-39 Albert Rd, Melbourne, Vic 3004 (☎ 03-9866 5660; fax 03-9866 4569)
France
    78 Champs Élysées, 75008 Paris (☎ 01 53 76 08 75; fax 01 53 76 08 77)
Germany
    Flughafen, Berlin/Tegel Apt, Counter Nr B1/05a, Berlin (☎ 030-8875 6127; fax 030-8875 6130); 60549 Frankfurt am Main Flughafen, Terminal 2, Building 149, Hall E, Room 5318 (☎ 069-6958 2511; fax 069-6958 2514)
Ireland
    Town Centre Mall, Swords, Co. Dublin (☎ 01-8406 295; fax 01-8400 498)
Russia
    Povorskaya 24, 121069 Moscow (☎ 095-203 7502; fax 095-291 1207)
Sweden
    Arlanda Airport, PO Box 187, 19046 Stockholm (☎ 08-5936 0905; fax 08-5936 0909)
USA
    443 Park Ave South, Suite 1006, New York, NY 10016 (☎ toll-free 800-7113 958; ☎ 212-679 0966; fax 201-8909 007)

Estonian Air, LAL and Rīga Airline tickets are all sold in the UK by Flight Representation (☎ 01293-535 727, 01293 534 735; fax 01293-553 321) of Ocean House, Hazelwick Ave, Three Bridges, Crawley, West Sussex RH10 1NP.

Rīga Airline tickets are sold in Russia by the Russian state airline, Transaero Airlines, (☎ 0578-0537/38/39) K-340 Airport, Sheremetyevo 1, 103340 Moscow.

FINLAND
Estonia
Finnair and Estonian Air both fly from Helsinki to Tallinn, and vice versa, at least once a day. The flight is only 30 minutes but

often ends up being no quicker than a hydrofoil (which is much cheaper) because of the time spent getting to and from the airports. The cheapest returns are around US$110 with either airline, providing you stay a Sunday night in Helsinki. Finnair has a return youth fare of around US$85, bookable no more than seven days before you fly. ELK flies to Turku twice weekly for US$278 return; it also has a youth fare for US$162 return.

Latvia & Lithuania

Finnair flies Helsinki-Rīga-Helsinki five times a week, and Air Baltic flies Rīga-Helsinki-Rīga six times a week. An Apex return ticket, with the Sunday night rule, from Helsinki is around US$250 with Finnair, and substantially more with Air Baltic. LAL, in co-operation with Finnair, flies five times weekly between Helsinki and Vilnius. You can also fly to Helsinki from Kaunas with Air Lithuania.

SWEDEN
Estonia

SAS has daily flights both ways between Stockholm and Tallinn, and Estonian Air flies the same route 12 times a week. The return fare with SAS, booking seven days in advance and adhering to the Sunday rule, is US$250. The youth fare is US$248 return with no restrictions. Estonian Air's cheapest single/return fares are US$370/248.

Latvia

SAS and Air Baltic have daily Stockholm-Rīga-Stockholm flights. The cheapest returns from Stockholm are around US$250 with SAS, providing you stay a weekend in Stockholm. SAS also has youth fares on this route. Air Baltic's return Rīga-Stockholm fare (seven days in advance and Sunday rule) is US$353. Transeast Airlines has three direct flights weekly between Jönköping, in central Sweden, and Rīga. The company also has three further flights a week to Billund, in Denmark, that also stop at Jönköping.

Lithuania

SAS and LAL both fly three times weekly each way between Vilnius and Stockholm. Air Lithuania also has twice weekly flights between Kaunas and Kristianstad via Palanga. There are also daily flights with SAS and four times weekly flights with LAL to Copenhagen, from where SAS connects with main Swedish cities. Stockholm-Vilnius returns start about US$460 on SAS (with a three day stay in Stockholm). The SAS return youth fare is US$398.

DENMARK
Estonia

Estonian Air makes direct flights between Tallinn and Copenhagen two times a week, taking 1½ hours; SAS flies there 12 times weekly. Estonian Air's cheapest Tallinn-Copenhagen fare is US$364 (seven days advance purchase and Sunday rule); its one-way fare is US$512.

Latvia

Air Baltic flies twice daily to Copenhagen while SAS has a daily flight. The cheapest SAS returns from Copenhagen are US$464. A return Air Baltic ticket from Rīga to Copenhagen is US$466. Air Baltic's daily flight to Geneva also stops at Copenhagen. Transeast Airlines has flights three times a week to Billund in Denmark via Jönköping in Sweden.

Lithuania

There are daily flights with SAS and four weekly flights with LAL to Copenhagen. The cheapest returns from Copenhagen on SAS are US$400, and the return youth fare is US$322. Single/return fares with LAL are US$195/356.

Kaliningrad

SAS has flights four times a week between Copenhagen and Kaliningrad. A return ticket booked seven days in advance and staying a Sunday in Kaliningrad is US$355.

POLAND

Estonia

Lot flies between Warsaw and Tallinn three times a week, the journey taking 2½ hours.

Latvia

Air Baltic and Lot both fly twice a week from Warsaw to Rīga and vice versa.

Lithuania

Between LAL and Lot there are flights every day between Vilnius and Warsaw. LAL flies every day, except Thursday and Sunday; Lot flies every day, except Saturday. An Apex Vilnius-Warsaw return with LAL is US$110. In Warsaw find out whether your flight will leave from the domestic or the international airport terminal. They're far enough apart to make you miss your plane if you turn up at the wrong terminal at the last minute.

GERMANY

In addition to the scheduled flights mentioned here, charter flights may be an economical option from Germany to any

Air Travel Glossary

Apex Apex (advance purchase excursion) is a discounted ticket which must be paid for in advance. You must purchase the ticket at least 21 days in advance (sometimes more), be away for a minimum period (normally 14 days), and return within a maximum period (90 or 180 days). There are penalties if you wish to change it.

Baggage Allowance This will be written on your ticket: usually one 20 kg item to go in the hold, plus one item of hand luggage.

Bucket Shop An unbonded travel agency specialising in discounted airline tickets. Flight availability varies widely, so you'll not only have to be flexible in your travel plans, you'll also have to be quick off the mark as soon as an advertisement appears in the press.

Bumped Just because you have a confirmed seat doesn't mean you're going to get on the plane – see Overbooking.

Cancellation Penalties If you have to cancel or change an Apex ticket there are often heavy penalties involved; insurance can sometimes be taken out against these penalties. Some airlines impose penalties on regular tickets as well, particularly against 'no show' passengers.

Check In Airlines ask you to check in a certain time ahead of the flight departure (usually 1½ hours on international flights). If you fail to check in on time and the flight is overbooked, the airline can cancel your booking and give your seat to somebody else.

Confirmation Having a ticket written out with the flight and date you want doesn't mean you have a seat until the agent has checked with the airline that your status is 'OK' or confirmed. Meanwhile you could just be 'on request'.

Discounted Tickets There are two types of discounted fares – officially discounted (see Promotional Fares) and unofficially discounted. The lowest prices often impose drawbacks like flying with unpopular airlines, inconvenient schedules, or unpleasant routes and connections. A discounted ticket can save you other things than money – you may be able to pay Apex prices without the associated Apex advance booking and other requirements. Discounted tickets only exist where there is fierce competition.

Economy Class Tickets Economy class tickets are usually not the cheapest way to go, though they do give you maximum flexibility and they are valid for 12 months. If you don't use them, most are fully refundable, as are unused sectors of a multiple ticket.

Full Fares Airlines traditionally offer first class (coded F), business class (coded J) and economy class (coded Y) tickets. These days there are so many promotional and discounted fares available from the regular economy class that few passengers pay full economy fare.

Lost Tickets If you lose your airline ticket an airline will usually treat it like a travellers' cheque and, after inquiries, issue you with another one. Legally, however, an airline is entitled to treat it like cash and if you lose it then it's gone forever. Take good care of your tickets.

No Shows No shows are passengers who fail to show up for their flight, sometimes due to unexpected delays or disasters, sometimes due to simply forgetting, sometimes because they made more than one booking and didn't bother to cancel the one they didn't want. Full-fare passengers who fail to turn up are sometimes entitled to travel on a later flight. The rest of us are penalised (see Cancellation Penalties).

Baltic state. Baltisches Reisebüro, Greif Reisen, Ost-Reise Service and Schnieder Reisen have all offered charters in the past. Lufthansa has open-jaw youth fares combining Baltic capitals at similar rates to there-and-back youth fares.

Estonia

Lufthansa has three flights a week to/from Frankfurt and Estonian Air has four (each airline flying on different days). Regular return fares from either end with both airlines start at around US$465.

Latvia

Lufthansa flies Frankfurt-Rīga-Frankfurt daily and Hamburg-Rīga-Hamburg daily, except Saturday; Air Baltic has daily flights to Frankfurt and Hamburg. An independent German airline, Hamburg Airlines, flies to/from Berlin (Tempelhof) and Hamburg four times a week. Air Baltic's return fares from either Germany or Latvia generally begin around US$390. Lufthansa's cheapest return fare is US$513 provided you purchase the ticket three days in advance and stay in Frankfurt on a Sunday night. It has a youth

---

Open-Jaws A return ticket where you fly out to one place but return from another. If available this can save you backtracking to your arrival point.

Overbooking Airlines hate to fly empty seats and since every flight has some passengers who fail to show up (see No Shows) airlines often book more passengers than they have seats for. Usually the excess passengers balance those who fail to show up but occasionally somebody gets bumped. And guess who it is most likely to be? The passengers who check in late.

Promotional Fares Officially discounted fares, like Apex fares, which are available from travel agents or direct from the airline.

Reconfirmation At least 72 hours prior to departure time of an onward or return flight you must contact the airline and 'reconfirm' that you intend to be on the flight. If you don't do this the airline can delete your name from the passenger list and you could lose your seat. You don't have to reconfirm the first flight on your itinerary or if your stopover is less than 72 hours. It doesn't hurt to reconfirm more than once.

Restrictions Discounted tickets often have various restrictions on them – advance purchase is the most usual one (see Apex). Others are restrictions on the minimum and maximum period you must be away, such as a minimum of 14 days or a maximum of one year. See Cancellation Penalties.

Stand-By A discounted ticket where you only fly if there is a seat free at the last moment. Stand-by fares are usually only available on domestic routes. To give yourself the best possible chance of getting on the flight you want, get there early and have your name placed on the waiting list. It's first come, first served.

Sunday or Weekend Rule Applies to some return tickets – you must spend one Sunday or weekend in your destination before returning.

Tickets Out An entry requirement for many countries is that you have an onward or return ticket, in other words, a ticket out of the country. If you're not sure what you intend to do next, the easiest solution is to buy the cheapest onward ticket to a neighbouring country or a ticket from a reliable airline which can later be refunded if you do not use it.

Transferred Tickets Airline tickets cannot be transferred from one person to another. Travellers sometimes try to sell the return half of their ticket, but officials can ask you to prove that you are the person named on the ticket. This is unlikely to happen on domestic flights, but on an international flight tickets may be compared with passports.

Travel Agencies Travel agencies vary widely and you should ensure you use one that suits your needs. Some simply handle tours while full-service agencies handle everything from tours and tickets to car rental and hotel bookings. A good one will do all these things and can save you a lot of money, but if all you want is a ticket at the lowest possible price, then you really need an agency specialising in discounted tickets. A discounted ticket agency, however, may not be useful for other things like hotel bookings.

Travel Periods Some officially discounted fares, Apex fares in particular, vary with the time of year. There is often a low (off-peak) season and a high (peak) season. Sometimes there's an intermediate or shoulder season as well. At peak times, when everyone wants to fly, not only will the officially discounted fares be higher but so will unofficially discounted fares, or there may simply be no discounted tickets available. Usually the fare depends on your outward flight – if you depart in the high season and return in the low season, you pay the high-season fare. ∎

fare for people under 25 which is US$485 return.

Lithuania

Lufthansa has daily flights to Frankfurt (Main). The German independent airline, Hamburg Airlines, flies three times weekly to Hamburg and Berlin (Temelhof), and twice weekly to Saarbrücken. The cheapest fares are offered by LAL which flies to Berlin (Tegel) and Frankfurt (Main) five times a week. Apex returns on the LAL Berlin route are around US$300, departing from either end. Returns to/from Frankfurt or Hamburg start at around US$418. Air Lithuania also has flights to Hamburg, to/from Kaunas airport.

Kaliningrad

The Russian state airline, Aeroflot, flies to Hamburg twice a week.

THE UK

Estonian Air flies Tallinn-London-Tallinn four times weekly and LAL flies from Vilnius daily, except Thursday and Sunday. Estonian Air's return flight is around US$390; LAL's starts at around US$350.

From Rīga you have more choice of who to fly with. Air Baltic flies to/from London twice weekly; the independent Latvian airline, Rīga Airlines, has flights daily, except Wednesday and Saturday; and, as of April 1997, British Airways (BA) flies London-Rīga-London four times weekly. BA also offers open-jaw fares to tour operators, meaning it is possible to fly with BA to Helsinki and fly back with it to London from Rīga. BA's published fare is US$310 (£199) but tour operators often get lower rates. In early 1997, Air Baltic's London-Rīga return flight was US$331, the only restriction being a minimum weekend stay and purchasing the ticket seven days in advance. Rīga Airlines' fare for a round trip is US$252 with no restrictions. Both airlines offer special deals every so often.

Flying with SAS, there are flights via Copenhagen to each of the Baltic capitals from London, Manchester, Edinburgh and Glasgow. The big advantage of SAS is that it offers student and youth fares; a return from Vilnius to London was US$315 in early 1997. Other air routes to the Baltics from Britain include via Warsaw with Lot, via Frankfurt with Lufthansa, and via Vienna with Austrian Airlines.

For all three Baltic capitals, the fares offered by specialist agents are often cheaper than the airlines' own. Some of the best are on SAS or Finnair flights via Scandinavia, or with Lufthansa via Frankfurt. Regent Holidays, for instance, has open-jaw returns to Vilnius or Tallinn on Lufthansa for US$353; and a standard London-Vilnius return with Lithuanian Airlines for around US$340. Campus Travel has a return to Rīga with Finnair for US$395; Trailfinders has return Rīga flights for US$420, and STA Travel has the same return with SAS for US$450.

As of 1 November, 1997, the departure tax from UK airports to non-EU destinations, ie the Baltic states, will double from £10 to £20.

ELSEWHERE IN EUROPE

Other direct flights to/from other European countries include:

Amsterdam-Tallinn
    Estonian Air, six times weekly
Amsterdam-Vilnius
    LAL, three times weekly
Budapest-Kaunas
    Air Lithuania, twice weekly
Geneva-Rīga
    Air Baltic, daily
Istanbul-Vilnius
    LAL, three times weekly
Larnaca-Vilnius
    LAL, twice weekly
Paris-Rīga
    Air Baltic, twice weekly
Paris-Vilnius
    LAL, three times weekly
Prague-Kaunas
    Air Lithuania, twice weekly
Prague-Rīga
    ČSA, four times weekly
Rome-Vilnius
    LAL, twice weekly
Vienna-Rīga
    Austrian Airlines, three times weekly
Vienna-Vilnius
    Austrian Airlines, three times weekly

Zürich-Kaunas
   Air Lithuania, twice weekly

RUSSIA, TRANSCAUCASIA & CENTRAL ASIA

There are up to four flights daily between Moscow and each of the Baltic capitals including Estonian Air and the Russian state airline Aeroflot from Tallinn, Aeroflot and Rīga Airlines from Rīga, Aeroflot and LAL from Vilnius, and Aeroflot from Kaliningrad. In Moscow all flights use Sheremetevo I airport, except Kaliningrad flights which use Vnukovo.

The three Baltic state airlines also fly up to seven times a week between Tallinn, Rīga and Vilnius. Estonian Air also flies to St Petersburg three times weekly and Aeroflot flies five times a week from Kaliningrad to St Petersburg and vice versa. You can also get to and from dozens of other places in Russia, Transcaucasia or former Soviet Central Asia via a connection at Moscow with Aeroflot or one of its successors – you should be able to book all the way through in one go. Some direct flights pop up but they're on/off affairs so far.

In early 1997, LAL had Vilnius-Moscow single/return flights for US$120/220; Estonian Air was offering single/return Moscow fares from Tallinn for US$376/258. Its single/return fare to St Petersburg is US$162/322. In Russia go to Aeroflot offices for tickets to the Baltics; you need your passport to buy a ticket.

BELARUS & UKRAINE
Estonia

Estonian Air flies Tallinn-Minsk-Tallinn and Tallinn-Kiev-Tallinn three times weekly. One-month singles/returns are US$320/210 for Minsk.

Latvia

Air Baltic flies Rīga-Minsk-Rīga and Rīga-Kiev-Rīga three times weekly. A Rīga-Minsk fare is US$335 single and US$295 return, providing you stay in Minsk for a weekend. A return with no restrictions is US$650. The small independent airline,

Aerosweet, also flies to Kiev, three times weekly.

Lithuania

Air Kiev flies Kiev-Vilnius-Kiev three times weekly.

Kaliningrad

Aeroflot flies once weekly to/from Kiev.

MIDDLE EAST

The independent Latvian airline, Latpass, flies to Tel Aviv once a week and LAL operates a twice weekly Dubai-Vilnius service.

NORTH AMERICA

There are no longer any direct flights between the Baltics and North America; all flights go via Scandinavia. There are also plenty of connections through countries near the Baltics on Finnair, SAS, Lot, CSA, Lufthansa and so on, plus some charter possibilities. Or you can fly to Scandinavia or Warsaw and finish the trip by sea or overland.

At the time of writing, Finnair was offering returns to/from New York for US$795, undercutting most other airlines by about US$300; while KLM had return trips from Toronto for US$850, dropping to US$550 out of season. Generally speaking, the best deals seem to be on offer in New York from firms that specialise in the Baltics. Baltic Tours and Baltic American Holidays can both do return fares to the Baltic capitals for around US$700, increasing to about US$1000 in summer.

The weekend edition of the Polish newspaper *Nowy Dziennik* has lots of ads for flights from the USA to Poland, and there are several Polish travel agencies in Manhattan, Brooklyn, Chicago and elsewhere. There's a lot of competition on US-Scandinavian routes which should keep prices down; you should get a New York-Stockholm return for US$500 to US$600 low season, US$700 to US$800 high season. Airhitch can get you a single stand-by fare from the USA to Europe for around US$160 to US$270 depending where you start in the USA. Call Council

Travel for information on courier flights – two to three months in advance, at the start of the calendar month.

AUSTRALIA

There are no direct scheduled flights from Australia to the Baltics. Aeroflot flies from Sydney to Moscow for US$1200 to US$1300 return. Another airline flying to both Australia and the Baltics is Lufthansa. Among the specialist agents, Gateway Travel offers return fares from Sydney, Melbourne or Brisbane to the Baltics from around US$1200 to US$1600. Well Connected Travel offers return fares with Singapore and Scandinavian Airlines from Sydney, Melbourne, Brisbane, Adelaide and Perth starting at US$1775. Or you could fly to Scandinavia, Warsaw or Moscow then finish the trip by sea or overland. Discounted return fares to Scandinavia on mainstream airlines – through a reputable agent like STA – range from around US$1200 (low season) to US$1600 (high season).

ASIA

There are no direct flights between Asia and the Baltics. Some of the cheapest flights from Asia are with east European airlines, such as via Moscow using Aeroflot, via Prague with CSA, or via Warsaw with Lot. Helsinki with Finnair and Stockholm with SAS are other possible routes.

Land

BUS

With a few exceptions, buses are the cheapest but least comfortable method of reaching the Baltic states. There are direct buses from Denmark, France, Germany, Norway, Poland, Sweden, Finland, Russia and Belarus. From much of the rest of Europe you can reach the Baltics with a single change of bus in Warsaw, though buses from Warsaw into Lithuania do have a couple of potential snags. One is that some of the buses between Warsaw and Vilnius can get booked

up. The other is the delays on the border (which are even worse when leaving Lithuania). Motorists have had to queue as long as four days at the border between Ogrodniki (east of Suwałki, Poland) and Lazdijai (Lithuania); and the second border point, on the road from Suwałki, Szypliszki and Budzisko (Poland) to Kalvarija and Marijampolė (Lithuania), is no better. Scheduled buses seem to be spared the very long waits that some private motorists have to endure and generally get through in two to four hours.

If you're thinking of taking a bus across this border, it pays to find out how long it will *really* take to reach its destination. Ask other travellers, youth hostel workers, and Lithuanian or Polish embassies as well as bus companies. In general you should book as far ahead as you can for any bus into or out of any of the Baltic states.

Bus Passes & Youth Tickets

If you are an ISIC holder or have a Euro<26 card, you are entitled to a 10% discounted fare on all Eurolines buses. And given all three Baltic states now have a Eurolines office to call their own, this saving can be well worthwhile. In Tallinn the Eurolines office (☎ 2-6410 100; fax 2-6410 101) is at Lasekodu 46; South Estonian Travel (☎ 27-476 346; fax 27-474 553), on the second floor of Tartu bus station, is the office in Tartu; in Rīga (☎ & fax 7211 158) it's at Aspazijas bulvāris 26; and in Vilnius (☎ & fax 22-635 467) at the bus station at Sodų 22.

None of the three Baltic states are yet to be included among the cities covered by the Eurolines pass, which offers one or two months unlimited travel between specified cities in Europe. However, this is expected to change shortly.

Poland-Lithuania

The Polish state tourist company, Orbis, runs a fairly reliable and comfortable service nightly from Warsaw (Varšuva in Lithuanian) to Vilnius and back. The overnight trip takes about 11 hours. The fare is US$15 one-way or US$26 return either way. In Warsaw you can get tickets from the Orbis head office (☎ 022-260 271; fax 022-273 301), ulica Bracka 16, 00-028 Warsaw, or at other offices including ones at ulica Pulawska 31 and ulica Marszalkowska 142 (open daily, except Saturday and Sunday). In Vilnius, tickets are sold at the international ticket desk in the bus station.

There are a further four daily buses each between Vilnius and Warsaw, and an extra bus on Monday and Wednesday. The scheduled nine hour trip costs US$15 to US$20 one-way – departures and tickets from Warsaw Central bus station or Vilnius bus station. The international (*miedzynarodowa*) ticket window at Warsaw Central bus station is closed on Saturday afternoon and all day Sunday.

The Varita bus company in Vilnius (☎ 22-730 219, 2-733 793; fax 2-723 884), next to the Lietuva hotel at Ukmergės 12a (open weekdays from 9 am to 6 pm), operates one bus daily from Vilnius to Poznan (17 hours, US$32.50/57.50 single/return) in Poland. The bus stops at Druskininkai in Lithuania and in Poland stops en route at Warsaw (10 hours, US$16.50/31.50), Lodz (12½ hours, US$20/37 single/return) and Konin (15 hours, US$25/45). For information and tickets in Warsaw contact OPEK (☎ 02-6253 895) at Warsaw Central bus station; in Poznan go to Eurostop (☎ 061-530 343, 331 897), ulica Glogowska 10.

Other buses, between Poland and Vilnius bus station, include:

Białystok-Vilnius
7½ hours; two daily; US$8.70 or US$12
Gdańsk-Vilnius
12 hours; one nightly; US$17.50
Gdynia-Vilnius
13½ hours; one bus nightly on Tuesday and Thursday; US$17.50
Kėntrzyn-Vilnius
7½ hours; one nightly (via Suwałki); US$8
Suwałki-Vilnius
4½ hours; three direct buses daily and one bus every Monday and Friday (via Olsztyn); US$6.50 to US$7.50

Buses between Poland and other places in Lithuania include:

Augustów-Druskininkai:	two daily
Gdańsk-Olsztyn-Suwałki-Kaunas:	one daily
Suwałki-Druskininkai:	one daily
Suwałki-Kaunas:	one daily
Warsaw-Kaunas:	one nightly

Poland-Belarus

There are buses from Warsaw Central bus station to Brest, Grodno and Minsk daily. These might be useful if you want to approach Lithuania through Belarus.

Poland-Estonia

There is a twice weekly bus between Warsaw and Tallinn (17 hours) operated by the Estonian bus company Mootor Reisid/Eurolines (☎ 2-6410 100; fax 2-6410 101), Lasekodu 46, EE-0001 Tallinn, and the Tallinn Bus Company (☎ 2-532 277; fax 2-6509 509), Kadaka tee 62a, EE-0026 Tallinn. In Warsaw you can get tickets at the Central bus station (see Poland-Lithuania). In Tallinn you can get tickets from the bus station – either from the international desk on your left as you enter (open daily from 8 am to 11.45 pm) or from the Eurolines office (open weekdays from 9 am to 6 pm).

Poland-Latvia

A Warsaw-bound bus departs daily from Rīga bus station at 6 pm, arriving in Warsaw Central bus station at 8 am the following morning. Tickets can be bought in Rīga from the Nordeka bus company (☎ 462 521, 468 814), Dzirciema 121. It also has an International Passage booking office (*Starptaukisko Reisu kase*) inside the main ticket hall at Rīga central bus station (open weekdays from 9 am to 1 pm, 2 to 6 pm, and Saturdays from 9 am to 1 pm, 2 pm to 7.30 pm), from where you buy tickets for immediate departures and in advance. In Warsaw you can get tickets from the bus station.

Poland-Kaliningrad

In 1992 a number of bus services started up between north-eastern Polish towns and Kaliningrad, operated jointly by König Auto of Kaliningrad (☎ 22-430 480) and various Polish companies. Initially these were only open to Polish and Russian residents, but now anyone can use them. Tickets can be bought at Kaliningrad bus station from the ticket window for Poland (see Getting There & Away in the Kaliningrad chapter). Current routes are:

Bartoszyce-Bagrationovsk-Kaliningrad: 4¼ hours, once daily each way, US$6, Polish operator: PKS
Elblag-Braniewo-Mamonovo-Kaliningrad: four hours, twice daily each way, US$5 Elblag-Kaliningrad, US$3 vice versa, Polish operator: ZKS Olimpia, ulica Agrikola, Elblag (☎ 0-50-24503)
Gdańsk-Elblag-Braniewo-Mamonovo-Kaliningrad: five hours, twice daily each way, US$7 Gdańsk-Kaliningrad, Polish operator: PPKS, ulica Wałowa 19, Gdańsk (☎ 0-58-316276)
Olsztyn via Bartoszice: four hours, six times daily each way, one bus daily via Olsztyn and Warsaw to Łodz, Polish operator: PKS

Western Europe
A bus trip through Poland is probably the cheapest way into the Baltics from western Europe.

Direct Buses From Vilnius, there is one direct weekly service between Vilnius and Paris, stopping at Kaunas, Strasbourg, Metz and Reims en route. It leaves Vilnius at 8 pm on Sunday, arriving in Paris at midnight the following night. It returns from Paris on Tuesday. A single/return fare is US$112/166.

Another bus runs every Sunday from Vilnius to Saarbrücken in Germany. The journey takes around 35½ hours and costs US$97.50 for a single ticket and US$146 for a return. Stops in between include Dresden (22 hours; US$73/131 single/return), Frankfurt Main (30 hours; US$81/131), and Hamburg (34 hours; US$97.50/146). In Vilnius tickets for both buses are sold by the Varita bus company in Vilnius (☎ 22-730 219, 22-733 793; fax 22-723 884), next to the Lietuva hotel at Ukmergės 12a (open weekdays from 9 am to 6 pm). The Vilnius Eurolines office (☎ & fax 635 467) at the bus station also sells tickets for the Paris bus. In April 1997, Eurolines plans to run a direct bus from Vilnius to Göteborg, via Tallinn, Norrköping, Jönköping and Borås.

From Tallinn there are a number of direct Eurolines buses to western Europe. Some of these buses stop in Kaunas, Panevėžys (Lithuania) or Rīga (Latvia). The Tallinn-Paris bus departs from Tallinn every Sunday at 7 am, passes through Kaunas at 4.35 pm and arrives in Paris the following morning at 7.30 am. A single/return from Tallinn is US$125/229; from Kaunas US$109/197. The Tallinn-Stuttgart bus leaves Tallinn on Monday and Friday at 7 am, passes through Pärnu at 8.50 am, Rīga at noon, Kaunas at 4.35 pm and stops at Berlin and Frankfurt en route to Stuttgart. The entire journey is 37 hours and a single/return from Tallinn is US$111/182. On Wednesday and Saturday, the Tallinn-Cologne bus leaves at 7 am, via Pärnu, Rīga, Panevėžys, Kaunas, Berlin, Hanover, Essen and Düsseldorf. A single/return ticket for the 36 hour trip costs US$108/194. The once weekly Tallinn-Munich service (Sunday departure, 7 am) also stops at Pärnu, Rīga, Panevėžys, Kaunas and Berlin.

Eurolines buses to Scandinavia include the Tartu-Tallinn-Stockholm-Oslo service and the Tartu-Tallinn-Stockholm-Jönköping-Göteborg service. Both run every six or eight days. A single/return from Tallinn or Tartu to Göteborg is US$47/79; fares to Oslo are about US$10 more. There are also some Tartu-Tallinn-Stockholm-Copenhagen buses weekly, via Norrköping, Göteborg and Helsingør.

Tickets for all these buses are sold at any Eurolines ticket office.

Via Warsaw From many other cities in Europe you can get a bus to Warsaw and pick up another bus or a train from there into Lithuania. There are useful youth or student discounts on some international European buses (see Bus Passes & Youth Tickets). Buses leave from London four times a week; the trip takes one to 1½ days and costs around US$45 single and US$63 return. For contact numbers for various operators, travel information and direct bookings contact the Polish travel office, Polorbis (☎ 0171-637 4971; fax 0171-436 6558) at 82 Mortimer St, London W1N 7DE. Traveller's Check-In at

35 Woburn Place, London WC1, is another sales point for bus tickets to Poland.

In Warsaw you can get tickets for buses to the west both at the Central bus station and at Orbis offices (see Poland-Lithuania).

Other international buses are run by Eurolines (☎ 0171-730 0202; 01582-404 511) of 52 Grosvenor Gardens, London W1, which is a major European bus line with continent-wide connections and agents in many cities including: Amsterdam (☎ 020-6275 151); Barcelona (☎ 093-490 4000); Berlin (☎ 030-301 2028); Brussels (☎ 02-217 0025); Budapest (☎ 01-1172 562); Cologne (☎ 221-135 252); Copenhagen (☎ 033-251 044); Frankfurt (☎ 069-230 735); Hamburg (☎ 040-2804 538); Lyon (☎ 04-72 41 09 09); Milan (☎ 02-80 11 61); Munich (☎ 089-54 58 700); Paris (☎ 01-49 72 51 51); and Prague (☎ 02-2421 3420). See the Bus Passes & Youth Tickets section for a listing of Eurolines' Baltic agents.

Belarus

Remember that if you travel through Belarus you will need a Belarus visa – see Visas & Embassies in the Facts for the Visitor chapter.

Services (all run both ways) include:

Minsk-Vilnius-Chernyakhovsk-Kaliningrad: 11½ hours; daily
Minsk-Vilnius-Kaunas: six or nine hours; twice daily
Minsk-Vilnius-Klaipėda-Palanga: 11 hours; daily
Minsk-Daugavpils-Rīga: 12 hours; daily
Minsk-Vilnius-Rīga: 10 hours; daily
Minsk-Vilnius: 4 hours; twice daily

Russia

All three Baltic states have bus links with Kaliningrad, although only Estonia has bus links with the Russian motherland. From Tallinn, Eurolines runs one bus nightly to Kaliningrad, via Rīga, Šiauliai and Sovietsk (15 hours). A single Tallinn-Kaliningrad fare is US$17; from Rīga it costs US$9.50. From Rīga, there is one other bus to Kaliningrad, also via Šiauliai (10 hours), operated by the Nordeka bus company. From Vilnius, there are two or three buses daily, taking eight to nine hours and costing US$8 to US$25. A

number of buses also travel along the Curonian Spit between Klaipėda and Kaliningrad.

There are two buses daily between Tallinn and St Petersburg, departing from Tallinn bus station at 7.30 am and 4 pm, passing through Narva at 10.45 am and 7.15 pm, arriving in St Petersburg at 3.20 pm and 11.50 pm. A single/return fare from Tallinn is US$10/20. Departure in St Petersburg is from bus station No 2 on the corner of Ligovsky prospekt and Obvodny kanal. There are also nightly buses both ways between St Petersburg and Tartu (eight hours, US$10) and between St Petersburg and Pärnu (10 hours, US$13).

Finland

Eurolines runs a daily Tartu-Tallinn-Helsinki-Tampere bus, departing daily from Tartu at 8.10 am, catching the noon ferry from Tallinn and arriving in Helsinki at 5 pm and Tampere at 7.50 pm. Tickets are sold in Tallinn and Tartu at the Eurolines offices in the central bus stations.

TRAIN

Travelling by train can be an interesting way of reaching the Baltic states – cheaper than flying and generally less boring than by bus. Two of the world's most memorable rail journeys figure among the approaches to the Baltic states: the Trans-Siberian and the briefer – but unforgettable – Suwałki-Šeštokai railway from Poland to Lithuania.

If you plan to do a lot of train travel around Europe get the *Thomas Cook European Timetable*, it's updated monthly, gives full intercity timetable listings and indicates where reservations are necessary or supplements payable. It covers as far east as Moscow (the *Thomas Cook International Timetable* continues across Siberia and Central Asia) and is available from Thomas Cook outlets around the world.

Rail Passes & Youth Tickets

The Baltic states are not, at present, included in the Inter-Rail, Eurail, ScanRail or Nordturist rail passes, so if you're travelling with one of these you won't get any benefits in the Baltics. There are rail passes available for the Baltic states and Kaliningrad alone, but you need to buy them before you arrive. See the Getting Around chapter for details.

The Baltic states and the Kaliningrad Region are not included in the Wasteels/BIJ (Billets Internationales de Jeunesse) ticket network either. Wasteels/BIJ tickets are sold in the Baltic states, however, only for western European destinations from Warsaw onwards, meaning you still pay the full fare between the Baltic states and Warsaw. Student and Youth travel offices, and some travel agencies, sell tickets and can give you more information. The Student and Youth travel office in Vilnius for example, sells single Warsaw-Berlin tickets for US$25.

Germany

There is one daily train from Daugavpils and Vilnius to Berlin – the Berlin-St Petersburg train which passes through the two Baltic cities en route. The St Petersburg train leaves Berlin-Lichtenberg at 11.02 pm and reaches St Petersburg's Warsaw Station some 35½ hours later. It travels via Warsaw Central (nine hours from Berlin); Białystok in Poland (12 hours); and Grodno in Belarus (17 hours). It arrives in Vilnius (21 hours later) at 8.56 pm; and Daugavpils, Latvia (24 hours). A through-carriage for Rīga is uncoupled twice weekly at Vilnius where it waits a few hours before being hitched to another train to reach Rīga 33½ hours after leaving Berlin. The return journeys follow similar schedules, though precise times change fairly often. Another possibility is to travel to Warsaw first and then take a direct train to Kaunas, Rīga or Tallinn (see Poland).

Since these trains pass through Belarus you also have to pay US$20 to US$50 for a Belarus transit visa. See Visas & Embassies in Facts for the Visitor for more information. At the Poland-Belarus border the train sits motionless for hours – apart from an incredible amount of lurching, vibrating and clanking – while the bogeys are changed to fit the broader gauge tracks of the former Soviet Union. You'll probably be checked by at least four different sets of officials as you go through Belarus – so don't hope for much sleep!

From Kaliningrad, every Monday, a through-carriage to Warsaw is hitched to the Gdynia-bound train (see Poland), which makes a direct connection in Warsaw with the St Petersburg-Berlin train. A single Kaliningrad-Berlin fare is US$117.

Poland

There are direct trains between Poland and all three Baltic states and the Kaliningrad Region.

The Baltic Express The daily *Baltic Express* (Balti Ekspress) between Warsaw and Tallinn began in summer 1993 and is now the top train in the Baltics. It uses the Suwałki-Šeštokai route between Poland and Lithuania, which means everyone has to transfer to a different train at Šeštokai because the gauge changes there. The route is Warsaw-Białstok-Suwałki-Šeštokai-Kaunas-Šiauliai-Rīga-Valga-Tartu-Tallinn (22 hours). The Tallinn-Warsaw fare is US$50 in compartment class and US$30 in non-sleeping accommodation.

Although the *Baltic Express* does not stop at Vilnius, it stops at Kaunas, where you can change to another train for Vilnius (of which there are plenty) or Klaipėda. The Warsaw-Kaunas fare is around US$40 in compartment class and US$20 in non-sleeping accommodation. You can get timetable information at Warsaw Central, Tallinn or any of the train stations en route. In early 1997 the timetable looked like this:

Northbound
Depart Warsaw Central 2.42 pm; Białystok 4.53 pm; arrive Suwałki 6.54 pm (all Polish time)
Depart Suwałki 7.04 pm Polish time (8.04 pm Lithuanian time); arrive Šeštokai 9.57 pm Lithuanian time (8.57 pm Polish time)
Depart Šeštokai 10.17 pm; Kaunas 12.09 am; arrive Šiauliai 2.40 am; Rīga 5.20 am; Tartu 9.28 am; arrive Tallinn 11.55 am (all Lithuanian time)

Southbound
Depart Tallinn 5.45 pm; Tartu 8.15 pm; Rīga 12.25 am; Šiauliai 3.12 am; Kaunas 5.50 am; arrive Šeštokai 7.25 am (all Lithuanian time)

Depart Šeštokai 7.45 am Lithuanian time (6.45 am Polish time); arrive Suwałki 8.35 am Polish time (9.35 am Lithuanian time)
Depart Suwałki 8.48 am; Białystok 10.50 am; arrive Warsaw Central 1.12 pm (all Polish time)

Šeštokai-Suwałki Unless you are a complete glutton for punishment, there is no longer any need to even attempt to travel this legendary 50 km stretch of track linking Lithuania with Poland. Following the huge success of the *Baltic Express*, enabling travellers to get from Tallinn to Warsaw on a single service, it is doubtful the one remaining Šeštokai-Suwałki border crossing service will remain for much longer.

The one daily Šeštokai-Suwałki train departs at 12.10 pm (Lithuanian time) and arrives in Suwałki at 1.50 pm (Polish time). On its return journey, it leaves Suwałki at 8.40 am (Polish time) and arrives in Šeštokai at 11.30 am (Lithuanian time). From Suwałki there are a couple of Warsaw trains or combination of trains (such as a Suwałki-Sokóka train) that will get you to Warsaw in the end. At Šeštokai, there is a daily Vilnius train that connects with the Šeštokai-Suwałki service, however, not with the *Baltic Express*. Its departure times (Lithuanian times) are:

Depart Vilnius 7.54 am; Kaunas 9.38 am; arrives Šeštokai 11.33 am
Depart Šeštokai 12.03 pm; Kaunas 2.01 pm; arrive Vilnius 3.32 pm

Tickets for each leg of the journey (Vilnius-Šeštokai, Šeštokai-Suwałki, Suwałki-Warsaw) can only be bought at the point of departure. Expect to queue at each departure point for a ticket and don't be surprised if you end up missing the only train going your way that day. If you get on a train without a ticket, you will be fined heavily. If it is a toss up between the ticket or the train though, get the train! (For a personal account of the Suwałki-Šeštokai experience, see A Day on Mars aside in the Eastern & Southern Lithuania chapter.)

Other Trains There are two daily trains between Warsaw and Vilnius, via Grodno in Belarus, one of which is covered by the Berlin-Warsaw-Vilnius train (see Germany). The other is a direct Warsaw-Vilnius train which has the same Belarus visa requirement as well as the same bizarre bogey-changing operation.

Kaliningrad A regular train service runs between Gdynia and Kaliningrad, via Gdańsk, using western European gauge all the way. This train departs daily from Kaliningrad at 6.25 pm, arriving in Gdańsk at 10.06 pm and Gdynia at 10.38 pm. On the return journey it departs from Gydnia at 6.32 am, Gdańsk at 7.04 am, and arrives in Kaliningrad at 12.42 pm. A single fare from Kaliningrad to Gdańsk/Gdynia is US$14/15.

Every Monday from Kaliningrad, a through-carriage for Warsaw is hitched to the Gdynia-Kaliningrad service; it arrives in Warsaw the following morning at 5.32 am. It returns the same day, arriving back in Kaliningrad on Wednesday. This service also connects with the St Petersburg-Berlin train (see Germany). A single Kaliningrad-Warsaw fare is US$31.

Western Europe
If you're coming from west of Germany, you can reach the Baltics with a change of train in either Berlin or Warsaw. There are direct services to Warsaw from London, Paris and elsewhere. From countries south of Germany you can head for Warsaw, or for Prague, Budapest or Sofia and take a train to Vilnius through Ukraine. Tickets to Vilnius bought in western Europe will route you through Belarus. See the earlier Germany section, and Visas & Embassies in the Facts for the Visitor chapter for comments on Belarus visas.

London-Vilnius takes a little under two days with a change of trains in Warsaw. The basic single 2nd class fare is US$185 as far as Warsaw and a couchette to Warsaw is US$24; Warsaw to Vilnius is around US$60 in compartment class.

Russia
The old Soviet rail network still functions,

with little change, over most of the former Soviet Union. Trains linking Moscow and St Petersburg with all the main Baltic cities enable you to combine the Baltics with a Trans-Siberian trip or other Russian or Central Asian travels. For information on types of train, classes of accommodation, how to understand timetables and so on, see the Getting Around chapter.

All the services mentioned here will have compartment-class *(kupeynyy)* sleeping accommodation, but some will lack either the more expensive soft class *(myagkiy or lyuks)*, or the cheaper reserved-place class *(platskartnyy)*.

Fares from Moscow to the Baltics are around US$25; if you are making a round trip from the Baltics to Russia, ask for a round-trip ticket before you set off to save queueing in Russia.

Services from Russia to the Baltics and Kaliningrad include:

Moscow (Belorussia station)-Kaliningrad
    19 to 29 hours; two trains daily, one via Minsk in Belarus
Moscow (Belorussia station)-Kaunas
    13 hours; three trains each way daily, two terminating at Kaliningrad, one at Kaunas
Moscow (Rīga station)-Rīga
    16 hours; two trains each way nightly (up to 23½ hours)
Moscow (St Petersburg station)-Tallinn
    16 to 20 hours; the Tallinn Express each way daily via Narva (16 hours), one train via Pskov and Tartu (20 hours)
Moscow (St Petersburg station)-Tartu
    17 hours; one train each way daily
Moscow (Belorussia station)-Vilnius
    13 hours; three trains each way daily, two terminating at Kaliningrad, one at Kaunas
Pskov-Kaliningrad
    14 hours; one train each way daily, terminating at St Petersburg
Pskov-Kaunas
    10 hours; one train each way daily, terminating at Kaliningrad and St Petersburg
Pskov-Rīga
    six hours; one train each way, terminating at St Petersburg
Pskov-Tallinn
    6½ hours; one train each way daily, terminating at Moscow

Pskov-Tartu
    four hours; one train each way daily, terminating at Tallinn and Moscow
Pskov-Vilnius
    eight or nine hours; four trains daily, terminating at Kaliningrad, Chernivtsi, Berlin or St Petersburg
St Petersburg (Warsaw station)-Kaliningrad
    19½ hours; one train each way daily, via Pskov, Daugavpils, Vilnius and Kaunas
St Petersburg (Warsaw station)-Kaunas
    15½ hours; one train each way daily, terminating at Kaliningrad
St Petersburg (Warsaw station)-Rīga
    10 or 11 hours; one train each way
St Petersburg (Warsaw station)-Tallinn
    8½ to 9¾ hours; two trains each way nightly, often heavily booked
St Petersburg (Warsaw station)-Vilnius
    14 hours; four trains each way daily terminating at Kaliningrad, Chernivtsi, Berlin and Truskaveca, via Daugavpils
Voronezh-Rīga
    13 hours; one train daily on odd days, via Daugavpils

Other places in the Baltics with direct rail services to/from Russia include: Daugavpils and Rēzekne in Latvia (Moscow, Pskov, Chernivtsi); Sigulda in Latvia (Pskov, St Petersburg); Narva in Estonia (St Petersburg, Moscow); and Valga and Võru in Estonia (Pskov, St Petersburg).

Ukraine

The daily St Petersburg-Chernivtsi train departs from St Petersburg at 3.45 pm, departs from Daugavpils (Latvia) at 1.04 am, arrives in Vilnius at 4.02 am, departs from Vilnius at 4.22 am, and arrives in Chernivtsi at 11.32 am. On the return journey it leaves Chernivtsi at 1.10 am, arrives in Vilnius almost 24 hours later at 12.28 am, leaves Vilnius at 12.51 am, departs from Daugavpils at 4.05 am and arrives in St Petersburg at 3.25 pm.

The Kharkov-Kaliningrad train also stops at Vilnius. On its journey to Kaliningrad, it departs from Vilnius on even days at 1.50 am; to Kharkov it departs from Vilnius on odd days at 1.21 am. On certain days of the month (at the time of writing, days 2, 6, 10, 14, 18, 22 & 26), a through-carriage to

Odessa is hitched onto the train at Kaliningrad.

From Kaliningrad, there is also a train to Simferopol. On even days a through-carriage to Simferopol is hitched on to the Kaliningrad-Moscow train, which departs from Kaliningrad at 9.40 am.

A direct Lvov-Rīga train departs every Tuesday and Friday from Rīga at 10.15 am, arriving in Lvov 21 hours later. The return train departs from Lvov at 6.50 am.

Belarus

The old Soviet rail network still functions between the Baltic states and Belarus. Timetables often list only the start and end points of a train's journey. Services include:

Grodno-Vilnius
    3½ hours; one train daily
Minsk-Kaliningrad
    10 hours; four trains each way daily; terminating in Kaliningrad, Moscow or Gomel or Kharov
Minsk-Rīga
    eight hours; one train on even days, terminating Rīga northbound, Gomel southbound
Minsk-Vilnius
    3½ hours; four trains each way daily; terminating Vilnius or Kaliningrad northbound; Moscow southbound

China & the East

If you have the time and inclination for it, the Trans-Siberian railway will carry you much of the way between the Baltics and eastern Asia, Australasia, or even Alaska. The 9297 km Trans-Siberian (proper) runs between Moscow's Yaroslavl station and Vladivostok on Russia's Pacific coast. In summer at least, there are steamers between Vladivostok and Niigata in Japan. Straight through without stopping, the ride takes 5½ to 6½ days, but you can break it at places like Irkutsk, Ulan-Ude and Khabarovsk and make side-trips to beautiful Lake Baykal and interesting regions like remote Yakutia or Buddhist Buryatia. Branches of the Trans-Siberian with their own names are the Trans-Mongolian which goes via the Mongolian capital, Ulaan Baatar, to Beijing; and the Trans-Manchurian which goes to Beijing via Harbin and north-east China.

The cost of a Trans-Siberian trip varies enormously, depending, among other things, on which direction and what class you travel, what time of year, where you book, who you book through, and the overall geopolitical situation. Through a western travel agent, expect to pay US$600 or more all the way from Moscow to Beijing or Vladivostok and more if you include the boat to Niigata. From Beijing to Moscow, CITS (China International Travel Service) offers tickets for US$312 in hard class, but book well in advance as these trains, especially the Trans-Mongolian, are currently very popular with Russian and Chinese business folk who compete for tickets and like to conduct business from the carriages.

There are almost as many variations of a Trans-Siberian itinerary as there are Trans-Siberian travellers, and equally as many ways of setting up a trip. Lonely Planet's *Russia, Ukraine & Belarus* travel survival kit has lots of Trans-Siberian ideas and detail, while a comprehensive resource is *The Trans-Siberian Rail Guide* by Robert Strauss & Tamsin Turnbull (Compass Star Publications, London, 4th edition with update addendum for March 1997). Also useful is Bryn Thomas' *Trans-Siberian Handbook* (Trailblazer Publications, UK).

CAR & MOTORCYCLE

Having your own vehicle has the great advantages of convenience and comfort in the Baltic states. One option is to rent a car for all or part of your stay, but this is costly – and it could also work out being cheaper to take your own vehicle. If you do take your own vehicle get it in good condition before you start off, and carry a large petrol can, supplies of engine oil and some basic spares. A fire extinguisher, first-aid kit and warning triangle are also advisable. Motoring clubs like Britain's AA and RAC are worth checking with for information on regulations, border crossings, and so on – as are Baltic states' embassies and, if you're going to drive in the Kaliningrad Region, worldwide branches of the Russian state tourist company, Intourist. For information and tips on driving once you're in the Baltic states see the Getting Around chapter.

Documents

You need to bring your vehicle's registration document. If you can get it in the form of an international motor vehicle certificate, which is a translation of the basic registration document, so much the better. Motoring associations should be able to provide one. An International Driving Permit (also obtainable from motoring associations) is recommended, but if you don't have one, your own licence (if from a European country) will suffice in most situations. Estonia is the only Baltic state with compulsory accident insurance for drivers, and even these payouts are low, so you really need comprehensive insurance in case of damage done by another driver.

At the time of writing, the Green Card – a routine extension of domestic motor insurance to cover most European countries – is valid in Estonia, but *not* in the other two Baltic states or Russia, so you must organise insurance separately. If you have difficulty getting this through your regular insurer, try Black Sea & Baltic General Insurance (☎ 0171-709 9202) of 65 Fenchurch St, London EC3M 4EY. Insurance policies with limited compensation rates can be bought at the Latvian and Estonian borders. Insurance is not yet compulsory in Lithuania. Remember that you'll also need appropriate documentation for all the countries you pass through on the way to or from the Baltics – motoring associations should be able to advise you.

Scandinavia

If travelling from Scandinavia, you can put your vehicle on a ferry or drive to the Baltics through Russia.

Ferries There are three vehicle-ferry crossings daily from Helsinki to Tallinn run by the Finnish-Estonian joint venture, Tallink. A one-way deck fare is US$18, a car costs US$30 one-way, and a motorcycle is US$10. Tallink also offers a special US$69 package

deal for a car and two to four passengers. Silja Line also takes vehicles on the two Tallinn-Helsinki daily ferries it operates; a car costs around US$40. From Stockholm there are direct services to Tallinn and Rīga but, at the time of writing, you'll save quite a lot on ferry fares if you sail with Viking Line from Sweden to Finland, then take a second ferry from Helsinki to Tallinn. Taking a car on the Stockholm-Tallinn/Stockholm-Rīga ferries costs around US$50/90 one-way. See the following Sea section for more on these services.

Cargo ferries between Fredericia in Denmark and Klaipėda (Lithuania), and Copenhagen and Klaipėda, offer a few car and passenger spaces at very reasonable prices.

Through Russia From the Finnish/Russian border at Vaalimaa/Torfyanovka to St Petersburg is about 220 km; from St Petersburg to the Russian/Estonian border at Ivangorod/Narva is 140 km. You could do it in a day but there's little point coming this way unless you want to look at St Petersburg on the way through. Don't delay on the Finland-St Petersburg road as it's said to be plagued by bandits.

See Facts for the Visitor for information on Russian visas.

Germany & Poland

Bringing a vehicle into the Baltics from the south is less straightforward than from Scandinavia. At present there are three main ways of doing it, with Kaliningrad offering a future fourth possibility.

Ferries – Germany The ferries between Kiel and Klaipėda (Lithuania), a voyage of 30 hours, get booked up months ahead. The Mukran-Klaipėda link is cheaper and quicker (18 hours) but with even smaller capacity. See the Sea section for details.

Ferries – Kiel The three ferries *Vilnius, Kaunas* and *Palanga* sail between Klaipėda and Kiel six times weekly (in total), although this could soon become a daily service. Each carries up to 40 cars as well as between 100 and 200 passengers. Return fares range from about US$200 for a simple seat to US$1000 for a luxury double cabin. Taking a car on a single/return trip is US$147/250.

Poland-Lithuania The border between Ogrodniki (east of Suwałki, Poland) and Lazdijai (Lithuania) was virtually closed during the Soviet era, but opened up with Lithuanian independence. Since then it has become notorious for interminable delays, making a mockery of the much talked-about 'Via Baltica' – a proposed fast road route from central to northern Europe through Poland and the Baltic states. A second border has since opened on the road from Suwałki, Szypliszki and Budzisko (Poland) to Kalvarija and Marijampolė (Lithuania), but this is reputed to be no better. Queues at both crossing points are longer and more chaotic on the Lithuanian side than the Polish side, so it should be easier to enter Lithuania than leave it! There is a reported danger of highway robbery on the Polish side of both borders.

A two km queue on the Lithuanian side is short, and movement is extremely slow due to the number of people trying to smuggle cheap cigarettes, alcohol and textiles into Poland and the extreme lack of urgency among border officials. In a car you can wait anything from four hours to four days. In 1993, the Lithuanian embassy in Tallinn admitted that 'no legal or moral norms' applied at the Lazdijai crossing, after an Estonian children's choir was held up for two days there. In short, seriously sound out the situation before you even consider crossing the Poland/Lithuania road borders.

Through Belarus For a couple of years after independence, it was claimed that a happy alternative to the direct Poland-Lithuania crossing was to go via Belarus from Poland to Lithuania, the most direct route being from Białystok, Poland, to Grodno in north-west Belarus, then to Merkinė, Lithuania.

However, since mid-1996, the situation at Lithuania's road borders with Belarus have become almost as hellish as those it shares with Poland. Not only will you probably have to wait in line for a good few hours – you also have to pay between US$20 to US$50, because you'll need a Belarusian transit visa. These can only be obtained in advance from a Belarusian embassy; no visas are issued at road borders. Other possible routes for suckers for punishment prepared to risk this not-so-rosy option include Brest-Lida-Vilnius or Brest-Minsk-Vilnius.

The UK
Ferries DFDS Baltic Line, which handles the cargo ferries running from Fredericia and Copenhagen in Denmark to Klaipėda (Lithuania), offers through fares for a limited number of cars and passengers from Harwich to Klaipėda, with a change of ferry at Esbjerg onto the Fredericia/Copenhagen-Klaipėda lines. A return fare from Harwich, including taking a car on board, is around US$390. See Sea section for details.

BICYCLE
Bicycles can be carried cheaply on the ferries from Scandinavia and Germany to the Baltic states, but of course the passenger fare depends on which route you take – see the Sea section for details. Overland riders through Poland face the same choices as drivers – see the Car & Motorcycle section.

HITCHING
Look upon hitching as a method of getting part-way to or from the Baltics; it's fairly widely practised in Finland, Germany and Poland, but Sweden and Denmark aren't so good for hitching. Many German towns have organisations called Mitfahrzentrale which put people willing to pay for lifts together with drivers willing to take them. If you're considering hitching from Poland to Lithuania, take advice on safety as there have been reports of highway robbery on roads leading to the Polish side of the borders. You reportedly can't cross the Ogrodniki-Lazdijai border as a pedestrian – you must be in a car. Keep in mind that hitching is never a totally

safe way of travelling. Even though we explain how to do it, we don't recommend it.

Sea

The number of ferries to the Baltic states has mushroomed since 1990, and you can now sail direct from Finland to Estonia; Sweden or Germany to Latvia, Lithuania and Estonia; Denmark to Lithuania; and Poland and Germany to Kaliningrad. This can be one of the most enjoyable ways to reach the Baltic states. The Helsinki-Tallinn route has so many competing services that you should have no difficulty getting a passage any day, but some of the other services – notably EstLine from Stockholm and the cargo ferries to Denmark – can get booked up far in advance. Schedules and fares change quite frequently and it is always a good idea to double-check both when you are planning your trip.

FINLAND
Estonia
A small fleet of varied shapes and sizes now ferries nearly two million people each year back and forth across the 80 km Gulf of Finland between Helsinki and Tallinn. There are fewer services from September to April, but at least five or six crossings are made each way every day. Ships cross in four hours, hydrofoils in two. In Helsinki they all sail from the large Southern Port (Eteläsatama), which has four different terminals. There is a 24 hour ferry information line (☎ 09-173 335 55) in Helsinki. You can also get tickets from other outlets, including those mentioned in the rundown of main services that follows. Prices change fairly frequently. There's a travel tax of about US$5 on tickets bought in Finland.

Tallink Tallink runs the large passenger and vehicle ferries the *Tallink*, *Vana Tallinn* and the *Georg Ots*, the only direct transport link in the Soviet era between the Baltic states and the west and rebuilt in 1992-3. All three ferries make one crossing in each direction daily, sailing time being four hours. In Tallinn they depart from Terminal A. Service is year round with extra services possible in the summer. A single deck fare is US$18 (students US$13), a car is US$30, a motorcycle US$10, and a berth in a cabin for two to four people is US$26. Buffet lunch or dinner is US$15. Cabins can also be booked overnight in Helsinki before or after the crossing for US$24 a night.

Tallink also operates two hydrofoils, the *Laura* and *Liisa*, which make six crossings between Tallinn and Helsinki each way daily between June and September. A single fare for a deck passenger is US$20 and the trip takes two hours.

Helsinki ferry departures are from the Olympia Terminal. You can get tickets there within two hours of departure, otherwise from the Tallinn office (☎ 09-2282 1121; fax 09-635 337) nearby at Eteläranta 14, 00131 Helsinki. The hydrofoils use the Magazine Terminal (Makasiiniterminaali) in Helsinki; tickets are available at the terminal or Tallink office. Travel agents worldwide also sell tickets. For Tallink's main booking offices in Tallinn, see Getting There & Away in the Tallinn chapter.

Silja Line The Silja Line operates two ferries daily between Tallinn and Helsinki, the *Wasa Queen* and the *Silja Festival*. Sailing time is four hours and both depart from Terminal A in Tallinn. Fares vary depending on which ferry you take at what time and on what day, with fares being more expensive if you sail on Saturday. Fares start at US$30 for a single deck passage; US$39/41/54 for a berth in a four/three/two-person cabin; and US$107/183 for a berth in a luxury double/single cabin. Lunch costs an extra US$12 and dinner US$19.

Helsinki ferry departures are from the Olympia Terminal. Tickets can be bought here within two hours of departure. For information in Helsinki call ☎ 800-74 552, 09-180 4531. The Baltic Tours travel agency is the line's official agent in Estonia.

Eestin Linjat The *Alandia* ferry, operated by Eestin Linjat, sails once daily back and forth from Tallinn to Helsinki. Sailing time is 3½ to four hours and it departs/arrives in Tallinn at Terminal D.

Tickets are sold in Helsinki from its offices (☎ 09-228 8522; fax 09-228 5222) at Keskukatu 1, Reisisadama Lääneterminaal; or at Fabianinkatu 9 (☎ 09-669 944; fax 09-669 990). In Tallinn, you can buy them from Eestin Linjat's offices in Terminal D (☎ 2-6318 676) at Lootsi 13, or Terminal A (☎ 2-6318 606; fax 2-6318 690) at Sadama 25.

Viking Line The *Viking Express* is a sleek, 450 seat jet catamaran operated by Viking Line. It ploughs its way between Tallinn and Helsinki six times a day in summer and three times daily in winter. Sailing time is 1¾ hours each way, and it docks at Terminal C in Tallinn. A one way crossing for a deck passenger is US$27.

In Helsinki it uses the catamaran harbour at the Makasiini Terminal. For information in Helsinki contact its office at the terminal (☎ 09-123 577, 09-123 51).

Viking Line is represented by Estravel travel agency in Estonia. It also has an office located at Terminal C (☎ 2-6318 623; fax 2-6318 629).

Cruises You can take 24-hour or half-day cruises from Helsinki to Tallinn on Tallink, Eestin Linjat, or aboard Silja Line's luxurious *Sally Albatross*. These are basically floating parties for Swedes and Finns. In 1996 EuroCruises offered a nine-day cruise on the *Kristina Regina* for US$2199, starting in Helsinki and calling at Tallinn, Rīga and Klaipėda, Gdańsk in Poland and Copenhagen. Contact any travel agency in Helsinki; in Tallinn, Estravel arranges a variety of cruises including the frighteningly popular 'Ladies Cruise' aboard *Sally A*.

SWEDEN
Estonia
There are direct sailings daily from Stockholm to Tallinn; alternatively you can go via Finland with Viking or Silja Line, which needn't take much longer and can sometimes work out cheaper.

EstLine The two Estline ferries *Regina Baltica* and *Mare Balticum* sail daily between Tallinn and Stockholm in summer. Only one sails in winter – meaning a ferry only departs from Tallinn every second day. Departures are from the Tallinnterminalen at the Frihamnen in Stockholm, and from the EstLine terminal B, which is next door to the main ferry terminal in Tallinn, at Sadama 29. Sailing time is around 13 hours.

A single/return deck ticket is US$53/80 every day except Saturday when it is around US$66/88. Children up to 11 are half price and students pay approximately two-thirds of the full price. A basic berth in a two/four-person cabin without an en suite bathroom or window is around US$35/16. If you're looking for a window and private bathroom you have to pay for a more expensive cabin on the third deck. A single/double is around US$66/132. A sea view is even more costly – US$272 for the whole cabin (sleeps two). Breakfast/dinner is an extra US$7/19.

EstLine runs a free transfer bus from Tallinn train station and some of the major hotels in Tallinn to its ferry terminal. In Stockholm it also operates a commuter bus between the ferry port and town centre; passengers have to pay a small fee.

In Stockholm, you can book tickets through EstLine's office (☎ 08-667 0001; fax 08-660 602) at the Tallinnterminalen, Frihamnen, S-11556 Stockholm; or through travel agents worldwide. For information call Stockholm ☎ 08-666 046, 08-666 045.

EstLine gets heavily booked so make your reservation a month or two ahead if possible. See Getting There & Away in the Tallinn chapter for EstLine offices and ticket agents in Tallinn.

Viking & Silja Lines You can combine a voyage between Sweden and Finland on Sweden's Viking Line with a Helsinki-Tallinn passage to travel between Sweden and Estonia. Viking Line sails once or twice daily to/from Stockholm to Helsinki, and to/from Stockholm to Turku (Finland). The crossings take 10 to 15 hours and some are made in vast 2500-capacity ships like the *Isabella* and *Mariella*, which would be better described as floating pleasure palaces. On both ferries, it costs around US$10/21 to take a motorcycle/car on board.

Basic deck passenger fares are US$20 Stockholm-Turku, and US$23 Stockholm-Helsinki; if you want to spend the night in a cabin it is an extra US$39/63 respectively. There are Inter-Rail, student, and pensioner discounts of about one-third on non-Friday sailings. Viking Line sails from the Stadsgården pier at Stockholm and the Katajanokan terminal in the South Harbour, Helsinki. For information ring Stockholm ☎ 08-452 40 00 (fax 08-452 40 30), or Helsinki ☎ 09-123 51 (fax 09-123 5461).

If you're travelling from the Baltic states to Sweden, you can buy Viking or Silja Line tickets in Estonia or Latvia to avoid Finnish travel tax. See Getting There & Away in the Tallinn and Rīga chapters.

From Saaremaa During the Soviet regime a ferry stopped at Roomassaare on Saaremaa en route between Rīga and Slite in Götland. In summer 1996, attempts to revive this service failed due to lack of demand but there is talk of trying one more revival in 1997. The overnight ferry, which will carry vehicles as well as deck passengers, is likely to sail twice weekly between Rīga and Slite, the journey taking 16 to 17 hours. For tickets and information contact the tourist information centre in Kuressaare (see Information under Kuressaare in West Estonia & the Islands chapter) or Transline BT in Rīga.

Cruises In 1991, the Ånedin Linjen-owned *Baltic Star* made twice weekly cruises between Stockholm and Veere harbour (☎ 245-76 236), on the north-west coast of Saaremaa. Since 1995 no ferry has connected the two ports but it will resume in summer 1997. A 36 hour cruise with a day spent touring Saaremaa will cost around US$300 to US$600. For tickets and information contact Baltic Tours in Tallinn or Kuressaare, or Ånedin Linjen in Stockholm (☎ 08-24 79 85; fax 08-10 07 41), at Vasagatan 6, S-11181 Stockholm.

Latvia

An overnight passenger and vehicle ferry sailing twice weekly between Rīga's sea-passenger port, at Eksporta 1, and Slite on Götland is expected to start operating as of summer 1997. Provisional fares from Rīga are about US$70 return for a double berth and US$60 for a car. From Rīga a ferry also runs to Stockholm.

ScanSov Line The ferry *Rus*, operated by the Swedish company ScanSov, sails between Rīga and Stockholm, the journey taking 17 hours. It leaves Rīga on Monday, Wednesday and Friday at 5 pm and arrives in Stockholm the following morning at 9 am. The Polish-built ferry fits 412 passengers; on-board facilities include sauna, conference halls, bar, restaurant and nightclub. A berth in a basic double/triple/four-person cabin is US$80/60/50. Prices include dinner and breakfast.

Departures are from the Balticterminalen at the Frihamn, Stockholm. In Rīga ferries arrive/depart from the sea-passenger port at Eksporta 1. Tickets are sold through the agents for ScanSov, LS Rēdereja (☎ 7220 172; fax 7212 775), Pils 8/10, Rīga. Most travel agencies also sell the ferry tickets.

Lithuania

From Århus The cargo ferry *Šiauliai* sails between Klaipėda and Århus three times weekly. If it has room, it will take a limited number of passengers and cars which, needless to say, get booked up very quickly. Book as many months in advance as you can! In Kiel tickets are sold by LITA Shipping GmbH (☎ 0431-209 760; fax 0431-201 395), Ostuferhafen 15, D-24149 Kiel. Tickets can be booked in the UK through Regent Holidays (see Travel Agencies earlier in this chapter). In Lithuania, contact Krantas Shipping (☎ 26-365 444; fax 26-365 443; email krantaspass @klaipeda.omnitel.net), Perkėlos 10, LT-5804 Klaipėda.

From Malmö The cargo ferry *Dan Minerva* sails from Klaipėda to Malmö four times weekly. A limited amount of car and passenger space is available but you have to book far in advance. Ticket bookings can be made through the ferry operator, DFDS Baltic Line. In Sweden its office (☎ 040-284 800; fax 040-284 878) is at Bjurögatan 15, Box 50122, S-20211 Malmö. In Klaipėda its office (☎ 26-310 598; fax 26-310 596) is at Kareivinių 2-7, LT-5800 Klaipėda.

GERMANY
Estonia
Kiel A weekly cargo ferry runs between Kiel and Tallinn, departing from Tallinn/Kiel on Tuesday/Friday and arriving in Kiel/Tallinn on Thursday/Monday. It might be worth contacting the operating company, Travend, as cargo ferries do sometimes offer cheap car and passenger places if there is space. For information in Kiel call ☎ 04313-055 8202 (fax 04313-055 8222), in Tallinn call ☎ 2-6503 527 (fax 2-6503 507).

Travemünde From Germany there is the twice weekly Tallink-Hansaway service, departing from Travemünde and arriving in Tallinn 1½ days later. A berth in a cabin for four costs from US$127, a double cabin costs US$228 and a budget couchette (only available in summer) costs US$97. Bookings are through the Tallink offices or through Baltic Tours' city office in Tallinn (see Getting There & Away in the Tallinn chapter).

Another option is to sail to Helsinki and take a Germany-bound ferry from there. Silja Line's *Finnjet*, sailing between Travemünde and Helsinki, is claimed to be the fastest passenger ferry in the world. It sails nine to 12 times a month, making the trip in 22 hours or so, and costs around US$160 one way. There's also the *Translubeca* vehicle ferry sailing Lübeck-Helsinki-Lübeck three times a fortnight – and there are several Germany-Sweden ferries if you want to go that way round.

Latvia
Travemünde There's a weekly ferry between Travemünde and Rīga, taking 38 hours for a minimum of US$200 one-way. Contact Transline BT (see Getting There & Away in the Rīga chapter for details).

Lithuania
Kiel Three ferries, the *Vilnius*, *Kaunas* and *Palanga* sail between Klaipėda and Kiel six times weekly in total although this could soon become a daily service. Each ferry carries up to 40 cars as well as between 100 and 200 passengers. Return fares range from about US$200 for a simple seat to US$1000 for a luxury double cabin. Taking a car on a single/return trip is US$147/250.

These ferries enable motorists to avoid the clogged-up Polish-Lithuanian borders, but you may need to book several months in advance. In Kiel tickets are sold by LITA Shipping GmbH (☎ 0431-209 760; fax 0431-201 395), Ostuferhafen 15, D-24149 Kiel. Tickets can be booked in the UK through Regent Holidays. In Lithuania, contact Krantas Shipping (☎ 26-365 444; fax 26-365 443; email krantaspass@klaipeda.omnitel.net; http://www.omnitel.net/krantas), Perkėlos 10, LT-5804 Klaipėda.

Mukran A ferry sails every two days between Mukran and Klaipėda, a journey of 18 hours. A single berth ticket in a six person cabin is US$93 (plus US$8 harbour tax) in Mukran. A round trip costs US$166 (plus US$16 harbour tax). Cars on a single/return trip are US$146/266. In Germany, tickets are sold by the Schnieder Reisin travel agency or by Deutsches DFR (☎ 0381-458 4672; fax 0381-458 4678) in Rostock. In Klaipėda contact the Ost Reise Service (☎ 26 254 354), Naujoji Sodo 1.

Kaliningrad
Rostock In early 1997 a weekly ferry sailed on the Baltic-Meteor line between Kaliningrad and Rostock, departing from Kaliningrad on Friday at 5 pm and leaving Rostock on Tuesday at 7 pm. For ticket bookings and information in Germany contact a Baltic-specialist travel agent. In Kaliningrad contact the ferry agent, Inflot (see Boat

under Getting There & Away – Kaliningrad, in the Kaliningrad Region chapter).

DENMARK
Lithuania
From Fredericia & Copenhagen The *Dana Corona* operated by DFDS Baltic Line is a cargo ferry which sails between Klaipėda and Fredericia twice weekly, a journey of 34 hours. DFDS also operates the *Dana Minerva*, which sails four times weekly from Klaipėda to Copenhagen, from where it continues to Malmö in Sweden. Both ferries offer a limited amount of car and passenger space. Tickets, which should be bought as far in advance as possible, can be bought at any DFDS office worldwide and most travel agents. Offices include DFDS Baltic Line (☎ 075-912 955; fax 075-912 975) in Denmark at Sobjerg, DK-7000 Fredericia; in Lithuania (☎ 26-310 598; fax 26-310 596), Kareivinių 2-7, LT-5800 Klaipėda.

Kaliningrad
In early 1997 a Polesye line ferry was scheduled to sail daily between Kaliningrad and Elbląg from 15 August to 15 October. A second daily ferry was scheduled between Kaliningrad and Krynica Morska.

OTHER COUNTRIES
DFDS Baltic Line offers a limited amount of through fares from Harwich (UK) to Klaipėda (Lithuania), with a change of ferry at Esbjerg (Denmark). A Harwich-Klaipėda return with a car is US$390. For ticket information in the UK contact DFDS Baltic Line's office (☎ 01376-562 595; fax 031376-565 582) at Coggeshall Bypass, Coggeshall CO6 1TL, Essex. Alternatively try Regent Holidays (see list of travel agencies earlier in this chapter).

From the UK and the Netherlands, Scandinavian Seaways sails to Sweden. At the time of writing there were no ferry services from Russia.

SAILING YOURSELF
The Baltic states – particularly Estonia with its many islands and deeply indented coast –

are now attracting hundreds of private yachts a year, mainly from Finland and Scandinavia. The EYU, the Estonian Yachting Union (☎ & fax 2-237 288; fax 2-238 344), at Regati puiestee 1, EE0019 Tallinn, is a useful contact. The EMTA, the Estonian Marine Tourism Association (EMTA; ☎ & fax 2-6411 417), at Pikk 71, EE-0001 Tallinn, recommends the following guest harbours:

Estonian mainland
Pirita (☎ 2-238 033), Lohusalu (☎ 2-715 573) and Ess Kalev (☎ 2-239 154) near Tallinn; Haapsalu (☎ 247-45 582); Rohuküla (☎ 247-256 140); Virtsu (☎ 247-75 660); Pärnu (☎ 244-31 420)
Estonian islands
Lehtma (☎ 246-99 214), Heltermaa (☎ 246-94 252) and Orjaku (☎ 246-92 127) on Hiiumaa; Sviby on Vormsi; Nasva (☎ 245-75 140), Roomassaare & Triigi (☎ 245-55 574), Veere (☎ 245-56 701) on Saaremaa; Kuivastu (☎ 245-98 446) on Muhu; Kihnu; Ruhnu (☎ 245-70 156)

Customs facilities are available at Pirita, Dirhami, Haapsalu, Kuivastu, Kunda, Lehtma, Narva-Jõesuu, Nasva, Paldiski-Nord, Pärnu, Ruhnu, Roomassaare, Triigi, Vergi and Veere. Approaches to Orjaku, Triigi, Mõntu, Kihnu and Ruhnu should only be made in daylight.

The EYU and EMTA both offer useful information, harbour-berth booking, and visa services for yachties. In Helsinki contact the Estum Sailing Agency (☎ 09-629 299; fax 09-629 390), at Vuorimiehenkatu 23a, SF-00140 Helsinki.

It's also possible to rent yachts in all the Baltic states – see the Getting Around chapter.

Organised Tours

With independent travel in the Baltics now fairly straightforward, there's no need to take a tour or package just to get there or to help you get around. A tour is unlikely to take you anywhere you couldn't easily reach yourself. But if you want to stay in the better hotels all the time a package may save you money.

From Britain, Regent Holidays runs tours, typically costing US$1555 for 12 nights, to the three Baltic capitals and trips to Saaremaa, Cēsis and Nida. It's also a good firm to contact for one-off special interest tours or if you are simply seeking someone with some Baltic expertise. The art-tour specialist Martin Randall offers one-week northern capital tours encompassing Tallinn, Rīga and Helsinki for US$2015. Architectural buffs should look no further than specialist ACE which offers a one-week architectural tour of Estonia for US$1242 and plans a similar tour of Lithuania in 1997.

Germany's Baltic-specialist travel agents are well abreast of developments. Schnieder Reisen offers an eight day tour to Rīga for around US$840, a 12 day bus tour of the three Baltic states for US$1332, and a four day tour to Kaliningrad for US$845. There are also organised self-drive trips which include a ship passage to the Baltics and back, accommodation, and, if you want, a hire car laid on. Greif Reisen has some of the less expensive regular tours and includes parts of Poland in some of them.

From the USA, Union Tours offers five-day, one Baltic capital packages. It is happy to arrange two city packages back to back though, giving you a 10 day two-city tour.

Five day tours start at around US$1000. Rates go up by about US$200 in high season. Baltic Tours has quite a big range of Latvian and Lithuanian packages with 10 to 12-day trips.

From Australia, Well Connected Travel arranges 18-night tours of eastern Europe, taking in the three Baltic capitals en route. In 1997 it is also arranging a Baltic sea cruise, and in 1998, a special tour to the Vilnius annual summer music festival in July.

Intourist, the Russian state travel company, still does Baltic tours. For information, contact its many branches worldwide.

Leaving the Region

You do not have to pay any departure taxes when leaving any of the Baltic states.

When leaving the Kaliningrad Region you might be asked to show the customs declaration form you filled in upon entering the country. Make sure you are not carrying more money than you declared; if you are, then that is probably the last you will see of it. Russian customs officers have no qualms about confiscating cash.

Getting Around

Buses and trains go just about everywhere throughout the Baltic states although services are infrequent to the more off the beaten track places. Both are cheap, if fairly slow. Since distances are small, flying is rarely a necessity – though it can be fun. Driving or riding your own vehicle is an attractive option if you can afford to bring or rent a motor vehicle, or have the time to tour by bicycle. It also makes some of the region's most beautiful – and remote – places far more accessible, enabling you to discover spots that a 'chug-chug' bus or train just would not get you to in a limited amount of time.

Buses are quicker than trains and on the whole slightly cheaper. Other factors you should take into account include the frequency of service, departure times, and comfort. On trains you can stretch your legs out more, although, for some obscure reason, you cannot open the carriage windows, which can make things stuffy (and sometimes smelly depending on your travelling companions). You stand equal chances of freezing or baking, depending on whether the heating is turned on or not. If you have to travel overnight, however, sleeping accommodation on a train is definitely more comfortable than on a bus. In compartment class, you can rent clean linen from the carriage attendant who will also serve you tea (both of which you pay extra for).

Services are reliable although schedules and fares do change slightly every few months.

Borders

Gone are the days when you had to wait for hours on end at road borders between Estonia and Latvia, and Latvia and Lithuania. Public buses get priority over private vehicles and cross the border immediately. Occasionally a surly border guard who hops on board to check passengers' passports can

be a hindrance, especially if you (or another passenger) do not have the necessary visa.

Latvian border guards still insist on violently stamping all western passport; they are also the least aware of who needs visas and can sometimes be troublesome. Estonian borderguards not only stamp every western passport but insist on dragging passengers off the bus in to their offices, even if it is 3 am and -25° outside, so they can key your passport data into their computer.

Lithuanian borderguards are completely nonchalant about the whole affair; they don't bother stamping passports anymore and generally don't even wake you to check your passport if you are sleeping. Most of them even smile.

If you are travelling by car, don't be alarmed by the km or more tailback of lorries waiting in line that you will see as you approach most border crossings. At every border there are separate queues for cars and lorries. You should only have to wait in line behind three or four cars usually, depending on the time of day. The whole procedure should not take more than 30 minutes or so. At the Latvian and Lithuanian borders, you also have to deal with the unnecessarily complicated affair of obtaining a variety of stamps on a little scrap of paper that is given to you by a borderguard when you enter the border zone and taken away from you by another borderguard when you leave. The reasoning behind this is yet to be fathomed.

Trains usually chug across the borders without stopping. Customs and immigration checks are dealt with while in motion but some still stop.

The Kaliningrad Region has road borders with Lithuania at Panemunė/Sovietsk, between Kybartai (Lithuania) and Nesterov, and on the Curonian Spit along the Klaipėda-Zelenogradsk road. It is only Belarus' road borders with Lithuania at Šalčininkai, Medininkai and Lavoriškės which are open to westerners. Queues also build up at the

Narva/Ivangrodod border between Estonia and Russia. All these borders are tightly controlled. You need a visa in advance to cross these points (none issued at land borders) and you can expect to wait in line up to an hour regardless of whether you are travelling by bus or car. Entering the Kaliningrad Region or Belarus, you are also required to fill in a declaration form, specifying how much cash (in any currency) and what valuables you are taking in to the country. No one appears to check whether you are lying or not though.

The Poland-Lithuania border crossings at Lazdijai and Kalvarija are to be avoided if possible owing to some delays and other shenanigans. Don't let anyone persuade you to do a slight detour through Belarus instead; you will be delayed just as long and have to fork out for a Belarusian visa.

Information

Most bus and train stations in towns and cities have information windows whose staff generally speak a little English. Occasionally, they charge (per question!) for their services. Throughout Estonia, and in Vilnius and Rīga, there are local information English-speaking hot-lines you can call to find out transport schedules. Some quality city guides in the capitals and other cities print the latest flight, bus and train schedules, updated every two months (see Newspapers & Magazines in the Facts for the Visitor chapter). Updated schedules for all three Baltic states can also be accessed on the Internet:

Estonia
   http://www.ciesin.ee/ESTCG/timetables.html
Latvia
   http://www.inyourpocket.com/ritrans.html
Lithuania
   http://neris.mii.lt

Timetables

Most bus and train stations have large, comprehensive timetables posted up in the main ticket hall. A rare few need some careful decoding. In Estonia you can buy a pocket-size, easy to use train timetable which lists all services in and out of Estonia. Flyers listing the timetables for a variety of bus routes are also freely distributed at most bus stations around the country. At Rīga bus station, you can buy a bus timetable covering all routes in Latvia but so far you cannot get your own copy of the train timetable. Lithuania has yet to print off any timetables full stop.

All timetables list departure and arrival times. Others list the return journey schedules, and the number of minutes a train waits in your station or the time a bus or train left the place it began its journey. The number of the train, which is worth taking note of, is generally included on timetables. Always study the small print on timetables too as many buses or trains only run on certain days or between certain dates.

AIR

There are plenty of scheduled flights between the three Baltic capitals (see relevant city and town Getting There & Away sections for details), but fares are expensive. Domestic flights between the major cities in the Baltics are completely reliable and stable though.

There are no flights between Kaliningrad and any of the Baltic states. From Rīga, you can fly to Minsk in Belarus.

BUS

There are good bus services throughout the region. Direct buses link the four major cities – Tallinn, Rīga, Vilnius and Kaliningrad – and there are plenty of other cross-border services between main towns.

Buses are slow – snail-slow. Don't be fooled by 'express' or 'fast' buses as they travel at the same snail's pace, but just make less stops along the way. This can be quite handy though, given that some buses do follow roundabout routes, adding several hours to a journey. On a few routes there are small microbuses, holding round about 15 passengers, which officially make less stops. Remember, that on these buses the driver is quite happy, upon request, to make unofficial stops along the way – meaning the bus can end up stopping more times and taking longer than a regular 'big bus'.

Buses used for local journeys, up to about two hours long, offer few comforts. Dating way back to some time in the prehistoric Soviet era, many of these buses appear to only be fit for the scrap heap. To ensure semi-survival, avoid window seats in rainy, snowy or very cold weather; travel with someone you're prepared to snuggle up to for body warmth; and sit in the seat allocated to you to avoid tangling with a merciless babushka who wants *her* seat that *you're* in!

Some buses travelling between the three Baltic states are equal to any long distance coach you'd find in the west. Eurolines has its appointed agents in each Baltic capital. Its buses do not have leaking windows and tout a heating system that functions and can be moderated. Some buses between Vilnius and Tallinn even have an on-board toilet and a hot drinks dispenser.

In all buses, you can carry your luggage on board with you, unless it is too large – in which case you can ask the driver to stash it in the underneath baggage compartment for a small fee.

Tickets

Ticket offices/windows selling national and international tickets are clearly marked in the local language and occasionally in English too. Tickets are always printed in the local language and easy to understand once you know the words for 'seat', 'carriage' and 'bus stop' (see Language Guide at the back of the book).

For long distance buses originating from where you intend to leave, tickets are sold in advance. For local buses to nearby towns or villages, or for long distance buses that are in mid-route ('in transit'), you normally pay on board. This may mean a bit of a scrum for seats if there are a lot of people waiting.

Costs

Fares vary little between the different countries. For a 100 km trip you pay around US$2 in Latvia and Lithuania, US$3 in Estonia,

and US$4 in the Kaliningrad Region. Fares do differ slightly between bus companies, between regular and 'express' buses, and between different times of day.

TRAIN

The Baltic states and the Kaliningrad Region are fairly well covered by railways although services have been drastically cut in recent years. Like buses, trains are slow and cheap – except for those travelling between the three Baltic cities and towns, which are rapidly increasing in price.

The railway network is one area of Baltic life that is dominated by Russian speakers. Tickets are now printed in the local language though. The Russian names for types of train and classes of accommodation are given below (also see Language Guide).

Routes

There is no longer any direct train between Vilnius and Tallinn, and there are few trains between Rīga and the other two Baltic states capitals.

The daily *Baltic Express* between Tallinn and Warsaw is the most important line through the Baltics. It runs from Tallinn, through Tartu, Valga, Šiauliai, Radviliškis and Kaunas en route to Šeštokai where it switches tracks and continues to Warsaw, via Suwałki and Białystok.

The Rīga-St Petersburg train stops at Sigulda, Cēsis, Valmiera, Lugaži, Valga and Võru, then Pechory (Petseri) on its way to St Petersburg. The Tallinn-Moscow *(Tallinn Express)* train makes stops at Rakvere, Jõhvi and Narva on its way to the Russian border.

Other lines include Tallinn-Narva; Tallinn-Pärnu; Tallinn-Tartu; Tallinn-Viljandi; Rīga-Ventspils; Rīga-Rēzekne; Rīga-Liepāja; Rīga-Daugavpils; Vilnius-Daugavpils-Rēzekne (some terminating at St Petersburg); Vilnius-Druskininkai; Vilnius-Ignalina; Vilnius-Kaunas; Vilnius-Kaliningrad; and Vilnius-Klaipėda. There are several other local railways fanning out from the main cities.

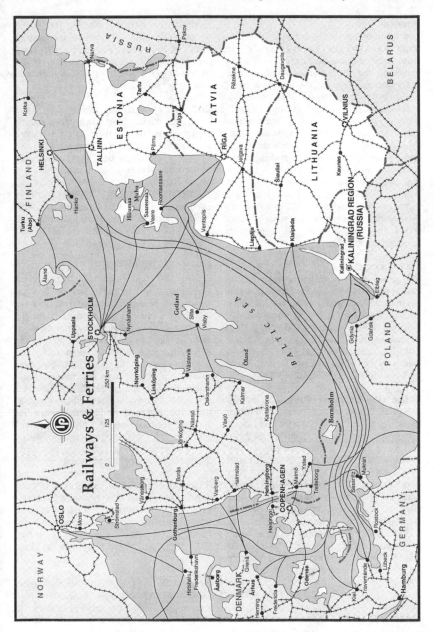

Types of Train

The basic distinction is between long distance trains, which link main towns and cities and stop at a limited number of stations between, and local trains, which stop at every station. There are just three main types of long distance trains: 'fast' *(skoryy)*, 'passenger' *(passazhirskiy)*, and 'diesel' *(dizel)*. 'Fast' trains are not so much fast as less slow than the others, but the only ones to be found in the Baltic states or Kaliningrad Region are some of those travelling to or from Russia, Ukraine or Poland – though you can, of course, use these for trips just within the Baltic region. Local trains are usually described as 'suburban' *(prigorodnyy)* – even though some of them travel 100 km or more – or sometimes 'electric' *(elektrichka)*.

Train Passes

Rail passes offering unlimited travel or discounts on fares have yet to become of much use in the Baltic region, mainly because fares are still considered so low by western standards that in many cases, you'd have to do a ridiculous amount of travelling to warrant getting a pass in the first place. See Rail Passes & Youth Tickets in the Getting There & Away chapter for more information.

Baltic Rail Explorer Pass This offers unlimited 2nd class rail travel in the three Baltic states and the Kaliningrad Region at US$38 for seven days, US$56 for 14 days, or US$75 for 21 days, and includes any sleeping and bedding supplements. It's sold by Campus Travel branches and other student travel offices in the UK, and in continental Europe by outlets of Eurotrain, the discount youth rail-ticket specialist. The card is available to ISIC holders and people under 26. At the time of writing, the sale of these cards was suspended (problems with Lithuanian Railways we were told); they were expected to be on sale again from 1 March, 1997.

Classes

There are four main classes of train accommodation, only some of which will be found on any one train. In descending order of comfort and cost, they are: soft class *(myagkiy)*, compartment class *(kupeynyy)*, 'reserved-place' *(platskartnyy)*, and general seating *(obshchiy)*.

Soft Soft class is only available on some 'fast' trains. Compartments have upholstered seats and convert to comfortable sleeping – lockable – compartments for two or four people. Your beds are usually made up for you. Myagkiy may also be called 1st class, *lyux* or *spalny vagon* (SV), which means 'sleeping carriage'. Latvian Railways even has one club class compartment, consisting of a bedroom with a double bed, kitchen and bathroom starting at around US$1500.

Compartment Compartment class is the equivalent of a western couchette, with plastic seats and an inside lock on the door which can be reassuring to use if you are travelling alone. Clean, starched linen and blankets are provided for the bunks at an extra charge (usually around US$2 in the local currency), which is collected by the carriage attendant once on board. 'Fast' and 'passenger' trains have compartment carriages and you can get places in them even if you're not travelling at night; in daytime they provide a numbered seat in a space that shouldn't be too crowded. Compartment and reserved-place classes together are sometimes referred to as 2nd class or 'hard' *(zhyostkiy)* sleeping accommodation.

Reserved-Place These carriages have three tiers of hard bunks in sections that are partitioned, but not fully closed off from each other. Travelling in them is certainly a communal experience and can be pretty grubby and stuffy. They're normally only found on 'passenger' trains.

General Seating This is the only class on local trains and usually on 'diesel' trains too. It also appears on some 'passenger' trains. It consists of unreserved bench-type seating.

This is what you'll travel on if you train it from Rīga to the seaside in Jūrmala.

Tickets

Tickets can be bought in advance at most stations (see relevant city and town Getting There & Away sections). If you are travelling compartment class and don't want to spend the night with a stranger, you have one costly option – buy all four tickets in the compartment.

If you are travelling on a long distance train between the Baltics and elsewhere, you give your ticket to the carriage attendant when you get on the train. You have to get on at the carriage specified on your ticket. The attendant returns the ticket to you about 15 minutes before you arrive at your final destination (a handy 'alarm clock' if you're on an overnight train and need waking).

Costs

Fares vary slightly between countries. In general seating you can go 100 km for about US$3 in Estonia, US$2 in Latvia, US$2.50 in Lithuania, and US$3 in the Kaliningrad Region. Once you get into compartment class though, fares start rising – 100 km costs about US$9 in Estonia, US$7 in Lithuania, Latvia and the Kaliningrad Region. Generally, soft class costs about twice as much as compartment class, while reserved-place fares are between general seating and compartment class fares, but nearer general seating.

CAR & MOTORCYCLE

Driving or riding in the Baltic states can be an enjoyable experience. The main roads linking the cities and towns are good, traffic is not as congested as in the west, and distances are not too great. In remoter areas there are a fair few gravel roads and dirt tracks, but with a wide range of locally available, quality road maps with the different grade roads marked, you can easily avoid the rougher roads if you don't feel your suspension is up to it.

There are 24 hour petrol stations run by western oil companies such as Statoil, Shell and Neste along all the major roads, selling a permanent supply of western-grade petrol, including unleaded (the days of chronic fuel shortages are long gone). In some remote parts of the Baltic states and in much of the Kaliningrad Region, you still find locally run stations which only sell regular 93 and 95-octane petrol. Western-made cars will run happily on both. Pumps are marked A-93 or A-95 and you pay for the petrol before you fill up. Wherever you are, it is still a good idea to take a spare petrol can with you and keep it full. Most towns have service stations and the number of outlets selling parts for western makes of car are spreading rapidly.

You can take your own vehicle to the Baltics from the west by ferry from Finland, Sweden, Denmark or Germany; or by road from Poland, Belarus or Russia (see Borders above). Alternatively you can rent a car in Estonia, Latvia or Lithuania, but this is not cheap.

Road Rules

The whole region drives on the right. In Lithuania and the Kaliningrad Region, driving with any alcohol at all in your blood is illegal – don't do so after even a sip of a drink. In Estonia a blood-alcohol level of 0.002% (which means you still can't drink!) is the legal limit; in Latvia it is marginally higher at 0.05%. Seat belts are compulsory for drivers and front-seat passengers. Speed limits in built-up areas are 50 km/h in Latvia and Estonia, and 60 km/h in Lithuania and the Kaliningrad Region. Limits outside vary from 90 to 110 km/h. In Estonia you always have your headlights switched on when driving on highways, even during the day! In Lithuania, you have to have them on during the day – wherever you are driving, be it a city, village or open highway – for a period of about four weeks starting from 1 September (apparently timed to coincide with the 'going back to school' rush). In Latvia, the same rules apply as in the west, ie switch them on when you really need them to see!

Traffic police are fearsome beings who no longer need any 'reason' to ask you to pull over. Expect to be asked to stop at least twice on a trip between Rīga and Vilnius. Traffic police are particularly stringent about speeding. Fines are collected on the spot by the police officer who books you. Fines vary dramatically and the only way you can ensure an officer is not adding a little pocketmoney for himself on to the official fine is to ask for a receipt.

It is possible to 'bargain' a fine down, ie you get no receipt and the officer pockets the entire fine. In Latvia, the fine for exceeding the speed limit by up to 20 km per hour is around US$10, up to 50 km per hour around US$15, and more than 50 km per hour anything up to US$100. If you do not have enough cash to pay immediately, your passport and car documents can be confiscated until you have paid the fine at the police station stipulated by the penalising officer. Traffic police rarely accept US dollar bills as payment.

Parking meters are starting to crop up in the capital cities. If you do not feed the meter with the required amount, your car will be wheel-clamped.

There is a fee of 5 lati (US$10) an hour to drive into the Old Town of Rīga from 9 am to 6 pm, when it drops to 3 lati (US$6) an hour; and there is a similar entrance fee for Tallinn Old Town. Driving in to the Old Town in Vilnius is free. Motorists also have to pay a small entrance fee to drive in to Latvia's and Lithuania's prime seaside resorts, Jūrmala and Palanga. Most national parks also demand an entrance fee from motorists.

Take care with trams, trolleybuses and buses in towns. Passengers may run across the road to catch them while they're still in motion. Traffic behind a tram must stop when it opens its doors to let people in and out. Trolleybuses often swing a long way out into the road when leaving a stop.

Rental
The three Baltic capitals are the easiest places to rent cars although there are small outlets elsewhere. Avis, Hertz and Europcar all have offices in the capitals. Most top-end and many middle-range hotels, and tourist information centres also arrange rentals, often acting as agents for the above companies. You usually need to pay with a major credit card. If you are driving across all three Baltic states, it is cheaper to rent a car in Vilnius. Some car rental companies, such as Avis and Hertz, allow you to hire a car in one city and drop it off in another.

The major car rental agencies only have western manufactured cars to rent, typically Toyota, Volvo and Ford. They all offer a variety of different packages and weekend deals and it is worth asking about all the possibilities before you decide which option to take. Deals apart, expect to pay around US$90 (unlimited mileage) a day in Estonia, US$120 a day in Rīga, and around US$70 a day with unlimited mileage in Vilnius.

You cannot rent a car in the Kaliningrad Region as, by law, drivers have to own their cars. You can hire a car with a local driver but this makes travelling very expensive (see Getting There & Away in the Kaliningrad Region chapter). You can drive a car hired in one of the other Baltic states in the Kaliningrad Region. Just make sure you have your paperwork in order.

See city and town Getting There & Away sections for specific information on car rental firms.

Documents
If you're renting a car you need a passport and a suitable driving licence – normally an International Driving Permit but a national licence from a European country is often acceptable. Some rental companies have minimum ages (usually 19 or 21, but 22 at some places in Estonia) and stipulate that you must have held your licence for at least a year. A major credit card is almost essential too, as some companies insist on it as the method of payment. Even if they don't, you'll have to leave a very large deposit or make a heavy cash prepayment. See the Car & Motorcycle section in the Getting There & Away chapter for more on licences and on other documents you need if you bring your own vehicle.

Security

Take normal precautions when you leave your vehicle unattended – lock it and don't leave anything of any value in it. Western vehicles will attract attention. There are fenced-in parking lots in many towns which are worth finding if you're not staying in a hotel with lock-up facilities (see Crime under Dangers & Annoyances in the Facts for the Visitor chapter).

BICYCLE

The flatness and small scale of the Baltic states and the light traffic on most roads make them good cycling territory. On the Estonian islands particularly, you will see cyclists galore in summer. Most bring their own bikes but there are also a few places where you can rent a bicycle – including Kärdla, Rīga, Rēzekne (Latgale), Vilnius and Palanga for local use, and Rīga, Vilnius, Sigulda and Valmiera for touring. Cyclists should certainly bring waterproof clothing, and perhaps a tent if you're touring since you may not find accommodation in some out of the way places.

The Estonian Ecotourism Association (☎ 2-6316 809; fax 244-43 779; email ecotourism@www.ee; http://www.ee/ecotourism), PO Box 84, EE3600 Pärnu, and the Tourist Club of Latvia (☎ 7221 731, 7221 113; fax 7227 680) at Škārņu iela 22, LV-1350 Rīga, both organise small-group cycle tours with a guide and all equipment provided if you need it.

The Estonian Ecotourism Association arranges a seven day cycling tour of Saaremaa, covering 45 to 70 km a day. It costs US$178 including farmhouse accommodation. Bicycle rental is a further US$40. Also on its agenda is a four day tour of Hiiumaa (US$331) and a five day tour of west Estonia, starting in Haapsalu and taking in the Rumpo peninsula and Vormsi island en route. It costs US$240, not including bicycle rental. Bookings can be made for these tours through the association's Pärnu head office via email or fax; or through one of its agents in Estonia or overseas.

The Tourist Club of Latvia offers a nine day riding itinerary round Vidzeme and Latgale (eastern Latvia) plus three days in and around Rīga, with accommodation in a mixture of cheaper hotels, tents and farmhouses. All food, equipment and an English-speaking guide are provided, for US$670 per person (maximum eight people).

HITCHING

Hitching is never entirely safe in any country in the world, and we don't recommend it. Travellers who decide to hitch should understand that they are taking a small but potentially serious risk. However, many people do choose to hitch, especially in the Baltic states where, locally, it is a popular means of getting from A to B. If you do hitch, travel in pairs and let someone know where you are planning to go. It is customary to pay your share of the petrol.

BOAT

Combined passenger and vehicle ferries sail from the Estonian mainland to the islands of Muhu (which is linked by a road causeway to Estonia's biggest island, Saaremaa), Hiiumaa and Vormsi. In summer there are also ferry services between Saaremaa and Hiiumaa, and between Saaremaa and Vilsandi island. Full details of all these services are in the West Estonia & the Islands chapter.

It's possible to take boat trips to the islands of Saarnaki and Hankatsi, off south-east Hiiumaa, and to Abruka and Vahase off Saaremaa's western coast. From Pärnu, you can take boat excursions to the Kihnu and Ruhnu islands – see the South-West Estonia chapter.

In Lithuania during summer, a hydrofoil service plies daily along the Nemunas river and the Curonian Lagoon between Kaunas and Nida, with some sailings to Klaipėda too.

Yacht

Private yachting is an increasingly popular way of getting around the Baltic coasts – particularly Estonia's with its many islands and bays. Yachts can be rented with or without a skipper from the Pirita marina (☎ 2-238 003; fax 2-238 044), Regati puiestee 1, Tallinn EE-0019. For advance information and advice you can always contact the Estonian Yachting Union (☎ 2-237 288; fax 2-238 344). The Pärnu yacht club (☎ 244-31 420; fax 244-42 950), Lootsi 6, Pärnu, and the Andrejosta yacht centre (☎ 323 261, 329 282), at Eksporta 1a, Rīga, also rent yachts.

The Estonian Marine Tourism Association (EMTA; ☎ & fax 2-6411 417), Pikk 71, EE-0001 Tallinn, publishes an annual *By Pleasure Boat to Estonia* guide which has a whole bunch of useful addresses as well as information and maps of Estonian harbours, and details of local sea rescue operations including shortwave radio channel listings and telephone numbers of the different regional emergency rescue services. The EMTA also sells updated navigation charts of the Estonian coast; they are also sold at most harbours in Estonia, and in Finland from the Estum Sailing Agency (☎ 09-629 299; fax 09-629 390), Vuorimiehenkatu 23a, SF-00140 Helsinki.

See Sailing Yourself in the Getting There & Away chapter for information on recommended harbours in Estonia.

LOCAL TRANSPORT
Bus, Tram & Trolleybus
A variety of trams, buses, and trolleybuses (buses run by electricity from overhead wires) provide pretty thorough public transport around towns and cities in the Baltic states and the Kaliningrad Region (the exception is Lithuania where there are no trams). All three types of transport get frighteningly crowded, especially during the early morning and early evening rush hour when so many people cram themselves in that the doors don't even shut properly (in Kaunas, some 400 students from the university squashed into one bus as a publicity stunt to highlight the need for more services!).

Trams, trolleybuses and buses all run from about 5.30 am to 12.30 am, but services get pretty thin in outlying areas after about 7 pm.

In Estonia, and the Kaliningrad Region, the same ticket is good for all three types of transport. In Lithuania and Latvia, you need different tickets for each type of transport. In all three countries, you pay for your ride by punching a flat-fare ticket in one of the ticket punches fixed inside the vehicle. Tickets are sold from news kiosks displaying them in the window and by some drivers (who are easier to find). Buy five or 10 at once. Weekly and monthly travel passes are also available. The system depends on honesty and lends itself to cheating, but there are occasional inspections with fines of up to US$10 levied on the spot if you're riding without a punched ticket.

Travelling on all trams, trolleybuses and buses requires a certain etiquette. If you are young, fit and capable of standing on one foot for the duration of your journey, do not sit in the seats at the front – these are only for babushkas and small children. Secondly, plan getting off well ahead of time. The moment the bus/tram rolls away from the stop prior to the one you are getting off at, start making your way to the door. Pushing, shoving, stamping on toes and elbowing is, of course, allowed. Thirdly, feel free to take anything you like on any form of public transport – squawking chickens will barely raise a second glance.

All airports are served by regular city transport as well as by taxis.

A further type of city transport is the route-taxi (Estonian: *liinitakso* or *marsruuttakso*; Latvian: *maršruta taksometrs*; Lithuania *mašrutinis*; Russian: *marshrutnoe taksi*), though most visitors needn't bother about it. These are minibuses that will drop you anywhere along their fixed routes for a flat fare.

Train
Suburban trains serve the outskirts of the main cities and some surrounding towns and villages. They're of limited use as city transport for visitors as they mostly go to residential or industrial areas with little to see. But some are useful for day trips to destinations outside the cities.

Taxi

Taxis are plentiful and usually cheap, as officially they cost 4 EEK (US$0.31) a km in Estonia, 0.20 lati (US$0.40) a km in Latvia, and 1.20 litų (US$0.30) a km in Lithuania. In the Kaliningrad Region, the only official rate is an hourly one (US$10). Absurd prices are often asked of unsuspecting foreigners. Former state-run taxis – often large Volga cars, usually sporting a little chequered strip on the side – tend to be more honest than private enterprise taxis with no recognisable insignia.

To avoid rip-offs, insist on the meter running, if it works that is. If not, agree on a fixed price before you set off. In some places, such as Vilnius, it is substantially cheaper to order a cab by phone.

ORGANISED TOURS

There are a lot of single city, two or three city, country, island and so on tours and excursions available in the Baltic states. Most are advertised by travel agencies. More alternative four or five-day tours with farmhouse accommodation aimed at the independent traveller are organised by the Estonian Ecotourism Association (see Bicycle above for contact details) and the Country Traveller Association (Lauku Ceļotājs), Kuģu 11, LV-1048 Rīga, Latvia (☎ 7617 600, 7617 024; fax 7830 041).

The Estonian Ecotourism Association offers skiing tours of the Haanja Uplands in south-east Estonia (US$175 including ski rental); a Hiiumaa nature tour (US$310); trekking tours in Lahemaa National Park (US$301) and Karula National Park (US$232); and a Muhu island tour taking in yachting, fishing and boating (US$238).

The Country Traveller's tours in Latvia include a 'Sea and Cities' tour (US$425), and a stud farming tour for horse enthusiasts (US$270).

Estonia

Facts about Estonia

Estonia (Eesti) is the northernmost of the three Baltic states. Helsinki is just 80 km away across the Gulf of Finland, making Tallinn, the capital, a good starting point for a trip through the region. Even before independence, Estonia had strong links with Finland and was popular with Finnish tourists. The Finns who hop across from Helsinki still outnumber other visitors.

Estonia's past lingers in the medieval heart of Tallinn, which is a highlight of any visit to the Baltic region. Tallinn is the hub of Estonian life, but Tartu, the second city; Lahemaa National Park; and the islands off the west coast are among other appealing destinations.

This chapter contains information specific to Estonia. For a more general introduction to the history, geography and culture of the Baltic states, see Facts about the Region at the front of the book.

HISTORY

Since independence in 1991 Estonia has matured both economically and politically.

The country held its first general election under the new constitution in 1992, choosing the conservative Fatherland party with nationalist, anticommunist and free-market policies that were clear enough but more moderate than those of some of its rivals. In May 1993, Estonia (along with Lithuania) was one of the first ex-Soviet states to be admitted to the Council of Europe. Estonian fears that Russia might return in force eased somewhat when the last Russian garrisons withdrew in 1995.

Estonia's border dispute with Russia

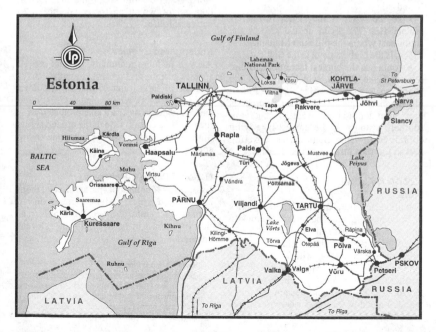

ended in 1997. Russia recognised Estonian independence, but Estonia had to give up its claim to two frontier areas, namely a slice of land east of the Narva River and a larger area of the Setumaa region around Pechory (Estonian: Petseri), across Estonia's existing south-east border.

GEOGRAPHY

Estonia is the smallest Baltic state, at 45,200 sq km – slightly bigger than Switzerland or Denmark. It borders Russia in the east and Latvia in the south. Tallinn is on the north coast. Islands make up nearly 10% of Estonian territory; the biggest are Saaremaa and Hiiumaa to the west. Some 44 per cent of the country is forested, and 22 per cent is wetland, with peat bogs which in places are six metres deep.

Northern Estonia faces the Gulf of Finland, the narrow eastern arm of the Baltic that leads into St Petersburg. Much of Estonia's west coast is shielded by its islands.

Like the other Baltic states, Estonia is mainly flat. The main upland area is the south-east where the hill Suur Munamägi, at 317m, is the highest point in the Baltic states.

Estonia has the biggest lakes in the Baltic region; Lake Peipus, which straddles the Estonian-Russian border, is the fourth biggest in Europe, at 3548 sq km (though its maximum depth is only 15m). Võrtsjärv, in southern Estonia, is the biggest lake lying entirely within the Baltic states, covering 270 sq km (but just six metres deep).

FLORA & FAUNA
Flora
Estonia's rich flora includes 1470 varieties of indigenous plant. The forests are mostly pine and spruce, with silver and dwarf birch, aspen, speckled and black alder the most common species. Oak, willow, linden and maple are also found. Many species of rare northern orchids, most of which are protected, can be found in western Estonia's wooded meadows, formed where trees have been felled.

One of 10,000 wild boar in Estonia

Fauna
Estonia has rich populations of large European mammals. There is more information about these in the Facts about the Region chapter. Roe deer, wild boar and elk are commonly hunted and may appear on the menu in more expensive restaurants. Exotic species, introduced for their fur, include the North American muskrat, mink and raccoon dog, all of which are potential threats to native wildlife.

Endangered Species
As well as large mammals, Estonia has 10 species of rare and protected amphibian. A number of large raptors, including golden eagle (250 pairs), white tailed eagle, spotted eagle and eagle owl, are also protected as is the rare black stork. One of the unique sights of the Estonian forest is the European flying squirrel.

National Parks & Reserves
Estonia has four national parks, three of them established since independence, and a number of nature reserves. More information on them can be found in the relevant chapters.

Lahemaa National Park
    Estonia's oldest national park (founded in 1971) comprises 1120 sq km of typical Estonian coast and unspoiled hinterland east of Tallinn – beaches, rivers, lakes, waterfalls, walking trails; park centre at Viitna

Karula National Park
  founded in 1993, 103 sq km of southern forest and lakeland

Soomaa National Park
  founded in 1993, protects a 367 sq km expanse of mid-Estonian swamplands and flat meadows

Vilsandi National Park
  small islands off western Saaremaa – bird sanctuary; closed to visitors

Biosphere Reserve of the West Estonian Archipelago
  two large inhabited islands, Saaremaa and Hiiumaa, two smaller islands, Muhu and Vormsi, and surrounding islets – shelters rare grey and ringed seals, black storks, cranes, boar, lynx, marten and raccoon dog

Endla State Nature Reserve
  around the lake Endla järv, east of Paide – boggy area, nature trails

Matsalu State Nature Reserve
  on west coast – wetland and major water bird habitat; visitor centre; guided trips available

Nigula State Nature Reserve
  in the south-west near Latvian border – bog

Väinameri Nature Reserve
  islets off south-east Hiiumaa – bird and plant habitat; permit needed

Viidumäe State Nature Reserve
  on Saaremaa – forested area around the island's highest point; observation tower

GOVERNMENT & POLITICS

Estonia's constitution was approved in June 1992 by a referendum. The law-making body is a 101 seat parliament called the Riigikogu (National Council), elected every four years. The head of state is the president, but the government is headed by the prime minister, who is nominated by the president and has to be approved by a majority in the Riigikogu. The prime minister chooses the cabinet.

The first elections under the new constitution were held in September 1992. The Fatherland Alliance won a narrow majority after campaigning under the slogan 'Cleaning House', which meant removing from power those who were associated with communist rule. Fatherland's leader, a 32 year old historian called Mart Laar, became prime minister. The alliance later formally united as the Fatherland (Isamaa) Party. Its stated policies include free-market economics, privatisation, reduction of state bureaucracy and monopolies, and liberalisation of the citizenship law.

In presidential elections held at the same time as those for parliament, Arnold Rüütel, the former head of Estonia's Soviet government, and president under the semi-democratic system in place since 1990, won most votes (42%) but did not get an overall majority. The system was then changed to allow the Riigikogu to elect the president. Its choice was the writer and former foreign minister, Lennart Meri, who won a second term in 1996. He remains the only still point on Estonia's fluid political scene. Since independence, government has passed through the hands of a series of coalitions with no single party gaining a clear majority. Seven governments were formed and three parliaments elected between 1991 and 1997, a pattern which seems likely to continue.

Estonian political parties come and go and critics say most are over-committed to narrow ideologies and sectional interests at the expense of national progress. All have been dogged by various scandals, including the Coalition Party-Rural People's Party government led by Tiit Vahti, which collapsed in early 1997 after being accused of misusing environmental funds. In March 1997, the non-partisan Mart Siimann was sworn in as prime minister at the head of a minority government made up of five Coalition Party MPs, two Rural People's Party ministers, one Progressive MP and six non-partisan members. Siimann, a former managing director of the private TV channel RTV, has a reputation as a diplomatic administrator, and his government is tipped to have a fair chance of surviving until general elections in March 1999. His confirmation was backed by 72 of Estonia's MPs, with only the Pro Patria and Moderate parties voting against him.

Siimann's government has made Estonia's relationship with the European Union its top priority. Two out of three Estonians favour joining the EU, and the government aims to harmonise all Estonian laws with EU guidelines within five years. Land and property reform, pensions, and reshaping the civil

ESTONIA

service also are on the agenda. Siimann promised the economy would remain open and that plans to make it easier for foreigners to invest in Estonian land and property would continue. Main players in the Estonian parliament include the centre-left Coalition group, the Rural People's Party, the right of centre Reform Party, the left leaning Centre Party, the Moderates, and the fiercely nationalist Pro Patria.

Citizenship

People who were citizens of the pre-1940 Estonian Republic (and their descendants) are automatically citizens. Other people, basically, must have lived in Estonia for two years after 30 March, 1990, and be able to write, read, and converse in the Estonian language. Applications take a year to go through. Only citizens may vote in parliamentary elections. The citizenship rules were approved by the referendum in 1992 and made law by the Riigikogu in 1993. Around 12,000 Russian-speakers applied for Estonian citizenship in 1996, but as many as 120,000 applied for Russian passports.

ECONOMY

Estonia is the outstanding economic success story of the Baltic region, making a remarkable transition to free market capitalism with an annual growth rate of 3% by 1995, and inflation dwindling to around 25% in 1996. Official unemployment is only 3.4%. The freely convertible kroon (EEK) replaced the virtually valueless Soviet rouble in 1992. Linked to the German mark at DM1 = 8 EEK, it has proved surprisingly resilient. Between 1993 and early 1994 the government privatised most state-owned enterprises with fairly positive results. Only a few privatised firms went under, and most held their own. Exceptions were the construction sector (in 1994 more than half of Estonia's construction companies were loss makers), co-operatives where shares were owned by the staff (80% were loss makers in 1994), and management buy-out enterprises. Privatisation continues. Employment increased by more than 25% between 1993

and 1995, but wages remain low. At the beginning of 1997 the government refused to raise the minimum monthly wage to 1200 kroons (US$100), and the average monthly salary is only US$238.

Estonia proved more willing than its neighbours to bite the free trade bullet, and has virtually no customs tariffs and minimum restrictions on foreign investment. As a result, investment poured into the country. Between 1992 and 1995 foreign firms invested US$700 million, US$250 million in 1995 alone. Some 22% of this came from Finland and 20% from Sweden. Two thirds of investment has gone into the Tallinn region, and the Estonian Investment Agency is now trying to direct money elsewhere. In terms of the number of people employed, food production and clothing have become the fastest growing sectors of the economy, but the metal and woodworking sectors have also picked up. The transitional economy created opportunities for many small and medium-sized enterprises. Many of these are headed by energetic young graduates who had little scope for promotion under the old regime.

The post-Soviet chaos has also left many people homeless, especially in Tallinn, where as many as 10,000 people suffer that fate. In the harsh winter of 1996-97 some were given temporary shelter in Soviet-era bomb shelters.

POPULATION & PEOPLE

Only around 62% of the approximately 1.5 million people living in Estonia are ethnic Estonians. About 30% of the population is Russian, and about 3% is Ukrainian. These ethnic populations are not evenly distributed throughout the country. About half the people of Tallinn, for instance, are Russian, and the industrial towns of north-east Estonia are overwhelmingly Russian populated.

The Estonians themselves are one of the Finno-Ugric peoples, an ethno-linguistic group whose members are scattered from the Arctic to central Europe, halfway across Siberia, and along the River Volga. This sets them apart from the Latvians and Lithuanians, who are Indo-European. It's reckoned that the ancestors of the present Estonians reached Estonia from the east from about 2500 to 2000 BC. Within the Finno-Ugric group, the Estonians are closely related to such peoples as the Finns, the Lapps, the Karelians (who live in Finland and neighbouring parts of Russia) and the Livs, who used to inhabit much of coastal Latvia but are now reduced to tiny numbers and are on the verge of extinction as a separate people. Other Finno-Ugric peoples include the Samoyeds along the Russian shores of the Arctic Ocean; the Ostyaks and Voguls, east of the Urals; the Magyars (Hungarians); the Votyaks and Zyryans, west of the Urals; and the Mordvins and Cheremis, along the Volga.

Woman in traditional Estonian dress
(Ruhnu region)

An estimated 60,000 Estonians live in Russia, many of them in the Setumaa region which was formally ceded to Russia under the 1997 treaty. It remains to be seen whether substantial numbers of them will choose to move to independent Estonia. Around 80,000 live in other countries, mainly as a result of emigration around the turn of the 20th century and following the outbreak of WWII. The main overseas Estonian communities are in North America and Sweden but there are others in Britain, Australia and elsewhere.

ARTS
Literature
Estonian literature began with the poems of Kristjan Jaak Peterson in the early 19th century. The national epic poem *Kalevipoeg* (Son of Kalev) was written between 1857 and 1861 by Friedrich Reinhold Kreutzwald, who was inspired by Finland's *Kalevala*, a similar epic created a few decades earlier. Kreutzwald put together hundreds of Estonian legends and folk tales to tell the adventures of the mythical hero Kalevipoeg, which end with his death and his land's conquest by foreigners, but also hope for a future freedom. Kalevipoeg must have travelled pretty widely round Estonia, as there's barely a big boulder in the country which wasn't apparently once tossed by him or a lake he didn't once jump across.

Lydia Koidula (1843-86) was the poet of Estonia's national awakening, while Eduard Vilde (1865-1933) was an influential turn-of-the-century novelist and playwright. Oskar Luts is reckoned to be a kind of Estonian Mark Twain for his school and childhood tales including *Kevade* (Spring), written in 1912-13. Anton Hansen Tammsaare is considered the greatest Estonian novelist for his *Tõde ja Õigus* (Truth and Justice), written between 1926 and 1933. A five volume saga of village and town life, it explores Estonian social, political and philosophical issues.

More recently the novelist Jaan Kross has won acclaim for his historical novels in which he managed to tackle contemporary Soviet-era subjects. His best known book,

The Czar's Madman, has been translated into English – see Books in the introductory Facts for the Visitor chapter. Another leading novelist is Arvo Valton who, like Kross, spent some time as an exile in Siberia. His *Masendus ja Lootus* (Depression and Hope) deals with that experience.

Estonia also has a number of outstanding contemporary poets. Jaan Kaplinski has had two collections, *The Same Sea in Us All* and *The Wandering Border*, published in English. His work expresses the feel of Estonian life superbly. Paul-Eerik Rummo is considered by many to be the leading Estonian poet – a judgement which predates his elevation to the post of Minister of Culture in 1992. Kross and Kaplinski were also elected to parliament the same year – and both have been mentioned as Nobel prize candidates.

Music

Rock thrives in Estonia and there are big annual festivals. Estonian musicians seem very open to foreign influence – Ultima Thule and Compromise Blue, the country's longest-running bands, owe much to American rock and blues, progressive rock virtuoso Peeter Volkonski sings in Russian and Greek as well as Estonian, and the Johanson Brothers show a strong Irish folk-rock influence. Kukerpillid and Justament are two top folk bands, and other leading Estonian combos include the U2-style Mr Lawrence and the folk rockers Jääboiler.

Arvo Pärt, the Baltics' most widely acclaimed serious composer, returned to his native Estonia in 1996 after 16 years of exile in Germany. His works are chiefly choral and classified as 'minimalist'. Veljo Tormis, another leading Estonian choral composer, writes striking music based on old runic chants. His best known works include the difficult to perform *Curse Upon Iron* and *The Ingrian Evenings*.

The Estonian Rudolf Tobias wrote influential symphonic, choral and concerto works around the turn of the century.

Visual Arts

Kristjan Raud (1865-1943), who illustrated *Kalevipoeg*, was a leading figure of the 19th century in Estonia. Contemporary Estonian art leans towards geometrical abstraction. Leading exponents include Raul Meel, Leonhard Lapin and Siim-Tanel Annus.

RELIGION

Only a minority of Estonians profess religious beliefs, but religion provides another division between ethnic Estonians and the Russian-speaking community. Historically, Estonia was Lutheran from the early 17th century, while Russia was and is once again Orthodox. The government's decision to register an Estonian branch of the Orthodox Church (founded in 1947 and linked to the Greek Orthodox Patriarch in Istanbul rather than to Moscow), caused some resentment among Russian Orthodox worshippers.

Facts for the Visitor

This chapter contains visitor information specific to Estonia. For more general information on travelling in the Baltic states and details on obtaining visas for Russia and Belarus, see the introductory Facts for the Visitor chapter at the front of the book.

HIGHLIGHTS

Tallinn's Old Town with its winding, cobbled streets and gingerbread façades is a definite high point of any trip to Estonia.

Equally memorable are the fairly untouched islands of Hiiumaa and Saaremaa – two spots of remarkable solitude and beauty where you can retreat into nature, stroll through pretty fishing villages or take a boat trip to Estonia's lesser explored islands. The tiny island of Kihnu, with its traditionally dressed peoples and thriving folklore tales, is another place island lovers should not miss out on. In northern Estonia is the Lahemaa National Park, and in the south-west, the Soomaa bogs where you can paddle in traditional Estonian canoes.

Split between Estonia and Russia is Setumaa, the tiny land of the Setus where a language and traditions all of their own are still very much part of daily life.

TOURIST OFFICES

Estonia boasts a wide network of tourist information offices at home and abroad. They are co-ordinated by the Estonian Tourist Board (☎ 372-6411 420; fax 372-6411 342; email info@turism.ee), Pikk 71, EE0001 Tallinn, Estonia. Their representatives overseas include:

Canada
  Orav Travel, 5650 Yonge St, North York, Ontario M2M 4G3 (☎ 416-221 4164; fax 416-221 6789)
Finland
  Baltic Tourism Information Centre, Merimiehenkatu 29, SF-00150 Helsinki (☎ 09-637 783; fax 09-637 887)

Germany
  Baltic Tourism Information Centre, Woldsenstrasse 36, D-25813 Husum (☎ 048-413 004; fax 048-412 109)

Estonian embassies, consulates and Baltic-specialist travel agencies in western countries are also useful sources of information (see Getting There & Away at the front of the book).

There are efficient tourist information centres all over Estonia, each of which has a home page on the Internet (see relevant chapters for details). Offices include:

Haapsalu (☎ 247-45 248; email info@haapsalu.turism.ee)
Jõhvi (☎ 233-22 306)
Kärdla on Hiiumaa (☎ 246-91 377; email info@hiiumaa.turism.ee)
Kuressaare on Saaremaa (☎ 245-55 120; email info@oesel.turism.ee)
Lake Peipus' north shore (☎ 233-93 378; email info@iisaku.turism.ee)
Narva (☎ 235-60 184)
Otepää (☎ 276-55 364); email info@otepaa.turism.ee)
Paide (☎ 238-50 400; email info@paide.turism.ee)
Pärnu (☎ 244-45 639; email info@parnu.turism.ee)
Rõuge (☎ 278-59 245; email info@rauge.turism.ee)
Tallinn city office (☎ 2-6313 940; email info@tallinn.turism.ee)
Tallinn harbour office (☎ 2-6318 321)
Tartu (☎ 27-432 141; email info@tartu.turism.ee)
Viljandi (☎ 243-34 444; email info@viljandi.turism.ee)
Võru (☎ 278-21 881; email info@werro.turism.ee)

Most Estonian national parks and nature reserves operate an information centre at their headquarters.

EMBASSIES & CONSULATES

Estonian diplomatic missions across the world include:

Australia
  Consulate: 86 Louisa Road, Birchgrove, NSW 2041 (☎ 02-9810 7468; fax 02-9818 1779; email eestikon@ozemail.com.au)

Austria
Embassy: Marokkanergasse 22/6, Wien 1030, Österreich (☎ 1-718 07 29; fax 1-718 07 29 15; email saatkond@estemb.or.at)
Belarus
Consulate: Varvasheni 17, Minsk (☎ 017-234 59 65; fax 017-210 12 60)
Belgium
Embassy: Avenue Isidore Gerard 1, 1160 Brussels-Auderghem, (☎ 02-779 07 55; fax 02-779 28 17; email saatkond@estemb.be)
Consulate: Charlottalei 34, B-2018 Antwerpen (☎ 3-231 16 60; fax 3-233 76 70)
Canada
Consulate: 958 Broadview Avenue, Toronto, Ontario, M4K 2R6 (☎ 416-461 0764; fax 416-461 0448; email estconsu@inforamp.net)
Denmark
Embassy: Aurehojvej 19, DK-2900 Hellerup-Kobenhavn (☎ 39-402 666; fax 39-402 630; email sekretar@estemb.dk)
Consulate: 4 Havnegade, DK-8000 Aarhus C (☎ 86-13 95 55; fax 86-19 34 55)
Finland
Embassy: Itäinen Puistotie 10, 00140 Helsinki, Suomi (☎ 09-622 02 60; fax 09-622 02 610; email sekretar@estemb.fi)
Consulate: Kasarmikatu 28, Helsinki (☎ 09-622 02 640; fax 09-622 02 810)
France
Embassy: 14 Boulevard Montmartre, 75009 Paris (☎ 01 48 01 00 22; fax 01 48 01 02 95; email saadik@est-emb.fr)
Germany
Embassy: Fritz-Schäffer Strasse 22, 53113 Bonn (☎ 0228-914 790; fax 0228-914 7911; email bonn@estebonn.gihub.de)
Consulate: Badestrasse 38, 20143 Hamburg (☎ 040-450 40 26; fax 040-450 40 515)
Hungary
Consulate: 1113 Budapest, Bocskai ut 34/B VII.I, Magyarorszag (☎ 361-161 24 25; fax 361-266 56 99)
Latvia
Embassy: Skolas 13, Rīga (☎ 7820 460; fax 7820 461; email sekretar@riia.vm.ee)
Lithuania
Embassy: Tilto 29, Vilnius (☎ 22-622 030; fax 22-220 461)
Netherlands
Consulate: Snipweg 101, 118 DP Schiphol South, PO Box 7634, 1117 ZJ Schiphol Centre (☎ 020-316 54 40; fax 020 316 54 54)
Norway
Embassy: Frognerveien 8, section 83, 0257 Oslo (☎ 2-255 39 99; fax 2-255 37 85)
Poland
Embassy: Karwinska 1, 02-639 Warsaw, Rzeczpospolita Polska (☎ 22-44 44 80; fax 22-44 44 81)

Russia
Embassy: Malo Kislovski 5, 103009 Moscow (☎ 095-2905 013; fax 095-2023 830; email aem@avalon.rosmail.com)
Consulate: Bolšaja Monetnaja 14, St Petersburg (☎ 812-233 55 48; fax 812-233 53 09)
Sweden
Embassy: Storgatan 38, 1 tr, Box 14069, Stockholm 10440 (☎ 08-665 6550, 661 5810; fax 08-662 9980; email sekretar@estemb.se)
Switzerland
Consulate: 8 Chemin des Aulx, CH-1228 Plan-les-Quates, Geneva (☎ 22-706 11 11; fax 22-794 94 78)
Ukraine
Embassy: Kutuzovi prospekt 8, Kiev (☎ & fax 44-295 87 72; email saatkond@estemb.kiev.ua)
UK
Embassy: 16 Hyde Park Gate, London SW7 5DG (☎ 0171-589 3428; fax 0171-589 3430; email sekretar@estonia.gov.uk)
USA
Embassy: 2131 Massachusetts Avenue, NW, Washington DC 20008 (☎ 202-588 0101; fax 202-588 0108; email info@estemb.org; http//www.estemb.org)
Consulate: 630 5th Avenue, Suite 2415, New York, NY 10111 (☎ 212-247 7634, 247 1450; fax 212-262 0893)

CUSTOMS

Customs regulations vary between the Baltic states and are subject to change. See the introductory Facts for the Visitor chapter for more general points. In Tallinn, the Estonian customs department (☎ 2-6318 607) is inside the Ministry of Foreign Affairs at Rävala puiestee 9.

Alcohol & Tobacco

People aged 21 or over can bring in or take out, duty-free, 10 litres of beer; 200 cigarettes or 20 cigars or 250 grams of tobacco; and either one litre of strong alcoholic drinks (up to 58% volume) and one litre of mild alcoholic drinks (up to 21% vol), or two litres of mild alcoholic drinks. You'll be charged tax from 30 to 100% of the retail price for exceeding those limits.

The duty-free allowances for people aged between 18 and 21 years are the same except that no strong alcoholic drinks are allowed.

Money

Hard currency worth more than DM10,000 should be declared on arrival, and you cannot take out more than you brought in.

Other Items

There's duty on bringing in furs, fur articles, precious metals and jewellery above certain limits which few people will exceed.

Purchases up to a total value of 5000 EEK can be exported duty-free (except vehicles). Above that there's 100% duty. There are also export duties on foodstuffs exceeding 10 kg; coffee, tea, spices and seeds exceeding 3 kg; and gold and silver jewellery above the duty-free import limits. Some cultural objects such as paintings and sculptures, furs and fur articles over 500 EEK in purchase price also attract duty.

Works of art or of cultural significance (including antique books) that date from before 1945, but are less than 100 years old, are subject to a 50% customs duty; those older than 100 years attract 100% duty. They may only leave with written permission from the Ministry of Culture (☎ 2-448 501), Sakala 14, Tallinn.

You cannot import or export diamonds (except in jewellery); scrap and waste of precious metals or metals covered with precious metals; firearms; ammunition; drugs or dangerous chemical substances.

MONEY

Estonia's currency is the *kroon* (pronounced 'krohn'), commonly written as EEK which stands for Eesti Kroon (Estonian Crown) and distinguishes it from Swedish, Danish, Norwegian and other crowns. It is divided into 100 *sents* (cents).

The kroon is the only legal tender in Estonia. It was the first new Baltic currency to be introduced, in 1992, and has held its initial rate of 8 EEK to one Deutschmark, making it a stable currency by any standards. Exchange rates in early 1997 included:

Australia	A$1	=	10.47 EEK
Canada	C$1	=	9.69 EEK
Finland	1 Fmk	=	2.66 EEK
Germany	DM1	=	8.00 EEK
Sweden	1 SKr	=	1.76 EEK
United Kingdom	UK£1	=	21.87 EEK
United States	US$1	=	13.49 EEK

The kroon comes in one, two, five, 10, 25, 50, 100 and 500 EEK notes, each featuring a national hero on the front. There are coins of five, 10, 20 and 50 sents and, less commonplace, 1 EEK. Estonia's pre-WWII currency, displaced by the rouble in 1940, was also called the kroon but was an entirely different system.

NEWSPAPERS & MAGAZINES

The most popular Estonian papers are *Postimees* (strongest on culture and international news), *Paevaleht* and *Sõnumileht* (best for regional news), and the business paper *Äripäev*. They are published five or six times weekly with circulations of 50,000 to 90,000. *Eesti Ekspress* is a sensationalist colour weekly but equally popular. The fortnightly *Luup* is the closest you'll find to *Newsweek* in Estonian. A full listing of Estonian-language newspapers and magazines is online at http://www.zzz.ee.

Details of English-language newspapers and magazines published in the Baltics are given in Facts for the Visitor – Media at the front of the book.

RADIO & TV

Seven TV channels can be picked up in Tallinn and along the north coast of Estonia – state-run Eesti TV plus two other Estonian channels and four from Finland which broadcast a handful of English-language programmes. Among its mainly Estonian-language output, Eesti TV shows a few British programmes and some locally made Russian-language ones. News in Estonian is at 9.30 pm. Almost all hotels have satellite TV offering an onslaught of European programmes.

State-run Eesti Raadio broadcasts 10 minutes of local news in English on weekdays at 6.20 pm, and the half-hour *Estonia Today* magazine programme, which is also in English, on Monday and Thursday at

11.30 pm. Its frequencies are 103.5 FM and 5.925 MHz on short wave. The BBC World Service is available on 100.3 FM.

The independent Radio Kuku on 100.7 MHz FM has good music and some English-language news and features between 2 and 4 pm daily. Voice of America (70.28 Mhz) broadcasts daily from 7 to 11 am, and 10 pm to midnight. Top of the charts is Love Radio, a music station which runs a two hour jazz programme on Sundays at 6 pm. It broadcasts English-language news and weather reports daily on the half hour. Its frequency in Tallinn is 97.8 FM; in Tartu 98.6 FM; Pärnu 98.3 FM; Viljandi 97.9 FM; and Rakvere 98.5 FM.

Some of these radio stations have a home page on the Internet (http://www.zzz.ee).

PUBLIC HOLIDAYS & SPECIAL EVENTS

National holidays in Estonia include:

New Year's Day, 1 January
Independence Day (anniversary of 1918 declaration), 24 February
Good Friday – Easter Monday is also taken as a holiday by many people
May Day, 1 May
Võidupüha (Victory Day commemorating the anniversary of the Battle of Võnnu, 1919), 23 June
Jaanipäev (St John's Day), 24 June – taken together, Victory Day and Jaanipäev are the excuse for a week-long midsummer break for many people
Christmas (Jõulud), 25 December
Boxing Day, 26 December

Estonia has a long list of festivals and cultural events, especially in summer. Three major events are the national song festival, the midsummer celebrations, and the Baltika folk festival, next due in Tallinn in 1998. The All-Estonian Song Festival, which climaxes with a choir of up to 30,000 people singing traditional Estonian songs on a vast open-air stage to an audience of 100,000, is held every five years, next in Tallinn in 1999 (see Facts for the Visitor – Public Holidays & Special Events at the front of the book).

The Tallinn Culture Board (☎ 6404 607; fax 6404 606) and the city tourist information centre in Tallinn (see Tallinn –

Information) issue information on events in and around the capital. They include:

Tartu Ski Marathon – mid-February
Student Jazz Festival – an international festival attracting musicians from the entire Baltic region; Tallinn, mid-February
Day of the Setu Lace – a traditional Setu folk festival; Obinitsa near Võru, March 1
Kuressaare Theatre Days – Kuressaare, March
International Harpsichord Days of Music – Tallinn, April
Jazzkaar – an international jazz festival; Tallinn, April
Old Tallinn Days – Tallinn old-town festival; early or mid-June
Memme-taadi Days – a celebration of Estonian folk culture; Rocca al Mare Open Air Museum, Tallinn, mid-June
International Music & theatre festival FiESTa – Pärnu, late June
Tallinn Rock Summer – the Baltics' biggest three-day, international rock-music festival; at Tallinn Song Bowl, July
Viru Säru – folk festival; Palmse Manor, Lahemaa National Park, first weekend in July, in even-numbered years
Visual Anthropology Festival – film festival focusing on issues of cultural survival; Pärnu, July
International Organ Music Festival – concerts throughout Estonia, early August
Classical Music Festival & Country Music Festival – two separate weekend musicals; Pärnu, August
White Lady Festival – a week-long festival of cultural events climaxing with the appearance of Estonia's most famous ghost; Haapsalu, August
Day of the Setu Kingdom – a new king of the traditional Setu kingdom is appointed; Obinitsa near Võru, around 28 August
Lillepidu – international flower festival; Tallinn, early September
Time of Spirits – a period of quietness for remembering the past and the dead, when spirits are believed to be abroad; roughly for a month from 2 November
Winter Days – festivities through Tallinn Old Town, late December.

ACTIVITIES

See Activities under Facts for the Visitor at the front of the book for general information on activities in Estonia.

Summer Sports

The Käsmu Sea Museum in the Lahemaa National Park arranges sailing, rowing, and diving summer camps, as well as traditional one-log canoe building camps. You can also canoe in your own hand-built canoe across the bogs of the Soomaa National Park and go bog-walking in the Endla Nature Reserve. Toonus Pluss (☎ 25-255 702) in Võru arranges canoeing trips around the southern shores of Lake Peipus and other regions in south-east Estonia.

Winter Sports
You can ski and snowboard at the Kuutsemäe Sports Centre (☎ 276-54 041) and the Väike-Munamäe Sports Centre (☎ 276-55 036), both near Otepää in south-east Estonia. Arctic Cat (☎ 278-21 959) in Võru arranges motorised snow-bike expeditions.

FOOD & DRINKS
The Estonian diet relies heavily on red meat, chicken, sausage and potatoes. Fish appears most often as a smoked or salted starter. *Suitsukala* means smoked fish. Smoked trout *(forell)* is one good speciality. Estonian sausage varieties include *suitsuvorst* (salami) and *viiner* (frankfurter). At Christmas time, sausages of a different variety are prepared – made from fresh blood and wrapped in pigs intestine. Blood sausages *(verevorst)* and also blood pancakes *(vere pannkoogid)* are served in most traditional Estonian restaurants all year round however.

As well as the widespread Baltic *kotlett*, Estonia also has the *schnitsel*, a slab of meat – usually pork or beef – which is pounded, breaded then fried. Barley, rice and oatmeal porridges are also staples of any daily diet.

No one quite knows what the syrupy *Vana Tallinn* liquor is made from – it is sweet, sickly, very strong and an integral part of any Estonian table. It is best served in coffee, over ice with milk, or – if you feel up to it – with champagne.

General information on eating in the Baltic states is given in the introductory Facts for the Visitor chapter at the front of the book. The Language Guide at the back of the book includes words and phrases you will find useful when ordering food and drink.

Tallinn

HIGHLIGHTS

- Climb Toompea to observe the castle, cathedral and Tallinn from above
- Wind your way round the cobblestoned Old Town; don't miss the souvenir market in the city walls on Müürivahe
- Watch the world go by while enjoying a beer in an outside café on Raekoja plats
- Visit an 18th century noble's house to view Estonia's biggest and best art collection
- Train it to Paldiski to tour the former Soviet submarine base
- Stay up late to witness the white nights (summer only!)

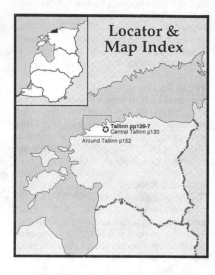

Locator & Map Index

Tallinn pp126-7
Central Tallinn p130
Around Tallinn p152

• *pop 442,000* • ☎ *(2)*

Tallinn fronts a bay on the Gulf of Finland and is dominated by Toompea, the hill over which it has tumbled since the Middle Ages. In few places in Europe does the aura of the 14th and 15th centuries survive intact as it does in Tallinn's Old Town jumble of medieval walls and turrets, needling spires, and winding, cobbled streets. The city is on a similar latitude to St Petersburg and shares the same warm summer 'white nights' and short, cold, dark winter days.

If you're seeking a glance at Estonia's Soviet past, forget looking in Tallinn. The city – with its cosy cafés, quality restaurants, and good, easy to find accommodation – is so 'western' that it has been dubbed by many a 'suburb of Helsinki'. All this and a coastal location makes Tallinn probably the most magnetic, not-to-be-missed hub in the whole of the Baltic states.

While a percentage of Tallinners are earning a better living than they used to, life for many is harder – witness the subdued, anxious people squeezing into trams or scouring the market for cheap food. Among Tallinn's less fortunate are many Russians who form about half its population. A visit to one of the drab apartment-block suburbs

where the Russians are congregated, such as Kopli or Lasnamäe, will show you a very different side of Tallinn from the carefully preserved charms of the Old Town.

HISTORY

The site of Tallinn is thought to have been settled by Finno-Ugric people about 2500 BC. There was probably an Estonian trading settlement here from around the 9th century AD, and a wooden stronghold was built on Toompea in the 11th century. The Danes under King Waldemar II (who conquered northern Estonia in 1219) met tough resistance at Tallinn and were on the verge of retreat when, so the story goes, a red flag with a white cross fell from the sky into their bishop's hands. Taking this as a sign of God's support, they summoned new energy and went on to win the battle; the flag became their national flag (see the Otepää section of the South-West Estonia chapter for the Estonian flag's true origins). The Danes set their own castle on Toompea. The origin of the name Tallinn is thought to be from *Taani linn* which is Estonian for 'Danish town'.

The Knights of the Sword took Tallinn from the Danes in 1227 and built the first stone fort on Toompea. German traders arrived from Visby on the Baltic island of Gotland and founded a colony of about 200 people beneath the fortress. In 1238 Tallinn returned to Danish control, but in 1285 it joined the German-dominated Hanseatic League as a channel for trade between Novgorod, Pskov and the west. Furs, honey, leather, and seal fat moved west; salt, cloth, herring and wine went east.

By the mid-14th century, when the Danes sold northern Estonia to the Teutonic Order, Tallinn was a major Hanseatic town with about 4000 people. A conflict of interest with the knights and bishop on Toompea led the mainly German artisans and merchants in the Lower Town to build a fortified wall to separate themselves from Toompea. However, Tallinn still prospered and became one of northern Europe's biggest towns. Tallinn's German name, Reval, coexisted with the local name until 1918.

The prosperity faded in the 16th century. The Hanseatic League had weakened; and Russians, Swedes, Danes, Poles and Lithuanians fought over the Baltic region. Tallinn survived a 37 week siege by Russia's Ivan the Terrible. It was held by Sweden from 1561 to 1710 until, decimated by plague, it surrendered to Russia's Peter the Great.

In the late 19th century a railway was built from St Petersburg, and Tallinn became a chief port of the Russian empire. Freed peasants converged on the city from the countryside increasing the percentage of Estonians in its population from 52% in 1867 to 89% in 1897. By WWI Tallinn had big shipyards, and a large working class in its population of over 100,000.

Tallinn suffered badly in WWII, with thousands of buildings destroyed during Soviet bombing in 1944. After the war, under Soviet control, large-scale industry was developed in Tallinn – including the USSR's biggest grain-handling port – and the city expanded fast, its population growing to nearly 500,000 from a 1937 level of 175,000. Much of the new population came from Russia, and new high-rise suburbs were built on the outskirts to house the new workers.

ORIENTATION

Tallinn spreads south from the edge of Tallinn Bay (Tallinna Laht) on the southern shore of the Gulf of Finland. At the city's heart, just south of the bay, is the Old Town (Vanalinn), which divides neatly into two parts: Toompea (the hill which dominates Tallinn) and the Lower Town, spreading out from Toompea's eastern side. The Lower Town is centred on Raekoja plats (Town Hall Square), and is still surrounded by most of its 2.5 km medieval wall. Around this old core is the New Town, dating from the 19th and early 20th century.

The tall slab of the Viru hotel, just outside the eastern edge of the Old Town, is a good landmark.

Maps

The accurate *Tallinn – City Plan* (1:25,000), published in 1996 (by the Jaņa Sēta Publishing House in Rīga, Latvia) with a street index and keys in Estonian, English and Russian, is sold for 35 EEK in most city bookshops and kiosks.

Available at the city tourist information centre (see Information – Tourist Offices) is the pocket-sized *Tallinn Map*, published in 1995 by the Tallinn-based Regio Map Publishers. It includes easy to handle maps of the Old Town (1:7400), the city (1:20,000) and the environs of Tallinn (1:170,000) as well as a 'phone directory' of museums, art galleries, hotels, restaurants, bars, cafés and even public toilets. At 15 EEK, it's well worth the investment – if only for that one time you're really desperate!

INFORMATION

Tourist Offices

There's an excellent tourist information centre (☎ 6313 940, 6313 942; fax 6313 941; email info@tallinn.turism.ee, http://www.tallinn.ee) situated at Raekoja plats 18, open

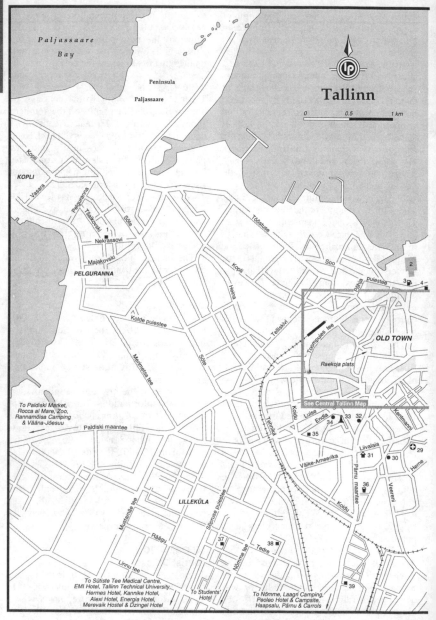

ESTONIA

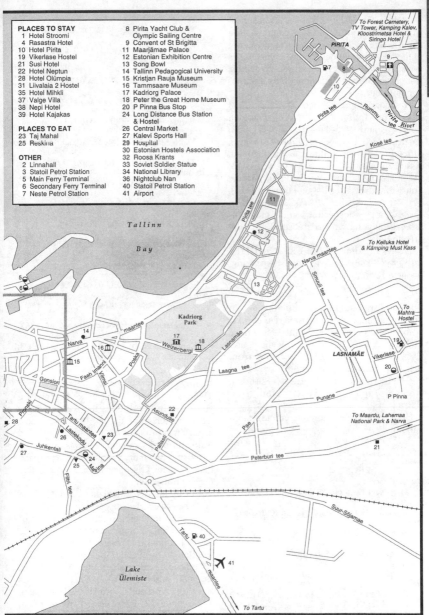

PLACES TO STAY
1 Hotel Stroomi
4 Rasastra Hotel
10 Hotel Pirita
19 Vikerlase Hostel
21 Susi Hotel
22 Hotel Neptun
28 Hotel Olümpia
31 Liivalaia 2 Hostel
35 Hotel Mihkli
37 Valge Villa
38 Nepi Hotel
39 Hotel Kajakas

PLACES TO EAT
23 Taj Mahal
25 Reskina

OTHER
2 Linnahall
3 Statoil Petrol Station
5 Main Ferry Terminal
6 Secondary Ferry Terminal
7 Neste Petrol Station

8 Pirita Yacht Club &
   Olympic Sailing Centre
9 Convent of St Brigitta
11 Maarjämäe Palace
12 Estonian Exhibition Centre
13 Song Bowl
14 Tallinn Pedagogical University
15 Kristjan Rauja Museum
16 Tammsaare Museum
17 Kadriorg Palace
18 Peter the Great Home Museum
20 P Pinna Bus Stop
24 Long Distance Bus Station
   & Hostel
26 Central Market
27 Kalevi Sports Hall
29 Hospital
30 Estonian Hostels Association
32 Roosa Krants
33 Soviet Soldier Statue
34 National Library
36 Nightclub Nan
40 Statoil Petrol Station
41 Airport

To Forest Cemetery,
TV Tower, Kamping Kalev,
Kloostrimetsa Hotel &
Siringo Hotel

PIRITA

Pirita tee

Rummu tee

Pirita River

Kose tee

Tallinn

Bay

To Kelluka Hotel
& Kämping Must Kass

Narva maantee

Smuuli tee

To Mahtra
Hostel

Kadriorg
Park

Weizenbergi

LASNAMÄE

Vikerlase

P Pinna

Narva

Faeh manni

Vimsi

Poska

Lasnamäe

Laagna tee

Punane

Gonsiori

Pronksi

Tartu maantee

Lastekodu

Juhkentali

Magina

Filtri tee

Asunduse

Pallasti

Pae

To Maardu, Lahemaa
National Park & Narva

Peterburi tee

Suur-Sõjamäe

*Lake
Ülemiste*

Tartu maantee

To Tartu

weekdays, from 9 am to 6 pm, and weekends, from 9 am to 4 pm. It books accommodation and theatre tickets; arranges sightseeing tours and city guides; mails letters, sells travel guides, films, souvenirs, postcards, stamps and phone cards; and offers a photo-copying service.

A second tourist office (☎ & fax 6318 321) is at Tallinn harbour. The Estonian Tourist Board (☎ 6411 420; fax 6411 432; email info@turism.ee), at Pikk 71, has an office in the same building as the Estonian Association for Travel Agents (☎ 6313 013; fax 6313 622) and the Estonian Marine Tourism Association (☎ & fax 6411 417). The latter publishes *By Pleasure Boat to Estonia*, a practical sailor's guide indispensable to anyone who arrives in Tallinn by private boat.

Express hotline (☎ 6313 222) and 1188 Info (☎ 8-1188) are free, English-speaking, phone information services.

Foreign Embassies & Consulates

Some nations cover Estonia from their embassies in nearby countries. These include: Australia, Albania, Iceland and Cyprus from Stockholm; Belgium from Brussels; New Zealand from Moscow; and the Netherlands, South Africa, Portugal, Greece, Japan and Switzerland from Helsinki.

Here is a list of foreign embassies in Tallinn:

Austria
    Pikk 58 (☎ 6313 294)
Azerbaijan
    Olevimägi 12 (☎ 601 891; fax 2-440 895)
Belarus
    Kuramaa 15-111 (☎ 6327 072; fax 6320 070)
Canada
    Toomkooli 13, (☎ 6313 570)
China
    Haigru 22 (☎ 477 325; fax 498 874)
Denmark
    Rävala 9 (☎ & fax 6313 120)
Finland
    Kohtu 4 (☎ 6311 441, 6314 444; fax 6311 351); Consulate: Uus 3-76, Tartu (☎ 431 240; fax 433 145)

France
    Toom-kuninga 20 (☎ 6311 368; fax 6311 385)
Germany
    Rävala 9, 7th floor (☎ 6313 970, 6313 976; fax 455 835)
Hungary
    Estonia 3/5 (☎ 6313 791; fax 6313 796)
Italy
    Müürivahe 3 (☎ 6311 370; fax 445 919)
Japan
    Harju 6 (☎ 6310 531; fax 6310 533)
Korea
    Väike-Ameerika 19 (☎ 453 990; fax 442 585)
Latvia
    Tõnismägi 10 (☎ 6311 366; fax 442 585)
Lithuania
    Uus 15 (☎ 6314 030; fax 6314 053)
Moldova
    Endla 33-3 (☎ 452 416)
Norway
    Pärnu 8 (☎ 448 014; fax 6313 001)
Russia
    Hobusepea 3 (☎ 443 014; fax 443 773)
Spain
    Estonia 7 (☎ 6466 166)
Sweden
    Pikk 28 (☎ 6405 600, 6405 640; fax 6405 695)
Switzerland
    Lai 27 (☎ 448 949; fax 6405 695)
UK
    Kentmanni 20, 2nd floor (☎ 6313 462, 6313 463)
USA
    Kentmanni 20 (☎ 6312 021/3/4; fax 6312 025; http://www.usislib.ee/usislib)

Money

There are currency exchanges everywhere you turn: in the airport, the sea passenger terminal, the train station, the central post office (window Nos 43, 44, 46 and 47) and inside all banks and major hotels, including the Viru (open daily from 8 am to 8 pm), the Palace, Pirita, Olümpia (open 24 hours), and the Central.

At Liivalaia 51, Liivalaia 12 and Aia 1 are branches of *Hansapank* which accept most currencies and credit cards. Branches of Tallinna Pank (Pärnu maantee 10 and Harju 13), Zhoupank (opposite the Barn hostel) and Põhja-eesti Pank (Pärnu maantee 12 and A Laikmaa) issue cash on Visa, MasterCard, Eurocard and Diners Club. There are ATMs accepting Visa at the Viru Hotel, Hansapank at Liivalaia 12, Põhja-eesti Pank at Pärnu maantee 12 and A Laikmaa.

SULEV KALAMÄE

JONATHAN SMITH

Top: Birch wood at Pirita, Tallinn, Estonia
Bottom: Walking along a street on Toompea, Tallinn, Estonia

JONATHAN SMITH

JONATHAN SMITH

JONATHAN SMITH

JONATHAN SMITH

Top Left: Old Town Hall Square, Tallinn, Estonia
Top Right: Boot & Alexandr Nevsky Cathedral, Tallinn, Estonia
Bottom Left: Ornamental urn on Toompea
Bottom Right: Street lamp on Kiriku, Old Town, Tallinn, Estonia

Travellers' cheques can be cashed at the Viru and Olümpia hotels' service bureaux and at branches of Põhja-eesti Pank. Estravel (see Travel Agencies) can replace lost American Express travellers' cheques or cards.

Post & Communications

The central post office is at Narva maantee 1 (open weekdays from 8 am to 7 pm, Saturday from 9 am to 5 pm). Stamps are sold at window No 40. Poste restante is kept for one month. Express Mail Service (EMS; ☎ 442 137) is also here. Telegrams and faxes can be sent from window No 45 (see introductory Facts for the Visitor for prices). Faxes can also be sent from the service bureaux at the Viru, Palace and Olümpia hotels.

Chip cards for public card telephones are sold at most hotels, kiosks, the tourist information centre and at the train and bus stations. The chip cards sold in the Viru and Olümpia hotels are only good for their in-house public telephones – these cards are not accepted by card phones outside these hotels.

If you are calling an analogue six digit number, dial ☎ 2 before the subscriber's number. You do not need a local telephone code if you are calling a seven-digit number from abroad. See Facts for the Visitor at the front of the book for details.

For Internet access contact Estpak Daea (☎ 6322 662; fax 6323 070) at Koorti 15, or log-in at the National Library (see Media) for 30 EEK an hour. If you subscribe to SprintNet, CompuServe or MCIMail you can access your account in Tallinn through Sprint (☎ 6312 286).

Travel Agencies

City tours, guided trips to provincial Estonia, and accommodation in other towns are all part of most travel agencies' stock in trade. Leading ones include:

Baltic Tours
    Aia 18 (☎ 6300 400; fax 6300 411); Laikmaa 5 (☎ 430 663; fax 6313 576); ferry terminal, Sadama 27 (☎ 6318 331; fax 6318 264); regional offices in Tartu, Elva and Kuressaare
Carol
    Lembitu 4 (☎ 454 900; fax 6313 918)

CDS Reisid
    Raekoja plats 17 (☎ 445 262; fax 6313 666; email cds@zen.estpak.ee)
Estonian Holidays
    Pärnu maantee 12 (☎ 6314 106; fax 6314 109; email holidays@holidays.ee); Viru väljak 4 (☎ 6301 930; fax 6302 900)
Estonian Youth Initiative Centre
    Västriku 6/10 (☎ 6552 614; fax 6552 614; email estyouth@saturn.zzz.ee)
Estravel
    Suur-Karja 15 (☎ 6266 206; fax 6266 262; email sales@estravel.ee; http://www.estravel.ee) Liivalaia 33 (☎ 6315 565); Narva maantee 9a (☎ 6302 202); Liivalaia 12 (☎ 6461 461); regional office in Tartu
Noorte Reisikubli
    Mustamae 59 (☎ & fax 6503 561; ☎ 528 427; email nrk@online.ee)
Tiit Reisid
    Narva maantee 27 (☎ 2-424 245; fax 6409 168); regional office on Hiiumaa

Bookshops

Rahva Raamat at Pärnu maantee 10, Lugemisvara at Harju 1, Viruvärava at Viru 23, and R&E at Pikk 2 have foreign-language selections. Raamatu Äri on Suur Karja has some second-hand English and German books, as does ARP at Voorimehe 9.

Media

The English-language *Tallinn This Week*, *City Paper* and *Shopping in Tallinn* (see Facts for the Visitor – Newspapers & Magazines at the front of the book) all have listings of places to stay and eat, things to see, entertainment and so on. The *Baltic Times* and the Finnish-language *Baltic Guide* run listings as well as a variety of topical culture and arts reviews.

The latest issues of foreign-language newspapers are plentiful in Tallinn. An impressive selection is sold in the Viru and Olümpia hotels and at the Finnish supermarket, Stockmann, close to the Olümpia at Liivalaia 53, which stocks the current affairs journals *Time* and *Newsweek* as well as glossy women's magazines.

The National Library, on the corner of Endla and Toompuiestee, has some English-language publications. See TV & Radio in the Estonia – Facts for the Visitor chapter for

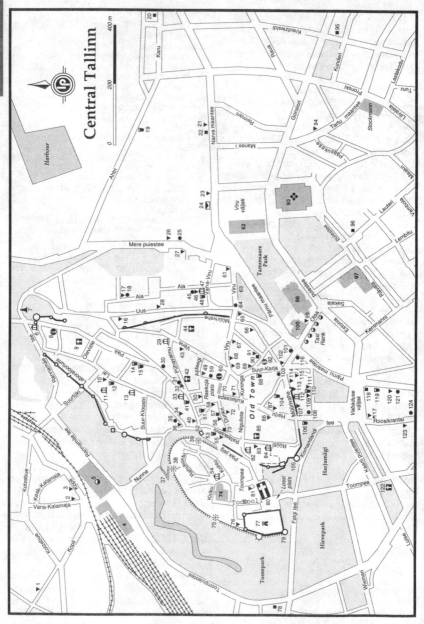

Central Tallinn

PLACES TO STAY
20 Dorell Hotel
22 Central Hotel
57 Hotel Eeslitall & Restaurant
62 Viru Hotel
73 Hotel Rataskaevu
78 Tallinn Hotel
90 The Barn
95 Hotel Kungla
96 Hostel Akmis
118 Palace Hotel & Pizzeria Margareta

PLACES TO EAT
1 Shalom
2 Peetri Pizza
3 Wagon lits
10 Teater
14 Tehas No 43
16 Sõti Klubi
17 Kaubahall
21 Primavera
23 Chick King
26 Ai Sha Ny Ya
27 Paan
28 Baar Vegan
32 Maiasmokk Restoran & Maiasmokk Kohvik
34 Peetri Pizza
36 Tiina
40 Grill Mexicana & Pizza Americana
43 Controvento
46 Chick Inn
49 Maharaja Restaurant
50 Vana Toomas
55 Vanaema Juures (Grandma's Place)
56 Papa Pizza
58 Karl Friedrich Restoran
61 Café Gallery (The Tube)
65 McDonald's
66 Mamma Mia
67 Mona Lisa
68 Kõver kõrts
69 Gnoom Grill
71 Kullassepa Kelder
72 Dunkri Restoran
76 Toomkooli
81 Kuller
83 Sub Monte Restoran
86 Wana Tunnel & Tallinn Business Centre

87 Hõbe Kass (Silver Cat) Café
89 Balti Sepik
91 Maitsekohvik
94 Ervin's Mexican Kitchen
99 Armanda Sandwicherie
102 Vesi Veski
105 Neitsitorn
107 Pizza Americana
109 Metropole
111 Wiiralti Café
113 Keldi Kauplus
114 Gloria Restoran
115 Leibur
117 Roosikrantsi
120 Peetri Pizza
123 Egeri Kelder

OTHER
4 Train Station
5 Local Bus Station
6 Great Coast Gate, Fat Margaret's, Fat Mararet Bastion & Sea Museum
7 Estonia Ferry Disaster Memorial
8 Estonian Tourist Board
9 Oleviste Church & Tower
11 Natural History Museum
12 Diesel Boots
13 Museum of Decorative and Applied Arts
15 Hell Hunt (Gentle Wolf)
18 Baltic Tours
19 Delkoltee
24 Central Post Office
25 Family Hotel Service
29 City Museum
30 Brotherhood of Blackheads & Oleviste Guild
31 Draakoni Galerii
33 State History Museum
35 Puppet Theatre
37 Patkuli Trepp
38 Lookout Point
39 Lookout Point
41 Art Café Opera and Jazz Café

42 Püavaimu (Holy Spirit) Church
44 Dominican Monastery & St Catherine's Church
45 Estline City Office
47 Fire-Fighting Museum
48 Bel Air
51 Voorimehe kelder
52 Pikk Jalg Gate Tower
53 Von Krahl Theatre Bar
54 Estonian Art Museum
59 CDS Reisid Travel Agency
60 Tourist Information Centre
63 Flower Market
64 Viru Gate
70 Town Hall
74 Toomkirik
75 Lookout Point
77 Toompea Castle
79 Pikk Hermann
80 Alexandr Nevsky Cathedral
82 Adamson-Ericu Museum
84 Archeological Museum
85 Niguliste Church
88 Nimeta Baar (The Bar with No Name)
92 Zhoupank
93 Kaubamaja
97 Sakala Conference & Cultural Centre
98 Estonia Theatre & Concert Hall
100 Estonia Drama Theatre
101 Bookshop
103 Estravel
104 Hollywood Club & Eldorado Bar
106 George Brownes
108 Kiek-in-de-Kök Tower
110 Ku Ku Club
112 Theatre & Music Museum
116 Estonian Holidays & Põhja-eesti Pank
119 Max Marine
121 Bus Ticket Office
122 Kaarli Kirik Church
124 Tallink Office

information on English-language radio broadcasts.

Photography & Video
Filmari, an agent for Fuji, at Suur-Karja 7, processes print film in a day for 35 EEK and a further 3 EEK for each print. Kodak Express, has outlets on A Laikmaa to the east of the Viru hotel and on the corner of Narva maantee and Pronksi. There's an instant photo booth inside the Viru shopping centre, at the bus station and inside the main ferry

terminal. Bring your own video tapes with you for your camcorder.

Laundry

There is a laundrette at Pärnu maantee 48 (opposite the Kosmos cinema) and at Liivalaia 26. Cost per machine (which takes a five-kg load) is around 50 EEK. An attendant is available to wash your clothes for an extra charge. Most major hotels also offer laundry and dry-cleaning services.

Medical Services

There is an emergency medical centre at Sütiste tee 19 in Mustamäe, a south-western suburb (☎ 525 652; open daily 24 hours), and another at Ravi 18, close to the Olümpia hotel (open weekdays 9 am to 6 pm). To call an ambulance dial ☎ 003.

Western in price, service and attitude are Tallinn's new, privately run medical centres: Medico Arstikeskus (☎ 444 231) at Hariduse 6, and Mäekalda Clinic (☎ 215 603) at Lanamäe 8, both open weekdays from 9 am to 5 pm. Baltic Medical Partners (☎ 6311 222) is at Tartu maantee 32.

Western medicines and hygiene products are sold in most pharmacies. Particularly useful is the Vanaturu Apteek in the Old Town on the corner of Vene and Vanaturu Kael (open weekdays from 9 am to 7 pm, Saturday 9 am to 4 pm). Tõnismäe Apteek (☎ 442 282) at Tõnismägi 5, prepares prescriptions, runs a night service and has an information counter (☎ 441 813) telling you where you can find a particular medicine (open Monday to Friday from 8 am to 9 pm). Another handy one to know about is the Kalamaja Apteek (☎ 601 585, 601 393) at the train station (open weekdays from 8 am to 8 pm, Saturday 9 am to 3 pm).

Tallinn water is reckoned to be safe to drink.

Left Luggage

There's a left-luggage room (*pakihoid*) in the main ferry terminal (open from 7 am to noon and 2 to 9 pm), in the basement at the bus station (open from 5 am to noon and 12.30 to 11.40 pm), and the one at the train station

(open from 5 am to midnight) will also take care of your bicycle for 10 EEK a day.

WALKING TOUR

A good place to start exploring old Tallinn is the twin towers of the **Viru Gate** in the east side of the Lower Town walls. Flower stalls line the eastern approach to the twin towers which are all that remain of the gate, once one of six entries in the Lower Town walls. From the gate continue along Viru to the corner of Vene (known as **Vana turg**); continue into **Raekoja plats**, the wide square which is the heart of the Lower Town. From here, climb the street Pikk jalg to **Toompea**. Use the **look-out points** off Toom-Kooli, Kohtu and Rahukohtu to get your bearings and decide where to go when you descend. Particularly interesting are the streets north of Raekoja plats in the Lower Town where you can walk north up Pikk to the **Fat Margaret** bastion, the northern bastion of the Lower Town, then return south along Lai.

RAEKOJA PLATS

Raekoja plats (Town Hall Square), dominated by the only surviving Gothic town hall in northern Europe, has been the centre of Tallinn Lower Town life since markets began to be held here in the 11th century (the last was in 1896). Today it's the place all Old Town streets lead to; a meeting place, and the setting for bustling outdoor bars and open-air concerts in summer.

The **Raeapteek** (Town Council Pharmacy) on the north side of the square is another ancient Tallinn institution; there has been a pharmacy or apothecary's shop here since at least 1422, and the present façade is 17th century. The building is currently under renovation and the Raeapteek is temporarily at Pikk 47.

Town Hall

Built between 1371 and 1404, the Town Hall was the seat of power in the medieval Lower Town. Its minaret-like tower is supposedly modelled on a sketch brought back by an explorer from the orient. **Vana Toomas** (Old Thomas), the warrior and sword weather vane at its top, has guarded Tallinn since 1530. The arches at ground level along the north side of the hall were a trading place in the Middle Ages. The interior of the hall is open weekdays from 10 am to 5 pm. Inside, the **Citizens' Hall** has an impressive vaulted roof, while the fine 1374 bench-ends in the **Council Hall** are Estonia's oldest woodcarvings. In the town hall cellar (Raekelder) is a small **museum** of Tallinn's history up to 1710 – open Wednesday to Sunday from 10.30 am to 5.30 pm. The old **Town Jail** (Raevangla, ☎ 448 767) at Raekoja plats 4/6 houses a commercial art gallery (open Thursday to Monday from 10.30 am to 5.30 pm).

NEAR RAEKOJA PLATS
Pühavaimu Church
An arch beside the Raeapteek on Raekoja plats leads into short, narrow Saia kang (White Bread Passage), at the far end of which is the 14th century Gothic Pühavaimu (Holy Spirit) church, used by Lutherans. Its clock is the oldest in Tallinn, with carvings dating from 1684, and the tower bell (1433) is the oldest in Estonia. Inside are a fine 1483 wooden altarpiece, 16th century carved bench-backs and a 17th century pulpit.

City Museum
A medieval merchant's home at Vene 17 (on the corner of Pühavaimu) houses the City Museum (Linnamuuseum, ☎ 441 829), devoted mainly to Tallinn in the 18th and 19th centuries. The museum is open daily, except Tuesday, from 11 am to 6 pm.

Dominican Monastery
At Vene 16 (Estonian for 'Russian', so named for the number of Russian merchants who used to inhabit this street), look for an 1844 Catholic church set back from the street with the Latin inscription 'Hic Vere Est Domus Dei' on its wall. A small door in the corner of the courtyard leads into the Dominican monastery (Dominiiklaste klooster, ☎ 444 606), founded in 1246. The monastery was home base for Scandinavian monks who played a big role in converting Estonia to Christianity and starting education in

Tallinn. Once wealthy, with its own brewery and hospital, the monastery was ruined by plunder during the Reformation in 1524-25 and by a fire in 1531; today it houses Estonia's largest collection of **stone carvings**. Music concerts are also held here. **St Catherine's Church** (Katariina kirik) on the south side of the cloister, once the biggest in northern Europe, has not been restored and is closed. The open areas contain a wealth of lovely 15th to 17th century stone carvings.

Niguliste Church
A minute's walk south of Raekoja plats, the early-Gothic north doorway of Niguliste church (named after St Nicholas of Bari, patron saint of sailors) proves the church's ancient origins – it was the hub of the 13th century German settlement – but most of Niguliste dates from the 15th century. It is now used for organ recitals and as a **museum of art** from medieval Estonian churches. It is open on Wednesday from 2 to 6 pm, and Thursday to Sunday 11 am to 6 pm, unless there's a concert on.

The foot of the small slope, on which Niguliste stands, looks like an abandoned demolition site. What you're looking at is the carefully exposed wreckage of the buildings that stood here before the Soviet bombing of Tallinn on 9 March, 1944. A sign in English facing Harju details the damage done to the city that night.

TOOMPEA
Toompea ('TOM-pe-ah'), the hill on which Tallinn is centred, is protected on the north, south and west by steep slopes, now with parks at their feet. In German times this was the preserve of the feudal nobility and bishop, looking down on the traders and lesser beings of the Lower Town. The most impressive – and until the 17th century the only – approach to Toompea is through the red-roofed **Pikk jalg gate tower** (dating from 1380) at the west end of Pikk in the Lower Town. From here Pikk jalg (Long Leg) slopes up the hill between high walls; where it curves right, a passage down to the left (beneath a 15th century gate tower)

emerges onto Lühike jalg (Short Leg), which leads down to Niguliste church.

According to Estonian legend, Toompea is the burial mound of Kalev, the heroic first leader of the Estonians, built by his widow Linda – herself commemorated by a statue in Hirvepark on the southern side of the hill.

Lossi plats

The 19th century Russian Orthodox **Alexandr Nevsky Cathedral** dominates Lossi plats at the top of Pikk jalg. In such a focal location it's an imposing testament to the Russian imperialist urge, but is rather out of place among its older neighbours.

A path leads down from Lossi plats beneath the uppermost stretch of the Lower Town wall into an open space where, in summer, artists set up their easels and paint portraits. One of the towers here, **Neitsitorn** (Virgin's Tower), has been turned into a popular café-bar, and has good views. Its name is ironic – it's said to have been a prison for medieval prostitutes!

Toompea Castle

Estonia's parliament, the Riigikogu, meets in Toompea Castle at the west end of Lossi plats. The seat of the government is in the same building. Nothing remains of the 1219 Danish castle here, but three of the four corner towers of its successor, founded by the Knights of the Sword in 1227-29, still stand. The castle's mainly Baroque appear-

Tall Hermann (Pikk Hermann to the locals)

ance dates from the 18th century when, under Catherine the Great, it was rebuilt and had its moat filled in. The finest of the towers is the 1371 **Pikk Hermann** (Tall Hermann) at the south-west corner, topped by the national flag. The two other surviving towers, plus most of the north wall of the old castle, can be seen from the yard of Toom-Kooli 13.

Toomkirik

Toompea is named after the Lutheran Toomkirik (Cathedral), founded in 1233, which is at the north end of Toom-Kooli. Most of this interesting building's existing structure dates from the 15th and 17th centuries (it was largely rebuilt after a fire in 1684) but the tower was built in 1779. Among other things, the church served as a burial ground for the rich and noble. Among the finest of the many **carved tombs** inside are those on the right as you approach the altar, including life-size figures of the 16th century Swedish commander, Pontus de la Gardie, and his wife. The Swedish siege of Narva, where de la Gardie died, is shown on the side of their sarcophagus. Also here are the tombs of two other Swedish commanders of the same period, Karl Horn and Otto Üxküll. The marble Greek-temple-style sarcophagus belongs to Admiral Samuel Greigh, an 18th century Scot who joined the Russian navy and became a hero of Russo-Turkish sea battles. Admiral Adam Johann von Krusenstern, a German Estonian who was the first Russian citizen to sail round the world, has another elaborate tomb.

Estonian Art Museum

Estonia's national art museum (Kunsti muuseum) boasts an impressive 59,000 items, many of which are on show in this 18th century noble's house at Kiriku plats 1 near the Toomkirik. The art museum dates to 1919 and is the largest in Estonia. It is open daily, except Tuesday, from 11 am to 6 pm.

Kiek-in-de-Kök

The tower south of Neitsitorn is the tall, stout Kiek-in-de-Kök, built about 1475. The name

Kiek-in-de-Kök is Low German for 'Peep into the Kitchen'; from the upper floors a watch could be kept over the entire Lower Town, even the kitchens. Kiek-in-de-Kök has several floors of maps, weapons, models of old Tallinn – and great views. Enter from Komandandi tee, on the outer side of the town wall. It is open Tuesday, Wednesday and Friday from 10.30 am to 5.30 pm, Saturday and Sunday from 11 am to 4 pm. Classical music concerts are hosted here at weekends.

LOWER TOWN (NORTH)
Pikk

Running north from Raekoja plats towards Tallinn port, the street Pikk (Long) is lined with the houses of medieval German merchants and gentry. Many were built in the 15th century, usually with three or four storeys, the lower two being living and reception quarters and the upper ones used for storage. Some top storeys still have the hatch to which goods were lifted by pulley.

Museum & Guild Buildings On Pikk are the buildings of several old Tallinn guilds (associations of traders or artisans, nearly all German dominated). At Pikk 17 is the Gothic doorway of the Great Guild, to which the most important merchants belonged. The building dates from 1410 and one of its fine vaulted halls retains its original appearance. Today it houses the State History Museum (Ajaloomuuseum, ☎ 443 446), devoted to Estonian history up to the mid-19th century. It's open daily, except Wednesday, from 11 am to 6 pm.

Pikk 20, on the east side of the street, with statues of Martin Luther and St Canute on the front, dates only from the 1860s, but the site had already housed St Canute's Guild for several centuries. Its members were master artisans. Pikk 24 and 26 are the adjoining buildings of the Brotherhood of Blackheads and the Oleviste Guild – both closed to the public except for concerts. The Blackheads were unmarried merchants who took their name from their patron saint, Maurice. His head is between two lions on one of the stone

reliefs on the building's façade (1597). The Oleviste Guild – probably the first guild in Tallinn – began in the 13th century, and developed a membership of mostly less important, non-German artisans and traders.

Oleviste Church Further north on Pikk, this church was the focal point of old Tallinn's Scandinavian population. It's dedicated to the 11th century king Olaf II of Norway but is linked in local lore with another Olaf, its legendary architect, who fell to his death from the tower. It's said a toad and snake then crawled out of his mouth. The incident is shown in one of the carvings on the eastern wall of the 16th century Chapel of Our Lady, adjoining the church, which shows a skeleton with a toad on its chest and a snake round its skull. The 124m **Oleviste tower** is a chief Tallinn landmark.

Fat Margaret At the north end of Pikk is the **Great Coast Gate**, the medieval exit to Tallinn port. It's joined to Fat Margaret (Paks Margareeta), a rotund 16th century bastion which protected this entrance to the town. Fat Margaret's walls are more than four metres thick at the base. Inside is the **Sea Museum** (Meremuuseum, ☎ 601 803), open daily, except Monday and Tuesday, from 10 am to 6 pm.

In the grounds stands a **white cross** in memory of the victims of the *Estonia* ferry disaster, Europe's worst peacetime maritime tragedy. A **monument**, entitled 'Broken Line', stands to the side of the cross and a three-metre-long granite table lists the 852 people who died when the popular Estline ferry sank in September 1994, en route between Stockholm and Tallinn.

Lai & Laboratooriumi

The street Lai (Wide) runs roughly parallel to Pikk. No 29, near the corner of Suurtüki, and No 23 opposite Vaimu, both have fine 15th to 17th century façades. The **Natural History Museum** (Loodusmuuseum, ☎ 444 223) occupies the back of a nice little courtyard at No 29 (open daily, except Tuesday, from 10 am to 5 pm).

ESTONIA

The **Museum of Decorative & Applied Arts** (Taideteollisuus-muuseum), in a 17th century barn at Lai 17, has a collection of excellent modern woven rugs, ceramics, glass, metal and leather work. It's open daily, except Monday and Tuesday, from 11 am to 6 pm. At Lai 28/30 is Tallinn's **Healthcare Museum** (Terveydenhoitomuuseum, ☎ 601 602), open daily, except Sunday and Monday, from 11 am to 5 pm.

Suur-Kloostri leads past the former St Michael's Convent to the longest standing stretch of the **Lower Town wall**, with nine towers marching back along Laboratooriumi to the north end of Lai.

EAST OF THE CENTRE
Kadriorg
Park & Palace The park at Kadriorg, two km east of the Old Town along Narva maantee, is pleasant and wooded, with oak, lilac, and horse chestnut trees. Together with the Baroque Kadriorg Palace (Kadrioru Loss), it was designed for the Russian tsar, Peter the Great, by the Italian Niccolo Michetti, soon after Peter's conquest of Estonia in the Great Northern War.

The palace, at Weizenbergi 37 along the road from the Kadriorg tram stop, was built between 1718 and 1736 with Peter himself laying an amazing three bricks! They were left bare for visitors to marvel at. The palace was the residence of the president of independent Estonia in the 1930s, and in the mid-1990s, became once more the president's home.

Behind the palace, at Mäekalda 2, is the cottage Peter the Great occupied on visits to Tallinn while the palace was being built. In summer it's open as the **Peter the Great Home Museum** (Peeter Esimese Maja-muuseum). You may examine his clothes and the boots he made. The wooden house at Koidula 12A, just west of the park, was the last home of the great Estonian novelist Anton Hansen Tammsaare, and now contains a museum of his work (open daily, except Tuesday, from 11 am to 6 pm).

Song Bowl The Tallinn Song Bowl (Lauluväljak), site of the main gatherings of Estonia's national song festivals, is a natural amphitheatre officially said to hold about 150,000 people. In September 1988 some 300,000 squeezed in for one sing-song during the Singing Revolution. The song bowl is on the left side of Narva maantee, a short distance past the fork where Pirita tee heads off to the left, up the side of Tallinn Bay.

Maarjamäe
Two km north of Kadriorg Park, at Pirita tee 56, Maarjamäe Palace (Maarjamäe Loss) contains the mid-19th-century-onwards section of the **Estonia History Museum** (☎ 237 071); it's open Wednesday to Sunday from 11 am to 6 pm. The neo-Gothic limestone palace was built in the 1870s as a summer cottage for the Russian General A Orlov-Davydov.

Pirita
Some 1.5 km beyond Maarjamäe, just before Pirita tee crosses the Pirita River, a short side road leads down to Pirita Yacht Club and the **Olympic Sailing Centre** (see Boat in the Getting Around chapter at the front of the book) near the mouth of the river. This was the base for the sailing events of the 1980 Moscow Olympics, and international regattas are still held here.

In summer you can rent rowing boats beside the road-bridge over the river. North of the bridge is the suburb of Pirita, six km from the city centre, with a **beach** backed by pine woods. Beside the river is the ruined **Convent of St Brigitta**, built in the early 15th century but destroyed in the Livonian War in 1577. It originally housed nuns of the Swedish-based Brigittine Order and in mid-1996, Brigittine nuns in Estonia (there are only five) were granted the right to return to the convent. Future plans for a new site, next to the limestone ruins, include a convent, nursing home and hostel. The convent ruins are open to visitors daily from 10 am to 6 pm in May, and 9 am to 11 pm from June to October. Entrance is 7/3 EEK for adults/students.

Forest Cemetery & TV Tower

Two km east of Pirita along Kloostrimetsa tee is the Forest Cemetery (Metsakalmistu) where many Estonian national heroes are buried including singer Georg Ots, writer Anton Hansen Tammsaare, and poet Lydia Koidula. A km further on is the 300m TV tower with, they say, views as far as Finland from the café halfway up.

Getting There & Away

Tram No 3 from anywhere along Pärnu maantee in the city centre, and No 1 along Narva maantee, go to the 'Kadriorg' stop right by Kadriorg Park. Bus Nos 1, 8, 34 and 38 all run between the city centre and Pirita, stopping on Narva maantee near Kadriorg Park, and at Maarjamäe. You can catch No 1 on Pärnu maantee in front of Tammsaare Park; No 8 at the Pronksi stop on Narva maantee, 350m east of the Viru hotel; and Nos 34 and 38 at the Viru väljak stop beside the main post office. No 34 goes on to the Forest Cemetery and TV tower. You could also walk along the seafront from Kadriorg to Pirita, although be warned that in summer the reek of decaying algae is not the most pleasant smell in the world.

WEST OF THE CENTRE

A giant flea-market-cum-car-boot sale, with many imported and, at best, semi-legal goods, is held on Saturday and Sunday until the early afternoon at Mustjõe, three km west of the Old Town on the north side of Paldiski maantee.

Rocca al Mare

About four km out along Paldiski maantee, Vabaõhumuuseumi tee branches right to Rocca al Mare, 1.5 km away, where wooden buildings from 18th and 19th century rural Estonia, including a windmill, farmstead and chapel, have been collected in the **Estonian Village Museum**. The site's Italian name (Rock by the Sea) was coined by a merchant who built his country house here in 1880. There are views back to the city and you can walk in the woods or down to the sea. Between May and September, the museum is open daily, except Monday and Tuesday, from 10 am to 5, 6 or 7 pm. On Sunday mornings there are folk song and dance shows. Every June, Rocca al Mare celebrates its *Memme-taadi days*, a colourful few days of traditional folk dancing, songs and craft fairs.

Zoo

Just past the Rocca al Mare turning, at Paldiski maantee 145, is the Tallinn Zoo with over 3500 animals of 370-plus species. While their living conditions are far from satisfactory, the zoo is commended for its imaginative animal-friendly schemes. At the time of writing the zoo was so keen to make its ibex mountain goats feel at home that it was pleading with local construction companies to help build a mountain by dumping their waste in the zoo (in case you're wondering what the heap of dirt and rubble opposite the elephants' cage is!). The zoo is open daily from 9 am to 7 pm.

Getting There & Away

Bus Nos 21 from the train station and 45 from Vabaduse väljak go to Paldiski market, Rocca al Mare and the zoo. Trolleybus No 6 and bus No 46 from Vabaduse väljak, and trolleybus No 7 from the train station, go to the market and zoo.

OTHER SIGHTS
Old Town Museums

The **Adamson-Ericu Museum** at Lühike jalg 3 is devoted to the art and crafts of Erich Karl Hugo Adamson (1902-68). It's open daily, except Monday and Tuesday, from 11 am to 6 pm.

For something a bit different look into the **Fire-Fighting Museum** (Tuletõrjemuuseum, ☎ 444 251) at Vana-Viru 14, open Tuesday to Saturday from noon to 6 pm; or the **Theatre & Music Museum** (Teatri-ja Muusika-muuseum, ☎ 442 884, 421 937) at Müürivahe 12 (open daily, except Monday and Tuesday, from 10 am to 6 pm). At Rüütli 10, there is an **Archeological Museum** (Arkeologiamuuseum, ☎ 444 805), open Thursday and Friday from noon to 4 pm.

Slightly east of the Old Town at Raua 8 is the **Kristjan Rauja Museum**, well worth a trip if you are interested in Estonian mythology. It is open daily, except Tuesday, from 11 am to 6 pm.

Exhibitions

Many of the museums stage temporary exhibitions along with their permanent displays, and there are also a couple of dozen specialist art galleries. Listings are published in *Tallinn This Week* and the Entertainment Guide of the *Baltic Times*.

Some of the best shows are at **Draakoni Galerii** (☎ 601 979) at Pikk 18 (concentrating on graphics), **Vaal** (☎ 443 764) at Väike-Karja 12, **Galerii Sammas** and **Kunstihoone Galerii** at Vabaduse väljak 6, **Shifara Galerii** (☎ 446 115) at Vana-Posti 7 (mainly classical art), **Linna Galerii** at Harju 13 (works by minority groups), and the **Raekoja Tarbekunsti Galerii** in the basement of the town hall at Raekoja Plats 1 (traditional Estonia arts and crafts including ceramics, hand-painted silk fabrics, glass and metal works, carpets and tapestries).

Trade fairs and exhibitions are held at the **Estonian Exhibition Centre** (☎ 238 697) at Pirita tee 28 and the **Sakala Conference & Cultural Centre** (☎ 444 492) close to the Viru hotel at Rävala 12.

Soviet Nostalgia

Rävala puiestee, a block south of the Estonia Theatre, was called Lenin puiestee in Soviet times and a statue of Lenin stood in the middle of it, between the corners of Lembitu and Lauteri. The building, overlooking Lenin's old standing place, at Rävala puiestee 9, which now houses the foreign ministry and some foreign embassies, was used as the Estonian Communist Party headquarters.

Still standing in its full glory – to the horror of many – is the monstrous **Maarjamäe Memorial** on the road to Pirita. The memorial to the 'liberation' of Estonia by the Red Army in 1944 is typically Soviet in both size and ugliness, yet so far has managed to remain unscathed.

Equally distasteful and the source of much hatred to Estonians – but the source of much pride to Russians living in Tallinn – is the statue of a **Soviet soldier** outside the Estonian National Library on Tõnismägi tee. After much heated debate, the municipality decided in 1996 to leave the soldier standing.

ACTIVITIES

See Facts for the Visitor at the front of this book for general information about activities in Estonia. Golf can only be played in the Baltics at the 18-hole Niitvälja Golf Club (☎ 771 690; fax 771 513) in Niitvälja, 34 km south of Tallinn on the road to Keila. It's open from April to November and it costs 300 EEK an hour, plus a further 90 EEK if you need to hire clubs. Other facilities include a café, bar, restaurant and sauna.

PLACES TO STAY

In summer it's worth trying to book ahead for most types of Tallinn accommodation, including the hostels. Tallinn tourist information centre (see Information – Tourist Offices) can provide you with an updated list of hotels in the city and outlying suburbs.

PLACES TO STAY – BOTTOM END
Camping

Most campsites are open at least from 1 June to 1 September. *Peoleo* (☎ 771 601; fax 771 463), 10 km from Tallinn on the Rīga road at Pärnu maantee 555, has 50 parking places, a great deal more tent spaces and saunas, showers and a small catering service. *Kloostrimetsa* at Kloostrimetsa maantee 6, also comes recommended. For sites out of town see the Around Tallinn section.

Hostels

The Estonian Hostels Association runs three hostels in Tallinn: the Mahtra, the Vikerlase and the Merevaik. Up-to-date information is available from the hostel headquarters (☎ 6461 457, 6461 455; fax 6461 595; email puhkemajad@online.ee) at Tartari 39. It also publishes a trilingual annual accommodation guide to Estonia in Estonian, English and Russian, giving full details (complete with a map of how to get there) of all the hostels it runs in Estonia. Bookings can be made through Helsinki or St Petersburg hostels (see Accommodation in Facts for the Visitor at the front of the book) or via its web page (http://www.planet-nc.com/eyh).

The *Vikerlase* (☎ 6327 781; fax 6327 715), at Vikerlase 15-148, six km east of the centre in the Lasnamäe suburb, has 15 or so basic two to three-bed family rooms with shared showers and toilets for 100 EEK per person. HI members get a 10 EEK discount. To get there take bus No 35 from the stop at Narva maantee 2 and get off 10 minutes later at the Pikri stop; cross the road and walk down Pikri, turning left onto Vikerlase at the end. To reach the *Mahtra* (☎ 218 828; fax 586 765), a further 10-minute journey by bus No 35, get off at the third stop after Pikri, at Mahtra 44 where the hostel is. Beds here cost 90 EEK a night; HI card holders pay 60 EEK. The *Merevaik* (☎ 529 604; fax 529 647) is a similar establishment with the addition of a common room and self-catering kitchens. The overnight fee is also 90 EEK. Take trolleybus No 2 or 3 from diagonally opposite the Palace hotel and get off at the Linnu tee stop. The hostel is 100m along the street at Sõpruse puiestee 182. All three hostels are open all year round.

Only open in summer are two privately run hostels. The central *Liivalaia 2 Hostel* (☎ 6461 130, 446 143), at Liivalaia 2, has beds in shared rooms for 90 EEK a night. Take tram No 3 or 4 to the Kino Kosmos stop. Close by is *Hostel Akmis* (☎ 454 964, 444 478) at Lauteri 3, home to commercial school students in winter. Prices start at 70 EEK.

Top of the range in location and reputation is *The Barn* (☎ 443 465), 30 seconds walk from Raekoja plats at Väike-Karja 1. Rooms with three or five bunk beds cost 160/150 EEK with/without bedding. A private double/family room costs 400/700 EEK. Breakfast costs an extra 25 EEK (a cheaper bet is to pop into the Balti Sepik bakery a few doors down at Suur-Karja 5 where excellent breads and pastries, still warm, are sold). Though not run by the Estonian Hostels Association, HI members are still entitled to

discounts on the nightly fee. Reception is open 24 hours.

Another excellent bet is the bus station! On the second floor, above the main ticket hall, the Estonian bus company Mootorreisi runs a small, but surprisingly comfortable *hostel* (☎ 425 150), complete with common room and TV. It has six double rooms for 120 EEK per person, two triple rooms for 80 EEK per person and one luxury room with two rooms and private shower for 400 EEK. All other rooms have a shared bathroom between two. Reception closes at midnight.

Private Homes

Several Tallinn-based agencies as well as several overseas organisations, can arrange homestays in Tallinn at various prices – see Accommodation in Facts for the Visitor at the front of the book.

Hotels

The drab 50 room *Hotel Neptun* (☎ 215 431) at Asunduse 15, 2.5 km south-east of the centre, has clean singles/doubles with bath for 150/240 EEK. Bus No 39 goes there from the corner of Tartu maantee and Pronksi. *Dorell* (☎ 6261 200, 585 414), at Karu 39 (take tram No 1 or 3 from the Viru stop to the Kreutzwaldi stop, walk back 10m and go through the arch on your right), has 17 sparse double rooms with shared toilets for 200 EEK a night.

Cheaper, but a fair way from the centre, is *Bris* (☎ 601 390; fax 601 575) at Tööstuse 50, which has 98 beds. Singles/doubles with shared bathrooms start at 100/220 EEK a night. Also good value is the *EMI Hotel* (☎ 6268 121) at Sütiste tee 21 in the south-western suburb of Mustamäe. It has 32 comfortable single/double rooms with shared showers for 80/120 EEK, and with private bath for 300/400 EEK. Take bus No 17 or 17a from Vabaduse väljak to the Tervise stop by the hotel.

The *Energia Hotel* (☎ 5287 131), east of Mustamäe at Elektroni, has 18 mediocre single/double rooms for 80/160 EEK. Take bus No 57 or 33 and get off at the Kerese stop.

South of the city centre at Nõmme tee 47 is the good value *Students' Hotel* (☎ 6552 679, 6552 663; fax 6552 666), probably the only hotel in Tallinn which welcomes dogs and cats as guests too. Two-room apartments for two people (and as many cats and dogs as you like) with private toilet and shower cost 200 EEK. Take bus No 17 or 17a to the Koolmaja stop or trolleybus No 2, 3, 4 or 9 to the Teadre stop.

The *Rasastra* (☎ 6551 665; fax 6551 664), close to the ferry terminal at Sadama 11, has 100 beds in double rooms with shared baths for 235 EEK. The handful of single rooms it has cost 149 EEK. Equally well located is the *Dzingel* (☎ 585 414; fax 585 411), five km from the centre at Männiku tee 89. Single/ double rooms with private bathroom cost 250/350 EEK and the hotel bar is open from 8 to 2 am. Take bus No 5 or 32 to the Viru stop. Within spitting distance of the Olympic Sailing Centre and Pirita Yacht Club is the cheap and not so cheerful *Siringo* (☎ 239 030) at Kloostrimetsa tee 29. It has 23 places, costing 120/350 EEK in single/double rooms.

PLACES TO STAY – MIDDLE
City Centre

One of the best hotels in this range is the little-advertised *Hotel Eeslitall* (☎ 6313 755) in the Old Town at Dunkri 4. Below is the popular Eeslitall restaurant, giving guests the chance to pop downstairs to the great courtyard for breakfast in the sun. Singles/doubles with private bath cost 350/485 EEK.

The small *Hotel Mihkli* (☎ 453 704) at Endla 23, 400m down the hill from Toompuiestee, has bright singles/doubles for 400/600 EEK and two luxury rooms (which translates as simply being decorated more recently) for 650 EEK. It's fair value but short on atmosphere despite the two stars it awards itself.

The large 300 bed, Soviet-built *Hotel Kungla* (☎ 6305 325; fax 6305 315) at the junction of Gonsiori and Kreutzwaldi, claims to have a three star rating and offers small, unrenovated singles/doubles with private bathrooms for 400/490 EEK. It also has a handful of renovated rooms – simply more beautiful (brass door knobs and the like) than the unrenovated ones – for 800/1000 EEK. Between 1 October and 31 December it is possible to get a bed for the night at the bargain rate of 75 EEK – in an unrenovated room of course.

The *Tallinn Hotel* (☎ 6264 111; fax 6264 101), at Toompuiestee 27 on the western edge of the Old Town, charges 450/600 EEK for singles/doubles, with suites at 800 EEK. Attempts have been made to brighten the place up and as with all the former Soviet hangouts, it offers an abundance of services ranging from massage and manicure to car rental.

Pirita

The 400 bed, two storey *Hotel Pirita* (☎ 6398 822, fax 6398 821) on the seafront at Regatii puiestee 1 at Pirita, six km north-east of the city centre, is bang next door to the Olympic Sailing Centre. The rooms are clean, modern, renovated and have balconies – those on the sea side look back across Tallinn Bay to the city centre. Prices are a bit on the steep side at 600/864 EEK for singles/doubles. It does have three/four-bed family rooms that are better value at 780/876 EEK, including free and unlimited use of the fitness centre (sporting an indoor swimming pool, a kids' pool, three saunas, two steam baths and a solarium). The *Galerie Bar* at the top of the building serves good meals. Bus No 8 from the train station and Nos 1 and 34 from the Pronksi stop on Narva maantee, 400m east of the Viru hotel, all stop on Pirita tee, a minute's walk from the hotel.

Other Suburbs

The *Hermes Hotel* (☎ 521 611; fax 6542 323), close to the EMI hotel at Sütiste tee 21 in the suburb of Mustamäe, is a small, cosy place overlooking a pine forest. Single/ double 'A' class rooms with private bath and glitzy furnishings are 320/499 EEK on weekdays and 425/606 EEK at weekends. The lower grade 'B' rooms are not as flash but just as serviceable – they cost 245/345

EEK during the week and 320/450 EEK on Saturday and Sunday.

South of Mustamäe in the district of Nõmme at Vabaduse 108 is *Kannike* (☎ 513 257; fax 6396 133), a fairly new, bright and modern hotel offering doubles/triples for 450/550 EEK and triples with sauna for 700 EEK. Close by is the *Alexi* (☎ 6700 096; fax 6506 221) at Sihi 49. It has six doubles for 500 EEK, including breakfast. Lunch and dinner are both available on request for 40 EEK.

South of the city centre at Nepi 10 is the aptly named *Nepi* (☎ 6551 665; fax 6551 664). All 12 rooms are equipped with shower and TV, and cost 350/500 EEK for singles/doubles. A junior suite is 550 EEK and a luxury suite, 600 EEK. Breakfast costs an extra 50 EEK. Take bus No 23 to the Kotka stop.

Five km north-west of the centre at Tšaikovski 11 in the suburb of Pelguranna on the Kopli peninsula is the *Hotel Stroomi* (☎ 6304 200; fax 6302 500) which was renovated in 1992 and has 150 clean rooms with private shower and cable TV for 350/490 EEK. As with most hotels in Tallinn, it also has a couple of token luxury suites for 760/1290 EEK as well as conference facilities, a hairdresser and car rental service. Bus No 3 from the Linnahall stop or Mere puiestee stops virtually outside the door.

One of the wackiest places in Tallinn is the *Susi Hotel* (☎ 215 541, 215 238; fax 6380 083) out of town at Peterburi tee 48. Saying that, it is one of the few places to have separate rooms for non-smokers and 'allergic visitors'. Fully-equipped double rooms for one/two people are 440/490 EEK. Dogs cost an extra 100 EEK. Facilities include a currency exchange, sauna, pool and fireplace room, bar-restaurant and the not-to-be-missed 'Green Spider' nightclub, open Monday to Thursday from midnight to 3 am.

The family-run *Valge Villa* (☎ & fax 6542 302) at Kännu 26/2, three km from the city centre, has four singles with shared bath for 300 EEK and two doubles with private bath for 550 EEK. A home-cooked breakfast is included in the price and the smiling landlady will quite happily cook you lunch or dinner if you so desire.

PLACES TO STAY – TOP END

There are two comfortable places on the outskirts that might interest motorists in particular. The Scandinavian-style *Peoleo* hotel (☎ 771 601, fax 771 463), 10 km south of the centre at Pärnu maantee 555, has 44 rooms with private bathroom and satellite TV. Singles/doubles cost 650/860 EEK. There's a good restaurant with a live band at night, a café, sauna, camping ground and trailer park (see Places to Stay – Bottom End). You can book through any Best Western office worldwide.

In a similar price bracket is the friendly, well-run *Kelluka* hotel (☎ 238 811, fax 237 398), eight km east of the centre at Kelluka tee 11. Bus No 5 from Pärnu or Narva maantee in the city centre reaches the Kelluka. Singles cost 530 EEK and small/large doubles are 590/700 EEK.

The cheapest of the most expensive city-centre hotels is the fairly new and friendly *Central Hotel* (☎ 6339 800; fax 6339 900) at Narva maantee 7. Singles/doubles cost 800/990 EEK and a luxury suite/apartment is 1600/1800 EEK.

The cheesiest of the most expensive is the *Viru Hotel* (☎ 6301 311, fax 6301 303) which is a massive hit with Finns, if no one else. Towering 22 storeys at Viru väljak 4 just east of the Old Town, the hotel dates from 1972 and was one of the better Intourist hotels in the USSR, despite the prostitutes and sullen service. Such Soviet joys are now a thing of the past for the Viru which boasts an OK nightclub in the basement, a fabulous panorama café on the top floor and a modern shopping mall. Comfortable pine-panelled rooms cost about 1200/1500 EEK.

Definitely the most chic is the exclusive *Hotel Rataskaevu* (☎ 441 939; fax 443 688), in the Old Town at Rataskaevu 7. Dating to 1850, it used to be reserved for government officials, and even today guests have to wait for the doorman to unlock the door. It's worth gritting your teeth though. Once inside, the decor is fascinating and well worth the

970/1180 EEK if you've got the cash. Equally prestigious is the 91 room *Palace Hotel* (☎ 6407 300; fax 6407 299) at Vabaduse väljak 3. The elegant, if not huge, rooms cost 2200/2800 EEK for singles/doubles. At weekends prices drop to 1400/2000 EEK. In Helsinki you can book through Arctia Hotel Partners (☎ 09-696 901; fax 09-698 958) of IsoRoobertinkatu 23-25, 00120 Helsinki; in other countries through Finnair Hotels or SAS Associated Hotels.

More modest but equally comfortable and favoured by cheeky budget travellers for its 24 hour currency exchange, 24 hour Café Boulevard and 95 EEK breakfast is the *Hotel Olümpia* (☎ 6315 333; fax 6315 675; email hotell@olympia.ee). The towering block which has its name flashing from the top is 700m south of the Old Town and a five minute walk from the long-distance bus station at Liivalaia 33. Simple singles/doubles are 1300/1600 EEK; business class rooms are 1900/2200, and luxury suites range from 2600 to 3700 EEK. The restaurant Elysée, Rendez-Vous brasserie, Kalev Pub and Bonnie & Clyde Nightclub are all favoured hotspots among visiting business people. The Olümpia is also famed in town for its 26th floor sauna!

A five star Holiday Inn hotel with 250 rooms is planned for a site close to the Sakala Conference and Culture Centre at Rävala 12.

PLACES TO EAT

Tallinn's eating-out scene has improved beyond recognition since the grim Soviet years when you had to bribe or barge your way into most restaurants. There are now countless quality restaurants to choose from offering an exotic array of cuisines from all over the globe. In fact, if you don't know where to look, it is quite difficult to track down good old traditional Estonian food – unlike Mexican, Indian or Chinese which is no problem!

For most of the restaurants it is best to make a reservation, especially at weekends. They practically all accept credit cards. New places open all the time.

Restaurants

Old Town Raekoja plats is the hub of Tallinn's dining scene. At No 8 is the *Vana Toomas* (☎ 445 818); a large, cheap, cellar restaurant serving a number of Estonian dishes. It's one of the few survivors from the Soviet era that can still hold its head up, even if the waiters are as cool as ever.

Just off Raekoja plats, at Dunkri 4, is *Eeslitall* (☎ 6313 755). Dating to the 16th century, the Donkey's Stable is a fairly calm, laid-back place with a good cellar bar and an enjoyable courtyard round the back. Most of the interior dates to 1991, including the wonderfully restored ceiling. It is open until 1 am and has a small vegetarian menu as well as excellent salad buffet. Opposite at Dunkri 5 is the little-acclaimed *Dunkri Restoran*, a fine, muralled building which looks far better from the outside. The bar and restaurant is open daily, 11 am to midnight.

A step back in time to Tallinn's Soviet delights can be had at a couple of great Estonian classics. The *Gnoom* grill (☎ 442 488) is a few steps from Raekoja plats at Viru 2. The traditional Estonian menu has, to some degree, been adapted to 'modern tastes' (such as Nordic roast for 98 EEK) but the old favourites, like cabbage schnitzel for 27 EEK, can still be had and the fine, spacious, 15th century stone interior is well worth a look. The upstairs café, serving slightly cheaper dishes, is open daily from 8 am to 9 pm. *Vanaema Juures* (Grandma's Place, ☎ 6313 927), off Raekoja plats in the opposite direction at Rataskaevu 12, was one of Tallinn's most stylish restaurants in the 1930s and still ranks today as Tallinn's most authentic Estonian restaurant. It is open daily from noon to 11 pm, except Sunday when it closes at 6 pm.

Kullassepa Kelder (☎ 442 240), tucked in the basement of an Old Town house off Raekoja plats at Kullassepa 9, is another old favourite. The *Sub Monte Restoran* (☎ 666 871), in a medieval cellar at Rüütli 4 by Niguliste church, is a more upmarket place (verging on the snotty) serving excellent international and Estonian fare. Meat or fish main courses are in the 100 EEK region.

Gloria Restoran (☎ 446 950) at Müüri-vahe 16, serves a glorious choice of fresh fish dishes and has live piano music. It is open daily from noon to midnight.

One of the first western-style restaurants to open in Tallinn, and still unrivalled, is the *Maharaja Restaurant* (☎ 444 367) at Raekoja plats 13, open from noon to 5 pm and 7 pm to 2 am. The Indian dishes it serves are authentic and worth the 250 to 300 EEK per head you'll end up paying.

On the opposite side of the square, in a peach-coloured painted house at Raekoja plats 5, is the upmarket *Karl Friedrich Restoran*, ideal for a calm and tranquil business lunch in a classical setting. It is open daily from noon to 11 pm.

Spaghetti lovers should head straight for the Baltics' best Italian restaurant, *Controvento* (☎ 440 470), tucked down an alleyway off Vene 12. The salads are heavenly, the carbonara authentically creamy, and the decor inside the old granary a sheer delight. Main dishes start at 60 EEK. It's open daily from 12.30 to 2.30 pm and 6.30 to 10.30 pm.

An equally good bet is *Grill Mexicana* (☎ 6564 006) at Pikk 1/3 which dishes out mammoth portions of hot nachos with lashings of sour cream and guacamole for 74 EEK, taco salad for 75 EEK and mugs of sangria for 20 EEK.

A few doors north at Pikk 16 is one of Tallinn's most respected establishments. *Maiasmokk Restoran* (☎ 601 250), above the Maiasmokk kohvik (see Cafés), still adheres to many a pre-independence ritual, including the finely dressed doorman to greet you as you enter (this one smiles, however). Salads start at 22 EEK, soups at 12 EEK, and it's open from 11 am to 10 pm.

Close by at Lai 23 there's the *Teater* cellar-restaurant (☎ 6314 518), a smoke-filled, funky restaurant serving mammoth portions of jambalaya, gumbo and filling daily specials for 67 EEK and often crowded with drunken Finns. It is open daily from 11 am to midnight. It serves some vegetarian dishes as does the informal *Baar Vegan* in the Old Town at Uus 22. For dinner in a medieval water tunnel, try *Wana Tunnel* inside the

Tallinn Business Centre at Harju 6 (open 1 pm to midnight).

Up on Toompea, there are a couple of good places. The old favourite *Toomkooli* (☎ 446 613) at Toom-Kooli 13 looking out over western Tallinn, remains as popular as ever for its fantastic views of the city. The choice of food is wide though the portions aren't huge. Weightier appetites should opt for one of the 'hunter's' meals. It is open daily from noon to 11 pm. *Kuller* (☎ 442 841), close to the cathedral at Piskopi 1, is a smaller, more intimate place serving fried chicken fillet with apricot sauce for 75 EEK, smoked trout on toast for 35 EEK and a mind-boggling 'turist' house special for 110 EEK. It's open from 11 am to midnight.

Elsewhere *Roosikrantsi* (☎ 6404 499) close to the Palace hotel at Vabaduse väljak, is an exceedingly upmarket, elegant restaurant serving a tantalising range of meat and fish dishes as well as the creamiest soups in town.

Next to the Central hotel at Narva maantee 7 is the cheaper – and more cheerful – *Primavera* (☎ 6339 891), a brightly-lit Italian restaurant serving typical pasta dishes like carbonara and bolognese for around the 55 EEK mark.

Paan, close to the Viru Hotel at Mere puiestee 5, is a must for late-night eaters. With just 28 seats, this exclusive bistro serves mouthwatering French-inspired fare and is the only place in town open daily from noon until 6 am.

Fun places, funky in decor and favourable on the wallet, include *Ervin's Mexican Kitchen* (☎ 6312 736), not far from the bus station at Tartu maantee 50 and *Egeri Kelder* (☎ 448 415) at Roosikrantsi 6. Ervin dishes up a variety of Tex Mex dishes as well as lots of tequila, beer and flamenco dancers. It is open weekdays from noon to 11 pm and on weekends from noon to 3 am. Egeri Kelder specialises in Hungarian food and is probably the best place in town if you're a vegetarian. A full three-course meal costs no more than 50 EEK. Another pretty kosher place is *Shalom* (☎ 441 195), a Russian-run restaurant behind the train station, dishing out a limited range of Jewish cuisine.

Close to the bus station there are a couple of choices – the *Taj Mahal* (☎ 6410 746) at Tartu maantee 81 has good vegetarian dishes and other acceptable Indian dishes for no more than 100 EEK per person. Don't be put off by the shabby exterior. *Reskina* (☎ 424 389) at Filtri tee 5 is an oriental restaurant; look for the flashing neon lights at the far end of the bus station. Delicacies include frogs' legs for 99 EEK, lobster for 250 EEK and pancakes with caviar for 129 EEK. Budget travellers should try the excellent seljanka for 19 EEK. Note that there's an extra 2 EEK charge for bread. It's open daily from noon to midnight.

Five minutes' walk from the ferry terminal is another touch of Asia. *Ai Sha Ny Ya* (☎ 441 997) at Mere puiestee 6, claims to be a Chinese restaurant; the odour wafting through the restaurant smells Chinese even if the food leaves you in doubt as to its ethnic origin.

Tiina, close to the train station at Nunne 18, serves traditional Estonian fare. It's open daily from noon to 2 am.

Upmarket restaurants boasting expensive a la carte menus can be found in all the major hotels and at the *Šoti Klubi* (Scottish Club, ☎ 6411 666) at Uus 33.

Cafés

Exploring Tallinn's thriving *kohvik* (café) scene is great fun. In summer, the entire length and breadth of Raekoja plats buzzes with temporary open-air cafés and bars, all of which sell light snacks, hotdogs, traditional kotlett and lots of Saku beer.

Close to Raekoja plats at Suur-Karja 17/19 is *Vesi Veski*, a small but chic café with high, steel tables, bar stools and scrumptious coffee and cakes for around 7 EEK. It is open daily from 9 am to 7 pm, except Sunday when it opens at 10 am. *Balti Sepik* at Suur-Karja 5 is another top place for the sweet-toothed. Here you can drink coffee standing up, accompanied by complimentary bread with home-made honey (open daily from 8 am to 8 pm). For the best

Danishes in town make your way to the nearby *Wiiralti* café at Vabaduse väljak 10, buzzing with life from 8 am to 8 pm.

Maitsekohvik, tucked down a sidestreet off Väike-Karja at Sauna 1, is the Baltics' only gourmet coffee-house – and well worth every kroon. A simply delectable range of mouthwatering coffees includes such devilishly naughty but nice concoctions as banana nut, Irish creme, chocolate and raspberry, and vanilla almond. It sells its beans for 25.90 EEK per 100g as well as coffee by the cup.

The popular *Hõbe Kass* (Silver Cat) café at Harju 6 has a limited selection of good, inexpensive hot food including sardelid (spicy sausage) and omelettes for 16 EEK. It's open daily from 8 am to 10 pm, except weekends, when it opens at 10 am.

Considered a favourite for years is the *Maiasmokk Kohvik* (Sweet-Tooth Café) at Pikk 16, which has a place of honour as the most elite café during Estonia's pre-WWII period of independence. Today this old-style tearoom tends to be filled with old men and women who have obviously been frequenting the place for years. Admittedly the cakes are worth a return trip. It is open daily from 8 am to 7 pm.

Two late-night cafés worth frequenting any time of day are the *Café Boulevard* inside the Olümpia hotel, and the *Metropole* on Vabaduse väljak. The Boulevard is open 24 hours and serves an endless supply of freshly baked pastries, cakes and filled croissants as well as a special night menu from 11 pm to 6 am. The Metropole, next to the legendary members-only *Ku-Ku Club*, is one of the hippest places in town. Open from 8 am to 6 am, this establishment has rapidly become an early morning hang-out for Tallinn's nightclubbing scene and is a great meeting place. The vast outside summer seating overlooking a parking lot is a particular delight.

No longer as much in favour as it used to be, although still far from quiet, is *Café Gallery*, known locally as *The Tube* – because it is a tube! Opposite the flower market at Viru 27a, it serves filled baguettes for 22 EEK, shrimp salad for 28 EEK and mussels for 25 EEK.

For fun on a different level, sample a quick lunch at *Wagon lits*, across from the train station at Kopli 2 (open from 8 am to 10 pm). It's decked out with bits of trash from the old Soviet railways, while the steel stools have brakes as seats.

For Italian ice cream look no further than *Mamma Mia* at Müürivahe 52 which opens daily from 10 am to 10 pm.

On Toompea there's at least one place worth the hike. The *Neitsitorn*, in one of the old towers of the city wall, serves good hõõgvein (mulled wine), coffee and snacks from 11 am to 10 pm. A hike in another direction is *Fat Margaret's* at the north end of Pikk maantee by the Old Town limits. This maritime coffee and light snacks place, inside a 16th century bastion, has a great wooden interior and terrace offering panoramic views of the city.

Pizzerias

Pizza joints are springing up all over the place in Tallinn. The cleanest, quickest and most stylish is *Mona Lisa*, close to the flower market at Viru 18. A regular pizza is 23 EEK and a more adventurous vodka-sauce pizza, 25 EEK. Extra toppings include eggplant, broccoli and zucchini. The upstairs casino is open from 10 pm to 6 am.

The most hip is *Pizza Americana* (☎ 6564 006) in the Old Town at Pikk 1, at Müürivahe 2 and inside the Viru shopping centre. Deep-pan pizzas come in 'normal' or 'large' sizes which range from 55 to 155 EEK depending on your choice of toppings. The chicken, shrimp, peach and blue cheese one is particularly tasty – and pricey (155 EEK).

Pizzeria Margareta inside the Palace hotel and *Papa Pizza* (☎ 6466 238) in the Old Town at Dunkri 6 and at Pärnu maantee 326, are both good value. Margareta serves 30 cm wide pizzas starting at 40 EEK. Tallinn's Papa offers 16 types of pizza from 25 EEK as well as pastas, soups and salads. He also does take-away. Both open daily from 11 am to 11 pm.

Peetri Pizza has outlets dishing out thin-crust pizzas all over town: at Kolpi 2c by the train station and at Liivalaia 40 (both open from 11 am to 10 pm); at Lai 4 (open 10 am to 9 pm) and Pärnu maantee 22 (open 10 to 4 am). For a 24 hour take-away service try its pizza outlets in the Kadaka or Laagri petrol stations (☎ 6796 708) or the petrol station at Pirita (☎ 239 152).

Fast Food

McDonald's, at Viru 24 and Sõpruse 200b (both open daily from 8 am to midnight), is impossible to miss. Before its arrival, there was only *Carrols*, a Finnish chain doling out reportedly moist burgers, crisp fries and 'Big Carol' meals for 45 EEK from outlets in the Viru shopping centre (open from 9 am to 8 pm), at Paldiski maantee 98 (open daily from 10 am to 11 pm) and on the Rīga road at Pärnu maantee.

Tucked in the old city walls opposite the taxi rank on Otsa tee is the *Armanda Sandwicherie*. Open 24 hours, the small kiosk dishes out burgers for 12 EEK and a variety of filled baguettes starting at 25 EEK. There is another 24 hour kiosk-cum-café opposite the Palace hotel.

Chick King, opposite the Viru hotel on Narva maantee, specialises in chicken. The least greasy options include chicken bouillon for 5 EEK and surprisingly tasty jacket potato wedges for 8 EEK. It is open daily from 7 am to 10 pm. *Chick Inn*, next to the Estline office at Aia 59, is as tacky as the name suggests (open from 9 am to 9 pm).

Self Catering

A good source of basic foodstuffs and fresh fruit and vegetables is the *kaubahall* (shopping hall) on Aia, near the Viru gates. Unbeatable for its imported products is the Finnish-run *Stockmann* supermarket, close to the Olümpia hotel, at Liivalaia 53 (open weekdays from 10 am to 9 pm and weekends from 10 am to 8 pm). Tallinn's central *market* is at Puru põik 2 (open daily from sunrise until 4 pm). There is a 24 hour store, *Roosa Krants*, at Pärnu maantee 36.

Bakeries worth visiting include *Leibur* at Suur-Karja 18; the cake shop inside the *Vesi*

Veski café at Suur-Karja 17/19 and *Balti Sepik* at Suur-Karja 5. The *Keldi Kauplus* grocery store at Müürivahe 16 is open daily from 8.30 am to 10.30 pm.

ENTERTAINMENT

Large multilingual posters listing what's on where are plastered up at every major street corner in the Old Town, including the corner of Kullassepa and Niguliste, the corner of Vene and Vana Turg, and next to the Viru gates. The *Baltic Times* runs weekly entertainment listings.

Pubs, Bars & Nightclubs

Flyers for warehouse groove all-nighters and other one-off events are splashed all round the Old Town. Here is a list of pubs and bars:

Amsterdamas
  Pärnu maantee 16 – cosy bar serving Saku beer and a variety of light bar snacks such as marinated eel and salmon caviar
Art Café Opera and Jazz Café
  Pikk 11 – sports a great open-air terrace; huge food, drink and cocktail menu including a variety of orgasms
Diesel Boots
  Lai 23 – a touch of the American life
George Brownes
  Harju 6 – self-conscious, Irish pub with a piano bar serving food upstairs
Hell Hunt (Gentle Wolf)
  Pikk 39 – Irish pub with live music entertaining a dwindling crowd
Karja kelder
  Väike-Karja 1 – old-style beer bar
Kõver kõrts
  Viru 8 – traditional beer bar a touch more modern than the rest
Voorimehe kelder
  Voorihemme 4 – Old Town courtyard bar with two billiard tables
Nimeta Baar (The Bar with No Name)
  Suur-Karja 4/6 – Tallinn's top bar, packed every night, and not just with foreign clientele; be sure to read the guest book. Open daily until 3 am
Rio
  Pärnu maantee 59 – Russian-run pool hall with Russian and European pool tables (Russian tables are bigger with smaller holes); one game is 20 EEK. Open daily until 3 am

Tehas No 43 (Factory No 43)
  Pikk 43 – dates to 1807; formerly a beer factory run by British beer trader Albert le Coq until it was shut down during the 1940 Soviet occupation. Open at weekends until 4 am
Veinide Pöönine (wine attic)
  22nd floor, Viru hotel – European-style 'enoteca' selling wine by the glass or bottle at retail price in an Italian-inspired setting; the best view of Tallinn you will ever find
Von Krahl Theatre Bar
  Rataskaevu 10 – great if you don't mind sweating a little; from late May to September it has a terrace bar to take off some of the heat. Open until the early hours

Here is a list of nightclubs for those who want to see the dawn breaking over Fat Margaret:

Bel Air
  Vana-Viru 14 – often has excellent live bands; admission can be pricey; Thursday and Saturday is solely House and Jungle beats. Open at weekends until 4 am
Bonnie & Clyde
  Liivalaia 33 – upmarket club inside the Olümpia hotel; hefty entrance fee. Open weekends until 4 am
Café Amigo
  Viru väljak 4 – upmarket club in the basement of the Viru hotel; popular with Finns
Dekoltee
  Ahtri 10 – large warehouse-style joint in a former Soviet factory; avoid if you have a strong aversion to techno
Green Spider
  Peterburi tee 48 – out of town club with wild cabaret shows involving lots of naked flesh
Hollywood Club & Eldorado Bar
  Vana Posti 8 – Tallinn's hottest spot for the city's bright young things; entrance fee from 40 to 60 EEK depending on the time/your sex/if you're in the elite-member-gang or not; casino, pool tables and lots of slot machines too
Ku-Ku Club
  Vabaduse väljak 8, ☎ 445 864 – the hippest place in town; a members-only club which has long been recognised as la crème de la crème of Tallinn's clubbing scene, attracting an elite mix of the city's most artistic and bohemian (even the President is a member). No sign outside; look for the black door tucked in the porchway between the Metropole and the Wiiralti café
Max Marine
  Pärnu maantee 19 – large, impersonal western-style clubs with all the trimmings

Nightclub Nan
>Vineeri 4 – the newest club to take Tallinn by storm; has karaoke and a Chinese restaurant on top of its regular clubbing frills. Open daily until 5 am

Piraat
>Regati 1 – equally large, impersonal and full of hot young things

Cinema

Practically all cinemas show films in English. The main cinema *(kino)* in Tallinn, *Sõprus* (☎ 6314 394, 441 919; email bdg@bdg.online.ee), is slap-bang in the Old Town at Vana Posti 8. The *Kosmos* (☎ 448 455) is at Pärnu maantee 45, *Kaja* (☎ 532 110) is at Vilde tee 118 and *Eha* (☎ 431 649) is close to the bus station on Tartu maantee. More alternative showings, cult movies and other foreign-language films – in French and German particularly – are shown at the *Kinomaja* (☎ 448 466), close to the Viru gate at Uus 3.

Opera, Ballet & Theatre

Tallinn has several companies staging dramas (including translations of western plays) in repertory from September until the end of May. Everything is in Estonian (except at the Russian Drama Theatre).

Tallinn's main theatre, the *Estonia Theatre* at Estonia puiestee 4, also houses the Estonian National opera and ballet. The box office (☎ 6260 215, 6313 080) is at Estonia puiestee 4 (open daily from noon to 7 pm). Tickets cost 10 to 25 EEK and can also be bought in advance from the reception of the Viru hotel. Performances generally start at noon, 2 and 7 pm. Tickets for matinee performances are available one hour before the performance starts.

Other theatres include the Russian Drama Theatre (☎ 442 716) at Vabaduse väljak 5; the *Puppet Theatre* (Nukuteater, ☎ 441 252) at Lai 1; and the Von Krahli Theatre (☎ 446 462) at Rataskaevu 10 which is known for its fringe productions.

Classical Music

The Hortus Musicus Early Music Consort and the Estonia Philharmonia Chamber Orchestra and Choir are Tallinn's leading smaller musical ensembles. Adjoining the Estonia Theatre at Estonia puiestee 4 is the *Estonia Concert Hall* (Kontserdisaal, ☎ 443 198) where you'll hear classical music and choral works. Concerts are held two or three times weekly; although the resident Estonian State Symphony Orchestra breaks for a few weeks in summer. Tickets can be bought from the box office (☎ 443 198) inside the concert hall.

Chamber, organ, solo and other smaller-scale concerts are held in the Estonia Theatre café and several halls around town including the Town Hall (Raekoda) on Raekoja plats, the House of Blackheads (☎ 443 877) at Pikk 26, the Gate Tower (☎ 440 719) at Lühike jalg 9, and at the Kloostri Ait (☎ 446 221) at Vene 14. Chamber music concerts are held at Niguliste church (☎ 449 911) every Saturday at 4 pm. Some big events are held at the 4200 seat City Concert Hall (☎ 601 893) in the Linnahall at Mere puiestee 20 near the harbour. Tickets for the above venues are also sold at the Estonia Concert Hall box office and at the tourist information centre (see Information – Tourist Offices).

During the summer there are also numerous open-air concerts around town; again, the tourist information centre should know about them. *Eesti Kontsert* (Estonian Concert, ☎ 442 901; email concert@netexpress.ee; http://www.bcs.ee/concert) provides updated information of what's on where.

SPECTATOR SPORT

Tallinn's basketball team, Kalev, plays to capacity crowds at the Kalevi sports hall at Juhkentali 12. Ice hockey matches are played at the arena in the Linnahall. The Estonian soccer team gained a cult following in 1996 when it boycotted a World Cup qualifying home match against Scotland (to the horror of 700 Scottish fans who ventured to Tallinn for the game) in protest at a FIFA ruling that the stadium's lighting was inadequate. The team plays at the Kadriorg stadium, two km east of the Old Town.

THINGS TO BUY

Shopping in Tallinn is just like shopping anywhere else in the west (including the price you pay). Visit the Viru shopping centre, adjoining the Viru hotel at Viru väljak 4 for proof.

Traditional knitted jumpers, hats, gloves and socks are among the more unique buys to be had. All sizes and styles galore can be found at some stalls in the flower market close to the Viru gates on Viru, and along Müürivahe where the market runs along the city walls. Expect to pay about 450 EEK for a knitted jumper. The Estonian Folk Art and Craft Union runs an excellent shop at Viru väljak 4. The best place to buy traditional folk costumes is Kästitöö at Vana Posti 1.

Close to the market on the corner of Vana-Viru and Viru is Galerii Molen, one of Tallinn's most stylish craft shops with an 'art garage' in the basement. Graaf Art at Vaike Varja 6 has some fine paintings and ceramics. If you fancy some funky porcelain, pop into Helina Tilk on Voorimehe puiestee (look for the 'two pigs sign' outside), or NRS, next to the Metropole on Vabaduse väljak. Some unique designs can also be found at Galerii 2, close to Sub Monte at Lühike jalg 1. Top of the class in funkiness stands Keraamika at Pikk 33, a great little place where you can watch the potter at work amid a jungle of wild ceramics for sale. Leather goods can be found at Nahk Leather behind the town hall at Raekoja plats 6. Guess what Antique Photography at Hobuspeas 12 specialises in?

GETTING THERE & AWAY

This section concentrates on transport between Tallinn and other places in the Baltic states and Kaliningrad. See the Getting There & Away chapter at the front of the book for detail on ferry, flight, train and bus links with countries outside the Baltic states.

The Tallinn Information section has information on some useful travel agents.

Air

Estonian Air flies daily to/from Vilnius; Air Baltic and ELK fly three times weekly to Rīga. A return fare costs 2379 EEK if you buy the ticket seven days in advance and stay in Vilnius for a weekend. A return ticket midweek with a minimum two day stay is 5000 EEK. Estonian Air also does a one-way/return youth fare (valid if you're between 13 and 24) costing 1189/2378 EEK.

Air Baltic flies to Rīga on Monday, Wednesday and Friday. A return ticket adhering to the Sunday rule is 3780 EEK and a one-way is 1980 EEK. In Tallinn tickets can be bought from the SAS city airport office. ELK flies to Rīga on Tuesday, Wednesday and Thursday and offers discounts to students. A full price one-way/return ticket with no restrictions is 1220/2400 EEK. With discount, the same tickets cost 865/1860 EEK.

Pärnu-based company, Baltic Aeroservis, flies from Tallinn to Kuressaare (Saaremaa) twice weekly (Monday and Saturday). In mid-1996, the one-way/return fare was 440/750 EEK. Flying time was 45 minutes. By mid-1997, there should be flights between Tallinn and Kärdla (Hiiumaa). See West Estonia & the Islands – Hiiumaa for details.

Tallinn airport (☎ 6388 888; http://www.estnet.ee/tallinn-airport) is three km southeast of the city centre on Tartu maantee.

Airline offices in Tallinn include:

Estonian Air
    Vabaduse väljak 8 (☎ 446 382, 6313 302; fax 211 624)
    Endla 59 (☎ & fax 490 679)
    Airport (☎ 211 092)
Finnair
    Liivalaia 12 (☎ 6311 455)
    Airport (☎ 423 538)
Lufthansa
    Mündi 2 (☎ 448 862)
    Airport (☎ 215 557)
LOT
    Lembitu 14-11 (☎ 6466 051, 6466 052; fax 661 838)
SAS & Air Baltic
    Roosikrantsi 17 (☎ 6312 240/41)
    Airport (☎ 6388 553; fax 6388 354)

Bus

Buses to places within 40 km or so of Tallinn, and some buses to Pärnu, go from the local bus station beside the train station. Tickets for these services can also be bought here.

For detailed bus information and advance tickets for all other destinations, go to the long-distance bus station (Maaliinide Autobussijaam) at Lastekodu 46, one km along Juhkentali from the Olümpia hotel. Situated here is a large and easy to understand timetable, an information desk staffed by people who speak some English, a left luggage room and a café.

Tickets for domestic destinations are sold from the windows opposite the entrance to the ticket hall. Tickets to Latvia, Lithuania and international destinations are sold at the Eurolines office (☎ 6410 100; fax 6410 101), which is open weekdays from 9 am to 6 pm, or at the window on your left as you enter which is open longer (8 am to 11.45 pm).

Bus information is also available at the ticket office at Pärnu maantee 24, just down the street from the Palace hotel (only tickets to Berlin, Hamburg and Kiel can be bought here – see Getting There & Away at the front of the book). It's open from 8 am to 2 pm and 3 to 6 pm daily.

Services within the Baltic states to/from Tallinn include:

Haapsalu
    100 km, 2½ hours, 10 buses daily, 34 EEK
Kaliningrad
    690 km, 13½ hours, one bus nightly, 245 EEK
Kärdla
    160 km, five hours, six bus daily, 70 EEK
Kaunas
    575 km, 12 hours, one bus daily, 210 EEK
Kuressaare
    220 km, 4½ hours, seven buses daily, 90 EEK
Narva
    210 km, four hours, seven buses daily, 70 EEK
Pärnu
    130 km, 2½ hours, more than 20 buses daily, 46 EEK
Rakvere
    95 km, 1½ hours, 12 buses daily, 32 EEK
Rīga
    310 km, six hours, four buses daily, 112 EEK
Tartu
    190 km, three hours, more than 20 buses daily, 66 EEK

Viljandi
    160 km, 2½ hours, 4 buses daily, 54 EEK
Vilnius
    600 km, 12 hours, one bus nightly, 217 EEK
Võru
    250 km, 4½ hours, four to six buses daily, 78 EEK.

Train

The main train station is the Baltic station (Balti jaam) at Toompuiestee 35, just outside the north-west edge of the Old Town. Tram Nos 1 and 2 go from Kopli street at the back of the station and travel to the Linnahall stop near the ferry terminals, continuing to the Mere puiestee stop near the Viru hotel. Tram No 1 then heads east along Narva maantee to Kadriorg, and No 2 goes south down Tartu maantee to the Autobussijaam stop near the bus station.

There are two ticket halls – one, as you're facing the station, to the left, is for longer-distance trains including to Tartu, Narva and places outside Estonia (signposted *eelmüügi kassad)*, and another for 'suburban' trains *(linnalähedased rongid)*, which includes some going all the way to Viljandi. The long-distance ticket hall has an excellent information desk staffed by people who speak English. They also sell copies of the useful *Reisirongide Sõiduplaan* (Train Timetable) booklet.

The daily Tallinn-Warsaw *Baltic Express* (Balti Ekspress), leaving Tallinn at 17.45 pm at the time of writing, runs via Tartu, Valga, Rīga and Kaunas. There's also an overnight train from Tallinn to Rīga (and vice versa), taking 9½ hours and making the same intermediate stops. The Tallinn-Rīga fare in compartment class is about 298 EEK at the time of writing; the equivalent Tallinn-Kaunas fare is 465 EEK.

The main services within Estonia, with approximate fares in general seating, include:

Kloogaranna
    39 km, one hour, five trains daily, 10.80 EEK
Narva
    210 km, 3¼ to 4½ hours, five trains daily, 58 EEK

Paldiski
    48 km, 1¼ hours, seven trains daily, 13.20 EEK
Pärnu
    141 km, 2¾ to four hours, two trains daily, 38.80
    EEK
Tartu
    190 km, 2½ to 3¾ hours, five trains daily, 67
    EEK
Valga
    252 km, five hours, two trains daily, 42 EEK
Viljandi
    151 km, 2½ to 3¼ hours, three trains daily, 48
    EEK

Car & Motorcycle

There are 24-hour petrol stations run by the foreign oil companies, Neste, Statoil and Shell, at strategic spots within the city and along major roads leading to/from Tallinn. They all sport 24-hour shops selling a terrific range of imported sweets, chocolates and other junk-food delights.

Stations include the Norwegian-run Statoil on the corner of Sadama and Mere puiestee near the ferry port, and on Tartu maantee by the airport; and the Finnish-run Neste petrol stations at Pärnu maantee 141 and Regati puiestee 1, Pirita. Tallinn traffic police (☎ 6124 687) is close to the bus station at Lastekodu 31.

Car Rental Some car rental agencies have offices in each of the Baltic capitals, allowing you to hire a car in one city and drop it off in another. Recommended agencies include:

Avis
    Airport (☎ 6388 222; fax 6388 220); Liivalaia 33
    (☎ 6315 930; fax 6315 931)
Eurodollar
    Airport (☎ & fax 6388 071); inside the Viru hotel
    (☎ 6301 526; fax 6301 562)
Europcar
    Airport (☎ 6388 031); Magdaleena 3E (☎ 6502
    559; fax 6502 560)
Hertz
    Airport (☎ 6388 923; fax 6388 953; email
    hertz@online.ee)
Mootor Tourist Centre
    Long distance bus station (☎ 448 713; fax 6312
    781) – 40-seater bus rental

Tulika Rent
    Tulika 33 (☎ 6552 552; fax 6552 577) – bookings
    through Palace, Olümpia, Central and Peoleo
    hotels.
Travel Line
    Roosikrantsi 19 (☎ 6411 512; fax 6311 334) –
    mini-bus rental

Boat

Tallinn's main ferry terminal *(sadama)* is at the east end of Sadama, about a km northeast of the Old Town. This is used by almost all passenger shipping except EstLine, which has its own terminal next door at Sadama 29. The main terminal has a café, bar, shops, and left-luggage room. Tram Nos 1 and 2 and bus Nos 3, 4 and 8 go to the Linnahalli stop (by the Statoil petrol station) at the west end of Sadama, a five minute walk from all the terminals. A private shuttle bus costing 25 EEK runs every 15 minutes between the main terminal and the Viru, Palace and Olümpia hotels.

The shipping lines' main booking offices are:

Eestin Linjat
    Main ferry terminal (☎ 6318 606; fax 6318 690)
EstLine
    Aia 5a (☎ 666 579) and Sadama 29 (☎ 6313 636;
    fax 6313 633)
Silja Line
    Baltic Tours (☎ 6300 400; fax 6300 411) at Aia
    18 or Laikmaa 5 (☎ 430 663; fax 6313 576); or
    in main ferry terminal (☎ 6318 331; fax 6318
    264)
Tallink
    Sadama 4 (☎ 6409 800, 6409 808) and at main
    ferry terminal (☎ 6409 840, 493 091; fax 493
    000)
Viking Line
    Estravel at Suur-Karja 15 (☎ 6266 206; fax 6266
    262; email sales@estravel.ee); Liivalaia 33
    (☎ 6315 565); inside Tallinn Expo at Narva
    maantee 9a (☎ 6302 202); Liivalaia 12 (☎ 6461
    461)

You can also buy tickets from a number of travel agents around town.

Yacht Charter Yachts can be rented from the Pirita marina (☎ 238 003; fax 238 044). Also at the marina at Regati 1 is the Estonian Yachting Union (☎ 237 288; fax 238 344).

GETTING AROUND
The Airport
Tallinn Airport is on the Tartu road three km south-east of the centre. Bus No 22 runs every 20 to 30 minutes to and from the bus station, the Tallinn department store near the Viru hotel, Vabaduse väljak near the Palace hotel, and the train station. There is also an additional summer airport bus (No 90) that runs every 30 minutes calling at the Palace, Viru, Olümpia, Kungla and Tallinn hotels. A taxi from the airport to the city centre should cost around 50 EEK.

Bus, Tram & Trolleybus
The Old Town is best explored on foot (trams, buses and trolleybuses circumvent it, and cars have to pay to enter it). Buses, trams and trolleybuses will take you everywhere else from 5 or 6 am to about midnight. Tickets *(piletid)* are sold from street kiosks or can be purchased from the driver. Buy five or 10 at once.

Train
Few of the suburban rail services from the main station in Tallinn go to places of much interest in the city. The one line that may be useful heads south to Nõmme, Pääskula and Laagri. There are about 40 daily trains along this line from 5.20 am until a little after midnight. Most continue beyond the city bounds to Keila, Paldiski or Kloogaranna, but some only go as far as Pääskula.

Route-Taxi
From 3 pm to 1.30 am there are also route-taxis *(liinitaksod)*, minibuses with a flat fare of about 7 EEK (pay the driver). They drop passengers anywhere along their fixed routes. Their terminal is beside the Viru hotel. No 1 runs to Pirita.

Taxi
Taxis are supposed to cost a minimum of 4 EEK a km. Tallinn taxis are the best of the Baltics; drivers generally switch their meter on and adhere to prices agreed upon before-hand for longer journeys. There are ranks at the bus and train stations, at Viru väljak and

another outside the Estonia Theatre on the corner of Estonia puiestee and Otsa. A 24-hour taxi company to call is Tulika Rent (☎ 6552 552).

Around Tallinn

Countryside and unspoiled coast are not far from Tallinn and there are several places worthy of an outing if you have time.

WEST OF TALLINN
Beaches
The coast west of Tallinn is a favourite summer escape for city folk and the first long, sandy beach is at **Vääna-Jõesuu**, 24 km from the city centre. From the main coast road it's about 600m down a side track to the beach. The beach continues south across the mouth of the Vääna River, where there's a stretch of 30m cliff, one of the highest on the Estonian coast. The road runs right along the cliff top soon after the Naage bus stop. There are more beaches further west at **Lohusalu**, and at **Laulasmaa** and **Kloogaranna** on Lahepera Bay, all 35 to 40 km from Tallinn.

Paldiski
• *pop 4000*
The port of Paldiski, on the Pakri peninsula 50 km west of Tallinn, was founded by Russian tsar Peter the Great. It was turned into a nuclear-submarine base and training centre by his Soviet successors, with the islands of Suur-Pakri and Väike-Pakri, west of the peninsula, being used for bombing drills.

The peninsula was off-limits to civilians until 1994 when the secret military base was opened for the first time since WWII. The last Russian soldier finally pulled out in September 1995, after decommissioning the experimental nuclear reactor facility, marking the final withdrawal of Russian troops from Estonia. While the two reactors are now embedded in a concrete sarcophagus, the nuclear waste still poses problems for the Estonian authorities. The reactors

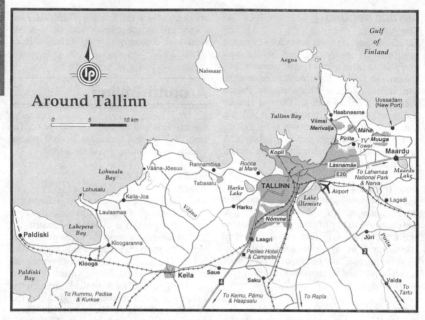

Around Tallinn

0   5   10 km

Gulf of Finland

Naissaar

Aegna

Tallinn Bay

Uussadam (New Port)

Haabneeme

Viimsi Merivalja

Mähe

Pirita

Muuga

TV Tower

Maardu

Kopli

Lohusalu Bay

Vääna-Jõesuu

Rannamõisa

Rocca al Mare

Lasnamäe

To Lahemaa National Park & Narva

Maardu Lake

E20

Lohusalu

Tabasalu

Keila-Joa

Harku Lake

TALLINN

Airport

Lagedi

Laulasmaa

Vääna

Harku

Lake Ülemiste

Lakepera Bay

Nõmme

Paldiski

Kloogaranna

Laagri

Jüri

Pirita

Peoleo Hotel & Campsite

Klooga

Paldiski Bay

Keila

Saue

Vaida

To Tartu

To Rummu, Padise & Kurkse

Saku

To Kernu, Pärnu & Haapsalu

To Rapla

functioned continuously from the early 1970s until 1989 and in 1994 a civilian died after stumbling upon radioactive materials – allegedly stolen from the disused base – on wasteground near Tallinn.

The withdrawal of the Russian navy severely affected the village. Most of the 10,000 ex-Soviet military based at Paldiski had left the military base by mid-1993, and former barracks and dwelling houses fell into ruin and were stripped of their fittings by local metal dealers. The impressive submarine training centre is now standing empty at the entrance of the town and plans to transform it into Estonia's police academy have not materialized. In late 1996 the local authorities dynamited the most run-down buildings. Paldiski's authorities are still hoping for an economic upturn; they boast of excellent ports (the harbour was cleaned of its scuttled patrol boats) and they speak with pride of their beautiful untouched beaches. A trip to the lighthouse on the north-western tip, passing through destroyed Soviet army barracks and sol-air missile sheds, is definitely worth the effort.

Padise

At Padise, about 15 km south of Paldiski on a back road between Tallinn and Haapsalu, is an atmospheric Cistercian monastery dating from the 14th to 16th centuries with a cemetery dating back to the 13th century. It was damaged in the Livonian War in the 16th century and again in a 1766 fire. Padise is four km west of Rummu on the route of Haapsalu-Rummu-Keila-Tallinn buses.

Places to Stay

Just 400m from the beach at Laulasmaa is the *Treppoja Hostel* (☎ 6461 457; fax 6461 595), run by the Estonian Hostels Association at Joa tee 10a in Laulasmaa. It has 90 beds in small, multi-bedded wooden cottages costing 90 EEK a night (open 15 May to 15 September). Another option is the four-storey *Laulasmaa Training and Holiday Centre* (☎ 2-715 521; fax 2-718 474). Singles/doubles with private bathroom cost 150/250 EEK including breakfast and a sea view.

Merihobu Bar & Camping (☎ 2-716 698) is 13 km west of Tallinn, 200m from the sea, at Rannamõisa. It has 100 places in cabins plus tent sites, showers, kitchen, tennis court, sauna and bar. The turning from the main road is just after Mere Tee bus stop which is just beyond Tabasalu village. Go 700m towards the coast.

Vääna-Viti Camping (☎ 2-713 315) is among forest 200m from Vääna-Jõesuu beach, 24 km from the city. It has tent places, a few cabins, kitchen and sauna.

Getting There & Away

CDS Reisid Travel Agency (See Tallinn – Organised Tours) arranges day trips to Paldiski. There are also suburban trains to Paldiski. Boat trips to the islands of Suur-Pakri and Väike-Pakri can be arranged through Kurkse marina (☎ 2-742 274, 2-742 810), in Kurkse on the southern shore of Paldiski Bay.

Buses travelling west along the coast, including Nos 108 and 126 to Rannamõisa, Vääna-Viti and Vääna-Jõesuu, go from the terminal beside Tallinn train station.

SOUTH OF TALLINN
Männiku & Kernu

Hotel Trap (☎ 2-721 958; fax 2-442 435), 10 km south of Tallinn at Männiku, is a modern, concrete building surrounded by pine trees with 32 rooms, all featuring private bathrooms. It arranges fishing trips and has two saunas.

At Kernu, 40 km south of central Tallinn on the road to Pärnu and Rīga, is the modern *Kernu Motel* (☎ 2-771 630), adjoining the Neste Eurostop petrol station with a 24 hour shop and bar. Doubles with/without private shower cost 250/400 EEK and a room for

four is 240 EEK. The classical Kernu Manor, complete with water mill dating to 1637, is nearby.

EAST OF TALLINN
Maardu

On Tallinn's eastern border, the Tallinn-Narva highway crosses the Maardu area which is an industrial wilderness thanks to phosphorite mining and other industries which raged unchecked here in the Soviet era. Phosphorite mining in Estonia was stopped in 1991.

As early as 1987, a 30-sq-km area to the east and south of Maardu Lake (which lies beside the highway) was declared the **Rebala Farming History Reserve**. Within this area are numerous traces of historic and prehistoric settlements and cultures including the Maardu manor founded in 1397, sites of pre-Christian cults, and 'sliding rocks' said to cure infertility in women who slide down them bare-bottomed.

Places to Stay & Eat

The Estonian Hostels Association runs the *Gabriel* hostel (☎ 2-233 223; fax 2-233 173) at Kallasmaa 3. Open all year round, it has 80 beds in double or four-bed rooms costing 45 EEK a night. Facilities include bar, restaurant and laundry.

Kämping Must Kass (Black Cat) (☎ 2-723 881) is delightfully situated in woods 400m south of the Tallinn-Narva highway at Kodasoo, 30 km east of Tallinn and 15 km east of Maardu. It provides room for 50 in two-person cabins, and also has tent sites and a café.

Housed in the smallest fortress in Estonia is *Kiiu Torn* (☎ 2-774 434), six km east of Maardu on the Narva road in the village of Kiiu. Built in the 16th century, the four-storey tower was restored in 1975 and is now a sweet little bar-cum-café famed throughout Estonia for its Kiiu egg liqueur.

North-East Estonia

- Explore the forests in search of European mink and brown bear at Lahemaa National Park
- Step back in time when you visit the restored manor at Palmse
- Marvel at the Sea Museum in the former Soviet coast guard barracks at Käsmu
- Hire a Lahemaa National Park guide and discover your own desert island
- See how fishermen lived and worked 400 years ago in the village of Altja
- Discover a Russian way of life in Narva

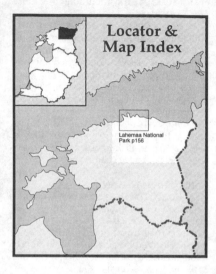

Locator & Map Index

Lahemaa National Park p156

You travel across north-east Estonia if you approach Tallinn from St Petersburg. Lahemaa National Park, about a third of the way from Tallinn to the Russian border, is well worth a visit. The border town of Narva is of interest chiefly for one or two historic remains and because it's one of the four main centres of Estonia's Russian minority (the others are Tallinn, Kohtla-Jarve and Sillamäe).

LAHEMAA NATIONAL PARK

Estonia's largest national park *(rahvuspark)*, Lahemaa (Bay Land), takes in a stretch of deeply indented coast with several peninsulas and bays plus 649 sq km of hinterland with more than a dozen lakes and numerous rivers and waterfalls. The park is a peaceful, unspoiled section of rural Estonia with a variety of attractive coastal and inland scenery. There's historical, archaeological and cultural interest as well as the natural attractions of the coast, forests, lakes, rivers, bogs and walking trails. About 26% of the park is human-influenced, 65% is forest or heath, and 9% is bog. Roads criss-cross the park from the Tallinn-Narva highway to the coast, and several parts of the park are accessible by bus.

When it was founded in 1971, Lahemaa was the first national park in the Soviet Union. Some 7% of its area is occupied by five closed reserves. By summer 1997, though, visitors should be able to apply for permission from the park to visit two of these reserves with a local guide – the Koljaku-Oandu reserve, an area of wet sea forest in the north-east of the park dating back 130 years; and Laukasoo reserve, a 7000 year old bog in the centre of the park.

Around 80,000 people visit the park every year, a small number of which go out of season when the park is transformed into a magical winterland of snowy shores, frozen seas and sparkling black trees. In 1996 the North Estonian Glint (see Geography section) was named as Estonia's National Monument.

Geography

The landscape is mostly flat or gently rolling, with the highest point just 115m above sea

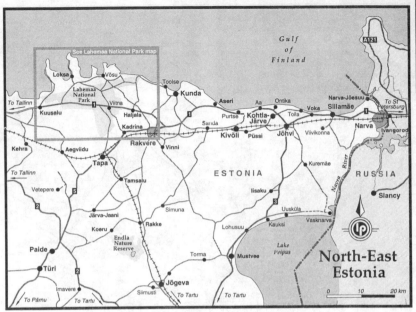

North-East Estonia

level. Geologically, much of the park is on the North Estonian limestone plateau whose northern edge, stretching east-west across the park, forms a bank up to 56m high known as the Baltic or North Estonian Glint. In parts, the bank is a short, barely noticeable slope; in other places it's a cliff. At Muuksi in the west of the park it forms a 47m high coastal bank (a site of Midsummer's Eve festivities). Rivers flowing over the bank become waterfalls, as at Nõmmeveski on the Valgejõgi river and Joaveski on the River Loobu. The Loobu and Valgejõgi are the park's major rivers.

Stone fields, areas of very thin topsoil known as 'alvars', and large single rocks known as 'erratic' boulders, brought here by glacial action, are typically Estonian features of the park. The biggest boulder (at 580 cubic metres) is the Majakivi (House Boulder), while the Tammispea boulder is the highest at 7.8m. The best known stone field is on the Käsmu Peninsula.

Flora & Fauna

Some 838 plant species have been found in the park (including 34 rare ones), plus 37 mammals (among them brown bear, lynx and European mink, none of which you're likely to see without specialist help), 213 birds (mute swan, black stork, black-throated diver and crane nest here), and 24 species of fish. Salmon and trout spawn in the rivers.

Information

Lahemaa National Park Visitors' Centre (Lahemaa Rahvuspark Külatuskeskus; ☎ 232-34 196; fax 232-44 575; email teet@lklm.envir.ee) is in a converted wagon-house and stable on the manor estate in Palmse, eight km north of Viitna in the south-eastern part of the park. Information, bicycle and car rental, and guides in several languages are available here, as is accommodation (see Places to Stay and Getting Around). The centre can also direct you to

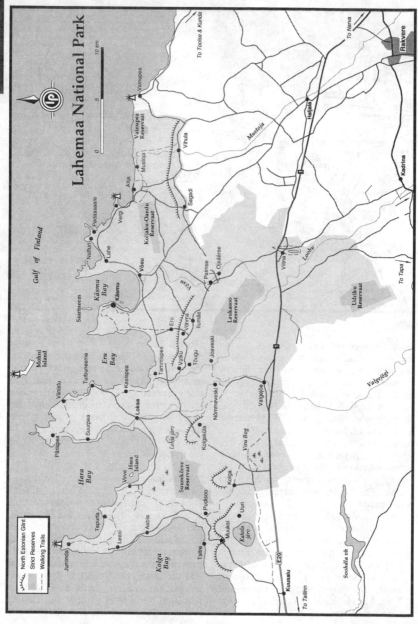

Lahemaa National Park

suitable fishing or bird-watching areas in the park. Between 13 May and 31 August, it is open daily from 9 am to 7 pm. From 1 to 30 September, it is open daily from 9 am to 5 pm; from 1 October to 12 May, Monday to Friday from 9 am to 2 pm.

Two further information points should be set up at Käsmu and Võsu by mid-1997. Käsmu Visitors' Centre (☎ 232-99 436, 232-34 196), immediately on your right as you enter the village from Viitna at Neeme tee 2, also arranges accommodation and guides.

Entrance to the park is free but visitors are encouraged to buy an annual visitors' permit for 15 EEK, the proceeds of which go towards the park's maintenance.

To reach the visitors' centre from Viitna, follow the road signposted for Võsu, almost directly opposite the main bus stop. Buses from Tallinn and Narva only stop at Viitna. In summer your best bet is to hitch the remaining eight km to Palmse although the visitors' centre can arrange for a car to meet you at the bus stop if you call in advance. It will cost you about 5 EEK per km.

Palmse

The restored manor and park at Palmse, eight km north of Viitna, is the showpiece of Lahemaa. In the early 13th century the Danish king gave the land to Cistercian monks from Gotland who had come to convert north-east Estonia. It belonged to the Baltic-German von der Pahlen family from 1677 until 1923 when the property was expropriated by the state and used as a holiday resort for the Estonian Home Guard (Kaitseliit). In Soviet times, Palmse gradually fell into disrepair until restoration began after the founding of the national park.

The existing buildings are restored versions of those that were built in the 18th and 19th centuries. The fine Baroque house, dating from the 1780s, is decked out with period furniture. It's open daily, except Monday, from 10 am to 3 pm (also closed on Sunday in winter). At other times you can walk around the estate without entering the manor house. Behind the manor house is a park, first laid out in medieval times, when

ponds were dug for fish breeding. The forest section of the park was added in the 19th century.

In the von der Pahlens' time, Palmse had, among other things, its own brewery, distillery, smithy, orchard, granaries, limestone quarry and water mill, many of which have been restored and are once more in use: the *ait* (storage room) is a summer exhibition hall, the *viinavabrik* distillery is a hotel and restaurant, the *kavaleride maja* (House of Cavaliers) which once housed summer guests, is a souvenir and book shop, and the wonderful *supelmaja* (bath house) must be one of the most romantic cafés in Estonia. The old granary, facing the manor on the opposite side of Võsu maantee, is the village school's canteen. Entrance to Palmse manor is 20/10 EEK for adults/students.

The Lahemaa area is rich in folk music and dance traditions. A small amphitheatre (across the lake behind the manor house) is the setting for the Viru Säru folk music and dance festival, held in the first week of July in even-numbered years, and for open-air concerts. Weekly classical music concerts are held in the manor.

Other Destinations

The small coastal towns of **Võsu** and, to a lesser extent, **Loksa**, are popular seaside spots in summer. Võsu has quite a long, sandy beach; Loksa has a ship repair yard with a mainly Russian workforce. There are also good beaches at Käsmu, an old sailing village across the bay from Võsu, and between **Altja** and **Mustoja**.

The former Soviet Coast Guard's barracks at **Käsmu** (Captains' Village) now shelters Käsmu Meremuuseum (Sea Museum, ☎ 232-99 136). From the end of WWII the entire stretch of the national park's coastal line was a military controlled frontier. A two-metre-high barbed wire fence was put up to ensure villagers did not access the beach or sea, and it was not until Estonia regained its independence in 1991 that fishers could freely go out in their boats. The museum has an excellent exhibition of Soviet propaganda as well as photographs and memorabilia tracing the history of the village. The museum is also making steps to re-establish **Käsmu Maritime School**, active between 1884 and 1931. The school arranges sailing, rowing, diving and canoe-building camps.

Many old wooden buildings still stand in the 400 year old fishing village of **Altja**, which retains much of its original appearance. The park has reconstructed traditional net sheds here and set up an open-air museum of stones along the coastline. Altja's *Kiitemägi* (Swing Hill), complete with traditional Estonian swings, has long been the centre of Midsummer's Eve festivities in Lahemaa. The restored *Altja kõrts* (Altja Pub) dates to the 1800s. Other coastal villages with an old-fashioned flavour are **Natturi** and **Virve**.

From Käsmu it is possible to cross over to **Mohni Island**. Inhabited by six families at the beginning of this century, the island is now home to a solitary lighthouse keeper who arranges guided tours of the island (see Getting Around). **Hara Island** was, up until 1992, a former Soviet submarine base and hence a closed area. The island was not marked on maps of the national park printed during Soviet times which also featured false roads running through the park. During the 1860s the island enjoyed a successful sprat industry and about 100 people inhabited it. Upon special request, park guides can take you to Hara Island (see Getting Around). **Saartneem** and **Alvi** are two other small islands which, when waters are low, it is possible to walk to – but only with a park guide.

Inland, old farm buildings still stand in villages like **Muuksi**, **Uuri**, **Vatku**, **Tõugu** and **Võhma**. On the small hill of Tandemägi, near Võhma, four stone tombs from the 1st century AD and earlier have been reconstructed after excavation. There are more old German manors at **Kolga**, **Sagadi** and **Vihula**. Now fully restored, Sagadi Manor houses a Forest Museum (☎ 232-98 642, 232-98 647). It is open daily (except Monday) between 15 May and 30 September from 11 am to 6 pm. Between October 1 and 14 May, the museum is only open for

advanced bookings. Entrance is 25/15/8 EEK for adults/pensioners/students. The manor's former grain dryer is now a café. The classical-style manor house at Kolga, dating to the 15th century but largely rebuilt in 1768 and 1820, is home to a luxury hotel and a la carte restaurant with the largest menu (over 300 dishes) in Estonia. Restoration work at Vihula is 80% complete and future plans include opening a hotel on the manorial complex.

Walking Trails

Apart from hikeable roads and tracks, the park has several nature trails including:

Altija
  a 3.5 km circular trail starting at 'Swing Hill' on the coast at Altija, taking in old fishing cottages, traditional net sheds and the open air museum of stones
Käsmu
  a four km circuit from Käsmu village, taking in coast, pine forest, 'erratic' boulders and the lake Käsmu järv; a longer route takes you to Eru
Palmse
  an eight km circuit starting at the visitors' centre and taking in the sights, sounds and smells of Palmse. An orientation map for this trail is available at the centre for 6 EEK
Viitna
  a seven km path starting at the visitors' centre and taking in lakes and forest
Viru Rapa
  a 3.5 km trail across the 1.5 sq km Viru Bog, starting at a car park on the road between Tallinn and Loksa
Virve
  a 3.5 km trail on the Juminda peninsula taking in the Majakivi boulder, on top of which 35 people can quite comfortably sit

Places to Stay

The Estonian Ecotourism Association (see introductory Facts for the Visitor – Accommodation) arranges accommodation in farmhouses throughout the park. The Lahemaa National Park Visitor Centre (see Information) at Palmse can find places to stay for 220 EEK per person, including breakfast, in 12 tourist farms spread no more than a day's walk apart around the park. A tent can be pitched at these farms for 25 EEK a night.

The park runs a *hostel* (☎ 232-34 108) 1.5 km south-east of Palmse at Ojaäärse. The 42 bed hostel in a restored farm dating to 1855, overlooks a lake and has shared rooms with six bunk beds for 80 EEK per person. There is a lakeside sauna and a common room with fireplace. It is open all year round. To reach it follow the road from Palmse to Sagadi and turn right down a wooded trail signposted Ojaäärse. If you prefer to go on foot, cut through the park from Palmse manor by following the river.

The *Merekalda Boarding House* (☎ 232-99 451), overlooking the sea in Käsmu at Neeme tee 2, has four double and two single rooms for 220 EEK per person. Rooms are beautifully furnished with clean shared bathrooms. Just ask for a sea view and you'll be in heaven. It also rents boats, water-bikes and sailboards for around 50 EEK an hour. If all the rooms are booked, you can try *Sireli Pansion* (☎ 232-99 422) a few doors down at Neeme tee 19.

In Sagadi your best bet is the restored Governor's House of *Sagadi Manor* (☎ 232 98 642; fax 232 98 647). For just 60 EEK a night it is possible to stay in a triple or four/six/eight bed room amidst some of the grandest surroundings in Estonia! A km south of Lõobu is the *Pallase Tallid* (Pallase Riding Stables; ☎ 252-365 62). It arranges four-day horse riding camps – camping being the optimum word – as well as fishing excursions, swamp walks and berry picking trips in the forest. Guests have to bring their own tents.

The *Viitna Motel* (☎ 232-93 651), in Viitna beside a lake which is suitable for swimming, has beds for 36 people. Singles/doubles cost 100/150 EEK. In Võsu, the *Mere* hotel (☎ 232-99 179), a large, unlovely Soviet-era building at Mere 21, has rooms with private bathroom for 250 EEK per person. The *Lepispea* campsite (☎ 232-99 199) in Võsu has 50 places.

Top of the range is the *Park Hotel Palmse* (☎ 232-34 167), inside the Palmse Manor distillery. Plush, pine-furnished single/ double rooms are 450/790 EEK including breakfast from April to October. From November to April prices fall by round about 100 EEK.

Places to Eat

The *Viitna kõrts*, almost opposite the eastbound-bus stop at Viitna, is a reconstruction of an 18th century St Petersburg stage house. The rustic-style restaurant is open daily from noon to 2 am; the shop and bistro, serving great early morning breakfasts, is open daily from 7 am to 8 pm.

For traditional Estonian dishes and revitalising mugs of Viru Õlu (beer) and bread with honey, try *Altja kõrts* in Altja. The pub prides itself on the traditional 'plain coast dwellers' food which it serves in the tavern room, originally reserved for the gentry of the village. Folk music accompanies most meals.

In Võsu, good cheap food for hearty appetites is served at the *Võsu Grill*, Mere 49. It is open daily from 10 to 1 am.

If you are staying at a tourist farm, don't miss the opportunity to sample some traditional home cooking. Just ask your host a day in advance.

Getting There & Away

Several Tallinn travel agents (see Tallinn – Travel Agencies) offer tours to the park, as does the Estonian Ecotourism Association (see introductory Facts for the Visitor).

Viitna To reach Viitna from Tallinn by public transport, take one of the 12 daily buses heading for Rakvere, 25 km beyond Viitna. These take an hour to Viitna, for 24 EEK. Tallinn-Narva and the Tallinn-St Petersburg buses don't stop at Viitna. From Narva to Viitna take a bus or train to Rakvere (about five of each daily taking two to 2½ hours), and then a bus to Viitna (nine daily, 20 to 30 minutes). From Tartu there's an early afternoon bus to Viitna (3½ hours, 64 EEK) and three daily buses to Rakvere (2½ to three hours, 48 EEK). The daily bus from Viitna to Tartu leaves at 6.43 am.

Other Destinations There are two buses daily from Tallinn to Käsmu and Võsu, leaving Tallinn around 9 am and 7 pm, making it possible to do a day trip from Tallinn to the park.

Getting Around

A bicycle or car is ideal. If you're not too pressed for time, walking is also a possibility, at least some of the time, as the distances are not too great. You can also use the buses running to the coastal villages (see Getting There & Away above) to get around the park.

The visitors' centre at Palmse rents out bicycles for 70 EEK a day, as do most of the tourist farms in the park. It also rents cars and minibuses which should be booked in advance. A car costs around 5 EEK per km and 20 EEK per hour. Petrol stations open 24 hours are at Kotka, Loksa and Viitna.

The visitors' centre provides guides for tours of the park in several languages including English, Swedish, Finnish and German. Guides for one to three people cost 210 EEK for two hours and 570 EEK for eight hours; for four to 10 people they're 270 EEK and 710 EEK respectively. For information on guided tours around the islands of Mohni, Hara, Saartneem and Alvi, contact the visitors' centre too.

Pallase Riding Stables (see Places to Stay) arranges walking, fishing and horse riding tours of the park and its surrounding areas. The Sea Museum at Käsmu (see Other Destinations) rents laser yachts for around 40 EEK an hour and simple rowing boats for 15 EEK. It also has a motor-boat for 12 people costing 350 EEK an hour which can take you across to Mohni Island.

LAHEMAA TO NARVA

Much of Estonian territory east of Lahemaa is blighted by industries developed in the Soviet era. Some 40% of Estonian industrial output is produced here. Extraction of oil shale and phosphorite has scarred the landscape from west of Kohtla-Järve to beyond the Russian border, though phosphorite production was stopped in 1991 after a four year public protest campaign that had been one of the seeds of Estonia's independence movement. A radioactive waste pond from the rare-earth-metal alloy plant at Sillamäe threatens to spill into the Baltic Sea. The towns in this north-eastern corner of Estonia have a predominantly Russian-speaking population.

The polluted town of **Kunda** is home to a mammoth cement plant which covers the entire town in an impressive grey dust blanket – day and night. Eight km west, on a headland at **Toolse**, are the evocative ruins of a castle built in 1471 by the Livonian Order as defence against pirates. At **Purtse**, 10 km north of Kiviõli, there's a picturesque, restored, 16th century castle open to visitors. The coast between Aa and Toila is lined by cliffs where it coincides with the edge of the Baltic Glint. At **Ontika**, north of Kohtla-Järve, these cliffs reach their greatest height of 55m.

Toolse Castle

Kohtla-Järve usually refers not only to the adjoining settlements of Kohtla and Järve but to a whole string of other towns and villages on or just south of the highway, from Kiviõli in the west to Jõhvi and Viivikonna in the east. This area, with a population of about 90,000, is the centre of large-scale extraction and processing of oil shale, a kind of combustible stone used as fuel for power stations around Narva. The Jõhvi tourism centre (☎ 233-22 306; fax 233-70 136; email info@johvi-turism.ee; http://www.estonia.ee/johvi), at Pargi 15, Jõhvi, is trying to promote tourism in the area.

Sillamäe, situated on the coast between

Top Left: Pikk Hermann, Toompea Castle, Tallinn, Estonia
Top Right: Kuressaare castle, Saaremaa, Estonia
Bottom Left: Bishop's Castle, Haapsalu, Estonia
Bottom Right: Kiek-in-de-Kök, Tallinn, Estonia

JOHN NOBLE

JOHN NOBLE

JOHN NOBLE

Top: 17th & 19th century houses, Pärnu, Estonia
Middle: Windmills at Angla, Saaremaa, Estonia
Bottom: Boats at Triigi, Saaremaa, Estonia

Kohtla-Järve and Narva, was built after WWII to support a military nuclear chemicals plant and metal plant which was barred to ethnic Estonians during Soviet times. Over 97% of its 20,000 population is entirely Russian-speaking and in 1995, it became the first town in Estonia to take advantage of a new language law passed allowing towns who have an ethnic minority of at least 50% to use their native language as the official administration language. Many street signs are bilingual.

NARVA
• *pop 80,000* • ☎ *(235)*

Estonia's easternmost town, Narva, lies on the Tallinn-St Petersburg road and railway, 210 km from Tallinn and 140 km from St Petersburg. Only the Narva River separates Narva from Ivangorod (Estonian: Jaanilinn) in Russia. With an industrial base that has particularly suffered from Estonia's economic problems, Narva had some of the highest unemployment in the country and was a centre of Russian political discontent for a few years following independence. Over 90% of the town's predominantly Russian-speaking population was not eligible for automatic Estonian citizenship after independence.

Occasional political strikes occurred, and talk of a 'special status' – even secession for Narva – surfaced from time to time in the first years of Estonian independence. Even today, the area raises controversy. Many state officials do not speak Estonian, and in early 1997 the government extended once again the deadline by which policemen in Narva and the Idu-Virumaa region have to pass the language proficiency test required for Estonian citizenship.

Strategically sited on a system of inland waterways, Narva was a Hanseatic League trading point by 1171. Later it became embroiled in border disputes between the German knights and Russia, and Ivan III of Muscovy built a fort at Ivangorod, on the other side of the river, in 1492. In the 16th and 17th centuries, Narva changed hands often between the Russians and Swedes. At the beginning of the Great Northern War in 1700, Russia's Peter the Great, having devastated the countryside around Narva, suffered a major reverse when the Swedes broke his siege of the town with a surprise winter attack. But the Russians came back to take the town four years later.

Independent Estonia between WWI and WWII included a strip of territory on the east bank of the Narva River which contained Ivangorod. This is probably why the modern 5 EEK note shows both Narva castle (on the left) and Ivangorod castle facing each other across the river.

Narva was almost completely destroyed in 1944 during its recapture by the Red Army. Afterwards it became part of the north-east Estonian industrial zone and one of Europe's most polluted towns, with two big power stations around it burning over 20 million tonnes of oil shale a year by 1990 and emitting an estimated 380,000 tonnes of sulphur dioxide and 200,000 tonnes of toxic ash.

About 12 km north of Narva is the rundown holiday resort, Narva-Jõesu, a pretty, but delapidated town, popular during Soviet times for its long white sandy beach backed by pine forests.

Orientation & Information
The main landmark, the castle, is by the river, just south of the bridge. The railway crosses the river a km south of the road bridge. The train and bus stations are next to each other on Vaksali. From them it's a half km walk north along Puškini to the castle.

The tourist information centre is at Puškini 13 (☎ 60 184; fax 60 181; email info@narva.turism.ee; http://www.estonia. org/narva). Narva's English-speaking Express Hotline (☎ 60 222) is useful out of office hours.

Things to See
Only a couple of Narva's fine Gothic and Baroque buildings survived its 'liberation' by the Red Army in 1944. The imposing **Narva Castle** at Peterburi 2, with its stout walls guarding the road bridge over the river, dates from Danish rule in the 13th century.

Across the waters, on the Russian side of the river, stands the matching fortress of Jaanilinn, forming an architectural ensemble unique in northern Europe. Restored after damage in WWII, Narva Castle houses the **Town Museum**, open daily, except Sunday and Monday, from 10 am to 6 pm. The Baroque **Old Town Hall** (1668-71) on Raekoja väljak, north of the castle, has also been restored. The Russian Orthodox **Voskresensky Cathedral** is situated on Bastrakovi, in front of the train station.

Places to Stay & Eat

The *Hotel Vanalinn* (☎ 22 486), at Koidula 6 just north of the castle in a renovated 17th century building, is one of the best things about Narva. There are 28 rooms, all with private bathroom. Singles/doubles are 400/600 EEK. The 160 bed Soviet-style *Hotel Narva* (☎ 22 700), at Puškini 6 just south of the castle, charges similar prices.

There are a few restaurants and cafés on Puškini and Peterburi, the best of which is the *German Pub* at Puškini 10. *Café Roldis* at Puškini 6 is best for light snacks. The most expensive is *Rondeel* inside the fortified wall of Narva Castle.

The *Narva-Jõesuu Health Resort* (☎ 71 311; fax 31 535) in the centre of Narva-Jõesuu overlooking the beach at Aia 3, is a huge, majestic building with singles/doubles for 200/300 EEK including breakfast. It also offers a delightful array of mud baths and other curative thrills.

Getting There & Away

There are seven daily buses from Tallinn to/from Narva (four hours, 70 EEK), passing through Rakvere and some continuing to Narva-Jõesuu. Daily Tallinn-St Petersburg buses stop at Narva at 10.45 am and 7.15 pm, passing back through Narva on the way back to Tallinn at 9.50 am and 7.50 pm. There are five buses daily to/from Tartu (3½ to 4½ hours, 64 EEK).

Five trains daily run from Tallinn to Narva and vice versa (3¼ to 4½ hours, 58 EEK), stopping at Rakvere on the way. Three of the trains terminate at Narva; one continues to St Petersburg and the other to Moscow.

KUREMÄE
• ☎ *(233)*

Formerly the site of ancient pagan worship, the tiny village of Kuremäe, 20 km southeast of Jõhvi, is home to the Russian Orthodox **Pühtitsa Convent** (☎ 92 124). Built between 1892-5, the magnificent nunnery with its five towers topped with green onion domes, is a place of pilgrimage for thousands of Russian Orthodox believers every year. Murals by the convent gate depict the Virgin Mary who, it is said, appeared to shepherds in the 16th century by an oak tree. The shepherds later returned to the tree to find an icon there which is now in the main church of the convent.

Today about 80 nuns and novices live in the convent and it is possible for visitors to stay overnight in one of the dormitories for 100 EEK a night including meals. Note that a strict vegetarian diet is followed and a religious service is held at 6 pm every evening. Rooms have to be booked in advance, either directly through the convent or through the Lahemaa Visitors' Centre. One bus daily runs from Tallinn to Kuremäe, leaving Tallinn at 5.25 pm and arriving in Kuremäe at 9 pm. The return bus leaves Kuremäe for Tallinn at 7.10 am.

LAKE PEIPUS (NORTH)
• ☎ *(233)*

There's a sandy beach along much of the northern shore of Lake Peipus, at its best at **Kauksi**, where the Narva-Jõhvi-Tartu road reaches the lake. At **Vasknarva**, where the Narva River flows out of the north-east corner of the lake, are ruins of a Teutonic Order castle.

At **Lohusuu**, on the lake 12 km west of Kauksi, a Russian fishing community has lived in harmony with Estonians for centuries. The Tartu road diverges from the sometimes desolate lake shore after passing a string of villages south of **Mustvee**. Much of this region is protected under the Kõrvemaa Landscape Reserve. There's a *camping site* (☎ 93 595) at Kauksi and another (☎ 93 234) at Uusküla, six km east along the lake shore. The Estonian Tourist Board operates a small information centre (☎ 93 378; email info@iisaku.turism.ee) at Tartu maantee 51 in Iisaku. For information on the southern part of Lake Peipus see the South-East Estonia chapter.

PAIDE
• *pop 11,000 ☎ (238)*

Paide lies on the main road between northeast and south-west Estonia, four km west of where that road crosses the Tallinn-Tartu road. Paide dates from 1260 when the German knights founded a fortress, whose main tower, Pikk Hermann, has recently been restored. The town centre has many 19th century classical-style buildings. There's also a tourism information centre (☎ 50 400; email info@paide.turism.ee; http://www.estonia.org/paide) at Pärnu 6 and an express hotline (☎ 71 222) which you can also call for information.

The **regional history museum** is at Lembitu 5. There's a small (12 beds), basic hotel, the *Paide Võõrastemaja* (☎ 21 227), at Telliskivi 8. The Kõrvemaa Landscape Reserve headquarters (☎ 41 167) is at Pärnu 75.

ENDLA NATURE RESERVE

The Endla Nature Reserve (Endla Looduskaitseala), covering a boggy area inhabited by beavers, begins south of Koeru, about 25 km east of Paide, and extends nearly 20 km east to include Lake Endla and the five-metre-deep spring (Estonia's deepest) from which the Oostungu River flows. The reserve, established in 1981, covers a total area of 8162 hectares.

The reserve headquarters (☎ 237-46 429) is in Tooma. It is possible to visit the reserve and follow a 1.5-km-long nature trail on boards across the bog, taking in two watch towers along the way. Guided tours are also available. All visits have to be arranged in advance through the headquarters.

South-East Estonia

HIGHLIGHTS

- Discover the history, life and traditions of Estonians at the National Museum in Tartu
- Hike up Toomemägi (Cathedral Hill) to see the ruined Gothic cathedral
- Check in to the luxury Dzhokhar Dudayev suite (if you're rich) at the Barclay Hotel and pay homage to the late Chechen rebel leader
- Enjoy cakes and coffee at the 17th century student café inside Tartu University
- Ski at Estonia's top winter sports resorts at Otepää and Haanja
- Witness the 'Berlin Fence' in Valga/Valka

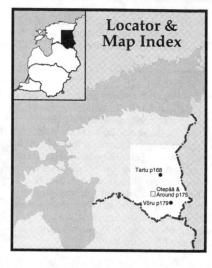

Locator & Map Index

Tartu p168
Otepää & Around p175
Võru p179

The focus of south-east Estonia is the historic university town of Tartu, Estonia's second largest city 190 km south-east of Tallinn. Beyond Tartu is an attractive region of gentle hills and lakes which includes the highest point in the Baltic states and some of Estonia's prettiest countryside – Estonia's prime ski resort in winter. The region is also home to the land of the Setus, an ethnic group whose ancient lands are now split by Estonia's border with Russia.

TARTU
• *pop 147,500* • ☎ *(27)*

Tartu, with its large number of students (8000) and active cultural life, is a small but busy place. Parks in the hilly city centre, and the river Emajõgi flowing through Tartu on its way from Võrtsjärv to Lake Peipus, give the town a pleasantly spacious feel.

Tartu was the cradle of Estonia's 19th century national revival and is the site of the country's original and premier university. The town managed to escape Sovietisation to a greater degree than Tallinn and retains a sleepy, pastoral air, being notable, not only for its university, but for its classical architecture stemming from a comprehensive rebuilding after most of the town burnt down

in 1775. Tartu is still regarded as Estonia's spiritual capital, and a measure of its importance is that all-Estonia song festivals often begin here. A big event in the local calendar is the Tartu ski marathon, a 60 km cross-country trek from Otepää made by hundreds of skiers in mid-February.

History
There was an early Estonian stronghold on Toomemägi hill around the 6th century AD. In 1030 Yaroslav the Wise of Kiev, ruler of the Russian ancestor-state Kievan Rus, is said to have defeated the Estonians and founded a fort here called Yuriev. The Estonians regained control, but in 1224 were defeated by the Knights of the Sword who placed a castle, cathedral and bishop on Toomemägi. The town that grew up between the hill and the Emajõgi became a successful member of the Hanseatic League. It was known as Dorpat – its German name – until the end of the 19th century.

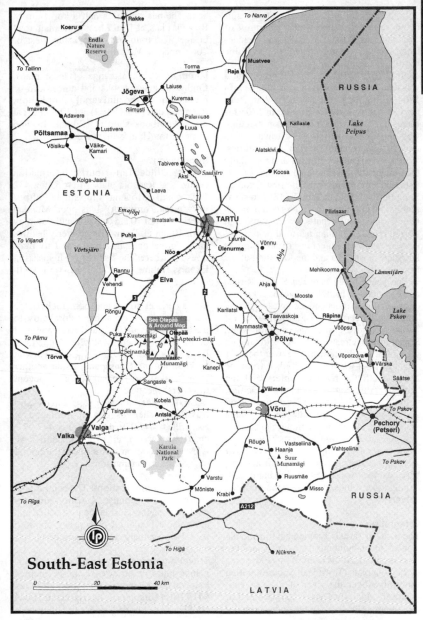

South-East Estonia

In the 16th and 17th centuries Dorpat suffered repeated attacks and changes of ownership as Russia, Sweden and Poland-Lithuania all vied for control of the Baltic region – though the period of Swedish control, 1625-1704, was one of peace and it was then that the university was founded. In 1704 during the Great Northern War, Peter the Great took Tartu for Russia. In 1708 his forces wrecked it and most of its population was deported to Russia. The town stayed under Russian control for over two centuries.

In the 19th century, Tartu – and especially the university – became the focus of the Estonian national revival. The first Estonian Song Festival, held in Tartu in 1869 to show that Estonian songs and singers could match their German counterparts, was an important step in raising Estonian national consciousness, as were the launching of an Estonian language newspaper and the founding of the first Estonian societies.

The peace treaty between Soviet Russia and Estonia by which the Russians acknowledged Estonian independence was signed in Tartu on 2 February, 1920. During WWII Tartu was severely damaged both when Soviet forces retreated in 1941 – blowing up the 1784 Kivisild stone bridge over the river – and in 1944 when they retook it from the Nazis. Both the Nazi occupiers and the Soviet regime committed many atrocities, with thousands dying. The Nazis massacred 12,000 people at Lemmatsi on the Valga road, where there's now a monument.

In the Soviet period Westerners were not allowed to stay overnight at Tartu because of the supposed security risk to a military air base near the town – a ban which hampered, among other things, the development of the university.

Orientation

The focus of Tartu is Toomemägi hill and the area of older buildings between it and the river Emajõgi. At the heart of this older area is Raekoja plats (Town Hall Square), with a footbridge over the river at its east end. Ülikooli, which runs across the west end of the square, is the focus of the main shopping area. The bus station is half a km south of Raekoja plats, at Turu 2 beside the main road bridge. The train station is 750m west of Toomemägi at Vaksali 6.

Maps An excellent range of local maps, English-language books and guides can be picked up at the university bookshop, Raamatupood (☎ 441 102) at Ülikooli 11; at the Teadra book shop at Ülikooli 1a; and from the tourist information centre.

Information

Tourist Office Tartu tourist information centre is at Raekoja plats 14 (☎ & fax 432 141; email info@tartu.turism.ee; http:// www.estonia.org/tartu). It is open Monday to Friday from 10 am to 6 pm, and Saturday from 10 am to 3 pm. The quarterly listings and information magazine *Tartu This Week* is also sold here. The Tartu English-speaking Express Hotline (☎ 487 222) is well worth calling.

Money Places to change cash include the Tartu Kaubamaja (department store) close to the bus station at Riia 2, and Hia Pank next door, which accepts travellers' cheques. Eesti Ühis Pank at Ülikooli 1, Era Pank at Ülikooli 1a and Hansapank inside another supermarket at Tehase 16, also accept travellers' cheques.

Lost American Express cards and travellers' cheques can be replaced at Estravel (☎ 447 979, 447 974; fax 447 977; email tartu1@estravel.ee) at Kompanii 2. An ATM giving cash on Visa is inside the central post office at Vanemuise 7.

Post & Communications The central post office is at Vanemuise 7. Chip cards for public telephones, inside the post office and at strategic points all over town, are sold here. Faxes can also be sent from here.

Travel Agencies Travel agencies that organise tours or arrange bookings include Estravel (see Money); Baltic Tours (☎ & fax 441 716) at Ülikooli 10; and Hermann Travel (☎ 441 222; fax 441 425) at Ülikooli 1.

South Estonian Travel (☎ 476 346; fax 474 553), on the second floor of the bus station, sells bus tickets for European destinations (see Getting There & Away at the front of the book) and tickets for ferries from Tallinn.

Raekoja Plats & Around

Raekoja Plats Many of Tartu's shops, restaurants and offices are on or near the square. The older streets are to its north, while the area to its south has been redeveloped since 1944, when it was flattened by Soviet bombardment. The square was rebuilt after a fire in 1775; its dominant feature is the finely proportioned **Town Hall** (1782-89), topped by a tower and weather vane, which its German architect, JHB Walter, based on the design of Dutch town halls. The buildings at Raekoja plats Nos 6, 8, 12 and 16 are also neoclassical, but No 2, one of the first to be built after the 1775 fire, is in an earlier style – late Baroque. No 18, formerly the home of Colonel Barclay de Tolly (1761-1818) – an exiled Scot who settled in Livonia and distinguished himself in the Russian army's 1812 campaign against Napoleon – is a wonderfully crooked building now housing the **Kirisilla Art Gallery**.

University The impressive main building of Tartu University (Tartu Ülikool) a block from the town hall at Ülikooli 18, with its six Corinthian columns, dates from 1803-09. It contains Tartu's **Classical Art Museum** (☎ 465 384) which is open weekdays from 11 am to 4.30 pm. The university departments, student residences and other buildings are scattered around the town. For more information visit the International Students Office (☎ 465 150, 465 152) at Ülikooli 18 or contact the university's information service (☎ 465 465) or public relations office (☎ 465 681; email proffice@ut.ee; http://www.ut.ee).

The university was founded in 1632 by the Swedish king, Gustaf II Adolf (Gustavus Adolphus), to train Protestant clergy and government officials. It was modelled on Uppsala University. A restored statue of Gustaf Adolf, unveiled by Carl XVI Gustaf of Sweden on his 1992 visit to Estonia, stands at the rear of the main university building. The university closed about 1700 because of the Great Northern War but reopened in 1802, developing into one of the Russian empire's foremost seats of learning, with an emphasis on science – which continues today. Those who worked here in the 19th century included physical-chemistry pioneer W Ostwald, physicists HFE Lenz and MH Jacobi, and natural historian Karl Ernst von Baer who, like the main building on Ülikooli, appears on the 2 EEK note.

The university's teaching language was originally Latin, then German for most of the 19th century, and then Russian until 1920, but that didn't stop it becoming the cradle of the Estonian national revival in the 19th century. In 1992 over 60% of the university's students were women. In 1996, international students made up 3.7% of the student population.

Other Sights North of the university on Jaani (the continuation of Ülikooli), the Gothic brick **Jaani Kirik** (St John's Church), founded in 1330 but ruined by Soviet bombing in 1944, has been under restoration for years. It has rare terracotta sculptures in niches around the main portal.

The nearby **Botanical Gardens** (Botaanikaaed), which were founded in 1803 on the corner of Lai and Vabaduse puiestee, are home to 6500 species of plants, including a large collection of palm trees housed in the 26m-high glasshouse. Between May and September, the gardens are open daily from 9 am to 5 pm.

Toomemägi

Toomemägi (Cathedral Hill), rising behind the town hall, was the original reason for Tartu's existence, having functioned on and off as a stronghold since the 5th or 6th century. It's the site of several important university buildings and a pleasant, tree-shaded park created when the university was revived in the 19th century. The approach to the hill from Raekoja plats is up Lossi, at the

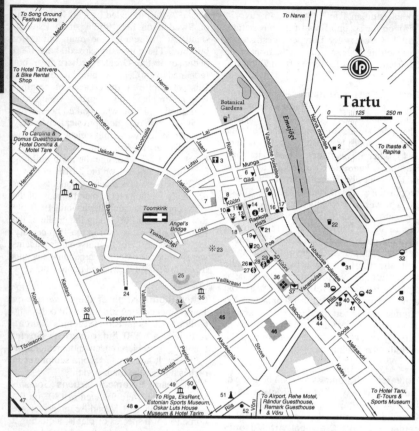

Tartu

0   125   250 m

foot of which stands a **statue** of Nikolai Pirogov (a Tartu University graduate who pioneered field anaesthesia in the 19th century) and the university's new humanities building. Lossi passes beneath the 1836-38 **Angel's Bridge** (Inglisild) with its Latin inscription 'Otium reficit vires' ('Rest restores strength').

Toomemägi's most imposing structure is the ruined brick Gothic **cathedral** (Toomkirik) on the top. Originally built by the German knights in the 13th century, it was rebuilt in the 15th century, despoiled during the Reformation in 1525, used for

a while as a barn, and partly rebuilt in 1804-07 when the university library was installed in the choir at its east end. The **university library** is now at modern premises in town on Struve between Tiigi and Vanemuise and its place is taken by the **Museum of University History**, open Wednesday to Sunday from 11 am to 5 pm. Entrance is 2 EEK.

North of the cathedral, on the top of the hill, are a couple of small 17th century Swedish cannons and a **sacrificial stone** of the ancient Estonians, standing by a small bridge in front of a rocky mound thought to

PLACES TO STAY		3	Jaani Kirik	33	Estonian National
2	Student Dorms &		(St John's Church)		Museum
	Canteen	4	City Museum	35	Art Museum
24	Park Hotel	5	KE von Baer House	36	Kaubamaja Shopping
26	Barclay Hotel		Museum		Centre
43	Hotel Tartu	7	University	37	Central Post Office
		9	Estravel	38	Central Bus Stop
PLACES TO EAT		10	Raamatupood	39	Kaubamaja
6	Gildi Grill		Bookshop		Department Store
8	Legend Klubi	15	Tourist Information	42	Bus Station & South
11	Rüütli Pub		Centre		Estonian Travel
12	Hommi kuhvlk	16	Kirisilla Art Gallery	44	Hia Pank
13	Bistroo	18	Town Hall	45	University Library
14	Rüütli Kelder	20	Illegaard	46	Vanemuine Theatre
17	Taverna	22	Atlantis Nightclub	47	Train Station
19	Central Restoran	23	Observatory	48	Tartu University
21	Bistroo	25	Old Anatomical Theatre		Housing Association
34	Peetri Pizza	27	Eesti Ühis Pank	49	Estonian Literature
40	Restoran Tarvas	28	Era Pank		Museum
41	McDonald's	29	Hermann Travel	50	Small Hall
		30	Teadra Bookshop	51	Weeping Cornflower
OTHER		31	Market	52	Estonian Agricultural
1	Zavood (Factory)	32	River Port		University

have been part of a defensive bastion but now known as **Musumägi** (Hill of Kisses). Nowadays students burn notes and drafts on the sacrificial stone after exams.

Also on this top part of the hill are **monuments** to the Estonian poet Kristjan Jaak Peterson and the Baltic-German natural scientist Karl Ernst von Baer, both of whom studied at Tartu University in the 19th century; and to Johann Karl Simon Morgenstern, founder of the university library.

On the eastern part of the hill, dating from the early 19th century, are the **observatory** (now also an astronomy museum open daily, except Tuesday) on the old castle site (a sculpture commemorates the 19th century astronomer Georg Struve) and the still functioning semi-circular **Old Anatomical Theatre**. The 1913 **Devil's Bridge** (Kuradisild) crosses the road on the south side of the hill, around which the street Vallikraavi follows the line of the old castle moat.

Other Sights

The **Estonian National Museum** (Eesti Rahva Muuseum, ☎ 421 311), tracing the history, life and traditions of the Estonian people, is at Veski 32 just west of Toomemägi. It's open Wednesday to Sunday from 11 am to 6 pm (entrance 6 EEK).

The **Estonian Agriculture Museum** (Eesti Põllumajandusmuuseum) (☎ 412 396), with a machinery collection that includes some of Europe's oldest steam tractors, alongside historical displays on dairy farming, grain growing and animal breeding, is in the village of Ülenurme, six km south of the town centre, just off the Võru road. It is open daily from 10 am to 4 pm.

The **City Museum** (Linnamuuseum, ☎ 422 022) at Oru 2, covering Tartu's history right up to the 19th century, is open daily, except Tuesday, from 11 am to 6 pm. The **Estonian Sports Museum** (☎ 434 602), open Wednesday to Sunday from 11 am to 5 pm, is at Riia 27A and there's an **Art Museum** (☎ 434 352) at Vallikraavi 14, open daily, except Monday and Tuesday, from 11 am to 6 pm.

The home of Karl Ernst von Baer at Veski 4 is now the **KE von Baer House Museum** (☎ 421 514), open weekdays from 9 am to 4 pm. On the literary side, there's the **Estonian Literature Museum** (Viron Kirjallisuusmuseo, ☎ 430 045) at Vanemuise 42, open weekdays from 9 am to 5 pm, and the **Oskar Luts House Museum** (☎ 428 060) at Riia 38, open daily, except Monday and Tuesday, from 11 am to 5 pm. Kreutzwald and Luts are also honoured by **statues** in the riverside park north of Raekoja plats.

In 1990 a monument of a **weeping corn-flower** was put up in front of the former KGB headquarters on Riia, almost opposite the main building of the **Estonian Agricultural University** (Eesti Põllumajandus Ülikool or just PU) to commemorate Estonian deportation and repression victims. The blue cornflower is Estonia's national flower.

The Song Festival grounds, also a site for 23 June bonfires, are in **Tähtvere-Park** at the north end of Tähtvere, two km north of the centre.

Entrance to most museums is free on Friday.

Places to Stay – bottom end

E-Tours (see Travel Agencies) arranges family accommodation for around 170/300 EEK for singles/doubles including breakfast. Prices drop by 10% after four nights. A number of other agencies including Family Hotel Service of Tallinn can also arrange private-home accommodation in Tartu (see Accommodation in the Facts for the Visitor chapter).

For a bed in student dorms at Narva 27, try *Tartu University Housing Association* (☎ 430 833) at Pepleri 14. It offers basic accommodation with no hot water for around 50 EEK. If the university housing director is not in, it is worth trying the hostels direct. The most central one is just across the river at Narva maantee 25. Just walk in and ask nicely if there is a room available. You will probably be told to go to the housing association office, but you may be able to persuade the staff to give you a room.

The only other cheap alternative in the centre is the *Hotel Tahtvere* (☎ 421 708) at Laulupeo 19. Small singles/doubles with private bathroom, TV and telephone are 120/160 EEK. A luxury double room with a fireplace costs 400 EEK.

Two km south of the centre is the *Hotel Tarim* (☎ 475 433; fax 473 357) at Rahu 8. It has 60 beds at 250/400 EEK for singles/doubles with private kitchen, bathroom and breakfast. Take bus No 4 from the bus stop on Riia and get off by the cemetery gates on Võru, just after you cross the railway; walk south and turn left onto Rahu. Also in the vicinity is the *Rändur Guesthouse* (☎ 475 691, 471 713) at Vasara 25, which has 40 places in singles/doubles starting at 50/70 EEK.

Carolina (☎ 422 070; fax 475 749) on the northern edge of town at Kreutzwaldi 15, has four single/double rooms equipped with private showers and TV for 200/400 EEK, including breakfast and transport to the centre. Close by at Tammsaare 8 is the *Domus Guesthouse* (☎ 422 575; fax 422 162) which has 35 places in nine apartments with shared kitchen and bathroom. Singles/doubles are 175/280 EEK and one/two room suites, 350/450 EEK.

Also good value is the *Rehe Motel* (☎ 412 234; fax 412 355) five km from the centre on the road to Võru. Singles/doubles/triples cost 250/380/540 EEK.

Places to Stay – middle

Directly opposite the bus station in a drab Soviet block is the *Tartu Hotel* (☎ & fax 432 091, 433 041). Singles/doubles/triples without private shower cost 350/600/740 EEK. Singles/doubles with shower start at 550/800 EEK. All prices include breakfast.

The *Park Hotel* (☎ 433 663; fax 434 382), in a beautiful woodland setting at Vallikraavi 23, has overpriced singles/doubles with shared bathroom for 200/500 EEK including breakfast. Prices rise to 500/600 for luxury rooms with private bathrooms.

Smaller and more cosy is the *Remark Guesthouse* (☎ 477 744, 477 420), just over two km from the centre at Tähe 94. Prices for its nine beds start at 400 EEK. The Remark is a single-storey white building on the corner of Tähe and Tehase, 1.5 km south of Riia – bus No 9 from the city centre stop on Riia goes there.

Hotel Domina (☎ 422 575; fax 422 588), slightly out of town at Tammsaare 8, has singles/doubles with shared bathroom for 240/400 EEK. Take bus No 5 or 6 from the train station.

The *Motel Tare* (☎ 99 145), beside a reservoir at Ilmatsalu, 10 km west of Tartu, has three double rooms at 175 EEK including breakfast.

Places to Stay – top end

The stylish *Taru Hotel* (☎ 441 177; fax 474 095) is on the edge of a housing estate at Rebase 9, 1.5 km south of the centre, but it's one of the top hotels in town, operated by the Finest group which runs Tallinn's Palace hotel. Comfortable and modern (though not huge) rooms cost 960/1240 EEK for singles/doubles, including breakfast. Rebase is west off Turu, 1.25 km south of the bus station. You can book in Finland through Arctia Hotel Partners (☎ 09-696 901; fax 09-698 958) of Iso-Roobertinkatu 23-25, 00120 Helsinki; in other countries through Finnair Hotels or SAS Associated Hotels.

Cheaper yet more exclusive is the *Barclay Hotel* (☎ 447 100; fax 447 101) at Ülikooli 8. The building, which dates to 1912, was taken over by the Red Army in 1944 and used as its headquarters until 1993. Extravagantly furnished singles/doubles start at around 900/1080 EEK, the most expensive of which is decked out as a luxury shrine to the late Chechen rebel leader Dzhokhar Dudayev who served as commander of a bomber unit of the Soviet air force for 10 years before moving back to Chechnya. Dudayev, who died in spring 1996, is greatly revered in Tartu for publicly assuring in 1991 that he'd refuse any military clampdown on the Estonian independence movement.

Just one km off the road to Rapina in Ihaste is the *Ihaste Hotell* (☎ 437 329; fax 485 664), a luxury hotel aimed at business people with conference facilities, a bar with tenpin bowling lanes and sauna with fireplace. Singles/doubles are 545/615 EEK. The hotel arranges horse riding trips at the nearby Ihaste equestrian centre.

Dzhokhar Dudayev – gave peace a chance

Places to Eat

For quick, cheap eating try the two *student canteens* at Tähe 4 and Narva 27, both open daily from 9 am to 3 pm. Here you can have a plate of potatoes, vegetables and mystery meat for around 12 EEK. Still cheap but far superior is the *Old Student Café* on the second floor of the main university building at Ülikooli 18. Housed in the original part of the university dating to 1632, this oldy-worldy café with worn wooden floors and a homely smell of baking, is a must. Omelettes cost 7 EEK, seljanka 9 EEK and the best cakes in town, 1 to 3 EEK.

The *Central Restoran* at Raekoja plats 3 is about as cheesy as the flashing lights strung round the courtyard outside. The set menu of the day for 35 EEK is not particularly tasty but it does the job if you're just out for a cheap fill (open daily from noon to midnight). *Rüütli Kelder* on the corner of Raekoja plats and Rüütli, still bears slight taints of its Soviet past but is busy nonetheless. It is open daily from noon to midnight, except Friday and Sunday when it opens at 2 pm.

For a complete blast from the past try the

Restoran Tarvas at Riia 2 opposite the bus station. Don't be deceived by the flashy sign beckoning you to come try its four-course 40 EEK meal.

Italian food is served at Raekoja plats 20, at the smart and formal *Taverna* where pasta costs 40 EEK with main dishes from 60 EEK. Vegetarian dishes are also included on its wide menu. It's open daily from noon to 6 pm, and 6.30 pm to 1 am; the entrance is actually just off the square, towards its east end.

Cheap, uninspiring Estonian 'fast food' such as schnitzel, kooreklops (meat in white sauce) and kotlett (meat cutlet) – all with fries for 20 EEK – can be eaten sitting down at the *Bistroo*, which has outlets at Raekoja plats 9 and Rüütli 2 (both open from 7 am to 10 pm). A *Peetri Pizza* outlet is at Tiigi 11 and *McDonald's* is opposite the bus station. Fun cafés worth a try for hamburgers, cakes and ice cream include *Hommi kuhvik* by the town hall on the corner of Raekoja plats and Ülikooli; and *Gildi Grill*, a large modern self-service joint in a basement on the corner of Gildi and Kompanii.

The *market*, is a source of fresh fruit, cheese and so on, is a block from the bus station on Vabaduse puiestee. A supermarket and department store are next to Restoran Tarvas at Riia 2.

Entertainment
Look at posters in the entrance of the main university building at Ülikooli 18 for what's on in the way of music and student theatre.

Theatre Tartu's Vanemuine Theatre, named after the ancient Estonian song-god, was the first Estonian-language theatre when founded in 1870. Today it's housed in a modern building at Vanemuise 6. Other events including concerts are also staged here. The theatre has a second, smaller hall higher up Vanemuise at No 45A near the corner of Kastani.

Bars & Nightclubs In a class of its own stands *Illegaard* at Ülikooli 5. Also an art gallery, this cellar bar-cum-café is the place to be seen at, so much so that after 5 pm it

becomes a members-only club (a year's membership costs 200/400 EEK for Estonians/foreigners). Also pretty hip at the time of writing was *Legend Klubi* at Küütri 2. Adjoining an art gallery too, the cellar-bar is crammed with antiques and fun relics including a motorcycle and a sewing machine.

Late night places to hang out include *Zavood* (Factory) at Lai 30, a fun bar open daily from 4 pm to 2 am and very popular with students. Overlooking the river Emajõgi at Narva 2 is the *Atlantis* nightclub which rocks until 4 am at weekends. The more sobre *Rüütli Pub* is just off Raekoja plats on Rüütli.

Getting There & Away
At the time of writing there were no buses between Tartu and Latvia or Lithuania. The *Baltic Express* train, linking Tartu and Šeštokai, stops at Rīga and Kaunas en route. Heading for Russia, there's a bus to/from St Petersburg and a train to Moscow. For buses to Sweden, Norway and Denmark see the Getting There & Away chapter.

Air Since 1994 there have been no scheduled flights from Tartu airport (☎ 432 304, 432 445). If you are a group of 10 or more, the state-owned airport is prepared to charter a flight to Tallinn or Helsinki. A one-way/return ticket to Tallinn costs 450/900 EEK at the last count; a one-way/return to Helsinki costs 2140/4280 EEK.

Bus More than 20 buses a day run to/from Tallinn (2½ to 3½ hours, 66 EEK). Tartu bus station has a left-luggage room *(pakihoid)* off the ticket hall on the ground floor and an information *(teated)* booth in the ticket hall. Other services to/from Tartu include:

Haapsalu
   5¾ hours, one bus daily, 92 EEK
Koidula (two km from Pechory)
   three hours, three buses daily, 38 EEK
Kuressaare
   eight hours, two buses daily, 122 EEK
Narva
   3½ to 4½ hours, five buses daily, 64 EEK

Pärnu
   three to 4½ hours, six buses daily, 64 EEK
Rakvere
   2½ to three hours, three buses daily, 48 EEK
St Petersburg
   7¾ hours, one overnight bus, 124 EEK
Valga
   1¾ hours, one bus daily, 64 EEK
Viljandi
   1½ to two hours, 13 buses daily, 124 EEK
Virtsu
   six hours, one bus daily, 98 EEK

Train Five trains depart daily for Tallinn
(3½ to four hours, 67 EEK). The daily
Tallinn-Šeštokai *Baltic Express* (Balti
Ekspress) departs from Tartu daily at 8.15
pm, stopping in Rīga and Kaunas en route,
and arriving in Šeštokai at 7.25 am. On its
northbound journey, the Baltic Express
leaves Šeštokai at 9.57 pm, and arrives in
Tartu at 9.28 am.

The Tallinn-Moscow *Tallinn Express*
(Tallinna Ekspress) stops at Tartu. It departs
from Tartu on even days at 6.42 pm and
arrives in Moscow the following day at 1.14
pm. On the return journey, it leaves Moscow
at 4 pm, arriving in Tartu the following day
at 8.17 am.

Three trains daily run from Tartu to Elva;
four trains daily to Valga also stop at Elva.
There are six trains daily to/from Põlva.

Getting Around
The Airport Bus No 12 runs between the
airport and bus station 14 times daily
between 6 am and 7.30 pm, a 25 minute trip.
The airport is seven or eight km south of the
city centre, a km or so west off the Võru road.

City Transport The central stop for city
buses is opposite the market, between Riia
and Vanemuise.

Car & Bicycle Rental EksRent (☎ 380 449)
at Riia 175 rents Ford Sierras and Escorts
starting at 200 EEK a day. A chauffeur is an
extra 25 EEK an hour. They are open weekdays from 10 am to 5 pm. Bicycles can be
rented from the Bike Shop next to the
Tähtvere Hotel at Laulupeo 21.

TARTU TO JÕGEVA
There are a number of places of interest on
(and not far off) the road from Tartu to
Jõgeva (population: 7000), 60 km north.
This is an alternative road route between
Tartu and Tallinn or Narva. Jõgeva and
Tabivere at the north end of **Saadjärv** – a six
km lake 20 km north of Tartu, which is one
of the beauty spots of the region, – are also
on the Tartu-Tallinn railway, with several
trains daily.

A large rock at **Äksi** on the west side of
Saadjärv is said to have been tossed there
from several leagues away by the legendary
Kalevipoeg, in a rock-throwing contest with
his two brothers.

Fourteen km north of Saadjärv is a fine
manorial park at **Luua**. In **Palamuse**, four
km beyond Luua, is a handsome, 13th
century three-naved, stone church. Also in
Palamuse is the **Oskar Luts House
Museum** which documents the life and work
of author Oskar Luts who grew up here and
wrote the *Kevade* (Spring), Estonia's most
loved novel of youth. **Kuremaa**, eight km
further north, has a lovely lake and sandy
beach, and a classical manor house with a
terraced park. Six km further north, at
Laiuse, are the fairly scanty remains of a
castle of the German knights, ruined in the
Great Northern War. Laiuse is on the road
from Jõgeva to Mustvee on Lake Peipus.

Places to Stay & Eat
The *Motel Kukulinna* (☎ 27-419 526), in a
manor dating back to 1299 at the south end
of Saadjärv, is known as having the best
outside tennis courts in the whole of Estonia.
It has four doubles at 180 EEK and three
triples at 210 EEK. Breakfast is available if
ordered and for other meals there's the *Restaurant Kukulinna*, open Tuesday to Thursday from 5 to 11 pm, Friday and Saturday
noon to 2 am, and Sunday noon to 11, am.
Boats and a sailboard can be rented.

LAKE PEIPUS (SOUTH)
Much of the southern half of the Lake Peipus
coast is marshy, but there are quite a number
of villages. Russian Old Believers, a sect of

the Orthodox Church persecuted for refusing to accept the liturgy and reforms carried out by Peter I and his successors, took refuge in **Kallaste**, the main town, in the 18th and 19th centuries and founded several of the coastal villages.

The island of **Piirisaar**, due east of Tartu, marks the south end of Lake Peipus. It used to be a refuge for young men fleeing from conscription into tsarist armies. Today the island is inhabited by 35 Russian fisher families. Fishers from the mainland village of Meerpalu are often quite happy to take you to the island for a small fee. The lake south of Piirisaar, Lämmijärv, narrows to only two km wide at Mehikoorma, where it may be possible to find a boat to Piirisaar. Further south, opposite Räpina, the waters widen out into Lake Pskov (Pihkva järv), which is mostly surrounded by Russian territory. The northern half of Lake Peipus is covered in the North-East Estonia chapter.

OTEPÄÄ
• *pop 2500* • ☎ *(276)*

The small hilltop town of Otepää, 44 km south of Tartu, is the centre of a pretty, rural area, part farmed, part forested, with many small hills and lakes. The district is popular among Estonians for country breaks and, in winter, is Estonia's major skiing resort and winter sports centre. It is protected under the Otepää Landscape Reserve, the largest reserve of its kind in Estonia.

Orientation & Information
The centre of town is the triangular main 'square', Lipuväljak, with the bus station just off its east corner. The post office is beside the bus station. The main road from Tartu enters Lipuväljak on its north corner. On Lipuväljäk you'll find the classical-style town hall, inside of which is Otepää tourist information centre (☎ 55 364; fax 61 214; email info@otepaa.turism.ee; http://www.estonia.org/otepaa). It is open all year round, on weekdays from 8.30 am to 4.30 pm. The headquarters of the Otepää Landscape Reserve (☎ 55 876) are at Kolga tee 28.

Zhoupank at Lipuväljäk 11 gives cash advance on credit cards and accepts travellers' cheques. Luggage can be left for 1 EEK an hour at Kauplus Kohvik, the café at the east end of the bus station.

Church
Otepää's pretty little 17th century church is on a small hilltop across the fields about 400m north-east of the bus station. The first church on this site was built in 1224. There's some fine timberwork and a large 1863 organ inside. It was in this church in 1884 that the Estonian Students' Society consecrated its new blue, black and white flag – which went on to become the flag of independent Estonia. Facing the church's west door is a small mound with a monument to Estonia's dead of the 1918-20 independence war.

Linnamägi
The tree-covered hill south of the church is the Linnamägi (Castle Hill), a major stronghold of the old Estonians in about the 10th to 12th centuries. There are traces of old fortifications on top, and good views of the surrounding country. Archaeological finds indicate that the area around the hill was inhabited as early as the 6th century.

Pühajärv
The islets and indented shore of 3.5-km-long Pühajärv (Holy Lake) on the south-west edge of Otepää, provide some of the area's prettiest views. The lake is circled by tracks and walkable roads. Its northern tip is just over two km along the Kääriku road from Otepää centre. The lake has a strangely mystical atmosphere that no doubt accounts for its name, and was blessed by the Dalai Lama when he came to Tartu in 1992 for a conference of unrepresented nations. The Dalai-Laama külaskaigu mälestusmärk (Dalai Lama Visit Memorial) stands on the east side of the lake. Pühajärv, legend has it, was formed from the tears of a mother whose five sons had all died in war. Its islands are their burial mounds. Pühajärv is the site of major midsummer Jaanipäev festivities every year.

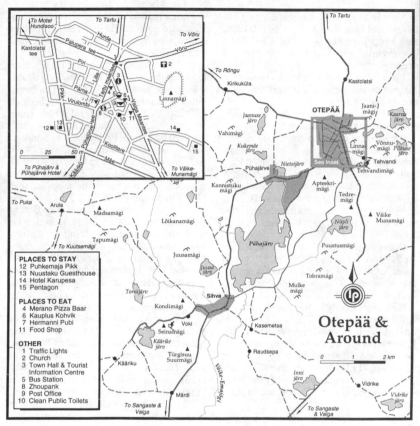

PLACES TO STAY
12 Puhkemaja Pikk
13 Nuustaku Guesthouse
14 Hotel Karupesa
15 Pentagon

PLACES TO EAT
4 Merano Pizza Baar
6 Kauplus Kohvik
7 Hermanni Pubi
11 Food Shop

OTHER
1 Traffic Lights
2 Church
3 Town Hall & Tourist
  Information Centre
5 Bus Station
8 Zhoupank
9 Post Office
10 Clean Public Toilets

Otepää &
Around

Activities

For some time now, Otepää has been the favoured winter sports centre in Estonia. Most skiing in this area is cross-country (the 60 km Tartu ski marathon begins at Otepää every February) but a ski jump looms out of the forest a km or two south of the town at **Apteekri-magi**, and there's downhill skiing available on **Kuutsemägi**, 12 km west, **Väike-Munamägi**, three km south-east of the town, and **Seinmägi**, 10 km to the south-west.

Among the top ski centres is the Kuutsemäe Sports Centre (see Places to Stay) overlooking Kuutsemägi. It charges 50 EEK for a one-day hill ticket on weekdays, and 90 EEK at weekends. Children smaller than 1.20m are free. Full ski equipment costs 70 EEK an hour or 300 a day; snowboards are 90 EEK an hour or 400 EEK a day. The centre also rents motor-sledges and arranges ski tuition. The slalom course and downhill slopes at Kuutsemägi are among the most favoured by Estonia's winter sportspeople.

The Väike-Munamäe Sports Centre (☎ & fax 55 036) at Väike-Munamägi charges 150 EEK for a one-day hill ticket valid from 9 am to 5 pm. An evening hill ticket valid from 4 pm to 8 pm is 110 EEK; a day and evening hill ticket valid from 9 am to 8 pm is 170 EEK. Full ski equipment is 100/80 EEK for a day/evening and 130 EEK for day and evening.

The Madsa Hostel (see Places to Stay) at Sihva, one km north of Seinmägi, also rents out ski equipment.

Places to Stay – in town

There are few places to stay in the centre. One option is the cheap *Nuustaku Guesthouse* (☎ 55 031; fax 461 205) at Pikk 45 which has 20 places in four small houses. A bed in a double/four-bed room costs 90/70 EEK. It also has a sauna which is 300 EEK for two hours. Prices do not include breakfast but there is a communal kitchen in each house.

Opposite at Pikk 43 is *Puhkemaja Pikk* (☎ 54 309). It has 24 beds in all (10 in one room) costing 100 EEK per person regardless of whether you sleep with one, two or nine other people!

Standing proudly at the other extreme is *Hotel Karupesa* (☎ 55 055; fax 27-44 11 66) on Tehvandi. Owned by the prestigious Finest hotel group, the newly opened hotel has luxurious single/double/triple rooms for 450/650/850 EEK including breakfast. Its a la carte restaurant is undoubtedly the finest – and most expensive – place to eat for miles around.

Places to Stay – out of town

One and a half km from Otepää centre is the 30 bed youth hostel, *Motel Hundisoo* (☎ 55 238, 55 934), open year-round at Kastolatsi tee 3. A bed in an unrenovated/renovated single room is 70/125 EEK. Both have shared bathrooms. From the traffic lights on Tartu maantee on the north side of Otepää, go 800m west down Palupera tee, then turn right on to Kastolatsi tee. The hostel is a cosy-looking, low, red-brick building on the left after half a km.

The *Pentagon* (☎ 55 431, 55 430), 1.25 km south-east of the centre, one of Estonia's top sports training centres, offers a bed in a shared room for 125 EEK. There is also a

sauna in a forest which you can rent. To reach the centre go to the far (east) end of the bus station, turn right along Valga maantee, then take the first left.

Out on the northern tip of Pühajärv, two km from the centre, is the *Pühajärve Hotel* (Holy Lake Hotel; ☎ 55 103). It is a large, rather institutional place with 180 beds at 170/290 EEK for singles/doubles from Monday night to Thursday night, and 220/390 EEK from Friday night to Sunday.

Sangaste Loss (Sangaste Castle; ☎ 91 343; fax 91 335), about 15 km south-west of the south end of Pühajärv and about 25 km from Otepää, is one of the most unusual places to stay in the Baltics. This fairy-tale brick castle, erected in Tudor-cum-Gothic style between 1874 and 1881, is said to be modelled on Britain's Windsor Castle. Singles/doubles are 350/395 EEK from Monday night to Thursday night and 450/495 EEK Friday night to Sunday night. Two buses daily run to Sangaste. Sangaste train station on the Tartu-Valga line is actually at Tsirguliina, 12 km from Sangaste.

There are a number of places to stay close to Otepää's slalom and cross-country skiing hot spots. Beyond the south end of Pühajärv, about 11 km from Otepää and just one km from Kääriku, another favoured downhill skiing area, is a *Tartu Ülikool Puhkebaas* (Tartu University Holiday Lodge; ☎ 55 196, 55 235). It has single/double rooms for 75/125 EEK.

Another of the most inviting places in winter is the *Kolga-Oru Motel* (☎ 55 213; fax 61 202), close to the Apteekri-magi ski jump on the eastern shores of Pühajärv. Singles/doubles are 500/650 EEK including private bathroom and breakfast. It has an Irish pub adjoining the motel and arranges horse riding for 200 EEK a day or 50 EEK for a one hour lesson.

The *Mäha Guesthouse* (☎ 54 003) at Mäha, about five km west of central Otepää, is a well-kept pine-panelled place with 30 beds in rooms holding three to five people. Showers are shared and a bed during the week is 130 EEK; at weekends 150 EEK. In summer it rents boats, bicycles and windsurfing equipment and, in winter, operates a small, night-lit slope served by a ski lift. To reach the guesthouse by car, fork right on to a dirt road soon after the Pühajärve Puhkekodu, then watch for the building and lake on the right (there's no sign) after about three km.

The *Kuutsemäe Sports Centre* (☎ 54 041) has shared accommodation in small cottages for 200 EEK per person on weekdays and 330 EEK at weekends. The price includes breakfast and a day ticket to the slalom hill (see Activities). One km from Kuutsemägi's slalom course and downhill slopes to the west of Pühajärv is the *Arula Motel* (☎ 54 763). Doubles with shower are 300 EEK including breakfast. It also has a sauna and swimming pool.

Places to Eat

Eating options are limited. The *Merano Pizza Baar* opposite the town hall at Tartu 1a slaps out cheap pizzas for 18 to 30 EEK. MTV blares in the background and it is the only place in town open from 9 to 5 am at weekends. *Hermanni Pubi* at Lipuväljak 10 serves a small range of light snacks and is open daily from noon to 1 am. If all else fails *Kauplus Kohvik*, the little café at the east end of the bus station has a nice choice of cakes.

Getting There & Away

Buses are Otepää's only public transport. To/from Tartu there are five or six direct buses (one hour and 10 minutes, 12 EEK). Avoid other buses going by Elva or Kanepi unless you fancy a roundabout trip.

There's a daily Tallinn-Otepää and vice versa bus via Tartu taking 4½ hours. Other places served by bus to/from Otepää include Kanepi and Valga three times daily; Kääriku, Võru, Sangaste and Pärnu twice daily; and Põlva and Viljandi once daily.

ELVA & VÕRTSJÄRV
• *pop 6500* • ☎ *(27)*

Elva, a small town in a hilly, forested landscape on the Tartu-Valga road, has two pretty lakes, Verevi and Arbi, in the middle of the town. In the depths of winter Lake Arbi becomes a skating rink. A handful of trains and a few buses daily go from Tartu to Elva. Baltic Tours travel agency (☎ 561 41) has an office at Pikk 2.

The eastern shore of Võrtsjärv, Estonia's second biggest lake (nearly 40 km long), is 35 km west of Tartu but only 15 km west of Elva.

Places to Stay & Eat

Motel Verevi (☎ 457 084), overlooking Lake Verevi in Elva at Raudsepa 2, has singles/doubles for 300/450 EEK. The bathroom is in the corridor.

The reportedly good *Motel Vehendi* (☎ 454 556; fax 434 288) is on the eastern shore of Võrtsjärv, due west of Elva and 43 km from Tartu. It's a converted old farmhouse, 600m from a swimming beach. There are six double/triple rooms at 360/430 EEK. Prices include breakfast and other meals are available if ordered. You can book through the Taru Hotel in Tartu.

Two km from Elva towards Rannu, a hamlet with a couple of pretty little lakes on the Elva-Vehendi road six km before Võrtsjärv, is the *Waide Motel* (☎ 457 119, 460 574). It has 11 double rooms including three with water beds, for 200 EEK per person including breakfast and a one-hour sauna. Facilities include fishing, rowing and paddleboat rental, bicycle rental, tennis, mini-golf and ski hire.

VALGA
• *pop 16,500* • ☎ *(276)*

The border town of Valga, contiguous with Valka in Latvia, is where the Rīga-Tartu road and the main railway from Rīga and the south enter Estonia. The only sites of interest include the 19th century Jaani kirik (St John's Church), and a local history museum (Valga Koduloomuuseum). An estimated 30,000 people were murdered at the Nazi death camp Stalag-351, in converted stables at Priimetsa on Valga's outskirts. The train station was built after the war by German prisoners. The headquarters of the Karula National Park is also in Valga (see

Paganamaa, Mõniste & Karula National Park later in this chapter).

One bus daily runs between Tartu and Valga (1¾ hours, 64 EEK) and four trains daily. The Baltic Express passes through Valga daily, as does a daily St Petersburg-Rīga train.

PÕLVA & TAEVASKOJA
• pop 7000 • ☎ (279)

Põlva lies in an attractive valley 50 km south-east of Tartu. Its typical country church dates from 1452.

Taevaskoja, seven km north of Põlva, is in the picturesque valley of the Ahja river which is noted for rapids and sandstone cliffs up to 20m high. You can walk up the river to Kiidjärve, six km north of Taevaskoja, where there's a working water mill built in 1909. At Karilatsi, 15 km north-west of Põlva on the Tartu road, is the **Põlva Museum of Peasant Life**. For updated information call the Põlva Express Hotline (☎ 95 222).

Places to Stay & Eat
The *Hotel Pesa* (☎ 90 086, fax 90 087), in Põlva at Uus 5, is a 1991 hotel with good service, good food in its own restaurant, and 24 singles/doubles with private bathroom and TV at 490/540 EEK. The *Põlva Restoran* and *Café Paus* at Kesk 10 provide other eating possibilities. A few doors down at Kesk 5 is the *Baar Kella*.

At Taevaskoja there's a youth hostel, the *Taevaskoja* (☎ 92 067), with 33 beds, two to four to a room, at 100 EEK per person. It's a wooden building, with showers and a sauna, about half a km east along the road from Taevaskoja train station. The hostel is open all year round.

Getting There & Away
From Tartu you can reach Põlva by bus (1¼ hours, 12 times daily, 16 EEK) or train (¾ to 1¼ hours, four daily).

The Tallinn-Moscow Tallinn Express stops at Põlva, departing from Põlva on even days at 7.23 pm and arriving in Moscow the following day at 1.14 pm. On the return

journey, it leaves Moscow at 4 pm, arriving in Põlva the following day at 7.33 am.

Taevaskoja is two km east of the Tartu-Põlva road, which is the nearest a bus would get you. There are three buses daily between Põlva and Võru, one between Põlva and Otepää and one between Põlva and Tallinn (4½ hours, 33 EEK).

VÕRU
• pop 16,977 • ☎ (278)

Võru, 64 km south of Tartu on the eastern shore of Tamula järv, is a simple provincial town and a possible base for visiting interesting points in Estonia's far south-east. The town was the home of Friedrich Reinhold Kreutzwald (1803-82), the father of Estonian literature for his folk epic *Kalevipoeg*. His home at Kreutzwaldi 31 is now the **Kreutzwald Memorial Museum**. In more recent years, Võru has become known in Estonia as the town which lost practically its entire town council in the 1994 *Estonia* ferry disaster. In front of the 18th century **Lutheran church** overlooking the central square, is a **granite monument** to the 17 officials from Võru who died while on a working retreat aboard the ill-fated vessel. Ten km south-east of Võru is Kütiorg, a popular lakeside resort and favoured spot for skiers and winter sports enthusiasts.

Võru tourist information centre (☎ & fax 21 881; email info@werro.turism.ee; http://www.estonia.org/werro) is at Tartu 31. The Hermes travel agency (☎ 21 326; fax 24 468) at Jüri 32a arranges tours, accommodation and skiing expeditions. Arctic Cat (☎ & fax 21 959) at Räpina 22 rents out motorised snow bikes and organises 100 km snow-safari tours. Toonus Pluss (☎ 25-255 702, 276-57 263) specialises in canoeing trips for all ages and abilities. Routes include from Võru to Räpina, Räpina to Tartu and Põlva to Värska.

Places to Stay & Eat
The tourist information centre and the Võru Farm Tourism Association (☎ 42 469, fax 22 928), part of the Estonian Ecotourism Association, at Liiva 11, arrange accommodation

in and around Võru. The *Hermes Guesthouse* (☎ 21 326; fax 23 231) at Jüri 32a has fully equipped singles/doubles/triples for 350/480/800 EEK. The *Wermo Guesthouse* (☎ 23 418) close to the Lutheran church at Koidula 6 has singles/doubles for 180/280 EEK. Bathrooms are shared between two rooms.

Huundijalg at Jüri 18b is a traditional beer bar-cum-contemporary pub serving great seljanka for 12 EEK as well as shashlik and other charcoal-grilled meats while you wait (open daily from 10 am to 11 pm). *Võru Kohvik*, inside the main post office building at Jüri 38, is a cosy cottage-style café serving a delicious array of freshly baked cakes and other light snacks.

Out of town is the *Võru Turismikeskus* (Võru Tourist Centre, ☎ 23 757, 58 581; fax 24 498), four km south of the centre at Männiku 43, which has single/double/triple rooms with private bathroom and balcony for 370/460/465 EEK including breakfast. It

also has double/triple/four-bed wooden cabins, available from June to September, for 180/240/280 EEK not including breakfast. The centre rents out canoes, water bikes and camping equipment.

At Kütiorg, *Motel Walla* (☎ 241-19 398, 241-22 364) has double rooms with private bath for 300 EEK. It arranges horse riding, canoe trips and hiking in summer, and in winter, downhill skiing.

Getting There & Away

There are seven or eight buses daily to/from Tartu via Kanepi (1½ hours, 22 EEK), four to six daily to/from Tallinn (4½ hours, 78 EEK), three daily to/from Põlva (4½ hours, 33 EEK), two to/from Otepää, and two to/from Pärnu (four to 4½ hours, 86 EEK).

Võru is about an hour from Valga by train, with four trains each way daily (16.20 EEK). There is a daily train to/from Rīga (four hours, 106.20 EEK) and St Petersburg (6½ hours, 111.40 EEK). Other stops on this

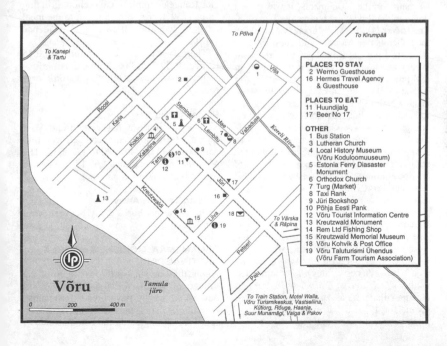

PLACES TO STAY
2 Wermo Guesthouse
16 Hermes Travel Agency & Guesthouse

PLACES TO EAT
11 Huundijalg
17 Beer No 17

OTHER
1 Bus Station
3 Lutheran Church
4 Local History Museum (Võru Koduloomuuseum)
5 Estonia Ferry Diasaster Monument
6 Orthodox Church
7 Turg (Market)
8 Taxi Rank
9 Jüri Bookshop
10 Põhja Eesti Pank
12 Võru Tourist Information Centre
13 Kreutzwald Monument
14 Rem Ltd Fishing Shop
15 Kreutzwald Memorial Museum
18 Võru Kohvik & Post Office
19 Võru Taluturismi Ühendus (Võru Farm Tourism Association)

Võru

Tamula järv

To Põlva
To Kirumpää
To Kanepi & Tartu
To Värska & Räpina
To Train Station, Motel Walla, Võru Turismikeskus, Vastseliina, Kütiorg, Rõuge, Haanja, Suur Munamägi, Valga & Pskov

Koreli River

0   200   400 m

route include Valga, Valmiera, Cēsis and Sigulda in Latvia, and Pechory (Estonian: Petseri) in Russia.

SUUR MUNAMÄGI & HAANJA

Suur Munamägi, 17 km south of Võru, is the highest hill in the Baltic states at just over 318m. It's part of the Haanja Upland lying between Võru and the Latvian border, which has three other hills over 290m. Suur Munamägi literally means Great Egg Hill, and indeed from a distance it looks not unlike the top of an eggshell. It's covered in trees, which makes it excusable that there's an ugly 29m observation tower which was plonked on its very summit in 1939.

The summit and tower are a 10 minute climb from the Võru-Ruusmäe road, starting about a km south of the village of Haanja. Near the start of the path is a **monument** to the dead of the Battle of Munamägi in Estonia's 1918-20 independence war. Like so many similar monuments, it was pulled down in the Soviet era but restored in 1988. The **tower** (☎ 78 847) is open from 10 May to 15 October on Monday and Tuesday from 10 am to 1 pm and from 2 pm to 7 pm. From Wednesday to Sunday it is open from 9 am to 8 pm.

The whole of this upland region forms the Haanja Nature Park, an area which is transformed into a bustling ski resort in winter, complete with two ski lifts and even an artificial snow generator! Over the next four years US$1.7 million will be invested in the resort. The mailing address for the park headquarters (☎ 21 209) is PO Box 37 Võrumaa Post, EE-2710, Võru.

Places to Stay

The Võru Farm Tourism Association and Võru tourist information centre offer rooms in farmhouses within a few km of Haanja (see Võru – Places to Stay). Recommended is the *Utsal Tourist Farm* (☎ 78 803) in Haanja village. It has seven places in shared rooms for 170 EEK a night, and lets you pitch your tent for a small fee.

Getting There & Away

There are a few buses a day from Võru to Haanja, just north of Suur Munamägi, or Ruusmäe. The Estonian Ecotourism Association arranges a number of fun eco-tours to the Haanja Nature Park, including bicycle treks and skiing trips (see Facts for the Visitor at the front of the book for details).

RÕUGE

• *pop 2360* • ☎ (278)

Ten km west of Suur Munamägi by dirt road, or reachable by paved road from Võru, the village of Rõuge stands on the edge of the Ööbikuorg (Nightingale Valley), so called for its singing spring nightingales, and strung with a chain of seven lakes. Suurjärv, near the village, is Estonia's deepest lake at 38m. Rõuge's Linnamägi (Castle Hill), by the lake Linnjärv, was an ancient Estonian stronghold in the 8th to 11th centuries. Nightingales gather near it in spring and there's a good view along the valley. Opposite Rõuge's simple village church, dating from 1730, there's a monument to the local dead of Estonia's 1918-20 independence war.

There is a tourist information centre in Rõuge (☎ 59 245; fax 22 669; email info@rouge.turism.ee; http://www.estonia.org/rouge).

Places to Stay

Võru Farm Tourism Association and Võru tourist information centre can help you find somewhere to stay for 120 to 175 EEK. The *Mae Tualu* tourist farm (☎ 59 150) in Rõuge has beds for 180 EEK a night.

Getting There & Away

There are a few buses a day between Võru and Rõuge.

PAGANAMAA, MÕNISTE & KARULA NATIONAL PARK

Along the Latvian border just south of the village of Krabi, which is some 20 km beyond Rõuge by paved road, Paganamaa (Devil's Land) is another scenic area with four lakes strung along the Estonian side of the border in the Piiriorg valley. The area forms the Paganamaa Landscape Reserve whose headquarters (☎ 31 841) are in Võru at Karja 17a. There's an observation tower and bathing spot at Liivajärv, one of the lakes.

Mõniste, on the Võru-Valga road and 15 km west of Krabi, has an open-air village museum (Mõniste Külamuuseum), open daily, except Monday, from 10 May to 1 October. It displays 19th century life on a southern Estonian farm.

About 12 km along dirt roads north of Mõniste is an area of round, wooded hills dotted with many small lakes which forms the **Karula National Park**. The highlight is Ähijärv, a three-km-long lake with several bays, inlets and promontories. This area can also be reached from Antsla, a similar distance to its north. The park headquarters (☎ 242-439 07) at Keskuse 16 in Valga provides information on the park.

VASTSELIINA CASTLE

The picturesque ruins of Vastseliina Castle (Vastseliina linnus), founded by the Germans on their border with Russia in the 14th century, stand on a high bluff above the Piusa River on the eastern edge of the village of Vahtseliina, five km east of the small town of Vastseliina. German, Russian and Swedish soldiers fought many battles over the centuries for control of this stronghold.

The castle stands behind a long, low 19th century inn building on the Meremäe road out of Vahtseliina. In the valley bottom, down to the left as you walk from the former inn to the castle, is the park of the old Vastseliina manor.

Vastseliina town has a big classical-style town hall in its centre.

Getting There & Away

To reach Vahtseliina turn east off the Võru-Pskov (Pihkva) road a km south of the southernmost turning to Vastseliina (which is just west of the road), and go two km. Several buses daily from Võru go to Vast-seliina and some, including most of those to

Misso, continue along the Pskov road to the Vahtseliina turning and beyond.

HINO JÄRV

Hino järv, two km south of Misso which is on the A212 Pskov-Rīga road, is one of southern Estonia's most picturesque lakes, with eight islands dotting its three km length. There are a few buses from Võru to Misso. Near Hino järv is the Kõõgumägi stronghold, a fortification likely raised by native tribes in the late 13th or early 14th century.

SETUMAA

Setumaa is the name of an area in far southeast Estonia, stretching over into Russia. Its people, the Setu, have a mixed Estonian-Russian culture and speak a dialect quite distinct from mainstream Estonian. Setumaa is particularly known for its women folk singers who improvise new words each time they chant their verses. All of Setumaa was in independent Estonia between 1920 and 1940 but the greater part of it is now in Russia. The town of **Pechory** (Estonian: Petseri), two km across the border in Russia, is regarded as the 'capital' of Setumaa. It is famed for its fabulous 15th century cave-monastery, considered one of the most breathtaking in Russia. The Sunday church service, held at 10 am, is well worth attending. Estonian Setumaa, roughly speaking, is the area east of a line extending north from Vahtseliina to the small town of Võõpsu, just east of Räpina near Lake Pskov. You need a Russian visa to go there – see Facts for the Visitor at the front of the book for details.

The town of **Värska** is known for its mineral water, drunk throughout Estonia, and its healing mud baths. **Võporzova** and **Tona** a few km north of Värska on the west side of Värska Bay, are classic Setu villages. In **Obinitsa** there is a Setu Museum (☎ 241-62 241) and a sculpture to the Setu 'Song Mother', both of which are well worth visiting. In **Võporzova** there's a monument to the folk singer Anne Vabarna who knew 100,000 verses by heart. Võporzova homesteads typically consist of a ring of outer buildings around an inner yard – a formation which has

The Day of the Setus

The Setus are a small Finno-Ugric tribe living in the (politically unrecognised) homeland of Setumaa, which is divided by the Estonian-Russian border. Today, as a result, 5000 Setus live in south-east Estonia and in Russia, where the Setumaa capital of Petseri (Pechory) stands, are a further 3000.

Peko, the pagan god of fertility, is as important to the Setus as the Russian Orthodox religion they adhere to. The 8000-line Setu epic *Pekolanõ* tells the tale of this macho god, the rites of whom are only known to men. The epic dates back to 1927 when the Setu's most celebrated folk singer, Anne Vabarna, was told the plot and spontaneously burst into song, barely pausing to draw breath until she had sung the last (8000th) line.

The Setus don't have a proper king: he sleeps night and day in his cave of sand, according to traditional Setu folklore. So, on the Day of the Setu Kingdom – proclaimed around 20 August each year – a *ülemtsootska* (representative) for the king has to be found. The Setus then gather around the statue of their 'song mother' in search of a singer worthy of being crowned the sleeping king's royal singer. Competitions of a less aesthetically pleasing nature are later held to find a strongman for the king.

The Setu king's dress, and the bread, cheese, wine and beer he eats and drinks are important too. On the same day that his kingdom is declared for another year, people from the Setu stronghold are selected to serve the king as his mitten and belt knitters, and bread, beer, wine and cheese makers.

And so completes the royal throne. Amid the day's glorious celebrations, traditional Setu songs are sung, dances danced and customary well-wishes exchanged. The women are adorned with traditional Setu lace and large silver breast plates and necklaces, said to weigh as much as two or three kilograms each. Later in the day respects are paid to the dead – any good Setu will tell you to never visit a grave without partaking in a small meal in front of it and leaving a small part of it behind on the gravestone for the deceased.

In 1996, the Setu community made steps to join the Unrepresented Nations & Peoples Organisation (UNPO), a worldwide organisation serving to unite unrepresented peoples such as Chechens, Kurds and Setus. The community was inaugurated as a member in early 1997. ∎

defensive purposes – while Tona's houses all face the lake from which its people derive their livelihood.

Traditional Setu holidays are still celebrated. The biggest feast of the year, Lady Day, falls on 28 August, close to which the Day of the Setu Kingdom is held. The Day of the Setu Lace is 1 March and midsummer celebrations are held on 6 July in accordance with the old calendar (see The Day of the Setus aside above).

Getting There & Away

The Hermes Reisid travel agency in Võru (see Võru – Travel Agencies) arranges day trips to the Pechory Monastery. Trips have to be booked about two weeks in advance to sort out a Russian visa for you.

There are three buses a day each way between Tartu and Värska, taking two hours via Räpina. Buses from Tartu do not cross the border into Russia – they stop at Koidula, two km from Pechory. Three buses daily make the two and a half hour journey, costing 38 EEK. From Võru, a Meremäe-Obinitsa bus departs daily at 5.55 am and 2.30 pm. On the return journey, the bus leaves Obinitsa 7.35 am and 4.10 pm.

The Tallinn-Moscow and St Petersburg-Rīga trains both stop at Pechory. You need a Russian visa to visit Pechory (see Facts for the Visitor at the front of the book for details).

West Estonia & the Islands

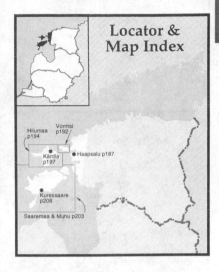

Locator & Map Index

Hiiumaa p194 · Vormsi p192 · Kärdla p197 · Haapsalu p187 · Kuressaare p208 · Saaremaa & Muhu p203

West Estonia is the most intriguing part of provincial Estonia. The large islands of Hiiumaa and particularly Saaremaa, with their trademark windmills, juniper groves, old-fashioned rural pace and coastal vistas stretching gently away into infinity, are close to the Estonian idea of an earthly paradise. They're also historically interesting and claim to enjoy more sunshine than the mainland. Less discovered, smaller islands – among them the Vilsandi National Park – and much of the mainland coast, including the historic town of Haapsalu and the Matsalu Nature Reserve – an important water bird sanctuary – are also rewarding to explore.

The Biosphere Reserve of the West Estonian Archipelago was set up in 1989 to protect the natural wonders of Saaremaa, Hiiumaa, Muhu, Vormsi and the hundreds of islets around them (see the Facts about Estonia chapter).

The whole region is extremely low lying. In fact when the Baltic Sea was formed about 7000 years ago most of the region still lay beneath the waves. A bit of Saaremaa and a small part of the mainland existed as land but Hiiumaa was still sea-bed. Since then the region has been gradually rising from the sea – currently by about three mm a year – owing to a slow lifting of the earth's crust.

Several travel agencies in Tallinn and the larger towns on the islands arrange tours to the west Estonian islands (see Travel Agencies in the Tallinn, Kärdla & Kuressaare sections). The Ecotourism Association also arranges some fun eco-tours here (see Facts for the Visitor at the front of the book).

HAAPSALU
• *pop 13,600* • ☎ *(247)*

Haapsalu stands on a peninsula jutting out into Haapsalu Bay, a 15 km inlet on Estonia's west coast. It has been the dominant settlement in west Estonia since the 1260s, when it was chosen as the centre for the Ösel-Wiek (Estonian: Saare-Lääne) bishopric, through which the Archbishop of Rīga controlled most of west Estonia and its offshore islands. During the 19th century this small sleepy town was a bustling spa resort, famous for its curative mud baths.

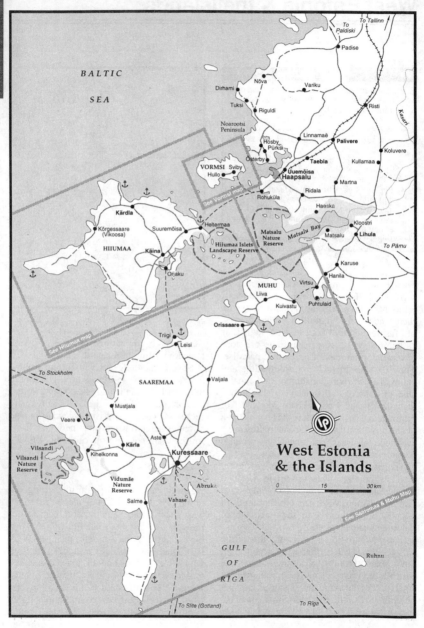

BALTIC

SEA

To Tallinn

To Paldiski

Padise

Nõva

Variku

Dirhami

Tuksi

Riguldi

Risti

Kasari

Noarootsi
Peninsula

Linnamäe

Hosby
Pürksi

Palivere

Koluvere

Österby

Taebla

Kullamaa

VORMSI Sviby

Üuemõisa
Haapsalu

Hullo

Martna

See Vormsi map

Ridala

Rohuküla

Haeska

Kloostri

Kärdla

Suuremõisa

Heltermaa

Lihula

Körgessaare
(Vikoosa)

Matsalu

To Pärnu

Hiiumaa Islets
Landscape Reserve

Matsalu
Nature
Reserve

Matsalu Bay

HIIUMAA

Käina

Karuse

Orjaku

Hanila

MUHU

Virtsu

Liiva

Kuivastu

Puhtulaid

See Hiiumaa map

To Stockholm

Triigi

Orissaare

Leisi

SAAREMAA

Valjala

Mustjala

Veere

Aste

Vilsandi

Kärla

Vilsandi
Nature
Reserve

Kihelkonna

Kuressaare

West Estonia
& the Islands

Vidumäe
Nature
Reserve

Abruka

0   15   30 km

Salme

Vahase

See Saaremaa & Muhu Map

GULF

OF

RIGA

Ruhnu

To Slite (Gotland)

To Riga

Today Haapsalu, with a fine castle and cathedral to remind us of its powerful past, is a pleasant place to stop for a few hours or a night on your way to or from Hiiumaa. It's also a good base for visiting Vormsi island, Noarootsi, Matsalu Nature Reserve or other places in west Estonia.

History

Following the Knights of the Swords' conquest of this region in 1224, the Ösel-Wiek bishopric, covering west Estonia and its offshore islands, was formed in 1228. For over 300 years the bishops ruled the region, except for a few areas on the islands and one small mainland area which belonged to the knights under a 1238 deal with the bishop.

Haapsalu became the bishop's residence in the 1260s and a bishop's fortress and cathedral were built soon afterwards. The town around it developed with Germans as merchants and artisans, Estonians and Swedes as the lower classes. At the start of the Livonian War in 1559 the last bishop sold his territory to the Danish king Frederick II who, in turn, gave it to his brother Duke Magnus. During the war, which lasted until 1583, west Estonia lost two-thirds of its population. During the 17th century most of the region ended up in Swedish hands and some of the war damage was reversed.

At the beginning of the 18th century the region fell under Russian control during the Great Northern War. In the 19th century Haapsalu became a spa when the curative properties of its shoreline mud were made known by Dr Carl Abraham Hunnius. Tchaikovsky and members of the Russian imperial family came for Haapsalu mud baths. A railway from Tallinn and St Petersburg was built in 1904-07 and a 216m-long covered platform, said to be the longest in the former Russian empire, was built at Haapsalu station to shelter eminent arrivals. The covered platform with its wooden lace ornaments and grand colonnade is now under state protection as an architectural monument. In the Soviet era the town's population more than doubled, but the development

> ### Swedish Influence
> West Estonia was home to most of Estonia's small Swedish population, who began settling along the coasts of the mainland and islands in the 13th century.
> In 1934, 5312 of Estonia's 7641 Swedes lived in this region, mostly as fishers and peasants. However, the Estonian Swedes left en masse for Sweden in 1944 before the Red Army occupied Estonia.
> It was partly in recognition of the region's historical link with their country that Sweden's King Carl XVI Gustaf and Queen Silvia came to Haapsalu in April 1992 on the first royal visit to independent Estonia. ■

took place away from the historic centre. A military air base nearby meant that Haapsalu was off limits for foreign tourists.

Orientation

The traffic lights at the crossroads, where the road from Tallinn reaches central Haapsalu, are a good landmark. The tourist information office and main hotel are just north of this junction on Posti, which leads to the castle and the heart of the Old Town a km further north. The bus station is half a km west along Jaama. Lihula maantee, south from the traffic lights, is the main road out of Haapsalu in that direction.

Information

Tourist Office The tourist information centre (☎ 45 248; fax 45 464; email info@ haapsalu.turism.ee; http://www. estonia.org/ haapsalu) is at Posti 39. Between May and September it opens daily, except Sunday, from 9 am to 6 pm. From October to April, it is open daily, except Saturday and Sunday, from 9 am to 3 pm. Out of hours, call Haapsalu Express Hotline (☎ 55 700).

Money You can change money in the Haapsalu Hotel and in some banks. Eesti Ühispank at Karja 27 and Zhoupank at Posti 41 give cash advances on credit card;

Tallinna Pank at Lihula 3 cashes travellers' cheques.

Post & Communications The post office is at Posti 1. It sells chip cards for the public card phones dotted all over town.

Travel Agencies Ritta Reisid (☎ 44 710) is at Posti 15. Haapsalu Travel Service (☎ 45 037; fax 44 335) at Karja 7 organises car rental for 500 EEK a day including mileage, and books accommodation all over Estonia. It also arranges a variety of tours including a day trip to Vormsi Island for 320 EEK, a three day tour of Estonian manor houses costing 1700 EEK and a one week cycling tour of west Estonia for 2840 EEK. It takes bookings for Estonian Ecotourism Association tours.

Castle & Cathedral
The focus of the Old Town and Haapsalu's main sight is the Episcopal castle (piiskopilinnus) dating to 1279 and surrounded by a circular wall, 803m in length and 10m high. Today, the castle – known as Bishop's Castle – is ruined, but one picturesquely turreted tower, most of the outer wall and some of the moat remain. In the castle grounds is a modern song stage, still in use.

Within the castle ruins stands a Roman-Gothic cathedral, considered to be Haapsalu's most impressive building and the largest single knaved church in the Baltics. Its integration into the episcopal stronghold from the very start (in the second half of the 13th century) shows just how lukewarm a welcome Christianity received when it was imported to these parts.

Today the cathedral is open to visitors at weekends from noon to 4 pm. It was badly damaged in 1563 during the Livonian War, restored in the first half of the 17th century by the Swedish owner of Haapsalu, Count Jakob de la Gardie, and badly damaged again by a fire in 1688 and a storm in 1726 which tore off its roof.

On the south-west side of the cathedral is a wooden statue of a mother holding a babe in arms – a memorial to those deported to

Siberia during WWII. Above the statue is Haapsalu's most famous window. Every August, at full moon, hundreds of revellers gather below this window to await the appearance of Haapsalu's ghostly White Lady, the lover of a monk from the castle. She was walled up within the castle walls for the sin of entering a male preserve.

Museum
Haapsalu's Läänemaa Museum is at Kooli 2, in the former town hall at the east end of Lossi plats, and was built in 1775. The museum gives an informative glimpse of the town's history from prehistoric times to the present. It's open Wednesday to Sunday, from 11 am to 5 pm.

Other Sights
The streets in the area round the castle are the hub of the Old Town. On Neidude is a former courthouse built in 1787 while the house at Saue 11 dates from 1782. Between Kooli and Jaani, east off Lossi plats, is the 16th century **Jaani kirik** (St John's Church).

On the shore north of here is a **park** with **Aafrikarand** (Africa Beach) at its east end, the 1905 **Kuursaal** (Spa Hall) at its west end, and a **promenade** that once led as far north as the **yacht club**. Sculptures dating to Haapsalu's most fashionable era are dotted along the promenade, including a sundial commemorating mud-cure pioneer Dr Carl Abraham Hunnius and the **Tchaikovsky bench**, put up in memory of the composer in 1940.

On the west edge of the town, beyond the train station, is the **Paralepa forest park** with a beach frontage good for walks. Also this way, near the former air base, are the ruins of **Ungru Castle** which, according to legend, had such fine gardens that even Peter the Great came to see them.

Special Events
In July the town plays host to a summer music festival and also 'Medieval Haapsalu', a three day music, arts and crafts festival. At the beginning of August is a blues music festival. The biggest event of the year is

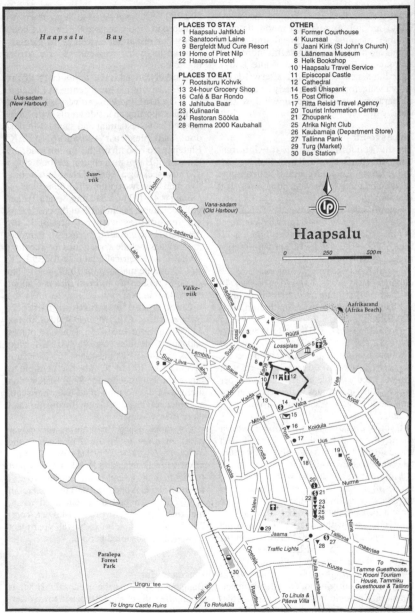

PLACES TO STAY
1   Haapsalu Jahtklubi
2   Sanatoorium Laine
9   Bergfeldt Mud Cure Resort
19 Home of Piret Nilp
22 Haapsalu Hotel

PLACES TO EAT
7   Rootsituru Kohvik
13 24-hour Grocery Shop
16 Café & Bar Rondo
18 Jahituba Baar
23 Kulinaaria
24 Restoran Söökla
28 Remma 2000 Kaubahall

OTHER
3   Former Courthouse
4   Kuursaal
5   Jaani Kirik (St John's Church)
6   Läänemaa Museum
8   Helk Bookshop
10 Haapsalu Travel Service
11 Episcopal Castle
12 Cathedral
14 Eesti Ühispank
15 Post Office
17 Ritta Reisid Travel Agency
20 Tourist Information Centre
21 Zhoupank
25 Afrika Night Club
26 Kaubamaja (Department Store)
27 Tallinna Pank
29 Turg (Market)
30 Bus Station

Haapsalu Bay

Uus-sadam
(New Harbour)

Suur-
viik

Vana-sadam
(Old Harbour)

Uus-sadama

Haapsalu

0   250   500 m

Väike-
viik

Aafrikarand
(Afrika Beach)

Rüütli

Lossiplats

Tamme Guesthouse,
Krooni Tourism
House, Tammiku
Guesthouse & Tallinn

Paralepa
Forest
Park

Ungru tee

To Ungru Castle Ruins   To Rohuküla

To Lihula &
Päeva Villa

Traffic Lights

Jaama

Valge Daami Päevad (Days of the White Lady) around August full-moon time. A number of musical, cultural and sports events are held, climaxing at full moon with a drama, *Valge Daam* (The White Lady), staged in the castle grounds. Afterwards the crowd waits for the White Lady to make her appearance at the cathedral window (she usually does).

Places to Stay

The tourist information centre (see Information) and the Haapsalu Travel Service (see Information – Travel Agencies) both arrange accommodation in private homes for 100 EEK a night.

The *Tamme Guesthouse* (☎ 57 550, 55 410), a five minute walk from the centre at Tamme 10a, is a small modern house with nine beds costing 150 EEK. The bathroom is in the corridor.

Smaller, but extremely comfortable, is the quaint wooden home of *Mrs Piret Nilp* (☎ 44 842, 45 339) at Luha 3a. A night in a single or shared room with shared bathroom costs 100 EEK.

Haapsalu Jahtklubi (Haapsalu Yacht Club; ☎ 45 582, fax 45 536), at Holmi 5A, just over a km north of the castle, offers cheap accommodation in jaded, wood-panelled rooms with two beds and a double bunk for 140 EEK per person. Bus No 2 comes to the nearby Holmi stop about every 45 minutes from Posti maantee.

If you're in a large group, try *Krooni Tourism House* (☎ 56 837; fax 44 294) at Lehise 8. The house sleeps 10 and you can only rent the entire thing for 900 EEK a night.

More upmarket is the *Päeva Villa* (☎ 45 244; fax 45 484) at Lai 7. The guesthouse has two buildings, one which is newer, plusher and more expensive than the other. The cheapest singles/doubles with private bathroom in the older building cost 250/400 EEK; and in the newer building 400/790 EEK.

Top of the range is Haapsalu's main hotel, *Haapsalu Hotel* (☎ 44 847; fax 45 191) at Posti 43. It is a bright modern establishment. Spacious single/double rooms cost 450/650 EEK between January and March, and

500/700 EEK from April to September. An extra bed in a room costs 200 EEK. The hotel runs a fine restaurant as well as the pleasant Monica lobby-bar and next door's Afrika nightclub.

Similarly priced is the *Tammiku* (☎ & fax 56 773), east of the town centre at Ehitajate 3a. It is a large, modern and very white hotel complex sporting an inside tennis court, conference halls, restaurant and sauna. Singles/doubles/triples cost 400/550/650 EEK. Ehitajate tee is south off the Tallinn road, 2.5 km east of Haapsalu's central traffic lights.

Those seeking a touch of Haapsalu's curative mud have two options. The *Sanatoorium Laine* (☎ 45 191) on Sadama beside Väikeviik lake, about 600m north of the castle, has singles/doubles with private bath for 250/380 EEK including breakfast. Pampering services include a one hour sauna costing 70 EEK, an electrical mud bath for 65 EEK and 25 minute massage for 70 EEK. Bus No 2 comes up here from Posti maantee about every 45 minutes.

Smaller and less institution-like is *Bergfeldt Mud Cure Resort* (☎ 45 830; fax 44 764) at Suur Liiva 15a. It has 16 places and singles/doubles cost 295/460 EEK. Mud baths are 140 EEK, massages 150 EEK and herbal baths 100 EEK. It is also possible to buy a six day voucher for 3820 EEK which includes a daily sauna, mud bath, massage, a choice of three different treatments and three meals a day.

For those using Haapsalu as a stopover point en route to Hiiumaa or Vormsi, the *Rohuküla Hotel* (☎ 57 601; fax 91 124) nine km west of Haapsalu at Rohuküla ferry port from where the island-bound ferries leave, is a handy place. A bed in an unrenovated room is 100 EEK; a bed in a renovated room, meaning you have a private shower, costs 250 EEK. The hotel also has an apartment equipped for disabled people.

Places to Eat

Bang next door to the Haapsalu Hotel is *Kulinaaria*, the cheapest place in town offering little frills but more than filling central-Asian style plov and hamburgers for around 9 EEK.

Handy for breakfast is the more upmarket *Café Rondo* at Posti 7. Freshly baked apple cakes cost 1.80 EEK, coffee is 3 EEK and cinnamon buns 2 EEK. It opens daily from 7 am to 7 pm, except on Saturday, when it opens at 9 am. The downstairs *Bar Rondo*, open Monday to Thursday from 11 am to 11 pm and Friday and Saturday from 11 to 2 am, is popular too.

The menu of *Restoran Söökla*, Posti 41, is small and unappealing but great if you're on a tight budget. The next door bar under the same management has a billiard table.

Meat eaters should try the brightly painted *Jahituba Baar* at Posti 29. A wholesome variety of smoked sausages, livers dipped in egg and meat cutlets for no more than 28 EEK are served from this cosy cabin-style wooden hut.

Considered one of the finest places in town is the *Rootsituru Kohvik* (Swedish Café) in front of the castle at Karja 3, although if you are looking for traditional Estonian cooking you'll leave disappointed. Everything comes served with extremely chunky French fries be it fried eggs, Vienna sausage or omelette. Pickled eel costs 35 EEK and a big sandwich with beef, fish and lettuce is 16 EEK. A pianist sometimes plays at weekends.

A small but well stocked 24-hour *grocery shop* is on the corner of Kalda and Karja maantee, not far from the castle. The *Remma 2000 Kaubahall* (supermarket) is close to the traffic lights at Lihula 3 (open daily from 9 am to 9 pm).

Getting There & Away

By car Haapsalu is an easy 105 km drive (about 1½ hours) from Tallinn along a good road. Otherwise you can reach it by bus. The bus station is at Jaama 1 inside the grandiose train station that is no longer in use; the ticket office is inside the main building of the Emperor's Pavilion.

Bus There are around 10 buses daily to/from Tallinn (1¾ hours, 34 EEK). Avoid the ones going via Keila (2¾ hours) or Nõva (3½ hours) unless you want a roundabout trip. Buses between Haapsalu and other main destinations include:

Kärdla
    2¾ hours, two buses each way daily, 40 EEK
Pärnu
    three hours, one or two buses each way daily, 42 EEK
Tartu
    5¾ hours, one bus each way daily, 92 EEK
Virtsu
    two hours, two buses each way daily, 20 EEK

Boat Ferries to the islands of Hiiumaa and Vormsi leave from Rohuküla, nine km west of Haapsalu. Information is given in the Hiiumaa and Vormsi sections.

Getting Around

Haapsalu is small enough for most people to walk around, unless perhaps you're staying up at the sanatorium or the yacht club, which you can reach by bus No 2, about every 45 minutes from Posti maantee. Bus No 1 runs almost hourly (though less often at weekends) between Lossi plats, the train station, and Rohuküla which is the harbour for ferries to Hiiumaa, and is several km out of Haapsalu. Bus No 1 timetables are posted at Lossi plats and the bus station. Bus No 3 goes about hourly between the bus station and the cinema in the Old Town, near the castle.

AROUND HAAPSALU
Taebla

A km south of the Haapsalu-Tallinn road, about 10 km from Haapsalu and two km west of Taebla, is **Ants Laikmaa majamuuseum** (☎ 96 688), the eccentric house of the artist Ants Laikmaa (1866-1942) who, among other things, walked more than 2600 km from Rīga to Düsseldorf in Germany (in six weeks apparently) to learn art there. His house has been turned into a gallery-museum which is worth a visit. It is open between May and September, Wednesday to Sunday from 10 am to 6 pm. Between October and April it closes at 4 pm.

Ridala

Ridala, nestled between the bays of Matsalu and Haapsalu, is 7 km south of Haapsalu on the Lihula road. The church at Ridala is typical of those built in west Estonia in the second half of the 13th century, the early years of the Ösel-Wiek bishopric. Tall and plain, these churches were based on the design of churches in Westphalia, Germany. The stonework of the west doorway is particularly fine, and there's some good wood carving inside including a 1650s pulpit made in Tallinn.

Also situated at Ridala are the remains of an ancient Estonian stronghold called Tubrilinn.

Places to Stay

The tourist information centre and Haapsalu Travel Service both arrange accommodation in Taebla and Ridala, with rooms at 130 to 160 EEK per person.

The *Käbi Motel* (☎ & fax 56 082) in Ridala has single/double rooms in wooden summer houses for 150/250 EEK. Triples and four-bed rooms cost 350/550 EEK. It also has five caravan places and space for 50 tents. Pitching up for the night costs 70 EEK. The sauna is 100 EEK an hour. The motel organises five-day treks into the forest.

Palivere Manor (☎ 94 374; fax 94 483), 7 km north-east of Taebla on the Haapsalu-Tallinn road at Palivere, is a wonderful old manor house dating to 1805 but completely refurbished in 1991. Doubles/triples on this fantastic rural homestead cost 250/270 EEK. Three communal showers are shared between 10 rooms. Horse riding or use of the gym is 100 EEK and the sauna is 50 EEK an hour.

Another getaway place close by is *Kiige Farm* (☎ & fax 95 492), 10 km north of Taebla at Linnamäe. At the small family homestead, a bed in a pretty wooden summerhouse costs 130 EEK while a bed in the main house with shared bath is 200 EEK. It arranges mushroom or berry picking treks in the forest, yachting and fishing trips.

Getting There & Away

Buses along the Tallinn-Haapsalu road will drop you at Taebla. Ridala is 20 minutes south of Haapsalu on the route of buses running to/from Lihula, Haeska or Puise.

TUKSI
• ☎ *(247)*

In a pine forest beside Estonia's northernmost stretch of open Baltic-facing coast, but somewhat removed from everywhere else at Tuksi is *Puhkeküla Roosta* (Roosta Holiday Village; ☎ 97 230, 57 665; fax 57 875). Managed by the Swedest Motel group, this comfortable and attractive Swedish-built holiday-cottage complex is open year round. The 34 wooden cottages are equipped with a mini-kitchen, living room, TV, phone, shower and verandah. Between January and April, and September to December, a cottage for two/four/six people costs 540/900/1260 EEK. In May it costs 660/1020/1380, and from June to August 960/1380/1740 EEK. A couple of cottages are kitted out for disabled people and there's a limited amount of caravan space. On site there is a restaurant, bar, sauna, tennis and mini-golf – and you can also rent a car, bicycle, sailboard or a rowing boat at competitive prices.

Not to be confused with Roosta, is *Roosi Farm* (☎ & fax 93 347, 93 381), a few km further north at Nõva. Singles/doubles in this private home within a stone's throw of the sea and forest cost 200/400 EEK. Caravans can park too. It also arranges yachting and fishing trips.

Getting There & Away

By road, Roosta is about 40 km north of Haapsalu and 130 km from Tallinn. Turn north off the main Tallinn-Haapsalu road seven km west of Palivere, and continue about 30 km through Linnamäe and Riguldi. Roosta will transfer up to eight people to/from Tallinn for around 700 EEK. It's well off the beaten track and the only buses that go there seem to be Haapsalu-Variku-Nõva-Dirhami buses which go once in each direction daily, except for Monday and Thursday, taking a painful 2¼ hours depending whether they go direct or via Nõva and Variku.

There's a harbour (☎ 97 221) at Dirhami, a few km further north.

NOAROOTSI
• *pop 900* • ☎ *(247)*

The Noarootsi peninsula is two km across the bay from Haapsalu but around 35 km away by road. Until the exodus of Estonian Swedes in 1944, it was populated mainly by Swedes for several centuries.

There's an old church from the Swedish era at **Hosby**, a fine manorial park at **Pürksi**, and views over to Haapsalu from the old Swedish village of **Österby**. The name Pürksi is a corruption of Birke, the name of the Swedish trading town to which it was linked. Though a peninsula now, Noarootsi was an island a few centuries ago. It has joined the mainland because of the gradual rise of the land in west Estonia (one to two metres in the last 1000 years).

Getting There & Away
There are two buses daily in each direction between Haapsalu and Österby via Pürksi, taking 1¼ hours.

VORMSI
• *pop 340* • ☎ *(247)*

Vormsi, Estonia's fourth biggest island at 93 sq km, lies just three km off the Noarootsi peninsula. Ferries, however, make a 10 km crossing to Sviby on Vormsi's south coast from Rohuküla, nine km west of Haapsalu. Like Noarootsi, Vormsi had a mainly Swedish population until 1944, when nearly all of the Swedes left. Nature is largely undisturbed and the whole of the peninsula sprawling to the south and the 30 islets embraced by Hullo Bay is protected as a nature reserve under the Biosphere Reserve of the West Estonian Archipelago which has its headquarters (☎ 57 593) in Haapsalu at Kiltsitee 12. The peninsula, known as 'Rumpo's Nose', is the only place where Arctic lichen grows south of the Arctic circle.

Things to See
Sixteen km from east to west and averaging six km from north to south, Vormsi is a good place to wander round by bicycle, but you could also take a car or walk. There are about 10 km of paved road.

Landmarks to head for include the 14th century church at **Hullo** (Vormsi's largest village) which has a fine Baroque pulpit and a collection of old Swedish-style wheel-shaped crosses in the graveyard; the southern **Rumpo peninsula** dotted with juniper stands; the lighthouse at **Saksby** on the island's western tip; and the 5.8m-high boulder, Kirikukivi (Church Rock), near **Diby** in the north-east.

Places to Stay
Suuremõisa Holiday Hostel (☎ 92 309) on the coast at Suuremõisa in the south-west and nine km from Sviby port, has two single, four double and one triple room. A bed for the night in a shared room with communal bath starts at 120 EEK and breakfast is extra. The hostel rents out bicycles.

At Rumpo there is the *Norrenda Pension* (☎ 92 341), a 'settlement' of 20 or so small wooden houses. A bed in a shared hut costs 200 EEK.

By far more unique and definitely a place that has to be booked in advance is the *Elle-Malle pansionaati* (☎ 92 338), inside a windmill at Hullo. The romantic double room inside the windmill costs 250 EEK. Single rooms inside a separate wooden cottage are 150 EEK. It also rents out bicycles, has a sauna, and meets guests arriving at Sviby port. All three places can be booked through the tourist information centre in Haapsalu.

Getting There & Away
The ferry leaves Rohuküla for Sviby three times daily from Monday to Thursday and Sunday; four times daily on Friday; and twice daily on Saturday. The return ferry departs an hour later and the journey takes 45 minutes. Between September and April, the ferry runs less frequently (twice daily on Monday, Wednesday, Thursday and Saturday; three times daily on Tuesday, Friday and Sunday).

ESTONIA

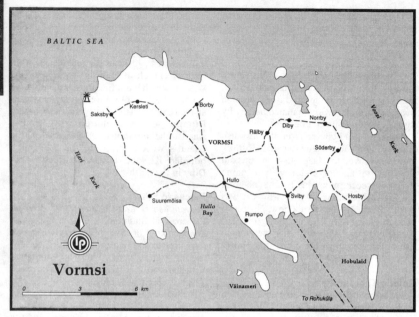

BALTIC SEA

Saksby
Kersleti
Borby
Norrby
Rälby
Diby
VORMSI
Söderby
Hari Kurk
Hullo
Suuremõisa
Hullo Bay
Sviby
Hosby
Rumpo
Voosi Kurk
Hobulaid

Vormsi

0   3   6 km

Väinameri

To Rohuküla

The ferry carries cars as well as bicycles and passengers. If you're taking a vehicle in summer or at a weekend, buy your outward ticket or reserve a place in advance (☎ 91 138) from the Rohuküla terminal as soon as possible. A one-way ticket for a foot passenger is 25 EEK. Pensioners and children pay 8 EEK. A ticket for a car and driver is 110 EEK on weekdays, and at weekends it is 137.50 EEK. A bicycle costs 10 EEK.

Haapsalu town bus No 1 runs hourly to Rohuküla from Lossi plats and the bus station, where its timetables are posted. All the Vormsi ferries wait for this bus except on Sunday morning . There are daily buses from Tallinn at 8 am and 4.10 pm, reaching Rohuküla two hours later. On weekdays a bus also leaves Tallinn at noon. From Rohuküla there is a daily bus to Tallinn at 9.50 am. On weekdays a bus also leaves at 7.05 am, on Sunday at 1.50 pm and on Monday, Wednesday, Friday, Saturday and Sunday at 6.05 pm.

MATSALU NATURE RESERVE

When birds die and go to heaven, they probably end up in Matsalu; or at least that is how the Estonian Ecotourism Association speaks of the bird (and bird-watcher's) paradise of Matsalu Bay. The deepest inlet in the west Estonian coast at over 20 km long, it is an important water bird habitat protected as the Matsalu Nature Reserve (Matsalu Looduskaitseala). The Reserve is considered a prime bird migration and breeding ground both in the Baltics and Europe, and has been a site of major research since 1970 when the Matsalu Ringing Centre was set up within the reserve, from which all bird ringing activities in Estonia are co-ordinated.

The 1.5 km long and half a km wide **Puhtulaid** peninsula, just a few km south of the reserve's southern border, is another important area for bird migration and breeding. Several hundred thousand velvet scoters, long-tailed ducks and barnacle and brent geese make a stopover here between mid-May and mid-June. There is an observation tower on the south tip of the peninsula and you can stay in Puhtu if you book in advance through the Puhtu nature reserve office (☎ 247-78 755).

At **Lihula**, bordering Matsalu Nature Reserve to the east, you can see the hillside ruins of a medieval castle, a manor house, a Russian Orthodox church dating to 1889, and a memorial stone to a battle in 1220 in which the local Estonians ejected the garrison placed here by an occupying Swedish king.

Matsalu's headquarters are at Penijõe, three km north of the Tallinn-Virtsu road, near Lihula. There is a small visitors' centre and a permanent exhibition with slide show (open daily, except Sunday, from 8 am to 5 pm). Bird-watching towers designed for visitors have been built at Penijõe, Kloostri, Haeska on the coast, and Keemu. The visitors' centre arranges tours of the reserve, including two-hour boat trips around the reed banks.

Places to Stay

The Matsalu Nature Reserve visitors' centre (☎ & fax 247-78 413) arranges accommodation in guesthouses at Haeska, Matsalu and Penijõe. *Haeska Boarding House* fits 25 to 30 people and costs around 90 EEK per person. *Matsalu Boarding House* has two double and one triple room. A bed in either costs 100 EEK. At Penijõe, there are eight beds, costing 75 EEK. They have to be booked in advance through the centre.

Haapsalu tourist information centre and Haapsalu Travel Service can make advance bookings at the reserve (see Haapsalu – Information). They also take bookings for the Estonian Ecotourism Association's four-day bird-watching tour of Matsalu.

VIRTSU
• ☎ (247)

The village of Virtsu, 135 km from Tallinn and 25 km south-west of Lihula, is the mainland terminus for ferries to Muhu island which is joined by a causeway to Saaremaa. The Virtsu ferry terminal (☎ 75 60) is where the main road ends, so you can't miss it. You can change money in the currency exchange in the terminal. The bar is open 24 hours.

Just back from the south side of the main road, down a side road about 600m from the ferry terminal, is a *kämping* with a few small cabins.

Getting There & Away

Buses between Virtsu and mainland towns include:

Haapsalu
two hours, two buses each way daily, 20 EEK
Pärnu
1½ to 2¼ hours, two to four buses each way daily, 22 EEK
Tallinn
2¼ to three hours, four to six buses each way daily, 34 EEK
Tartu
six hours, one bus each way daily, 98 EEK

Some of these are on the way to or from Kuressaare on Saaremaa. More on these, and information on the ferries, is given in the Saaremaa & Muhu section.

Hiiumaa

• *pop 11,500* • ☎ *(246)*

Hiiumaa, Estonia's second biggest island (1023 sq km) is quiet, sparsely populated, and gently beautiful with some lovely stretches of coast and pretty inland areas. Like nearby Saaremaa, Hiiumaa retains some of the atmosphere of pre-Soviet Estonia, being little touched by industry or Russian immigration. Low lying like the rest of Estonia (its highest point, 63m, is on the western Kõpu peninsula), Hiiumaa is not quite visible from the mainland, 22 km away. Its old name, Dagö (Swedish for 'Day Island'), allegedly comes from the fact that it used to take a day to reach it from the mainland.

Like Saaremaa, Hiiumaa was out of bounds to foreign tourists in the Soviet era but has rapidly caught up in the tourist stakes

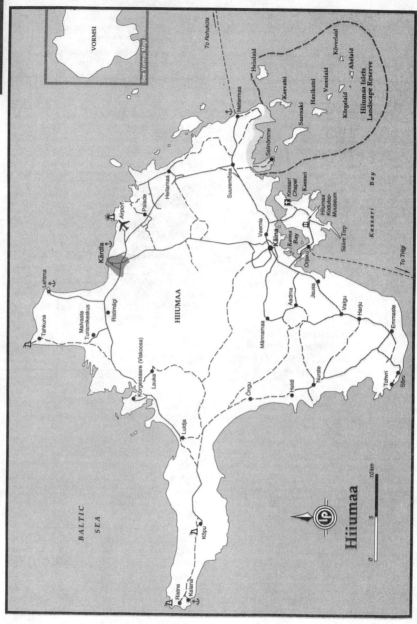

since! The island has a strong tradition of hospitality and if you're stuck in some out of the way place as the afternoon draws on, locals might offer you a bed.

Since 1994 Hiiumaa has adopted its own 'green label'. Hotel, restaurant, home owners and drivers of vehicles stick the small label depicting a small map of a green Hiiumaa in their windows to demonstrate their commitment to protecting their environment.

GETTING THERE & AWAY

A passenger and vehicle ferry service runs between Rohuküla on the mainland, nine km west of Haapsalu, and Heltermaa at Hiiumaa's east end. A few buses from Tallinn via Haapsalu run right through to Hiiumaa, with a ferry crossing included in the trip. Other buses will drop you off or pick you up at either ferry terminal. It's also common to hitch or ask for lifts off the ferries at either end.

At their closest, Hiiumaa and Saaremaa are just 5.5 km apart. There is a regular ferry crossing from Orjaku, 25 km south of Kärdla, to Triigi on Saaremaa. This service only runs between May and September though, and in winter months the quickest way to reach Saaremaa from Hiiumaa is – ridiculous as it may seem – to catch a bus to Tallinn and from there hop on a Kuressaare-bound bus.

The tourist information office and Tiit Reisid travel agency (see Kärdla – Information) in Kärdla can book all kinds of transport tickets in or out of Estonia.

Air

Estonian Air pulled out of flights between Tallinn and the islands in 1993. From the beginning of July to mid-August in 1996, a Tallinn-Stockholm flight run by the private Pärnu-based airline Baltic Aeroservis (see Pärnu – Getting There & Away) stopped at Kärdla airport (☎ 91 227, 91 217).

Ferry

Hiiumaa The crossing between Rohuküla and Heltermaa takes about 1½ hours. Ferries leave Rohuküla nine times daily between 6.30 am and 8.30 pm on Monday and Wednesday; and 12 times daily between 4.30 am and 11.15 pm on Tuesday, Thursday and Friday. On Saturday the last ferry sets sail at 6.30 pm; and on Sunday they run 10 times daily between 8.30 am and midnight.

On the return journey, ferries leave Heltermaa 10 times daily between 5.30 am and 8.20 pm on weekdays, with extra ferries leaving at 9.20 pm on Tuesday and Thursday, and at 9.20 and 10.20 pm on Friday. On Saturday, six ferries run between 6.30 am and 6.30 pm; and on Sunday, 11 ferries run between 6.30 am and 10.20 pm.

A one-way fare is 15/7 EEK for adults/children and pensioners. A ticket for a car including driver is 70 EEK on weekdays and 105 EEK on weekends. Bicycles cost 10 EEK.

You should reserve a place in advance if you're taking a vehicle, particularly in summer or at weekends. Outward tickets can be bought from Rohuküla terminal (☎ 247-91 138). Return tickets can only be bought from the Heltermaa ticket office (☎ 94 212 or 94 252) which is a small building on the right as you leave the pier. Ferry departure times are also posted in the bus ticket office at Haapsalu station.

Saaremaa From mid-May to mid-September a small ferry runs from Orjaku ferry terminal (☎ 92 127), 25 km south of Kärdla, to Triigi (☎ 245-73 203) on Saaremaa. The journey takes 1½ hours, and costs 45 EEK per person and 140 EEK for a car one-way. Sixteen cars and 80 passengers fit on the ferry.

In summer 1996, a ferry left Orjaku daily except Wednesday at 10 am and 6 pm with an extra ferry leaving at 2 pm from the beginning of June until mid-September. From Triigi on Saaremaa, ferries left daily, except Wednesday, at 8 am and 4 pm, an extra ferry leaving at noon between June and mid-September.

Ferry tickets should likewise be bought as far in advance as possible; either directly from the ferry terminals or from the Tiit Reisid travel agency in Kärdla or from Baltic

ESTONIA

Tours in Kuressaare. However, the tourist information offices in both places will only handle reservations.

Bus

Through-Buses – Hiiumaa There is one bus daily between Tallinn and Kärdla, stopping at Haapsalu, Heltermaa and Käina en route (4½ hours, 70 EEK). Two buses daily depart from Tallinn to Nurste (3½ hours), via Haapsalu, Heltermaa, Käina and Valgu.

Through-Buses – Mainland Three Tallinn-bound buses leave Kärdla daily; two more buses heading for Tallinn depart daily from Käina, stopping at Kärdla and Haapsalu en route.

Mainland – Rohuküla Haapsalu town bus No 1 runs about hourly to/from Rohuküla. Its timetables are posted at Lossi plats and Haapsalu station, its two main stops in the town. The buses running between Hiiumaa and Tallinn can also be picked up at Rohuküla.

GETTING AROUND

Paved roads circle Hiiumaa and cover several side routes. The tourist information centre in Kärdla has bicycles to rent, and AS Dagotrans (☎ 91 846, 91 289) at Sõnajala 11, rents bicycles and cars. There are petrol stations at Kärdla and Käina.

Buses, nearly all radiating from Kärdla, get to most places on the island, though in some cases not very often. Information on buses to and from the ferry port, Heltermaa, has been given under Hiiumaa, Getting There & Away. Hitching is fairly common on the roads to and from Heltermaa.

HELTERMAA TO KÄRDLA

At **Suuremõisa**, six km inland from Heltermaa, you can visit the chateau-like, late-Baroque manor and park, created in the mid-18th century, that used to belong to the rich baronial Ungern-Sternberg family. The nearby **Pühalepa Church** dates to the 13th century.

Legends surrounding a mound of rocks

known as the **Stones of the Ancient Agreement** (Põhilise leppe kivid), about a km north-east of the manor, suggest that they mark the grave of a ruler of Sweden. At Palade, 12 km north towards Kärdla, then a km north-east along a side road, is the **Soera Farm Museum** (Soera Talumuuseum) in a traditional long, low wooden building.

KÄRDLA
• *pop 4300* • ☎ *(246)*

Hiiumaa's 'capital' grew up around a cloth factory founded in 1829 and destroyed during WWII. It's a green town full of gardens and trees, with a sleepy atmosphere and little of great interest except that it's Hiiumaa's centre for services of all kinds.

Orientation

The town's main focus is Kesk väljak (central square), a long plaza half a km north of the main Heltermaa-Kõrgessaare road. About 700m further north along Võidu and Sadama, where the cloth factory used to stand, is another square, Vabriku väljak, with a park either side – to the east Linnapark, with the town's Lutheran church built in 1861-63, to the west Rannapark running down to the sea.

Information

Tourist Office Kärdla tourist information centre (☎ & fax 91 377; email info@info.hiiumaa.turism.ee; http://www.hiiumaa.ee) at Kesk väljak 1, prides itself on the wealth of information and practical help it provides. It rents bicycles (see Hiiumaa – Getting Around), arranges accommodation on the island and takes bookings for the Hiiumaa Guides Association which charges 75 EEK an hour. It also produces a number of refreshingly well written guides to the area.

Particularly noteworthy is *The Lighthouse Tour – Discover Hiiumaa by Car*, a 33-page driving tour of the island published in English, Swedish, Finnish, German and Estonian. The centre is open between mid-April to mid-September on weekdays from 9 am to 6 pm, and on weekends from 10 am to 4 pm. From mid-September to mid-April it is open weekdays from 9 am to 5 pm.

The Hiiumaa headquarters of the Biosphere Reserve of the West Estonian Archipelago (☎ 991 42) at Vabriku väljak 1, provides information on 'green' Hiiumaa.

Money Tallina Pank on the central square gives cash advance on credit card and cashes travellers' cheques.

Post & Communications The post office, at Posti 7, is open weekdays from 8 am to 4.30 pm, and on Saturday from 9 am to 1 pm.

Travel Agencies Tiit Reisid (☎ 96 454; fax 96 455; email tiitreis@pb.uninet.ee) on the central square close to the market arranges accommodation and tours round the island. It also books ferry tickets.

Est Dago travel agency (☎ & fax 96 566) at Vabaduse 13, arranges cheap accommodation for around 100 EEK a night and rents cars from 360 EEK a day. At weekends it arranges local culture evenings at a Hiiumaa farmstead costing 100 EEK including food and home-brewed beer.

Places to Stay
See the preceding Information section for details of travel agencies that can arrange accommodation in Kärdla or around the island. Est Dago travel agency runs a *hostel* (☎ 91 445) at Vabaduse 13. Singles/doubles with shared bath cost 90/160 EEK. A triple is 210 EEK and a room for four, 260 EEK. Breakfast is not included in the price but there is a small kitchen where you can prepare food. The reception is open 24 hours but after midnight you have to ring the bell.

The only other accommodation in Kärdla are two not particularly good value hotels. The *Padu Hotel* (☎ 98 034) at Heltermaa 22 has 10 double rooms with private bathroom for 400 EEK. The *Sõnajala Hotel* (☎ 99 336), two km from the centre at Leigri väljak 3, offers a bed in a double or triple room for 130 EEK a night. Breakfast costs an extra 40 EEK. The hotel also rents tents.

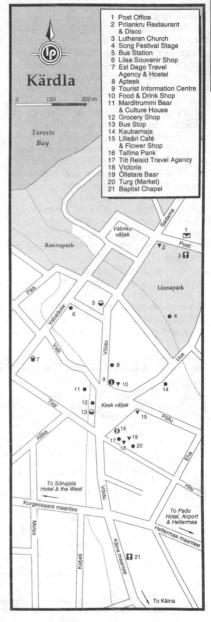

Kärdla

0   150   300 m

Tareste
Bay

1   Post Office
2   Priiankru Restaurant
    & Disco
3   Lutheran Church
4   Song Festival Stage
5   Bus Station
6   Liisa Souvenir Shop
7   Est Dago Travel
    Agency & Hostel
8   Apteek
9   Tourist Information Centre
10 Food & Drink Shop
11 Marditrummi Baar
    & Culture House
12 Grocery Shop
13 Bus Stop
14 Kaubamaja
15 Lilleäri Café
    & Flower Shop
16 Tallina Pank
17 Tiit Reisid Travel Agency
18 Victoria
19 Õlletare Baar
20 Turg (Market)
21 Baptist Chapel

ESTONIA

Places to Eat

Around the market area on the east side of the central square there are a couple of places: *Victoria*, behind the Tiit Reisid travel agency in a little wooden cottage, dishes up cheap and cheerful burgers and other grilled meats. Behind Victoria is *Õlletare*, another painted wooden hut which serves light snacks and is the main drinking hole in the village (open daily from noon to midnight).

More refined is *Lilleäri*, at the north end of the central square on the corner of Kesk väljak and Põllu maantee. The café inside the flower shop serves cakes and coffee for around 4 EEK. Another good option for smaller-sized meals and pizza is the *Marditrummi Baar* inside the Culture House, a large yellow building on the west side of the central square. Incidentally, if you're seeking the use of a public toilet, this is the place to go.

Top of the not so vast range is *Priiankru*, to the north of the bus station on the corner of Sadama and Posti maantee at Sadama 4. More traditional Estonian dishes include herring in sour cream for 15 EEK. European-style specialities include roast pork with

cheese for 40 EEK and pan-fried salmon in cream sauce for 59 EEK. It is open weekdays from noon to 10 pm and on weekends from noon until 4 am, with live music, dancing and billiards.

Getting There & Away

Direct bus/ferry connections between Kärdla, the mainland, and Saaremaa are dealt with in the Hiiumaa, Getting There & Away section. See Hiiumaa, Getting Around for bicycle and car rental possibilities. Kärdla's tiny bus station is at Võidu 1 about halfway between Kesk väljak and Vabriku väljak. This is either the terminus or a stop for most buses on the island and a timetable is posted inside.

TAHKUNA PENINSULA

The Tahkuna peninsula stretches eight km north into the Baltic Sea a few km west of Kärdla. At Tahkuna, the peninsula's north-west tip and Hiiumaa's northern extremity, there's a lighthouse. Next to the lighthouse stands a **memorial** to the victims of the *Estonia* ferry disaster. Facing out to sea, the nine to 12m-tall metal frame encases a huge

---

The Baltic Sea

The Baltic Sea is very low in salt as seas go, being fed by so many rivers and with only one narrow, shallow opening to the North Sea (between Denmark and Sweden) – a factor which also makes it relatively tideless. The Baltic is also a very young sea, having attained its present character only about 6500 years ago.

The Scandinavian ice sheet of the last ice age covered the whole Scandinavian-Baltic region as far south as the Polish-German coast till about 12,000 BC. The melting of the southern part of the ice sheet created what was the Yoldia Sea, which, by about 7500 BC, stretched from the North Sea across southern Sweden, southern Finland and most of the present Baltic (except the Gulf of Bothnia between Finland and Sweden), and along the Gulf of Finland to Lake Ladoga, east of St Petersburg.

By about 6500 BC, with the ice sheet almost completely melted, water levels dropped. This left a land bridge between Sweden and Denmark/Germany and, behind it, a freshwater 'lake' (Ancylus Lake) – which roughly covered the present area of (what we now know as) the Baltic Sea. The land bridge was breached around 4500 BC, opening up the Baltic to the open sea once more.

At that time nearly all of the Estonian islands and the western Estonian mainland, along with a slice of Latvia's west coast, were still under the sea. The earth's crust here has been gradually rising ever since – hence the proliferation of very low-lying islands off Estonia's coast and the flat, low nature of western Estonia. Currently the rate of rise is about one metre every 350 years. In a few more millennia, if this continues, Estonia's present islands will be part of the mainland and new islands will have appeared further offshore.

The Baltic Sea is called Läänemeri (Western Sea) in Estonian, Baltijas jūra in Latvian, Baltijos jūra in Lithuanian, and Baltiyskoe More in Russian. ∎

cross, from the bottom of which a bell is suspended; it only rings when the wind blows with the same speed and in the same direction as that fatal night in September 1994, which saw the *Estonia* go down. At Lehtma, the north-east tip, there's a harbour (☎ 99 214) suitable for yachts; and there are a number of pre-WWI fortifications on the peninsula. Northern Hiiumaa had a population of free Swedish farmers until the late 18th century, when they were deported to Ukraine. At Ristimägi there is a **Hill of Crosses**. The dune decked with handmade crosses near the main road about seven km west of Kärdla, marks the spot where the last 1200 Swedish people living on Hiiumaa performed their last act of worship before being deported from the island in 1781. Since then it has become a tradition for first-time visitors to Hiiumaa to lay a cross at the hill.

Places to Stay
The *Malvaste Turismikeskus* (Malvaste Tourist Centre) (☎ 91 525, 91 445), 2.5 km north of the Kärdla-Kõrgessaare road from a turning 10 km from Kärdla, consists of a house with year-round accommodation for 30 people, summer 'camping' cabins for 50, and tent spaces. It's in the forest, 15 minutes walk from a sandy beach. Rooms in the house cost 190 EEK plus 95 EEK for each extra person up to four. The summer cabins house four people and cost 380 EEK each and a tent site is 20 EEK. Rooms can be booked in advance through the tourist information centre in Kärdla.

Getting There & Away
Several buses a day go along the main road from Kärdla to the Malvaste turning, a 15 minute ride. Buses heading for Viskoosa, Luidja or Kalana are the ones to look for.

WESTERN HIIUMAA
The harbour village of **Kõrgessaare**, 20 km west of Kärdla, is also known as Viskoosa (particularly on bus timetables) because of an unsuccessful artificial silk mill built here by a Belgian company called La Viscosa just before WWI.

At **Kõpu**, a little over halfway along the western Kõpu peninsula, is Hiiumaa's best known landmark – the inland Kõpu lighthouse said to be the third oldest continuously operational lighthouse in the world. A lighthouse has stood on this raised bit of land since 1531 to warn ships away from the offshore Hiiumaadal sandbank. The present white limestone tower, built in 1845, is 37m high and can be seen about 55 km away. A second lighthouse stands at the west end of the peninsula near **Ristna** (Stockholm is just over 200 km west of here). It was brought to Hiiumaa by freighter together with its sister lighthouse that now stands at **Tahkuna**, on the north tip of the island. The Tahkuna lighthouse, built in Paris in 1874, is 40m tall and it is possible to climb to the top if you can get the key from the lighthouse keeper. This area was the scene of battle between German and Russian troops in WWII, the official Soviet story being that the Soviets bravely fought to the bitter end, the last man climbing to the top of the lighthouse and flinging himself off while still firing at the Germans. Further west of the lighthouse near Ristna, lie the deserted and rotten ruins of the former barracks of the Soviet border guards.

Places to Stay
Kärdla's tourist information centre arranges accommodation in Kõpu. *Pihla Farm* (☎ 93 431) in Kõpu offers 12 places costing 180 EEK per person including a hearty breakfast. It also rents boats and bicycles.

Eight km west of Kõpu in the village of Kalana is the equally good value *Lautri Hostel* (☎ 93 444). A bed in a shared room costs about 100 EEK. The hostel is within one km of the beach and rents boats and fishing gear.

Getting There & Away
Kärdla buses run several times most days to/from Kõrgessaare (Viskoosa) and Luidja at the start of the Kõpu peninsula, and two or three times a day to/from Kalana near the end of the peninsula. Kalana is about 1½ hours from Kärdla.

KÄINA & KÄINA BAY BIRD RESERVE

Hiiumaa's second biggest settlement – not quite big enough to merit the label 'town' – is a fairly nondescript place, apart from the ruins of a fine 15th century stone church, wrecked by a WWII bomb, near the main road in the middle of the village. During the Soviet regime, the authorities built a grey faceless building on top of the church cemetery, sparing the headstones of just two graves. On the western edge of Käina is the house-museum of Rudolf Tobias, composer of some of the first Estonian orchestral works around the turn of the century.

The main appeal of the town is its idyllic location in the south of the island near the shore of Käina Bay, an important bird reserve which is virtually cut off from the open sea by the twin causeways to Kassari island. During the hot summer months a large part of the bay dries up and becomes nothing more than a mud field. About 70 different species breed at Käina Bay. The Hiiumaa headquarters of the Biosphere Reserve of the West Estonian Archipelago (see Kärdla – Information) publishes a variety of leaflets which take you through specified nature trails within the reserve.

Four km from Käina, at Vaemla on the road to Kassari is a small wool factory, Hiiu Vill (☎ 92 121), which still uses original 19th century weaving and spinning machines to produce some fine traditional knitwear.

Places to Stay

The *Hotel Liilia* (☎ 92 146; fax 92 546), at Hiiu 23 in Käina, is Hiiumaa's best hotel. Its 13 rooms, all with private bathroom and satellite TV, cost 590/770 EEK for singles/doubles. The Liilia has a restaurant with an Estonian and international menu including fish and vegetarian options. There's also a bar.

A cheaper option is the *Lõokese puhkekeskus* (☎ 92 107; fax 92 269), at Lõokese 14. It has a hotel and hostel on the same site. Singles/doubles in the hotel are 300/500 EEK. In the hostel, double rooms cost 280 EEK with a shared bath and 320 EEK with a private bath. A family room

kitted out for two adults and two children costs 480 EEK.

The Estonian Hostels Association runs a small six bed hostel in the private home *Heido* (☎ 92 485; fax 92 470) in Käina at Luige 8. A bed for the night costs 250 EEK including breakfast. The hostel is open 24 hours and you can horse ride here.

Puulaid Camping and Lodge (☎ 92 126, 97 629), four km south of Käina on the road to Orjaku, has beds in shared summer houses for 100 EEK. Breakfast is 40 EEK. There are 35 beds in total and the price list is beautifully illustrated with pictures for all to understand. You can rent bicycles, paddle and rowing-boats for 16 EEK an hour, and binoculars and fishing rods for 10 EEK an hour. To go yachting or fish at sea you have to negotiate with the captain.

Two km further south from Puulaid and five km from Orjaku ferry terminal is the *Tuuliku Guest House* (☎ 97 373, 91 944; fax 91 753) at Jausa. This family guesthouse with five double rooms and one triple and quadruple offers excellent value for money. Beds cost 150 EEK a night including breakfast. It also rents out bicycles and cars, and has a yacht you can hire to launch from the beach, just 400m away.

Getting There & Away

A good paved road runs 20 km across the island from Kärdla to Käina. There are five or six buses between Kärdla and Käina on weekdays, a few less on weekends. Some are heading south or west to Aadma, Valgu, Tohvri, Nurste or Õngu. Buses also run to Kassari.

KASSARI

The eastern half of the eight-km-long island of Kassari is thickly covered with mixed woodland. At each end it's linked to the mainland by a causeway which supports a paved road. There's a harbour and ferry terminal at Orjaku (☎ 92 127) at the west end of the island from which ferries ply their way across to Saaremaa (see Hiiumaa – Getting There & Away).

Southern Kassari narrows to a promontory

with some unusual vegetation and ends in a thin, three km spit of land whose tip, Sääre Tirp, is five km from Kassari's single main road. It's well worth making the trip to Sääre Tirp and allowing enough time to savour the unusual environment.

Just inland of the main road, a short distance west of the Sääre Tirp turning, is the single-storey **Hiiumaa Koduloomuuseum** (☎ 97 121), formerly servants' quarters on the Kassari estate, with a large collection of artefacts and exhibits on Hiiumaa's history, nature and ethnography. It is open daily, between May and September, from 10 am to 5.50 pm.

Another enjoyable walk, ride or drive is to a pretty, whitewashed 18th century **chapel** at the east end of Kassari. A sign 'Kassari Kabel 2' directs you down a dirt road from the easternmost point of the island's paved road. In fact it's just 1.5 km to the lovely little 18th century chapel which stands among trees, with a graveyard around it. A path continues nearly two km to a small bay in Kassari's north-east corner.

Getting There & Away
Only a few buses go to Kassari. By changing buses in Käina (maybe with a bit of a wait) you can get from Kärdla to Kassari and back most days, but the times certainly aren't very convenient. Alternatively it's a six or seven km walk (or hitch) to the middle of Kassari across either causeway from the main Valgu-Käina-Heltermaa road (which is used by buses), or about 10 km from the middle of Käina.

SOUTHERN HIIUMAA
The main paved road from Käina runs southwest through Valgu and Harju, villages separated from the coast by a three-km-wide marshy strip. Harju has two restored windmills. At Emmaste the main road turns north-west to end at Haldi just past Nurste. Hamlets and isolated farmsteads dot the west facing stretch of coast and its hinterland. The southern tip of Hiiumaa around the harbour of Sõru is bleaker with few trees. North of Haldi, dirt roads continue through Õngu to

the western Kõpu peninsula and to Luidja, the end of the paved road west from Kärdla.

Getting There & Away
There are buses from Kärdla and Käina to Valgu, Harju, Emmaste, Tohvri (in the south near Sõru), Nurste and Õngu every day.

HIIUMAA ISLETS LANDSCAPE RESERVE
Saarnaki, Hanikatsi, Vareslaid, Kõrgelaid and other islets off south-east Hiiumaa form the Hiiumaa Islets Landscape Reserve. The reserve is a breeding place for some 110 bird species, including avocets, eider ducks, goosanders, greylag geese, as well as a migration halt for swans, barnacle geese and other species. Over 600 plant species – almost half Estonia's total – grow here including the rare red helleborine, wild apple and shining geranium.

Saarnaki and Hanikatsi, the two largest islands measuring 131 and 83 hectares respectively, were inhabited until the 1960s or 70s. They were depopulated, like many other Estonian coastal villages, because of Soviet bans on seagoing boats, which meant people could no longer earn a living from fishing.

Bird fauna on the islands has been carefully monitored since 1974. A number of observation towers have been built within the reserve, including one close to the Hiiumaa Nature Reserve headquarters (☎ 94 299) at Salinõmme on the mainland. It is possible to spend a night on Saarnaki or Hanikatsi islands but you have to get permission from the reserve centre first. It can arrange for a guide to take you by boat to the islands.

Saaremaa & Muhu

• *pop 42,000* • ☎ *(245)*

Mainland Estonians say Saaremaa, the country's biggest island at 2668 sq km, is 'like the old Estonia'. Soviet industry and immigration barely touched the place, and it retains the appearance and old-fashioned pace of agricultural pre-WWII Estonia, even though its famous windmills (which numbered 800 in the 19th century) no longer work and its 'typical' reed-thatched roofs aren't so typical any more.

Saaremaa has always had an independent streak and was usually the last part of Estonia to fall to invaders. Its people have their own customs, songs and costumes, speak Estonian with a strong accent and never spoke much Russian at all. They brew a clear, dark beer widely reckoned to be the best in Estonia. They don't respect mainland Estonia's Kalevipoeg myth, for Saaremaa has its own legendary hero, Suur Tõll, who fought numerous battles around the island with devils, fiends etc.

Though Saaremaa has long been a popular Estonian summer holiday retreat, during the Soviet era it was closed to foreigners, and even mainland Estonians needed an invitation to visit because of the siting of an early warning radar system and rocket base here. The island today is a thinly populated place of unspoiled rural landscapes with wooden farmsteads dotted among the forests that still cover nearly half the land. Saaremaa is flat but has a deeply indented 1300 km coast of bays and peninsulas (and some sandy beaches). There are many remains from its intriguing past including pre-German strongholds, fine fortress-like early churches, windmills and, not least, the attractive old capital, Kuressaare, which has a mighty castle. Though known for its juniper groves, Saaremaa is also home to four-fifths of Estonia's roughly 1300 other plant species, many of which are contained in the Vilsandi National Park and a number of other nature reserves.

In recent years, Saaremaa has become an almost painfully popular tourist resort, especially with Finns who flock there in droves for a cheap break. Many have already purchased their own little holiday home on Estonia's most sought after island, while the rest pour into Saaremaa's few hotels, motels and tourist farmsteads. Saaremaa is joined by a causeway to the neighbouring island, Muhu, to which ferries run from Virtsu on the mainland.

Historically the name Saaremaa (islandland) sometimes referred to the whole archipelago of Estonia's western islands, and the same ambiguity goes for its old name Ösel. In Swedish *Ö* means island and *sel* means sieve. 'Island-sieve' could, perhaps with little imagination, mean 'archipelago'.

HISTORY

Human settlement on Saaremaa dates to the 4th millennium BC. The early coastal settlements now lie some way inland owing to the rising of the land by about 15m in the last 5000 years. In the 10th to 13th centuries AD Saaremaa and Muhu were the most densely populated parts of Estonia. Denmark tried to conquer Saaremaa in the early 13th century but failed, and it wasn't until 1227 that the Knights of the Sword subjugated it. The knights and the church divided the islands between them in 1238. The knights got Muhu and relatively small eastern and northwestern parts of Saaremaa, setting up their headquarters at Pöide in eastern Saaremaa. The Haapsalu-based bishop of Ösel-Wiek got the rest of Saaremaa, making Kuressaare his stronghold on the island.

Saaremaa rebelled against German rule in 1236-41, 1260-61, and again in 1343 when the Germans were thrown off the island and the knights' castle at Pöide destroyed. In 1345 the Germans returned and forced the islanders to surrender.

All Saaremaa became a Danish possession in 1573 during the Livonian War, and in 1645 it was transferred to Sweden by the Treaty of Brömsebro. It was taken by Russia in 1710 during the Great Northern War and made part of the Russian province of Livonia, governed from Rīga. Saaremaa was occupied briefly by Germany from 1917 to 1918 before Estonia became independent.

GETTING THERE & AWAY

The usual way of reaching Saaremaa from mainland Estonia is the ferry service across the seven km strait between Virtsu on the mainland and Kuivastu on the east coast of

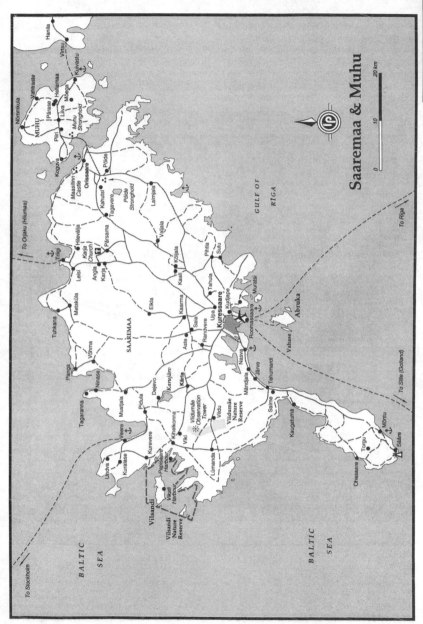

Saaremaa & Muhu

Muhu. Buses from Tallinn, Pärnu and Tartu run right through to Saaremaa, with a ferry crossing included in the trip. These are the most straightforward buses to use, especially in summer when direct buses are given first priority on the packed ferries. Other buses will drop you off or pick you up at either ferry terminal. It's not unusual for people to hitch lifts off the ferries at either end.

Between mid-May and mid-September it is possible to reach Saaremaa directly from Hiiumaa via a ferry which runs from Orjaku, 25 km south of Kärdla on Hiiumaa, to Triigi port, on the north coast of the island.

At the time of writing it was not known whether a proposed ferry service between Rīga, Roomassaare on the south coast of Saaremaa and Slite on the Swedish island of Gotland would actually run. However, cruises between Stockholm and Veere will be resumed in 1997. See Getting There & Away at the front of the book for information on these services.

There are twice-weekly flights from Tallinn to Kuressaare.

From Saaremaa mainland, you can charter private boats to the islands of Abruka and Vahase, off the south coast, and Vilsandi to the west.

Air
Baltic Aeroservis flies to Kuressaare from Tallinn twice weekly. See Tallinn – Getting There & Away for details.

Ferry
Muhu The crossing between Virtsu ferry terminal (☎ 247-75 520) on the mainland and Kuivastu ferry terminal (☎ 98 432) on Muhu takes about 25 minutes. Ferries leave Virtsu 12 times daily between 7 am and 10.30 pm daily, with four additional sailings on Saturday.

On the return journey, ferries leave Kuivastu 11 times daily with six extra sailings on Saturday and two extra on Sunday.

A one-way fare is 10/4 EEK for an adult/child or pensioner; 50 EEK for a car and 10 EEK for a bicycle. Each ferry takes about 25 vehicles including trucks and buses. During summer it is essential to reserve a place for your car in advance and buy your return ticket back to the mainland as soon you arrive in Saaremaa. The Maardi travel agency in Kuressaare (see Kuressaare – travel agencies) handles ferry bookings.

Hiiumaa From mid-May to mid-September a ferry runs from Triigi port on the north coast of Saaremaa to Orjaku on Hiiumaa (see Hiiumaa – Getting There & Away).

Rīga A twice-weekly ferry is planned between Roomassaare port on Saaremaa and Rīga for summer 1997. See Getting There & Away at the front of the book for details.

Yacht
Saaremaa is extremely popular with visiting yachties. Probably the best harbour facilities are at the Nasva Yacht Club (Nasva Jahtklubi; ☎ 75 140, fax 55 257), nine km west of Kuressaare. See Getting There & Away chapter at the front of the book for a list of other harbours on the island.

Bus
Through-Buses – Mainland Seven direct buses daily travel each way between Tallinn and Kuressaare (4½ hours, 90 EEK). There are two buses daily to/from Tartu (4¼ hours, 62 EEK) and one bus daily to/from Pärnu (eight hours, 122 EEK).

Other Buses If the through-buses don't suit you, you can get separate buses to and from the ferry, perhaps using one of the through-buses for part of its trip only. There are five buses daily between Virtsu and Saaremaa; and a five times daily bus service each way just between Kuivastu and Kuressaare – a 1½ hour trip timed to connect with ferry arrivals and departures.

GETTING AROUND
There are around 400 km of paved roads on Saaremaa and many more of reasonable dirt road. Hitching is not uncommon on the main routes (but there's not much traffic on minor roads). Buses from Kuressaare get to many

places and you could use them to make day trips to several parts of the island. Information on buses to/from the ferry port of Kuivastu can be found under Saaremaa, Getting There & Away.

MUHU

Muhu is the third biggest Estonian island and is famous for its painstakingly worked folk costumes. Near the main road about halfway across the island is the 13th-14th century **Liiva church**, with some unusual ship murals. Just east of the road, shortly before the 2.5 km causeway to Saaremaa, is the **Muhu stronghold** of the old Estonians. It was here that the islanders surrendered to the Knights of the Sword on 3 February, 1227, marking the end of Estonian resistance to the German invasion. The nearby **Eemu Tuulik** (windmill) houses a small museum which sells its milled flour. **Koguva** on the western tip of Muhu, six km off the road, is an exceptionally well preserved old-fashioned island village and all its 105 houses are protected as an open-air museum. They were mostly built between 1880 and 1930 but some date from the mid-18th century.

Places to Stay

The Estonian Ecotourism Association arranges farmhouse holidays on the island. The *Kuivastu Hotel* (☎ 98 429; ☎ & fax 98 171) about 200m from Kuivastu ferry terminal, provides a good stopover point. Double rooms in the big white building immediately on your left as you leave the terminal cost 330 EEK a night, including breakfast. A cheaper option is *KämpingPiiri*, about 150m from the main Kuivastu-Kuressaare road in Piiri village. It has two small wooden houses; one for four costs 150 EEK. A small kitchen, bathroom and sauna is inside the main house, a short walk away.

At Hellamaa, the first village you hit on the main Kuivastu-Kuressaare road, the *Tihuse turismitalu* (☎ 98 750, 98 043) arranges three-hour horse treks round the island for 240 EEK. A bed in one of 20 simple wooden cottages, each with two or three beds, costs 210 EEK per person not including breakfast.

Tammisaare Tourism Farm (☎ 98 789), tucked away in the tiny village of Mõega, offers accommodation for up to 160 people in a rural setting for about 110 EEK per person. Most idyllic of all is *bed & breakfast* (☎ 98 627) at a grand old farmhouse, built in 1910 in the open-air museum of Koguva. Although thoroughly renovated, the traditional wood burning stoves have been retained in all the rooms. A place in a single/double/triple or family room for four costs 200 EEK including a hearty breakfast. Children under 12 are half price.

Top of the farmhouse range is *Lõo Farmhouse* (☎ 244-43 618) in Vahtraste, 13 km north of Kuivastu. The entire farmhouse is 1000/5000 EEK a night/week. It also rents bicycles, cars, boats and fishing tackle. Reservations for all three can be made through the tourist information centre in Kuressaare (see Kuressaare – Information).

Getting There & Away

You can use the Kuivastu-Kuressaare buses, or hitch, to reach the points along the main road. There are occasional buses to Koguva too.

EASTERN SAAREMAA

The causeway from Muhu reaches Saaremaa near Orissaare on the north-east coast. The main road to Kuressaare goes past Tagavere and Valjala.

Orissaare is the second biggest settlement on Saaremaa. The German knights built the Maasilinn castle just north of Orissaare in the 14th to 16th centuries. It was blown up in 1576 but there are ruins to see. Three km south of the main road, **Pöide** was the German knights' headquarters on Saaremaa. Their fortress was destroyed in 1343 in the St George's Night Uprising, but Pöide church, built by the Germans in the 13th and 14th centuries a short distance east of the road, remains a starkly imposing reminder of their influence. There's another early German church dating to the 1230s at

Valjala, just off the main Kuivastu-Kuressaare road, 25 km out of Kuressaare.

Kaali

The **meteorite crater** at Kaali (2.5 km north of the Valjala-Kuressaare road from a turning 10 km from Valjala) is over 100m wide and maybe 30m deep. It was blasted into existence by a meteorite about the 8th century BC. For the islanders living here today, this magnificent, haunting lake – nothing more than a water-filled crater, in fact – remains a source of great mystery and pride, a fact quickly revealed by their love for exaggerated tales of Lake Kaali's spectacular beginnings. At nearby Kõljala there's a classical 17th-19th century manor house.

Angla, Karja, Triigi & Tuhkana

This group of places in the northern part of eastern Saaremaa can be reached from Kuressaare or from other places in the east, to which they're linked by several paved roads. If you are arriving on the ferry from Hiiumaa, this is the perfect spot to explore immediately.

Angla, 40 km from Kuressaare on the main road to the north coast, is the site of the biggest and most photogenic grouping of **windmills** on Saaremaa – five of them of various sizes, none now in use, lined up together on the roadside. Opposite the windmills is the turn-off to **Karja church**, two km east which, with the blank, fortress-like gaze of its façade, is one of the most evocative of Saaremaa's 13th-14th century German churches. There's a fine crucifixion carving on one of its walls. The church incidentally is not in Karja hamlet which is two km south of Angla on the Kuressaare road.

North of Angla the road continues 5.5 km to Leisi, from where it's 3.5 km to the **harbour** of Triigi on Triigi laht, a picturesque bay on Saaremaa's north coast with views across to Hiiumaa. To reach Triigi turn right in the middle of Leisi, then turn left (north) after two km and go 1.5 km.

There's a sandy beach at Tuhkana, three km north of Metsküla, which is 10 km west of Leisi, mostly by unpaved roads.

Kaarma

There's another fine **13th century church** and almost equally old **parsonage** *(pastoraat)* at Kaarma, 12 km north of Kuressaare. On the other side of the main road from the church are the remains of an old **Estonian stronghold**. Kaarma is a centre of dolomite mining, one of Saaremaa's very few industries.

Places to Stay

Kuressaare tourist information centre arranges accommodation in Orissaare, Pöide, Valjala, Angla, Karja, Triigi, Tuhkana and Kaarma. Mere Farmstead Tourism (see Kuressaare – Travel Agencies) arranges accommodation of all price ranges (35 EEK for roughing it in a tent to 850 EEK for sheer luxury) in tourism farms all over the island. It caters for the disabled as well as people on special diets.

Orissaare offers some cheap options. At Ranna 11, a *hostel* (☎ 95 149) inside the village school has 80 beds available between May and August for 40 EEK per person. From the beginning of September until the end of April, the hostel has 10 double rooms to let, costing 100 EEK per room. *Kämping Kadakas* (☎ 95 297), on the south side of Orissaare at Kuivastu 44, has room for 28 people in four-bed wooden cabins. A bed for the night costs 80 EEK but don't expect any mod-cons – including hot water!

In Triigi harbour is a small, two-room, four-bed *summerhouse*. A bed for the night, including breakfast, is 190 EEK. Advance bookings through the Mere travel agency (☎ 54 461) in Kuressaare are essential. More basic accommodation can be found at *Triigi Majutus* (☎ 73 203), next to the port. A bed in a single/double/triple room costs 140/120/100 EEK and a shower/sauna costs 10/40 EEK. Again, book in advance as it only has seven places.

Just a few km south of Triigi at Hilevälja is *Välja* (☎ 73 720, 73 291), a modern outbuilding of an 1876 farmhouse offering bed & breakfast for 300 EEK per person. It also has a mini-bus for hire.

Getting There & Away

Buses between Kuressaare and the mainland usually take the main road passing within a km of Valjala, while the local Kuressaare-Kuivastu service takes the more southerly road through Laimjala and within a km of Pöide. There are several buses daily between Kuressaare and Orissaare, taking about 1¼ hours, and several, mostly in the morning, between Orissaare and Kuivastu.

Up to seven buses daily run between Kuressaare and Leisi, a trip of about an hour, passing right by Angla windmills and close to Karja church. Those via Pärsama go right by Karja church. Those via Eikla will probably go through Kaarma, which is also served by buses 4½ hours apart in morning and early afternoon, via Aste.

Kaali is halfway between the Kuressaare-Valjala and Kuressaare-Leisi roads, two to three km from each, so you could use a bus along either road to get within walking distance.

KURESSAARE

• *pop 17,000* • ☎ *(245)*

Much of Saaremaa's capital, on the island's south coast 80 km by road from Kuivastu on Muhu, retains its historic appearance and atmosphere.

A castle was founded at Kuressaare (originally named Arensburg) in the 13th century as the Haapsalu-based Bishop of Ösel-Wiek's pied-a-terre in the island part of his diocese. The settlement that grew around it was given the rights of a town in 1563 by Duke Magnus, the Danish noble to whom it passed from the church in the mid-16th century. Kuressaare became Saaremaa's main trading centre, developing quickly after passing into Swedish hands in 1645. In the 19th century it became a health spa because of the curative properties of its coastal mud. In the Soviet era Kuressaare was named Kingisseppa, after Viktor Kingissepp, an Estonian communist of the 1920s.

Orientation

The road from Kuivastu and the mainland enters Kuressaare as Tallinna, passing southwestward through modern suburbs to the central square Kesk väljak. Kuressaare castle and its surrounding park, which reaches down to the coast, are 500m beyond Kesk väljak, along Lossi. The bus station at Pihtla tee 25 is within a short walk of Kesk väljak and the castle.

Information

Tourist Office Kuressaare's tourist information office is inside the old town hall at Tallinna 2 (☎ & fax 55 120; email info@oesel.turism.ee; http://www.estonia.org/oesel). It sells maps and guides, arranges accommodation, books boat trips and island tours, and sorts out car and bicycle rental. Between May and September, it's open daily, except Sunday, from 9 am to 6 pm. Between October and April, it is open weekdays from 9 am to 5 pm.

The Saaremaa headquarters of the Biosphere Reserve of the West Estonian Archipelago (☎ 577 68) at Kalevi 10 provides information on the natural side of things. Kuressaare's Express Hotline (☎ 53 220) operates 24 hours and calls are free.

Money Tallinna Pank on the corner of the central square and Kohtu gives cash advance on credit cards and cashes travellers' cheques. It is also possible to change cash at Kuressaare Maapank – the building with a 'Pank' sign at Tallinna 27, almost opposite the bus station – and at Hansapank on the west side of the central square. The currency exchange inside Jurka, a liquor shop next door to Hansapank on the central square, offers the best exchange rates (open daily Monday to Saturday from 10 am to 9 pm, Sunday from 10 am to 7 pm).

Post & Communications The post office is at Torni 1. There are public card telephones both inside and outside the post office as well as at strategic points around the town.

Travel Agencies Mardi travel agency (☎ 54 875, fax 56 241), which you will find inside the old fire station at Tallinna 4, and Baltic

ESTONIA

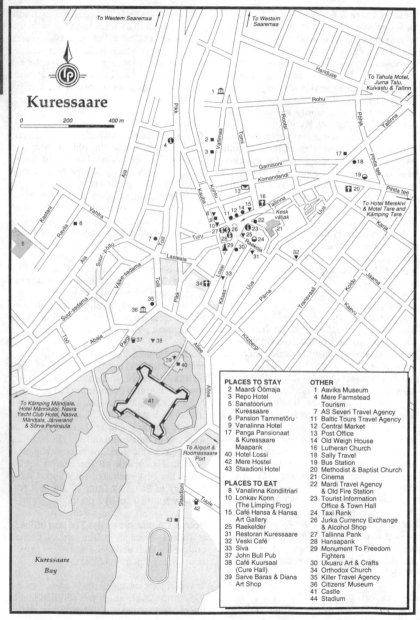

Kuressaare

0   200   400 m

To Western Saaremaa

To Western Saaremaa

To Tahula Motel,
Jurna Talu,
Kuivastu & Tallinn

To Hotel Merekivi
& Motel Tare and
Kämping Tare

To Kämping Mändjala,
Hotel Männikäbi, Nasra
Yacht Club Hotel, Nasva,
Mändjala, Järverand
& Sõrve Peninsula

To Airport &
Roomassaare
Port

Kuressaare
Bay

PLACES TO STAY
2 Maardi Öömaja
3 Repo Hotel
5 Sanatoorium
   Kuressaare
6 Pansion Tammetõru
17 Vanalinna Hotel
17 Panga Pansionaat
   & Kuressaare
   Maapank
40 Hotel Lossi
42 Mere Hostel
43 Staadioni Hotel

PLACES TO EAT
8 Vanalinna Konditriari
10 Lonkav Konn
   (The Limping Frog)
15 Café Hansa & Hansa
   Art Gallery
25 Raekelder
31 Restoran Kuressaare
32 Veski Café
33 Siva
37 John Bull Pub
38 Café Kuursaal
   (Cure Hall)
39 Sarve Baras & Diana
   Art Shop

OTHER
1 Aaviks Museum
4 Mere Farmstead
   Tourism
7 AS Severi Travel Agency
11 Baltic Tours Travel Agency
12 Central Market
13 Post Office
14 Old Weigh House
16 Lutheran Church
18 Sally Travel
19 Bus Station
20 Methodist & Baptist Church
21 Cinema
22 Mardi Travel Agency
   & Old Fire Station
23 Tourist Information
   Office & Town Hall
24 Taxi Rank
26 Jurka Currency Exchange
   & Alcohol Shop
27 Tallinna Pank
28 Hansapank
29 Monument To Freedom
   Fighters
30 Ukuaru Art & Crafts
34 Orthodox Church
35 Killer Travel Agency
36 Citizens' Museum
41 Castle
44 Stadium

Tours (☎ & fax 55 480) at Tallinna 1, can fix you up with a variety of accommodation, tours in several languages, and other services.

Mere Farmstead Tourism (☎ & fax 54 461; email lii@evk.oesel.ee; http://www.ee/ecotourism) at Pikk 60, specialises in countryside tourism on the island and arranges accommodation in a variety of idyllic farmhouses off the beaten track as well as cycling, fishing and horse riding tours. It is also one of two official agents for the Estonian Ecotourism Association.

Arensburgi Reisid (☎ 57 660, 56 400), inside the main building of the bus station, arranges boat trips to Abruka while the Killer travel agency (☎ 54 354; fax 55 480) at Pargi 3, specialises in trips to Vilsandi.

The Castle

Kuressaare castle stands at the south end of the town, on an artificial island with four pointed bastion corners, ringed by a partly filled moat which is surrounded by a park. It's very well preserved and definitely one of the most impressive castles in the Baltic states.

A castle was founded on this site as the bishop of Ösel-Wiek's island base by the 1260s, but the mighty square fortress of locally quarried dolomite that stands today at the centre of several rings of fortification was not built until 1338-80. It was designed as an administrative centre as well as a stronghold. The more slender of its two tall corner towers, Pikk Hermann at the east, is separated from the rest of the castle by a shaft crossed only by a drawbridge, so it could function as a last refuge in time of attack.

Interior The inside of the castle is a warren of chambers, halls, passages and stairways which will meet anyone's fantasies about Gothic fortresses. It houses the **Saaremaa Regional Museum** (Saaremaa Koduloo-muuseum) and is open daily, except Monday and Tuesday, from 11 am to 7 pm. Entrance is 20/10 EEK for adults/students. On the ground floor look for the hypocaust (hüpokaust) on the south-west side – a furnace which fed a medieval central heating system. Nine ducts conveyed warm air to the chapter house one floor above; there you'll find nine corresponding holes in the floor, which could be opened and shut as comfort demanded.

Exterior The wall around the outer edge of the castle island was built at the end of the 14th century, and the cannon towers added later. The greatest of the cannon towers, completed in 1470, is at the island's north corner. The bastions and moat were created by the Danes in the 17th century. There's a former gunpowder cellar in the south bastion.

Park The shady park around the castle moat and running down to Kuressaare Bay was laid out in 1861 and there are some fine wooden resort buildings from the turn of the century in and around it, notably the 1889 Kuursaal (Spa Hall). There's a **Citizens' Museum** (Linnakodaniku Muuseum) at Pargi 5, open daily, except Monday and Tuesday, from 10 am to 6 pm.

Other Sights

Town Centre Kuressaare's other best old buildings are grouped round the central square Kesk väljak, notably the **town hall** (linnavalitsus) on the east side with a pair of fine stone lions at the door, and the **weighhouse** opposite it on the corner of Kohtu,

Kuressaare Castle – the best-preserved medieval fortress in the Baltics.

both 17th century Baroque. There's a hand-some **Lutheran church** at the north-east end of Kesk väljak, and an **Orthodox church** on Lossi.

At Vallimaa 7 there is **Aaviks Museum**, dedicated to the life and works of outstanding linguist Johannes Aavik (1880-1973) and his musically-talented cousin, Joosep Aavik (1899-1989). It is open Wednesday to Sunday from 11 am to 6 pm. In the small square on the corner of Lossi and Kauba is a **monument** dating to 1928 in honour of the islanders who died during their fight for independence.

Beaches The best beach in the Kuressaare area is Järverand at Järve, about 14 km west, a couple of km past Mändjala. On the way – at Nasva – there's a yacht harbour with a few yachts for charter. There's also a beach at Sutu, 12 km east. Salme, Torgu, or Sääre buses from Kuressaare go to Järverand.

Special Events
In March, Kuressaare hosts its annual theatre days. At the beginning of June, the town celebrates the beginning of the season, followed closely by Midsummer day celebrations on the eve of 23 June.

In summer, classical and folk music concerts are held at the open-air stage in the grounds of the castle and inside the Kuursaal. Fortnightly schedules are listed at the tourism information centre and on flyers round town. In August there is a chamber music festival.

Places to Stay – in town
Between May and September, trying to find somewhere to stay is horrendous. The place swarms with visitors and prices soar sky high. Booking as early as April does not even guarantee the room of your choice for June, July or August. Nightly rates drop by 50% from October when the town dies until another year.

The tourist information centre, Baltic Tours and Mardi travel agencies all arrange accommodation in private flats in town for around 120 EEK per person. Family Hotel Service of Tallinn (see Accommodation in Facts for the Visitor at the front of the book) also has options in Kuressaare.

The Estonian Hostels Association runs a small hostel with six beds at Tuule 3. To stay at the *Mere Hostel* (☎ 59 431; fax 56 929) it costs 150 EEK a night.

Good value is the *Maardi Öömaja* (☎ 57 436; fax 56 056), run by students from the Kuressaare trade school, at Vallimaa 5a. From the front it seems to be a grey, faceless building, but round the back (where the entrance is), it is brightly painted with graffitti-style murals. From mid-May to mid-September, singles/doubles/triples with shared bath in the hostel cost 100/150/200 EEK. The price does not include breakfast. In the hotel, singles/doubles/triples cost 240/380/525 EEK including breakfast. From mid-September to mid-May, the hostel is closed and hotel prices drop by 50%. The students also run the good hotel restaurant, Kass, boldly decked out in the Estonian national colours.

Next door to the Maardi is the *Repo Hotel* (☎ 55 111; fax 55 552) at Vallimaa 1a, a modern house with little character offering singles/doubles with private bath, cable TV, radio and telephone for 370/520 EEK including breakfast. Between October and May, rooms cost 100 EEK less.

The *Panga Pansionaat* (☎ 57 989; fax 57 990) close to the bus station at Tallinna 27 is a small, modern place where good, clean rooms with spotless, shared showers and toilets cost 200/400 EEK for singles/doubles. It has 20 places in total.

Given its prime location, the *Hotel Lossi* (☎ 54 443), a dark-red painted wooden house at Lossi 27 (on the island crossed by the road over the castle moat), is exceedingly good value. Clean singles/doubles with shared bathrooms cost 220/440 EEK. Just make sure you book months ahead if you really want to stay here.

Equally well placed but not quite so affordable is the luxurious *Vanalinna* (☎ 59 889; fax 55 309) just footsteps from the central square at Kauba 8. Prettily painted in pink and white, Kuressaare's most modern hotel has singles/doubles/luxury suites for 450/665/800 EEK. From October to April prices fall to 350/450/550 EEK. Tour groups get slightly better rates. It has an excellent in-house restaurant.

A short walk to the centre of town through pretty woodland is the *Staadioni Hotel* (☎ 55 202; fax 56 499) close to the castle and stadium at Staadioni 1. Singles/doubles cost 400/525 EEK.

In a similiar price bracket is the *Sanatoorium Kuressaare* (☎ 59 250; fax 59 304), behind the hospital at Kastani 20. Singles/doubles cost 350/550 EEK between May and September; 250/350 EEK from October to April. An overnight voucher, including a bath in mud or some other curative treatment and a bed for the night, costs 450 EEK.

A couple of blocks away is the *Pansion Tammetõru* (☎ 59 638; fax 54 772) at Ravila 2a. Singles/doubles with private bathroom in the recently built bungalow cost 350/450 EEK.

Places to Stay – out of town

These places are mainly aimed at people with their own vehicles, though some are on bus routes.

Mere Farmstead Tourism (☎ & fax 54 461) at Pikk 60 has farmhouses to let in a number of inspiring locations all over the island. For an advance copy of its summer catalogue write to it at Pikk 60, EE-3300 Kuressaare, Saare County, Estonia. Farmhouse accommodation is also arranged by the Estonian Ecotourism Association.

Jurna Talu (☎ 53 453) at Upa, six km from Kuressaare on the Kuivastu and Tallinn road, is a beautifully renovated farmhouse offering rooms for 250 EEK. You have to share the bathroom with your neighbours but the wholesome breakfast more than compensates. Extra meals cost 100 EEK and you can rent a bicycle for 15 EEK an hour.

One km further east on the same road at Tahula is the *Tahula Motel* (☎ 57 410), an excellent, modern place with friendly staff. Good, clean double/family rooms with private bath on the more spacious first and second floors cost 490/590 EEK. Smaller single/double rooms with low attic ceilings on the third floor cost 300/420 EEK. Its summer café hosts regular folk programs and can arrange picnics with Estonian folk music.

Kämping Mändjala (☎ 55 079; fax 54 035), open in June, July and August in woods behind a beach at Mändjala, 11 km along the coast road west of Kuressaare, has wooden cabins close to the sea for 120 EEK per person. Each cabin fits two, three, four or five people. Pitching a tent costs 40 EEK in total and parking a campervan for the night is 140 EEK. Other facilities include a restaurant, bar, café, volleyball, basketball, fireplace and sauna. The showers and toilets are a five minute walk from the sleeping area. Buses from Kuressaare to Torgu or Sääre (running three times a day) go to the Mändjala bus stop, about half a km past the site.

The *Hotel Männikäbi* (☎ 75 106; fax 54 772), about 600m past Kämping Mändjala, has spacious rooms with private bath and TV for 400/620 EEK including breakfast. It's 300m off the road; the turning is just past the Mändjala bus stop.

Motel and Kämping Tare (☎ 90 125; fax 57 584) near the beach at Sutu, 13 km east of Kuressaare, takes 25 people in sizeable rooms at 300 EEK for a double. A place in a triple or four-bed room costs 100 EEK. Unheated double wooden cabins cost 150 EEK while campervans are 110 EEK and pitching a tent 20 EEK. There is also a field shower and kitchen.

The 50 bed *Hotel Merekivi* (☎ 57 744) at Kudjape, three km east of the town centre, was built in 1991 and charges 645 EEK for a double room with private bathroom. It also has a restaurant and bar.

Rapidly establishing itself as Saaremaa's most elite hang-out is the *Nasva Yacht Club Hotel* (☎ 75 100; fax 55 257), situated nine km from Kuressaare at Nasva harbour. Surrounded by the sun, sea and sand – a truly scenic backdrop for a fleet of yachts – it really is an idyllic place to stay. Plush singles/doubles cost 400/700 EEK and luxury suites, 1000 EEK.

ESTONIA

Places to Eat

For freshly baked, traditional Estonian breads and cakes look no further than the very pink and green *Vanalinna Kondiitriari* next to the Vanalinna Hotel at Kauba 6. Post-modern in decor and a minimalist menu consisting of purely calorie-laden plates, this is a must for anyone with a sweet tooth.

Coming in second on the sweet side is *Café Hansa*, inside an art gallery on central square at Tallinna 9. It is small and cosy and serves delicious muffins as well as home-made soups and light snacks.

The cheap fast food joint *Siva* at Lossi 3 serves filling meat and potato-style meals on plastic plates for no more than 10 EEK. Equally fast in service is *Lonkav Konn* (The Limping Frog), Kuressaare's Irish pub at Kauba 6 offering pub grub and live music at weekends. Estonian-style shepherd's pie topped with lots of sour cream is 25 EEK (open daily from 10 to 3 am).

For the ultimate Saaremaa dining experience try *Raekelder* on the corner of Tallinna and Raekoja. The waiters, all of which appear to be exclusively young handsome men, wear traditional costume – bloomers and all! The grilled beef fillet in black bread sauce for 50 EEK and the fried cheese in rum sauce are both tasty.

The *Café Kuursaal* (Spa Hall) inside a former turn of the century health resort at Pargi 2, in a park opposite the Bishop's Castle, has been around so long it has become a bit of an institution with tour groups. Unfortunately the food is not quite as impressive as the setting. The *John Bull Pub*, also overlooking the castle on Pargi, is pretty naff; try the more rustic, country-style *Sarve Baras* opposite the Lossi Hotel and castle in the basement of the Diana art shop instead. The *Veski café* inside an old wind-mill at Parna 19 serves Saaremaa beer. Discos are held on the tiny third floor at weekends. For the ultimate room with a view try a coffee in the *Tower Café* in the parapet of the castle. It is only open in summer.

Things to Buy

Top quality juniper-wood beer mugs, leather goods, dolomite, hand knitted sweaters and other Saaremaa textiles are sold at the Ukuaru art and crafts shop at Lossi 9, and at the central market just off town hall square. The Hansa Art Gallery at Tallinna 9 sells paintings, sculptures and other locally produced art pieces.

Getting There & Away

Direct bus/ferry connections between Kuressaare, the mainland and Hiiumaa island are covered in Saaremaa – Getting There & Away. Kuressaare's bus station at Pihtla tee 25 is the terminus for most buses on the island and schedules are posted inside.

Getting Around

Kuressaare airport is at Roomassaare, three km south-east of the town centre. Bus No 2 runs about 15 times daily to/from the central Kesk väljak. There's a taxi rank on Raekoja, just off Kesk väljak. Taxis charge 4.50 EEK per km.

Sally Travel (☎ 56 760) at Tallinna 30 rents out cars and six and 18-gear bicycles from 17 EEK an hour. AS Kumar (☎ 59 094) at Rootsi 7 and AS Severi (☎ 57 118) at Pikk 4 rent cars and bicycles.

WESTERN SAAREMAA
Viidumäe Nature Reserve

Founded in 1957, Viidumäe Nature Reserve covers an area of 1194 hectares, the highlight of which is a tall observation tower on Saaremaa's highest point (54m) at Viidumäe, about 25 km west of Kuressaare. The tower, about two km along a dirt road off the Kuressaare-Lümanda road at Viidu, offers a panoramic view of the surrounding habitat of the reserve as well as the forested and coastal wonders of the island itself. Viidumäe is essentially a botanical reserve, its favourable climate and conditions making it home to rare plant species such as the blunt-flowered rush, the Saaremaa yellow rattle and the white-beam.

Guided tours of the reserve are available through the reserve's headquarters (☎ 76 321, 76 462; email talvi@viidu.oesel.ee) in

Viidu. The mailing address is Viidu, PO Lümanda, EE-3335 Saaremaa.

Viki & Kihelkonna

At Viki on the Kuressaare-Kihelkonna road, about 30 km from Kuressaare, an old farm has been preserved as the Mihkli Talumuuseum (Mihkli Farm Museum). Kihelkonna, three km beyond, has a tall, austere, early German church. The village is also home to the Vilsandi National Park headquarters (see Vilsandi & Vilsandi National Park). There's a fishing harbour, usable by yachts, at Veere on the east side of the Tagamõisa peninsula north of Kihelkonna.

Karujärv

About 10 km east of Kihelkonna, but reachable by paved road from Kuressaare through Kärla, Karujärv is a popular forest lake with islands and indented shores. Dejevo, by the road near its north shore, is a Russian village built for Soviet military families who were stationed on Saaremaa.

North Coast

The 22m cliff known as Panga pank (bank) or sometimes Mustjala pank, at Panga on the north coast is Saaremaa's highest cliff.

Sõrve Peninsula

More cliffs, such as the Kaugatuma pank and Ohesaare pank, rear up along the west coast of the 32 km south-western Sõrve peninsula. There are good views from the lighthouse at Kaugatuma. Tehumardi at the neck of the peninsula, shortly west of the beach at Järve (see Kuressaare), was the site of a fierce night battle in October 1944 between retreating German troops and an Estonian Rifle Division. There's a big sword monument there now. About halfway down the narrow peninsula are remains of the Lõpe-Kaimri defence line also from WWII. Mõntu on the east coast has a small harbour usable by yachts in daylight. From Sääre at the peninsula's southern tip it's possible to see the Latvian coast, over 25 km away, in clear weather. Situated here are a lighthouse and coastal artillery positions built by the Red Army early in WWII.

Places to Stay

Fifteen km north of Veere at the coastal village of Undva, on the most northern tip of the Tagamõisa peninsula north, is *Pühassoo Talu* (☎ 56 873, 56 100). A place in a four-bed room in a delightful reed-roofed granary is 130 EEK. Pitching a tent costs 30 EEK. It also rents out bicycles/boats for 50/30 EEK an hour.

At Kuralase, seven km from Veere, is the *Loode Tourist Farm* (☎ 56 227). Bed & breakfast in one of the thatched log houses, some dating to 1779, is 150 EEK. Tents can be pitched for 40 EEK. It also arranges horse riding and fishing. The authentic Saaremaa smoke-sauna is 300 EEK.

Among the trees on the east side of Karujärv lake, *Kämping Karujärv* (☎ 72 681) is a basic place with cabins at 85 EEK per person. Pitching a tent is 25 EEK and parking a campervan is 120 EEK. There is a small outside song stage, a mini golf course and horse riding at weekends.

Kämping Tagaranna (☎ 79 743) is a modern Swedish-built place consisting of five comfortable double cabins, with shared showers and toilets, on the north coast about 10 km north of Mustjala. The cost is 180 EEK per person. It has four mountain bikes to rent.

At Ninase, about eight km north of Mustjala on the same road, is *Ninase Puhkekülasse* (☎ & fax 79 743), a pleasant place from which to explore the neighbouring fishing villages. A double wooden cabin is 300 EEK. Less authentic is the newly constructed Scandinavian-style *Ninase Vacation Village* (☎ 79 743), open between mid-May and mid-September. It rents bicycles, windsurfing equipment and arranges fishing trips.

Mere Farmstead Tourism and Kuressaare tourism information centre arranges accommodation on the Sõrve peninsula (see Kuressaare – Places to Stay).

Getting There & Away

There are several buses daily to/from Kihelkonna (about an hour) by various routes. A number of buses also run daily to Karujärv which are possible to use for day trips. Be sure to check the time of your returning bus when you arrive as buses do have a tendency to deviate from the supposedly set schedules.

VILSANDI & VILSANDI NATIONAL PARK

Vilsandi, west of Kihelkonna, is the largest of 161 islands and islets off Saaremaa's western coast which are protected under the Vilsandi National Park. It covers an area of 18,155 hectares (including 161 tiny islands) and is an area of extensive ecological study. The breeding patterns of the common eider and the migration of the barnacle goose have been monitored particularly closely in the park.

Six km long and in places up to three km wide, Vilsandi is a low, wooded island, the small islets surrounding it being abundant with currant and juniper bushes. Up to 247 bird species are observed here, and in spring and autumn there is a remarkable migration of waterfowl – up to 10,000 barnacle geese stop over on Vilsandi in mid-May and the white-tailed eagle and osprey have even been known to drop by.

The prime time to visit the island is from the beginning of May to mid-June. In summer a small boat runs twice daily on Tuesday and Friday from Papisaare on the mainland to Vikati on Vilsandi. The one-way fare is 25 EEK. In July, if the waters are sufficiently shallow, an old bus ploughs its way across from Papisaare to Vakati instead, a one-way journey taking about 20 minutes.

Overnight accommodation for 15 people in shared rooms is available at the biological station on Vilsandi for 75 EEK per person.

Places in the hostel or on the boat from the mainland have to be booked in advance through the national park headquarters (☎ 23 007, 76 604, 76 554) at Kihelkonna. The Killer travel agency in Kuressaare also arranges trips to the island (see Kuressaare – Travel Agencies).

ABRUKA & VAHASE

Known as a 'Mecca for naturalists' by Estonians, the 10.6 km sq island of Abruka and neighbouring Vahase lie six km from Roomassare, off Saaremaa's south coast. Part of the island is a botanical-zoological reservation and deer, although now endangered, also inhabit the island. Today about 30 people live on Abruka. The class register at the small island school listed nine pupils at the last count. In summer two boats – a mail boat and a private boat – provide the only regular link between the island and the mainland. In the depths of the Baltic winter it's possible to walk across the ice to Saaremaa.

Between mid-May and mid-September, the *Abruka Centre* (☎ & fax 57 412) on the island provides farmhouse accommodation for nine people at 150 EEK a night. Tents can also be pitched. The family running the centre rents out bicycles, arranges horse riding, provides hearty home-cooked meals at an extra charge and can also pick you by boat from Roomassare port. Boat trips to Abruka and accommodation can only be booked in advance. The Arensburgi Reisid travel agency also arranges trips to Abruka and Vahase (see Kuressaare – Travel Agencies).

South-West Estonia

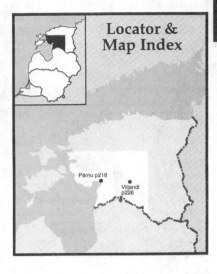

Locator & Map Index

Pärnu p218

Viljandi p226

The main town of south-west Estonia, the coastal resort Pärnu, really comes alive at summer festival times – when it positively buzzes! The rest of the year it's a quiet but amiable place worth a halt if you're not in a hurry (and don't have an aversion to men in shiny tracksuits). Elsewhere in the region you might explore the isolated coast west of Pärnu, canoe on the wild bogs of the Soomaa National Park, trail the Nigula bogs, or venture to the remote islands of Kihnu or Ruhnu.

PÄRNU

• pop 51,526 • ☎ (244)

Pärnu, dubbed 'the summer capital of Estonia' by party goers, is 130 km south of Tallinn on the main road to Rīga. In the Soviet era the pleasures of the long, sandy beach of the country's leading summer resort sadly were greatly reduced by pollution which rendered swimming inadvisable. New water-purification equipment removed any health risk by 1993, according to local environmental authorities. Still, 40% of the town's waste continues to flow directly into the Pärnu River. Meanwhile, Pärnu is making energetic efforts to attract visitors in other ways, by hosting a succession of festivals every summer, among other things. And indeed, while not exactly the 'Estonian Las

Vegas' that some in the tourist business like to imagine, Pärnu rocks at festival times – so much so that finding somewhere to stay if you have not booked in advance can be quite a mission.

History
Stone Age objects from around 7500 BC found at Pulli, near Sindi on the Pärnu River about 12 km inland, are the oldest human artefacts found in Estonia. At that time the mouth of the river was at Pulli and the site of Pärnu was still sea-bed.

There was a trading settlement at Pärnu before the German crusaders arrived, but the place only entered recorded history when the Pärnu River was fixed as the border between the territories of the Ösel-Wiek bishop (to the west and north) and the Livonian knights (to the east and south) in 1234. In 1251 the bishop even came to live on his bank of the river here, promoting the church to a cathedral, but he moved north to Haapsalu after

ESTONIA

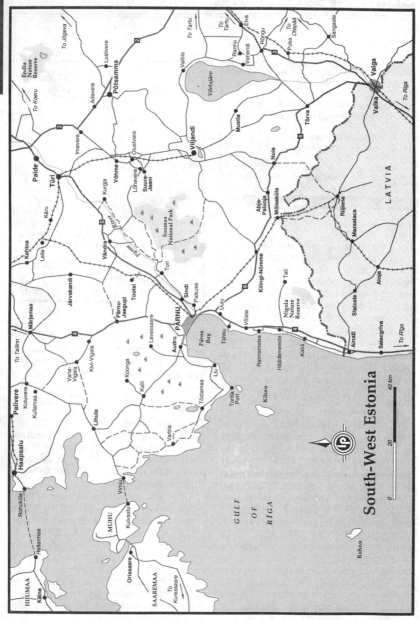

South-West Estonia

a Lithuanian raid in 1263. Meanwhile the knights had built a fort on the east side of the river. The town that grew up around the knights' fort, joined by rivers to Viljandi, Tartu, and Lake Peipus, became the Hanseatic port of Pernau in the 14th century. (Sinking water levels have since cut this link.) Pernau/Pärnu had a population of largely Lübeck origin till at least the 18th century. It suffered wars, fires, plagues, and switches between German, Polish, Swedish and Russian rule down the centuries – apparently taking an upswing in the 17th century under Swedish rule but having its trade devastated by the Europe-wide blockades that accompanied the Napoleonic wars.

From 1838 the town gradually revived as a resort, mudbaths proving a draw, as well as the beach and relatively good weather. By the late 1930s Pärnu was attracting Swedes and Finns as well as local visitors. Only the resort area was spared severe damage in 1944 as the Soviet army drove out the Nazi occupiers, but many bits of the old town have since been restored.

Orientation

Pärnu lies either side of the estuary of the Pärnu River, which empties into the northeast corner of the Gulf of Rīga, known as Pärnu Bay. The southern half of the town, a roughly 1.5-km-wide neck of land between the river and the bay, is the centre of activity. The central square is on the corner of Ringi and Rüütli, with the bus station half a block to the north on Pikk, and the old town with its relatively narrow streets stretching to the west. Rüütli is the main shopping street. Southward towards the sea the streets are younger and wider, opening out into a wide, treed park backing the beach.

Maps Maps of Pärnu and surrounding areas can be picked up at the Looming bookshop at Rüütli 41 or at the tourist information centre.

Information

Tourist Office The tourist information centre (☎ 40 639, 45 533; fax 45 633; email info@parnu.turism.ee; http://www.estonia.org/parnu) is at Munga 2. The English-speaking Express Hotline (☎ 39 222) is on line 24 hours.

Money Tallinna Pank at Rüütli 55 will exchange travellers' cheques and give a cash advance on Visa, Diners Club, Eurocard and MasterCard, as will the Põhja-Eesti Pank at Munga 2 next to the tourist information centre.

Eesti Ühispank at Rüütli 40a, on the north side of the square and close to the bus station, cashes travellers' cheques and gives cash advance on credit cards; it also has a Visa ATM. The Pärnu hotel has a 24 hour currency exchange.

Post & Communications The main post office, open weekdays from 8 am to 7 pm and weekends from 9 am to 3 pm Saturday and Sunday, is at Akadeemia 7.

Travel Agencies Eha Reisid Travel Agency (☎ 45 105) at Hospidali 6 is the leading agent for selling boat tickets between Tallinn and Helsinki. Wris (☎ 31 456) inside the Hotel Pärnu at Rüütli 44 is also a reputable travel agent. Atlas (☎ 42 032) at Rüütli 40 and Reiser Travel Agency (☎ 44 556; fax 44 566) at Rüütli 29 are the best travel agencies to get you to the islands of Ruhnu and Kihnu.

Media 'Everyone has fun!' according to Pärnu Radio on 100.3 MHz which has news bulletins on the hour alternately in Estonian, Russian, English and Finnish.

Left Luggage There's a left-luggage office (pakihoid) in the bus station opposite the bus parking lot. The white wooden cabin is open weekdays from 8 am to 7 pm (with a munch break from 1 to 1.45 pm) and on Saturday from 8 am to 1 pm.

Town Centre & Old Town

The old area stretches about 700m west of the central square along streets like Malmö, Rüütli and Kuninga. The oldest building in Pärnu is the **Red Tower** (Punane Torn) on

ESTONIA

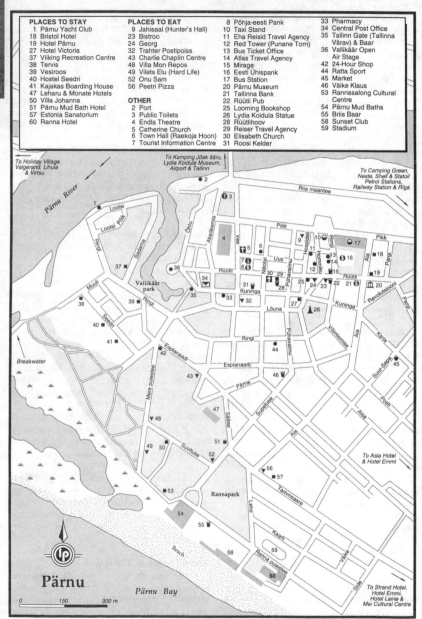

PLACES TO STAY
1   Pärnu Yacht Club
18 Bristol Hotel
19 Hotel Pärnu
27 Hotel Victoria
37 Viiking Recreation Centre
38 Tervis
39 Vesiroos
40 Hostel Seedri
41 Kajakas Boarding House
47 Leharu & Monate Hotels
50 Villa Johanna
51 Pärnu Mud Bath Hotel
57 Estonia Sanatorium
60 Ranna Hotel

PLACES TO EAT
9   Jahisaal (Hunter's Hall)
23 Bistroo
24 Georg
32 Trahter Postipoiss
43 Charlie Chaplin Centre
48 Villa Mon Repos
49 Vilets Elu (Hard Life)
52 Onu Sam
56 Peetri Pizza

OTHER
2   Port
3   Public Toilets
4   Endla Theatre
5   Catherine Church
6   Town Hall (Raekoja Hoon)
7   Tourist Information Centre

8   Põhja-eesti Pank
10 Taxi Stand
11 Eha Reisid Travel Agency
12 Red Tower (Punane Torn)
13 Bus Ticket Office
14 Atlas Travel Agency
15 Mirage
16 Eesti Ühispank
17 Bus Station
20 Pärnu Museum
21 Tallinna Bank
22 Rüütli Pub
25 Looming Bookshop
26 Lydia Koidula Statue
28 Rüütlihoov
29 Reiser Travel Agency
30 Elisabeth Church
31 Roosi Kelder

33 Pharmacy
34 Central Post Office
35 Tallinn Gate (Tallinna
    Värav) & Baar
36 Vallikäär Open
    Air Stage
42 24-Hour Shop
44 Ratta Sport
45 Market
46 Väike Klaus
53 Rannasalong Cultural
    Centre
54 Pärnu Mud Baths
55 Briis Baar
58 Sunset Club
59 Stadium

Pärnu

Pärnu Bay

0   150   300 m

Hommiku. Originally bigger, this was the south-east corner tower of the medieval town wall, of which no more remains. At one stage the tower was used as a prison. The ground floor is a small museum, open daily, except Sunday and Monday, from noon to 5 pm. Upstairs is an art shop.

Two blocks west, on Pühavaimu, is a fine pair of large **17th century houses** joined by a columned structure built in 1877. The in-between bit also has the date 1741 which was when the Pärnu merchant Hans Dietrich Schmidt, who owned both older wings in the 18th century, founded his general store.

One block further west, on Nikolai on the corner of Uus, is the former **Town Hall** (Raekoja Hoon), a yellow and white classical edifice originally built in 1788 as the home of the town police chief. The grey and white Art Nouveau north wing with its little spire, opposite the corner of Malmö, was added in 1911.

Across Nikolai from the main town hall building there's a half-timbered house dating from 1740, and a block down the street on the corner of Rüütli is the Baroque Lutheran **Elisabeth Church**, also from the 1740s, named after the Russian empress of the time. Another block west at the corner of Uus and Vee, the Russian Orthodox **Catherine Church** (Ekatarina kirik) from the 1760s is named after another Russian empress, Catherine the Great.

Heading to the far west end of Rüütli, you'll find an embankment along an inlet of water from the river. This is a stretch of Pärnu's **Swedish ramparts** overlooking the **moat** which defended the west side of the old town. Where the rampart meets the west end of Kuninga it's pierced by the tunnel-like **Tallinn Gate** (Tallinna Värav), one of three gates in the ramparts that the Swedes built as part of their 17th century strengthening of Pärnu's defences.

Heading back east along Kuninga, there's a **17th century house** at No 21, with a shoe hanging from its eaves which is said to have been lost by Sweden's King Carl XII in 1700. Nearby is an 18th century stone warehouse at Kuninga 24 and an 18th century house at

Kuninga 28. The **Hotel Victoria** at Kuninga 25, a fine 1930 Art Nouveau building, stands on the site of the old Swedish Rīga Gate. Kuninga ran from the Tallinn Gate to the Rīga Gate. In Koidula väljak, the park opposite the hotel, stands a symbol of Pärnu – the **statue of Lydia Koidula**, the poet of Estonia's national revival whose likeness appears on the 100 EEK note. There's also a **Lydia Koidula Memorial Museum** (☎ 41 663) at Jannseni 37 in Ülejõe on the north side of the river, open Wednesday to Sunday from 11 am to 5 pm.

Pärnu Museum (Pärnu Rajoonide Vaheline Koduloomuuseum) (☎ 43 464) is on the corner of the central square at Rüütli 53, open Wednesday to Sunday from 11 am to 5 pm.

Resort Area

The resort area begins just south of the old town and most of it is closed to vehicles. A band of green parkland known as Rannapark backs the long, wide beach. From its northern end you can walk along the two km breakwater at the mouth of the river, but take care with the tides.

The eye-catching classical structure at the sea end of Supeluse is the mud baths, which are still operating. Bus No 1 comes to the Rannasalong stop here from Pärnu post office. Just to the west is the Rannasalong Cultural Centre.

Mud Baths

No trip to Pärnu is complete without a mud bath. Standing royally on the sea front at Ranna 1 is the town's most sought after mud baths, dating to 1927. At Pärnu Mud Baths (☎ & fax 41 295) bathers can choose from a selection of mud to wallow in, be it 'local' or 'electric' mud, costing 80 EEK for about 40 minutes. 'General' mud is an extra 20 EEK. See also Pärnu Mud Bath Hotel and Estonia Sanatorium in Places to Stay.

Places to Stay – bottom end

The tourist information centre arranges accommodation in private homes in and around the centre of Pärnu for 100 EEK a night. It also sorts hotel bookings.

Some of the cheapest beds in town can be

found at the friendly *Kajakas* boarding house (☎ 43 098; fax 42 181), a km from the bus station at Seedri 2. The reception has been painted in recent years although the rooms could do with a quick lick. Singles/doubles/triples with shared bath are 140/220/300 EEK and a room for four with shared bathroom is 390 EEK. Breakfast is 30 EEK extra.

The neighbouring *Hostel Seedri* (☎ 43 350; fax 43 960) at Seedri 4 and the slightly more upmarket *Vesiroos* (☎ 43 534; fax 43 963), round the corner at Esplanadi 42a, are both approved by the Estonian Hostels Association. The Seedri has 86 beds. Doubles/triples/quads are 220/290/345 EEK including a meagre breakfast which is not served until 10 am (and even then you have to make a point of asking for it). The Vesiroos sleeps 35 and has an outside pool, free for hotel guests. Doubles/triples are 450/630 EEK including breakfast.

The *Hotel Laine* (☎ 39 111; fax 43 442) at Laine 6a has two singles and nine doubles with shared bathroom for 170/260 EEK.

Also good value are the seven rooms available at *Pärnu Yacht Club* (☎ 31 420; fax 42 950) overlooking the harbour at Lootsi 6. Small singles/doubles with private bathroom cost 200/320 EEK and breakfast is 25 EEK. The club arranges car rental, theatre tickets and yacht rental, the price of which is negotiable with the captain. It also has parking space for four caravans.

Pärnu Mud Bath Hotel (☎ 42 040) is on Supeluse, 500m north of the Pärnu Mud Baths. Singles/doubles cost 220/340 EEK, a family room is 350 EEK, and a night stay with two treatments is 380 EEK.

There are three camping grounds around Pärnu. *Holiday Village Valgerand* (☎ 64 231), also run by the Seedri and Vesiroos, is 10 km west of central Pärnu among pleasant pine woods by the sea. It opens from mid-May to the end of September and has 40 reasonably sized two or four-person cabins for 125/180 EEK. Turn south off the Lihula road six km from Pärnu then go three km. An overnight fee for pitching a tent is 60 EEK.

Kämping Jõek ääru (☎ & fax 41 121) is in Sauga, 10 km north of the Pärnu River. A place in a four/five-person bungalow is 65/75 EEK. It charges 50 EEK to pitch a tent and 100 EEK to park a campervan. Campers can use the tennis courts, volleyball, basketball courts, football pitch and mini-golf of the adjoining Sauga School.

Two km from the centre overlooking the Pärnu River is *Camping Green* (☎ 43 776; fax 43 442) at Suure-Jõe 50b. A place in a two-person summerhouse is 75 EEK and breakfast is an additional 20 EEK. It also has a tennis and basketball court, a fitness hall and can arrange fishing and rowing (open between June and September).

Places to Stay – middle

Definitely one of the best choices in the 300 to 400 EEK range, despite being oddly placed at Laine 2 in a housing estate two km east of the town centre, is the *Hotel Emmi* (☎ 22 043, fax 45 472). It's small, friendly and modern with singles/doubles at 300/420 EEK including private bathrooms and a big breakfast. From the centre take bus No 7, 19 or 21 from the post office.

The ugly concrete hotel block 500m from the beach at Sääse 7, the *Leharu* (☎ 45 895; fax 40 064) and *Monate* (☎ 41 472; fax 44 656), is also slightly more appealing than the exterior suggests. The Leharu is on the fourth floor and the Monate, on the fifth, with rooms in the Monate being slightly cheaper. Singles/doubles with private bath and breakfast in the Monate are 280/395 EEK; at the Leharu they are 300/420 EEK. Prices at both drop to 210/310 EEK between October and the end of May.

Equally drab from the outside but brighter inside is the *Asia* (☎ & fax 43 186), on the east side of town at Asia 39. Its name is not derived from the street but from the 'real Indian and Chinese savouries' it apparently serves in its restaurant. However, our taste buds certainly weren't aroused. Reasonably comfortable doubles/triples with private bath are 450/525 EEK.

The *Estonia Sanatorium* (☎ 40 558; fax 44 571) is at Tammsaare 6 and, as well as mud baths, prides itself on its medicinal herbal teas and luxurious indoor swimming pool. Doubles cost 460 EEK including breakfast and a variety of cures.

Two hotels which have hiked up their room rates following renovations are the *Strand* (☎ 39 333; 24 276), a five minute stroll to the beach at Tammsaare 27D; and the *Hotel Pärnu* (☎ 78 911) overlooking the bus station at Rüütli 44. Plush singles/doubles at the Strand are 670/790 EEK and the hotel's piano bar and Moonshiner nightclub are reportedly pretty hot. Other facilities include laundry service, massage, manicure, indoor swimming pool and outside tennis courts. Singles/doubles at the Pärnu are 690/890 EEK. Some rooms are pretty characterless despite their revamp.

Similarly priced is the *Viiking Recreation Centre* (☎ 31 293; fax 31 492) close to the beach at Sadama 15. Built in 1993, it is a bright, modern complex with a sauna, pool, gym, solarium and tennis courts. Pleasant wooden-floored singles/doubles are 580/880 EEK.

Close to the beach area at the southern end of town, is the delightful *Villa Johanna* (☎ 38 370; fax 38 371), a quaint wooden cottage with a country-style decor. Small single/double rooms are 520/680 EEK with larger rooms costing 660/840 EEK.

Places to Stay – top end

The *Hotel Victoria* (☎ 43 412; fax 43 415) in the town centre at Kuninga 25, is considered among the top hotels in the Baltic states. The 21 singles/doubles are as tasteful and comfortable as you'd expect, with satellite TV, minibar, bathroom etc. The hotel is part of the Best Western chain. Also run by the Victoria is the *Bristol* (☎ 31 455), next door to the Hotel Pärnu at Rüütli 45. Singles/doubles are both cost 750/990 EEK. Prices include breakfast and a sauna.

The top hotel in Pärnu, built in the 1930s, is the elegant and beautifully renovated *Rannahotell* (☎ 44 312, 42 955; fax 44 533), a stunning white mansion reposing quietly on the sea front at Ranna puiestee 5, run by the prestigious Palace Hotel in Tallinn. Completely luxurious singles/doubles are 1080/1380 EEK.

Places to Eat

A block west from the bus station at Rüütli 43 is the *Georg*, a clean cafeteria offering soups and salads for 8 EEK and hot dishes such as the ubiquitous viinerid (frankfurter) and schnitsel (hamburger) for around 25 EEK.

Handily placed in the centre of town on the corner of Rüütli and Ringi is an outlet of the *Bistroo* fast food chain. It has been around for years but it is clean, serviceable and not to be frowned upon. You can eat here daily from 9 am to 7 pm for around 20 EEK.

The *Trahter Postipoiss* at Vee 12 is a 19th century post office converted into a tavern-restaurant with a limited menu of meat and vegetarian dishes (open daily 11 am to midnight). A sign outside says that you can play blackjack here. The bar-cum-restaurant *Jahisaal* (Hunter's Hall) at Hospidali 6 serves a variety of game dishes as well as a wide range of beers and is open daily from noon to 1 am.

At Esplanadi 10, once Communist Party headquarters, is the *Charlie Chaplin Centre* (☎ 42 753), a cinema, bookshop, cultural centre and great coffee shop, open daily from 10 am to 6 pm.

The entire beach area is dotted with cafés, kiosks and fast food stands. Establishments worth a longer visit include the *Villa Mon Repos* at Mere 14. It is a cosy restaurant in a pretty pink and white wooden house with red roof overlooking the sea, and is one of the

If Vilnius can have a Frank Zappa statue, Pärnu can pay homage to Charlie Chaplin.

ESTONIA

few places serving good enough value food to draw in the locals. Its outside seating is a hot spot on summer evenings.

Close by is the funky art café-cum-gallery, *Vilets Elu* (Hard Life) at Mere 22, run by the same people as the trendy Illegaard in Tartu. It opens daily from 10 am to 2 am and is all the rage. Also in the beach area, at Tammsaare tee 6, is *Peetri Pizza* with outdoor terrace seating and a takeaway service. For the 24 hour fast food option, try *Onu Sam* on the corner of Supeluse and Suvituse. There are no tables or chairs but given the number of hungry people waiting in line for the 15 EEK 'sam' burgers and hot dogs, the lack of furniture is clearly just a technicality. Close by is the *Baar*, a small bar serving light snacks (open daily from 11 am to 10 pm). The restaurant in the Victoria hotel has a special vegetarian menu.

The *market* is on the corner of Karja and Suur-Sepa.

Entertainment
The tourist information centre distributes an annual *Pärnu Cultural Calendar* which lists dates, times and venues of over 75 events in Pärnu. It sells tickets for most cultural events too. The culture department of Pärnu town council (☎ 41 252; fax 44 167; email kultuur@lv.parnu.ee) is surprisingly tuned in and welcomes people to its office at Nikolai 8.

Theatre & Classical Music Pärnu Town Orchestra holds classical concerts every weekend in summer. Venues include the *Mai Cultural Centre* (☎ 24 144) at Papiniidu 50 and the *Vallikäär Open Air Stage* (☎ 40 194) at Õhtu 1a. The Mai Cultural Centre also shows films daily between May and September. Performances at the *Endla Theatre* (☎ 30 692) start at 6.30 pm.

Bars *Roosi Kelder* at Kuninga 18 is a traditional Estonian bar serving lots of beer in a dimly lit cellar. Close by, above the Tallinn Gate is tucked the tiny *Tallinn Gate Bar*, a

small and fun bar above the arch which rarely gets packed despite its size.

The *Väike Klaus* pub at Supeluse 3 has a smart wooden interior, lots of flags and other promotional trash hanging around and a covered terrace outside so it can still make money when it rains.

At Rüütli 29 is the *Rüütlihoov*, a beer bar with a great courtyard adorned with photos by the entrance showing lots of punters having fun. Further down at Rüütli 45, is the *Rüütli Pub*, yet another of the many let's pretend we're Irish pubs to open in the Baltics.

Nightclubs Pärnu's clubbing scene rocks, the highlight of it being the massively renovated and very flashy *Sunset Club* (☎ 38 000) which spills out onto the beach at Ranna 3 (open until 5 am at weekends). Less hip is *Mirage* (☎ 44 670), opposite the Irish pub, at Rüütli 40 (open daily until 4 or 5 am). Both sport casinos too. There is also a nightclub, *Venus*, inside the Pärnu Hotel, and in the Strand, a wildly popular cocktail bar.

Getting There & Away
Air Pärnu has an airport on the northern edge of town, west off the Tallinn road. The private company, Baltic Aeroservis (☎ 41 235; fax 45 036) at Raua 5, operates three flights a week from Pärnu to Kihnu island; and twice weekly flights to Kuressaare on Saaremaa, stopping at Ruhnu island en route. Flights to Kihnu leave at 10 am on Tuesday, Thursday and Saturday. Flying time is 15 minutes and a one-way/return fare is 60/120 EEK. Flights to Kuressaare depart at 9 am on Wednesday, arriving at Ruhnu island 30 minutes later and in Kuressaare, 20 minutes later. A one-way/return fare to Ruhnu is 100/200 EEK; to Kuressaare 200/400 EEK.

Bus The terminal (☎ 41 554) for overland buses is at the north end of Ringi, just off Pikk. The ticket office, a red brick building open from 4.45 am to 9 pm, is a short distance south on the opposite side of Ringi. More than 20 buses daily make the 130 km trip to/from Tallinn (two hours, 46 EEK). Other buses to/from Pärnu include:

Haapsalu
three hours, one or two buses each way daily, 42 EEK
Kaliningrad
11 hours, two overnight buses each way daily, 144 EEK
Kuressaare
4¼ hours, one bus each way daily, 62 EEK
Otepää
3½ to four hours, two buses each way daily, 48 EEK
Rakvere
4½ hours, one bus each way daily, 66 EEK
Rīga
3¾ hours, one bus each way daily terminating in Vilnius and two others in transit each way daily, 64 EEK
St Petersburg
10 hours, one overnight bus each way daily, 162 EEK
Tartu
three to 4½ hours, six buses each way daily, 64 EEK
Viljandi
1¾ to 2¼ hours, five buses each way daily, 34 EEK
Vilnius
9½ hours, one overnight bus each way daily, 170 EEK
Virtsu
1½ to 2¼ hours, two to four buses each way daily, 22 EEK

Train Two trains a day run each way between Tallinn and Pärnu (2¾ to four hours, 38.80 EEK). Pärnu station is five km east of the town centre along the Rīga road, at Riia 116. There's a central ticket office on the south side of Rüütli between Hospidali and Hommiku.

Car & Motorcycle The Neste, Shell and Statoil petrol stations along Riia maantee are all open 24 hours and have western-grade leaded and unleaded petrol. Europcar (☎ 33 365; fax 33 367) at Tallinna 89a has cars to rent, starting at 1138 EEK a day. Cars from Tulika Rent start at 560 EEK a day; the Rannahotell, Strand, Pärnu and Viiking hotels and Pärnu Yacht Club are its agents.

Bicycle You can rent bicycles from Ratta Sport at Ringi 14a (open weekdays from 10 to 6 pm, Saturday from 10 am to 3 pm).

Boat It's possible to take a ferry or private boat trip from Pärnu to Kihnu and Ruhnu islands (see sections on those islands). Pärnu Yacht Club (Pärnu Jahtklubi) (☎ 31 420; fax 42 950) at Lootsi 6 has a harbour with a customs point and passport control, making it suitable for visiting yachts. Harbour dues are 110 EEK a night.

Getting Around
A main local bus stop in the town centre is the Sidesõlm stop on Akadeemia in front of the main post office. There's a taxi stand on the corner of Pikk and Ringi, to the side of the bus station. State-run taxis (☎ 40 190, 41 240) can also be booked in advance.

AROUND PÄRNU
Lavassaare
Railways are used in the peat extraction industry at Lavassaare in an area of bogs 25 km from Pärnu, and there's a **railway museum** close to the peat fields with a couple of little old steam engines and narrow-gauge trucks. To reach Lavassaare turn north off the Lihula road 13 km west of central Pärnu, then go 12 km or so north.

Tori
There has been a **stud farm** at Tori, 20 km north-east of Pärnu on the Pärnu River, since 1856 when attempts began to breed bigger, stronger Estonian farm and cart horses. There's a horse-breeding museum here too, in a 25 year old house.

Kurgja
At Kurgja, on the Pärnu River 15 km east of Vändra and 65 km north-east of Pärnu, there's a **farm** still operated by 19th century methods and machinery. It was founded in 1874 by Carl Robert Jakobson – a much revered leader of the Estonian national movement – as a model farm with the latest ideas in crop rotation, cattle feeding and so

on. Here too is a museum to Jakobson, who was also an educationalist and edited the radical newspaper *Sakala*. If you should ever possess a 500 EEK banknote you can see what he looked like.

PÄRNU TO THE LATVIAN BORDER

The M12 highway from Pärnu to the Latvian border, a 65 km stretch, runs through forest much of the way, usually two or three km inland. The border on the older road along the coast itself from Häädemeeste, 40 km from Pärnu, is no longer operational.

Things to See

Konstantin Päts, the president of independent Estonia before WWII, was born at **Tahku**, 20 km down the coast from Pärnu. His statue here was the first **political monument** to be restored in post-Soviet Estonia. Estonia's biggest dunes line the coast at **Rannametsa**, about three km north of Häädemeeste.

The **Nigula bog** (Nigula raba), just north of the Latvian border about 10 km east of the M12 highway, is protected by the Nigula Nature Reserve. The bog is a treeless peat bog filled with pools and hollows, in the western part of which there are five 'bog islands'. It is also an important bird breeding area, golden eagles and black-throated divers being occasional visitors to the bog which is home to 144 bird species.

Places to Stay

The *Nigula Nature Reserve* (☎ 244-92 470, ☎ & fax 244-91 664; email agu@nigula.tartu.ee) at Pärnu 2 in Kilingi-Nõmme, arranges daily visits to the bog where you can follow a 3.2 km long trail along wooden planks placed on top of the bog. It also arranges accommodation in a guesthouse at Vanajärve for 40 people near the reserve. The Estonian Ecotourism Association arranges farmhouse accommodation in and around the reserve.

The *Valge Hotel* (White Hotel) (☎ & fax 244-37 367) is the Las Vegas-style mansion which appears like a mirage about 25 km

from the Latvian border in Häädemeeste. Singles/doubles are 400/530 EEK.

Lepanina Motel (☎ 244-98 477; fax 244-40 230), 10 km south of Häädemeeste, accommodates 131 people in the main building and 46 in summer cottages. Singles/doubles with shared bathroom cost 180/300 EEK; triples 400 EEK and rooms for four/five, 480/560 EEK.

Lemme Kämping (☎ 244-98 415; fax 244-98 430) in Kabli has one-place cabins for 52 EEK a day. Pitching a tent costs 15 EEK and two/three-person summer cottages are 140/180 EEK.

KIHNU
• *pop 550* • ☎ (244)

Six-km-long Kihnu island, in the Gulf of Rīga 40 km south-west of Pärnu, is one of the most traditional places in Estonia, with colourful striped skirts still worn every day by most of the women. There are three main villages plus a school, church, and combined village hall-cum-bar in the centre of the island. Kihnu people are among the few Estonians who follow the Russian Orthodox Church.

Many of the island's first inhabitants, centuries ago, were criminals and others exiled from the mainland. Kihnu men traditionally made a living from fishing and seal hunting. The most famous of them was the sea-captain, Enn Uuetoa (better known as Kihnu Jõnn), who became a symbol of lost freedom for Estonians during the Soviet period when they were virtually banned from the sea. Kihnu Jõnn, said to have sailed on all the world's oceans, drowned in 1913 when his ship sank off Denmark on what was to have been his last voyage before retirement. He was buried in the Danish town of Oksby but in 1992 his remains were brought home to Kihnu and reburied in the island's church.

There's a museum near the church, and a lighthouse, shipped over from Britain, in the south with good views of the whole island from its top. After WWII a fishery collective was established on the island. Fishing and cattle herding continue to be the mainstay of employment for Kihnu's inhabitants.

Getting There & Away

Pärnu tourism information centre, and the Atlas and Reiser travel agencies (see Pärnu – Information) all arrange trips to the islands of Ruhnu and Kihnu.

The Kihnurand Travel Agency (☎ 69 924, 43 580) in Kihnu arranges boat trips to the island from the mainland. A day excursion costs 175 EEK including a traditional lunch of freshly smoked fish. It also arranges farmhouse accommodation in Kihnu for 129 EEK per person, boat rental for 20 EEK an hour, fishing trips for 600 EEK and folk concerts for 900 EEK. A walking tour of Kihnu is 135 EEK and a driving tour in an open-air truck, 175 EEK.

Air Baltic Aeroservis has flights three time a week from Pärnu to Kihnu. See Pärnu – Getting There & Away for details.

Ferry A passenger boat and a small ferry makes the crossing from Torilla port (☎ 244-96 312), 50 km south-west of Pärnu on the mainland, to Kihnu port (☎ 69 932).

The year-round ferry departs to/from Kihnu twice daily on Monday, Wednesday, Thursday, Friday and Sunday. A one-way fare is 20/60 EEK for a person/car and the journey takes 1½ hours. The ferry is sometimes cancelled in rough weather.

Between June and August, the passenger boat *Vesta* departs from Torilla twice daily on Tuesday, Friday, Saturday and Sunday; from Kihnu it leaves twice daily on Tuesday, Saturday and Sunday. The journey is 40 minutes and a one-way fare is 39 EEK.

From Pärnu there are two buses daily to/from Torilla.

RUHNU
* *pop 68* • ☎ *(245)*

Ruhnu island, a little smaller than Kihnu, is 100 km south-west of Pärnu and nearer to the Latvian than the Estonian mainland. For several centuries Ruhnu had a mainly Swedish population of 200 or 300 but most left on 6 August, 1944, to avoid the advancing Red Army, abandoning homes and animals. Ruhnu has some sandy beaches and

a 1644 **wooden church** which is the oldest wooden building in Estonia. It's flat but there's a forest of 200 to 300-year-old pines on its eastern dunes.

Getting There & Away

For organised trips to the island, see Kihnu – Getting There & Away. Baltic Aeroservis runs a weekly flight from Pärnu to Ruhnu. See Pärnu – Getting There & Away for details.

VILJANDI
* *pop 24,000* • ☎ *(243)*

Viljandi is a quiet country town 160 km south of Tallinn en route to Valga on the Latvian border. It's a green, hilly and pretty place on the north shore of the four-km-long lake Viljandi järv, over which there are good views. Many houses here are decorated with small turrets, windmills or bay windows.

The Knights of the Sword founded a castle at Viljandi (known in German times as Fellin) when they conquered this area in the 13th century. The town around it later joined the Hanseatic League, then was subject to the usual comings and goings of Swedes, Poles and Russians.

Orientation & Information

The centre of town is about half a km back from the lake shore. The central square is Kesk väljak, where Tartu meets Lossi, leading south to the castle park on the edge of the centre. The bus station is half a km north of the centre on Tallinna, past the main post office at Tallinna 11. The market is at the west end of Turu, which leads west off Tallinna just south of the post office. The train station is 750m west of the centre along Vaksali, at Metalli 1.

Viljandi tourist information centre (☎ 34 444; fax 33 093; email info@viljandi.turism. ee; http://www.estonia.org/viljandi) is inside the Hetika Travel Agency at Kauba 12. Ühispank at Vaksali 2, gives cash advance on credit card and has a 24-hour ATM accepting Visa and MasterCard, as does Zhoupank opposite the centre.

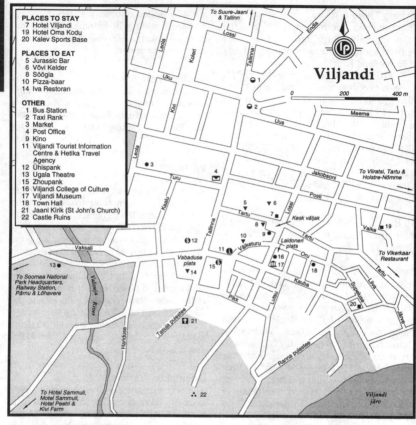

PLACES TO STAY
7 Hotel Viljandi
19 Hotel Oma Kodu
20 Kalev Sports Base

PLACES TO EAT
5 Jurassic Bar
6 Võvi Kelder
8 Söögia
10 Pizza-baar
14 Iva Restoran

OTHER
1 Bus Station
2 Taxi Rank
3 Market
4 Post Office
9 Kino
11 Viljandi Tourist Information
 Centre & Hetika Travel
 Agency
12 Ühispank
13 Ugala Theatre
15 Zhoupank
16 Viljandi College of Culture
17 Viljandi Museum
Town Hall
21 Jaani Kirik (St John's Church)
22 Castle Ruins

Things to See

The ruins of **Viljandi Order Castle** overlook the lake from a hill in the castle park, just south of the town centre. The corner tower known as **Villu Kelder** is named after the leader of a 14th century Estonian rebellion who died a captive in it. Also in the castle park are the medieval **Jaani kirik** (St John's Church) and a **suspension footbridge** built in 1931.

There are few other pre-19th century buildings. An exception is the 18th century **Town Hall** (Raekoda) in the centre. The **Viljandi Museum** is in a classical building

on Laidoneri plats, the old market square. The **Viljandi College of Culture** is next door. The surprisingly large **Ugala Theatre** (☎ 34 617) at Vaksali 7 near the little Valuoja River is Estonia's most modern theatre.

Places to Stay & Eat

Viljandi's cheapest option, *Kalev Sports Base* (☎ 54 870), is close to a lake at Ranna 6, and has 93 places. A bed in a double/triple/four-bed room with shared showers costs 50 EEK a night.

The top hotel is *Hotel Oma Kodu* (☎ 54 414; fax 33 590) in the centre at Väike 6.

Singles/doubles/triples are 350/520/660 EEK. The Soviet-era *Hotel Viljandi* (☎ 53 852), at Tartu 11 has 26 rooms with private toilet and shower at around 150/350 EEK for singles/doubles. It also has grottier rooms with shared bathrooms for 80/100 EEK.

Hotel Peetri (☎ 98 234; fax 98 299), a horse-breeding centre 12 km south-west of Viljandi in Heimtali, has singles/doubles for 300/600 EEK. It arranges horse riding, calash and winter sleigh rides.

In town, *Söögia* at Tartu 8 is a small, cosy café decked out with lace table cloths and serves a small selection of home cooking including delicious soups for 7.80 EEK. Light snacks are served at the *Võvi Kelder* at Tartu 11, an Irish-style bar where 'Guinness welcomes you' as you walk in. *Jurassic Bar* at Tartu 1c has great outside seating in the summer and holds discos at weekends.

Getting There & Away
There are four buses daily to/from Tallinn (2½ hours, 54 EEK). Other services include seven buses daily to/from Pärnu (two to 2½ hours, 34 EEK) and three daily to/from Tartu (1½ to two hours, 24 EEK) by various routes. There are also one or two buses a day to/from Valga, Kuressaare, Otepää and Haapsalu. Three trains run daily to/from Tallinn (2½ hours to 3¼ hours, 48 EEK).

AROUND VILJANDI
At **Lõhavére** on the east side of Suure-Jaani on the Viljandi-Vändra-Pärnu road, is the site of the fortress of Lembitu, the 13th century Estonian leader who put up most resistance to the invading Knights of the Sword. **Vaibla** is a bathing beach at the north end of Võrtsjärv, just off the Viljandi-Tartu road. The Viljandi-Valga road crosses an area of slightly higher ground known as the **Sakala kõrgustik** (Sakala heights).

At Olustvere, 30 km from Viljandi in the northern part of the Sakala upland, is **Olustvere Manor**, a 1730's manor house with a water-mill, distillery and English-style gardens housing the Olustvere tourist centre (☎ 74 280) and a riding centre. It is

also possible to camp here. Three buses daily run between Viljandi and Olustvere.

Soomaa National Park
Although embracing Estonia's largest area of swamps, flat meadows and waterside forests, Soomaa National Park (Soomaa: literally 'land of wetlands'), covering an area of 36,700 hectares north-east of Viljandi, is primarily made up of four bogs – Valgeraba, Öördi, Kikepera and Kuresoo, the peat layer of which measures seven metres in places. The bogs are split by tributaries of the Pärnu River, the spring flooding creating a fifth season for the inhabitants of this boggy land where the waters can rise to five metres in March and April.

Up to 36 different mammal species inhabit the surrounding forests, among them the wolf, lynx, brown bear, elk, wild boar and otter. Thousands of birds migrate to Soomaa every year.

The only way to explore the national park, ridden with small waterways, is by canoe or by haabja, a traditional Finnish-Ugric single-tree boat carved from aspen and used for centuries as the only means of fishing, hunting, hauling hay and simply getting around.

Historically witches lived on the bog to isolate themselves. According to Estonian folklore, it is the evil will-o'-the-wisp who leads people to the bog, where they are forced to stay until the bog gas catches fire, driving the grotesque bog inhabitants out for all to see.

The headquarters of Soomaa National Park (☎ 31 448, 52 265; fax 52 461) at Paargi 1 in Viljandi, provides information on the park. The Estonian Ecotourism Association arranges two and five-day canoeing trips through the park. It is also possible to contact the host farm (☎ 66 405; fax 43 779) at Saarisoo directly. It arranges accommodation, canoe and haabja trips, bog expeditions and fishing holidays. It also offers one-log boat building courses, at the end of which you test out your haabja on the bog, of course.

Latvia

Facts about Latvia

Latvia (Latvija) is sandwiched between Estonia and Lithuania. Rīga, its capital, is on the Baltic coast and is Latvia's chief visitor magnet. It is the biggest, most vibrant city in the Baltic states. Several other attractive destinations lie within day trip distance of Rīga – including the coastal resort Jūrmala, the Sigulda castles overlooking the scenic Gauja river valley, and the Rastrelli palace at Rundāle. And now that Soviet-era restrictions are no more, there's plenty of off the beaten track country to explore – such as the dune-lined coast and historic towns of Kurzeme (western Latvia) or the remote uplands of the eastern half of the country.

This chapter contains information specific to Latvia. For a more general introduction to the history, geography, people and culture of the Baltic states, see Facts about the Region at the front of the book.

HISTORY

Since independence, Latvia (like its neighbours) has dropped out of the front-page news. Elections to its first post-independence parliament were held in June 1993.

The centre-right moderate nationalist party Latvijas Celš (Latvian Way), led by Valdis Birkavs, formed a governing coalition with the Latvijas Zemnieku Savieniba (Latvian Farmers' Union) and Birkavs became the country's first prime minister. Guntis Ulmanis of Latvijas Zemnieku Savieniba, a great-nephew of the pre-WWII leader Kārlis Ulmanis, was elected president. In August 1994 the last Soviet troops withdrew. Meanwhile, Latvia's road to capitalism was by no means smooth. Ambitions to become the 'Switzerland of the Baltics' took a knock when the country's biggest commercial bank, Bank Baltija, went spectacularly bust, taking the investments of 200,000 depositors with it. The banking crisis spread to affect a number of other banks which had been playing fast and loose with investors' money, and by the time the bloodletting was over 40% of Latvia's banking system had disappeared. Rīga's

231

dream of becoming a Baltic Zurich now seems impossible.

Borders

Influenced by Estonia's example in settling its border dispute with Russia, some Latvian politicians by 1996 were canvassing a compromise solution, with Latvia reluctantly ceding the Abrene (Russian: Pytalovo) region – a 15 km wide, 85 km long sliver of territory down its north-east border, immediately south of the Pechory region, which was incorporated into Russia in 1944 – in return for formal Russian recognition of Latvian independence. Latvia also disputes its maritime borders with Estonia (where the issue is fishing rights) and Lithuania (where the dispute is fuelled by offshore oil finds).

GEOGRAPHY

Latvia, the middle Baltic state, is 63,700 sq km in area – a little smaller than the Irish Republic. Unlike the other two Baltic states, which are fairly compact in shape, Latvia is a lot wider from east to west than from north to south. A good half of Latvia's long, sweeping coast faces the Gulf of Rīga, a deep inlet of the Baltic Sea which is shielded from the open sea by the Estonian island of Saaremaa.

Latvia borders Estonia in the north, Russia and Belarus in the east, and Lithuania in the south. Rīga lies on the Daugava River, just inland from the Gulf of Rīga. Latvia has four regions: Vidzeme, the north-east; Latgale, the south-east; Zemgale, the centre; and Kurzeme, the west.

The Vidzeme Upland in eastern Latvia is the largest expanse of land with an elevation over 200m in the Baltics, with Latvia's highest point, Gaizina kalns (311m), topping it. The Latgale Upland in south-east Latvia reaches 289m at Lielais Liepukalns. The Kurzeme Upland in south-west Latvia manages only 184m at Krievu kalns near Priekule.

ECOLOGY & ENVIRONMENT

Latvia's pollution problems were given a high profile in the years of protest immediately before independence, when they were seen as one more aspect of Soviet misrule and (by some politicians) as a handy stick to beat the Russians with. Now that the environment is Latvia's own responsibility, they are being addressed – and downplayed. New sewage treatment facilities for the capital mean swimming in the Gulf of Rīga is less of a health hazard than it was, and financial assistance from Scandinavia and Germany has helped to reduce the pollution generated by industrial centres including Daugavpils and Liepāja. The government aims to solve the problem of drinking water pollution within the next few years. Tourism is still in its infancy, and tourist numbers aren't sufficient to pose a real environmental hazard anywhere in the Baltics, but the Latvian government seems aware that maximising the benefits of tourism will mean careful management of both urban and rural environments.

NATIONAL PARKS & RESERVES

Latvia has a single national park and a number of nature reserves. More information is provided in the relevant chapters.

Gauja National Park
    920 sq km straddling the Gauja valley east of Rīga – castles, lovely valley scenery, wildlife centre, walking trails; park administration at Sigulda
Grīņi State Nature Reserve
    south of Pāvilosta in Kurzeme – bog area
Krustkalni State Nature Reserve
    south of Madona in eastern Latvia
Moricsala State Nature Reserve
    northern Kurzeme – part of the lake Usmas ezers and its shores
Slītere State Nature Reserve
    northern tip of Kurzeme – coast and hinterland
Teiči State Nature Reserve
    south-east of Madona – large bog area

GOVERNMENT & POLITICS

The Latvian political scene is a complex mosaic. More than 30 parties seek election (the old Communist Party is banned, but there are several post-Communist groups), and government by coalition is the norm. Latvia's 100-seat parliament, the Saiema, was first elected in June 1993 by proportional representation – parties were required to win 5% of the vote to be represented in the Saiema. The first post-independence coalition lurched from crisis to crisis, with Maris Gailis replacing Valdis Birkavs as prime minister and leader of the Latvian Way alliance in September 1994. Gailis in turn was given the coup de grace a year later in the aftermath of the Bank Baltija crash.

By the time of the October 1995 elections, the original four main parties had mutated into 19, with 1111 candidates running for office (a year later there were 34 parties). Nine parties cleared the five per cent hurdle to enter the Saeima. Andris Skele (acceptable because he had no party of his own) emerged after three rounds of voting as prime minister leading a cross-spectrum alliance of six parties. Two former prime ministers were given cabinet posts – Birkavs as foreign minister, and Gailis as minister of environmental protection and regional development. Guntis Ulmanis won a second term as president in June 1996. In late 1996, Skele weathered a confidence vote with 65 MPs supporting his proposals for independent Latvia's first balanced budget. Opposition politicians had denounced plans to shift some of the fiscal burden from central to local government. They also claimed Skele's plan to appoint regional prefects in place of elected regional governments was a step towards a more authoritarian regime.

ECONOMY

Latvia replaced the Soviet rouble with its own Latvian rouble in 1992 and introduced the Latvian lats in 1993. It has since held its value against major currencies. Inflation is around 20%, official unemployment stands at 7%, and the average Latvian earns US$185 a month.

Privatisation got off to a slow start, with the first 300 industrial enterprises going on sale in 1995 and 200 more listed for privatisation in 1996. Some 20 per cent of the population works in agriculture, but farming's importance to the economy is shrinking (from 21.1% of Gross Domestic Product in 1990 to only 9.8% in 1995) and

the government is committed to making farming more efficient, which could mean job losses.

Since 1990 manufacturing industry too has dwindled quickly (from 34.5% of GDP to 19.2%), while the service sector has expanded dramatically (from 31.9% to 57.2% of GDP). The main beneficiaries of the economic revolution have been young technocrats and entrepreneurs, while for many Latvians money remains tight.

Foreign trade began to pick up in 1995, with western European trading partners replacing the defunct Soviet Union, but the 1995 banking crisis threw the entire economy into reverse. Since then the financial sector has been watchdogged more closely. In 1996 the Bank of Latvia shut down five undercapitalised commercial banks.

By late 1996 the economy seemed to be making a recovery, and the government is now seeking increased foreign investment (which totalled US$180 million in 1995), clarifying its commitment to the free market.

POPULATION & PEOPLE

Of Latvia's total population of 2.7 million just 52% are ethnically Latvian. Russians account for 34% of the total population, Belarusians 4.5%, and Ukrainians 3.5%. Latvians are a minority in all seven of Latvia's biggest cities including the capital, Rīga, which has a predominantly Russian population.

The Latvians and Lithuanians are the two surviving peoples of the Balt branch of the Indo-European ethno-linguistic group. The Balt peoples are thought to have spread into the south-eastern Baltic area around 2000 BC from the region which is now Belarus and neighbouring parts of Russia. (The term *Balt*, derived from the Baltic Sea, was first used last century to describe these peoples.) Those people who stayed behind were assimilated, much later, by Belarusian or Russian Slavs (who are ethnically the Balts' nearest relatives). By the 13th century the Balts were divided into a number of tribal kingdoms.

The Latvians are descended from those tribes who were settled on the territory of modern Latvia, such as the Letts (or Latgals), the Selonians, the Semigallians, and the Cours. The Latgals, Semigallians and Cours gave their names to Latvian regions: Latgale, Zemgale and Kurzeme. The Selonians were settled between the Daugava River and northern Lithuania. During succeeding centuries of foreign rule these tribes (and to a large extent the Finno-Ugric Livs who inhabited northern coastal regions of Latvia) lost their separate identities and became merged in one Lettish, or Latvian, identity.

Up to 200,000 Latvians live in western countries as a result of emigration around the turn of the 20th century and during and after WWII. There are approximately 100,000 Latvians in the USA, 33,000 in Australia, 18,000 in Canada, 12,000 in Germany, and 10,000 in Britain.

Citizenship

Citizens of the pre-1940 Latvian Republic and their descendants – including about 300,000 non-ethnic Latvians (mainly Russians) – are automatically citizens of modern Latvia. Other residents, roughly 35% of the population, were not allowed to vote in the 1993 elections.

Citizenship rules, finalised in 1994, state that would-be citizens must have lived in Latvia for at least five years, speak Latvian, and must take a loyalty oath. Former Soviet soldiers settled in Latvia after demobilisation are barred from citizenship, as are former Soviet secret service employees.

EDUCATION

Education is central to Latvia's efforts to create a modern economy and a modern democracy. With fluent Latvian a requisite for citizenship, providing facilities for Russian-speaking adults as well as school age children could be a vital tool in integrating the Russian community into the new Latvia, but there seems little evidence of government commitment.

Instead, education has become a political football. In 1996-97, as part of its budget-balancing act, the government made local authorities responsible for education budgets, but without saying where they were to find the money. This prompted protests from local government and demonstrations by teachers. On a more positive note, a graduate law school scheduled to open in Rīga in July 1997, with funding from Sweden and the EU, will take up to 100 students from Latvia, Lithuania and Estonia, supplying the Baltics for the first time with properly qualified lawyers.

ARTS
Literature

Latvia's national epic – *Lāčplēsis* (The Bear Slayer), written by Andrējs Pumpurs in the mid-19th century – is based on traditional Latvian folk stories. The hero struggles against his enemy, a German Black Knight, only to drown in the Daugava River at the moment of final triumph. The anticipated rebirth of Lāčplēsis, however, leaves hope for new freedom. The first Latvian novel, *Mērnieku Laiki* (The Time of the Land Surveyors), written in the 1860s and 70s by the brothers Reinis and Matiss Kaudzīte, has become a classic for its humorous portrayal of Latvian characters.

The towering figure in Latvian literature is Jānis Rainis (1865-1929), who Latvians say might have the acclaim of a Shakespeare or Goethe had he written in a less obscure language. Rainis' criticisms of social and political oppression led to him spending much of his life in exile in Siberia and Switzerland. His leading works, all written in the first quarter of the 20th century, include the plays *Uguns un nakts* (Fire and Night) on the Lāčplēsis theme and *Jāzeps un viņa brāļi* (Joseph and his Brothers), and the poetry volumes *Gals un sākums* (The End and the Beginning) and *Piecas Dagdas skiču burtnīcas* (Dagda's Five Notebooks). Rainis' wife, Aspazija, was also a leading poet, playwright and social critic.

Rūdolfs Blaumanis (1863-1908) wrote psychologically penetrating novelettes and comic and tragic plays; among them, *Skroderdienas Silmačos* (Tailor's Days in

Silmači) is still one of Latvia's most popular plays. Anna Brigadere (1861-1933) wrote much loved tales of rural life and fairy-tale dramas. Kārlis Skalbe (1879-1945) was another major writer of fairy tales.

Music & Dance

Rock is very popular in Latvia and, like Estonia, there are big annual festivals (see Public Holidays & Special Events). Award-winning mainstream rockers Rebel, working on their third album as this book went to press, are among the leaders – they were formed out of Dr Blues, a band which had been on the scene since the late 80s. Andrey Yahimovich, who fronts Latvia's longest-running band, Cement, is another survivor – the band has been going since 1985 and plays a mix of rhythm and blues and urban ballads. Acoustic blues is represented by Hot Acoustic, formed in 1994, while the eccentric Karl (no last name) and Cuckoo-Bite contribute a new wave sound to the Rīga club scene.

The National Opera House, reopened in 1996 after renovation, is the home of the Rīga Ballet, which during the Soviet years produced Mikhail Baryshnikov and Aleksander Godunov among others. The Latvia Philharmonic is highly regarded. The song composers Joseph Wihtol (Jāzeps Vītols) and Alfrēds Kalniņš are important early 20th century figures in classical music. Contemporary classicists include internationally renowned conductor Mariss Jansons, winner of the Latvian 1995 Grand Prix in music, and eclectic composer Imants Kalniņš. Kalniņš, a graduate of the Latvian State Conservatory, has written everything from film scores to symphonies and operas. He is also the godfather of Latvian rock, founding the country's first rock band, Menuets, in the mid-70s.

Visual Arts

Jānis Rozentāls was really the first major Latvian painter. Around the turn of the century he painted scenes of peasant life and portraits, with some influence from Impressionism and Art Nouveau. Vilhelms Purvītis and Jānis Valters were the outstanding landscape artists of the time. Both – especially Purvītis – were influenced by Impressionism. Olegs Tillbergs is one of the most interesting modern Latvian artists. He collects and assembles garbage and other unwanted materials. Ivars Poikans is another contemporary artist to watch for. Karlis Rudēvics, a leading figure in Latvia's 15,000-strong Gypsy community, is known for his translations of Gypsy poetry and for his striking paintings inspired by Gypsy legends.

Facts for the Visitor

This chapter contains visitor information specific to Latvia. For general information on travelling in the Baltic states and details on obtaining visas for Russia and Belarus see the introductory Facts for the Visitor chapter at the front of the book.

HIGHLIGHTS

Apart from the obvious destination of Rīga – which is a particular must for anyone into partying, architecture or markets – the other highly recommended spot in Latvia is the Gauja valley. For the most adventurous, the ideal way to experience the scenery is to take a canoe trip down the Gauja river from Valmiera, but for those pushed for time a day's hiking from Sigulda is a pleasant alternative.

More off the beaten track is the Kurzeme region. Taking your time to explore this coastal tip – the land of the Livs and a world apart from the rest of Latvia – is a magnetic experience that will draw you back time and again.

Once is enough for the vast former Soviet army barracks at Daugavpils – strolling through a 'town' where no one lives is eerie, bizarre and a poignant way of glancing at Latvia's not-so-happy past.

TOURIST OFFICES

Latvia has a small network of tourist offices overseas representing the Latvian Tourist Board (☎ 7327 542; fax 7229 945; http://www.eunet.lv), which is at Pils laukums 4, LV-1050 Rīga, Latvia. The overseas offices are in:

Austria
    World Trade Centre, room 530, A-1300 Vienna Airport (☎ 01-71110 6143; fax 01-71110 6144)
Finland
    Baltic Tourism Information Centre, Merimiehenkatu 29, SF-00150 Helsinki (☎ 09-637 783; fax 09-637 887)

France
    Visages Du Monde, 5 rue du Bellay F-75004, Paris (☎ 01 43 29 63 10; fax 01 43 26 84 74)
Germany
    Baltic Tourism Information Bureau, Woldsenstrasse 36, D-25813 Husum (☎ 048-413 004; fax 048-412 109)

Some of the tourist board's in-country information centres are more efficient than others and some also have no English-speaking staff.

There are official tourist centres in Rīga (☎ 7221 731); in Jūrmala (☎ 7-62 288); in Saulkrasti (☎ 951 141); in Salacgrīva (☎ 40-41 254); in Sigulda (☎ 971 345), in Cēsis (☎ 41-22 246); in Jēkabpils (☎ 52-20 950); in Kuldīga (☎ 33-22 259); in Liepāja (☎ 34-22 113); in Tukums (☎ 31-24 451); in Talsi (☎ 32-25 433); in Valmiera (☎ 42-33 660); and in Ventspils (☎ 36-24 777).

EMBASSIES & CONSULATES

Latvian worldwide diplomatic missions include:

Australia
    Consulate: 38 Longstaff St, Ivanhoe East, Vic 3073 (☎ 03-9499 6920)
Austria
    Embassy: 3-8 Wahringer Strasse, A-1090 Vienna (☎ 01-403 3132; fax 01-403 3112)
Belarus
    Embassy: Storazevskaja 15, Hotel Belarus, Room 1905, BY-220029 Minsk (☎ 017-2391 631; fax 017-2506 784)
    Consulate: Lenina 69, BY-210026 Vitebsk (☎ 021 236 58 54; fax 021 237 01 40)
Belgium
    Embassy: 158 Ave Molière, B-1060 Brussels (☎ 02-344 1682; fax 02-344 7478)
Canada
    Embassy: 112 Kent Street, Place de Ville, Tower B, Suite 208, Ottawa, Ontario K1P 5P2 (☎ 613-238 6014, 238 6868; fax 613-238 7044; email latvia-embassy@magmacom.com; http://www2.magmacom.com/latemb/)
Czech Republic
    Consulate: 3 Hradeshinska, PO Box 54, CZ-10100 Prague (☎ 02-242 32 454; fax 02-242 35 099)

Denmark
Embassy: Rosbaeksvej 17, DK-2100 Copenhagen (☎ 39 27 60 00; fax 39 27 61 73)
Estonia
Embassy: Tõnismägi 10, Tallinn (☎ 2-6311 366; fax 2-442 585)
Finland
Embassy: Armfeltintie 10, SF-00150 Helsinki (☎ 09-474 472 44, 09-474 472 33)
France
Embassy: 14 Boulevard Montmartre, F-75009 Paris (☎ 01 48 01 00 44; fax 01 48 01 03 71)
Germany
Embassy: Adenaueralle 110, D-53113 Bonn (☎ 0228-26 4242; fax 0228-26 5840)
Consulate: Königin-Luise Strasse 77, D-14195 Berlin (☎ 030-831 5877)
Italy
Embassy: Via Boncompagni 16, I-00187 Rome (☎ 06-428 1710; fax 06-494 1333)
Lithuania
Embassy: Čiurlionio 76, Vilnius LT-2009 (☎ 22-231 260; fax 22-231 130)
Poland
Embassy: Reteana 15-19, PL-02516 Warsaw (☎ 22-481 947, 22-481 946; fax 22-480 201)
Russia
Embassy: ulitsa Chaplygina 3, RUS-103062, Moscow (☎ 095-925 2703, 095-925 2707; fax 095-923 9295)
Consulate: Kuibyshev 31, St Petersburg (☎ 812-230 3374; fax 812-311 3182)
Sweden
Embassy: Odengatan 5, Box 19167, S-10432 Stockholm (☎ 08-700 6300; fax 08-140 0151)
Ukraine
Embassy: Desiatinna 4-6, UA-252025 Kiev (☎ 044-229 2745, 044-229 2360; fax 044-229 2745)
UK
Embassy: 45 Nottingham Place, London W1M 3FE (☎ 0171-312 0040; fax 0171-312 0042)
USA
Embassy: 4325 17th Street NW, Washington, DC 20011 (☎ 202-726 6757, 726 8213; fax 202-726 6785; email latvia@seas.gwu.edu; http://www.seas.gwu.edu/guest/latvia)

CUSTOMS

Customs rules vary between the Baltic states and are subject to change. Some general points are given in the introductory Facts for the Visitor. In Rīga, the Customs Department (☎ 7226 246) is at Valdemāra 1a.

Alcohol & Tobacco

People over 18 can bring in and take out one litre of alcohol and 200 cigarettes, 20 cigars or 200 grams of tobacco without paying duty.

Currency

You can import and export duty-free any amount of hard currency.

Other Items

You have to get special permission from the police department in the Interior Ministry (☎ 7208 618), at Stabu 89 in Rīga, if you want to import arms of any kind. Works of art or of cultural significance (including antique books) that date from before 1945, but are less than 100 years old, are subject to a 50% customs duty; those older than 100 years attract 100% duty. They may only leave with written permission from the relevant Ministry of Culture, at Pils 22 in Rīga (☎ 7214 100).

MONEY

Latvia's currency, the *lats* (plural: *lati*), was introduced in March 1993 alongside a transitional currency – the Latvian rouble (Latvijas rublis) – which was out of circulation by April 1993. The lats is divided into 100 *santīmi* (singular: *santīms*). Though it is a floating currency (not tied in value to any other) the lats has remained stable ever since it was introduced. Exchange rates in early 1997 included:

Australia	A$1	=	0.44 lati
Canada	C$1	=	0.41 lati
Finland	1 Fmk	=	0.11 lati
Germany	DM1	=	0.34 lati
Sweden	1 SKr	=	0.08 lati
United Kingdom	UK£1	=	0.93 lati
United States	US$1	=	0.57 lati

The lats is the country's only legal tender and comes in one and two lati coins, and five, 10, 20, 50, 100 and 500 lati notes. There are also one, two, five, 10, 20 and 50 santīmi coins.

NEWSPAPERS & MAGAZINES

The Latvian papers *Diena*, *Rīgas Balss*, and *Neatkariga Ciņa* are the leading newspapers, each published four or five days a week with

LATVIA

circulations of 25,000 to 60,000. All four have a separate Russian-language edition too. *SM-Segodņa* is a wildly popular Russian-language youth newspaper, and *Lauku Avīze* is a newspaper for rural areas. The evening newspaper, *Vakara Ziņas*, sells some 70,000 copies per edition. *Dienas Bizness* (Latvian) and *Bizness & Baltija* (Russian) are two equally popular weekly business newspapers.

Details of English-language publications available in the Baltics are given in Facts for the Visitor – Newspapers & Magazines at the front of the book.

RADIO & TV

There are two state TV channels, three private channels and some 20 private TV companies. Baltcom is a cable TV network which is user-pays during the day and free between 6 pm and midnight. It broadcasts 40 minutes of CNN in English on Saturdays at 7 pm. A number of pubs, bars and hotels, particularly in Rīga, show CNN and Eurosport on cable TV.

The BBC World Service can be picked up 24 hours a day on 100.5 FM. Latvian State Radio, Latvijas radio I, transmits daily short-wave broadcasts at 5935 kHz in English from 8 to 8.30 pm, and in Swedish from 9.30 to 10 pm. The most popular commercial channels are Radio Rīgai on 106.2 FM and Super FM on 104.3 FM.

PUBLIC HOLIDAYS & SPECIAL EVENTS

Latvian national holidays include:

New Year's Day – 1 January
Good Friday
Easter Day – (Easter Monday is also taken as a holiday by many)
Labour Day – 1 May
Mothers' Day – second Sunday in May
Ligo (Midsummer festival) – 23 June
Jāni or *Jānu Diena* (St John's Day) – 24 June
National Day (anniversary of proclamation of Latvian Republic, 1918) – 18 November
Christmas (Ziemsvētki) – 25 December
Second Holiday – 26 December
New Year's Eve – 31 December

Latvia shares a number of regular cultural events with Estonia and Lithuania, the most important of these being the national song festival (held every five years, with the next in 1999 in Estonia), the Baltika International Folk Festival (next in Rīga in 1997) as well as midsummer celebrations. See Public Holidays & Special Events in the introductory Facts for the Visitor chapter for more details. Major annual festivals include:

Gadatirgus – big arts and crafts fair; Open-Air Ethnography Museum, Rīga; first weekend in June
International Festival of Organ Music – Rīga; end of June
Rīga Summer – festival of symphonic and chamber music; Rīga; every even year in July
Jūrmala Pop Festival – a contest not a festival, intended for TV rather than for the public; Jūrmala; mid or late July
Rīga Rock Summer – a three day rock festival attracting international names; Mežaparks, Rīga; July
Opera Music Festival – Sigulda; July
Festival of Ancient Music – Bauska Castle; July
Liepājas Dzintars – rock festival; Liepāja; usually mid-August
Ascension Day – Roman Catholic processions, celebratory masses; Aglona; 14-16 August
Arsenāls – big international film festival; Rīga; mid or late September, even-numbered years
Lāčplēsis Day (Lāčplēšu Diena) – commemoration of dead heroes, named after Latvia's mythical warrior hero, whose name means 'Bear-slayer'; 11 November

ACTIVITIES

See Activities under Facts for the Visitor at the front of the book for general information on activities in Latvia.

FOOD & DRINKS

Latvians consume a lot of dairy products, eggs, potatoes, fish and grains; although you will also find plenty of meat in restaurants. *Šprotes* (sprats) crop up as a starter in many places. If they're *ar sīpoliem*, they'll be with onions. You may also find *siļķe* (herring), *līdaka* (pike), *zutis* (eel), *forele* (trout), or *lasis* (salmon). If fish is *cepts*, it's fried; if *sālīts* or *mazsālīts*, it's salted; and *kūpīnats* means it'll be smoked. Soups and sausage are also popular. *Žāvēta desa* is smoked sausage.

The sweet toothed won't be left disappointed. In summer and autumn good use is

Black Magic

It's black as ink, as thick as custard, as sharp as lemon, and has been produced in Latvia – and nowhere else – since 1755.

Its recipe remains a closely guarded secret: orange peel, oak bark, wormwood and linden blossoms are among some 25 fairy-tale ingredients known to stew in the wicked witch's cooking pot.

It steels the nerves, settles the stomach and stops Jack Frost from biting. A shot a day keeps the doctor away, so say most of Latvia's pensioners. In the 18th century it was administered to Catherine the Great when she was struck down by a mystery illness in Rīga. Two sips later she made an instant recovery – and left town.

Rīga druggist Abraham Kunze created the insidious concoction. Its name originates from *balsamon*, the ancient Greek word for a sweet-smelling medicinal balm or ointment. Its opaque ceramic bottle, labelled with a black and gold Rīga skyline, is reminiscent of the clay jars the potent liquid used to be stored in during the 18th and 19th centuries to keep it safe from the rays of the sun.

It is 45% proof and guaranteed to knock the hind legs off a donkey. Drink it with coffee or Coca-Cola. Down it with a shot of vodka if you dare.

That's what you call Rīga Black Balsams *(Rīgas Melnais Balzāms)*! ■

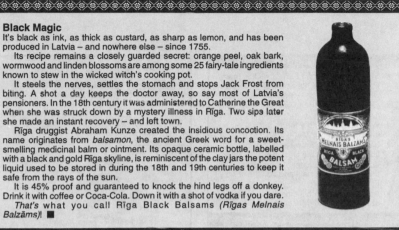

made of berries, freshly picked from the forest. Fruit pies and tarts *(kūka)* are abundant at these times of year. Cream is *krējums*, sour cream *skābais krējums* and is served with practically everything. Throughout Latvia you will find a mouthwatering choice of freshly baked cakes, breads and pastries from as little as 0.06 lati.

Latvia's leading beer is Aldaris. It comes in varying degrees of darkness and costs around 0.30 lati in kiosks (every kiosk stocks beer) and from 0.60 lati a pint in bars. Rīga champagne *(šampanietis)* comes in two varieties – sweet *(sausais)*, which is very sweet, and semi-sweet *(pussaldais)* and is dirt cheap at 2 lati a bottle. And it tastes OK. Not to be missed is Latvia's infamous Balzams, a thick, jet-black, 45% proof concoction that tastes strange, if not downright revolting. Apparently, it's best served with coffee or mixed with equal parts of vodka. The brown ceramic bottle it comes in is worth the 2 lati it costs (see Black Magic aside).

The Language Guide at the back of the book includes words and phrases you will find useful when ordering food and drink.

Rīga

HIGHLIGHTS

- Stroll the streets of Rīga's Old Town, taking the lift up the spire of St Peter's Church for an aerial view
- Shop at Central Market (take your own plastic bag)
- Witness the world's fourth-largest organ in action at Dome Cathedral
- Learn about the Soviet and Nazi occupations of Latvia at the Occupation Museum
- Look up at the fantastic *Jugendstil* architecture on Alberta iela and visit the nearby Fine Arts Museum
- See Brezhnev in his smashed-up 'Roller' at the Rīga Motor Museum

Locator & Map Index

Rīga p242
Jūrmala p268 Central Rīga pp248-9

• *pop 826,508*

Rīga has always been the Baltic states' major metropolis, with far more of a big-city atmosphere than anywhere else in the region. Set on a remorselessly flat plain divided only by the 500m-wide Daugava river, the city is less pretty – and less quaint architecturally – than Tallinn or Vilnius. But it has a touch more depth to its life than the other Baltic capitals, with far more of that hustle and bustle one expects of a capital. Like Vilnius and Tallinn, Rīga has its historic quarter – Vecrīga (Old Rīga).

Fewer than half of Rīgans are ethnic Latvians (40%). Most of the rest are Russians (44%), the majority of whom are not citizens. The fact that Latvians are a minority in their own capital and many Russians have spent their entire lives in Rīga but have remained non citizens, are both contentious issues, giving rise to an undercurrent of tension that can be felt as one strolls Rīga's streets.

HISTORY

There was a Latgal, or Liv, fishing village on the site of modern Rīga which Scandinavian and Russian traders and raiders had used as a stopover for centuries before German

traders from Lübeck and Bremen first reconnoitred the mouth of the Daugava in the mid-12th century. In 1201, Bishop Albert von Buxhoevden from Bremen founded the first German fort in the Baltics here, as a bridgehead for the crusade against the northern heathens. He also founded the Knights of the Sword, who made Rīga their base for subjugating Livonia. The first German settlements were at the southern end of today's Old Town. Colonists from north Germany followed, and Rīga became the major city in the German Baltic, thriving from trade between Russia and the west and joining the Hanseatic League in 1282. The city's coat of arms still combines the key of Bremen with the towers of Hamburg – the two cities most instrumental in its founding. Furs, hides, honey and wax were among the products sold westward from Russia through Rīga.

Rīga's bishop, elevated to archbishop in 1252, became the leader of the church in the lands the Germans conquered, ruling a good slice of Livonia directly and further areas of Livonia and Estonia indirectly through his bishops. But there was always a contest for power between the church, the knights (who controlled most of the remainder of Livonia and Estonia), and the German merchant-dominated city authorities, who managed to maintain a degree of independence from 1253 to 1420.

Rīga reached its early peak of prosperity around the beginning of the 16th century. Following the knights' collapse in the middle of that century, the city suffered attacks by Poles and Russians. After a brief spell of independence from 1561, it fell under Polish rule in 1582, then Sweden captured it in 1621; however both Sweden and Poland allowed it autonomy. During the Swedish period Rīga was, effectively, the second city of Sweden, and it was at this time that it first expanded beyond its fortified walls. In 1710 Russia took it from Sweden. Throughout this entire period, however, the old German nobility and merchants remained in real control.

In the Russian era Rīga grew into an important trading and industrial city, the capital of the province of Livonia. Its population jumped to 28,000 in 1794 and 60,000 by the 1840s. While the old part of the city remained a preserve of Rīga's approximately 30,000 Germans, around it grew suburbs of wider, straighter streets with wooden houses, inhabited by the largest Russian community in the Baltic provinces as well as a growing number of Latvians.

The city walls were pulled down between 1857 and 1863 to assist the free flow of commerce. Rīga developed into the world's busiest timber port and Russia's third greatest industrial city (after Moscow and St Petersburg). Russia's first cars were built here. Rīga was also renowned for the quality of the Lithuanian and Belarusian hemp and flax which it exported to the outside world.

Also in the 19th century, Latvians freed from serfdom in the countryside moved to the city and pushed into its trades, business, civil service and intellectual circles, forming about a quarter of the population by the

1860s. The Rīga Latvian Association, formed in 1868, became the core of the Latvian national awakening, inspiring a Latvian national theatre, opera, encyclopedia and, in 1873, the first Latvian song festival. The number of Latvians in Rīga grew until they formed about half the city's population of 500,000 on the eve of WWI. There were also significant communities of Jews and western merchants – the city's last mayor before the war, George Armitstead, came from an English merchant family.

Rīga was badly damaged in both world wars and was left with only 181,000 people at the end of WWI after evacuations and other ravages. The Germans departed after the Latvian land reform of the 1920s and Hitler's 'come home' call in 1939. In the Latvian independence era between the wars, Rīga was the centre chosen by western diplomats, journalists and spies to eavesdrop on Stalin's Soviet Union, and flourishing nightclubs, restaurants and intellectual life earned it the nickname 'Little Paris'.

During WWII, Rīga was occupied by the Germans from 1941 to 1944, and virtually all its Jewish community (estimated variously at 45,000 to 100,000) was exterminated. Thousands of Latvians left for the west towards the end of the war to avoid Soviet rule.

After the war, the city became the industrial and commercial powerhouse of the USSR's Baltic region and many thousands migrated here to work in the new industries. Rīga became the USSR's main source of railway engines and carriages, producing half its mopeds and a third of its washing machines, as well as trams, radios, telephone exchanges, robots and computers. The city sprawled outwards as large numbers of migrants arrived, and Rīga became known as the most western city in the USSR, with a liberal arts and music scene that attracted people from all over the Union.

ORIENTATION

Rīga sits on either side of the Daugava river, about 15 km inland from its mouth in the south-east corner of the Gulf of Rīga. The

LATVIA

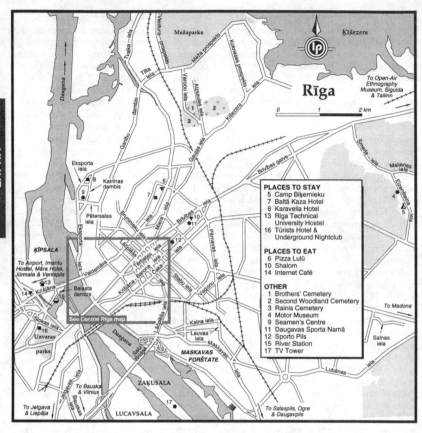

Rīga

PLACES TO STAY
5 Camp Biķernieku
7 Baltā Kaza Hotel
8 Karavella Hotel
13 Rīga Technical
   University Hostel
16 Tūrists Hotel &
   Underground Nightclub

PLACES TO EAT
6 Pizza Lulū
10 Shalom
14 Internet Café

OTHER
1 Brothers' Cemetery
2 Second Woodland Cemetery
3 Rainis Cemetery
4 Motor Museum
9 Seamen's Centre
11 Daugavas Sporta Namā
12 Sporto Pils
15 River Station
17 TV Tower

east bank holds almost all the interest. Old Rīga (Vecrīga), the historic heart of the city, stretches one km along this side of the river and 600m back from its banks.

Old Rīga's skyline is dominated by three steeples. From south to north these are: St Peter's (the tallest), the square bulk of the Dome Cathedral tower, and the simpler St Jacob's. Around most of the Old Town runs a wide band of 19th century parks and boulevards, and beyond that is New Rīga, beginning with the areas built up in the 19th and early 20th century, which have a mixed business and residential life. Further out are the newer, mainly residential suburbs and Soviet industrial enclaves.

The boundaries between these zones are clear to see if you trace the street running north-east from the Akmens Bridge (Akmens tilts) over the Daugava. First it cuts across the middle of the Old Town as a narrow, mainly pedestrianised artery called Kaļķu iela. Then, gaining the name Brīvības bulvāris (Freedom Boulevard), it widens to cross the ring of boulevards and parks and passes the Freedom Monument, an important landmark. At the towering Latvija hotel, 1.25 km from the river, it enters the new town and becomes Brīvības iela. Further out still, en route to Sigulda, Pskov and St Petersburg, it becomes Brīvības gatve. (In the Soviet era it was called Ļeņina iela from one end to the other.)

The train and bus stations are only a five minute walk apart on the south-east edge of Old Rīga. The ferry terminal is 600m north of Old Rīga.

Maps

The top spot for maps – not only for Rīga and Latvia but the rest of the Baltics too – is Jāņa Sēta at Elizabetes 83-85 (see introductory Facts for the Visitor for more details). It has an excellent 1:20,000 *Rīga City Map* with a smaller-scaled city centre map (1:7000) for 0.70 lati, as well as a large selection of road and city maps for the rest of Latvia. Lonely Planet guidebooks are sold here too.

The Latvian-Australian artist Aldis Tīlens, of Pilot Projekts (☎ 7225 337) at Šķūņu 19, publishes the alternative 'bird's-eye panoramic map' of Rīga.

INFORMATION
Tourist Offices

Although privately run, Rīga Tourist Information Bureau (☎ 7221 731, 7212 377; fax 7227 680), behind St Peter's Church at Skārņu 22, is the official tourist office. The staff here can arrange theatre and concert tickets, take hotel bookings, sell quality maps and city guides, and arrange city and country tours (see the introductory Facts for the Visitor chapter). There is also a wealth of information on everywhere else in Latvia also, as well as a small travel library set up by the Tourist Club of Latvia – which is also run from the bureau, and is synonymous with it. The bureau is open daily, except Sunday, from 9 am to 6 pm.

Another valuable information source is *Rīga In Your Pocket* (☎ 7220 580; fax 7223 416; email riyp@mailbox.riga.lv), Latvia's city guide, which has an office at Pils laukums 4, room 112. Bookings for some hotels can be made through RIYP's web site (http://www. inyourpocket.com/rihome.html).

Foreign Embassies & Consulates

Some countries cover Latvia from their embassies in nearby countries, including Iceland and the Netherlands from Stockholm, Australia from Copenhagen, New Zealand from Moscow, Ireland from Warsaw, and South Africa from Helsinki.

The following countries have representatives in Rīga:

Belarus
    Embassy: Jēzusbaznīcas 12 (☎ 7322 550)
Canada
    Embassy: Doma laukums 4, 4th floor
    (☎ 7830 141; fax 7830 140)
Denmark
    Embassy: Pils 11 (☎ 7226 210, 7210 433; fax 7229 218)
Estonia
    Embassy: Skolas 13 (☎ 7820 460; fax 7820 461; email sekretar@riia.vm.ee)
Finland
    Embassy: Kalpaka bulvāris 1 (☎ 7333 596; fax 7333 597)
France
    Embassy: Raiņa bulvāris 9 (☎ 7213 972; fax 7820 131)
Germany
    Embassy: Basteja bulvāris 14 (☎ 7229 096; fax 7820 223)
Israel
    Consulate: Elizabetes 2 (☎ 7320 739; fax 7830 170)
Italy
    Embassy: Teātra 9 (☎ & fax 7216 069)
Lithuania
    Embassy: Rūpniecības 22 (☎ 7321 519)
Netherlands
    Embassy: Teātra 9 (☎ 7220 110; fax 7223 388)
Norway
    Embassy: Zirgu 14 (☎ 7216 744; fax 7820 195)
Poland
    Embassy: Elizabetes 2 (☎ 7321 617; fax 7338 196)
Russia
    Embassy: Antonijas 2 (☎ 7332 151; fax 7830 209)
Sweden
    Embassy: Lāčplēša 13 (☎ 7286 276; fax 7288 501)
UK
    Embassy: Alunāna 5 (☎ 7338 126; fax 7338 132)
USA
    Embassy: Raiņa bulvāris 7 (☎ 7210 005; fax 7226 530)

Money

There are exchange offices at Rīga airport and dotted throughout the central area in hotels, banks, shops, street kiosks and elsewhere. Look for the sign saying *'Valūtas maiņa'*. The 24 hour Ahāts currency exchange in front of the train station offers acceptable rates but is not the safest place in town to change money.

Other 24 hour exchanges include Ahāts on the edge of Old Rīga at Basteja bulvāris 12, Marika at Basteja bulvāris 14 and another at Brīvības iela 90.

The ATM inside Rīgas KomercBanka at Smilšu 6. accepts Visa cards. ATMs for Eurocard and MasterCard can be found at the airport, the central post office, Saules Banka at Smilšu 16, the World Trade Centre at Elizabetes 2, the Hotel Metropole at Aspazijas bulvāris 36-38, the Latvija hotel, and in the Statoil petrol station at Krasta 101. Most major banks give cash advances on Visa, MasterCard and Eurocard.

Latvia Tours (☎ 7213 652) at Kaļķu 8 is the agent for American Express. It cannot cash travellers' cheques, but will issue them and replace any lost American Express cheques and cards. All the banks listed above change travellers' cheques and Eurocheques, although Saules Banka charges the lowest handling fee (1% of total sum).

Post & Communications

Rīga's central post office (☎ 7333 285), at Brīvības bulvāris 19, is open 24 hours and also has telephone services. The post office (☎ 7213 297) is at Stacijas laukums, immediately on your right as you come out of the train station, and is the best place to send large parcels from as they will wrap them for you. The express mail service (☎ 7211 226) is in the hall to your right as you enter. The post office is open weekdays from 8 am to 8 pm, Saturday from 8 am to 4 pm and on Sunday from 10 am to 4 pm.

There is a telephone, fax and telex office (☎ 7217 293) on Dzirnavu iela immediately behind the Latvija hotel, open Monday to Saturday from 9 am to 8 pm and Sunday

from 9 am to 7 pm. There is another in the post office next to the train station.

There is no city code for Rīga if you are dialling a seven digit number. If you are calling a six digit number in Rīga, however, you need to dial 2 before the number – all numbers in the Medical Services section already have the 2 added to their listed numbers, for your convenience. See Facts for the Visitor at the front of the book for details.

Email messages can be sent and received from the Internet Café (☎ 610 104), across the river (Vanšu Bridge) at Bezdelīgu 12. You can also access the Internet here. Online access is 1 lati an hour. The local access telephone number in Rīga for Sprint is ☎ 7223 816, 7223 817. LvNet Teleport (☎ 7551 133; fax 7553 261; email info@lvnet.lv), at Brīvības 204, and Latnet (☎ 7211 241; fax 7820 153; email darba@mii.lu.lv), at Raiņa 29, are two local Internet providers.

Travel Agencies

The Latvian Travel Agents Association (☎ 529 092; fax 7828 297) is at Šmerļa 3. Major travel agencies offering city and regional tours, and usually accommodation bookings, include:

Latvia Tours
    Kaļķu 8 (☎ 7213 652; fax 7820 020; email lt@mail.bkc.lv)
Rīgas Tūrisma Aģentūra
    Aspazijas bulvāris 28 (☎ 7220 368; fax 7216 727)
Travel Agency Satellite (TAS)
    Kaļķu 20 (☎ 7216 216; fax 7820 285)
Via Hansa
    Vāgnera 3 (☎ 7227 323; fax 7820 294)
Via Rīga
    Radisson-SAS Daugava hotel, Kuģu 24 (☎ 7061 171; fax 7061 172); K Barona 7-9 (☎ 7285 614; fax 7828 199)

Bookshops

English-language books are sold in every bookshop in town. Aperto Libro at K Barona 31 has textbooks, contemporary fiction, travel and guidebooks. Globuss at Vaļņu 26 is best for dictionaries and Penguin classics.

The biggest – and best – bookshop, Jāņa Rozes at Elizabetes 85a, stocks everything, including cassettes to learn Latvian with, children's books, encyclopedias, postcards and posters. It is open weekdays from 10 am to 7 pm and Saturday from 10 am to 4 pm.

Media
Rīga In Your Pocket, sold for 0.50 lati at most hotels and news kiosks, and *Rīga this Week* both run listings of places to stay, where to eat, things to see, entertainment and the like. The weekly Rīga-published *Baltic Times* also has an entertainment guide which includes cinema listings (see Media in the previous chapter).

You can get up-to-date British and German newspapers, the *International Herald Tribune*, *Time* and *Newsweek* at several places, including the Hotel de Rome, the Latvija hotel, the Hotel Metropole, and most bookshops. The United States Information Service (USIS; ☎ 7216 565), at Smilšu 7, has a reading room where you can read all the latest US publications for free.

Photography & Video
Kodak Express at Brīvības iela 40, opposite the Latvija hotel, sells Kodak film (including slide film) and other photographic supplies, including batteries, and will process print film in 24 hours. Bring your own camcorder film.

Laundry
There is an excellent laundrette, Miele (☎ 7217 696), at Elizabetes 85a, close to the train station. It is open 24 hours and offers service washes for around 5 lati. Tīrītava (☎ 7276 108), at Ģertrūdes 37, does dry cleaning, and is open weekdays from 8 am to 8 pm and on Saturday from 9 am to 4 pm.

Medical Services
Drinking tap water is not advisable unless you boil it first, as the foreign residents of Rīga do.

ARS Clinic (☎ 2-201 001, 2-201 007) at Skolas 5 offers a 24 hour English-speaking service and an emergency home service

(☎ 2-201 003). There is an emergency dental service at the A & S Health Centre (☎ 7289 516) on Lāčplēša 60. The AIDS Centre (☎ 2-529 895) is at Pilsoņu 13 and the Centre for Sexual Diseases (☎ 2-272 198) is at Aristīda Briana 2. Pharmacies stocking western drugs include Koblenz (open Monday to Saturday from 10 am to 9 pm and on Sunday from 10 am to 7 pm), at Dzirnavu 57; Drogas (open Monday to Saturday from 10 am to 9 pm), at Tērbatas 52; and Kamēlijas aptieka (open daily from 8 am to 8 pm), at Brīvības 74 . For 24 hour service, ring the bell at Kamēlijas aptieka.

Left Luggage
There is a 24 hour left-luggage room *(rokas bagāžas glabātuve)* downstairs in the long distance section of the train station. Small bags can be left here for 0.50 lati a day and large bags for 1 lati. The locker room (open 24 hours) is on the right as you walk towards the tracks. It costs 0.60 lati per locker. At the bus station the left-luggage room (open daily from 5 am to 11 pm) is to the left as you enter the main hall. At the airport it is behind the staircase to your right as you enter the arrival hall.

WALKING TOUR
The following walking tour is a good way to get an introductory feel for Rīga. It will take about three hours nonstop at a fairly leisurely pace, but you could make a day of it with pauses at museums, galleries, and cafés that take your fancy. Start with a look at the northern half of Old Rīga, which centres on **Doma laukums** (but don't forget to explore a few of the smaller, more crooked byways). Then make your way to the riverside and walk halfway over the **Akmens Bridge** for a view of Old Rīga from the river. Return to the southern half of Old Rīga and take the lift up the tower of **St Peter's Church** for a view of Old Rīga from above. Wander south out of Old Rīga to the **central market** on Prāgas iela, a focus of the city's modern life. Then head north-west (for about 600m) past the train station, another of the city hubs, to the **Freedom Monument**, set in the band of

LATVIA

boulevards and parks. Wander around the parks and, if you still have the energy, head out to the streets to their east to look at a more everyday, but still busy, section of the city. From here you can head to the **Jugendstil** (German Art Nouveau style of design) quarter, east of the Old Town.

OLD RĪGA

Many centuries-old German buildings survive in the Old Town – in places, whole squares or rows have stood since the 17th century or earlier. Old Rīga is a protected zone of narrow, crooked, now mainly pedestrianised streets, made prettier by restoration, and dotted with cafés and restaurants. Motorists have to pay 5 lati an hour to drive in the Old Town. Walking its streets is one of the chief pleasures of Rīga, but don't forget to keep looking up so as not to miss the playful statuettes and carvings that adorn many of the buildings. Kaļķu iela divides Old Rīga fairly neatly into two halves, each focusing on a towering church – the Dome Cathedral in the north, St Peter's in the south.

Dome Cathedral

The brick cathedral known as Rīgas Doms (from the German *Dom*, meaning cathedral) towers beside Doma laukums, the major open space within the Old Town, and is surrounded by an unusual brew of architectural styles. Founded in 1211 as the seat of the Rīga diocese, the Dome is now a church and organ concert hall. Church services are held at noon on Sunday. In the Soviet era they were banned; the first service for over 30 years, in 1988, was a major event of the *perestroika* era.

Architecturally, the Dome is an amalgam of styles from the 13th to the 18th century: the east end, the oldest, has Romanesque features; the tower is 18th century baroque; and much of the rest dates from a 15th century Gothic rebuilding. The floor and walls of the huge interior are dotted with old stone tombs – note the curious carved symbols on some of those on the north side, denoting the rank or post of the occupant.

JONATHAN SMITH

Organ recitals at Rīga's Dome Cathedral are a highlight of the city's cultural life.

Eminent citizens would pay to be buried as close to the altar as possible. In 1709, a cholera and typhoid outbreak, which killed a third of Rīga's population, was blamed on a flood that inundated the cathedral's tombs. The pulpit dates from 1641 and the huge organ (which has 6768 pipes and is believed to be the world's fourth largest) was built in the 1880s. Rīga's oldest museum, the **Museum of the History of Rīga & Navigation** (☎ 7212 051), founded in 1773, is housed in the cloister of the monastery next to the cathedral at Palasta 4. It's open daily, except Monday and Tuesday, from 11 am to 5 pm.

Rīga Castle

The castle, on Pils laukums, dates from 1330 when it was built as the Livonian Order's headquarters and served as the residence of the order's grand master. Today the castle – now painted canary yellow and home to Latvia's president – looks much younger following various modifications through the centuries, and not very castle-like from its inland side. You get a more turreted aspect from the river or the Vanšu Bridge. Part of the castle houses a **Museum of Foreign Art** (☎ 7226 467) which exhibits Latvia's largest treasury of art works dating back to the 15th century. The museum entrance is at Pils laukums 3. It is open daily, except Monday, from 11 am to 5 pm. The **Rainis Museum of Literature & Art History** (☎ 7227 901), tracing the history of national literature, is also here. It's open daily, except Sunday, from 11 am to 5 pm.

Old Rīga North – other sights

The red-brick Gothic **St Saviour's Church**, off Pils iela at Anglikāņu 2a, was built in 1857 by a small group of British traders on 30 feet of British soil brought over as ballast in the ships transporting the building material. During Soviet times, it served as a disco for Rīga's Polytechnic Institute. It still remains the property of the Church of England today. Services in English are held at 10 am every Sunday.

At Mazā Pils 17, 19 and 21 is a quaint row of houses known as the **Three Brothers** (Trīs brāli). No 17 dates from the 15th century, which makes it the oldest house in Latvia. No 19 houses Rīga's **Museum of Architecture** (☎ 7220 779), open weekdays from 9 am to 5 pm and Saturday from noon to 4 pm. At the end of Mazā Pils iela is Jēkaba iela, where the interior of tall **St Jacob's Church** (Jēkaba baznīca) maintains its original 13th century form. This church is the seat of Rīga's Roman Catholic archbishopric. Next door to St Jacob's at Jēkaba 11 is Latvia's **Parliament** (Saeima), a Florentine Renaissance-style building which was a focus of Latvian resistance to Soviet provocation in January 1991 and remained barricaded for over a year afterwards.

The picturesque **Swedish Gate** (Zviedru vārti), at the meeting of Torņa iela and Aldaru iela, was built onto the city walls in 1698 during the Swedish period and is the only remaining old-city gate. The round, peaked **Powder Tower** (Pulvertornis) at the end of Torņa iela is a 14th century original and the only survivor of the 18 towers in the city wall. Nine Russian cannonballs from 17th and 18th century assaults are embedded in the tower's walls. In the past it has served as a gunpowder store, prison, torture chamber, museum and students' party venue. Today, it houses the **Latvian War Museum** (Kara Muzejs, ☎ 7223 743), and is open daily, except Monday and Tuesday, from 10 am to 5 pm.

The 19th century Gothic exterior of the **Great Guild Hall** (Lielā Gilde), at Amatu 6, encloses a fine 1330 merchants' meeting hall, the Minsteres istaba, which is now the concert hall of the Latvian State Philharmonic. If you can't get in to look round the hall, consider attending a concert to see it. The yellow-painted **Cat House** on the other side of Meistaru iela at No 19 is the one you see pictured on all the postcards. At the beginning of this century, the Latvian owner of the house had statuettes made of the back ends of his two black cats – backs arched and tails up – on the building's topmost pinnacles facing the Big Guild Hall across the road as a gesture of defiance against the guild who refused him entry. The guild was strictly reserved for rich German traders. Following a lengthy court case, he was admitted on the condition that he turn his cats around to a more elegant position. A **plaza** with an outdoor art market opens out before it at the meeting of Meistaru iela and Kaļķu iela.

Latviešu strēlnieku laukums

The open space immediately east of the Akmens Bridge is known as Latviešu strēlnieku laukums (Latvian Riflemen Square). It is dominated by a big, dark-red statue of the said marksmen. The **Latvian Riflemen** were eight regiments formed in WWI to fight in the Russian imperial army. When the Russian Revolution rolled around, most of them supported the Bolsheviks. They provided a kind of palace guard for Lenin and formed key units of the Red Army during the Russian civil war – although some sided against the Bolsheviks in the concurrent Latvian independence war. During the Soviet era the riflemen were known as the Latvian Red Riflemen.

LATVIA

LATVIA

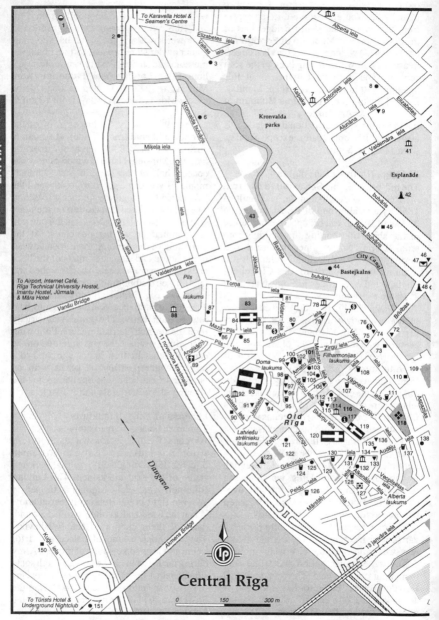

Central Rīga

0   150   300 m

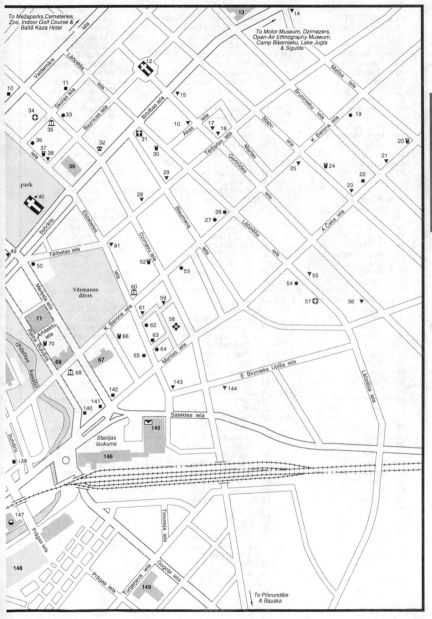

LATVIA

To Mežaparks,Cemeteries,
Zoo, Indoor Golf Course &
Baltā Kaza Hotel

To Motor Museum, Dzimezers,
Open-Air Ethnography Museum,
Camp Biķernieku, Lake Jugla
& Sigulda

Valdemāra iela
Lāčplēša iela
Skolas iela
Baznīcas iela
Brīvības iela
Bruņinieku iela
Matīsa iela
K. Barona iela
Stabu iela
Ģertrūdes iela
Tērbatas iela
Akas iela
Martas iela
Lāčplēša iela
A. Čaka iela
Blaumaņa
Elizabetes
Dzirnavu iela
K. Barona iela
Merķeļa iela
Arhitektu iela
Raiņa Bulvāris
(Pilsētas kanāls)
Marijas iela
E. Birznieka Upīša iela
Lāčplēša iela
Satekles iela
Timoteja iela
Prāgas iela
Prāgas iela
Turgeņeva iela
Gogoļa iela

park
bulvāris
Vērmanes
dārzs
Stacijas
laukums

To Pilsrundāle
& Bauska

13 14
12
11
10
34
35
33
36
37 38
39
31
30
15
10 17 18
25 24
19
20
21
22
23
29
28
26 27
61
52 53
55
54
57 56
60
59
61 58
62
63
66 64
65
68 67
69 70
71
143 144
142
141
140
145
146
139
147
148
149

LATVIA

Behind the statue is the **Occupation Museum** (☎ 7212 715), which gives an impressive account of the Soviet and Nazi occupations of Latvia between 1940 and 1964. The exhibition has been criticised as having a strong nationalist bias. However, it is informative, disturbing in parts and probably Rīga's most interesting museum. It is open daily from 11 am to 5 pm. There is talk of moving the Occupation Museum to another site and demolishing the building. The reason for this is the reconstruction of the **Blackhead's House** (Melngalvju nams) which is taking place behind the Occupation Museum. The Blackhead's House is a 14th century architectural gem built in 1344 for the Blackhead's guild of unmarried merchants (who also had an important house in Tallinn). It was destroyed in 1941 and is being rebuilt from scratch to mark Rīga's 800th birthday, which it celebrates in 2001.

From the square it is worth walking along the riverside a little way, or out onto the bridge. East of the square, at Grēcinieku 18, is **Mentzendorff's House** (☎ 7212 951), a 17th century dwelling showing how wealthy Rīgans once lived (open daily, except Monday and Tuesday, from 10 am to 5 pm). Further east is the interesting **Latvian Photography Museum** (☎ 7227 231) in an 18th to 19th century merchant's house at Mārstaļu 8. Among the exhibits are some unique photographs of 1920s Rīga. It is open Wednesday, Friday and Saturday from 11 am to 5 pm, and on Thursday from 1 to 7 pm.

St Peter's Church

The Gothic St Peter's Church (Pētera Baznīca) is the dominant feature of the southern half of Old Rīga. Don't miss the panoramic view from its famed spire, which has been built three times in the same baroque form: originally in wood in the 1660s; again in wood in the 18th century, after being burnt down by lightning; and most recently in steel between 1967 and 1973, after the church had been burnt to a shell in 1941 (by attacking Germans or the retreating Red Army depending on whom you consult).

A wooden church was built here in 1209, but the body of the existing building dates mainly from the 15th century – however, the fine stone of the western façade is 17th century. The body, like the spire, was badly damaged by the Germans – it was gutted and only the outer shell of stone remained, for many years in ruin, until the 1967-73 restoration. A lift takes you up the spire (1 lati). The church is open daily, except Monday, from 10 am to 7 pm.

Skārņu iela & Mārstaļu iela

A row of particularly pretty restored buildings faces the north side of St Peter's on Skārņu iela. No 10-16, originally a chapel of the Knights of the Sword's first Rīga castle built here in 1208, is now the absorbing **Museum of Decorative & Applied Arts** (Dekoratīvi Lietišķās Mākslas Muzejs, ☎ 7229 736). Full of fine Latvian work it is open daily, except Monday, from 10 am to 6 pm. The pottery and wall hangings are outstanding.

The building at No 22 dates back to the 15th century when it formed part of a convent. In 1592, the convent was converted into a home for widows by the then mayor, N Eke. The Rīga Tourist Information Bureau now has its offices inside No 22, while the rest of the original convent has been restored and turned into an upmarket hotel. Duck into the yard behind for a view of St Peter's rising above the roofs. Next door at No 24, **St John's Church** (Jāņa Baznīca) is a 13th to 19th century amalgam of Gothic, Renaissance and baroque styles. Be sure to look up and see the stone faces of two monks who,

LATVIA

so the story goes, were bricked alive into the wall during the building's construction.

Further south at Mārstaļu 2-4, on the corner of Audēju iela, is the 17th century **House of Johannes Reitern**, (a rich German merchant), with its elaborate stone carvings. Today it is a meeting house (and small exhibition hall) for journalists. At Mārstaļu 10, a **Protestant church** built between 1727-33, has a restaurant-cum-jazz club in its basement; and at Mārstaļu 21 is the baroque **House of Dannenstern**, another wealthy 17th century merchant.

Alberta laukums, a small square on the south edge of Old Rīga, was the site of Bishop Albert's original German settlement. There are several tall **medieval warehouses** on narrow streets which lead back into the Old Town from here – at Alksnāja 5, 7, 9 and 11 and Vecpilsētas 10 and 11.

PARKS & BOULEVARDS

East of Old Rīga's confined streets, the city opens out into a perfectly contrasting band of parks and wide boulevards laid out in the 19th century. Along the boulevards are many fine 19th and early 20th century buildings. Some of these belong to the eclectic school of design which drew on a multitude of past styles, while others are flamboyant examples of Jugendstil (German Art Nouveau), which crops up all over Rīga – in fact, the style survives here more so than in many German cities because of damage during WWII. Many of the ornate Jugendstil decorative motifs are on upper storeys. The old defensive moat, known as the **City Canal** (Pilsētas kanāls), snakes through the parks and marks the line of the old-city walls which were knocked down in the mid-19th century.

Freedom Monument

The central landmark of the park ring is the Freedom Monument (Brīvības piemineklis) on Brīvības bulvāris, near the corner of Raiņa bulvāris. Paid for by public donations, the monument was erected in 1935 in the style you could describe as 30s nationalism, on a spot where a statue of Peter the Great had stood. Topped by a bronze female

Liberty holding up three stars facing west, representing the regions of Latvia – Kurzeme, Vidzeme and Latgale – it bears the inscription 'Tēvzemei un Brīvībai' (For Fatherland and Freedom). During the Soviet years the Freedom Monument was off limits, and a statue of Lenin, facing the other way down Brīvības iela, was placed two blocks east. Lenin was removed on the night of 20 August, 1991, after the collapse of the Moscow coup attempt. In the late 1980s and early 90s the Freedom Monument became a focus of the Latvian independence movement, which started on 14 June, 1987, when 5000 rallied here illegally to commemorate the victims of Stalin's deportations. Several later rallies and marches focused on the monument, which still functions as an unofficial centre for animated political debate. Since 1992 the guard of honour that stood at the monument before WWII, has been revived. If the authorities were prepared to open up Milda (as the bronze statue is called) to the public, it would be possible to walk to the top for a breathtaking view of Rīga from the small window cut in her body.

North of Brīvības bulvāris

The mound called **Bastejkalns** (Bastion Hill) beside Basteja bulvāris is what remains of one of the bastions of Old Rīga's fortifications. Beside the paths either side of the canal, below Bastejkalns, stand five red stone slabs – **memorials** to the victims of 20 January 1991. Edijs Riekstiņš, Sergey Kononenko, Vladimir Gomanovich, Andris Slapiņš and Gvido Zvaigžne were all killed or fatally wounded here when Soviet special forces stormed the Interior Ministry nearby at Raiņa bulvāris 6. Slapiņš and Zvaigžne were members of the film crew of the Latvian documentary maker Jūris Podnieks. No one who has seen the films *Baltic Requiem* or *Post Scriptum*, or the documentary *Homeland*, will forget the last footage shot by Slapiņš that night or his gasped words 'keep filming...' as he lay dying.

Raiņa bulvāris was 'Embassy Row' during Latvian independence between the world wars and is approaching that status again, with the Stars and Stripes fluttering in front of No 7, France installed at No 9, and Germany at No 11. To the west, on K Valdemāra iela, opposite the corner of Basteja bulvāris, the **National Theatre** (1899-1902) is an interesting baroque building; Latvia's independence was declared here on 18 November, 1918. To the north, past the Congress Centre at K Valdemāra 5, at Elizabetes 2 was the Latvian Communist Party headquarters. It's now Rīga's **World Trade Centre** and also home to some foreign embassies.

The **Fine Arts Museum** (☎ 7325 021) at K Valdemāra 10a, on the north corner of the Esplanāde park, has permanent collections of Russian work downstairs and Latvian work upstairs, plus some interesting temporary exhibitions. It is open daily, except Tuesday, from 11 am to 6 pm. On the Kalpaka bulvāris side of the Esplanāde is the **Jānis Rainis Monument** to Latvia's national poet, who, Latvians say, would have been world famous if he'd written in a less obscure language than Latvian.

The domed 19th century **Russian Orthodox Cathedral** fronting Brīvības bulvāris was a planetarium under Soviet rule but has now been restored and is once more used as a church.

South of Brīvības bulvāris

There's a colourful **flower market** on the corner of Merķeļa iela and Tērbatas iela. The main building of **Latvia University** (Latvijas Universitāte), dating from 1866-1906, is at Raiņa bulvāris 9. Rīga's **National Opera House** (1860) at Aspazijas bulvāris 3, reopened for the first time since independence on 29 September, 1995, following a costly renovation.

NEW RĪGA

In many ways the heart of everyday Rīga life lies beyond both the Old Town and the park-boulevard ring, in the areas built up in the 19th and early 20th century. The **Central Market** (Centrālais tirgus) – housed in several WWI zeppelin hangars, south of the train station at the south end of Old Rīga –

always presents a lively scene and is a barometer of the city's standards of living.

In the combined residential, office and commercial streets east of Elizabetes iela, a number of low, wooden buildings survive from the 19th century. Here there are many impressive and flamboyant 19th and early 20th century buildings in Rīga's characteristic Jugendstil style. One of the best examples, designed by Mikhail Eisenstein, father of the renowned film maker, is at Elizabetes 10b, just north of the fine Arts Museum. Around the corner, on nearby **Alberta iela**, the buildings become even more fantastical. Alberta 12-9 is home to the **Jānis Rozentāls Memorial Museum** (☎ 7331 641), an Art Nouveau apartment, formerly home to the Latvian painter Jānis Rozentāls (1866–1916). It is open daily, except Tuesday and Wednesday, from 11 am to 5 pm.

Other specific landmarks to head for include the Russian Orthodox **Alexandr Nevsky Church**, built in the 1820s, at Brīvības iela 56; the Gothic **Old Gertrude Church**, built in 1865, at Ģertrūdes 8; or the towering Stalin era wedding cake-like **Science Academy** on Turgeņeva ielā.

Krišjānis Barons, the father of Latvian folk songs, lived the last years of his life at K Barona 3-5, which now houses the **Krišjānis Barons Memorial Museum** (☎ 7284 265). At K Barona 4 is the **Latvian Nature Museum** (☎ 7226 078), open daily, except Monday and Tuesday, from 10 am to 5 pm.

At Kraslavas 22, a **Cinema Museum** (☎ 7220 282) traces the history of Latvian movies (open daily, except Monday, from noon to 5 pm).

Rīga Ghetto

The Rīga ghetto in WWII was in the Maskavas suburb about a km south-east of the train station. It was a 750 sq m area bounded by Lāčpleša iela, Maskavas iela, Ebreju iela, Lauvas iela and Kalna iela. Before WWII many, but not all, of its inhabitants were Jews. There's little trace of the area's old character now.

LATVIA

About 5000 Jews had been among the thousands of Latvians deported to Siberia by the Soviet authorities from 1940-41. The city fell to the Germans on 1 July and new atrocities began that day with hundreds of Jews executed as 'retribution' for the Germans killed in the taking of the Old Town. Others were forced to scrub the bloodstains from the site of the battle with toothbrushes. A few days later 300 or more Jews were taken from the streets and locked in their synagogue. Grenades were then thrown through the windows and the building was set on fire. No one survived.

Several thousand more Rīga Jews were murdered before the remaining thousands (34,000 according to one Nazi account, but that doesn't tally with other figures for pre-war Rīga's total Jewish population) were herded into the ghetto in October 1941. Half-starved, they endured forced labour until most were taken and killed in Rumbula Forest, east on Maskavas, between 30 November and 8 December. Latvian collaborators as well as Germans were responsible for the holocaust – indeed the collaborators had a reputation for greater cruelty. Other Jews transported from Germany took some of the dead victims' places in the ghetto.

After the 1943 Warsaw-ghetto uprising, the Rīga ghetto, along with others, was liquidated on Himmler's orders, but those inmates capable of work were moved to the Kaiserwald prison camp in Mežaparks. Later they were brought back to other camps with the retreating German forces.

Today, the city's only remaining **synagogue** is at Peitavas 6-8. You can call in advance (☎ 7210 827, 7224 549) to sample kosher food in the synagogue. On the corner of Dzirnavu and Gogoļa iela there is a memorial marking the former site of the Jewish community's Big Choral synagogue. Rīga's **Jewish Museum** (☎ 7283 484, 7289 602), recounting the history of Latvia's Jewish population, is west of Brīvības iela at Skolas 6 (open weekdays from noon to 5 pm). The museum can arrange a three hour tour of Jewish Rīga and also sells *Fragments of the Jewish History of Rīga*, an excellent booklet (in English and German) with explanations and a map of the major Jewish sites in the Latvian capital.

OUTER SUBURBS
Motor Museum

Rīga Motor Museum (Rīgas Motormuzejs, ☎ 537 730) is at Eizenšteina 6, eight km east of the Old Town along Brīvības iela, then two km south. It is open daily, except Monday, from 10 am to 6 pm.

The museum was opened in 1989, but its seeds go back to 1975, when a Latvian car enthusiast, Viktors Kulbergs, saved a very rare 16-cylinder 1938 German Auto Union racer from being scrapped in a Moscow factory. The racer is now on show with 100 or so other eastern and western cars, motorbikes and bicycles, all packed into the two floors of this modern, purpose-built museum. The collection ranges from an 1886 Daimler Motorkutsche (a genuine horseless carriage – maximum speed 16 km/h) to a 1984 Cadillac Fleetwood limo. Motorcycle enthusiasts can drool over the 1942 Harley Davidson.

The star pieces of the collection though are the cars that once belonged to the Soviet luminaries Gorky, Stalin, Khrushchev and Brezhnev – complete with irreverent life-size figures of the men themselves. Stalin, pock-marked cheeks and all, sits regally in the back of his seven tonne, 6005 cc armoured limousine. The car has 1.5 cm-thick iron plating everywhere except on the eight cm-thick windows. It drank a litre of petrol every 2.5 km. Brezhnev sits, with appropriate surprise registering on his features, at the wheel of his crumpled Rolls-Royce Silver Shadow, written off in 1980 when he strayed from the safety of an official convoy into the path of a lorry.

To get there take bus No 21 from the Russian Orthodox Cathedral to the Pansionāts stop on Šmerļa iela in the suburb of Mežciems.

Latvian Ethnography Museum

The Latvian Open-Air Ethnography Museum (Latvijas etnogrāfiskais brīvdabas muzejs, ☎ 7994 510) is on the shore of Lake Jugla on the eastern edge of the city, at Brīvības gatve 440. Over 90 buildings from rural Latvia, mainly wooden and from the 18th and 19th centuries, have been assembled on a one sq km site here. They include churches, windmills and farmhouses from Latvia's different regions, and they're furnished with thousands of artefacts to provide a record of bygone country life. Services are held in the Usma church here every Sunday. On summer weekends, folk dance performances are given, and museum staff wear national costumes. There's also a big crafts fair in early June. The museum is normally open from 10 am to 5 pm daily from mid-May to mid-October – except on the last day of each month when it is closed. Take bus No 1 from opposite the Russian Orthodox Cathedral on Brīvības bulvāris.

Mežaparks & Cemeteries

Rīga's biggest park is **Mežaparks** (Woodland Park), about seven km north of the centre, beside lake Ķīšezers. Here you'll find playgrounds, lots of boats and jet skis to rent in summer. You'll also find the **Rīga Zoo** (☎ 518 409), the stage for the main concerts of Latvian song festivals, and pine woods.

South of Mežaparks are three cemeteries: the **Rainis Cemetery** (Raiņa kapi), where Jānis Rainis, his wife (the feminist poet Aspazija) and other Latvian cultural figures are buried; the large **Second Woodland Cemetery** (Meža kapi II), with a monument to the five dead of 20 January, 1991; and the **Brothers' Cemetery** (Brāļu kapi), originally designed as the resting place of Latvian soldiers who died in WWI and the independence war, and notable for its many monuments and sculptures. Later, WWII dead (including some Soviet troops who died reconquering Latvia, and some Communist Party members) were buried in the Brothers' Cemetery, but for much of the Soviet period the cemetery was off limits and allowed to fall into disrepair. In 1993 the Latvian parliament decided to restore the cemetery to its pre-Soviet state and moved the graves of

Latvia's remaining windmills recall the old-fashioned pace of pre-WWII agricultural life.

about 200 Communist Party members elsewhere.

GALLERIES

There are numerous art galleries around town, varying in quality and *Rīga In Your Pocket* lists them. Temporary exhibitions are regularly held at the contemporary arts centre, Arsenāls (☎ 7213 695), at Tirgoņu 1; the Latvian Exhibition Hall (☎ 7222 461) at Brīvības iela 31; and in the House of Johannes Reitern (☎ 7228 059) at Mārstaļu 2-4.

ACTIVITIES

See Facts for the Visitor at the front of this book for general information about activities in Latvia. Rīga has a golf driving range (☎ 7320 671) at K Valdemāra 143; and an indoor bowling alley in the Seamen's Centre (☎ 7321 375) at Katrīnas dambis 12. Rīga Technical University has outside tennis courts (☎ 322 920) at Kronvalda 3 which it rents out for 3 lati an hour and Andrejosta (see Getting There & Away – Yacht) has a sandy beach volleyball court which you can hire. In the depths of the Baltic winter you can ice skate on the outdoor rink (☎ 7551 334) at Ropažu 1.

ORGANISED TOURS

All of the major travel agents arrange city tours and day trips to other places in Latvia including Sigulda, Cēsis, the Open-Air Ethnography Museum and Rundāle. Bookings for trips arranged by Latvia Tours can be booked through the Hotel Metropole, Latvija hotel, or Hotel de Rome (see Information – Travel Agencies). The Latvian Hostels Association (LaJTMA – see Places to Stay) arranges a two hour bus tour of Rīga for 11 lati, as well as other budget tours.

The Country Traveller Association (see Places to Stay) arranges private guides; alternatively call the Rīga Association of Guides (☎ 7222 336).

SPECIAL EVENTS

Rīga hosts dozens of annual and one-off festivals of many different types each year. See Public Holidays & Special Events in the Latvia Facts for the Visitor chapter.

PLACES TO STAY – BOTTOM END
Camping

Rīga Tourist Information Bureau (see Private Homes) has information on camping sites around Rīga. In the suburbs there are some places to pitch your tent. *Dzirnezers* (☎ 951 415), 14 km north of Rīga on the road to Tallinn, offers magnificent views of Lake Dzirnezers from the small summerhouses it rents out, but there's no hot water. Campervans, tents and caravans cost 4 lati; beds in a summerhouse 7 to 9 lati. Electricity, hot water and showers are provided at *Camp Biķernieku* (☎ 7552 322, 7530 920), in a forest on the north-east edge of the city limits, at Eizenšteina 2. Pitching a tent is 3 lati. Take trolleybus No 7 from the centre and get off at the Biķernieku stop.

Hostels

The hostel scene in Rīga is less developed than in Tallinn: Places seem to appear and disappear quickly – check at the Rīga Tourist

Information Bureau (see Private Homes) for an update. Alternatively, try the Latvian Hostels Association (LaJTMA, ☎ 7217 544), at K Barona 32-11, which takes bookings for hostels elsewhere in Latvia and abroad (see the introductory Facts for the Visitor chapter for more details). In Rīga, LaJTMA runs four hostels. *Placis* (☎ 7551 271, 7551 824) at Laimdotas 2a has 80 places. Singles/doubles with shared bathrooms cost 3/6 lati. The reception is open 24 hours. To reach the hostel, take trolleybus No 4 from the Circus stop on Merķela iela to the Teika stop. *Turība* (☎ 7901 471) at Graudu 68 has 150 beds, split between singles/doubles/triples for 1.80/2.50/5 lati. Facilities are shared. Take trolleybus No 8 from Strēlnieku laukums to the Graudu stop. *Argo* (☎ 7225 895, 7225 298), east of the centre at Burtnieku 1, charges 3 lati per person a night. Take trolleybus No 16 to the Tālivalža stop. In the Soviet era high-rise suburb of Imanta, there is also a hostel – the *Imantu* (☎ 413 847), at Zolitūdes 30 – which has one double room and a handful of dormitories sleeping up to 15 people. A bed for the night is around 3 lati. To get there take bus No 53 from the Orthodox Church stop to the Rostokas stop or a Jūrmala train to the Imanta stop.

The Latvian University Tourist Club or *LUTK* (☎ 7223 114, 7225 298; fax 7820 113; email mountin@com.latnet.lv), in room 122 of the university building at Raiņa bulvāris 19 (open weekdays from 9 am to 6 pm), has singles/doubles/triples in the university youth hostel at Basteja bulvāris 10 (☎ 7220 703). It is best to book in advance as this place is always packed in summer. A bed in a double with communal showers and toilets costs 6 lati. A bed in a double (with toilet and wash basin) costs 12 lati. There are also three triples (with toilets) for 12 lati.

Alternative student accommodation includes *Rīga Technical University Hostel* (☎ 201 491, 203 395) on the other side of the river at Āzenes 22a. Rooms here are cleaner as they are not in such demand. A bed for a night in a shared room is 3 lati. Take trolleybus No 7 from the centre and get off one stop after Akmens Bridge.

Top Left: Art Nouveau architecture, Rīga, Latvia
Top Right: Guard by the Freedom Monument, Rīga, Latvia
Bottom Left: Dome Cathedral, Rīga, Latvia
Bottom Right: Freedom Monument, Rīga, Latvia

Left: St Peter's Church as seen from Old Rīga, Latvia
Right: Skārņu iela, Old Rīga, Latvia
Bottom: St John's Church, as seen from Old Rīga

Private Homes

Rīga Tourist Information Bureau (☎ 7221 731, 7212 377; fax 7227 680), behind St Peter's Church at Skārņu 22, can arrange accommodation in *private homes* in the Old Town for 7.50 lati a night. It also has four *luxury rooms* above its office. The small/large rooms with 'no church view' and shared facilities are 15/20 lati; larger rooms with a 'church view' are 25 lati. Book well in advance.

The Country Traveller Association (Lauku Ceļotājs, ☎ 7617 600, 7617 024; fax 7830 041) across Akmens Bridge at Kuģu 11 arranges *bed and breakfast* accommodation in Rīga for 15 to 20 lati a night as well as in *farmhouses* throughout Latvia. Advance bookings can be made through any of its European offices (see the introductory Facts for the Visitor chapter for details). The entrance to its Rīga office is actually on Uzvaras bulvāris and the office is on the 2nd floor.

Patricia (☎ 7284 868; fax 7286 650), at Elizabetes 22-6, offers rooms in private flats all over Latvia, including one next door to its Rīga office, which is a five minute walk from the train station. Rooms cost 7.50/10 lati with/without breakfast.

See Homestays under Accommodation in the introductory Facts for the Visitor chapter for further agencies which can provide rooms in Rīga and in other cities too.

Hotels

There are a handful of cheapies right by the train station. The best of the worst is *Aurora* (☎ 7224 479), opposite the station at Marijas 5. The rooms are small and tend to be very noisy. Singles/doubles/triples cost 3.40/5.80/6.30 lati. *Saulīte* (☎ 7224 546), just round the corner at Merķeļa 12, is one of the few cheap hotels in which rooms have been repainted in recent years. Singles/doubles cost 5/7 lati. Luxury rooms (which lack the garish colour schemes of the others) cost 15 to 20 lati depending on the degree of refurbishment. *Viktorija* (☎ 272 305; fax 276 209), one km north-east from the station at Čaka 55, is in a red light district but offers

fairly decent rooms with shared toilets and showers from 8 to 16 lati. *Baltija* (☎ 7227 461) at Raiņa bulvāris 33 is only for the absolutely desperate; the rooms are bare and in need of a lot of fresh air, and the shared showers and toilets are definitely a gamble. Singles/doubles cost 3.90/5.20 lati.

One place that gets good reports, but is tough to get a room at is *Arēna* (☎ 7228 583), slap bang in the Old Town at Palasta 5. The 45 bed hotel is full of clowns in winter (it's owned by the circus which reserves it for its acts between October and April), but in summer it is business as usual. Shared rooms are 2 lati per person.

Not so central is *Baltā Kaza* (☎ 378 135) at Ēveles 2, which is in a street off the north end of K Valdemāra. It has a couple of 10-bed rooms for 3 lati per person a night, and lots of doubles for 8 lati.

There are similar prices at two hotels in Rīga's outlying suburbs: the *Almina* (☎ 569 278), east of the centre at Ieriķu 2a, has four-bed rooms for 2 lati per person and doubles for 7 lati; some doors down at Ieriķu 20 is the *VEF* hotel which has a handful of rooms with shared facilities from 4 to 6 lati a night. To get to both hotels, take trolleybus No 18 or 23 from Čaka iela to the Stārķu stop.

Mežaparks (☎ 7557 988; fax 7557 964) at Sakses 19 in Mežaparks has simple doubles for 7 lati a night, complete with outstanding lake views. Take trolleybus No 2 to the last stop to reach one of Rīga's top cheap hotels.

PLACES TO STAY – MIDDLE

The *Laine* hotel (☎ 7288 816; fax 7287 658), centrally located at Skolas 11, is good value. On the 3rd and 4th floors of a run-down old building tucked in a courtyard off the main street, it has singles/doubles with a shared bathroom for 12/24 lati and singles/doubles with private bathroom for 22/35 lati. If you want to meet other travellers stay on the floor with the communal showers and toilets. Along similar lines is the *Radi un Draugi* (☎ 7220 372; fax 7242 239), in the Old Town at Mārstaļu 1. Owned by British-Latvians, it is clean and particularly popular with Brits. Singles/doubles cost 23.60/35.40 lati.

Another fair bet, although not as cheerful as the Laine or Radi, is the *Tūrists* hotel (☎ 615 455; fax 7860 008), a large former Soviet trade union and tourism hotel at Slokas 1, about a km west of the Akmens Bridge. Clean enough, but fusty, rooms with shared/private shower and toilet go for 14/30 lati a single, and 16/35 lati a double. Prices fluctuate depending on renovation levels. Take tram No 4 or 5 from the Grēcinieku iela stop by the Akmens Bridge and go three stops to the Rainberga bulvāris stop.

More pleasant – and slightly more expensive – is the *Karavella* (☎ 7324 597; fax 7830 187), a tower block at Katrīnas dambis 27 in the Pētersala area, two km north of the Old Town close to the ferry docks. It is a fairly modern hotel run by the Latvian Shipping Company, in the Seamen's Centre, with bright singles/doubles for 30/50 lati. It also has a bowling alley. Tram Nos 5 and 9 north along Aspazijas bulvāris and Kronvalda bulvāris in the city centre go to the Eksporta stop on the corner of Pētersalas iela and Katrīnas dambis, 500m south of the hotel.

Elias (☎ 518 117), close to lake Ķīšezers, out of town at Hamburgas 14, has seven large rooms costing 16 lati. Take bus No 9 from the central bus station or tram No 11 from K Barona iela. The *Saeimas deputātu* hotel (☎ 7332 132), well located at K Valdemāra 23, is clean, simple and has a great café-bar-cum-bistro next door. Singles/doubles are 16/24 lati. Book in advance for this one.

PLACES TO STAY – TOP END

Rīga has top hotels galore to choose from, meaning that there are always rooms available in this price bracket.

Slightly cheaper than the rest are Rīga's former Intourist hotels, all of which have seen a complete revamp (almost!) since Soviet Rīga's grey days. The monstrous *Latvija* hotel (☎ 7222 211, 7211 755; fax 7280 059; email admin@latvija.hotel.lv) is unmissable. Its Soviet-built ugliness towers 27 drab storeys into the sky at Elizabetes 55, and still sends shivers down the spines of many Latvians who were not allowed to set foot in the building in Soviet times. Rooms are moderately sized, the service fair, and the eating options manifold. Singles/doubles are about 85/100 lati; there are also more expensive VIP rooms (bigger with even more western furnishings). Views from the top floor restaurant are superb. The *Rīga Hotel* (☎ 7216 107, 7213 285; fax 7229 828; email vanda@hotel.riga.lv), also ex-Intourist although today harder to believe, is on the edge of Old Rīga at Aspazijas bulvāris 22. It is older (1956) and smaller (about 200 rooms) and slightly cheaper than the Latvija. Singles/doubles start at 55/80 lati and there are also some luxury suites to choose from. On the 3rd floor is the separately run *Eurolink* (☎ 7220 531; fax 7216 300) which awards itself four stars. Singles/doubles are around 50/70 lati. All rooms have cable TV.

Hotel Metropole (☎ 7225 411; fax 7216 140; email metropole@mail.vernet.lv), further down the street towards the station at Aspazijas bulvāris 36-38 was renowned as a centre of diplomatic intrigue and espionage in the 1930s. Singles/doubles cost from 39/44 lati and range up to 48/58 lati. The *Rīdzene* (☎ 7324 433, 7325 171; fax 7830 074; email hotel@ridzene.lv), at Reimersa 1, was run exclusively for Communist Party officials and other Soviet top dogs when it opened in 1984. Singles/doubles cost 77/85 lati.

Considered the top hotel since 1991 when it opened, the prestigious *Hotel de Rome* (☎ 7820 050; fax 7820 059) is in the heart of the Old Town at Kaļķu 28. Today it remains the mainstay for foreign business people. Singles/doubles cost 91/100 lati, luxury suites 125 lati and a suite fit for a president, 500 lati. It has a business centre inside and its à la carte restaurant, Otto Schwartz, is the most expensive in town. Equally fine, and also run by the same team, is the unique *Konventa Sēta* (☎ 7820 050; fax 7820 058), contained within the restored courtyards of a 15th century convent at Kaļķu 8. The 10 medieval buildings are each named after their original uses – in German and Latvian. Exquisitely furnished singles/doubles are

36/45 lati although prices are expected to rise. It also has 145 apartments within the complex, available for long-term rental (minimum 30 days).

Equally expensive but on the 'wrong' side of the river is the *Radisson-SAS Daugava* (☎ 7061 111; fax 7061 100; email radisson@com.latnet.lv), at Kuģu 24, across Akmens Bridge. It has great views of the Old Town skyline and all the facilities including a modern fitness centre, indoor swimming pool, sauna and a couple of restaurants. Singles/doubles start at 80/100 lati and breakfasts costs an extra 10 lati.

Māra (☎ 7901 316; fax 7901 315), on the road to the airport at Kalnciema 186, is part of the Best Western chain and has singles/doubles with all the mod cons for 65/75 lati.

PLACES TO EAT

Dining out in Rīga is substantially more expensive than in Vilnius or Tallinn. If you have the cash, however, the choice of where to dine is quite dizzying. Cheap and cheerful bars and cafés serving palatable dishes from non plastic plates are slowly starting to sprout in Rīga though – a couple probably opening up every month. During the summer months, in true Mediterranean style, the tables and chairs spill out onto Doma laukums (Dome Square), transforming it into a fun-packed plaza of cheap cafés, beer tents and late-night bars.

Restaurants

Old Town On and around Doma laukums there is a colourful variety of places to choose from. *Zilais Putns* (☎ 7228 214), at Tirgoņu 4, with an outside terrace overlooking 'the place to be seen' in summer, serves up a variety of higher-than-average priced dishes which are supposed to be Italian in origin. It does do some nice creamy soups though (open daily from 12.30 pm to 12.30 am). Next door is the contemporary Latvian beer bar *Alus Sēta* (☎ 7222 431) at Tirgoņu 6 (open daily from noon to 1 am), which serves mammoth portions of ribs, šašliks (kebabs) and other hunks of meat for around

5 lati a head. Don't just sit and wait for the waiter to come to you – order your food from the counter, buy your beer at the bar, and don't forget that all the salad garnishes cost extra.

On the north-east side of Doma laukums at Šķūņu 19 is *Možums* (7223 943), best known for its giant-sized lasagne for 4.95 lati. Beyond that, the somewhat clinical interior does little to attract punters after 6 pm when the place seems to empty for the night; it is open daily from 11 to 1 am.

A minute's walk from Doma laukums is one of Rīga's up-and-coming hot spots. Before independence, *Pūt,Vējiņi* (☎ 7212 291) was strictly reserved for government officials. Now, complete with an outside terrace in summer and a roaring fire in winter (the only one in Rīga), this funky restaurant, bar and café at Jauniela 18-22 is bustling with life. The small but select menu ranges from good old fish and chips, to a quick carrot and orange soup for 0.80 lati or a more lavish souvlaki for 2.90 lati. It is open daily from noon to around 4 am and has a cold courtyard in the shade in summer.

A minute's walk away in the other direction at Mazā Pils 11 is *Vērdiņš* (☎ 7221 339), a French-style restaurant boasting one of the best courtyards in Rīga and favoured as the best creperie in the Baltics. An excellent bean and watermelon salad costs 2.75 lati; sweet and savoury crêpes cost 2 to 3 lati (open daily from 10 am to 11 pm).

Rozamunde (☎ 7227 798) at Smilšu 8 is a Latvian-inspired place, dating from pre-independence times but massively revamped in recent years. Photos on the wall tell the story of the place and a Latvian opera trio sing while you eat. It is open daily from noon to 1 am and has outside seating in summer.

Heading towards St Peter's Church you pass *1739*, an upmarket Italian restaurant serving authentic pastas, meat dishes and soups for around 10 lati a head in a calm, refined atmosphere. It is open daily from noon to 11 pm. Close by at Jāņa 8-10, is *Kalanda* (☎ 7229 775), another elegant, but cheaper, restaurant serving traditional Latvian fare for no more than 5 lati a head;

LATVIA

it's open daily from 11 am to 11 pm. At its south end, Jāņa iela joins Mārstaļu iela. Here at no 6, is the *Asia* Chinese restaurant, not a bad choice for Chinese food, if you don't mind smelling as rank as the restaurant when you leave. It is open daily from noon to midnight.

Zivju (7216 713) at Vāgnera 4 is a very expensive fish restaurant offering a fine selection of oysters, lobster, shark and other fishy things. *Jana* at Šķūņu 16 is not quite as expensive, serving an unexciting array of European dishes. The caviar, however, is not bad. Both are open daily from noon to midnight.

Elsewhere One of Rīga's finest restaurants is *Symposium* (☎ 7242 545), a light and airy French-style bistro in a restored shopping mall at Dzirnavu 84-1. Home-made pasta starts at 5 lati and main dishes at 7 lati. It plays classical music, stocks a constant supply of English and German dailies, serves brunch and has outside seating in summer. It is open daily from 11 to 1 am. Also run by the same team is the equally popular *Osiris* (☎ 7243 002) at K Barona 31. It's open daily from 8 to 1 am.

Vincents (☎ 7332 830), at Elizabetes 19, inspired by the one-eared Vincent (Van Gogh), claims to have the best chef in town. He cooks up French-style dishes such as grilled chèvre (goat's cheese). In summer the restaurant has tables and chairs outside and serves barbecued meats, cooked in front of you. It is open daily from 11 am to midnight.

More off-beat is the Salvador Dali inspired *Andalūzijas Suns* (☎ 7287 282) at Elizabetes 81-85. The food is lavish, the decor almost industrial, and at weekends silent Charlie Chaplin films are screened while you eat. It is one of the few places to sport vegetarian dishes on its menu and it is open daily from noon to midnight.

There are a couple of high style, contemporary Latvian eating places worth a try. The *Imperial* (☎ 7228 223) at Brīvības iela 21 has a cabaret singer every night and is a regular haunt for wealthy Russians and expats (open daily from noon to 1 am). The upmarket *Lido* (☎ 7287 849) at Lāčplēša 53 – as opposed to the takeaway outlets which are also part of the same chain – serves mainly meat dishes, but has a good salad bar. It's open daily from noon to 11 pm. *Senā Rīga* (☎ 7216 869), at Aspazijas bulvāris 20, has live Latvian folk music every night and is a touch more rustic than the other; it's open daily from noon to 1 am. Expect to pay at least 12 lati a head in all three.

Orients (☎ 7280 936) at Blaumaņa 5a excels in eastern dishes such as plov (greasy fried rice with bits of meat) and dolma (stuffed vine leaves), all for around 2 lati. The *Chabad Lubavitch Centre* (☎ 7334 147) at Lāčplēša 141 specialises in kosher cuisine.

All the major hotels have restaurants too. The grill room inside the Radisson-SAS Daugava serves huge American-style grilled burgers and good nachos too, when it can get the chips in.

Cafés

A must, for anyone who missed the demise of the Soviet Union, is the Baltic's first purpose-built Soviet café *Mārrutku Maizītes* (Horseradish Sandwiches) at Krāmu 4, which is open daily from 10 am to 11 pm. Stale buns, plastic cups, drab walls and vodka at rock-bottom prices are all part of the deal.

Dishes are even cheaper at the *Hare Krishna Rāma & Svāmīdži's Space Station* at K Barona 56. It's open daily from 8 am to 8.30 pm, and between noon and 6 pm an entire soup and porridge meal costs just 0.40 lati.

Staburags (open daily from noon to 1 am), at Čaka 57, is a rustic Latvian joint serving great ribs, peas and lots of beer in a cheap, farmhouse setting.

Shalom at Brīvības iela 158 is the main hang-out for Rīga's Jewish community. *Dņipro* at Alunāna 6 is a Ukrainian café complete with Ukrainian newspapers. More authentic Ukrainian food, however, can be had at *Pie Kūma* (open daily from 11 am to 10 pm) at Čaka 65 .

Favoured for its exotic range of coffee and cakes is *Monte Kristo* at Ģertrūdes 27. It is open Monday to Saturday from 9 am to 9 pm and on Sunday from noon to 9 pm. Ice cream and milkshake lovers should try *Ice Queen* (open daily from 11 am to 11 pm) a few doors down at No 20.

Fredis, at Audēju 5 and Ģertrūdes 62, was a massive hit when it revolutionised the eating scene in the early 1990s – and it still is. US-style sub sandwiches, spaghetti bolognese and spicy salads can be eaten in or taken out for around 1 lati. It is open daily from 9 am to midnight. Also offering an eat-in or take-out service is the Mexican café *Nacho Nana*, almost opposite Fredis at Audēju 6. This one also stays open until midnight.

Other old favourites still as busy as ever include *Baltā Roze*, at Kaļķu 7/9, and the *Anre* café, at Aspazijas bulvāris 30, which has a tempting range of cakes and pastries. *Kolonāde*, under the watchful gaze of Milda at Brīvības 26, is actually a very nice café in a prime spot with a trendy terrace garden overlooking the opera house. It is known locally as 'the toilet' because it's next to a public toilet block.

Pizzerias & Fast Food

Opting for fast food no longer means steeling your stomach against cardboard fries and gritty burgers. *Lido*, at Ģertrūdes 54 and Brīvības 90, remains as popular as ever despite the grease. Another outlet is close to the Latvija hotel on the corner of Elizabetes and Tērbatas iela. All are open 24 hours, daily.

Of equal standing is *Sigulda*, on Brīvības bulvāris 21, where a quick lunch of pizza bread topped with a blob of tomato sauce and sprinkling of cheese can be eaten (while standing) for less than 1 lati. *Little Johnnys* (open daily from 8 am to 2 am), close to the train station at Elizabetes 91-93, also serves reasonable pizza slices. The menu at *American Fried Chicken*, at Tērbatas 33, comes as no surprise.

The best bet for pizza is *Pizza Lulū* on the corner of Ģertrūdes 27 and K Valdemāra 143-145. Run by a Canadian-Latvian team,

Lulū's is open daily from 8 am to midnight and serves up giant-sized pizza slices for 0.69 to 0.85 lati. Inferior joints include *Yankee Pizza* at Brīvības iela 70, and *American Pizza* at Brīvības iela 57. For 30 different species of pizza in a slightly more refined setting try *Lolo Pizzeria* (open daily from 11 am to 11 pm) close to the Latvija hotel at Elizabetes 51.

Pīrādziņi, close to the train station at Birznieka-Upīša 10, specialises in cheap traditional Latvian buns, pīrādziņi, ranging in price from 0.07 lati for a potato one to 0.13 lati for meat-filled ones (open weekdays from 8 am to 9 pm, weekends from 9 am to 8 pm). They're not messy, not greasy and ideal for your picnic basket. For freshly-filled baguettes and chocolate cake to take away, look no further than *Fredis* (see cafés).

You'll find *McDonald's* even if you don't want to; it is opposite the Hotel de Rome on the top end of the main Old Town drag at Basteja bulvāris 18.

Self-Catering

Rīga's colourful *central market* is housed in five great zeppelin hangars on Prāgas iela behind the bus station. It's open Tuesday to Saturday from 7 am to 6 pm and on Sunday and Monday from 7 am to 4 pm. Visiting the fresh meat hangar is not a particularly savoury experience however. The *Interpegro* grocery store opposite the train station is open 24 hours.

ENTERTAINMENT

Rīga has a lively entertainment and cultural scene. Two good what's-on poster sites are on the square where Kaļķu iela meets Meistaru iela in Old Rīga and on Basteja bulvāris opposite Smilšu iela. The *Baltic Times* and *Rīga In Your Pocket* list upcoming events.

Pubs, Bars & Nightclubs

There are plenty of them! And there are more and more springing up all the time. See *Rīga In Your Pocket* to get the latest offerings in the Baltic's clubbing capital.

Here is a list of pubs and bars:

Ala (The Cave)
Audēju 11 – pool tables in a cellar bar which has great live bands in the courtyard outside in summer. Open until 4 am

Citrons
Vāgnera 3 – a fairly new restaurant-cum-bar-cum-club serving great Mexican-style food in a post-modern setting; the hippest bands in town play here. Open weekdays until 3 am and until 5 am at weekends

Dublin
Vāgnera 16 – Rīga's second Irish pub; it's rather sedate and has not yet found the recipe for success

Jever Bistro
Kaļķu 6 – a German-style pub generally attracting foreign businessmen and pretty women keen to sell their wares

Karakums
Lāčplēša 18 – hip cellar bar where wild dancing is freely permitted; live bands. Open daily until 3 am

Kolonna
Šķūņu 16 – upmarket cocktail bar with an outside terrace on Doma laukums

Lido Alus Bārs
Dzirnavu 74 – traditional Latvian beer bar with waiters in medieval bloomers

NB
Šķūņu 9 – pool and billiard bar with lots of tables so everyone can play. Open daily from 9 to 5 am

Paddy Whelan's
Grēcinieku 4 – Rīga's first Irish pub; pints of Aldaris at a cheap 0.60 lati to appease the Latvian youngsters; most foreigners' first port of call; pub grub including fried British breakfasts until 4 pm

Pulkvedim Neviens Neraksta ('No one Writes to the Colonel')
Peldu 26-28 – an offbeat bar with a football table and packed dance floor which stays open until 5 am at weekends; when Paddy's closes everyone comes here

Roisin Dubh (Black Rose)
Grēcinieku 4, 2nd floor – run by the same team as Paddy's; beer is 0.30 lati more a pint to ensure the riffraff stays downstairs

Tim McShane's
Tirgoņu 10 – Rīga's third Irish pub; small and cosy and great pub grub

Here is a list of clubs:

808
A Kalniņa 8 – gay club close to the train station. Open Friday and Saturday only from 10 pm to 6 am

Bimini
Čaka 67-69 – once the city's only club; now it's clammering for clients, but great for a bop; free entrance for women

Cita Opera
Raiņa 21 – this club is in a cellar; it's yet to find its niche but it tends to go more for the live band touch

Groks Stacija
Kaļķu 12 – the place to go for a flashback to life under communism; a modern club decked out as a Soviet train complete with the cloakroom in a recreated train compartment and the DJ in the driver's cabin. Open daily until 6 am

Jockey Club
Elizabetes 49 – a popular haunt for businessmen and other lone guests in town; cabaret show with lots of almost-naked women

Reformātu Klubs
Mārstaļu 10 – upmarket jazz club in a restored church; book in advance to guarantee a table

Saksofons
Stabu 43 – the place to listen to great jazz in a tiny, smoke-filled cellar; more bohemian than the rest

Slepenais Eksperiments
Šķūņu 15 (entrance from Amatu) – industrial-designed club where the local art scene tends to gather. Open daily until 5 pm

Underground
Slokas 1 – Rīga's first western-style nightclub across the river; definitely for techno enthusiasts. Open nightly from 9 pm to 6 am

Zero Zone
Kandavas 27 – Rīga's flashiest club which has been firebombed a couple of times; snazzy laser show with a mainly Russian crowd

Cinema

Most of the major cinemas show the latest films in English with Latvian or Russian subtitles. An English-speaking telephone information service (☎ 367 777) can tell you what's on where. The cinemas it serves include the Daile Cinema (☎ 7283 990) at K Barona 31; Oskars (☎ 7283 990) at Skolas 2; Kino-52 (☎ 7288 778) at Lāčplēša 52-54. The artsy cinema above the Andalūzijas Suns (☎ 7287 282), at Elizabetes 81-85, screens a colourful variety of old B&W and contemporary art films. Kinogalerija (☎ 7229 030) at Jauniela 24 is the venue for the British Film Club on Tuesday and the French Film Club on Wednesday. Tickets cost 0.70 to 1.20 lati.

Opera, Ballet & Theatre

The Opera House, home to the highly rated Rīgas Balets (Rīga Ballet), where Mikhail Baryshnikov made his name, and the Latvian opera, has performances most nights with a break for a few weeks in July and August. Tickets costing 1 to 10 lati can be bought from the box office (☎ 7225 803) inside the opera house at Aspazijas bulvāris 3. It is open daily from 11 am to 7 pm with a one hour break from 3 pm. Tickets can also be booked in advance by phone (☎ 7228 240, 7225 747). To find out what is on, call ☎ 073 or ☎ 367 777.

Theatre is all in Latvian or Russian. The National Theatre (☎ 7322 759), at Kronvalda bulvāris 2, and the Dailes Teātris (Arts Theatre, ☎ 270 278), at Brīvības iela 75, stage plays in Latvian, and the Russian Drama Theatre (☎ 7224 660) is at Kaļķu 16. Like ballet and opera, theatre shuts up shop from around June to September.

Classical Music

The Latvia State Philharmonic is a local leader in the field, and there's an acclaimed national symphony orchestra, too, as well as lots of visiting orchestras, quartets and so on. Its main concert hall is in the Great Guild Hall at Amatu 6. The Dome Cathedral's acoustics, as well as its huge organ, are spectacular, and the frequent organ and other concerts are well worth attending. The ticket office (☎ 7224 432) is opposite the west door and schedules are listed there. There is another ticket office inside the 17th century Vāgnera Zāle (Wagner Hall), at Vāgnera 4, which is used for chamber and solo concerts. Both ticket offices are open daily from noon to 7 pm with a one hour break at 3 pm.

Circus

Rīga has the only permanent circus (☎ 7213 279) in the Baltics, at Merķeļa 4, and it's worth visiting for the bizarre nature of some of the acts (performing pigs and stubbornly non-performing domestic cats). The circus goes on holiday from June to September. Shows are twice daily on Friday, Saturday and Sunday.

SPECTATOR SPORT

Basketball (basketbola) and soccer are the most popular spectator sports – posters announce the big games. The Daugavas Sporta Namā (Daugava Sports House), which is at K Barona 107, is the big basketball venue.

THINGS TO BUY

Rīga has lots of craft and souvenir shops, some selling goods of quality. Among the better ones are Senā Klēts, at K Barona 28a, for Latvian national costumes; Gleznas un Grafikas, at Brīvības iela 52, for the best in pottery, leather goods and handmade jewellery; Daina, opposite the Latvija hotel on the corner of Brīvības and Elizabetes, for knitted socks and wooden candlesticks; Daiļrade, at Vaļņu 28, for great tablecloths and knitted jumpers; and Sakta, at Aspazijas 31, for Latvian flags and wooden jewellery. For amber go to the A&E Gallery off Doma laukums at Jauniela 17.

For paintings, drawings and imported Russian dolls, visit the craftspeople who set up shop daily in Filharmonijas laukums, the square where Meistaru and Zirgu iela cross.

If you're after some traditional Latvian Balzams or other local alcohols, be sure not to miss the Latvijas Balzams shop, opposite the train station at Marijas 1. For locally made honey try Latvijas Bite at Ģertrūdes 13. The irresistible Laima chocolate shop is at Vaļņu 28.

Centrs Universālveikals, near the Rīga Hotel, on the corner of Vaļņu iela and Audēju iela, is the main department store. The newly restored Berga Bazārs shopping mall, in a maze of courtyards off Dzirnavu 84/1, has some fine shops and galleries to browse in.

GETTING THERE & AWAY

Links with countries outside the Baltic states, which include ferries to/from Sweden and Germany, flights to/from several western and CIS cities, trains to/from Germany, Poland, Russia and Belarus, and buses to/from Poland and Russia are given in the introductory Getting There & Away chapter.

Air

Air Baltic flies five times a week to Vilnius and three times a week to Tallinn. The private Estonian charter ELK also has flights, three times a week, between Rīga and Tallinn.

Air Baltic's Rīga-Tallinn fare one-way is 83 lati in economy class and 135 lati business class. A business class return fare is 255 lati; an economy return with no restrictions is 160 lati; and a return ticket adhering to the Sunday rule (stopover Sunday night) costs 135 lati. The one-way Rīga-Vilnius fare is 55 lati; a return with a weekend stay is 73 lati while a return with no restrictions costs 115 lati. ELK's fares are cheaper – a one-way Rīga-Tallinn fare is 49 lati and a return is 95 lati. It also offers discounted fares for students – 35 lati one way and 74 lati return.

Air Baltic also flies three times weekly to Minsk, dropping off passengers at Vilnius en route (see Getting There & Away at the beginning of the book for details).

The airport is at Skulte, 14 km west of the city centre. For flight information, ring ☎ 7207 009, 7207 136.

Airline ticket offices in Rīga include:

Aeroflot
   Ģertrūdes 6 (☎ 278 774)
   Airport (☎ 7207 472)
Aerosweet
   Dzirnavu 18 (☎ 7332 674)
   Airport (☎ 7207 502)
Air Baltic
   Kaļķu 15 (☎ 7229 166, 7226 355)
   Airport (☎ 7207 401, 7207 402)
Austrian Airlines
   Kaļķu 8 (☎ 7216 309)
British Airways
   Airport (☎ 7207 096, 7207 097)
Czech Airlines (ČSA)
   Airport (☎ 7207 636)
Finnair
   K Barona 36 (☎ 7243 008)
   Airport (☎ 7207 010)
Hamburg Airlines
   Mārstaļu 12 (☎ 7227 638)
Latpass
   Pils laukums 2 (☎ 7227 263; fax 7227 738)
LOT
   Māza Pils (☎ 7227 234, 7227 263)
Lufthansa
   Airport (☎ 7207 183, 7207 381)

Rīga Airlines (RIAIR)
   Mellužu 1 (☎ 424 283)
   Airport (☎ 7207 325)
SAS
   Kaļķu 15 (☎ 7216 139)
   Airport (☎ 7207 055)
Transeast Airlines
   Airport (☎ 7207 771; fax 7207 772)

Bus

Buses to/from other towns and cities use Rīga's main bus station (*autoosta*, ☎ 7213 611) at Prāgas 1, behind the railway embankment just beyond the south edge of the Old Town. Up-to-date, handwritten timetables are displayed, with services listed under their final destination and the platform they depart from.

There is an information office at window No 1, which is in the main ticket hall. Comprehensive timetables for buses throughout Latvia are sold for 0.20 lati from window Nos 2 to 8.

Tickets for buses to Germany, Poland and France are sold at the International Passage booking office *(Starptautisko reisu kase)*, on your left, next to the currency exchange as you enter the ticket hall. It is open weekdays from 9 am to 1 pm, and 2 to 6 pm, and on Saturday from 9 am to 1 pm, and 2 to 7.30 pm.

Buses within the Baltic states and Kaliningrad service the following destinations:

Bauska
   65 km, 1½ hours, more than 20 buses daily, 1.10 lati
Cēsis
   90 km, two hours, 17 buses daily, 1.10 lati
Daugavpils
   230 km, four hours, four buses daily, 2 to 3 lati
Jelgava
   40 km, one hour, every half-hour daily, 0.50 to 0.65 lati
Kaliningrad
   370 km, nine hours, two buses daily, 5 lati
Kaunas
   280 km, 5½ hours, four buses daily, 3.55 lati
Klaipėda
   310 km, six to seven hours, two buses daily, 4 lati
Kuldīga
   150 km, three to four hours, one bus daily, 2 lati

Liepāja
220 km, 3½ hours direct, four to 4½ hours via Kalnciems, five to seven hours via Jelgava or Tukums; about 17 buses daily; 2.65 lati

Pärnu
180 km, 3½ hours, three buses daily, 3 lati

Rēzekne
245 km, 4½ hours, three buses daily, 3.60 lati

Šiauliai
130 km, 2½ to three hours, eight buses daily, 2 lati

Sigulda
50 km, one hour, 12 buses daily, 1.15 lati

Tallinn
310 km, six hours, four buses daily, 4.50 lati

Valmiera
120 km, 2½ hours, 12 buses, 1.15 lati

Ventspils
200 km, 3½ to five hours, 10 buses daily, 2.30 lati

Vilnius
290 km, six hours, five buses daily, 4.15 lati

Train

Rīga station (*centrālā stacija*; ☎ 233 095), on Stacijas laukums at the south end of the park-and-boulevard ring, is divided into two parts, side by side, for long distance trains (the bigger block, on the left as you face the station) and slower 'suburban trains' *(priepilsetas vilcienu)*, which travel to destinations up to 150 km away from Rīga.

Suburban At the time of writing, it was only 1.21 lati to some of the furthest flung places served by suburban trains, such as Valmiera or Mazsalaca. Some main suburban stations are also served by long distance trains on the way to places further afield. These trains are likely to be quicker, especially to the more distant suburban stations. Train fares within Latvia are 0.01 lati per km.

There are five suburban lines out of Rīga:

Dubulti-Sloka-Ķemeri-Tukums Line
This is the line to take for Jūrmala. About two or three trains an hour leave for each of Ķemeri, Sloka and Tukums II between 5.38 am and 11.36 pm. All call at Majori

Jelgava Line
One or two trains an hour go to Jelgava between 5.42 am and 11.31 pm. Some long distance trains to Ventspils, Šiauliai, Kaunas and Vilnius stop at Jelgava too

Ogre-Krustpils Line
This line follows the Daugava River inland to Krustpils, opposite Jēkabpils. Most trains only go as far as Ogre (11 between 5.05 am and 11.30 pm). A few others go on to Lielvārde, Aizkraukle or Krustpils. Long distance trains heading to Daugavpils, Rēzekne, Zilupe, Moscow and elsewhere also take this line

Sigulda-Cēsis-Valmiera Line
There are four trains daily to Sigulda, one to Cēsis and four to Valmiera. All call at Sigulda; Valmiera trains also call at Cēsis. The long distance train to St Petersburg also takes this line

Saulkrasti-Aloja Line
Two trains an hour leave for varying destinations, including Skulte and Vecāķi, between 6.14 am and 11.30 pm

Long Distance The timetable for departures *(atiešanas laiks)* listing the final destination, platform number, name of train and departure time is on the right hand side as you enter the main hall of the train station. Arrivals *(pienakšanas laiks)* are posted up on the opposite side.

Tickets for immediate and same-day departures are sold at the windows to the right as you enter the main hall. There is an information booth on the right of the entrance which is open weekdays from 7.30 am to 9 pm. To buy a ticket 24 hours or more before departure, go to the advance booking hall *(ieprikšpārdošanas kases)* at the south end of the suburban part of the station.

You can also call in advance and have your train ticket delivered to your home for a 1 lati fee (☎ 7216 664).

The daily Baltic Express between Tallinn and Warsaw comes through Rīga around midnight, southbound, and in the early morning, northbound. Its other stops include Kaunas, Šiauliai and Tartu. There is also one slower overnight train to/from Tallinn and to/from Vilnius via Kaunas and Šiauliai. Other long distance services from Rīga to places within the Baltic states include:

Cēsis
90 km, 1½ hours, one train daily terminating at St Petersburg

Daugavpils
225 km, 3¼ to four hours, seven trains daily (two terminating at Indra or Voronezh)

Liepāja
220 km, 4¾ to 5¾ hours, three trains daily
Rēzekne
235 km, 2¾ to four hours, two trains daily terminating at Moscow
Sigulda
50 km, 1¼ hours, one train daily terminating at St Petersburg
Valga
165 km, three to 3½ hours, one train daily terminating at St Petersburg
Valmiera
115 km, 2 hours, one train daily terminating at St Petersburg
Ventspils
200 km, 4¼ hours, three trains daily
Võru
215 km, four hours, one train daily terminating at St Petersburg

Car & Motorcycle

Some major western petrol companies, such as Neste, Shell, Statoil and Texaco, operate 24 hour petrol stations selling all types of western-grade petrol including unleaded and diesel all around Rīga and at strategic places around the country. Most western car dealers have showrooms and repair workshops in Rīga.

Between 9 am and 6 pm, all motorists have to pay a fee of 5 lati per hour to enter the Old Town. After 6 pm, the hourly rate drops to 3 lati an hour. You can also buy a yearly pass costing some equally ridiculous amount of money.

Car Rental Most travel agencies (see Information – Travel Agencies) act as agents for the major car rental firms and can take bookings. Major companies include:

Avis
Teātra 12 (☎ 7225 876)
Airport (☎ 7207 535)
Europcar
Basteja bulvāris 10 (☎ 7207 825)
Airport (☎ 7207 825)
Hertz
Kaļķu 15 (☎ 201 241)
Airport (☎ 7207 980)
Statoil
Ulmaņa gatve 117 (☎ 401 654)

Boat

Ferry Rīga's passenger port (☎ 7329 882) is at Eksporta 1, on the river about 1.5 km downstream (north) of the Akmens Bridge. Tickets for the weekly Travemünde and Slite ferry, and the planned Rīga-Saaremaa-Slite ferry are sold by Transline BT (☎ 7329 903, 7329 514; fax 7830 040) in the port at Eksporta 1a. Its office is open weekdays from 9 am to 5 pm. LS-Rēdereja (☎ 7220 172; fax 7212 775) at Pils 8-10 is the official agent for the Swedish run ferry to Stockholm which runs three times a week. Most major travel agencies also sell ferry tickets (see Information – Travel Agencies).

See the Getting There & Away chapter at the front of the book for information on these services.

Yacht Andrejosta, Rīga's yacht centre (☎ 7323 261, 7329 282), at Eksporta 1a, rents yachts from 9 lati a day or 15 lati for two hours. It has a mooring depth of up to four metres.

GETTING AROUND
The Airport

Rīga Airport (Lidosta Rīga) is at Skulte, 8 km west of the city centre. Bus No 22 runs about every 20 minutes between the airport and the stop on 13 janvāra iela opposite the bus station. Regular bus tickets (0.14 lati) are sold at the information booth (☎ 7207 009, 7207 136) in the departure hall. Taxi drivers should charge no more than 7 lati to take you to the city centre.

Bus, Tram & Trolleybus

A comprehensive tram, trolleybus and bus scheme showing all the routes is published in *Rīga In Your Pocket*. The usual ticket-punching system is used on buses, trams and trolleybuses but different tickets are used on each. Tickets cost 0.14 lati, and are sold at most news kiosks and from the driver. City transport runs daily from 5.30 am to 12.30 am.

Taxi

Officially, taxis charge 0.20 lati a km during the day and 0.30 lati between 10 pm and 6 am.

As a foreigner, you're sure to be ripped off. Insist on the meter running and if it doesn't work, agree on a fixed price before you set off. There are taxi ranks outside the bus and train stations and at the airport. You can call a taxi on ☎ 334 041; this costs 1 lati extra.

Bicycle

Rūķis (☎ 426 020) at Slokas 161, rents bicycles for 1 lati a day with a 30 lati deposit. It's open Monday to Saturday from 10 am to 7 pm, and Sunday from 10 am to 2 pm. Baltkonkorde (☎ 299 748) at Matīsa 141, offers deals from one day up to two weeks.

Around Rīga

SALASPILS

Between 1941 and 1944 an estimated 45,000 Jews from Rīga and about 55,000 other people, including Jews from other Nazi-occupied countries and prisoners of war, were murdered in the Nazi concentration camp at Salaspils, 15 km south-east of Rīga. Giant, gaunt sculptures stand as a memorial on the site which stretches 40 hectares. The inscription on the huge concrete barrier at the entrance reads 'Behind this gate the earth groans' – a line taken from a poem written by the Latvian writer Eizens Veveris, who was imprisoned in the camp. The centrepiece of the memorial is a six-metre-long block of polished stone bearing a metronome inside, ticking a haunting heartbeat which never stops.

Getting There & Away

From Rīga, take a suburban train on the Ogre-Krustpils line to Dārziņi (not Salaspils) station. A path leads from the station to the memorial (piemineklis) – about a 15 minute walk.

JŪRMALA

Jūrmala (Seashore) is the combined name for a string of small towns and resorts stretching 20 km along the coast west of Rīga. The beautifully fresh air and relaxed atmosphere have drawn holiday-makers in their droves since the 19th century. In Soviet times 300,000 visitors a year from all over the USSR flooded in to boarding houses, holiday homes and sanatoriums owned by trade unions and other institutions. Today Jūrmala's long, sandy beaches backed by dunes and pine woods and its shady streets lined with low-rise wooden houses are not quite so packed. Despite warnings you might hear about swimming in the sea, everyone does (just don't swallow mouthfuls of water). Beware of ticks too (see Health in the introductory Facts for the Visitor chapter).

Orientation

Jūrmala lies between the coast, which faces north, and the Lielupe river, which flows parallel to the coast, a km or two inland (it finally empties into the Gulf of Rīga just nine km west of the mouth of the Daugava). The main townships which make up Jūrmala are, from the east (Rīga) end: Priedaine (inland), Lielupe, Bulduri, Dzintari, Majori, Dubulti, Jaundubulti, Pumpuri, Melluži, Asari, Vaivari, Kauguri (on the coast) and Sloka (two km inland), and finally Jaunķemeri (on the coast) and Ķemeri (six km inland). All except Kauguri and Jaunķemeri have train stations. The busiest part is the four or five km between Bulduri and Dubulti, centred on Majori and Dzintari.

Majori's main street is the one km long, pedestrianised Jomas iela. Here you'll find cafés, ice-cream stalls, galleries, shops and bars. Streets and paths lead through the woods on the left (north) to the beach.

Maps

A pocket-sized Jāņa Sēta map of Jūrmala is published in Rīga In Your Pocket.

Information

There is a tourist information centre (☎ 7-64 493; fax 7-62 288) at Jomas 42, open in winter on weekdays only from 9 am to 5 pm and in summer at weekends too from 10 am to 3 pm. It stocks maps, books accommodation and arranges guided tours.

The post office is in front of the town hall at Jomas 2. There are public cardphones inside the telephone centre at Lienes 16-18

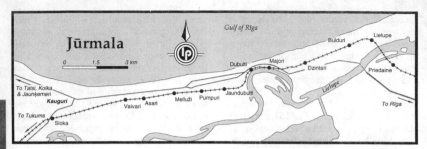

and on most street corners. You can change money and get cash advances on Visa and MasterCard from Komercbanka close to Majori train station at Jomas 30.

Things to See & Do

Walking the beach, dunes and woods and popping into a couple of cafés is reason enough to come to Jūrmala. The highest **dunes** are at Lielupe. Dubulti is the oldest of the Jūrmala settlements. In Majori, at Pliekšāna 7, north off Jomas iela, the poet Jānis Rainis' country cottage, where he died in 1929, is now a **museum** (☎ 7-64 495, 7-64 295) dedicated to him. It is open daily, except Tuesday, from 10 am to 5 pm. The **Art Gallery Fenikss** (☎ 7-62 429) is at Jomas 44 and is open daily from 11 am to 9 pm. A few doors down at Jomas 33 is the **Jūrmala Cultural Centre** (☎ 7-62 403), open daily from 10 am to 8 pm.

In Priedaine, at Lielais prospektas 24, there is the **Jūrmala Town Museum** (☎ 7-51 547) which shows how the seaside resort has developed since the 19th century. Dzintari (literally meaning 'pieces of amber') is home to a **Museum of Prison History** (☎ 7-54 536) at Piestātnes 6-8. Visits have to be pre-booked.

Places to Stay – bottom end

Jūrmala is a very spread-out place, so you may have to put in some legwork to find a room. Your best bet is to try the tourist information centre which can often guide you straight to accommodation in your price bracket.

Ella (☎ 7-63 978) at Rīgas 50-52 in Dzintari, is the place to camp. You can pitch a tent (6 lati) or rent a wooden cabin (18 lati). Beyond that there are two options: *Kempings* (☎ 7-62 3535), some five km west of Sloka at Kolkas 6 in Jaunķemeri; and another *Kempings* (☎ 7-67 554) three km west of Majori, at Upes 1 in Pumpuri. Both sites charge 2.50/3.50/4 lati a night for a single/double/triple wooden chalet. Washing facilities are in a separate block at both. The Pumpuri site also has a small hostel (☎ 7-67 554) with a few rooms for around 6 lati a night. To reach the hostel and camping site from Pumpuri station, walk 350m towards the coast along Kronvalda iela, cross over Strelnieku prospekts, then turn left along Dubultu prospekts after another 150m. The second road on your right will be Upes iela.

At Vaivari there's the reasonable looking *Tūristu Bāze Vaivari* (Vaivari Tourist Base), a solid three storey building in a secluded setting at Kauguru 49. From Vaivari station walk five minutes or so towards the coast until you reach the main road, Asaru prospekts. There's a sign to the tourist base, along a road that branches diagonally off Asaru prospekts, immediately west of the big red Vaivari Sanatorium. From the sign it's a few hundred metres to the tourist base.

Places to Stay – middle & top end

Many of Jūrmala's sanatoriums are in the quiet streets behind the beach, between Majori and Bulduri. Majori has two reasonable hotels. The smaller *Majori* (☎ 7-61 380; fax 7-61 377) is at Jomas 29, on the corner of Atrā iela, almost opposite Majori station. It is one of the more attractive blocks lurking in Jūrmala's concrete jungle. Singles/doubles with private bath cost 11/16 lati. The 250 room *Jūrmala* hotel (☎ 7-61 341, 7-61 340), in Soviet glass-and-concrete style at Jomas 47-49, charges 26/40 lati for singles/doubles, or 35/46 lati with a sea view.

In Soviet times, many visitors stayed in holiday homes or sanatoriums run by institutes, trade unions, factories and so on. Some of those intended for Communist Party highups are quite luxurious, and they're almost all open to whoever chooses to stay in them now. The *Zinatnes Nams* (☎ 7-51 205; fax 7-51 234) at Vikingu 3, five minutes walk from Lielupe station, has singles/doubles with private bath for 12.50/20 lati. It also has a restaurant, bar and tennis courts.

The *Rīgas Jūrmala* (☎ 7-62 295, 7-62 043) at Jūras 23-25 in Majori is a sight for sore eyes – the 98 room showpiece is right on the beach with its own swimming pool, sauna and tennis courts. Singles/doubles are 26/32 lati and there are luxury rooms which command a seaview for 46 lati.

The *Baltija* (☎ 7-62 338), also in Majori at Dzintaru prospektas 11, is decked out with all the facilities too – swimming pool, sauna and solarium. Singles/doubles start at 10/18 lati a night.

Places to Eat

Every second building on Jomas iela offers some eating option. More refined places include the Latin American, Cuban-run *Habanas* at Jomas 66, which serves not-very-authentic tacos and burritos for around 3 lati. In summer it hosts open-air concerts on the terrace; feel free to salsa on the street outside – everyone else does! It is open daily from 11 am to 11 pm – officially at least!

Just around the corner under the same Cuban management on Jauna iela is *Barbara*, a cosy, candle-lit bistro with a menu touting paella and tortilla for around 3.50 lati. It's open daily from 11 am to 11 pm.

The Middle Eastern *Orients* restaurant, which has an outlet either end of Majori at Jomas 86 and 33, is the most authentic of the lot and

worth the wait for a table. A table full of what Russians call zakuski – tasty salads, cold meats, smoked fish – followed by a hot šašlik or fish dish with vegetables, plus a couple of brandies, will set you back about 5 lati. It is open daily from 10 am to midnight.

Malibu, down a side street off Jomas iela at Konkordijas 13, serves a variety of huge Indian dishes, some of which are not as spicy as they should be but are still among the tastier meals to be had in Jūrmala. It is open daily from 10 am to 10 pm.

Sicilia at Jomas 77 serves thin Italian pizza daily from 10 am to 10 pm.

Entertainment

In summer there are discos several nights a week in and around Majori. Look for flyers on billboards down Jomas iela. The tourist information centre should be able to tell you what's on too. From June to August there's a summer season of concerts at the Latvia Philharmonic's Dzintari Koncertzāle (Concert Hall), at the (north) beach end of Turaidas iela.

Getting There & Away

Between 5 am and midnight, two to three trains an hour run from Rīga to Jūrmala along the Ķemeri-Tukums line (see Rīga, Getting There & Away). They all stop at Majori, but not always at every other station (40 minutes, 0.70 lati).

Cars driving into Jūrmala have to pay a toll of 1 lati a day. There are self-service machines at control posts either end of the seaside resort. A number of bicycle tracks run through the pine forests from Rīga to Jūrmala; ask at bicycle hire outlets in Rīga for details. In front of Rīga train station there is a special Jūrmala-bound taxi rank.

Getting Around

You can use the trains to go from one part of Jūrmala to another. There are also buses along the main roads. Cycling is a pleasant option. Veloviss (open daily from 11 am to 7 pm) at Jomas 75, rents bicycles for 1 lati an hour. Try the tourist information centre too.

LATVIA

Vidzeme

HIGHLIGHTS

- Cross the Gauja in a cable-car for the finest views of 'Switzerland' in Latvia
- Bomb down the Gauja valley in a bobsleigh made for four
- Follow in the footsteps of the Turaida Rose from Gūtmaņis Cave to the Daina Hill Song Garden
- View elk and wild boar at Līgatne Wildlife Park
- Enjoy an open-air concert in the grounds of Cēsis Castle
- Glide over the Gauja valley or hire a canoe instead

Vidzeme is the northern half of eastern Latvia, the country's most scenically varied region. The highlight of this region is the Gauja river valley (partly a national park) which contains some of the prettiest scenery in the Baltic states and is dotted with castles. There are three main towns in the park: Sigulda, Cēsis and Valmiera. Also in the region is the Vidzeme Upland, Latvia's highest region, and a long stretch of largely unspoilt coast along the Gulf of Rīga.

THE COAST

The main road from Rīga to the Estonian cities of Pärnu and Tallinn runs close to the shore of the Gulf of Rīga for much of the 115 km to the border. Soon after dividing from the Sigulda and Tartu road, 15 km from Rīga, it starts to run through some lovely wooded country, dotted with lakes and small villages with quaint churches.

One such village, **Baltezers** – a popular spot for midsummer celebrations – stands between two lakes, one on each side of the road. Most suburban trains on the Sigulda line stop at Baltezers station, three km south of the town.

Saulkrasti, 45 km from Rīga, is a popular summer escape for Rīga residents. As you approach the village at its south end, there is the cheap *Saulkrasti* restcamp (☎ 951 960) at Rīgas 26. There is a small tourist information office (☎ & fax 951 141) at Ainažu 12. A little further north, the road meets the open sea at a sandy beach on the north side of town.

Salacgrīva, at the mouth of the Salaca river, is where most northbound buses stop for a drink break. The tourist information office (☎ 40-41 254) is at Sila 2. **Ainaži** (derived from the Liv word *annagi* meaning 'lonely'), a small former shipbuilding town, is a km before the Estonian border. The main highway bypasses it inland (although you can still catch a glimpse of the town's wind power station), but buses usually detour along the old road into the town centre, where the old Maritime School is now a museum (Ainaži Jūrskolas Memorialais Muzejs), which is open daily, except Monday, from 10 am to 5 pm.

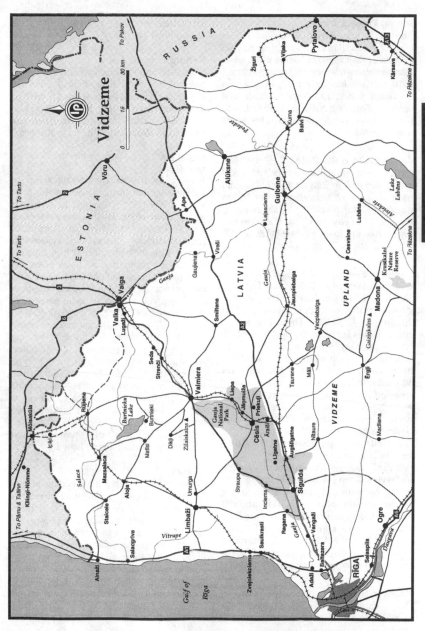

LATVIA

Getting There & Away

Buses north from Rīga to Pärnu and Tallinn follow this coastal road. Journey time is about one hour to Saulkrasti, 1¾ hours to Salacgrīva. There are also a few buses a day to Saulkrasti or Ainaži, either leaving from Rīga or places in the Gauja valley, like Sigulda, Cēsis and Valmiera. Suburban trains from Rīga run to Saulkrasti, but after that the Rūjiena line heads away from the coast.

MAZSALACA & RŪJIENA

There's some attractive scenery and a few spots renowned in Latvian folklore around the small town of Mazsalaca, about 55 km inland from Ainaži on the Salaca river. At Rūjiena, 7 km east of Mazsalaca, there is a tiny tourist information centre (☎ & fax 42-63 767) at Rīgas 12.

Things to See

In Mazsalaca there's a 13th century Lutheran church on the Rūjiena road on the east edge of town. At Rīgas 1 there is a **Woodcarving Museum** (☎ 42-51 945). The main spots that attract visitors are along the right bank of the river, to the west. About one km down river from the railway bridge, and two km from the town centre, is the **Werewolf Pine** (Vilkaču priede), reckoned to turn you into a werewolf if you crawl through its roots after muttering certain incantations under a full moon. The **Stairway of Dreams** (Sapņu kāpnes), about 300m north, is supposed to be able to tell young lovers how well suited they are. About a km down river from the Werewolf Pine, a spring flowing out of a rock at the **Devil's Cave** (Velna ala) is said to have healing properties. And about 800m further downstream, the sandstone cliff **Sound Hill** (Skaņais kalns) on the left bank of the river has some bizarre acoustic effects. In Rūjiena, at Rīgas 11a, is the **Adam Alksnis Museum** (☎ 42-63 385) displaying the works of the graphic artist and painter it is dedicated to.

Places to Stay

There's an old, basic *viesnīca* (*hotel*, ☎ 42-51 235) at Rīgas 17, not far from the river in Mazsalaca. At Rīgas 12 in Rūjiena is the *Talava* hotel (☎ 42-63 767).

Getting There & Away

Mazsalaca and Rūjiena are both on a suburban rail line from Rīga, though only one suburban train a day comes this far up. The daily long-distance train between Rīga and Ipiķi also reaches both stations. There are buses from Cēsis and Valmiera to Rūjiena.

SIGULDA
• *pop 11,800*

Known locally as the 'Switzerland of Latvia', Sigulda (formerly Segewold) is 53 km east of Rīga. Sigulda and its surrounds boast a string of medieval castles and legendary caves scattered along what is one of the prettiest stretches of the Gauja valley. It is probably the most popular day trips from the capital – for foreigners and locals alike.

Sigulda stands on the south edge of a picturesque, steep-sided, wooded section of the Gauja valley. It is the main gateway to the 920 sq km Gauja National Park (Gaujas nacionālais parks), which stretches northeastward almost to Valmiera, extending some distance either side of the Gauja valley. At Sigulda, you enter the park as you descend the hill from the town to the river. In addition to its tourist attractions, Sigulda is a minor health resort and a winter sports centre, with a bobsleigh run snaking down into the valley.

Every May, Sigulda plays host to an international hot-air ballooning festival.

History

Finno-Ugric Liv tribes inhabited the area as far back as 2000 BC, and by the 12th century they had built several wooden hilltop strongholds. But they were unable to prevent the German conquest in the early 13th century. In 1207, when the German crusaders were dividing up their spoils, the Gauja was chosen as the boundary in this area between the territories of the Knights of the Sword, who acquired the land south of the river, and of the Archbishop of Rīga, who acquired the north side. Both built castles in prominent positions – as much to guard against each other, one suspects, as against any local uprising.

After suffering numerous wars, particularly between the 16th to 18th centuries, Sigulda started to develop as a country resort with the building of the Pskov-Rīga railway in 1889. The Russian owner of the local estate, Prince Kropotkin, sold off land to wealthy Rigans to build their own country houses.

Orientation & Information

The national park visitors' centre (☎ 971 345), at Raiņa 15, sells maps of the park and Sigulda, arranges accommodation, guided tours of the park and even folklore evenings complete with campfire and national costume. It opens weekdays from 8.30 am to 5 pm and weekends from 10 am to 5 pm.

Unibanka (open weekdays from 9 am to 4 pm) at Rīgas 1 has a currency exchange, cashes travellers' cheques and gives cash advances on MasterCard and Eurocard. The post office is at Pils 2 and there is a 24 hour shop at Ausekļa 9. Maps and information booklets about the national park and town are sold at the kiosk, on your left after you exit the train station.

Sigulda Castles & Church

Little remains of the knights' stronghold (Siguldas pilsdrupas), built between 1207 and 1226 among woods on the north-east edge of Sigulda town. The castle hasn't been repaired since the Great Northern War, but its ruins are perhaps more evocative because of that. There's a great view through the trees to the archbishop's reconstructed Turaida Castle, on the far side of the valley.

On the way to the ruins (*pilsdrupas*) from the town, you pass the Sigulda church (Siguldas baznīca), which was built in 1225 and rebuilt in the 17th and 18th centuries, as well as the 19th century New Sigulda Castle (Siguldas jaunā pils), the former residence of Prince Kropotkin and now a sanatorium.

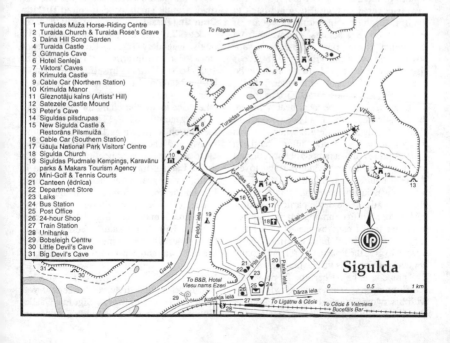

1 Turaidas Muža Horse-Riding Centre
2 Turaida Church & Turaida Rose's Grave
3 Daina Hill Song Garden
4 Turaida Castle
5 Gūtmaņis Cave
6 Hotel Senleja
7 Viktors' Caves
8 Krimulda Castle
9 Cable Car (Northern Station)
10 Krimulda Manor
11 Gleznotāju kalns (Artists' Hill)
12 Satezele Castle Mound
13 Peter's Cave
14 Siguldas pilsdrupas
15 New Sigulda Castle &
   Restorāns Pilsmuiža
16 Cable Car (Southern Station)
17 Gauja National Park Visitors' Centre
18 Sigulda Church
19 Siguldas Pludmale Kempings, Karavānu
   parks & Makars Tourism Agency
20 Mini-Golf & Tennis Courts
21 Canteen (ēdnīca)
22 Department Store
23 Laiks
24 Bus Station
25 Post Office
26 24-hour Shop
27 Train Station
28 Unibanka
29 Bobsleigh Centre
30 Little Devil's Cave
31 Big Devil's Cave

LATVIA

Krimulda Castle & Manor

On the north side of the valley, a track leads up from near the bridge to the ruined Krimulda Castle (Krimuldas pilsdrupas), which was built between 1255-73 and once used as a guesthouse for visiting dignitaries. A good way to reach the castle, or leave it, is by **cable car** which crosses the valley (west of Raiņa iela) every 15 minutes between 7.25 am and 6.25 pm, affording splendid views of the valley (0.5 lati one way). The big white building just west of the northern cable-car station is Krimulda Manor (Krimuldas muižas pils), built in 1854 and now a children's sanatorium.

Gūtmaņis' & Viktors' Caves

Below the viewing tower of Krimulda, immediately to the left of the castle as you face it, are some steep wooden steps. Walk down the 410 steps to the bottom and follow the wooden riverside path leading to **Gūtmaņis Cave** (Gūtmaņa ala), in the bottom of the north side of the valley. The cave is covered with graffiti going back to the 16th century – including the coats of arms of long gone hunters. The water from the stream flowing out of the cave is supposed to remove facial wrinkles. The cave is also meant to be named after a healer who allegedly cured the sick with water from it.

But this cave is most famous for its role in the tragic legend of the local beauty Maija, the Turaida Rose. Maija had been taken into Turaida Castle as a little girl when she was found among the wounded after a battle in 1601. She grew into a famous beauty courted by men from far and wide, but she loved Viktors, a gardener at Sigulda Castle. They would meet in this cave, halfway between the two castles. One day a particularly desperate Polish officer among Maija's suitors lured her to the cave by means of a letter forged in Viktors' handwriting. Maija offered to give the Pole the scarf from around her neck, which she said had magical protective powers, if he let her go. To prove the scarf's powers, she suggested he swing at her with his sword. Whether this was a bluff or she really believed in the scarf isn't clear.

Either way, the Pole duly took his swing, killing her, and then fleeing the scene.

Viktors' Cave (Viktora ala), a little further along the valley, was supposedly dug out by Viktors for Maija to sit and watch the castle gardens where he worked.

Turaida Castle & Around

The red-brick archbishops' castle (Turaidas pils), founded in 1214 on the site of a Liv stronghold, was blown up when lightning hit its gunpowder store in the 18th century. The restored structure is none too pretty, although the rebuilding has made it the most complete of the Sigulda area's old castles and (unfortunately) the most prominent feature on the southern escarpment of the valley. The castle is better viewed from afar, but the museum inside the 42m **Donjon Tower**, originally a last refuge from attack, offers an interesting account of the Livonian state from 1319 to 1561. It is open daily from 10 am to 5 pm, and admission is 0.5 lati.

On the path between the castle and the road, near the small wooden-spired **Turaida Church** (Turaidas Baznīcas) which dates back to 1750, two lime trees shade the grave of the legendary Turaida Rose. The headstone bears the inscription 'Turaidas Roze 1601-1620'. Viktors himself is said to have buried Maija and planted one of the trees, then disappeared without trace. Services take place in the church on the first Sunday of every month at 11 am. The hillside behind the church is known as Daina Hill (Dainu kalns) and shelters the **Daina Hill Song Garden**. The *daina*, or poetic folk song, is a major Latvian tradition, and the hillside is dotted with sculptures dedicated to epic Latvian heroes immortalised in the dainas collected by Krišjānis Barons. The whole castle area is open daily from 10 am to 5 pm.

Kārļa Hill (Kārļa kalns), facing Turaida Castle across the ravine which the road ascends, was another old Liv stronghold.

Walks

You'll get a good stretch of the legs if you walk to the main sites – Sigulda Castle, Gūtmaņis' Cave and the Turaida Castle area.

If you want goals for further exploration, there are many other historic sites and caves, with legends attached, up and down the valley. A good circular walk on the south side of the valley – about six km to and from Sigulda Church – is to the **Satezele Castle Mound** (Satezeles pilskalns), another Liv stronghold, then to **Peter's Cave** (Pētera ala), on a steep bank of the Vējupīte river, and onto **Gleznotāju Kalns** (Artists' Hill), which has a 12 km panorama.

On the north bank you could walk downstream from the bridge to the **Little Devil's Cave** (Mazā Velnala) and **Big Devil's Cave** (Lielā Velnala), then return along the top of the escarpment to Krimulda Castle – about seven km. The Little Devil's Cave has a **Spring of Wisdom** (Gudrības avotiņš). The Big Devil's Cave has black walls from the fiery breath of a travelling demon who once sheltered for a day here to avoid sunlight.

Ballooning & Bungee Jumping

To get a different perspective on things, you could always try a 43m bungee jump from the cable car which crosses the Gauja. Jumps take place in summer every Saturday and Sunday at 6 pm, courtesy of the Bungee Jumping Club of Latvia (☎ 926 482, 7551 181). The club also arranges jumps from a hot-air balloon in Sigulda as well as jumps-to-order from a variety of other stomach churning contraptions. *Nāc man līdzi* (☎ 7611 614; fax 786 0206), in Rīga, also arranges hot-air balloon rides over Sigulda for around 60 lati an hour.

Bobsleighing

The 1200m-long artificial bobsleigh track (☎ 973 813; fax 972 006), built for the former Soviet bobsleigh team, at Šveices 13, is one of the main attractions of the town. Part of the European luge championships are held here every January. You can try out the run for yourself for 1.50 lati per person. Between 1 May and 1 October, at weekends, you can take an exhilarating ride round the 16-bend track in a wheeled bob (3 lati). If

LATVIA

Canoe & Bicycle Trips

Vidzeme's Gauja and Salaca rivers are both good for canoeing – in particular the 220 km stretch of the Gauja between Vireši and Sigulda, which flows through some of Latvia's best scenery with nothing more hazardous than some fairly gentle rapids. There are riverside tent-camping sites dotted along this whole stretch, and above Valmiera the river flows through almost entirely unspoilt country.

You can set up a Gauja canoe trip through the Tourist Club of Latvia in Rīga, or the Makars Tourism Agency in Sigulda (see Activities in the Facts for the Visitor chapter at the front of the book for contact details), or other organisations.

The Tourist Club of Latvia is particularly good value. It offers three basic trips depending on your preparedness (and enthusiasm), ranging from one to 10 days: Cēsis-Sigulda (one day), Valmiera-Cēsis (three days out of Rīga, two spent on the river), and Sigulda-Vireši (10 days, nine days spent on the river). The cost per person, including equipment and food, transport to/from Rīga, and overnight accommodation in the Sporta Bāze Baiļi (see Valmiera, Places to Stay), or in riverside camps en route, is around US$40 a day. The club can also arrange tailor-made tours for groups with special interests or needs.

The Sporta Bāze Baiļi, with which the Tourist Club works closely, rents canoes and bicycles for touring, for around US$16 to US$20 a day. It also rents out all the gear you could possibly need to ensure as comfortable a trek as possible: tents (US$2 to US$3 a day), life belts (US$2 a day), raincoats (US$1.20 a day), mats (US$1.20 a day) and water cans (US$1.20 a day). You can hire a guide to take along with you for US$10 a day.

The Makars Tourism Agency arranges one to three-day water tours in two to four-person boats from Sigulda, Līgatne, Cēsis and Valmiera, ranging in length from three to 85 km. The tours cost US$16 to US$88 per boat including equipment, transportation to/from the tour's starting point, and camping site fees for up to four people. The agency also hires out bicycles for US$10 a day, two to three-person canoes for US$16 a day, inflatable boats for two people for US$8 a day, and 12-person rafts for US$30 a day. ∎

your stomach is not up to it, you can always opt for a ticket to the viewing tower for 0.30 lati, offering panoramic views of the run snaking into the valley.

Other Activities

The Makars tourism agency (☎ 973 724; fax 972 006) at Peldu 1 rents out skis and can also arrange a one day cross-country skiing tour. In summer it arranges canoeing, rafting and boat trips (see Canoe & Bicycle Trips aside). The Senleja hotel (see Places to Stay) also arranges skiing trips.

Turaidas muža (☎ 974 584), at Turaidas 10, organizes various horse riding activities, including treks and horse-drawn carriage rides (5 lati for half an hour) around the national park. At the north end of Parka iela there is a mini-golf course and tennis courts (☎ 223 808).

Places to Stay

The national park visitors' centre (see Information) can guide you to one of 19 special campsites set up in the park.

At *Siguldas pludmale kempings & karavānu parks*, run by the Makars tourism agency (see Other Activities), at Peldu 1, you can pitch a tent for 1 lati a night plus a further 1 lati for each person who sleeps in it. It also rents out tents/inflatable mattresses for 2/0.10 lati a night. If you have a car/caravan, it costs 1/2 lati to park it for the night. The campsite also arranges accommodation in *private homes* in and around Sigulda for 5 to 12 lati per person. Advance bookings can be made in Rīga through Durbe (☎ 7226 931; fax 7226 765) at Perses 2.

The *Senleja* hotel (☎ 972 162), originally built for Soviet groups in the 1950s, is in the valley below Turaida Castle at Turaidas 4. It has clean, basic singles/doubles for 10/17 lati. The hotel nightclub is open at weekends from 9 pm until the last guest leaves. *B & B* (☎ 973 724) in town on Brieža iela, has a handful of singles costing 4 lati a night. The *Bobsleigh Centre* (see Bobsleighing) has singles/doubles for 4/5 lati. A red-brick building close to the bobsleigh run at Beržu

1a houses a small family-run hotel with no name (☎ 974 965).

Viesu nams Ezeri (☎ 973 009; fax 973 278), a few km south of Sigulda in Ezeri, offers modern doubles with private bath for 25 lati. It arranges horse riding and skiing in winter.

Places to Eat

Laiks at Pils 8 (☎ 971 450) is by far the best place around – and also the trendiest. Various dried fauna decorates the ceiling and there's a pool table, darts, one-armed bandits (slot machines) and air hockey. It is open daily from 8 to 2 am.

Another bar-cum-restaurant which has proved a massive hit since it opened is the *Bucefāls* bar, at Brieža 93, which offers a combination of live music, Latvian beer and tasty food. It also stays open until the early hours.

Restorāns Pilsmuiža (☎ 971 395), inside New Sigulda Castle at Pils 16, overlooks the ruins of the old castle and is open from noon to 2 am. Ask the waiter for the key to the castle tower which dates back to 1937 and offers panoramic views of the Gauja valley.

For dirt cheap food try the Soviet-style *canteen (ēdnīca)* next to the department store at Leona Paegles 3. Just don't expect to be able to work out exactly what type of meat you're eating. It's open daily, except Sunday, from 9 am to 6 pm. There's a second ēdnīca opposite the entrance to the castle grounds that is open daily, except Sunday, from 10 am to 8 pm.

The *Turaida Café*, in the Turaida Castle grounds, is open daily from 10 am to 8 pm and serves reasonable snacks in a pretty location.

Getting There & Away

To/from Rīga there are 12 buses daily (two hours, 1.15 lati). There are nine local trains daily on the Rīga-Sigulda-Cēsis-Valmiera line (1¼ hours, 0.53 lati). The Rīga-St Petersburg train also stops at Sigulda (1¼ hours, 1.21 lati).

Getting Around

Walking is a good way to get around, as the atmosphere is fairly leisurely here. But you can save your legs by taking the cable car, which crosses between Krimulda and the west end of Raiņa iela, or bus No 12 which runs from Sigulda bus station to Turaida and Krimulda a few times a day. The bus departure times are posted at the bus station. It takes about 50 minutes for the round trip to Krimulda and back. Get off at the Senleja stop for Gūtmaņis' Cave.

Makars tourism agency (see Other Activities) rents bicycles for 1/5 lati an hour/day.

LĪGATNE & AROUND

The stretch of the Gauja valley between Sigulda and Cēsis is in the heart of the national park, and there are a number of things to see and do even if you're not in a canoe – which is about the best way to experience the Gauja.

On the south side of the river, about 15 km north-east of Sigulda, there's a Latvian wildlife park (Līgatnes atpūtas parks) with elk, beaver, deer, bison and wild boar in sizeable open-air enclosures in the forest. A five km motor circuit and a network of footpaths link a series of observation points, and there's a 20m-high observation tower with a fine panorama. The wildlife park is part of an 'Intensive Recreation Zone' within the national park, and one of the recreations is **horse riding** – the Delta stables (☎ 7173 714) rents horses and arranges treks through the park. There's also a 2.3 km **botanical path** marked out along here, as well as a **wild nature trail** and a **fairy-tale trail**, which leads you through a fantastical path of some 90 wooden sculptures.

Several sections of steep bank line the Gauja either side of Līgatne. These would hardly rate a second glance in some parts of the world, but in a flat country like Latvia they're a big deal – and they get names. The one on the north bank, almost opposite the wildlife park, is called **Katrīna**.

If you're continuing to Cēsis from the wildlife park you don't have to return to the main road. Instead, you can head on through the settlement around **Līgatne paper factory**, which locals proclaim is the biggest paper factory in Latvia. Three or four km

past the factory is a former **Communist Party holiday home** – which is hardly surprising considering the beauty of the area. Here the road ceases to be paved and you have about 12 km of dirt and gravel before you reach the main road again, via Karļi.

Places to Stay

There are several campsites, intended for hikers and canoeists, along the banks of the Gauja between Sigulda and Cēsis. They're mostly on the north bank, but there's one opposite the Katrīna bank at Līgatne – and there are a couple more on the Amata between Zvārtas Iezis and the Gauja. The national park visitors' centre (see Sigulda – Information) can tell you where they are.

Getting There & Away

Public transport to the area is poor. The nearest bus stop to the wildlife park is Gaujasmala, two km from the entrance, near the final turning to the park. Five buses daily are scheduled from Cēsis to Zvārtas Iezis, but this service, too, is erratic. You can always get a bus or suburban train to the Līgatne main road village or to Ieriķi, then walk or maybe hitch.

CĒSIS
• *pop 20,000* • ☎ *(41)*

About 30 km north-east of Sigulda up the Gauja valley is the historic city of Cēsis (formerly Wenden) which was once the headquarters of the Livonian Order and a member of the Hanseatic League.

Today it is heralded as Latvia's most Latvian town, and is home to the country's oldest breweries. Every year, around July, a major beer festival is held attracting beer drinkers and revellers from all over Latvia. Open-air concerts are often held in summer in the castle grounds.

Orientation & Information

The bus and train stations are together on the eastern fringe of the central area. Raunas iela, running almost straight ahead from the far side of the bus yard as you exit the train

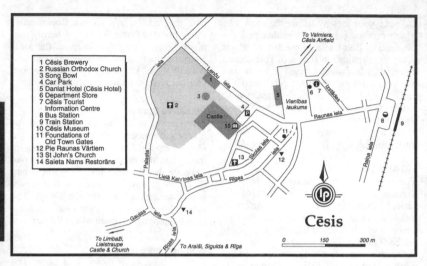

1 Cēsis Brewery
2 Russian Orthodox Church
3 Song Bowl
4 Car Park
5 Danlat Hotel (Cēsis Hotel)
6 Department Store
7 Cēsis Tourist
   Information Centre
8 Bus Station
9 Train Station
10 Cēsis Museum
11 Foundations of
    Old Town Gates
12 Pie Raunas Vārtiem
13 St John's Church
14 Saieta Nams Restorāns

To Valmiera,
Cēsis Airfield

Vienības
laukums

Raunas iela

Castle

Palasta

Lielā Katrīnas iela

Rīgas

To Limbaži,
Lielstraupe
Castle & Church

To Araiši, Sigulda & Rīga

Cēsis

0   150   300 m

station, leads to the main square, Vienības laukums, which, together with the older streets down to the left, constitutes the town centre. If you cross Vienības laukums and take the street heading downhill on the far side you soon reach the castle, on your left.

Cēsis tourist information centre (☎ 22 246; fax 34 432), at Uzvaras boulevard 2, sells maps and arranges accommodation in private homes. Note that seven digit telephone numbers in Cēsis do not require a local telephone code.

Castle, Museum & Park

Cēsis Castle (Cēsu Pils) was founded in 1209 by the Knights of the Sword, who later became the Livonian Order. Its dominant feature is two stout towers at the west end, looking over the castle park. To enter, you need to visit the extensive Cēsis Museum (Cēsu Muzejs) which is housed in the adjoining 18th century 'new castle', a yellow and white building at Pils 9. It's open daily, except Monday, from 10 am to 5 pm. In the attractive park below the castle there is a small song bowl, a lake and a Russian Orthodox church. Beside the park, on the far side from the church, is the Cēsis brewery.

Old Town

The old part of town, with a few narrow, crooked streets of mainly wooden buildings extends south from the bottom end of Vienības laukums. Just off this square, at the top of Rīgas iela, the foundations of the old town gates have been excavated and left exposed. Nearby, at Rīgas 7, is the old town hall and guard house dating back to 1767.

The main landmark of the old town is St John's Church (Svēta Jāṇa baznīca), on Skolas iela, which dates back to 1287, though its original Gothic form has been altered down through the centuries. Its towers date back to 1853 and the church has some fine stained glass. Several masters of the Livonian Order were buried by the north wall, near the altar.

Lielstraupe Castle & Church

Standing picturesquely beside the Brasla river at Straupe, about 25 km west of Cēsis, and the same distance north of Sigulda, Lielstraupe Castle and church (Lielstraupes pils un baznīca) date back to the 13th and 14th centuries – though they look more recent. There are four daily buses from Rīga and Valmiera, and the odd bus runs from

Cēsis at weekends. You can also approach Straupe from Līgatne, by taking the ferry across the Gauja there.

Activites

Cēsis Flying Club (Cēsu Aeroklubs, ☎ 22 639, 9-353 309) offers flying lessons for 40 lati an hour and gliding for 4 lati an hour with an extra 6 lati charge for every tow you need (to get you up). It also arranges aerial sightseeing trips that cost 40 lati for the entire aircraft (of four passengers).

To reach the airfield, follow Valmieras iela north out of town. The airfield is about 2 km along this road.

Places to Stay & Eat

The Rīga Tourist Information Bureau (see Rīga – Places to Stay) has information and takes bookings for campsites in the Cēsis area. *Piparini Kempings* (☎ 22 379), at Dzirnavu 52-54, has 41 riverside places for tents and campervans, as well as three rooms in the main building costing 1.50 lati a night. *Ungurs Kempings* (☎ 22 869, 33 219), 15 km from Cēsis in Ungurs, has cheap double rooms to let and rents boats.

In Cēsis, the fine *Danlat* hotel (☎ 22 392, 7894 122; fax 7894 121), at Vienības laukums 1 (known locally as the Cēsis hotel), is under Danish management and is one of the most homely, comfortable hotels in provincial Latvia. Singles/doubles are 22/30 lati and the hotel arranges guided walking tours, car and minibus rental, as well as fishing and canoeing trips. The in-house *restaurant* serves strictly Latvian cuisine and is undoubtedly the top place to eat in town.

Other eating options include the *Saieta Nams Restorāns* at the bottom of Rīgas iela and, at the top end of Rīgas iela, *Pie Raunas Vārtiem* which has a good cellar café.

Getting There & Away

Some 15 buses daily run to/from Rīga (two hours, 1.10 lati) and 10 to/from Valmiera. There are also daily services to/from Saulkrasti, Limbaži, Ainaži, Valka, Rūjiena, Madona, Jaunpiebalga and Alūksne.

There are five local trains daily to/from

Rīga (1¼ to two hours, 0.93 lati). The Rīga-St Petersburg train also stops here.

VALMIERA
• *pop 28,000* • ☎ *(42)*

Valmiera, a similar sized town to Cēsis about 30 km further north up the Gauja valley, just outside the national park, is less historic than Sigulda or Cēsis – most of Valmiera's (formerly Wolmar) old town burnt down in 1944 – but is still an interesting place on an attractive bend of the Gauja, with some useful accommodation possibilities.

Orientation & Information

The focus of matters is the road bridge over the Gauja, in the middle of town. Stacijas iela leads south from the bridge (after 100m or so) to the bus station, opposite the corner of Cēsu iela, and the train station after two km. The centre of town is on the north side of the bridge. The area rebuilt since WWII is ahead and to the left as you come off the bridge, while the little historic area is to the right, above the end of the bend of the Gauja. The market is at Tērbatas 8a, near the centre – go north from the square in front of St Simon's Church and turn right after crossing the small Ažkalna river.

Valmiera's extremely efficient tourism information centre (☎ 33 660; fax 32 447) is next door to St Simon's Church, at Lāčplēša 2. It sells maps, arranges accommodation in and around Valmiera, and has a seemingly endless supply of information on the area.

Things to See

From the north side of the Gauja bridge go to the right along Rīgas then Bruņinieku iela. The small historic area stands here on a point of land between the Gauja and a tributary called the Ažkalna. The tall **St Simon's Church** (Svētā Sīmaņa Baznīca), on the square opposite the theatre, was founded in 1283. It has a fine 19th century organ. A little further along the street are the ruins of the **castle** founded by the Livonian Order, also in 1283. At the end, at Bruņinieku 3, is the **Regional Museum** (☎ 32 733), with a collection of limited interest, however it's a good source of information on the district. It is open daily, except Monday, from 10 am to 5 pm. **Valmiera Drama Theatre** (☎ 23 300) is on Lāčplēša iela. Performances start at 1 and 6.30 pm.

There's an observation tower on the hillock called **Valterkalniņš**, just above the meeting of the Ažkalna and the Gauja. Across a small bridge over the Ažkalna, a loop of land surrounded by the Gauja has been preserved as a woodland **park**.

Activities

The Sporta Bāze Baiļi has touring bicycles for rent, has its own mountain bike tracks and is a base for canoe trips on the Gauja – see the following section and the Canoe & Bicycle Trips aside.

In summer it also rents out boats and arranges horse riding treks, while in winter it is transformed into Latvia's top ski resort. The centre also sports a 200m-long artificial ski slope, enabling ski fanatics to ski all year round. It rents out skis, boots, etc for around 0.30 lati an hour and also provides lessons.

Places to Stay & Eat

At the *Sporta Bāze Baiļi* (Baiļi Sports Centre) (☎ 21 861; fax 27 277; email baili@valmiera.lanet.lv), on the eastern outskirts of Valmiera, there are a number of accommodation options: self-contained wooden chalets for nine/six/four people costing 32/20/16 lati a night, a single/double room in the main building for 7/10 lati a night, or a space for your tent for 1 lati a night plus 0.60 lati per person. Breakfast costs an extra 1.30 lati and campers can hire bedding for 0.40 lati, or a three/10 person tent for 1/1.50 lati. On site, there is also a sauna, a steam bath and showers (0.02 lati a minute). The centre rents out three-person canoes (8 lati), and three/six-person rafts (8/15 lati), as well as all the gear – life belts, raincoats, water cans etc. Bookings can be made at the centre, through the Rīga Tourist Information Bureau (see Rīga – Information) or LaJTMA (see Rīga – Hostels). To reach Baiļi, go about 1.5 km south along Stacijas iela from the Gauja bridge, then turn left (east) along Kauguru iela and go about two km, mainly through woodland. The centre is easily identifiable by its tall artificial ski jump.

The small private hotel *Irina* (☎ 25 345), at Palejas 8b, has three doubles and a single (all share a bathroom) and cost 10 lati per person a night. The family run hotel also has a sauna.

The *Motelis Pakavs* (☎ 33 060), close by at Beātes 5, is another new establishment offering six doubles with private bathrooms and TV for one/two people for 13/20 lati. It has an in-house *café* and bar.

The main restaurant in town is the *Dzirnezers* at Rīgas 4. More cosy *cafés* are dotted along the same street.

Getting There & Away

There are about 12 buses daily to/from Rīga (2½ hours, 1.15 lati), and 10 buses to/from Cēsis; there are also services to/from Rūjiena, Mazsalaca, Valka, Dikļi and Burtneiki.

```
1   Irina Hotel
2   Motelis Pakavs
3   Market
4   Drama Theatre
5   Dzirnezers
6   Tourism Information Centre
7   St Simon's Church
8   Shop & Gallery
9   Regional Museum
10  Castle Ruins (Pilsdrupas)
11  Observation Tower
12  Bus Station
```

Valmiera

There are four local and four long distance trains daily to/from Cēsis, Sigulda and Rīga (1¾ to three hours, 1.21 lati).

AROUND VALMIERA

The **Strenči Rapids** on the Gauja, four km below the town of Strenči and 15 km north-east of Valmiera, is reckoned to be the most scenic stretch of the entire river, with steep, high banks. **Zilaiskalns** (Blue Hill), 14 km west of Valmiera, and **Lake Burtnieku**, about 23 km north, off the Mazsalaca road, are other local beauty spots. There's a lookout tower on top of Zilaiskalns. In **Burtnieki**, bordering the southern edge of the lake, there is a **Horse Breeding Museum** (☎ 56 444) which captures life as it was on a traditional Vidzeme farmstead. You can go horse riding here and there is also a campsite. Lying midway between Zilaiskalns and Burtnieku is **Dikļi**, a tiny village which would be pretty much ignored were it not for the fact that it hosted Latvia's first song and dance festival way back in 1864. The **Museum of the First Song Festival** (☎ 41 456) opens upon request!

VALKA

• *pop 7780* • ☎ *(47)*

Valka, about 45 km north-east of Valmiera on the road and railway to Tartu in Estonia, is the Latvian (and smaller) part of the twin towns of Valga/Valka – which were divided between Latvia and Estonia when the republics were declared in 1920. Valka in Latvia was allocated 142 buildings. There is the **Valka Museum of Local Studies** (☎ 22 198) at Rīgas 64, and a *viesnīca* (☎ 22 378) at Tirgus 2.

Today the border, marked by a fence, once again divides the twin cities with several border posts. Motorists have to make a five km detour to drive from one town centre to the other – yet, they're just 200m apart. The main train station is on the Estonian side but trains stop (in the middle of nowhere) on the Latvian side too.

VIDZEME UPLAND

Between Cēsis and Madona, 80 km to its south-east, is the part-forest, part-farmed Vidzeme Upland (Vidzemes Augstiene), which is at its hilliest approaching Madona. Latvia's highest point, the 311m Gaiziņkalns, is 10 km west of Madona.

There are a number of lakes in the upland, and the Gauja rises on the south side of Elka kalns near Māli. The Gauja basically flows in a big circle – first east through Jaunpiebalga and Lejasciems, then north past Vireši and Gaujiena (where there's a ruined 13th century castle) to form the Latvian-Estonian border for a stretch, before turning south-west through Strenči and Valmiera.

The Rīga-Rēzekne-Moscow trunk road crosses the upland from west to east and goes through Madona, but the north-south route from Cēsis to Madona (through Taurene and Vecpiebalga) is probably more scenic. In Madona, there's a *viesnīca* (☎ 22 606) at Saieta laukums 10. The Rīga-Pskov-St Petersburg road crosses to the north of the upland, it's here that you'll find a *Kempings*, near Alūksne, 17 km south of the road not far from the Estonian border.

Getting There & Away

Buses reach into and cross the upland from Cēsis, Valmiera and Sigulda to the north, from Rēzekne to the south, and from Rīga to the west.

Latgale

HIGHLIGHTS

- Stand where the pope stood at Latvia's leading Roman Catholic shrine in Aglona
- Canoe round Latvia's 'lake district' in the Latgale Upland
- See where Latvian poet Jānis Rainis was born in Dunava
- Blast yourself back to the past with a visit to a 19th century fortress at Daugavpils

Locator & Map Index

Daugavpils
p286

The south-east area of Latvia is called Latgale. Named after the Latgal (Lettish) tribes who inhabited the region at the time of the German invasion in the 12th century, it's the main bastion of Roman Catholicism in Latvia – having been under Polish control from 1561 to 1772.

The Latgale Upland, in the far south-east corner, is a scenic lake district, with Rēzekne prominent among the medium-sized towns around its fringes. Daugavpils, to the south-west, is Latvia's second biggest city and has a mainly Russian population. The Daugava river flows from Daugavpils to Rīga. A number of dams and hydroelectric schemes create artificial lakes along its length, and there are a few towns of minor significance. Relatively few visitors come to this part of Latvia.

DAUGAVA VALLEY

The road and railway from Rīga to Daugavpils follow the north bank of the Daugava fairly closely. At **Lielvārde**, 50 km from Rīga, and **Aizkraukle**, 80 km out, there are ancient castle mounds *(pilskalns)* of the pre-German inhabitants. The one at Aizkraukle is large and impressive. At **Koknese**, 95 km from Rīga, there's a 13th century knights' castle right on the river bank. At **Krustpils**, 140 km from Rīga, the railway divides and the main line heads east

(away from the river) towards Rēzekne and Moscow, while the branch continues on up the river to Daugavpils. Krustpils forms a single town with **Jēkabpils** on the south bank. Krustpils has a 13th century castle and a 17th century church.

In Jēkabpils, there is a church dating back to 1769, and a **History Museum** (☎ 52-31 750), at Brīvības 169-171, which has a musical history section and an open-air ethnographic section.

There are a couple of places to stay, including a *Motelis* (☎ 52-21 708), at Rīgas 33, on the east edge of town. The tourist information centre (☎ 52-31 391) is in town at Pasta 29.

Līvāni, some 28 km further south-east on the Rīga-Daugavpils road, is a pretty little village to make a fleeting stop at on the way. **Dunava**, 27 km further south-east on the same road, is the birthplace of Latvia's great poet Jānis Rainis, and as such, the village is said to be 'the cradle of the poet's soul'. The

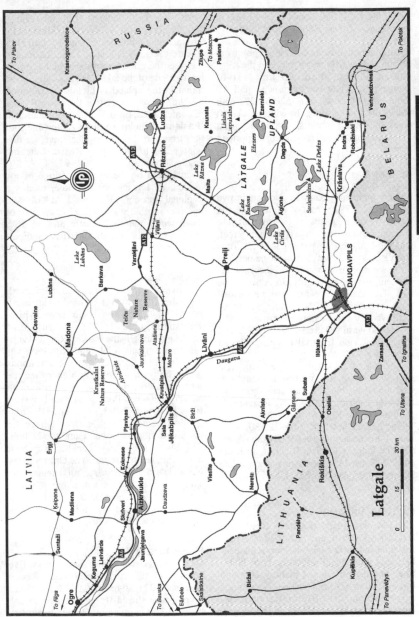

LATVIA

Latgale

Rainis museum 'Tadenava' (☎ 52-52 522) in the village recounts Rainis' childhood days here.

An alternative route to Daugavpils from Jēkabpils, is via **Gārsene**, close to the Lithuanian border, about 50 km east of Daugavpils. In Gārsene there is a small, 10 room hotel (☎ 52-68 616, 52-68 637) with places for 1 lati a night. In winter a ski lift takes you up the gentle slopes of the Saara Hills and you can also rent skiing equipment here.

RĒZEKNE
• *pop 42,385* • ☎ *(46)*

The predominantly Russian populated town of Rēzekne, 235 km east of Rīga, forms the north-western gateway to the Latgale Upland. Atbrīvošanas aleja is the main street, and most interesting part of town. It runs from Rēzekne II train station in the north to the bus station in the south, and incorporates the central square (roughly) in between the two. The **statue of Māra**, standing gloriously in the centre of the square, was twice destroyed by the Soviet authorities in the 1940s and wasn't re-erected until 1992. The inscription 'Vienoti Latvijai' means 'United Latvia'.

Rēzekne I train station, in the south-west of town, is on the Vilnius-Daugavpils-Pskov-St Petersburg line and sees about five trains in each direction daily. Rēzekne II station is on the Rīga-Moscow line.

The *Latgale* hotel (☎ & fax 22 180) overlooks the central square at Atbrīvošanas aleja 98. The Latgale Tourism Business Institute (☎ 23 518; fax 23 709), at Atbrīvošanas aleja 90, rents bicycles and boats, and arranges horse riding.

LATGALE UPLAND

The Latgale Upland (Latgales Augstiene) stretching south and south-east from Rēzekne is Latvia's lake district, a plateau-like area with literally thousands of lakes. They're mostly clean and shallow, although **Lake Drīdzs** (Dridzu ezers) is Latvia's deepest at 65m. **Lake Rāzna** (Rāznas ezers) covering 55 sq km has been Latvia's biggest

lake since Lake Lubāns (Lubānas ezers), further north-west, was partially drained by the Soviet authorities. Some of Latgale's prettiest scenery is around Lake Rāzna and between there and **Ezernieki**, which is on the eastern side of the lake Ežezers. The highest point in the upland is **Lielais Liepukalns** (289m), three km east of the Lake Rāzna-Ezernieki road. From the Catholic church at **Pasiene**, eight km south of Zilupe and four km from the Russian border, there's a fine view across to the plains of Russia stretching endlessly eastward.

In **Ludza** on the northern fringe of the region, 25 km east of Rēzekne, there's a regional museum at Kuļņeva 2. At **Krāslava** on the southern fringe, 45 km east of Daugavpils, there's a castle and an 18th century Catholic church which has a staggering 12 altars.

Aglona Basilica

The twin-towered white church, 8 km north from the village of Aglona (and 35 km north of Krāslava) on the main Daugavpils-Rēzekne road crossing the western part of the lake district, is the leading Roman Catholic shrine in Latvia. The church, which was built in 1699, is engulfed by an enormous grass courtyard – probably bigger than the whole of Aglona village put together – which was created when Pope John Paul II visited the church in 1993. The equally disproportionately-large pulpit where he addressed thousands who came to see him, still stands, as does the regal archway built at the entrance to the site. The church today is Latvia's most important pilgrimage site. Thousands gather here – some pilgrims coming long distances on foot – for Ascension Day (15 August) and a candlelight procession the night before.

Places to Stay

On the northern shores of Lake Ciriss, five km north of Aglona village, is *Arkada Kempings* (☎ 53-22 687; fax 53-21 123) which has 80 places in shared wooden chalets by the lake for 2.50 lati a night. Here you can fish or rent rowboats and paddle boats. It also has a traditional Latvian lakeside sauna.

On top of Sauleskalns (Sun Hill), 15 km north of Krāslava near Lake Dridzs, is the *Sauleskalns* hotel, a former tourist base during Soviet times. There should also be opportunities for wild camping here.

Otherwise there are the hotels at Rēzekne and Daugavpils, plus the basic *Saka* hotel (☎ 56-21 241), at Raiņa 19, in Krāslava and the *Ezerzeme* (☎ 57-22 490), at Stacijas 42, in Ludza. As you approach the town from Zilupe, there is a *Motelis* (☎ 57-25 498) at Latgales 251. Patricia of Rīga (see Rīga – Places to Stay) may be able to book *private home* accommodation.

Getting There & Away

A car or bicycle, or even a canoe (see Activities), is the ideal way to get around the Latgale Upland, as public transport is limited. There are a handful of buses daily between Rēzekne and Ludza, and several daily between Daugavpils and Krāslava, Aglona and Ludza.

Train Two or three trains run daily (in each direction) along both the northern fringe of the district, on the Rēzekne-Ludza-Zilupe line, and along the southern fringe, on the Daugavpils-Krāslava-Indra-Robežnieki line. Aglona station, on the Rēzekne-Daugavpils line, is 10 km north-west of Aglona village.

DAUGAVPILS

• *pop 122,000* • ☎ *(54)*

Daugavpils, Latvia's second biggest city, dates from 1275 and has a chequered past in which it has, at various times, been called Dünaburg by Germans, Borisoglebsk by Russians and Dvinsk by Poles. Today it's predominantly a drab, post-WWII Soviet creation – strangely interesting to visit for the view it gives you of another side of Baltic reality. It's also a gateway to the Latgale Upland. Situated on the north bank of the Daugava, 225 km upstream from Rīga, Daugavpils had 40,000 inhabitants before WWII – about two-thirds of them were Latvians and one-third Russians or Poles. Now just 10-15% of them are Latvians with Russian seemingly being the only language used in shops, bars and on the street. The massive shift in population is a result of industries located here during the Soviet period, which attracted mainly Russian workers. Because many of the industries were large, specialist, all-union plants performing a single service for the whole USSR – like the 4000 people devoted to making bicycle and tractor chains and 3500 to repairing one particular type of railway locomotive – Daugavpils has suffered badly from the break-up of the Soviet Union and is more economically depressed than other Latvian towns.

Orientation

The train station is at the east end of mostly pedestrianised Rīgas iela (formerly Leņiņa iela) which leads to the city's centre, focused on the Latvija hotel, 800m west. The bus station is on the corner of Viestura iela (which crosses Rīgas iela halfway between the station and the hotel) and Lāčplēša iela, two blocks south of Rīgas iela. The Daugava river skirts the south of the city centre and the main road bridge over it is at the west end of Imantas iela, one block south of Lāčplēša iela.

Information

The privately run tourist information, Relax Tour'D (☎ 27 525; fax 28 122), at Parādes 11, is slightly useful. A better bet is to pick up a copy of the slim, packed-with-ads *Daugavpils Guide-Book* – which at least has a good pocket-size town map in it – from the reception of the Latvija hotel. The Mari Tūrisma Firma (☎ 29 773) inside the hotel arranges bus tours, mainly for tour groups.

There are left-luggage rooms in the train and bus stations. Rīgas Komercbanka, on the corner of Rīgas iela and Cietokšņa iela, has a currency exchange, cashes travellers' cheques and gives cash advances on Visa. It also sells phonecards.

LATVIA

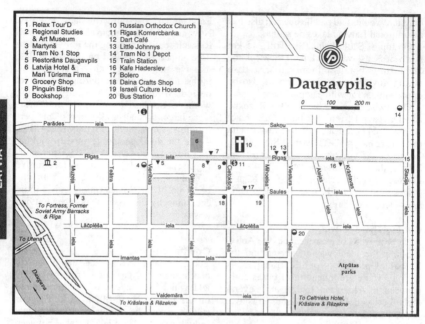

1 Relax Tour'D	10 Russian Orthodox Church
2 Regional Studies & Art Museum	11 Rīgas Komercbanka 12 Dart Café
3 Martynš	13 Little Johnnys
4 Tram No 1 Stop	14 Tram No 1 Depot
5 Restorāns Daugavpils	15 Train Station
6 Latvija Hotel & Mari Tūrisma Firma	16 Kafe Haderslev 17 Bolero
7 Grocery Shop	18 Daina Crafts Shop
8 Pinguin Bistro	19 Israeli Culture House
9 Bookshop	20 Bus Station

Daugavpils

City Centre

The downtown area is a typical Soviet city centre of straight streets arranged in a strict grid, a couple of large squares, the odd park and a mixture of pre-WWII and Soviet era buildings. The ugly Latvija hotel is the dominant landmark. There's a Russian Orthodox church next to it across Cietokšņa iela. The **Regional Studies & Art Museum** (Novadpētniecības un Mākslas Muzejs), open daily, except Monday, from 11 am to 5.30 pm, is 3½ blocks west of the hotel at Rīgas 8 inside a fine Art Nouveau house. Entrance for adults/students is 0.15/0.30 lati.

River, Fortress & Former Soviet Army Barracks

The most remarkable feature in Daugavpils is a huge fortress *(cietoksnis)* on the northwest side of town, just past the railway bridge. It was built by the Russians in 1810, and was occupied by the Soviet army until 1993. A monument by the entrance road states (in Russian) that the Tatar poet Musa Jalil languished here from September to October 1942, in what was then the Nazi concentration camp Stalag 340.

You can walk to the fortress along a fairly quiet riverside road – two km from the west end of Imantas iela. The old Soviet turnstile and checkpoint at the main entrance to the inner compound is still intact. An elderly caretaker is the only sign of life here and far from trying to stop you entering the forlorn wasteground, he's more than happy to answer (in Russian) any questions you have.

During the Soviet era, the barracks housed some 6000 army personnel including 2500 army cadets attending the engineering school based within the fortress. Future plans for the boarded-up buildings and desolate parade areas include using them as a police academy. Half of the old living quarters are actually occupied today, mainly by pensioners and those in need of state assistance who moved in following the troops' withdrawal.

Places to Stay

In true post-Soviet era style, the *Latvija* hotel (☎ 20 950; fax 22 237), a big concrete-and-glass block on Rīgas iela, charges a variety of room prices reflecting the extent – or not – of renovations. The 3rd class doubles/triples (which means the rooms haven't been touched for at least 20 years) cost 6 lati per person per night. The 2nd class singles/doubles, which the hotel describes as 'half-improved', are 12/30 lati. While the 1st class rooms, meaning all four walls have been repainted a pretty pastel colour, are 12/40 lati. All its prices include the most revolting breakfast you'll eat during your stay in the Baltics.

The *Celtnieks* hotel (☎ 32 510) on the 3rd floor of a yellow building on the east side of town at Jelgavas 7, has 60 beds – the entrance to the hotel is around in Strādnieku iela. A place in a shared room is 2 lati a night. The staff do not speak English.

Places to Eat

Among a fairly wide run-of-the-mill selection of small restaurants and cafés, there are a couple of real goodies. *Kafe Haderslev*, close to the train station at the east end of Rīgas iela, sports a post-modern brick and steel decor and serves light snacks daily between 10 am and 10 pm. *Bolero*, in a fine *Jugendstil* house halfway up Saules iela, has huge glass windows overlooking the street and a great salad bar. It's open daily from 11 am to midnight.

For a touch of old Soviet grandeur complete with live music while you eat, try *Martynš* on Muzeja iela. The caviar (4.32 lati) and the pork with cheese (1.37 lati) are both very edible – and 100 times better than the breakfast you'll have had. Also serving good cheap food, amid faded Soviet grandeur, is the self-service *café* at the train station. Just be sure to put your dirty crockery on the trolley in the corner when you've finished.

Less tempting options include the *Pinguin* bistro, at Rīgas 28, and *Little Johnnys*, a couple of blocks east on Rīgas iela. There is an excellent *grocery shop* selling fresh breads and pastries behind the Latvija hotel on Rīgas iela, which is open daily from 9 am to 9 pm.

Getting There & Away

Bus Four buses daily run to/from Rīga (four hours, 2 to 3 lati). Other main bus services, all several times daily, are to/from Krāslava, Dagda, Jēkabpils and Rēzekne. Buses also run at least twice daily to/from Aglona and a few days a week to/from Cēsis and Valmiera.

Train Daugavpils is reached by Rīga-Indra and Rīga-Voronezh as well as Rīga-Daugavpils trains. In total there are seven trains daily each way between Rīga and Daugavpils (3¼ to four hours, 2.25 lati). Daugavpils is also on the Vilnius-Pskov-St Petersburg line with four trains daily in each direction (Vilnius three to 3½ hours, St Petersburg 11 to 13 hours). Other trains runs to Šiauliai (four or five hours) and Kaliningrad (nine to 12½ hours). See the Getting There & Away chapter for more on services beyond the Baltic states.

Getting Around

Tram No 1 runs from Stacija iela, a block north of the train station, to the central square in front of the Latvija hotel. Tickets costing 0.07 lati are sold at the train and bus stations or by the driver.

Zemgale

HIGHLIGHTS

- Stroll round Bauska's 15th century castle and visit the museum inside
- Witness one of Rastrelli's next best creations after the Winter Palace in St Petersburg – Rundāle
- Delve into the family vault of the Duke of Courland in the Baroque Palace at Jelgava

Zemgale is the region of central Latvia west of the Daugava river, between Rīga and the Lithuanian border. The region is low lying (below sea level in parts) and has a vast network of waterways – most of them flowing into the Lielupe, which enters the sea between Rīga and Jūrmala – making it Latvia's most fertile farming area.

Zemgale is named after the Baltic Zemgal (Semigallian) tribes who lived here before the 13th century German conquest. The Semigallians, in fact, held out longer against the Germans than any other people living in the area which is now Latvia and Estonia, not being subdued until 1290. From the 16th to the 18th century, Zemgale (along with the Kurzeme region) formed part of the semi-independent Duchy of Courland.

Most places in Zemgale can be reached on day trips, if quite lengthy ones, from Rīga. You pass through the region if you're travelling between Rīga and Lithuania. The main road to Vilnius and Kaunas passes through Bauska, while the rail link goes through Jelgava.

IECAVA

Iecava is a small, nondescript town 45 km south of Rīga on the road to Bauska and Vilnius. However, six km north of Iecava, on the east side of the road, is the *Brencis* (☎ 39-28 033, 39-23 866), a modern hotel aimed at foreigners and wealthier locals which is cen-

trally located to explore the Zemgale. It boasts a sauna (8 lati an hour), bistro, billiard room, bar and 24 hour restaurant. Doubles with private bath cost 17 lati – if you want a TV it's an extra 4 lati a night. The motel is set slightly back from the main road amid some trees. Look for the sign at night – it is the only light for miles around so you can't miss it.

BAUSKA
- *pop 11,702* • ☎ *(39)*
Bauska is a country town, with a small textile industry, 65 km south of Rīga on the main Rīga-Vilnius road. It's a staging post on the way to Rundāle but worth a stop in its own right, primarily to see its large castle. Every year, in July, a festival of ancient music is held in and around the castle.

Orientation
The town centre is on the south side of the main road bridge over the Mēmele river. The

Top: 13th century knight's castle, Koknese, Latvia
Middle: Gauja river, Latvia
Bottom: Winter scene, near Rīga, Latvia

JONATHAN SMITH

JONATHAN SMITH

COLIN RICHARDSON

GABRIELIUS ŽEMKALNIS

Top Left: Clock tower, near west end of Cathedral, Vilnius, Lithuania
Top Right: Statue of pre-war Lithuanian president Antanas Smetona, Central Lithuania
Bottom Left: Gedimino Tower, Vilnius, Lithuania
Bottom Right: Old Town Hall, Kaunas, Lithuania

bus station is a km from the bridge on the road out towards Vilnius – 500m straight up the hill (Kalnu iela), then round to the left along Zaļā iela.

Information

The castle administration (☎ 23 797, 23 793), at Kalna 16, provides some information even though it is not an official tourist office. A map indicating the main things to see in town is sold at the reception of the Bauska hotel. The post office is next to the bus station at Slimnīcas 9. The market is at Rūpniecības 11.

Things to See

One km from the town centre, on a hillock between the Mēmele and Mūsa rivers and on the western edge of town, is **Bauska Castle** (Bauskas Pilsdrupas). From the bus station, walk towards the centre along Zaļā iela then branch left along Uzvaras iela beside the park at the top of Kalna iela. You can also approach the castle along any street westward off Kalna iela. The castle was built between 1443 and 1456 as a stronghold for the Livonian knights and occasioned the first mention of Bauska in historical documents, though the place had been a Zemgal settlement

LATVIA

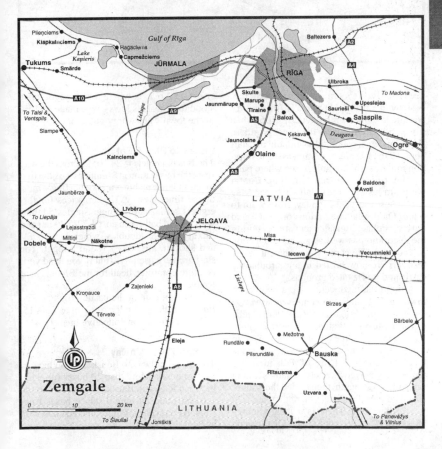

Zemgale

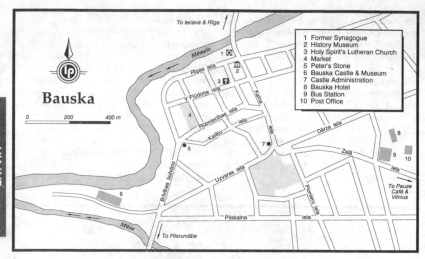

LATVIA

1 Former Synagogue
2 History Museum
3 Holy Spirit's Lutheran Church
4 Market
5 Peter's Stone
6 Bauska Castle & Museum
7 Castle Administration
8 Bauska Hotel
9 Bus Station
10 Post Office

previously. It's an imposing edifice, destroyed during 16th and 17th century warfare but always rebuilt, until 1706, when it was blown up during the Great Northern War. This time, restoration work did not start until 1976. Despite the impressive restoration job, it is still possible to see where parts of the old castle remain. The **Castle Museum** inside is open daily between May and October, except Monday, from 9 am to 6 pm. On display are various objects found during archaeological excavations during the restoration as well as a small collection of 16th and 17th century art. Ancient music festivals are now hosted in and around the castle and its elevated grounds.

Around the town centre are a number of low-rise 18th and 19th century houses. On the corner of Kalēju and Rūpniecības iela, **Peter's Stone** still stands – the story goes that at the start of the Great Northern War, in 1701, Peter I ate his dinner on this stone together with the King of Poland. After dinner they played a variety of games testing each other's strength, then buried their silver spoons under the stone, where they are said to still be today. There is a local **History Museum** (☎ 22 197) at Kalna 6. On the same

street, at No 2, is where a synagogue once stood for Bauska's Jews – who made up 15% of the town's pre-war population.

Places to Stay & Eat

The *Bauska* hotel (☎ 24 705), across the way from the bus station at Slimnīcas 7, is the first to admit it has no hot water or heating – most of the time anyway. Higher prices for foreigners still stand; simple singles/doubles with shared bathroom cost 4.72/5.49 lati and 'luxury' singles/doubles, which have a TV and shower, are 5.90/6.37 lati a night. The staff are very friendly – but if you need your creature comforts, head for the Brencis near Iecava.

There's a *café* in the castle grounds. The *Pauze*, on the east edge of town at Zaļā 15, dishes out 'agrarian collective breakfasts'.

Getting There & Away

There's no railway to Bauska so you have to rely on buses. More than 20 buses run daily between Rīga and Bauska (1½ to 1¾ hours, 1.10 lati) and all long-distance buses from Rīga to Panevėžys, Vilnius and Kaunas, stop at Bauska.

PILSRUNDĀLE

The 18th century Rundāle Palace (Rundāles Pils), 12 km west of Bauska, is the architectural highlight of provincial Latvia and a popular day trip from Rīga. It was designed and built in two phases (one in the 1730s and the other in the 1760s) for Baron Ernst Johann von Bühren (1690-1772), Duke of Courland, by Bartolomeo Rastrelli, the baroque genius from Italy who created many of St Petersburg's finest buildings including the Winter Palace.

Modern restoration work began in the 1970s after the palace had fallen into some disrepair, with most existing period furnishings being bought or donated. Parts of the palace still remain somewhat dilapidated, especially obvious when compared to the parts which have been truly restored. A walk through the extensive, but sadly neglected gardens around the back of the palace makes

you feel like you've walked onto a movie set, where (literally) the bare minimum has been done to create the right illusion in front of the camera.

Of the palace's 138 rooms, some 40 are open to visitors. The main reception rooms, upstairs in the east wing, are the most splendid, with marble and gilt wall decorations that conjure up the same opulence as the great tsarist palaces in Russia. These date from the second phase of work. The Gold Room (Zelta zāle) was the throne room; its ceiling paintings display the baron's virtues as a ruler. The White Room (Baltā zāle) was the ballroom. The main staircase in this wing, with multiple mirrors in its walls, is perhaps the outstanding original Rastrelli creation here, reminiscent of his wonderful Jordan staircase in the Winter Palace. Decorative work by the Italians Francesco Martini and Carlo Zucchi and the German J M Graf,

LATVIA

From Russia with Love

How the Italian master Bartolomeo Rastrelli came to build this splendid palace in such a remote corner of Europe, which wasn't even part of the Russian empire at the time, is a curious little tale. It begins with the marriage in 1710 of Anna Ioannovna, a niece of Russia's Peter the Great, to Frederick, Duke of Courland – no doubt an affair of state as Russia clawed its way into Poland's sphere of influence. In 1730, following Peter the Great's death, Anna of Courland found herself crowned empress of Russia, and she appointed the Baltic German baron Ernst Johann von Bühren (Latvian: Bīron) to handle her affairs of state.

Von Bühren had been something of a failed adventurer in Courland and Russia before becoming Anna's chief adviser (and lover) a few years before she succeeded to the Russian throne. With more interest in the trappings than the exercise of power, Anna handed over much of the management of the empire to von Bühren and a small clique of German advisers. Von Bühren's apparently heavy-handed and corrupt style soon made him unpopular with the Russian nobility, but as long as Anna ruled Russia, the baron's star waxed. When he decided he needed a new home to go with his new status, Anna dispatched Rastrelli to Courland, and in 1736 work began on the summer palace for von Bühren, at Rundāle. It proceeded quickly with as many as 1000 people working on it at one time.

In 1737 the Duke of Courland died heirless and, thanks to Russian influence, von Bühren was handed the dukedom. He then began work on an even grander Rastrelli-designed palace at Jelgava, intended as his main residence. Rundāle was put on the back burner – and came to a halt altogether in 1740 when Empress Anna died and von Bühren's enemies took their revenge, forcing him into exile for the duration of Empress Elizabeth's reign in Russia. Only in 1763 – with a German, Catherine the Great, now on the Russian throne – was von Bühren allowed to return and finish Rundāle, also restoring the parts that had decayed in his absence.

This time Rastrelli brought the Italians Francesco Martini and Carlo Zucchi, who had worked on the St Petersburg Winter Palace, to do the ceiling paintings. J M Graf, who had worked on Prussian royal palaces in Berlin, came to do the elaborate wall decorations. In contrast to Rastrelli's initial baroque work, this second phase at Rundāle, completed in 1768, was in the newer rococo style. Von Bühren was then able to enjoy the palace until 1795 when, in the third Partition of Poland, Courland became Russian territory, and Catherine gave Rundāle to one of her favourites, Subov. Von Bühren managed to shift most of the fixtures and fittings to some of his other estates in Germany. ∎

brought in during the second phase, is also found in the duke's apartments in the central part of the palace.

On the ground floor of the east wing you can visit the palace kitchens, while the west wing was for the duchess's apartments. Part of the kitchen is now a restaurant. The ground floor of the palace also houses a museum of 15th to 20th century applied art from Latvia, Russia and western Europe.

Between May and October the palace and park (☎ 39-62 274) are open daily, except Monday and Tuesday, from 10 am to 6 pm, and in the winter months from 1 am to 5 pm.

Getting There & Away

Rundāle Palace is a km or so south off the Bauska-Eleja road. Unless you're on a tour or have your own transport, the best way to reach it is to first get to Bauska. From Bauska you need a bus that's going to Pilsrundāle – not just Rundāle, which is about 2.5 km further west.

There are also a couple of buses a day between Pilsrundāle and Jelgava, 33 km north-west, so it's possible to approach it from there too.

JELGAVA
• *pop 75,000* • ☎ *(30)*

Jelgava, 42 km south-west of Rīga, is the biggest town in Zemgale. From the 16th to 18th centuries, Jelgava (then called Mitau), was the capital of the Duchy of Courland and its little overseas empire. Afterwards, it was the capital of the Russian province of Courland and a place of renowned society and hospitality where gentry would gather in winter.

Unfortunately, a lot of old Jelgava was wrecked in the two world wars, and it's not such an exciting place any more. Only lovers of Rastrelli architecture should stop here, and then only to see the 300 room **baroque Palace** of the Dukes of Courland. On the eastern side of town, the palace is beside the main river bridge on the Rīga road, a 750m walk from the central square. The palace has been restored a number of times during the 20th century, major works being undertaken after it was severely damaged in 1919 and during WWII. Today the palace (☎ 40 617) houses the family vault of the Dukes of Courland, originally displayed in Rundāle Palace. It is open daily, except weekends, from 10 am to 4 pm. There's a pleasant park on the town side of the palace and a few more old buildings in the streets south and east of the main square.

Getting There & Away

Buses run every half-hour between Rīga and Jelgava (one hour, 0.50 to 0.65 lati).

One or two suburban trains an hour run from Rīga to Jelgava, and vice versa, between 5.42 am and 11.31 pm. Some long-distance trains between Rīga and Ventspils, Šiauliai, Kaunas and Vilnius, also stop at Jelgava.

Kurzeme

HIGHLIGHTS

- Take a trip up the Rīga-Kolka coast road savouring the white-sand beaches en route
- Dip your toes in the water at Cape Kolka where the Gulf of Rīga and Baltic Sea meet and have a picnic of traditional freshly baked *platmaize* on the beach
- Explore the fishing villages on the Livonian Coast
- Visit Dundaga Castle and discover the real 'Crocodile Dundee'
- Stroll among the world's most northern vineyards in Sabile
- Admire the wacky sculptures at Pedvale Open-Air Art Museum

LATVIA

The western region of Latvia, with coasts on both the Baltic Sea and the Gulf of Rīga, is known as Kurzeme (English: Courland; German: Kurland). Though Liepāja and Ventspils on the Baltic Sea are sizeable ports, Kurzeme as a whole is one of Latvia's most sparsely populated regions, with the northern part still heavily forested. The landscape is basically flat – Krievukalns on the Kursa Upland (Kurzemes augstiene), in the south, is Kurzeme's highest point at 184m. The coastline, comprising beautiful white sandy beaches, is untouched and home to Latvia's smallest ethnic minority, the Livs, who speak a language of their own and adhere to their own traditions.

In many ways Kurzeme is a region apart from the rest of Latvia, with its off-the-beaten-track location and distinct history. The region became sadly famous as the 'Courland Fortress' for the fight Latvian troops (who suffered heavy losses in the struggle) put up against the Red Army, which had succeeded in reconquering the whole of the Baltic states – except Courland – when Germany signed its unconditional surrender in Berlin in 1945.

Kurzeme is named after the Cours (Latvian: Kursi; German: Kuren), a Baltic tribe who lived here before the 13th century German invasion. They were quite an adventurous lot who would raid Scandinavia from time to time – and even, occasionally, join forces with the Vikings to attack Britain. Their leader, Lamekins, accepted Christian baptism and made a separate peace with the pope in 1230 in order to avoid rule by the German knights of Livonia – the knights, however, refused to accept this arrangement and eventually subjugated the Cours in 1267.

The Cours themselves ceased to exist as a separate people during the subsequent centuries of foreign rule, but Courland remained an important region when invading European and Scandinavian powers established their colonies. When the Livonian Order state collapsed under assault from Russia's Ivan the Terrible in 1561, the order's last master, Gotthard Kettler, salvaged Courland

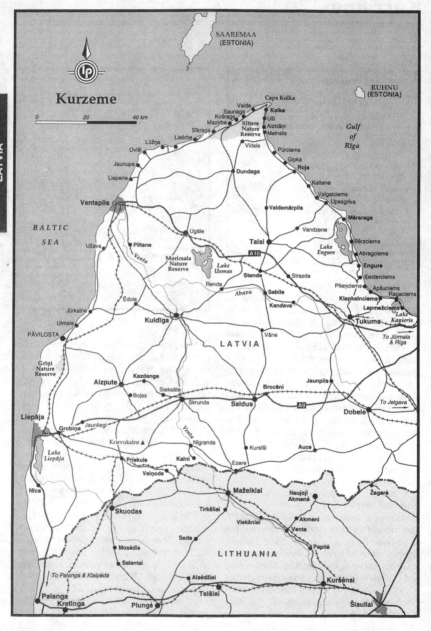

and neighbouring Zemgale as his own personal fiefdom. Though owing allegiance to Poland, this Duchy of Courland, as it was known, was largely independent. Its capital was Jelgava (then called Mitau) in Zemgale. Duke Jakob, its ruler from 1640 to 1682, developed a sizeable and well known navy, merchant fleet and shipbuilding industry, and purchased two far flung colonies – Tobago in the Caribbean (from Britain) and an island in the mouth of the Gambia River (from local African chiefs). He even laid plans to colonise Australia! His son Duke Frederick tried to make Jelgava into a 'northern Paris' and married into the Russian royal family. The duchy was swallowed up by Russia in 1795 and governed as a province of the tsarist empire. It became part of independent Latvia after WWI.

TUKUMS
• *pop 21,156* • ☎ *(31)*
The small town of Tukums is just north of the Rīga-Ventspils road, 65 km west of Rīga. It has a church built in 1670, an old castle mound and a **Regional Studies & Art Museum** (Novadpētniecības un Mākslas Muzejs, ☎ 23 652) with a good collection of 1920s and 30s Latvian art and a picture gallery which sells some quality oils and watercolours. There are good views reaching as far as the Gulf of Rīga, from Milzukalns (113m), five km north-east. The tourist information centre (☎ 24 451; fax 22 237), at Pils 15 in the town centre, can help with information or arrangements for travel in Kurzeme. There is one hotel, the *Tonuss* (☎ 25 956) at Rīgas 20a.

Getting There & Away
You could combine a visit to Tukums with one to Jūrmala, since they're both on the same suburban rail line from Rīga. About one train an hour comes to Tukums. Tukums I station, the first you reach coming from the east, is nearer the town centre than Tukums II where the trains terminate. Some buses from Rīga to Talsi, Ventspils, Liepāja and elsewhere call at Tukums.

TALSI
• *pop 13,226* • ☎ *(32)*
The peaceful, pretty country town of Talsi, a few km north of the Rīga-Ventspils road, 115 km from Rīga, is the cultural and economic centre of northern Kurzeme and as such, is a good base for exploring the area. During medieval times it was the centre of many wars with the Livonian Order, and up until the 12th century it was the heart of the Courland kingdom.

Orientation
A shallow valley runs north-south down the middle of Talsi making it surprisingly hilly for such a flat region. There are two lakes in the valley, one on the south edge of town (Lake Talsu), and a bigger one (Lake Vilku) towards the north. The town centre is at the top of the valley's western slope, with the central square at the meeting of K Valdemāra iela and Lielā iela. From here Lielā iela slopes down the valley and up the eastern slope. To reach the central square from the bus station, walk a block south down Dundagas iela to the first traffic lights, go left along Puškaiša iela then take the second turning to the right which is K Valdemāra iela – altogether about 700m.

Information
An occasionally unhelpful tourism information centre is inside the Talsi hotel (☎ 22 689, 23 224) – See Places to Stay & Eat. You can change money at Latvijas Unibanka, down the hill on Lielā iela, or at Sakaru Banka on the corner of Lielā and Ezera iela. The post office (open daily from 8 am to 6 pm except Sunday) is at Lielā 4 from where telephone calls can be made. The market is at Ezera 7, north off Lielā iela in the bottom part of town.

Things to See
There's not a great deal to do except wander round and enjoy the quiet atmosphere and scenery. The lakes are good focal points. Talsi has quite a lot of one or two-storey wooden buildings dating from the 19th century. Along Lielā iela, as you start to go

LATVIA

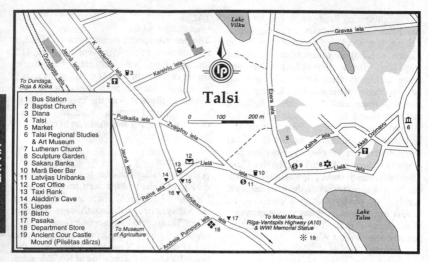

1   Bus Station
2   Baptist Church
3   Diana
4   Talsi
5   Market
6   Talsi Regional Studies
    & Art Museum
7   Lutheran Church
8   Sculpture Garden
9   Sakaru Banka
10 Marā Beer Bar
11 Latvijas Unibanka
12 Post Office
13 Taxi Rank
14 Aladdin's Cave
15 Liepas
16 Bistro
17 Pasaka
18 Department Store
19 Ancient Cour Castle
    Mound (Pilsētas dārzs)

up the east side of the valley, there is a **Sculpture Garden** although the creations dating to the Soviet era have been removed from their pedastals. A **Lutheran Church** dating back to 1403 is at the top of the hill on the same side of town. A block past the church, the small **Talsi Regional Studies & Art Museum** (Talsu Novadpētniecības un Mākslas Muzejs, ☎ 22 770) at Rožu 7, is open daily, except Monday, from 11 am to 6 pm. A **Museum of Agriculture** (☎ 20 143) is south-east of the town centre at Celtnieku 11. It is open weekdays from 8 am until 5 pm. Rising above Lake Talsi on the west side of the town is Pilsētas dārzs, an ancient Cour castle mound and now home to **Freedom Sun**, a large statue of a young man sitting Buddha-style, overlooking the lake. It was erected in 1996 in remembrance of Latvia's freedom fighters.

Places to Stay & Eat
The *Talsi* hotel (☎ 22 689, 23 224) at Kareivju 16 is the only hotel in the city. It's a Soviet era block of 95 rooms on four or five floors and, despite talk of renovation, has absolutely no air of westernisation about it. The rooms are clean but the water smells foul, making you wonder if it is actually worth paying the extra asked for hot water. Singles/doubles with cold water cost 10/15 lati. Singles/doubles with hot water cost 18/24 lati. Breakfast in the *café-bar* is extra.

A better alternative if you have your own transport is *Motel Mikus* (☎ 92 226), 5 km from Talsi on the Rīga-Ventspils highway. Clean comfortable double rooms cost 18 lati. The *restaurant* is also worth eating in.

In Talsi the best place for a real meal is *Pasaka*, at Brīvības 12, which is open daily from 11 am to midnight. Huge slabs of karbonāde (meat crumbed and fried) topped with a choice of cheese, mushrooms or other vegetable mixtures, and costing no more than 3 lati, seems to be the speciality at this small cottage-restaurant surrounded by hanging trees. Unfortunately the toilet is of the outside variety.

Cheaper, lighter snacks are dished up at *Bistro* (open daily from 9 am to 7 pm), at Brīvības 2, and at the more popular *Liepas* (open daily from 7 am to midnight), opposite the taxi rank in the centre of town at Lielā 1. Nothing costs more than 1 lati and they don't seem to mind if you buy cakes in the adjoining shop to dunk in your 0.20 lati cup of coffee either. Be sure to try the platmaize, a delicious sponge cake topped with curd, particular to this region.

Those looking to drink rather than eat could try *Diana*, on the 2nd floor of the cinema building at K Valdemāra 30, which is open daily from 10 am until 1 am, or the definitely more hip *Marā Beer Bar* (Pagrabs) at Lielā 16. It's open daily from 11 am until 11 pm.

Getting There & Away

The only long distance public transport is bus. The bus station is at Dundagas 15, on the road leading north out of Talsi towards Dundaga and Valdemārpils.

To/from Rīga there are six buses daily to Talsi (three hours, 2 lati). Most buses are in transit to/from Ventspils and make stops en route. Other daily bus services to/from Talsi include Jelgava (three hours); Kuldīga (two or 2½ hours); Liepāja (4½ hours); Sabile (45 minutes); and Ventspils (1½ to two hours).

NORTHERN KURZEME

You could also visit the remote northern tip of Kurzeme in a day trip from Talsi, the nearest accommodation base, or on the way to/from Rīga and Talsi or even on the way to/from Ventspils. LaJTMA (see Accommodation – Rīga in the introductory Facts for the Visitor chapter) arranges treks in the region.

The Rīga-Kolka Coast Road

The west coast of the Gulf of Rīga is an idyllic stretch of pretty fishing villages, deserted white sand beaches and lush pine forests full of hidden wonders. The area remains fairly undiscovered and is well worth taking your time to explore.

Leaving Rīga, follow the Liepāja highway (A9) for a short while before cutting onto the coastal road. This area is dotted with cemeteries and memorials to the thousands of soldiers who died here during WWI and WWII. There is a **WWI Soldiers' Cemetery** (Pirma pasaules kara brālu kapi) eight km from Rīga on this road. Turn left at the red

sign and follow the dirt track for two km. Unkempt and off limits to visitors during the Soviet era, the memorial garden to the 1240 Latvian Riflemen killed in their fight against the Germans is slowly being restored to its full glory. A further 50m along the Rīga-Liepāja highway is a **WWII Soldiers' Cemetery** (Otrā pasaules kara brālu kapi). The graves in memory of 47 Red Army soldiers who died here during WWII are vandalised, although some attempt has been made to stick the smashed headstones back together. **Ložmetejkalns**, a WWI battlefield, is 10 km further along this road. Turn left at the sign for Ložmetejkalns and follow the dirt track through the woods for four km. Climb the 89 steps of the wooden watchtower for breathtaking views of the **Tīruļu Swamp**, the site of some gruesome battles between the Latvian Riflemen and the Germans. The stone monument to the left of the tower is in memory of the 167 Latvian soldiers who died in battle here on 23 December, 1916.

At **Lapmežciems**, a delightful fishing village overlooking Lake Kaņieris, three km east of Jūrmala, you'll find the *Zivju Fish Restaurant* where the day's catch can be fried. It is on your right opposite the bus stop as you enter the village. Two km north of **Apšuciems**, is *Apšuciems Camping* (☎ 31-43 146, 31-25 358). A bed in a shared unheated wooden hut is 2 lati a night (after two nights, 1 lati a night). Shared facilities include showers with hot water and a Finnish bath. Linen is included.

Lake Engure, two km north of the fishing village of Engure, is Latvia's third largest lake and a major bird reservation. *Stagars Hotel* (☎ 31-61 240, 31-61 208), inside Engure village community centre at Jūras 62, arranges boating and bird-watching trips on the lake. Singles/doubles with shared/private bathroom are 2.50/5 lati. To find it look for the 'Holsten' beer sign above the Muca Kafejnīca-Bārs on your left as you enter. The hotel reception is at the bar.

For a cheap but complete getaway there must be few places better than *Vecupe Kempings* (☎ 31-61 740, 31-61 409), three km north from Engure and a km inland from the coast amid extensive pine forests. A bed in one of the delightful unheated/heated wooden summerhouses costs 6/15 lati, including linen. It also has tennis courts, Turkish baths, a sauna, basketball court, bar and café. For camping by the sea try *Abragciems Kempings* (☎ 31-61 644, 31-61 668), 200m further on than the Vecupe turn-off on the main coastal road. Despite its seaside location, the site is not nearly so idyllic but it does rent paddle and rowing boats.

Roja, 120 km north of Rīga, is a pretty fishing town, the history of which can be found at the small **Fishery Museum** (☎ 32-69 594) at Selgas 33, on your right as you enter the town. The most interesting exhibits are those which relate to the development of Roja's collective fishing farms and state fish cannery in the 1950s. Further along the main street and just past the harbour at Jūras 6 is the *Roja Hotel* (☎ 32-69 380, 232-60 209). Singles/doubles cost 18/23 lati. The *café-bar* is open 24 hours.

Kolka & Cape Kolka

Kolka is Kurzeme's most northerly village, standing on the Gulf of Rīga just south of Cape Kolka (Kolkasrags), which is the dividing point between the gulf and the Baltic Sea. The village itself is not as pretty as others on the coast but its dramatic coastal positioning on the tip of the cape is reason enough to spend time here strolling along the sandy beaches, over dunes and through forests. During the Soviet era the area was a military reserve, out of bounds to civilians. The former military lookout post, manned by first Soviet, then Latvian soldiers, now appears to be abandoned.

The cape itself (the Latvian *rags* translates literally as horn) is the point where the line of beach and dunes changes direction – making it possible to stand with one foot in the Gulf of Rīga and the other in the Baltic Sea. It's marked by a bright orange, three square metres, futuristic sculpture – a dramatic contrast to the naturally wild, barely touched surrounding landscape. A few km

off the cape there's an island with a lighthouse.

To reach the cape from the centre of Kolka, follow the main road through the village and turn right at the T-intersection. The shore is 400m further along the dirt track. Before leaving the village, stock up on provisions at the *Partikas Veikals* shop, immediately on the right as you enter Kolka from the south. Its freshly baked platmaize, a local speciality, makes for the perfect picnic on the cape.

Slītere Nature Reserve & the Livonian Coast

Made up of spectacular dunes and forests, the Slītere Nature Reserve (Slīteres Valsts Rezervāts) begins at Cape Kolka and continues (between five and 10 km inland from the coastline) 26 km further west along the Baltic coast. In addition to a vast array of flora the reserve also includes deer, elk, buzzards and beaver. You'll need a permit to explore the reserve, however, the coast road goes right through it. Some coastal villages, including Kolka, are excluded from the reserve while others are included. Part of the reserve boundary runs close to the line of the 15-km-long, 35m-high Slītere Cliff. The Mazirbe-Dundaga and Kolka-Vīdale-Dundaga roads both ascend (or descend, depending which way you're going) the cliff line, with a lookout tower on the former.

The Livonian Coast is made up of 14 fishing villages stretching from Pūrciems, 11 km north of Roja on the Rīga-Kolka coast road, to Lūžņa, 49 km south-west of Kolka along the Kolka-Ventspils coast road. These villages are preserved under Latvian law, and it is forbidden to open a hotel, restaurant or other commercial enterprise in them. This is to protect the culture and national identity of the last remaining groups of Livs – the Finno-Ugric people who inhabited the coastal regions on the east and west sides of the Gulf of Rīga at the time of the 13th century German invasion. A small number of Livs still inhabit the area today although many, especially younger generation Livs, have left their homeland for other cities in

Latvia and quickly assimilated into the surrounding Latvian culture and language. Today, while only 120 people are registered as Liv nationals in their passports, the Liv language is making a slight revival. Many homes along the Livonian Coast still do not have telephones – the first of 48 telephone lines were only installed in the area in August 1996.

The Kolka-Ventspils Coast Road

The villages dotted along the northernmost stretch of this strip are worth exploring, if only to witness first-hand the simple, quiet life led along the Livonian coast. Nestled among a natural wilderness of sea, sand and breathtakingly beautiful beaches and pine forests, it's as if time has stopped for the inhabitants of these villages.

In the tiny village of **Vaide** there is little to see except to wonder at the simple wooden houses, many of which do not have electricity, cut off from the world of hi-tech gadgets. Elk bones hang from the street signs, most of which point to individual houses. **Košrags** is worth visiting for its similar 18th century buildings.

Considered the mainstay of the Livonian Coast, **Mazirbe**, 18 km south of Kolka, is home to the **Livonian People's House** where national Livonian costumes and other exhibits explaining the history of the Livs are on display. For proof that the Livonian language is still alive and well pick up a copy of the Livonian language newspaper *Livli* while you are here. As you enter the village, there is a public card telephone on the right. The inscription inside the booth, installed in August 1996, reads: 'The installation of this payphone is the first step in the telephonisation of the Liv shore.' On the beach is the shell of a traditional **Liv fishing boat**.

Dundaga

At Dundaga, a village set among three lakes, 20 km in from the Gulf of Rīga coast via Vīdale, and 40 km north of Talsi, there is a huge **statue** of a crocodile. Considered the centrepiece of the village, the three-metre-

long concrete crocodile, which lazes on a bed of stones, was given to Dundaga by the Latvian Consulate in Chicago in September 1995. The statue is in honour of Arvids von Blumenfelds, a Latvian born in Dundaga but forced to flee his hometown for Australia during WWII, where he spent his days hunting crocodiles in the outback. The story goes that the film *Crocodile Dundee* was based on this Dundaga hero. As you enter Dundaga from the north, the crocodile is on your left, on the corner of Talsu and Dinsberga iela.

To visit the **castle**, built in 1249, follow Dinsberga iela to the top of the hill and turn left. The castle is 100m further along, through a stone archway on the right. Legend has it that a fair maiden made the mistake of intruding upon a gnomes' wedding and as punishment she was walled up alive. She continues to haunt the castle appearing when the moon is full. The castle is open Monday from noon to 4 pm, Wednesday 10 am to 3 pm, and Friday 10 am until 2 pm. Guided tours (☎ 32-42 093, 32-42 142) are also available.

Getting There & Away

Private transport is easily the most convenient, but there are buses too. If travelling by bus, always try to check return schedules before you set out. From Rīga, three buses daily go direct to Kolka along the coast road, passing through Mērsrags and Roja.

From Kolka there are two buses to Mazirbe, both of which pass through Vaide, Saunags and Pitrags.

THE ABAVA VALLEY

The Abava river from around Kandava to its confluence with the Venta is a popular canoe route; the Tourist Club of Latvia (see Activities in the introductory Facts for the Visitor chapter) can arrange trips here. It's also quite possible for land-bound travellers to visit the area.

In **Strazde**, 20 km south of Talsi on the Rīga-Ventspils highway, there's a similar image of the orange sculpture at Cape Kolka.

LATVIA

This sister sculpture, which appears like a mirage in a green field rising up on the right as you approach the village from Talsi, is painted red and entitled Zaļē Saule (Green Sun).

Kandava

Split in two by the Abava river, Kandava is a charming historic town, 20 km south of Strazde and five km south of the main Rīga-Ventspils highway. It's full of cobblestone roads, many of which have been or are being relaid, and quaint wooden houses. The ruins of a **Livonian Order castle** and a mound once fortified by the ancient Cours appears on your right as you enter the village from the east. From the top of the mound, there is an excellent view of the fine **stone bridge** over the Abava river. Dating back to 1875, it is considered one of the oldest bridges in Latvia. The simple **Lutheran Church**, overlooking the village, dates back to 1736 and is renowned for its baroque pulpit. The church is closed from October to May but it is possible to arrange an excursion in advance (☎ 31-31 607, 231-31 750).

The *Pils Bārs*, inside a pretty green and white cottage below the castle ruins, serves coffee and some decent snacks. It has a wonderful fireplace in winter and sunny terrace in summer.

Plosti Tourist Centre (Tūristu mītne Plosti; ☎ 31-32 431, 31-31 349), nine km west of Kandava on the road to Sabile, sells guides and maps on the area, arranges boating and canoeing on the Abava river, and rents bicycles. A bed in a wooden summerhouse by the river is 1.50 lati a night. You can also pitch your tent here. The reception is open 24 hours. If you are coming by bus, get off at the Plostkrogs bus stop, 50m further down the road.

Sabile & Pedvāle

At Sabile, 14 km downstream (a few more if you're following the twists and turns of the river), is another ancient fortification mound and a 17th century church. This sleepy, cobbled-street village is famed however for

its vineyards – it's listed in the *Guinness Book of Records* as having the most northern vineyard in the world. A Council of Europe flag (Latvia became a member of the council in February 1996) marks **Vīna kalns** (Wine Hill), rising above the village to the south. Unfortunately it is impossible to buy locally produced wine in Sabile.

Just 1.5 km from Sabile on the north bank of the Abava river is the **Pedvāle Open-Air Art Museum** (☎ 32-52 249). An ancient Cour settlement dating back to 1230 which was later developed as a country estate by the Firkspedvāle family, the 200 hectare open-air museum is listed as an endangered landmark by World Monuments Watch. Many of the sculptures, installations and paintings are in memory of those deported to Siberia and the graves of many Latvian soldiers who died during WWII can be found on the estate. Many of the estate's rambling outbuildings are now used as exhibition halls and the main house, in desperate state of disrepair but absolutely delightful nonetheless, serves as an information centre and dormitory. A bed in the attic costs 2 lati a night and pitching a tent in the grounds costs 0.50 lati per person. You can also arrange horse riding and hire fishing gear here. A full meal in the adjacent *Ēdnīca Dāre* (canteen) is no more than 2 lati and is open daily from 9 am until 11 pm.

Renda

The **Abavas Rumba** is a small, pleasant waterfall four km downstream from Sabile, close to the Sabile-Renda road. While the **Rendas Rumba**, just off the Abava at Renda, 20 km below Sabile on a tributary called the Ivanda, is claimed to be Latvia's highest natural waterfall, it falls a staggering two metres!

Getting There & Away

This area is best explored by car but it is possible to travel by bus too. From Rīga five buses daily pass through Kandava, Sabile and Renda. Kandava train station is seven km north of the town.

VENTSPILS
• *pop 44,221* • ☎ *(36)*

Ventspils (former German name: Windau), 200 km west of Rīga, is an industrial town and Latvia's busiest port. Despite the various horror stories surrounding the town's alarming pollution record (2% of children dying in their first year, gas masks being issued to survivors, and the like), the centre of town appears reasonably clean, pretty and a pleasant place to visit.

History
There was a Cour settlement here before the Livonian Order founded a castle in 1244. Ventspils was in the Hanseatic League from the 14th to the 16th centuries, and in the 17th century Duke Jakob of Courland based his navy here. After a spell in the doldrums the town revived with the arrival of a railway from Rīga in the early 20th century.

In the Soviet era its ice-free harbour brought it considerable – if unwelcome – importance and attracted a gas pipeline, oil and gas storage terminals, oil and chemical terminal, and ammonia and fertiliser plants. These industries attracted a new workforce mainly from non-Latvian parts of the USSR – 33% of the population is Russian.

Orientation
The Venta river flows up the east side of the town then turns west for its final 2.5 km to the sea. The central area of Ventspils is south of the river, about 1.5 km in from the coast. The old part, nearest the river, is a bit of a maze. Its main street is Pils iela, running roughly east-west, parallel to the river and about 200m south of it. This was the real town centre until the Soviet navy took over the riverside area, and a new centre was created around Ganību iela and Kuldīgas iela, 750m or so further south. The bus station, on Lauku iela, is about 300m south of the eastern part of Pils iela. The train station is on the Rīga road, two km east of the centre, across the river.

Maps Jāņa Sēta in Rīga publishes an excellent Ventspils Town Plan (1:25,000) which

is sold in most bookshops. The bilingual guide *Ventspils*, published by the Latvian Encyclopedia Publishers (1996), includes detailed town and harbour maps, and three walking routes. It is also sold in bookshops.

Information
There is a tourist information centre (☎ 24 777, 26 823) at Annas 13, however, the staff barely speak English. The Tobago tourist firm (☎ 24 003) at Raiņa 16 arranges tours of Ventspils and the Livonian shore.

Latvija Unibanka, round the corner from the bus station at Kuldīgas 3, has a currency exchange and gives cash advances on Visa, MasterCard and Eurocard. As does the Rīga Komercbanka, on the corner of Platā and Lielā Dzirnavu iela. There is a currency exchange inside the lobby of the Dzintarjūra hotel (open daily from 8 am to 8 pm). The main post office is on Jūras iela, opposite the corner of Andreja iela, 100m east of Kuldīgas iela. There are a bunch of public cardphones on the corner of Platā and Ganību iela.

The Gaisma Bookshop at Jūras 10 stocks maps and postcards. The Dina Salons, close to the tourist information centre at Sofijas 8, is a quality souvenir shop, and there is a very good antique shop next to the bookshop.

Old Town
All the main points of interest in the Old Town are along the length of Pils iela, with a few detours here and there. You can reach Pils iela by turning right out of the bus station, left at the end of Lauku iela, and then take the first right (Sofijas iela). After 150m this brings you to the **Evangelical Lutheran church**, on the right. Cross over Pils iela, just past the church, and continue straight along Tirgus iela to the **market** which is on your right. Immediately past the market, turn right along Skolas iela, which becomes Plostu iela, and leads, after about 250m, to a pretty little **Russian Orthodox church**.

At Akmeņu 3 is a **History & Art Museum** (Ventspils Vēstures un Mākslas Muzejs, ☎ 22 031). Just under half a km further west

LATVIA

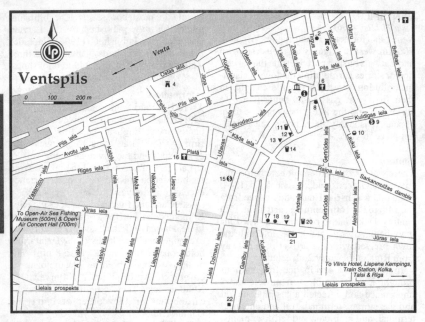

1	Russian Orthodox Church
2	Market
3	Castle
4	Livonian Order Castle
5	History & Art Museum
6	Evangelical Lutheran Church
7	Tourist Information Centre & Hotel
8	Dina Salons
9	Latvija Unibanka
10	Bus Station
11	Landora Bars
12	Pičērija Kaija
13	Little Johnnys
14	Aladdins
15	Rīga Komercbanka
16	Baptist Church
17	Gaisma Bookshop
18	Antique Shop
19	Kafēnica Kurzeme
20	Holivuda Naktsklubs
21	Post Office
22	Dzintarjūra Hotel

Seafront & Parks

Ventspils' sandy, dune-backed **beach** stretches south from the river mouth, about two km west of the town centre. Some locals swim there. You can reach it along Viļņu iela (or Medņu iela) which branches off Vasarnīcu iela – or take bus No 10 along Lielais prospekts from the Dzintarjūra hotel.

Breakwaters poke a km or so out to sea from the mouth of the river to form Ventspils' **Sea Gates**, with a narrow entrance which makes it treacherous for shipping if there's any sea running. Since Latvian independence in 1991 it has been a popular pastime to walk or cycle from the north end of the beach to the lighthouse at the end of the southern breakwater – a previously illegal activity. There are good river views, and you can see the oil storage terminal on the north side of the river mouth.

Vasarnīcu iela, parallel to the beach about 700m inland, runs through an area of greenery and parks. Towards its south end, on the

along Pils iela are the ruins of the 13th century **Livonian Order castle.** The oldest streets in Ventspils are to the west of the castle.

corner of Riņķu iela, is the Ventspils **Open-Air Sea Fishing Museum** (Ventspils Jūras Zvejniecibas Brīvdabas Muzejs, ☎ 24 467), which has a collection of venerable fishing craft and related and not-so-related items, including an old windmill. Between May and August, it is open daily, except Monday and Tuesday, from 11 am to 6 pm. Between September and April it closes at 5 pm. A little further south on Vasarnīcu iela there's an **open-air concert hall**. Bus Nos 6 and 11 both come down here, about hourly, from Lielais prospekts opposite the Dzintarjūra hotel.

Places to Stay & Eat
Liepene Kempings (☎ & fax 22 375), 10 km north of Ventspils on the road to Kolka, has 24 places in wooden chalets in a pine forest by the sea.

Ventspils tourist information centre runs the small *Ratsnams* hotel (see Information), which is directly above its office and overlooking a cobbled old town square. A single with a private bathroom is 6 lati, and doubles/triples with shared bathrooms are 4/3 lati per person. Book in advance if you want to guarantee a bed for the night.

The Soviet era *Dzintarjūra* (Amber Sea hotel, ☎ 22 719), at Ganību 26, offers doubles with shared/private shower for 15/33 lati. Singles with shared bathrooms are 6 lati. The *café* adjoining the hotel is open daily from 7 to 3 am and inexpensive.

The only other option is the *Vilnts* hotel (☎ 68 686) across the river on the northern edge of town. Apparently the Latvian Fisherman's Association (☎ 21 320, 22 833), at Riņķu 2, at the harbour, has a few rooms to let.

Kafēnica Kurzeme (open daily from 8 am to 11 pm), a modern coffee shop with glass tables, sparkling furnishings and lots of mirrors, is the best place to eat. Stuffed peppers, chicken with vegetables and a wide choice of salads, starting at around 2 lati, are beautifully displayed in a refrigerated cabinet. The coffee shop is opposite the post office. The equally modern *Picērija Kaija*, on the corner of Lielā and Kuldīgas iela, is

another good bet. It's open daily from 10 am to 9 pm. Next door at Lielā 2 is the *Landora Bars*, a fun eating and drinking place decorated with fishing nets and other bits of junk from the sea.

Little Johnnys, at Kuldīgas 20, dishes up kotletes (meat balls) for 0.75 lati, karbonāde for 0.76 lati and slices of pre-cooked pizza for 0.23 lati.

The *Holivuda Naktsklubs* on the corner of Jūras and Andreja iela is open at weekends until 6 am. The adjoining *café* is open daily from 9 am to 8 pm. *Aladdins*, opposite Little Johnnys on Kuldīgas iela, is a games bar which is open 24 hours.

Getting There & Away
Bus Ten buses daily run to/from Rīga (3½ to five hours, 2.30 lati), a couple of which go via Kuldīga and others via Talsi. Other daily services include 12 to/from Liepāja (3¼ to 3¾ hours, 2.15 lati); eight to/from Kuldīga (1½ hours, 0.80 lati); four to/from Talsi (1½ hours, 1.30 lati); and four to/from Jelgava (4¾ to 5½ hours, 2.90 lati).

Train Three trains daily run to/from Rīga (4¼ hours, 3 lati). There's also one train daily each way to/from Liepāja, taking 3½ hours.

Getting Around
For a bus from the train station to the town centre, turn right on your exit from the station and walk up to the roundabout, then turn right and walk down to the bus stop opposite the end of the railway tracks. Any bus from here will go to the centre. The main taxi rank is opposite the post office on the corner of Andreja and Jūras iela.

VENTSPILS TO LIEPĀJA
There are high sandstone cliffs and a lighthouse on the coast at **Užava**, 21 km south of Ventspils. **Pāvilosta**, 70 km from Ventspils, is a small port at the mouth of the Saka River. Between these two places the road runs fairly close to the coast most of the way. The railway stays well inland for the entire 125 km from Ventspils to Liepāja.

KULDĪGA
• *pop 14,575* • ☎ *(33)*

Kuldīga, 150 km west of Rīga and 55 km south-west of Ventspils, is the most picturesque and historic town in Kurzeme. Set on the Venta river, it has a number of old buildings and some pretty cottage gardens.

History
Kuldīga was an important settlement of the Cours and probably their capital at the time of the 13th century German invasion. Later Kuldīga (then called Goldingen) became an important stronghold of the Livonian Order. When the Duchy of Courland was founded in 1561, Kuldīga was briefly its capital. It suffered in the Great Northern War, at the beginning of the 18th century, and never really regained its former importance.

Orientation
The Venta river flows up the east side of town and is crossed by the bridge that leads out to the Rīga road. The old part of the town centre is within 500m or so west and south-west of the bridge. The newer part of the centre focuses on Pilsētas laukums, a further 500m west along Liepājas iela. The bus station is on Stacijas iela, a km walk south-east of the old part.

Maps Jāņa Sēta publishes a Kuldīga Town Plan, available at the tourist information centre. The Latvian Encyclopedia Publishers produce a Latvian-English guide, *Kuldīga*, which has a good history section on the town as well as maps and walking routes.

Information
The tourist information centre (☎ 22 259) is at Pilsētas laukums 5 and is open daily, except Sunday, from 10 am to 6 pm. The 91 Latvia Holidays travel agency (☎ 22 721) inside the Kursa hotel, arranges guided tours. The post office is at Liepājas 34. The department store is on the north side of Pilsētas laukums, and there are other shops along Liepājas iela.

Old Town
A central point to start exploring from is **Rātslaukums**, the old town-hall square, where Pasta, Tirgu, Liepājas and Baznīcas streets all meet. Kuldīga's **oldest house** stands here on the northern corner of Pasta iela – its '1670-1742-1982' sign tells the dates of its construction, reconstruction and renovation. The wooden building on the southern corner of Pasta iela, at Rātslaukums 5, is the **17th century town hall**. At the south end of the square is the town hall built in 1860 in Italian Renaissance style – now it's a library. A short way off Rātslaukums, on the north side of Liepājas iela, there's a big **18th century granary**. Down Raiņa iela, off Liepājas iela, is the Roman Catholic **Holy Trinity Church** (Svētās Trisvienības baznīca), built in 1640, with an ornate baroque/rococo interior including a fine 16th century sculpture of the Madonna and child. On Smilšu iela, a block north of Liepājas iela, about halfway to Pilsētas laukums, there's quite an attractive **Russian Orthodox church**.

From Rātslaukums, Baznīcas iela leads north to the Lutheran **St Katrīna's Church** (Svētās Katrīnas baznīca), which was built in 1655 and rebuilt in the 1860s and 1960s. The wooden altar and pulpit date from 1660 and the large organ, which has 996 pipes, from 1712. In Soviet times this church was used as a museum.

East of St Katrīna's, a bridge leads across the Alekšupīte, a small tributary of the Venta, beside a **water mill** built in 1807. In front of you as you cross this bridge is the site of the **Livonian Order castle**, built in 1242 but ruined in the 18th century. The **castle watchman's house** at Pils 4 was built in 1735 to protect what remained of the castle ruins. Legend has it that the house was the site of executions and beheadings and the stream flowing behind the house glistened red with the victims' blood. Today all that remains of the castle are a few mounds and ditches, now mostly overgrown and partly occupied by a **sculpture garden**. Also in the grounds, on Pils iela, which runs along the top of the high bank of the Venta River, is the **Kuldīga Regional Museum** (Kuldīgas Novada Pētīšanas Muzejs; ☎ 23 364, 24 618). The building was constructed in Paris in 1900 to house the Russian pavilion at the World Exhibition and was later dismantled and shipped in pieces to Kuldīga. The museum is open daily, except Monday, from 11 am to 5 pm.

Venta River & Kuldīgas Rumba

From Pils iela there's an excellent view of the Venta and the bridge, which was built in the 1870s. A short distance upstream of the bridge, directly below the castle, is the well known Kuldīgas Rumba waterfall, only a metre or two high but stretching the whole width of the river, and pretty enough to be big news in a flat country like Latvia, where any waterfall is a rarity. It is also said to be the widest waterfall (275m) in Europe. The spot is popular for fishing and swimming, and when there's not too much water flowing you can walk across the top of the fall – altogether, a refreshing place to end a walk round the old part of Kuldīga.

The Venta at this point is 258 km from its source in north-west Lithuania and 88 km from its mouth at Ventspils.

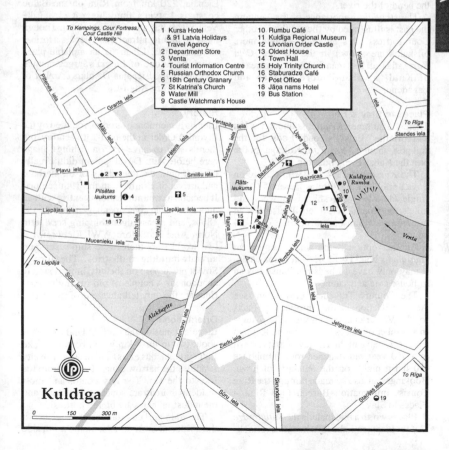

1	Kursa Hotel & 91 Latvia Holidays Travel Agency
2	Department Store
3	Venta
4	Tourist Information Centre
5	Russian Orthodox Church
6	18th Century Granary
7	St Katrina's Church
8	Water Mill
9	Castle Watchman's House
10	Rumbu Café
11	Kuldīga Regional Museum
12	Livonian Order Castle
13	Oldest House
14	Town Hall
15	Holy Trinity Church
16	Staburadze Café
17	Post Office
18	Jāṇa nams Hotel
19	Bus Station

Kuldīga

0   150   300 m

Cour Fortresses

The large old castle hill *(pilskalns)* 2.5 km north of Kuldīga town centre, on the west bank of the Venta, was the fortress of Lamekins, the Cour who ruled much of Kurzeme before the 13th century German invasion. Legend has it the castle was so staggeringly beautiful – copper pendants hanging from the roof glistened in the sunlight and tinkled in the wind – that invaders were magnetically drawn to it. You can get to the hill by following Ventspils iela then Virkas iela, north from the town centre, then taking the right fork off Virkas iela to follow the bend of the river.

The strategic importance of the Venta in the past is illustrated by the number of other Cour fortress sites along it – three more pilskalns are shown in the *Latvijas Ceļu Karte* atlas, all less than 30 km (downstream) of Kuldīga, near Padure, Zlēkas and Lagzdene.

Places to Stay & Eat

There's a summer *Kempings* about 1.5 km east off the Ventspils road. Look for the signpost about 13 km from Kuldīga, 500m past the Nabas Ezers bus stop.

The *Kursa* hotel (☎ 22 430), a 37 room Soviet era block at Pilsētas laukums 6, has singles/doubles with shared showers and toilets for around 10/20 lati. It also has an in-house café and bar, which are open 24 hours.

Another option is the small, family run *Jāņa nams* hotel (☎ 23 456) at Liepājas 36. It may only have 14 beds but it also has an in-house café and sauna.

The Country Traveller Association (see Accommodation in the introductory Facts for the Visitor chapter) arranges *B&B* stays in a number of places in and around Kuldīga for 5 to 15 lati a night. The jewel in its crown is a 350 year old thatched-roof farmhouse (10 lati a night) on the outskirts of town. Bookings can also be made through the Rīga Tourist Information Bureau (see Rīga – Places to Stay).

Places worth a bite include the *Staburadze Café* at Liepājas 8, the *Rumbu* café overlooking the Kuldīgas Rumba on Pils iela, which serves a mediocre assortment of light dishes in an absolutely idyllic location, and *Venta* at Pilsētas laukums 1. There is a disco-cum-bar (☎ 22 766) at Baznīcas 32.

Getting There & Away

There are no trains to/from Kuldīga, only buses. Five run daily to/from Rīga (three to four hours, 2 lati). Other daily services include one to Liepāja and eight to Ventspils.

LIEPĀJA

• *pop 115,000* • ☎ *(34)*

Liepāja, 220 km from Rīga on the Baltic coast, is Latvia's third biggest city. Like Ventspils it has an ice-free harbour. Though lacking in big attractions Liepāja (former German name: Libau) is an amiable place which hosts one of Latvia's largest annual rock festivals, Liepājas Dzintars (Amber of Liepāja), every August.

History

Liepāja is mentioned as being founded by the Livonian Order in the mid-13th century, but there's said to have been a fishing village here before that. Development didn't really take off until the deepening of the harbour and arrival of a railway in the 19th century. It became a communications centre, with an undersea cable to Copenhagen laid in the 1860s, and a passenger shipping service to North America before WWI. Between the two world wars there were ship repair and aircraft-building industries. The former Soviet naval base on the city limits is today abandoned. A couple of old rusting submarines are the only telltale signs of its past.

Orientation

Liepāja stands on the neck of land (which is about two to three km wide) between Lake Liepāja (Liepājas ezers) and the sea. The city straddles the narrow canal flowing from the lake to the sea. The city centre and most residential areas are south of the canal, and the industrial areas are on the north side.

The train and bus stations are together at the north end of Rīgas iela, on the north side of the canal, about a km from the main bridge. The main street through the city centre begins on the south side of this bridge and runs south until it eventually meets the main road south to the Lithuanian border. It goes through a variety of names starting as Lielā iela, then Tirgoņu iela and finally Kuršu iela. Liepāja's beach stretches a long way south from the canal, one to 1.5 km west of Lielā or Tirgoņu iela.

Information

The tourist information centre (☎ 22 113, 26 039) is at Rīgas 3 and can provide a fair selection of information as well as arrange tours of the city. An equally good information source is the Liepāja Tūristu Klubs (☎ 26 403), 'Līgo', at Graudu 34, just south of the corner of Kurmajas prospekts. It also arranges city and beach tours.

There are left-luggage lockers in the combined bus and train station. The post office is on the corner of Pasta iela and Radio iela, a block west of Lielā iela.

City Centre

The large Lutheran **Holy Trinity Church** (Svētās Trisvienības baznīca), on the east side of Lielā iela 300m further south, was built between 1742-58 and has a fine interior. Other main buildings on Lielā iela include the Liva hotel a little further along, and the **Teacher Training Institute** (Liepājas Pedagogiskais Institūts) on the west side.

About 700m from the bridge, Lielā iela becomes **Tirgoņu iela**, which is pedestrianised. More interesting are the busy main **market** (*tirgus*) and **flea market** (*mantu tirgus*), a block further south on the same street (here called Kuršu iela). Across Kuršu iela from the markets is the Roman Catholic **St Joseph's Cathedral** (Svēts Jāzepa katedrāla).

Beach Area

Between the main street and the beach, the architecture is mostly wooden two storey houses, some of quite original design – a neighbourhood that must once have been

1 History & Art Museum
2 Liepāja Tūristu Klubs
3 Post Office
4 Theatre
5 Holy Trinity Church
6 Klubs UTT
7 Pīle
8 Teacher Training Institute
9 Liva Hotel
10 Kurzeme Department Store
11 St Joseph's Cathedral
12 Markets
13 Church

To Military Port, Train & Bus Stations & Tourist Information Centre

To Beach

Kurmajas prospekts

To Beach & Feja Hotel

Liepāja

0   150   300 m

LATVIA

attractive and may become so again, but is for the moment rather shabby. You can reach the beach by following Jūras iela west from the north end of Lielā iela, by the bridge. Jūras iela becomes Kurmajas prospekts, which leads to the beach. Graudu iela, beside the Teacher Training Institute on Lielā iela, also leads to the start of Kurmajas prospekts.

On the north side of Kurmajas prospekts is the **Liepāja History & Art Museum** (Liepājas Vēstures un Mākslas Muzejs, ☎ 22 327, 22 604) Its collection includes some carved amber ornaments 1500 years old. Between May and September it is open daily, except Monday and Tuesday, from 11 am to 7 pm. From October to April it closes at 5 pm. At the end of Kurmajas prospekts is a big **monument** to sailors and fishers who have died at sea. The beach, backed by dunes and a park strip, is long, clean and sandy. However no one seems to swim here – which may have something to do with reports that several hundred thousand tonnes of toxic waste and unexploded bombs were dumped off Liepāja by the Soviet navy after WWII.

Places to Stay

Liepāja's old Soviet ghetto is alive and very well as evidenced by the *Liva* (☎ 20 121) at Lielā 11. It charges 3/4 lati for basic singles/ doubles with shared bathroom. Room rates then ascend in scale depending on the extent to which rooms have been renovated. Top of the range luxury singles/ doubles with private bath and contemporary furnishings are 18/21 lati a night.

More expensive is the privately run family guesthouse, *Feja* (☎ 22 688; fax 27 667), at Kurzemes 9. Singles/doubles with all the mod cons are 26/34 lati with a couple of luxury suites for 38/50 lati. The hotel entrance is actually on Peldu iela.

Places to Eat

By far the most hip hang-out – serving great food too – is *Klubs UTT* at Baznīcas 3-5. It has a sunny courtyard with lots of outside seating in summer and buzzes both day and night. Another place which people in the know claim is cool is the *Pīle* at Brīvzemnieka 38. Food here is just as cheap and cheerful.

Don't forget the main market on Kuršu iela as a source of fresh food. There's a smaller market just off Rīgas iela, the approach road to the bus and train stations.

Getting There & Away

You'll probably have to make a connection in Liepāja if you're travelling from Kurzeme to Lithuania or vice versa. Buses are the only cross-border transport although there are trains between Liepāja and Rīga and Ventspils. Liepāja's train station, at the north end of Rīgas iela, doubles as a booking hall for the buses, whose terminus is immediately outside.

Bus Some 17 buses make the journey between Rīga and Liepāja daily (3½ hours direct, four to 4½ hours via Kalnciems, five to 5½ hours via Jelgava, and seven hours via

Tukums; 2.65 lati). Other services to/from Liepāja include:

Kaliningrad
    7½ or 9½ hours, two buses daily, 5 lati
Klaipėda
    2¾ hours, two buses daily, 3 lati
Kuldīga
    two hours, one bus daily, 1.20 lati
Palanga
    1¾ hours, two buses daily, 3.50 lati
Talsi
    4½ hours, one bus daily, 3.10 lati
Ventspils
    3¼ to 3¾ hours, 12 daily, 2.15 lati

Train There are three daily trains to/from Rīga (4¾ to 5¾ hours, 2.20 lati); and one daily train to/from Ventspils, taking 3½ hours.

Getting Around

There is only one tram route. Tram No 1 from Rīgas iela outside the train and bus stations will take you straight down the main street. If you get off in front of the Kurzeme department store on Lielā iela, shortly beyond the Liva hotel, you'll be just about in the centre of town.

SKRUNDA
• *pop 2,800* • ☎ *(34)*

Skrunda, 58 km east of Liepāja, was a military town during the Soviet era. It was home to the USSR's most western early warning radar station, ever alert to track incoming nuclear missiles. When the bulk of the Russian force withdrew from Latvia in mid-1994, some 500 military personnel stayed at Skrunda to run the radar station (five km north of town), which will remain operational under Russia's control until August 1998. Much to Moscow's annoyance, the Latvian authorities – amid a national party of fireworks and champagne – blew up a disused 19 storey tower block on the radar site in May 1995. It was done to 'celebrate' the fifth anniversary of Latvia's declaration of independence and was followed by a rock festival, Rock against Militarism. This is now an annual event.

AROUND SKRUNDA

At Siekstāte, eight km west of Skrunda on the road to Aizpute, there is a **Milk Museum** (piena muzejs, ☎ 34-34 122), which is actually set on a farm and traces the development of dairy farming in Latvia between 1861 and 1940. It is open daily, except Monday, from 10 am to 6 pm.

Bojas, 25 km west of Skrunda and six km south of Aizpute on the road to Kalvene, is the setting for a **Forest Museum** (Meža muzejs, ☎ 34-12 054, 12 921). While its 17 rooms outline the story of how people lived in the forest in times gone by, they also provide a colourful guide to the flowers and fauna of Latvia. It is a pleasant place to wallow in nature and accommodation is available on site, but it's best to book in advance – call the museum number for accommodation.

LATVIA

Lithuania

Facts about Lithuania

Lithuania (Lietuva), the southernmost Baltic state, is in many ways the most vibrant, as it showed the world by its daring, emotional drive for independence. Lithuania owes much to the rich cultural currents of central Europe; with neighbouring Poland it once shared an empire stretching from the Baltic Sea almost to the Black Sea, and it still shares the Roman Catholicism which sets it apart from its Baltic neighbours.

Vilnius, the historic, lively capital, is the obvious base for visitors. But Lithuania has other sizeable cities such as Kaunas, briefly its capital this century, and the seaport Klaipėda, formerly the German town Memel. Other intriguing places include the Curonian Spit on the coast, the strange Hill of Crosses near Šiauliai, and the forests and castles of the south.

This chapter contains information specific to Lithuania. For a more general introduction to the history, geography, people and culture of the Baltic states see Facts about the Region at the front of the book.

HISTORY

Ironically, after forming the vanguard of the Baltic states' independence drive, Lithuanians promptly voted the former Communists of the LDDP (Lithuanian Democratic Labour Party), born from the democratic, pro-independence wing of the old Lithuanian Communist Party, back into power in the first post-independence general election in 1992. The last Russian garrisons left Lithuania in 1993 and in the following year Lithuania joined NATO's 'Partnership for Peace' programme. However, full NATO membership seems remote. The *litas*, Lithuania's own currency, replaced the rouble in March 1993.

A new constitution was approved in a referendum held at the same time as the general election. Under its terms, popular elections for a president, the head of state, were held in February 1993 and were won by Algirdas Brazauskas, the leader of the LDDP (he remained in office in 1997). In May 1993, Lithuania joined the Council of

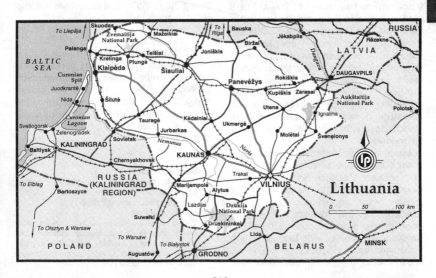

Europe. In 1995, a huge banking crisis rocked the entire economy.

Under prime minister Mindaugas Stankevičius, the LDDP governed until November 1996, when the Conservative party, chaired by independence leader Vytautas Landsbergis, was elected with 70 seats – not quite enough for a majority in the 141 seat parliament. The new government faced an uphill task convincing Lithuanians that government could be trusted; a survey in 1996 revealed that only one in 10 expressed any respect for parliament or government. They had a good deal more faith in the press, which has been outstandingly outspoken since independence. Investigative journalists blew the banking crisis wide open and have exposed a number of corrupt politicians.

By 1996 Lithuania had settled some of its border squabbles and had settled relations with Kaliningrad. Security on the Belarus border, where smuggling is big business, remains a worry, and Lithuania also has a dispute with Latvia over the maritime border.

GEOGRAPHY

Lithuania is the biggest of the three Baltic states, covering an area of 65,200 sq km. It borders Latvia in the north, Belarus in the south-east, and Poland and the Kaliningrad Region in the south-west. Vilnius lies in the south-east of the country, an oddly off-centre location explained by the fact that Lithuania used to stretch much further to the south and east than it does now. Its four main regions are Aukštaitija (Upper Lithuania), the east; Žemaitija (Lower Lithuania), the west; Dzūkija, the south; and Suvalkija or Sūduva, the south-west.

Lithuania's Baltic coast extends only about 100 km, half of which lies along the extraordinary Curonian Spit (Lithuanian: Neringa; Russian: Kurshskaya kosa) – a sandbar 98 km long and up to 66m high, but nowhere more than four km wide. It's the most unusual natural feature of the Baltic states and well worth a visit. Behind Neringa is the wide (up to 35 km) Curonian Lagoon, one of a series of lagoons protected by sand-

bars round this south-east corner of the Baltic Sea. It has a single narrow opening to the sea at its north end, by the Lithuanian port of Klaipėda.

Lithuania is a predominantly flat country, though it has two broad bands of territory which often exceed 150m above sea level. One is down the whole eastern quarter of the country, straddling the border with Belarus. It reaches its highest levels in the Medininkų Upland in the south-east (where the country's highest point, Juozapinės at 294m, is located) and the Švenčionių Upland in the north-east. The second band is the Žemaitija Upland which spreads over much of the north-west and reaches a height of 234m.

ECOLOGY & ENVIRONMENT

The Ignalina nuclear power plant in Lithuania – 120 km from Vilnius – has reactors of the same type as the Chernobyl reactor in Ukraine, scene of the nuclear disaster in 1986, but Lithuania depends on it for much of its electricity. In 1996, Ignalina's technical director gave visiting journalists a 'firm guarantee' that the plant would not become another Chernobyl, but some experts rate it among the world's most dangerous nuclear installations.

NATIONAL PARKS & RESERVES

Lithuania has five national parks and a number of nature reserves dotted throughout the country. The highlight is the Kuršių Nerija National Park on the outstanding Neringa sandspit. More information on some of the parks can be found in the regional sections.

Aukštaitija National Park
   300 sq km in north-east Lithuanian lake district near Ignalina – lakes, rivers, forest, walking, canoeing; park centre at Palūšė
Dzūkija National Park
   550 sq km of the Varėna-Druskininkai forest in south Lithuania – forests, historic settlements on Nemunas river at Merkinė and Liškiava; park headquarters at Marcinkonys, accommodation at spa town of Druskininkai

Kuršių Nerija National Park
    180 sq km on the Neringa sandspit south of Klaipėda – a special environment of high dunes, pine forests, beaches, lagoon and sea coasts; park headquarters at Smiltynė

Trakai National Park
    80 sq km around Trakai, west of Vilnius – lakes, castles, historic town

Žemaitija National Park
    200 sq km in north-west Lithuania – forests, Lake Plateliai, Žemaicių Kalvarija Catholic shrine centre

Čepkeliai Nature Reserve
    85 sq km on Belarus border south of Marcinkonys – Lithuania's biggest marsh, bird habitat, forest

Kamanos Nature Reserve
    36 sq km, west of Naujoji Akmenė in north-west Lithuania near Latvian border – upland bogs, bird, plant and mammal habitat; limited access

Viešvilė Nature Reserve
    32 sq km, west of Jurbarkas, south-west Lithuania – river basin, forest and marshland

Žuvintas Nature Reserve
    54 sq km around Žuvintas Lake near Marijampolė, south-west Lithuania – important bird and plant habitat

GOVERNMENT & POLITICS

Lithuania's parliament is the Seimas. It has 141 seats. The head of government is the prime minister, who is nominated by the president (but has to be approved by the Seimas). Early in 1996 LDDP prime minister Adolfas Šleževičius was sacked after it was revealed that he had shrewdly whipped his savings out of the Innovation Bank just before it was closed. He was replaced by Laurynas Mindaugas Stankevičius, but the LDDP's days were numbered. In November 1996, the Conservative Party caused an upset, winning 65 seats, and forming a centre-right coalition with the LKDP (Lithuanian Christian Democrat Party), a natural ally, which won 16 seats. Conservative election promises included fighting corruption and cutting taxes by 10%. The LDDP was whittled down to 12 MPs, while the moderate Centrist Union won 13 seats and the leftist Social Democrats 12. In addition, the Lithuanian Democratic Party won two seats, eight smaller parties gained one seat each, and there were four independent MPs.

The turnout for the two rounds of elections in October and November 1996 was low. Only 40% of those eligible voted in the second round. Pessimists saw this lack of electoral interest as a potential threat to democracy. Optimists viewed it as a sign of political maturity.

Citizenship

By the citizenship law of December 1991, all residents who lived in Lithuania before 3 November, 1989, were granted citizenship. People who have moved there since will have to stay 10 years before they can become citizens. Non-ethnic Lithuanians have to pass a language test to get jobs dealing with the public.

ECONOMY

Lithuania is the economic under-achiever of the three Baltic states, with higher inflation (around 35% in 1996) and unemployment (officially estimated at 8.3%) and lower earnings. The average monthly salary in 1996 was US$160, and the economy was headed for close to zero growth after growing by 3% the previous year.

The banking crisis was a pivotal element in Lithuania's poor economic performance. In 1995, nine smaller banks failed and the government bailed out two larger institutions. In December, things reached crisis proportion with the two biggest banks, Litimpex and Innovation Bank, being closed. Inexperience, undercapitalisation, mismanagement and alleged corruption were blamed. The government mounted a damage-limitation exercise, guaranteeing some deposits to shore up confidence, but around 400 million litų went astray.

Another factor was the continuing rule of politicians and bureaucrats who were steeped in the thinking of the Soviet era and slow to accept the free market. The first round of privatisation of state-owned enterprises was virtually restricted to Lithuanian buyers, and Lithuania has generally proved a less attractive foreign investment magnet than its neighbours. More positively, low wages and a central location make it an

LITHUANIA

attractive base for companies looking to trade with Russia and other former Soviet republics, the government aims to reduce taxation to attract investment and a second round of privatisation has been opened to international bidders.

POPULATION & PEOPLE

Lithuania has the most ethnically homogenous population of the three Baltic states, with Lithuanians accounting for 80% of the 3.68 million people. About 9% are Russian and 7% Polish.

The modern Lithuanians are the descendants of the Balt tribes who inhabited roughly the area of modern Lithuania. They are thought to have spread into the south-eastern Baltic area, along with other Balt tribes who settled modern Latvia, Poland and the Kaliningrad Region, from the south and east about 2000 BC. By the 13th century the tribes in Lithuania were basically two groups – now referred to as Lithuanians (in the south-east) and Samogitians (in the northwest).

Some of the Yotvingians or Sūduviai, a Balt people who lived in the region which is now south-west Lithuania and north-east Poland, were assimilated by the Lithuanians. Another Balt people, the Old Prussians, who inhabited the area that became known as East Prussia (the modern Kaliningrad Region and neighbouring areas of northern Poland) were almost exterminated (and were finally assimilated) by the Germans who conquered their territory in the 13th century.

The Lithuanian diaspora is by far the biggest of any of the peoples of the Baltic states, mainly due to emigration for political and economic reasons in the 19th and early 20th century and also around the time of WWII. More than three million Lithuanians live abroad, including an estimated 800,000 in the USA with the main concentration in Chicago. Other Lithuanian communities are scattered all around the world including Canada, South America, Britain and Australia. Some 150,000 were sent to Siberia after the Soviet invasion of 1940.

ARTS
Literature

The first major fiction in Lithuanian was the poem *Metai* (The Seasons) by Kristijonas Donelaitis, describing the life of serfs in the 18th century. A high mark in the 19th century was Antanas Baranauskas' poem *Anykščių šilelis* (Anykščiai Pine Forest), written in 1860-61, which uses the forest as a symbol of Lithuania and bemoans its cutting down by foreign landlords.

From 1864 Lithuanian literature was severely handicapped by Russia's insistence on the Cyrillic alphabet for Lithuanian publishing. Jonas Mačiulis, known as Maironis, was the poet of the Lithuanian national revival. His nationalist, romantic *Pavasario balsai* (Voices of Spring), published in 1895, was the start of modern Lithuanian poetry. Vincas Mykolaitis-Putinas, a priest who left the priesthood in the 1930s, is probably the leading literary figure of the 20th century. He wrote poetry as well as prose but his outstanding work is *Altorių šešėly* (In the Altars' Shadow), a three volume novel.

Lithuania's intimate relations with Poland down the centuries give it a share of the credit for some of the best of Polish literature, too. Several major Polish writers grew up in Lithuania and regarded themselves as partly Lithuanian. Among them are Adam Mickiewicz, the inspiration of 19th century Polish nationalists, whose great poem *Pan Tadeusz* begins: 'Lithuania, my fatherland...', and the contemporary writers Czesław Miłosz (winner of the 1980 Nobel prize) and the novelist Tadeusz Konwicki. Miłosz, a poet, essayist and critic who has, among many other things, translated Lithuanian *dainas* into French and written about the Soviet occupation of the Baltic states in the last chapter of *The Captive Mind*, which looks at ways in which intellectuals sell out to oppressive communist regimes.

Music

Lithuania is the jazz headquarters of the Baltics, and Vilnius has a good little live-jazz scene. Two musicians you should particularly look out for are the sparkling pianist

Gintautas Abarius and the more cerebral saxophonist Petras Vyšniauskas.

The romantic and folk influenced Mikalojus Konstantinas Čiurlionis is probably Lithuania's, and the Baltic states', leading composer from earlier periods. Two of his major works are the symphonic poems *Miške* (In The Forest) and *Jūra* (The Sea), written between 1900 and 1907, but he also wrote a lot of piano pieces.

Visual Arts

Mikalojus Konstantinas Čiurlionis (1875-1911) achieved international recognition with his romantic and symbolic paintings in gentle, lyrical tones. A depressive genius, he was also a major composer. There's a good book on his life and work by the former Lithuanian president Vytautas Landsbergis. *M K Čiurlionis – Time and Content* is well illustrated with many of Čiurlionis' paintings, scores, letters and writings as well as Landsbergis' account of Čiurlionis' rather tragic life and absorbing times.

Two artists who achieved major standing, though their work is not specifically Lithuanian, were the Vilnius-bred Jews Isaak Levitan (a landscape painter who holds an important place in Russian 19th century art) and Jacques Lipchitz (a 20th century sculptor). Contemporary artists to look out for include Romas Dalinkievičius who composes pictures based on old runic symbols, and Saulius Vaitiekūnas, director of the Vartai Gallery in Vilnius, who makes elegant jewellery and sculptures from pebbles and boulders inlaid with precious metals. Konstantinas Bogdanas, who during the Soviet era cast heroic bronzes of Communist heroes, celebrated the new artistic freedom by creating a stone bust of weirdo musician Frank Zappa, which now stands outside Vilnius' academy of arts.

Some 19 km north of Vilnius, at a site claimed to be the exact geographic centre of

Pietà – woodcarving of Madonna and child

Europe, an international group of sculptors led by Gintaras Karosas has created a unique sculpture park museum which hosts an annual sculpture symposium.

Folk Art

An interesting Lithuanian folk-art tràdition is that of carving large wooden crosses or suns, saints' figures or weathercocks on tall poles and placing them at crossroads, in cemeteries or village squares, or at the sites of extraordinary events. Vincas Svirskis (1835-1916) is reckoned to be the master of this form; there's a fine collection of his carvings in the State Museum in Vilnius. In the Soviet period, such work – with its religious overtones – was banned, but it survived to amazing effect at the Hill of Crosses near Šiauliai.

Film

Audrius Stonys (born 1966) has made a number of intimate documentaries which have been shown at festivals worldwide.

Facts for the Visitor

This chapter contains visitor information specific to Lithuania. For more general information on travelling in the Baltic states and details on obtaining visas for Russia and Belarus see the introductory Facts for the Visitor chapter at the front of the book.

HIGHLIGHTS

The Old Town of Vilnius – the largest Old Town in eastern Europe – is a chocolate box of three-storey baroque and classical buildings. No less enchanting is the coastal region of the Curonian Spit, a magnificent world of windswept sand dunes and pine trees. The less discovered coast, on the eastern shores of the Curonian Lagoon in western Lithuania, and the Aukštaitija National Park in northern Lithuania, are two other remote areas that remain blissfully untouched. Not quite so easy to reach, but the perfect representation of the Lithuanian spirit, is the Hill of Crosses near Šiauliai. The fantastical Orvydas Garden in the Žemaitija National Park is a moving tribute to those that were persecuted under Stalin's regime.

Savouring the unique atmosphere and friendliness of Lithuania's ethnic street carnivals and theatre festivals is an unbeatable highlight for many.

TOURIST OFFICES

Lithuania has a small network of tourist offices, co-ordinated by the Lithuanian Tourist Board (☎ 22-622 610; fax 22-226 819; email vtd@ktl.mii.lt; http://www.ktl.mii.lt/visitors/strukt.htm), Ukmergės 20, LT-2600 Vilnius.

Its representatives overseas include:

Finland
    Baltic Tourism Information Centre, Merimienhenkatu 29, SF-00150 Helsinki (☎ 09-637 783, fax 09-637 887)
Germany
    Baltic Tourism Information Bureau, Woldsenstrasse 36, D-25813 Husum (☎ 048-413 004; fax 048-412 109)

USA
    Vytis Tours, 40-24 235th St, Douglaston, NY-11363 (☎ 718-423 6161, 800-778 9847; fax 718-423 3979; email vyttours@gnn.com

Within Lithuania, official tourist information centres include: a city office in Vilnius (☎ 22-620 762); in Kaunas (☎ 27-204 911); in Klaipėda (☎ 26-213 977); in Šiauliai (☎ 21-430 795); in Alytus (☎ 235-385 565); in Nida (☎ 259-52 345); in Palanga (☎ 236-57 125); in Druskininkai (☎ 233-51 777); and in Trakai (☎ 238-51 934).

Most national parks and nature reserves also operate an information centre at their headquarters. See regional sections for details.

EMBASSIES & CONSULATES

Lithuanian diplomatic missions worldwide include:

Australia
    Consulate: 40B Fiddens Wharf Rd, Killara, NSW 2071 (☎ 02-9498 2571)
Belarus
    Embassy: Varvasheni 17, BY-220029 Minsk (☎ 017-234 7784)
Belgium
    Embassy: Rue Maurice Lietart 48, B-1150 Brussels (☎ 02-772 27 50)
Canada
    Embassy: 130 Albert St, Suite 204, Ottawa, Ontario K1P 564 (☎ 613-567 5458)
Czech Republic
    Embassy: Pod Klikovkou 2, Smichov, Prague 5 (☎ 02-521 858, 526 698)
Denmark
    Embassy: Bernstorffsvej 214, DK-2920 Charlottelund, Copenhagen (☎ 02-636 207)
Estonia
    Embassy: Uus 15, EE-0100 Tallinn (☎ 2-6314 030)
Finland
    Embassy: Raohankatu 13a, SF-20180 Helsinki (☎ 09-608 210)
France
    Embassy: 14 Boulevard Montmartre, 75009 Paris (☎ 01 48 01 00 33)

Germany
Embassy: Argelanderstrasse 108a, D-53115 Bonn 1 (☎ 0228-914 910, 914 9113)

Italy
Embassy: Via po 22, I-00198 Rome (☎ 06-855 9052)

Latvia
Embassy: Rūpniecība 22, Rīga LV-1010 (☎ 7321 519)

Norway
Embassy: Drammensveien 43, N-0244 Oslo (☎ 022-55 81 50)

Poland
Embassy: aleje Szucha 5, Warsaw (☎ 02-625 3368)

Russia
Embassy: Borisoglebsky pereulok 10, RUS-121069 Moscow (☎ 095-291 2643)

Sweden
Embassy: Strandvagen 53, S-11523 Stockholm (☎ 08-667 1134)

Ukraine
Embassy: vulitsya Gorkoho 22, UA-252024 Kiev (☎ 044-227 1042)

UK
Embassy: 17 Essex Villas, London W8 7BP (☎ 0171-938 2481)

USA
Embassy: 2622 16th St NW, Washington, DC 20009 (☎ 202-234 5860)

CUSTOMS

Customs regulations vary between the Baltic states and are subject to change. Some general pointers are given in the introductory Facts for the Visitor chapter. In Vilnius the customs department (☎ 22-226 415) is at Jakšto gatvė 1/25.

Alcohol & Tobacco

You can import duty-free one litre of alcoholic drinks over 40% volume and two litres of wine or champagne.

Money

There is no limit to the amount of hard currency you can bring in or take out. You no longer have to declare it on entry or exit.

Other Items

Lithuania limits the export of amber, but a few necklaces as souvenirs or gifts should be OK providing their value doesn't exceed US$250. You need to get a Culture Ministry

permit, and pay 10% to 20% duty, to export artworks over 50 years old. For further information contact the Committee of Cultural Heritage (☎ 22-724 005) at Šnipiškių 3, Vilnius.

MONEY

Lithuania introduced its own currency, the *litas* (plural: *litų*), on 25 June, 1993. The litas is divided into 100 *centų* (singular: *centas*). It is Lithuania's only legal tender, and a fully convertible currency that has managed to hold to the rate of 4 litų to US$1, which it was valued at when introduced.

In early 1997 exchange rates were:

Australia	A$1	=	3.11 litų
Canada	C$1	=	2.88 litų
Finland	1 Fmk	=	0.78 litų
Germany	DM1	=	2.35 litų
Sweden	1 Skr	=	0.52 litų
United Kingdom	UK£1	=	6.48 litų
United States	US$1	=	4.00 litų

The litas comes in one, two, five, 50 and 100 litų notes; and in one, two, five, 10, 20 and 50 centų coins. It replaced the *talonas* (coupon), the transitional currency used in Lithuania during the phasing-out of the Russian rouble.

NEWSPAPERS & MAGAZINES

The most popular Lithuanian newspaper is *Lietuvos Rytas*, favoured for its many advertisements, classifieds and entertainment listings. Other popular dailies include *Respublika* and *Lietuvos Aidas*, which both sell over 100,000 copies. The smaller, 'Financial Times-pink' *Verslo Žinios* is a biweekly business newspaper with an English-language summary. Details of English-language newspapers and magazines published in the Baltics are given in the introductory Facts for the Visitor chapter.

RADIO & TV

Lithuanian TV is the state television station. There are also a number of commercial channels, but those likely to be of most interest are Tele-3 and Baltic TV, which screens

LITHUANIA

CNN news in English daily at midnight and World Net every day at 1 pm.

M1, the first private radio station to broadcast in Soviet times, remains as popular as ever, along with the equally fun-loving commercial channel, Radiocentras, which can be picked up on 101.5 FM. You can find M1 on 106.8 FM or at http://www.tdd.lt/m1 on the Internet. Other popular music channels include Ultra Vires (103.1 FM), Lithuanian Radio (102.6 FM) and Hansa (105.1 FM).

In Vilnius, Voice of America (VOA) broadcasts in English on 105.6 FM. It has regular news broadcasts every half-hour. The BBC World Service is available 24 hours a day on 100.1 FM while French-speakers can listen to Radio France Internationale (RFI) at 98.3 FM. Znad Wilii is an independent Polish-Russian language channel, found on 103.8 FM.

PUBLIC HOLIDAYS & SPECIAL EVENTS

Lithuania's national holidays are:

New Year's Day, 1 January
Independence Day (Nepriklausomybės diena; anniversary of 1918 independence declaration), 16 February
Good Friday and *Easter Monday*
Mothers' Day, first Sunday in May
Statehood Day (commemoration of coronation of Grand Duke Mindaugas, 13th century), 6 July
All Saints' Day, 1 November
Christmas (Kalėdos), 25 & 26 December

Lithuania's most important cultural events include the national song festival, Midsummer celebrations and the Baltika folk festival. For background to these events see Public Holidays & Special Events in the introductory Facts for the Visitor chapter.

For detailed information on most cultural events, contact the Lithuanian Folk Culture Centre in Vilnius at Radvilaitės 8 (☎ 22-612 594; email pjurkus@ktl.mii.lt; http://neris.mii.lt/heritage/lfcc/lfcc.html). Other popular annual cultural events in Lithuania include:

Horse Races – on Lake Sartai in Dusetos, near Utena, if the lake is frozen, otherwise in the town; first Saturday of February

Užgavėnės (Mardi Gras) – animal, bird and beast masquerades in towns and villages of Žemaitija
St Casimir Day – Lithuania's patron saint's day, 4 March, with the Kaziukas crafts fair in Vilnius around this date
Birštonas Jazz Festival – three day jazz event with top Lithuanian and foreign musicians; Birštonas, late March, even-numbered years
International Jazz Festival – a four day festival attracting top jazz musicians from all over the world; Kaunas, April
Life Theatre Festival – a week-long theatre festival attracting avant-garde theatre companies from Europe; Vilnius, May
Vilnius Summer Music Festival – a week-long summer festival of street theatre, dancing, masked parades and craft fairs in the streets of Vilnius' Old Town; July
Žemaičių Kalvarija Church Festival – thousands of pilgrims from all over Lithuania flock to the Žemaičių Kalvarija to celebrate the week-long church festival; first week of July
Vilnius City Days – three days of musical and cultural events in theatres, concert halls and in the streets of Vilnius; mid-September
Vilnius Jazz Festival – one of eastern Europe's leading contemporary jazz gatherings, so they say; Vilnius, autumn (usually October)
Vėlinės (All Souls' Day) – commemoration of the dead with visits to cemeteries; 2 November

ACTIVITIES

For information on general activities in Lithuania see the introductory Facts for the Visitor chapter.

FOOD & DRINKS

Dairy products and potatoes are mainstays of the Lithuanian diet. Common dairy products include *varškė* (curd) and *grietinė* (sour cream). Pancakes are particularly popular, and there are special names for various types including: *blyneliai* (small pancakes), *varškėčiai* (curd pancakes), and *bulviniai blynai* which are pancakes made with grated potato. Common Lithuanian starters include *silkė* (herring), *šprotai* (sprats), mushrooms and salads. Soups are also very popular. Particularly unique is *šaltibarščiai*, a cold beetroot soup, garishly-pink in colour, served with boiled potatoes and really quite delicious.

One traditional meal, of which it is definitely a case of once tried, never forgotten, is *cepelinai*, Lithuania's infamous Zeppelin, which is an airship-shaped parcel of a glutinous substance alleged to be potato dough, with a wad of cheese, meat or mushrooms in the centre. It comes topped with a sauce made from onions, butter, sour cream and bacon bits. Another 'good-old-potato' favourite is *kugelis*, grated potatoes and carrots baked in the oven and served with sour cream. *Virtinukai* are small, ravioli-like dumplings which are stuffed with cheese, curd, fruit, mushrooms or meat. The old standby, *balandėlė*, is a tasty stuffed cabbage roll. *Troškinys* is a type of meat stew-cum-soup.

Lithuanians are the first to create a new dish to mark a special occasion. Particularly noteworthy is *šakotis* – a metre-tall, Christmas-tree shaped cake covered with long spikes (made from a rather dry, sponge cake mixture), which is generally served at weddings. Christmas is another major culinary feast. Dinner on the 24th consists of 12 different vegetarian dishes (no meat is allowed), one of which is *kūčiukai* – cubed biscuits made from regular dough and poppy seeds and served in poppy seed milk.

Beer is *alus* in Lithuanian and the best local brands such as Utenos and Kalnapilis are served in most restaurants and bars. *Utenos porteris* is a good, hard-hitting dark ale. Lithuanians also drink mead *(midus)*, such as Žalgiris and Suktinis, which are as much as 60% proof, and *gira*, made from fermented grains or fruit and brown rye bread. The more sober-minded should look out for *stakliskes*, a honey liqueur.

General information on eating in the Baltic states is given in the introductory Facts for the Visitor chapter at the front of the book. The Language Guide at the back of the book includes words and phrases you will find useful when ordering food and drink.

LITHUANIA

Vilnius

HIGHLIGHTS

- Hike up Gediminas Hill, visit the tower, and hike back down again to tour the cathedral
- Witness a town without inhabitants when you visit the former Soviet army barracks in the Northern Township
- Stroll round the Old Town and see Pilies' street sellers, the Gates of Dawn and the university
- Discover what Napoleon wanted to take back to Paris with him when you visit St Anne's Church
- See the cells where Lithuanians were interrogated, tortured and shot by the KGB at the Museum of the Genocide of the Lithuanian People

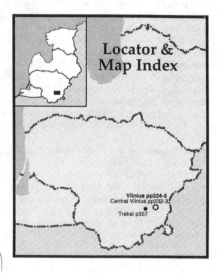

Locator & Map Index

Vilnius pp324-5
Central Vilnius pp332-3
Trakai p357

LITHUANIA

• *pop 574,000* • ☎ *(22)*

The greenest and prettiest of the three Baltic capitals, Vilnius lies 250 km inland on the Neris river, among a series of small hills. While Tallinn is arguably the most picturesque of the three cities and Rīga the most metropolitan, Vilnius is the most fun! Its people are warmer and less reserved, and life, on the whole, less formal. Vilnius also has a more international flavour than the other capitals – partly because of the influence of the big Lithuanian diaspora and partly because it has always been more open to central Europe and the outside world, especially through Catholic Poland, in whose history it has a prominent place and of which it was actually a part as recently as 1939.

Vilnius' Old Town – with its varied array of central-European Catholic architecture contrasting with the German influence on the other Baltic capitals – is the largest Old Town in eastern Europe. A church spire can be seen from every one of its winding streets, which, coupled with its countless hidden courtyards, are intriguing to explore. Vilnius' modern history is dramatic – there are

reminders of its once flourishing Jewish community, all but wiped out in WWII, and of its pivotal role in the campaign for Baltic independence from the USSR.

HISTORY

Legend has it that Vilnius was founded in the 1320s when the Lithuanian grand duke, Gediminas, camping here on a hunting trip, dreamt of an iron wolf that howled with the voices of 100 wolves – meaning that he must build an impregnable city, as mighty as the howl of 100 wolves. In fact, the site had been occupied at least 1000 years before and may well have been a political and trade centre before Gediminas' time.

Fourteenth century Vilnius was built on Gediminas Hill, with its upper and lower castles and townspeople's houses all protected by a moat, walls and towers against the knights of the Teutonic Order, who attacked at least six times between 1365 and 1402.

The knights' defeat by joint Lithuanian-Polish forces at Grünwald, in 1410, ushered in a period of prosperity in which Vilnius extended south from Gediminas Hill into what's now the Old Town, and many Gothic buildings went up.

Merchant and artisan guilds were formed. The castles were rebuilt, and the cathedral founded inside the lower one. Following attacks by Tatars from the south, a 2.4-km-long defensive wall was built, between 1503 and 1522, around the new part of town, south of Gediminas Hill.

Sixteenth century Vilnius was one of the biggest cities in eastern Europe, with a population of around 25,000. It blossomed with fine buildings in the late-Gothic and Renaissance styles as the Lithuanians Žygimantas I and II occupied the Polish-Lithuanian throne. Polish Jesuits founded Vilnius University in 1579 and made the city a bastion of the Catholic Counter-Reformation. Lithuania sank into a subordinate position in the Polish-Lithuanian state in the 17th century, and Vilnius gained a place in Poland's 'golden age'. Under Jesuit influence, baroque architecture made a big impact.

Nineteenth century Vilnius became a refuge of Polish and Polonised Lithuanian gentry dispossessed by the region's new Russian rulers, which made it a focus of the Polish national revival, in which the Vilnius-bred poet Adam Mickiewicz was a leading inspiration. The 1830-31 and 1863-64 Polish uprisings didn't take off here, but Vilnius University was closed by the tsarist authorities in any case.

In the second half of the century the city grew quite quickly as railways arrived and industry developed. Vilnius had also become a very important Jewish city, with around 70,000 or 80,000 Jews in its 160,000 population at the turn of the century, earning it the nickname 'Jerusalem of Lithuania'. Meanwhile the Polish influence was so strong that the first language of most of the non-Jewish inhabitants, even if they regarded themselves as Lithuanian, was Polish. At the same time, many Poles and Jews emigrated to the USA.

In the 20th century, Vilnius has changed hands about a dozen times. Germany occupied it for over three years in WWI. When the subsequent, confused, Soviet/Polish/Lithuanian fighting died down, Vilnius found itself in an isolated corner of Poland, cut off from trade with both Lithuania and Russia.

Economically it went backward. Nevertheless, it developed into a prominent centre of Jewish culture. Vilnius was now, essentially, a Polish and Jewish city, with its streets named in Polish, and Lithuanians a small minority in the population – though perhaps not quite as small as the 1% claimed by Polish statistics of the time!

Stalin handed Vilnius to Lithuania after the Red Army walked into Poland in 1939, but WWII saw another three-year German occupation. Nearly all the Vilnius Jews were killed in its ghetto or in the nearby Paneriai forest.

Vilnius' population fell from 209,000 to 110,000, and the city was badly damaged in the six day battle in which the Red Army recaptured it towards the end of the war.

Many of its Poles – including virtually all the middle and upper classes – moved or were deported to Poland between 1945 and 1958. Those who stayed in Vilnius were mostly Belarusian speakers of peasant origins, whose communities had been Polonised in the 19th century, at least to the extent of worshipping in Polish-speaking Catholic churches.

The new residential and industrial suburbs which sprang up around the city after WWII were filled by Lithuanians who moved in from the countryside and by immigrant Russians and Belarusians. Russians account for about 19% of the city's population today, Poles for some 4% and Belarusians, less than 1%.

Vilnius was the chief focus of Lithuania's push for independence from the Soviet Union in the late 1980s and early 1990s. Particularly dramatic and tragic events took place here in January 1991, when Soviet troops trying to destabilise the situation stormed the city's TV installations, killing 13

LITHUANIA

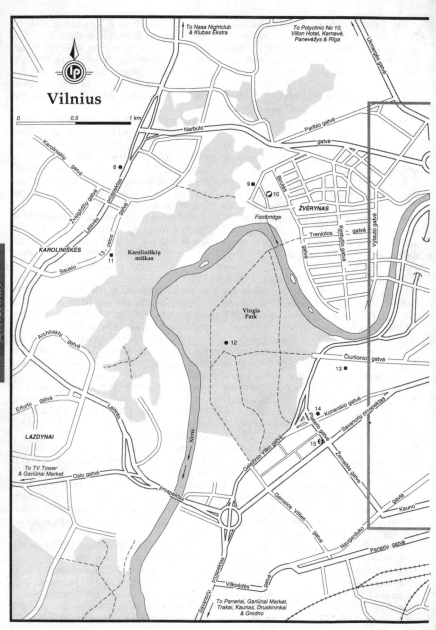

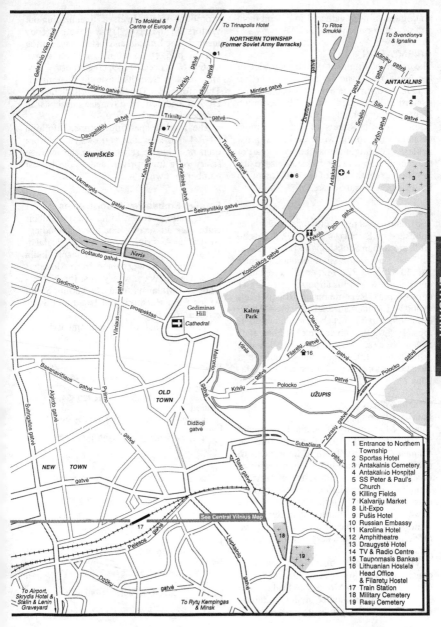

1 Entrance to Northern
   Township
2 Sportas Hotel
3 Antakalnis Cemetery
4 Antakalnio Hospital
5 SS Peter & Paul's
   Church
6 Killing Fields
7 Kalvarijų Market
8 Lit-Expo
9 Pušis Hotel
10 Russian Embassy
11 Karolina Hotel
12 Amphitheatre
13 Draugystė Hotel
14 TV & Radio Centre
15 Taupomasis Bankas
16 Lithuanian Hostels
   Head Office
   & Filaretų Hostel
17 Train Station
18 Military Cemetery
19 Rasų Cemetery

among the crowds gathered to defend them and wounding many more.

ORIENTATION

The centre of Vilnius is on the south side of the Neris river, and its heart is Cathedral Square, an open square with the cathedral on its north side and Gediminas Hill (Gedimino kalnas) rising behind it. South of Cathedral Square are the streets of the Old Town (senamiestis); to the west, Gedimino prospektas cuts straight across the newer part of the centre. The train and bus stations are just beyond the south edge of the Old Town, 1.5 km from Cathedral Square.

Maps

Top quality road maps, city maps and atlases published by Briedis (☎ 220 970), at Bokšto 10-9, are sold in bookshops and at the *Vilnius In Your Pocket* tourist information centre (☎ 260 875; fax 222 982; email viyp@post. omnitel.net) at Vilnius airport (open daily 11 am to 4 pm). Recommended Briedis maps include a Lithuanian Road Map (1:400,000) and another of Vilnius Old City and its environs (1:15,000), both costing 8.40 litų. Jāṇa Sēta in Rīga (see Maps – Rīga) publishes an assortment of Lithuanian maps, available at most bookshops, many hotels and petrol stations.

INFORMATION
Tourist Offices

Vilnius Municipality Tourism Department (☎ 620 762, 628 169; fax 616 622) at Vilniaus 25, room 306, third floor, plans to open a 'real' tourist information centre at Pilies 42, offering a full range of services including accommodation bookings, guided tours and car rental. Until the centre is open (it was due to be functioning by Easter 1997), visitors are welcome at the Vilniaus gatvė office, which unfortunately has little practical help on offer.

Vilnius County tourism information centre (☎ 616 867; fax 226 118), at Gedimino 14 (open Monday to Friday from 9 am to 6 pm), is another, mainly administrative office, which is geared more to promoting Vilnius overseas than helping out visitors on the spot. Try a private agency instead: The Lithuanian Hostels Association runs a budget travel information office (☎ 696 627; fax 220 149; email root@jnakv. vno.soros.lt) from its hostel at Filaretų 17. The Information Bureau (☎ 224 140; fax 211 255) at Didžioji 13 advertises itself as an independent tourist office.

The English-speaking hotline, Infolinija (☎ 704 000), can tell you everything from train and theatre schedules to the average salary of a tram driver, and is the hottest number in town.

Foreign Embassies & Consulates

Some nations cover Lithuania from their embassies in nearby countries, including: Australia, Austria, Brazil, Egypt, Iceland, Japan and Spain from Copenhagen; India from Minsk; New Zealand from Moscow; Ireland from Warsaw; Cyprus, the Netherlands and Malaysia from Stockholm; South Africa from Helsinki; and Israel and Switzerland from Rīga.

Here is a list of foreign embassies in Vilnius:

Belarus
    Muitinės 41 (☎ 263 828; fax 263 443)
Canada
    Gedimino 64 (☎ 220 898; fax 220 884)
Denmark
    Kosciuškos 36 (☎ 224 545; fax 290-30 110)
Estonia
    Tilto 29 (☎ 620 030; fax 220 461)
Finland
    Klaipėdos 6 (☎ 221 621; fax 222 463)
France
    Didžioji 1 (☎ 222 979; fax 223 530)
Germany
    Sierakausko 24 (☎ 650 272, 263 627; fax 231 812)
Italy
    Tauro 12 (☎ 220 620; fax 220 405)
Latvia
    Čiurlionio 76 (☎ 231 260; fax 231 130)
Norway
    Poškos 59 (☎ 726 926; fax 726 964)
Poland
    Smėlio 20a (☎ 709 001; fax 790 007)
Russia
    Latvių 53/54 (☎ 721 763; fax 723 877)

Sweden
    Jogailos 8 (☎ 226 467; fax 226 444)
UK
    Antakalnio 2 (☎ 222 070; fax 727 579)
USA
    Akmenų 6 (☎ 223 031; fax 267-06 084)

Money

Vilnius' best 24 hour exchange is on your left as you exit the train station at Geležinkelio 6 (☎ 630 763). Another is on the ground floor of the Lietuva hotel at Ukmergės 20.

The central post office (see Post & Communications) cashes travellers' cheques and Eurocheques. Vilniaus Bankas at Gedimino 12 and at the airport also accept travellers' cheques, offer cash advances on Visa and have an ATM at each branch accepting Visa cards. MasterCard and Eurocard holders can get cash advances at the currency exchange next door to Vilniaus Bankas at Gedimino 12. Branches of Taupomasis Bankas (Pilies gatvė, Vilniaus gatvė and on the corner of Savanorių prospektas and Žemaitės gatvė) all have ATMs accepting MasterCard and Eurocard.

The numerous Snoras Bankas ATMs, housed in bright blue glass cages all over town, only accept local bank cards but they should give cash advance on Visa, Master-Card and Eurocard soon.

Post & Communications

The central post office (☎ 616 759) at Gedimino 7 (open weekdays from 8 am to 8 pm and on weekends from 11 am to 7 pm) has telephone and telegraph facilities too. The Lietuva hotel has a fax service which is open 24 hours a day but it is expensive. The best service is said to be at the telegraph centre at Universiteto 14, also open 24 hours.

Express mail can be sent with the state Express Mail Service (EMS) at Vokiečių 7; DHL Worldwide Express (☎ 725 144) at Vytauto 6-4; Federal Express (☎ 614 654) is at Geležinio Vilko 12-52; and UPS (☎ 226 111) at Vasario 16-osios 2a.

Non-commercial email messages can be sent and received free of charge from the Open Lithuania Fund (☎ 227 905; fax 227

825; email fondas@headof.osf.lt or rimas @kic.osf.lt). You can also send messages and access the Internet from the Skliautai Cyber Café (☎ 622 426; email svl@ktl. mii.lt) in the Old Town at Ašmenos 10. The hourly online rate is 7 litų. The Sprint access code in Vilnius is ☎ 224 180. Omnitel (☎ 623 851; email info@post.omnitel.net), at Jakšto 24, is a local Internet provider.

Travel Agencies

Most travel agencies in Vilnius can book accommodation, tickets and other services within Lithuania and the Baltics. Major ones include:

Baltic Travel Service
    Subačiaus 2 (☎ 220 151, 220 220)
Booking Centre
    Šeimyniškių 12 (☎ 727 921; fax 721 815)
Gintarinė sala
    Vokiečių 8 (☎ 223 223; fax 223 213)
Lithuanian Holidays
    Kudirkos 7-16 (☎ 632 915; fax 233 975)
Lithuanian Student and Youth Travel
    Basanavičiaus 30, room 13 (☎ 220 220; fax 222 196)
Lithuanian Tours
    Šeimyniškių 18 (☎ 723 931; fax 721 815)
Viliota
    Basanavičiaus 15 (☎ 652 238)
West Express
    Stulginskio 5 (☎ 222 500; fax 619 436)

Bookshops

Penki Kontinentai (Five Continents), at Stulginskio 5, stocks a good range of English-language textbooks, Lithuanian phrasebooks and dictionaries. The university bookshop, Litera, at Šv Jono 12, has a large selection of foreign-language books as well as great postcards. Rūtos Knygos, in room 13 at Daukanto 2, offers a two-for-one book exchange. There are a couple of less impressive bookshops on Gedimino prospektas: Knygos at Gedimino 62 and Aura at Gedimino 2.

Media

The best single investment you can make is a copy of the English-language city guide *Vilnius In Your Pocket*, updated five times a year and as good as any available publication of its type (4 litų from kiosks, hotels, currency exchanges etc). *Lithuanian Weekly* is a weekly English-language newspaper which covers events in Lithuania (1.50 litų from bookshops). The weekly Rīga-based *Baltic Times* has a better coverage of Lithuanian events though. The German-language *Baltische Rundschau*, published monthly, is available locally for 2.40 litų. Excellent features can be found in *Lithuania in the World*, a superb glossy which is, in fact, Lithuanian Airlines' in-flight magazine but available in most bookshops and kiosks. The Lithuanian business biweekly *Verslo Žinios* has brief news summaries in English and good information on its web site (http://www.omnitel. net/Business and Economy/vz).

Jerusalem of Lithuania is a small, independent newspaper, published in Yiddish, Lithuanian, Russian and English, and available at the Jewish Museum.

See Media in Facts for the Visitor at the front of the book for more on some of these publications.

Western newspapers, one day old at most, are sold at practically every bookshop in town. For details of English-language TV and radio broadcasts see the Lithuania Facts for the Visitor chapter.

The British Council library in the House of Teachers at Vilniaus 39 has British papers and magazines. The American Center (☎ 220 481), at Pranciškonų 3-6, has a reading room where you can scan the latest American newspapers and news magazines, and the Open Society Fund's reading room, at Šv Jono 5, is another good bet.

Photography & Video

Kodak Express, in a courtyard at Šv Jono 13, does one-hour processing and sells some Kodak film and other supplies. Polaroid Express, in the bookshop at Gedimino 13, develops passport photos in one minute. Fuji has outlets at Gedimino prospektas; in the Iki Commercial Centre at Žirmūnų 68; and at Pilies 23/15. Bring your own video tapes with you for your camcorder.

Laundry

Baltoji Kojinė at Saulėtekio 33 is open daily from 10 am to 7 pm. Palūstrė at Savanorių 11a accepts washing daily from 7 to 11 am and home delivers between 3 and 7 pm. Dry cleaning is possible at Virkštis (☎ 456 654) at Vairo 18 and at the Italian-run Joglė at Jasinskio 16.

Medical Services

There are two private clinics offering an English-speaking, western service. The Baltic-American Medical and Surgical Clinic (☎ 742 020), inside Vilnius University Antakalnio hospital at Antakalnio 124, is open weekdays from 9 am to 5 pm, but also offers a 24 hour emergency service. A less expensive option is the Medical Diagnostic Centre (☎ 709 120, 709 121) at Grybo 32, it's open weekdays from 8.30 am to 8.30 pm. A recommended dental service is AS Klinika (☎ 225 919) at Sėlių 18a.

The German-Lithuanian pharmacy at Didžioji 13, open weekdays from 9 am to 7 pm and Saturday from 10 am to 5 pm, stocks the best range of western medicines. Gedimino Vaistinė (☎ 624 930), at Gedimino 27, offers 24-hour emergency service. For an ambulance, call ☎ 03.

Left Luggage

There is a small left-luggage room *(saugojimo kamera)* at the main ticket hall of the bus station, and another in the train station basement.

WALKING TOUR

The **Cathedral Square** (Katedros aikštė) is a good starting point for an initial exploration. Have a look in the **cathedral** and then walk up the path through the park, next to the square, to **Gedimino Tower** (Gedimino bokštas) on top of **Gediminas Hill** (Gedimino kalnas). From the top of the tower there are views over the entire city – the Old Town stretches to the south, Gedimino prospektas cuts west through the newer part of the centre, **Three Crosses Hill** (Trijų kryžių kalnas) stands to the east, and the river stretches north.

From here, walk back down to Cathedral Square and hike up in to the Old Town along Pilies gatvė. This street, together with Didžioji gatvė and Aušros Vartų gatvė, forms the main single axis of the Old Town.

Try to save some time for a walk along Gedimino prospektas, through the newer part of central Vilnius to the **Parliament**. From here you could stroll in **Vingis Park** (Vingio parkas) or cross the river to the north to visit the **State Museum**. Another area you shouldn't miss is north and east of the cathedral – where you'll find museums, Three Crosses Hill and **SS Peter & Paul's Church**. If time is short, the little money you'd spend on a cab to the TV Tower, the Soviet army barracks and Gariūnai market is also well worth it.

GEDIMINAS HILL & CATHEDRAL SQUARE

Gediminas Hill and, below it, Cathedral Square are the focal points of the city. The Old Town stretches to their south; Gedimino prospektas leads west across the New Town.

Gediminas Hill

This mound, which rises 48m behind the cathedral, was the natural bastion that early Vilnius was founded on. Walk up the path through the park from Cathedral Square. Gedimino Tower – the single, brick tower flying the national flag atop the hill – was part of the 14th century defences of the upper of the two Vilnius castles. On top of the tower is an **observation platform**. Inside is the **Vilnius Castle Museum** (Vilnius pilies muziejus), open daily, except Monday and Tuesday, from 11 am to 6 pm. It has exhibits on old Vilnius that show you the extent of the castles, the upper of which has been partly renovated in recent years and the lower, excavated.

Cathedral Square

Cathedral Square, the open space at the foot of Gediminas Hill dominated by the white bulk of Vilnius Cathedral, was the scene of some of the mass gatherings during Lithuania's independence campaign. In the 19th century, markets and fairs were held here. Before that, the square and the cathedral were within the precincts of the lower castle, destroyed by the Russians in the early 19th century. A moat ran round what is now the square's perimeter – roughly where Vrublevskio and Šventaragio streets are today – and ships could sail almost up to the cathedral door. Within the moat was a ring of walls and towers, the only remaining parts of which are the **clock tower**, standing alone near the west end of the cathedral (a favourite rendezvous point in the city), and a few excavated remains behind the cathedral.

At the east end of the square stands a brand new **statue** of Grand Duke Gediminas and his horse. The statue to the city's founder is a source of much love and hatred to local residents, not least because the duke wields a sword even though he was never a warrior. Press reports claiming that the pedestal on which the statue stands (carved from Ukrainian granite) emits abnormally high levels of radiation as a result of the Chernobyl disaster have done little to help matters. Apparently, it is 'not wise' to stand within a metre of the statue for more than three consecutive days.

When the foundations for the statue were being dug, an archaeological site was uncovered leading to the discovery of a centuries-old **ritual stone** believed to have been used for pagan offerings. The municipality plans to display it in Cathedral Square. Behind Gediminas stretches Sereikiškės and Kalnų parks leading to the Hill of Crosses.

Cathedral This important national symbol was used as a picture gallery during the Soviet era. It was reconsecrated in 1989, and mass is celebrated daily, once again, in Lithuanian and sometimes in Polish.

The site was originally used for the worship of Perkūnas, the old Lithuanian thunder god. The first wooden cathedral was built here in the 13th or 14th century. A grander edifice was constructed under Grand Duke Vytautas in the 15th century. It was initially in Gothic style, but has been rebuilt so often, as architectural fashions have changed, that its old form is unrecognisable.

LITHUANIA

LITHUANIA

Paganism vs Christianity

Czech bishop Albert Waitiekus, the first Christian missionary to venture into the Baltics, came here at the end of the 10th century. Unfortunately for him, he happened to wander into a Baltic forest dedicated to the pagan gods – and was killed – leaving paganism to run rife in the region for another two centuries.

Quite a lot is known about the pre-Christian religions of the Latvians and Lithuanians, who shared similarities as members of the Balt group of peoples. Less is known about the religion of the old Estonians, who came from the entirely different Finno-Ugric religious tradition.

Paralleling the importance of Latvian and especially Lithuanian among Indo-European languages, the old Latvian/Lithuanian religion apparently shares many similarities with Vedic ideas from India and ideas from ancient Iran. There are also similarities between the metrical structure of the Baltic folk rhymes known as *dainas* and the verses of the old Indian sacred text the *Rig Veda*.

To the old Latvians and Lithuanians the sky was a mountain and many of the leading gods lived on it, among them: Dievs the sky god, Saule the sun god (a female), Perkūnas (Latvian: Pērkons) the thunder god (who seems to have been particularly revered) and Mēness the moon god. There was also an earth mother figure called Žemyna in Lithuania and Zemes māte in Latvia. In Latvia the Christian Virgin Mary seems to have taken on many of the attributes of Žemyna, and the two figures seem to be combined in the mythological figure of Māra. Also important were Laima the goddess of fate, the forest goddess (Meža māte in Latvia, Medeinė in Lithuania), and the guardian of wizards and sages (Latvian: Velns; Lithuanian: Velnias), who was transformed into the devil in the Christian scheme of things. Many lesser deities presided over natural phenomena and objects, or human activities.

Today, there are still pagans in the Baltic region who adhere to this system of belief. In Latvia, the Dievturība (pagan followers) are but a handful, however, in Lithuania it is a different story. Lithuania was the only part of Europe not christianised by the end of the 12th century and existed as the last European stronghold of paganism until 1385. Today, the pagan gods are enjoying a marked revival in worshippers.

The Romuva movement has congregations in Vilnius and Kaunas as well as among Lithuanian communities overseas in Canada and the US. It is named after an ancient temple site near Chernahovsk (in today's Kaliningrad Region) that attracted Lithuanian, Latvian and Prussian worshippers alike prior to Christianity's arrival in the Baltics. The movement works towards rekindling Lithuania's ancient spiritual and folklore traditions. Romuva was founded as an organised pagan revival movement in 1967, banned under the Soviet regime in 1971, and revived again under the jurisdiction of the 'Society for Ethnic Lithuanian Culture' in 1988. ∎

The most important restoration was done between 1783 and 1801, when the outside was completely redone in the classical style that remains today. The five-metre **brass statues** of St Helene, St Stanislav and St Casimir on top of the cathedral, are replicas of the original wooden versions added in 1793. They were destroyed under Stalin's regime in 1956. The saints were resurrected in late 1996 following a mammoth seven-year fund raising effort. Helene, who holds a nine-metre-long gold cross, and her saintly companions have become a distinctive landmark, clearly visible from the far west end of Gedimino prospektas.

The statues on the south side facing the square are of Lithuanian dukes, those on the north side are of apostles and saints. The interior retains more of its original aspect,

though the entrances to the side chapels were harmonised in the late 18th century.

The chief showpiece is the **Chapel of St Casimir**, at the east end of the south aisle, which was created in 1623-36 with a baroque cupola, coloured marble and granite on the walls, white stucco sculptures, and fresco scenes from the life of St Casimir, a 15th century grand duke who is the patron saint of Lithuania. The remains of several members of the old Polish royalty and high nobility lie beneath the chapel.

Museums

The **Lithuanian History & Ethnography Museum** (Lietuvos Istorijos ir Etnografijos muziejus), in a long, low, old arsenal building 100m north of the cathedral, takes you from prehistoric amber ornaments to the pre-

WWII independence period. There are good sections on costume and folk art. It's open daily, except Tuesday, from 11 am to 6 pm.

The **Decorative & Applied Arts Museum** (Taikomosios dailės muziejus, ☎ 221 813), in another old arsenal at Arsenalo 3 at the northern foot of Gediminas Hill, has an exceptional collection of furniture, tapestries, jewellery and ceramics from the 15th century onwards. Don't miss the 20th century work upstairs. The museum is open daily, except Monday and Tuesday, from noon to 6 pm.

OLD TOWN

The area stretching 1.5 km south from Cathedral Square was built up in the 15th and 16th centuries, and its narrow, winding streets, hidden courtyards and amazing number of old churches retain the feel of bygone centuries. The Old Town's main axis is along Pilies, Didžioji and Aušros Vartų gatvė. Its approximate boundary, starting from Cathedral Square, runs along Stuokos-Gucevičiaus, Liejyklos, Vilniaus, Trakų, Pylimo, Bazilijonų, Šv Dvasios, Bokšto, Maironio, Radvilaitės and Šventaragio streets – an area of roughly one sq km.

Pilies gatvė

Pedestrianised Pilies gatvė (Castle Street) is the main entrance to the Old Town from Katedros aikštė, with a little gaggle of bright tourist shops and a daily craft market strung along its length. Until the 19th century the street was divided from what's now the square by the lower castle wall which ran across its north end. Only a gate in the wall connected the two. Notice the 15th to 17th century brickwork of Nos 4, 12 and 16 towards the north end of the street.

Vilnius University

The central buildings of the university form most of the block between Pilies gatvė and Universiteto gatvė. Founded by Jesuits in 1579 on the instigation of the Polish king, Stefan Batory, in the Counter-Reformation, the university was run by Jesuits for two

centuries and became one of the greatest centres of Polish learning. It produced many notable scholars in the 17th and early 19th century, but was closed by the Russians in 1832 and didn't reopen until 1919. Today it has about 14,000 students and the library houses five million books.

Each autumn, during the 'University Theatre festival', alternative dramas and plays are staged around 12 linked courtyards, which can be entered by numerous passages and gates from the surrounding streets. The southern gate on Šv Jono gatvė brings you into the Didysis or Skarga Courtyard, where you'll find **St John's Church** (Šv Jono bažnyčia), which was founded in 1387 well before the university arrived. It now has an outstanding 18th century baroque main façade and a fine interior. Its 17th and 18th century **bell tower**, standing separately on the south side of the courtyard, is a distinctive feature in the Vilnius skyline. The galleries around three sides of this courtyard are in the early 17th century Mannerist style, which formed the transition from Renaissance to baroque.

The arch through the 16th century building opposite St John's leads to the Pocobuto Courtyard, with an old two-domed **observatory** whose late 18th century façade is adorned with reliefs of the zodiac. The other main courtyard, reached through the passage from the north side of the Didysis Courtyard, is the Sarbievijus Courtyard.

Daukanto aikštė

The exit from the university's Sarbievijus Courtyard to Universiteto gatvė brings you out opposite the former Bishops' Palace – now the **President's palace** – on Daukanto aikštė, rebuilt in the classical Russian empire style early in the 19th century. Once the residence of Vilnius bishops, the palace was later used by Russian governors and, during the Napoleonic Wars, by both Napoleon when he was advancing on Moscow and by his Russian adversary, General Mikhail Kutuzov, when he was chasing Napoleon back to Paris. In Soviet times it became the

LITHUANIA

LITHUANIA

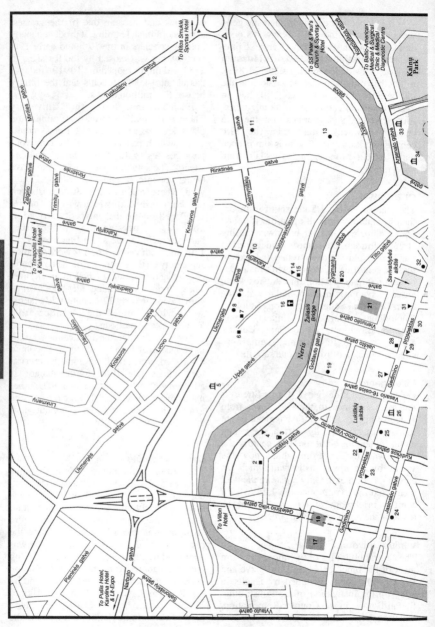

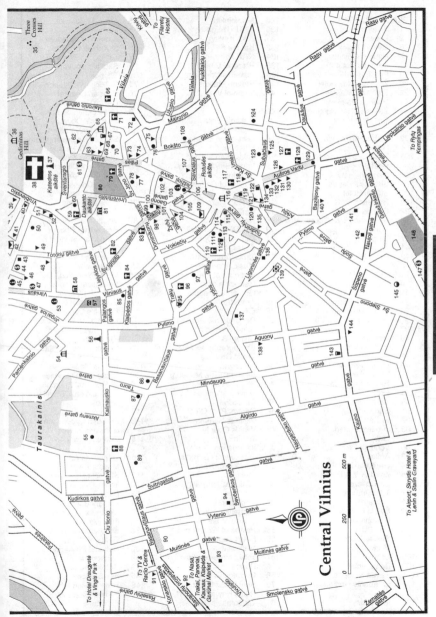

Central Vilnius

LITHUANIA

LITHUANIA

'Art Workers' Culture Palace' (Menininkų rūmai) and, after housing the French embassy for a while and following massive renovation work, is now the president's palace.

The baroque **Holy Cross Church** (Šv Kryžiaus bažnyčia) at the north-west corner of the square was used as an organ-concert hall until it was given back to the church recently.

East of Pilies gatvė

Mickiewicz Museum The old rooms of the Polish romantic poet Adam Mickiewicz (1798-1855), at Bernardinų 11, are now the Adam Mickiewicz Memorial Apartment (☎ 620 148). Mickiewicz (known as Adomas Mickevičiaus by any good Lithuanian!) grew up near Vilnius and studied at its university from 1815 to 1819 before being exiled, in 1824, for anti-Russian activities. Much of his work, which inspired Polish nationalists through the 19th century, is set in the Vilnius region. It's a measure of how intertwined Lithuanian and Polish history are that Mickiewicz's poem, *Pan Tadeusz*, which ranks as Poland's national romantic epic masterpiece, begins: 'Lithuania, my fatherland...'!

St Michael's & St Anne's Churches Opposite the east end of Bernardinų gatvė, at Volano 13, is the 17th century St Michael's Church (Šv Mykolo bažnyčia, ☎ 616 409), now an architecture museum. Members of the noble Sapieha family, which had it built, are mummified in the vaults beneath.

Across Maironio gatvė stands the fine, brick, 16th century St Anne's Church (Šv Onos bažnyčia, ☎ 611 236), the jewel of Lithuanian Gothic architecture with its sweeping curves and delicate pinnacles. Napoleon reportedly wished he could take it back to Paris with him 'in the palm of his hand'. The buildings adjoining St Anne's, including the austere church behind it which is currently being renovated, were part of a mostly 16th century **Bernardine monastery** (like St Michael's) and also part of the Old Town's defensive wall.

Didžioji gatvė

Rotušės aikštė Didžioji gatvė (Main Street) is the southward continuation of Pilies gatvė. Towards its south end it widens into Rotušės aikštė (Town Hall Square), which was, for a long time, one of the centres of Vilnius life. Markets were held here from the 15th century, when this was a crossroads from which roads led to Kraków and Rīga. The old Town Hall in the middle of the square has stood since at least the early 16th century, but its classical exterior dates from 1785-99. The **Contemporary Art Centre** (Šiuolaukinio Meno Centras, ☎ 221 981), behind the Town Hall at Vokiečių 2, displays avant-garde art. At Vokiečių 20, in a courtyard, is the extensively renovated **Evangelical Lutheran Church**, dating back to 1553 today it is home to Vilnius' tiny protestant community. Under the Soviet regime a concrete floor divided the church into a workshop and a basketball court.

St Casimir's Church The oldest baroque church in Vilnius is the large St Casimir's (Šv Kazimiero bažnyčia, ☎ 221 715), at Didžioji 34, which was built by the Jesuits in 1604-15. Its dome and cross-shaped ground plan, influenced by the Jesuits' Il Jesu Church in Rome, defined a new style for 17th century Lithuanian churches. Under tsarist rule St Casimir's was taken over by the Russian Orthodox Church and given an onion dome, which was removed in 1942. Under Soviet rule it spent two decades as a museum of atheism.

Aušros Vartų gatvė

North End Aušros Vartų gatvė – a street famed for its amazing cluster of churches of different denominations – leads south from St Casimir's. At No 73 near its north (lower) end, on the west side, there's a fine late-baroque archway known as the **Basilian Gates**, forming the entrance to the decrepit Basilian monastery complex. On the east side of the street, just above the 16th century house that now contains the Medininkai restaurant, is the big, pink, domed, 17th century **Orthodox Church of the Holy Spirit** (Šv

LITHUANIA

Dvasios cerkvė), the chief Russian Orthodox church of Lithuania. The amazingly preserved bodies of three 14th century martyrs – SS Anthony, Ivan and Eustachius – lie in a chamber at the foot of a flight of steps in front of the altar (you can even see their feet peeping out). The Catholic **St Teresa's Church** (Šv Teresės bažnyčia), further south on the east side above the Orthodox Church of the Holy Spirit, is early baroque (1635-50) outside and more elaborate late baroque inside. Below its entrance is a sinister chamber for the dead – which would make for an awkward sight should a wedding procession meet a funeral party coming out of the cellar.

Gates of Dawn At the top of Aušros Vartų gatvė, the Gates of Dawn (Aušros Vartai) are, in fact, themselves a single gate tower – the only one of the original nine in the town wall that's still intact. The gate was lucky to survive the Soviet era; this is the start of the Minsk-Moscow road and the Soviet authorities had planned to run a highway from the centre of Vilnius, which would have meant levelling the Gates of Dawn. Shortly before the gate, a door on the east side of the street opens onto a staircase that leads up to a little 18th century chapel directly over the gate arch. This houses a supposedly miracle-working **icon of the Virgin**, reputed to have been souvenired from the Crimea by Grand Duke Algirdas in 1363, though more likely dating from the 16th century. It is particularly revered by the deeply Catholic Polish community, to whom the chapel is known as the Ostrabramska, and is said to be one of eastern Europe's leading pilgrimage destinations. A replica of the icon adorns a chapel in St Peter's in Rome. Locally, it attracts a constant bustle of people coming, going and saying prayers, as well as a good few poverty-stricken pensioners begging for whatever people will give them. The icon was repainted in the 17th or 18th century. Notice the quite different appearances of the northern and southern faces of the tower. One of the few surviving lengths of the Old Town wall leads east from here.

Artillery Bastion
If you follow the old wall round from the Gates of Dawn on to Šv Dvasios gatvė, then continue north, you reach the Artillery Bastion (Artilerijos bastėja, ☎ 612 149) at Bokšto 20. This 17th century fortification, with a collection of old weaponry and armour, is open as a museum daily, except Monday and Tuesday, from 11 am to 5 pm.

Jewish Vilnius
One of Europe's most important Jewish communities once flourished in the Old Town of Vilnius. A few years ago there was hardly any outward sign of this, so thoroughly had the Soviet authorities obliterated its memory, after the Nazis had annihilated the Jewish community itself. Between the 1950s and 70s even the city's Jewish graves were desecrated – tombstones were used as paving stones and the main Jewish cemetery became the Sports Palace. A commemorative stone stands in front of the palace today. Since independence the city council has started returning tombstones to the existing Jewish community and has built some memorials in places so discreet that no one knows about them. A national Jewish Museum opened in 1989 (the first in the former USSR) and detailed information on Vilnius' Jewish past is much easier to come by as a result. In mid-1996, following years of bickering, Germany agreed to pay DM2 million to Lithuania to compensate the holocaust survivors and other victims of Nazi persecution.

History Jews lived in Vilnius almost from its founding by Gediminas, who invited them here. Their numbers apparently reached 3000, in a city population of 15,000, in the mid-17th century. In the 18th century it was a Vilnius rabbi and scholar, Gaon, who led the opposition to the widespread Jewish mystical movement Hassidism. In the 19th century the Vilnius Jewish community grew, and the city became a centre of development of the European Jewish language, Yiddish. The famous landscape artist Isaak Levitan and, later, the sculptor Jacques Lipchitz were

Vilnius Jews. Despite emigration, the city's Jewish population peaked on the eve of WWI at nearly 100,000 out of a total of 235,000.

Between the world wars, with Vilnius a provincial outpost of Poland, the Jewish community of 60,000 to 80,000 faced discrimination and poverty, but Vilnius blossomed into the Jewish cultural hub of eastern Europe. In 1925 it was chosen ahead of the other Yiddish centres, Warsaw and New York, as the headquarters of the Yiddish-language scientific research institute YIVO (which stood west of the Old Town on what's now Vivulskio gatvė, opposite the end of Šviesos gatvė). Jewish schools, libraries, literature and theatre flourished. There were over 100 synagogues and prayer houses and six daily Jewish newspapers.

Jewish Quarter & Ghettos The Jewish quarter lay in the streets west of Didžioji gatvė. Today the street names Žydų (Jews) and Gaono are among the few explicit reminders of this. The main synagogue, founded in the 16th century, and its famous library stood just about where the west end of Žydų gatvė is now, with a nursery school on its site. Today there is a school here.

Virtually all Vilnius' Jewish organisations, except communist ones, were dissolved when the Soviet Union took over eastern Poland in September 1939. Many Jewish leaders were deported. Meanwhile Polish Jews fleeing the Nazis arrived here as refugees. Vilnius fell to the Nazis two days after their invasion of the USSR on 22 June, 1941. About 35,000 Jews – almost half those in the city – were murdered in Paneriai forest (see the Around Vilnius section) in the next three months, before a ghetto was established in a small area north of Vokiečių gatvė, which was the heart of the Jewish quarter. This first ghetto was liquidated after 46 days and its inhabitants killed at Paneriai; a larger one, south of Vokiečių gatvė, lasted until the general liquidation of ghettos on Himmler's orders in 1943, when 26,000 people were killed at Paneriai and 8000 transported to

Estonia. The single gate of the main ghetto stood at what's now the south end of Rūdininkų gatvė, today marked with a commemorative plaque bearing a detailed map of the former ghetto. There is another identical plaque along Stiklių gatvė. About 6000 Vilnius Jews escaped, one way or another. Survivors say that Lithuanian sidekicks acted at least as cruelly and mercilessly in the Vilnius holocaust as their German masters.

The central reservation on Vokiečių gatvė and the roadway down its eastern side were created after WWII in place of buildings of the Jewish quarter that had stood there previously. The contrast between the old buildings on the west side of the street and the Stalin-era ones on the east is clear. Sources differ on whether the original buildings were destroyed by Nazi or Soviet hands.

Jewish Museum Today there are about 5000 or 6000 Jews in Vilnius, most newcomers since WWII. One of the few ghetto survivors still here has helped to found the admirable Lithuanian State Jewish Museum (Lietuvos valstybinis žydų muziejus, ☎ 620 730), which currently has two sections near each other, both open from 10 am to 5 pm Monday to Friday. The branch at Paménkalnio 12 (actually up the first little street on the south side of Paménkalnio gatvė as you go from Pylimo gatvė) provides a general record (with many photographs) of Vilnius' Jewish history and the holocaust in Lithuania. The branch at Pylimo 4, which is also the Jewish Community Centre (☎ 613 105), contains relics of the great synagogue, blown up along with its adjoining library in 1944. Another branch of the Jewish museum opened in Druskininkai in 1996 (see Eastern & Southern Lithuania – Druskininkai). Funds permitting, the museum publishes a small newspaper, *Jerusalem of Lithuania*, available in Yiddish, Lithuanian, Russian and English.

Synagogue Modern Vilnius' only synagogue (☎ 612 523) is at Pylimo 39. It was originally built in 1894 for the wealthy, and massively renovated in 1995. It survived because the Nazis used it as a medical store.

Old Town – west

There are no less than four sizeable Catholic church-and-monastery complexes, all created by different monastic orders, within 200m of the corner of Vilniaus and Dominikonų streets. All date chiefly from the 17th and 18th century baroque era. Among them, the **Holy Spirit Church** (Šv Dvasios bažnyčia), at the corner of Dominikonų and Šv Ignoto streets, is now one of Vilnius' chief Polish churches. Once attached to a Dominican monastery, it has a splendid gold and white interior. The twin towers of **St Catherine's Church** (Šv Kotrynos bažnyčia), at Vilniaus 30, were once part of a Benedictine monastery, and are considered landmark of Vilnius.

The other monasteries are the **Jesuit Noviciate** with **St Ignatius' Church** (Šv Ignoto bažnyčia) on Šv Ignoto gatvė and the **Franciscan monastery** on Trakų gatvė. The fine little **St Nicholas' Church** (Šv Mikalojaus bažnyčia), on Šv Mikalojaus gatvė, is much older – it is Lithuania's oldest Gothic church, dating from 1320 (before Lithuania's conversion) and was founded by German merchants.

Radvilos Palace, the 17th century residence of Jonušas Radvila (1612-55) at Vilniaus 41, houses part of the **Lithuanian Art Museum** along with portraits of 165 members of the Radvila family. It is open daily, except Monday, from noon to 6 pm.

EAST OF GEDIMINAS HILL

Worth exploring in this area, is the charming run-down quarter of Užupis. The tiny little church on Užupio Polocko doubled as a home/workshop to the Cathedral's three saints for some five years while they were being rebuilt.

Three Crosses

The Three Crosses (Trys kryžiai) overlooking the Old Town from, funnily enough, Three Crosses Hill (Trijų kryžių kalnas), just east of Gediminas Hill, are long-time land-marks of Vilnius. Crosses are said to have stood here since the 17th century in memory of three monks who were martyred by crucifixion on this spot. The current crosses (painted white), erected in 1989, are replicas of the three that were knocked down and buried by the Soviet authorities after WWII. You can walk up to them through Kalnų Park from Kosciuškos gatvė.

SS Peter & Paul's Church

The outside of SS Peter & Paul's Church (Šv Petro ir Povilo bažnyčias), at the east end of Kosciuškos gatvė, may be plain, but the interior is a sea of sparkling-white baroque stucco that has been moulded into thousands of sculptures and reliefs of plants, animals, and real and mythical people – broken here and there by touches of gilt, paintings and coloured statues. Most of the decoration was done by Italian sculptors between 1675 and 1704. The church was founded by the Lithuanian noble, Mykolas Kazimieras Pacas, whose tomb is on the right of the porch as you enter.

Rasų & Military Cemeteries

Vilnius' Rasų and Military cemeteries face each other on either side of Sukilėlių gatvė, south-east of Vilnius Old Town. Founded in 1801, Rasų cemetery is the resting place of Vilnius' most elite artists and politicians etc. More interesting, however, is the small, unkempt military cemetery opposite, where just the heart of the Polish Marshal Jósef Piłsudki, responsible for Poland's annexation of Vilnius in 1921, lies. His mother shares his heart's grave. His body is buried in Kraków.

NEW TOWN

The area known as the New Town (naujamiestis) stretches 1.5 to two km west of the cathedral and the Old Town. It was mostly built in the 19th century.

Gedimino prospektas

The main street of modern Vilnius runs west from the cathedral to the river. Its 1.75 km length is dotted with shops, a theatre, banks, hotels, offices, the government, ministries, parliament and a few park squares. Laid out in 1852, it has had 11 name changes since, reflecting the nationalities and political tendencies of Vilnius' rulers. The Russian tsarist authorities named it after St George, the Poles after Mickiewicz, the Soviet rulers first after Stalin, then Lenin. The three saints, gazing down the entire length of the prospektas from the top of the cathedral, are a major landmark.

Savivaldybės aikštė The city hall is on the east side of this square at the corner of Vilniaus gatvė; the seat of the government occupies the north side. Above Vilniaus gatvė, down towards the river, is the large modern Opera & Ballet Theatre.

Lukiškių aikštė The ministry of foreign affairs and the former KGB building surround Lukiškių aikštė, formerly called Lenin Square due to the statue of Lenin which used to stand in the centre (see Soviet Nostalgia). The large building facing this square, at Gedimino 4, used to be the headquarters of the Lithuanian KGB (and during the Nazi occupation, the Gestapo). Part of it is now used as the State Prosecutor's office; the remaining part is the **Museum of the Genocide of the Lithuanian People** (☎ 622 449). The museum guides are all former inmates and will show you round the cells where they were tormented (open weekdays from 10 am to 4 pm). If you want a tour, it is best to call in advance.

Parliament Only a few slabs now remain as reminders of the barricades erected at the west end of Gedimino prospektas, in January 1991, to protect Lithuania's parliament (Seimas) from marauding Soviet troops. Thousands of people gathered inside and outside the building on 13 January, 1991, just as they gathered at the TV & Radio Centre and the TV tower. The barricades to the north of the parliament building, were left in place until December 1992, when the last Russian soldier left Vilnius.

The classical building next to parliament

is the **National Library**. Trolleybus No 7 from the train station, or No 3 from the Gedimino stop on Vrublevskio gatvė near the cathedral, will take you along Jasinskio gatvė, a block south of Gedimino prospektas. For parliament, get off at the Tiltas stop just before the river or the Liubarto stop just after it.

South of the River

The Soviet-era **Palace of Weddings** (Santuokų rūmai) is in the park off Kalinausko gatvė at the top of Taurakalnis. Opposite the Palace of Weddings, on Basanavičiaus gatvė, is the **Romanovs' Church**, an interesting Russian Orthodox church built in 1913. A little further down Basanavičiaus gatvė, at No 42, is a daily flower market (open 24 hours). A **Kenessa**, a traditional prayer house belonging to the Karaites, Lithuania's smallest ethnic minority who adhere to the Law of Moses, is west of Jasinskio at Liubarto 6.

At Kalinausko 1, outside a medical clinic, stands a 4.2m-high bronze bust memorial to the American rock 'n' roll legend **Frank Zappa**, who died from cancer in 1993 when he was in his mid-50s. The bust, said to be

Frank Zappa memorial

LITHUANIA

Beginning with B

'We want to show the world how a little nation fought for its independence; show how dear, how valuable, independence itself is.'
Juozas Aleksiejūnas, Tour Guide, Museum of the Genocide of the Lithuanian People.

Juozas Aleksiejūnas is 76. He is a tour guide at the Museum of the Genocide of the Lithuanian People, housed in the former headquarters and prison of the KGB in Vilnius. He is also a former inmate of this house of horrors where blood still stains the walls of the cramped cells in which prisoners lived and died.

Aleksiejūnas joined the partisan resistance movement in 1944, almost immediately after Soviet rule was re-established in Lithuania and the other Baltic states. As one of the country's estimated 40,000 'forest brothers', he roamed the forests in the Molėtai area, 75 km north of Vilnius, with his five other 'brothers'. His official task was to steal identity forms from the local passport office to pass on to fellow partisans.

On 26 March, 1945, he was betrayed. In a bloody battle in which two of his brothers were shot, he was arrested by the KGB and taken to Utena where he was tried in court for carrying out anti-Soviet activities. Less than an hour later he was found guilty and imprisoned. Four days later he was moved to the KGB prison in Vilnius, notorious for its high security and inhumane disciplinary measures.

Between 1944 and 1953, 200,000 Lithuanians passed through the Soviet prisons in Lithuania. The one in Vilnius was used for equally sinister purposes by the Gestapo during the Nazi occupation; its execution ward, various torture chambers, and nine-metre-square cells where up to 20 prisoners were kept at any one time, all remain today.

Aleksiejūnas was interrogated and tortured for a week. 'How many of you are there?' and 'who is your leader?' were the key questions fired at him. Prisoners did not have names. They were called 'Beginning with A', 'Beginning with B' and so on to ensure prisoners knew as little about each other as possible. Inmates who attempted to converse were sent to an isolation cell, stripped to their underwear and rationed to 300 grams of bread and half a litre of water a day.

Inmates who refused 'to talk' to KGB officers during interrogation were sent to the infamous 'soft cell'. Its walls were heavily padded to muffle the hideous human cries and the sound of beatings. Prisoners were put in straitjackets and forced to sit in the pitch-black, silent cell until their spirit broke. Aleksiejūnas survived the soft cell hell.

After three days in the 'wet room' he lost consciousness. This eight-by-10 metre punishment cell had a sunken floor covered with cold water, which turned to ice in winter. In the centre of the cell was a circular, slippery-metal pedestal, 30 cm in diameter, which was the prisoners' only refuge from the wet floor. Before the KGB left the building in 1991, it boarded up the prison's two wet cells. They were found beneath a false floor in the prison library when the building was opened as the Museum of the Genocide of the Lithuanian People in 1992. The remains of prisoners who were shot have since been found buried in Tuskulenai park, a popular picnic spot in Vilnius until 1994 when the KGB graveyard was discovered. The park is now known as the 'killing fields'.

Juozas Aleksiejūnas was later moved to Vokiski prison in Vilnius. On 29 June, 1945, he was deported to Vorkuta, Siberia, where he spent five years in a hard labour camp followed by a further five years in a high security prison. In 1955, he was released on parole. But he was not allowed to leave Vorkuta and had to report twice a month (which he did for nine years) to the prison's special commander. His Lithuanian wife, Jane, whom he had married in 1943 (but barely seen or been in contact with since), joined him in Vorkuta where their first son was born. The Aleksiejūnas family was allowed to return home to Vilnius in 1963. ■

the first of its kind in the world, was erected in 1995 by the Lithuanian Frank Zappa fan club after a long dispute with various authorities, who found the whole idea completely preposterous!

Vingis Park

Just over a km south-west of parliament, at the west end of Čiurlionio gatvė, is the pleas-ant, wooded Vingis Park (Vingio parkas). It is surrounded on three sides by the Neris and has a big stage, which is the usual setting for the Lithuanian Song Festival. If you don't want to walk all the way from the city centre, take trolleybus No 7 from the train station or No 3 from the Gedimino stop on Vrublevskio gatvė, near the cathedral, to the Kęstučio stop (the second after the bridge over the river), then walk over the footbridge from the end of Treniotos gatvė.

TV & Radio Centre

Like the more distant TV Tower, the TV & Radio Centre at the corner of Konarskio gatvė and Pietario gatvė, near the south-east edge of Vingis Park, was stormed by Soviet tanks and troops in the early hours of 13 January, 1991. A group of wooden crosses stand outside the centre as a memorial to the many martyrs of Lithuania's independence campaign.

North of the River

North of the river stretches Vilnius' Soviet-era suburbs, typical to any sizeable town in the Baltics. Fine specimens of **Soviet housing architecture**, dating from the Khrushchev to Gorbachev eras, can be found here. **St Raphael's Church** (Šv Rapolo bažnyčia), on the north side of the Žaliasis tiltas (Green Bridge) over the Neris, has quite a fine baroque interior.

Beyond the Lietuva hotel on Ukmergės gatvė is the **Lithuanian State Museum** (Lietuvos valstybės muziejus), open daily, except Monday and Tuesday, from 11 am to 7 pm. In the Soviet era this was the Revolution Museum of the Lithuanian Soviet Socialist Republic. **Antakalnis Cemetery**, off Karių kapų gatvė in the northern region of Antakalnis, is said to be one of the most beautiful graveyards in eastern Europe. Those who were killed by Soviet special forces outside the parliament on 13 January, 1991, are buried here, along with the seven border guards also killed by Soviet forces at the Medininkai border crossing with Belarus in 1991. A sculpture of the Madonna cradling her son in her arms stands in memorial to them. On All Saints' Day (1 November) hundreds of people light candles by the graves in respect to the dead.

TV TOWER

Vilnius' 326m-high TV Tower (Televizijos bokštas) is in the suburb of Karoliniškės, across the river west of Vingis Park, at Sausio 13-osios gatvė. Here, on 13 January, 1991,

Soviet special forces (OMON), tanks and troops killed 12 people and wounded many more as they fought through the crowd that had gathered to defend the tower after the troops' disruptive activities of the previous days. Lithuanian TV kept broadcasting until the troops came through the tower door. It announced: 'The tower and studios are being attacked by the Red Army. But we will celebrate victory in the end.' A few carved wooden crosses and candles now stand as memorials to the victims. Every year, on 13 January, hundreds of people light candles at this spot to pay tribute to the people who were killed. The tower now houses a small exhibit on those who died, and a restaurant offering panoramic views of the city.

To get to the tower, visible from parts of the city centre, take trolleybus No 16 from the train station or No 11 from Lukiškių aikštė to the Televizijos Bokštas stop on Laisvės prospektas. A visit here also takes you into the heart of some of Vilnius' Soviet-era high-rise suburbs.

SOVIET NOSTALGIA

The Soviet special forces responsible for the 13 January crackdown on the TV tower were stationed at the **Northern Township** in Vilnius, just a couple of kilometres from the centre in the northern suburb of Žirmūnai. The barracks was home to the 107th Motorized Rifle Brigade until 31 December, 1992, when the Red Army pulled out of Vilnius. Today the barracks are empty, serving only as an unwanted reminder of the Soviet occupation.

Attempts to turn the 63 hectare site into a 'free economic zone' business park have failed and there is little hope of any future development. The former checkpoint at Apkasų 8 is now an 'automobilu Dalys' and the officers' canteen behind is a small supermarket. The former officers' mess is today's city morgue.

About one km south of the barracks, wedged between Žirmūnų gatvė and the Neris river, is Tuskulenai park, a former picnic spot that is now known as the **Killing Fields**. An estimated 800 people were shot and buried here by the KGB following the Soviet reoccupation of Lithuania in 1944. Among the victims were many partisans who put up an armed resistance against Soviet rule from their positions in the surrounding forests. The secret graveyard was only discovered in 1994. The park is now fenced off to the public while an investigation takes place. When it is completed a memorial to the partisan struggle will be put up in the park.

To get to the killing fields, take trolleybus No 8, 12, 17 or 18 to Žirmūnai and get off at the stop after the roundabout on Žirmūnų gatvė. To reach the Northern Township, continue one more stop.

Lenin's statue lies in bits, along with his communist mate Stalin, outside the Dailės Studija on the main road to the airport at Dariaus ir Girėno 25. Up until 1991 Lenin's statue occupied a prime spot in the centre of Lukiškių aikštė. When it was taken down from the pedestal, Lenin's legs broke, leaving him dangling legless in mid-air from the crane.

EXHIBITIONS

Many of the museums host a variety of temporary art exhibitions. *Vilnius In Your Pocket* and the Entertainment Guide of the *Baltic Times* run listings of what exhibitions are on where. The cultural department of the French embassy in Vilnius publishes a bimonthly magazine, with parallel text in French and Lithuanian, which contains useful exhibitions, events and entertainment listings.

Lithuanian and some foreign avant-garde artists are exhibited at the **Contemporary Art Centre** (Šiuolaukinio Meno Centras, ☎ 221 981) at Vokiečių 2 in the Old Town. Far funkier and less 'touristy' is **Langas** (☎ 221 505) at Ašmenos 8; **Arka** (☎ 221 319) at Aušros Vartų 7; **Vartai** (☎ 222 949) at Vilniaus 39 (in the House of Teachers); and the **Russian Cultural Centre Gallery** (Rusų Kultūros Centro Galerija, ☎ 223 236) at Bokšto 4/2.

Some interesting exhibitions are also held at the **Photographic Society Gallery** at Didžioji 19; and at the Polish art gallery, **Znad**

Willi, at Išganytojo 2/4. Trade fairs and exhibitions are held at Lit-Expo (☎ 454 500), east of the city centre at Laisvės 5.

The **Centre Culturel Français Oscar Milosz** (☎ 222 979), a new cultural centre run by the French embassy in Vilnius will open at Didžioji 1 in October 1997. Given the embassy's innovative repertoire to date, look out for some highly original and experimental exhibitions.

MARKET

Gariūnai is the big free-for-all market held daily, except Monday, up to about 11 am, just off the Kaunas road, on the western fringe of Vilnius. All imaginable goods (mostly legal) are sold here, as well as a staggering selection of second-hand vehicles of all shapes, sizes and origins.

Minibuses marked 'Gariūnai' or 'Gariunų Turgus' ferry shoppers from the train station road every morning. By car take a turning marked 'Gariunai', 11 km along Savanorių prospektas from Vilnius centre.

ACTIVITIES

See Activities in Facts for the Visitor at the front of the book for more general details on activities in Lithuania. Specific to Vilnius, is Boulingo Klubas (☎ 235 500) at Jasinskio 16, the Baltics largest 12-pin bowling centre, which also features American and Russian pool tables. It's open Monday to Thursday from noon to 2 am, and on Friday to Sunday from 11 to 3 am. There is a table tennis club (☎ 226 622) at Jasinskio 6; open daily from 10 am to 10 pm. High flyers can try skydiving for 50 litų a jump with the Vilniaus Aeroklubas (☎ 674 488) or go ballooning with the Lietuvos Oreivių Draugija (☎ 220 511), in the Old Town at Leijyklos 2.

ORGANISED TOURS

Most travel agencies, hotels and the Lithuanian Art Museum (☎ 220 166, 628 639) arrange city tours.

SPECIAL EVENTS

Vilnius hosts a number of festivals. Ones particularly Lithuanian in flavour include

Užgavėnės, a pagan carnival celebrated on Shrove Tuesday (in February) to mark the end of winter; the Kaziukas craft fair held in the Old Town around 4 March to celebrate St Casimir's Day; and Lygiadienis, another pagan carnival that takes place in March on Spring Equinox.

PLACES TO STAY – BOTTOM END

Camping

There is a campsite, 25 km east of Vilnius on the road to Minsk, at Rukainiai. Here, at *Rytų Kempingas* (☎ 651 195), you can stay in small wooden summerhouses by the river as well as pitch a tent. Doubles/triples cost 40/50 litų and luxury huts cost 105/135 litų. It is only open in summer.

Hostels

The *Lithuanian Hostels Association* (Lietuvos Nakvynės Namai, ☎ 696 627; fax 220 149; email root@jnakv.vno.soros.lt) has its head office at the *Filaretų Hostel* at Filaretų 17 in the Užupis area, one km east of the Old Town. It has 15 rooms with two to 10 beds in each. Beds in a double room cost 32 litų including linen and breakfast. If you stay more than one night the rate drops by 4 litų and HI members get a 25% discount. To get to the hostel take bus No 34 from outside the bus and train stations, and get off at the seventh stop. Bookings for other hostels run by the association in Lithuania can also be made here. Don't be deceived by old signs around the station area pointing to a Lithuanian Hostel office at Kauno 1a; this office closed long ago.

Vilnius University Student Representation (Vilniaus Universiteto Studentų Atstovybė or VUSA, ☎ 614 414; ☎ & fax 617 920), in the Pocobuto courtyard of the main university building at Universiteto gatvė 3, offers rooms in student blocks – which are about a 20 minute trolleybus ride from the city centre. Rooms with a shared shower and toilet cost 16/20 litų. Book and pay in advance at the VUSA office. The *Teacher's University Hostel* (☎ 230 704; fax 262 291), on the west edge of the Old Town at Vivulskio 36, has singles/doubles costing

50/56 litų. Euro<26 card holders are entitled to 10% discount at both places.

A cheap but rough alternative worth considering is *Vilnius train station* where you can sleep in a standing carriage overnight for 15 litų including linen – very popular with traders from Poland and other CIS countries. The 'reception' (☎ 692 472), marked 'Budinti', is on your right as you enter the main ticket hall.

Private Homes

Litinterp (☎ 223 850; fax 223 559; email litinterp@post.omnitel.net), at Bernardinų 7-2, arranges B&B accommodation in the Old Town for 60 litų a single or 100 litų for a double. It also arranges accommodation in Klaipėda, Nida, Palanga and Kaunas; and rents cars and bicycles. Bookings can be made through the Internet (http://www.omnitel.net/litinterp).

Also providing private accommodation, but at more expensive rates, are *Vilniaus Kalvos* (☎ & fax 220 894) at Ašmenos 10 with singles/doubles for 80/120 litų, and *Trečjasis aukštas* (☎ 220 918, 222 973; fax 222 963), at Gedimino 41-3, which has singles/doubles for 100/140 litų. *Lobis* (☎ 737 162), at Mečetės 4, finds apartments for short stays from 120 litų a night, as can *Vingriai* (☎ 222 950) at Vingrių 19. The *Information Bureau* (see Information – Tourist Offices) can find you a bed for the night although its main speciality is finding short and long-stay apartments to rent.

Several organisations based elsewhere can also arrange homestays in Vilnius – see Accommodation in Facts for the Visitor at the front of the book.

Hotels

A convenient place to stay close to the train and bus station – and best value for the budget conscious – is *Žvaigždė* hotel (☎ 619 626) at Pylimo 63. Most of the customers are from Russia, Central Asia or Caucasia and the staff at reception only speak Russian, however. Doubles/triples with shared bathroom cost 18/15 litų per person and a room with four/five beds is 13 litų per person.

LITHUANIA

Hotel Gintaras (☎ 634 496), on Naujoji gatvė in front of the train station (its official address is Sodų 14), is a former Soviet ghetto which has made attempts to brighten up its appearance in recent months. Only unrenovated rooms remain cheap; singles/doubles start at 39/59 litų and rise to 100/160 litų, depending on how much has been renovated. As with everything in close range of the station, security is not the best here.

Two km north-east of the cathedral at Bystričios 13, is the *Sportas* hotel (☎ 748 953), a large, decaying Soviet-era hotel where you can get a very basic single/double/triple/quad with bathroom and TV for 47/61/60/75 litų. Take trolleybus No 2, 3 or 4 from the Gedimino stop, on Vrublevskio gatvė near the cathedral, five stops to the Minskas stop, on Antakalnio gatvė, now walk east along Tramvajų gatvė and turn left (north) along Grybo gatvė at the end, after two blocks. Bistryčios gatvė is then the first on the right.

Five km north of the centre in the Žirmūnai district, among the woods near the river at Verkių 66, is the *Trinapolis* (☎ 778 913; fax 762 605). Its single rooms for 40 litų a night with a bathroom or 20 litų a night without are popular among hardened travellers. Trolleybus No 5 from the train station or No 5 or 6 from the Universalinė Parduotuvė stop, on the north side of the Žaliasis bridge, will take you within 10 minutes walk of the hotel. Get off when they diverge to the right off Verkių gatvė. At the airport try the *Skrydis* hotel (☎ 262 223; fax 262 135) which offers a 25% discount if you stay for more than five days. The normal rate for basic singles/doubles without bathrooms is 70 litų and for triples, 75 litų. Look out for some much-needed renovation work here in the future.

PLACES TO STAY – MIDDLE

Some travel agencies in Vilnius can get you into some of the better hotels at short notice – and at a cheaper nightly rate than if you go to the hotel direct.

Blasting yourself back to Vilnius' Soviet past generally guarantees you a fair night's sleep for a price that won't break the bank,

although prices at former Soviet ghettos could rise as some embark upon renovations of sorts.

Old Town & Gedimino prospektas

One which has definitely not changed for some 35 years is the *Neringa* hotel (☎ 610 516; fax 614 160) at Gedimino 23. Singles/doubles with shared bathrooms for 280/360 litų are simply furnished, complete with some of the ugliest colour schemes you're likely to encounter. Top-floor rooms are to be transformed into luxury suites with a price tag to match. A few Soviet-era hangovers also remain at the *Draugystė* (☎ 236 711; email hotel draugyste@post.omnitel.net), once the top hotel for Communist Party officials, 2.25 km west of the centre at Čiurlionio 84. Rooms are equally lacking in finesse but the glass elevator and rooftop bar offer brilliant views of Vingis Park. Singles/doubles start at 200/220 litų.

The *Žaliasis Tiltas* (Green Bridge) has 70 quite pleasant, clean rooms with TV and private bathroom, split between two sites: Vilniaus 2 (☎ 615 460; fax 221 716), which was once a Communist Party hangout, and Gedimino 12 (☎ 615 450; fax 221 716), which has the added perk of a brand new in-house café overlooking the main street. Room rates start at 175/245 litų.

Good value are the cheaper rooms in the attic of *Centrum* hotel and business centre (☎ 232 770; fax 232 760), a 10 minute walk from the Old Town at Vytenio 9/25. This sparkling hotel with lots of glass and blue steel is becoming increasingly popular with western business people and tourists. Singles/doubles start at 180/260 litų and the larger rooms go for 320/440 litų.

North of the River

The face of Vilnius' largest and ugliest hotel, the *Lietuva* (☎ 726 090; fax 722 130; email lietuva@aiva.lt), at Ukmergės 20, has changed a little since Soviet times when western visitors were obliged to stay here. It is still ugly, but only from the outside. Extensive renovations have transformed it into a reasonable hotel offering all the facilities –

sauna, swimming pool, beauty parlour, a choice of restaurants and more – attracting tour groups in their droves. Singles/doubles are not badly priced at 300/360 litų; rooms on the 17th VIP floor are almost double the price. The hotel has a 24 hour currency exchange, popular Jet-Set nightclub and unbeatable news kiosk selling western daily newspapers.

Just as popular with tour groups is the tower block next-door, which is the *Naujasis Vilnius* (☎ 726 756; fax 723 161; email hotelnv@is.et). Unrenovated singles/doubles with private bathrooms are still good value at 200/240 litų and the in-house restaurant gets very good reports. The more expensive rooms on the sixth and seventh floors are all renovated to five star western standards.

Smaller, more cosy middle-range hotels include the Swedish-run *Victoria* (☎ 724 013; fax 724 320) at Saltoniškių 56, which has comfortable singles/doubles with private bathrooms for 230/300 litų a night. Singles/doubles at the *Pušis* (☎ 721 863; fax 721 305), within walking distance of Vingis Park at Blindžių 17, cost 100/140 litų. Slightly more expensive but worth it for its magnificent location inside a 'palace' is the *Pilaitė* (☎ 752 292; fax 752 269) at Kalvarijų 1. Singles/doubles are quite small and there are only 10 of them, but they are quite reasonable at 240/320 litų.

PLACES TO STAY – TOP END

Vilnius' top hotels tend to have few rooms, and are often booked out months ahead.

Old Town & Gedimino prospektas

Tucked away down the Old Town's cobbled streets, there are a handful of really delightful little family-run places which are hard to fault. Among the most exclusive is the *AAA Mano Liza Guest House* (☎ 222 225; fax 222 608), overlooking a pretty green square at Ligoninės 5. Its eight rooms are beautifully furnished, complete with real double beds (most hotels simply push two singles together), a decent-sized desk, TV and en

suite bathroom. Each room is individually priced but the cheapest is 320 litų.

Close by, in a courtyard off Aušros Vartų, is *Grybas House* (☎ 619 695; fax 222 416). It has six suites, ranging in price from 440 to 560 litų depending on the window view (the courtyard view is the most expensive). Breakfast is served in the cosy cellar bar and the host family arranges city tours in English.

The German-managed *Mabre Residence Hotel* (☎ 222 087; fax 613 086) at Maironio 13 is in a former Orthodox monastery, near St Anne's Church, which has been converted into a 23 room hotel. Singles/doubles cost 300/340 litų. The Mabre team also runs the equally prestigious *City Park* hotel (☎ 223 515; fax 617 745) at Stuokas-Gucevičiaus 3. Despite its prime location opposite the cathedral, none of the rooms has a 'cathedral view'. A simple single/double with all the mod cons is 300/360 litų and an even more spacious luxury room costs 600 litų.

Outstripping them all in price and prestige, however, is the *Stikliai* hotel (☎ 627 971; email stikliai@mail.tipas.lt). Vilnius' pride and joy, it is tucked down a picture-postcard cobbled street in the heart of the Old Town at Gaono 7. Singles/doubles cost a staggering 560/640 litų but are actually well worth it if you have the cash.

One to look out for is the promised *Radisson-SAS* hotel, set to open by late 1997 in the former Astorija hotel, which dates back to 1901. Since the mid-1990s this classical building overlooking St Casimir's Church in the Old Town at Didžioji 35 has stood sadly neglected. The new hotel will open with 60 rooms, possibly extending to 150 within two years, and will house a bar, restaurant and business centre.

North of the River

If you're into basketball stay at the *Šarūnas* (☎ 723 888; fax 724 355), east of the Žaliasis bridge at Raitininkų 4, built by Lithuanian basketball god Šarūnas Marčiulionis. True fans can even gaze adoringly at – or smell – his discarded sports shoes that hang in the hotel bar along with the rest of his team's unwanted footwear. Singles/doubles cost 280/329 litų.

Handy if you're in town for an exhibition at Lit-Expo is the *Karolina* hotel (☎ 268 934; fax 269 341), which has the only indoor tennis courts in town as well as a top Chinese restaurant. Singles/doubles with all the perks cost 280/320 litų.

Out of Town The 75 room *Villon* hotel (☎ 505 200; fax 651 385), a Lithuanian-British joint venture on the Rīga road, 19 km north of Vilnius, outstrips anywhere in the city for facilities; it's just the out-of-town location which is not the greatest. Set between two lakes, it has a restaurant, night-club, casino, swimming pool, fitness centre, riding, sauna, fishing, boating, hairdresser and a shuttle bus to/from the city. Singles/doubles are 232/368 litų.

PLACES TO EAT

Dining out in Vilnius is a rich and rewarding experience. Unlike the other Baltic capitals, the dramatic influx of western-style restaurants serving ethnic cuisines from all over the world has done little to thwart Lithuania's traditional kitchen. Local dishes at a variety of prices are still easy to come by in Vilnius, making any trip to the Lithuanian capital that much more fun.

It is substantially cheaper to eat out here than in Rīga or Tallinn. A decent main course can still be had for around US$4. Note that new places are opening all the time.

Restaurants

Lithuanian For the most authentic Lithuanian experience you're ever likely to encounter anywhere, look no further than *Ritos Smuklė* (☎ 770 786), north of the city centre at Žirmūnų 68. The owner, Rita Dapkutė, is an American-Lithuanian who worked for Vytautas Landsbergis in the independence period and 'freelanced' for the KGB with the approval of the CIA. Her restaurant serves strictly Lithuanian fodder made from strictly Lithuanian produce, meaning that Coca-Cola, Marlboro cigarettes and Soviet-introduced champagne are completely banned. The traditional ale peas, garlic bread and beet broth with 'ears' are all yummy and while, in true Lithuanian style, you occasionally have to drain off the grease before you attempt to eat what you've ordered, it all adds to the enjoyment of the experience! Wild folk bands play every weekend. It's open daily from 11 am to 2 pm. To get there take bus No 12 from outside the cathedral and get off at the Žirmūnai stop.

Overlooking the cathedral at the east end of Gedimino prospektas, is *Literatų Svetainė* (☎ 611 889), one of Vilnius' glorious pre-independence restaurants which is still going strong. It's open daily from noon to midnight and is well worth a visit. Apparently it was from here that the Polish-Lithuanian poet and Nobel prize winner, Czesław Miłosz, watched the Red Army march into Vilnius in June 1940. *Gryčia*, a minute's walk away on the corner of Tilto and Vrublevskio gatvė, is a small, modern restaurant serving country-style dishes in a wooden interior. It serves traditional gira (a drink made from brown rye bread) instead of contemporary alcoholic drinks and is one of the few places in town with disabled access. It opens daily from 11 am to 11 pm.

Set in a maze of cellars in the Old Town at Stiklių 8 is another classic – although vegetarians might be better to avoid it as a large, stuffed bear does watch you dine! *Lokys* (the Bear, ☎ 629 046) serves a variety of wholesome meat and game dishes, including the wild boar that is the house speciality. You pay extra for bread, and dishes are strictly weighed and listed on the handwritten menu in grams. The blynai (pancakes) with cheese or chocolate are absolutely delicious – and cheap at 9 litų. Another cellar establishment, with fair food at similar prices and a great interior, is the *Medininkai* at Aušros Vartų 4. The place was all the rage during the Soviet era and, while its popularity died a speedy death following independence, in recent months it has made a comeback among tourists seeking a blast from the past.

A modern-day Lithuanian restaurant which has been packed since it opened in

1996 is *1901 Užeiga* at Aušros Vartų 11. Crammed with relics, this sitting room-style restaurant with one of the best summer courtyards (could almost be Portugal!), serves great stuffed chicken for 11 litų and 'cold noses' (sweet ravioli in sour cream) for 8 litų among other things. It is also one of the best places in town for a porridge breakfast (open weekdays from 8 am to midnight and weekends 11 am to midnight).

For giant-sized cepelinai try *Stikliai Aludė* (☎ 222 109) at Gaono 7. Run by the legendary Stikliai team responsible for opening the first co-operative café in the former Soviet Union (it's now closed), this upmarket beer-bar-cum-restaurant serves traditional Lithuanian dishes amid a contemporary setting. Expect to pay at least 35 litų for a main course.

Other Cuisines For a cheap and cheerful meal guaranteed to fill there are two obvious options. Both are British-run and have been packed since they revolutionised the dining scene in 1995. *The PUB* (open daily from 8 am to 2 am), in the Old Town at Dominikonų 9, dishes up shepherd's pie, lasagne, Lithuanian black garlic bread, shaslik, and a whole host of other mammoth-sized meals for around 10 litų. More upmarket is *Prie Parlamento* at Gedimino 46 whose specialities include steaks for 18 litų and yummy chocolate brownies and crumbles for 9 litų.

Offsetting these is a host of colourful off-beat eating places, each of which compete to be the most outrageous. *Savas Kampas* at Vokiečių 4 sports the most daring colour scheme, serving delicious salads for 7 to 12 litų and great mozzarella-stuffed pancakes topped with a spicy tomato sauce for 11 litų (open daily from noon to 3 am).

Metaxa at Gedimino 32a (open weekdays from 10 am to midnight and weekends from noon to midnight) and *Gero Viskio Baras* at Pilies 28 (open daily from 10 am to midnight), are run by the same Lithuanian team that also happens to be Lithuania's biggest liqueur importer. Both are equally fun and serve the best salads and stuffed chicken (with pears, ham or cheese) in town.

Bix, at Etmonų 6, was formed by the Lithuanian hard-rock band Bix. At the time, its avant-garde, industrial-style decor was almost as shocking as its menu – 'chicken with promise to fly', 'chew chew pig' and 'ecstasy' are just some of their delights.

The most hard-hitting of them all is the military-inspired *NATO's* at Pasažo skg 2 (open daily from noon to 3 am). 'When muses and arms are silent, it is NATO's that inspires' it claims. The black interior with various military memorabilia splattered over the walls may have inspired NATO's secretary-general to pop in during an official visit to Vilnius in spring 1996.

The first fun place to open in Vilnius, *Ritos Sléptuvé* at Goštauto 8, run by the same Rita who runs Ritos Smuklė, retains the same glorious retro-US-meets-USSR style, but it's no longer as hot as it used to be. The menu features breakfast dishes, chilli, salads, steaks, lasagne and other pastas, and pizzas – including true Chicago-style deep-pan pizzas which take 45 minutes to cook and must be at least four inches thick (open daily 7.30 am to 2 am).

Vilnius also boasts a fine array of more formal, expensive restaurants. The most widely known are the Stikliai establishments. The restaurant of the *Hotel Stikliai*, next to the Stikliai Aludė at Gaono 7, specialises in French cuisine as well as the customary caviar-pancake dishes for which they are so well known; *Ponių Laimė*, at Gedimino 31, seems to feature a bit of everything; *Capriccio Italiano*, inside the Šarūnas hotel, is Italian orientated; and *Geltona Upė* (☎ 222 875), at Stiklių 18, serves Chinese fare. All four are lavishly furnished, cost at least 100 litų a head and are open daily from noon to midnight. Other Chinese restaurants serving less refined meals at a lesser price include the *Auksinis Drakonas* (Golden Dragon, ☎ 262 701) at Aguonų 11, which is open daily from noon to 10 pm, and the *Sidabrinis Drakonas* (Silver Dragon, ☎ 221 296) at Didžioji 40, which is open daily from 11 am to 11 pm.

For expensive German fare, try *Idabasar* (☎ 628 484) at Subačiaus 3. A typical meal in the upstairs restaurant is about 100 litų a head; in the downstairs 'cellar bar' it is slightly cheaper. Both open daily from 11 am to midnight.

Traditional Hungarian dishes are served in the cellar of *Trys Draugai* (☎ 222 455), also in the Old Town at Pilies 25a. The 'Three Friends' is actually spread over three levels, covering a variety of other ethnic cuisines (as well as Hungarian) – the origins of the other cuisines dependant on what ingredients have been imported to Lithuania that month. It is open daily from noon to midnight.

Another place relying pretty much on imported products is the Mexican *Vidudienis* (☎ 628 089) at Gedimino 5. The funky interior sports different furnishings in each of the four halls – ranging from a pretty raunchy calf-skin look, to a fantastical 'Alice in Wonderland' garden feel. The menu is equally salacious with main dishes costing around 35 litų. Don't get excited by the word 'spicy' – it simply translates as lots of garlic (open daily from noon to 5 am).

A couple of run-of-the-mill, expensive places mainly frequented by a Russian nouveau riche crowd include the *Raudona-Juoda* (Red-Black, ☎ 620 685) restaurant at Gedimino 14; and *Markus ir Ko* (☎ 623 185) on Antokolskio gatvė. A favourite for its fish dishes is *Juodasis Riteris* (Black Knight, ☎ 611 070) at Pilies 16. All three open daily from noon to midnight.

Practically all of the larger hotels have decent restaurants too.

Cafés

Afrika, halfway between the cathedral and the Gates of Dawn at Pilies 28, is bright, cheerful and popular with the local art scene. Its sliced meat cooked on a spit (gyros) is particularly good, along with its delicious home-made soups for 4 litų and staggering choice of salads for around 5 litų (open daily from 9 am to 8 pm).

Kavinė F, further up Pilies gatvė at Aušros vartų 5, has some of the best cakes and pastries in town; aside maybe from *Kaktusas*, on the outskirts of the Old Town at Totorių 3, which serves the widest and freshest range of sweet-toothed temptations in town. The coffee at the 'cactus' is thick, strong and served weekdays from 9 am to 9 pm, and weekends from 11 am to 9 pm.

For Lithuanian cuisine at dirt-cheap prices try *Koldūninė Ravioli*, close to the Kalvarijų market at Kalvarijų 13, where you can sample meat or cheese stuffed ravioli cushions (koldūnai) for around 7 litų. *Litotė*, down a side street off Vilniaus gatvė at Labdarių 4, open daily from 11 am to 9 pm, is extremely popular locally for the mammoth portions it serves at rock bottom prices. You can eat to full capacity (and still leave food on your plate) for no more than 10 litų.

Equally popular is *Gabi* in the Old Town at Mykolo 6. You are not allowed to smoke here but that does not seem to deter the people who pour in every lunchtime to fight for a table. The plov (fried rice with meat and vegetables), for 8 litų, is particularly good, but it tastes better without the tomato ketchup they douse over it (unless you specifically state otherwise!).

The clean and modern *Baltų Ainiai* at Savičiaus 12 (off Didžioji gatvė), has lots of blynai (pancakes), good coffee, and cepelinai too. You cannot light up here either.

Vegetarians have a couple of choices, both of which are also extraordinarily cheap and quite decent too. The Hare Krishna canteen, *Vediniai Valgiai*, close to the train station at Kauno 2/21, serves wholesome dishes for around 7 litų (open weekdays from 10.30 am to 6 pm). The second-floor *Erš Kėtuogė*, inside a health centre on Bernardinų gatvė, offers a daily special for around 6 litų as well as a choice of salads, beanburgers and stews. Complimentary pumpkin seeds are on every table and you can also get gira here.

For a touch of Polish Vilnius, try *Znad Wilii*, inside a Polish art gallery at Išganytojo 2/4 (open daily from 11 am to 6 pm). Another little-known gem is the Caucasian *Achtamar*, close to the Basinavičiaus flower market at Konarskio 1. It is a tiny place which specialises in a variety of freshly flame-grilled šašlykas (chunks of meat on a spit), cooked to your taste in a little courtyard round the back. The really tasty dolma (stuffed vine leaves) served with a 'lethal' garlic sauce are worth a try too. It opens daily from 10 am to 10 pm.

Pizzerias & Fast Food

The Italian-run *Venezia* (☎ 221 432) at Pilies 16, serves pizza, as good as anywhere you'll find, for around 15 litų, as well as a good range of tasty pasta dishes and soups. The rich and meaty soup is quite superb and well worth the 6 litų. It also makes pizza to take away (open daily from 8.30 am to midnight). It has another outlet, *Roma*, not far from the bus station at Pylimo 21b, which is reportedly not as good.

Overlooking the river, next to the Pilaité hotel, is the *Pulčinela* pizzeria at Kalvarijų 1, which serves pizza with an imaginative range of toppings to tempt your tastebuds including peaches and pineapples. It opens daily from 10 am to 11 pm.

Despite its Italian-sounding name, *Pizzeria Milano* in the Old Town at Rūdininkų 14, offers little to get excited about. It's open daily from 10 am to midnight, does takeaway too and is generally empty.

For home delivered American-style pizza, the faithful Rita of Sleptuvė and Smuklė is your best bet. Her delivery service *Ritos Virtuvė* (☎ 620 589), which offers the full range of pizzas served in the Sleptuvė, runs daily from 10 am to 2 am

McDonald's is impossible to miss. There are outlets opposite the train station and close to the cathedral at Gedimino 15 (both open daily from 8 am to midnight), as well as drive-in stations on the main Rīga-Vilnius roads at Ukmergės 177 and on Kareivių 15 (both open daily from 8 am to 11 pm). Two more outlets will open by the end of 1997.

Submarinai, another Rita venture, is a kiosk on the corner of Gedimino prospektas opposite the cathedral, which does superb takeaway hot chicken submarine sandwiches for 10 litų.

Self Catering

Šviežia Duona, at Savanorių 6, is the best place for traditional Lithuanian rye bread (bočių). Fresh milk straight from the cow's udder, home-made honey and smoked eel are just some of the culinary delights to be found at *Kalvarijų market* at Kalvarijų 6 (open daily, except Monday, from 7 am to noon). There is a smaller market on Bazilijonų gatvė (not far from the train station).

French-owned *Iki* supermarkets, which stock every importable and local product imaginable, have outlets on Žirmūnų 68 and Architektų 43/31, among others. The one at Žirmūnai has an authentic French bakery inside. For locally produced and imported alcoholic drinks try *Mineraliniai Vandenys* located next to the Metaxa restaurant at Gedimino 32.

ENTERTAINMENT

Given the generally casual and laid-back attitude of Vilnius' going-out scene, there is often a fine line between restaurants, bars and even clubs! Top drinking (as well as eating) holes include The PUB, Prie Parlamento and Bix (see Places to Eat).

A contemporary cultural centre complete with bar and club is planned for the old cinema building on the corner of Didžioji and Savičiaus.

Here is a list of bars and clubs:

Armadillo
  Gedimino 26 – Tex-Mex pool hall; open daily until 5 am
Geležinis Kablys
  Kauno 5 – known locally as the 'Hook House' because of the very large hook that is suspended outside; plays strictly live music; open daily, except Monday and Tuesday, until 6 am
Indigo
  Trakų 3/2 – the newest club in town with all the makings of a hip 'n' groovy London club: retro canteen on the ground floor, dancefloor on the second, cocktail bar on the third and chessboard-painted tables in the courtyard outside; open weekdays until 3 am and weekends until 5 a
Klubas Ekstra
  Laisvės 55 – out-of-town alternative club with a steel decor; open until 6 am at weekends
Langas
  Ašmenos 8 – live jazz or rock concerts kick off most evenings at 8 pm

LITHUANIA

Max Dance World
Justiniškių 64 – avoid if you're not into techno; a bit out of town; open until 3 am at weekends
Ministerija
Gedimino 46 – mainstream nightclub in the cellar of Prie Parlamento; *the* place to be seen; Sunday afternoon jazz sessions from 2 to 4 pm and cheaper students night every Monday; open daily from 11 to 4 am. (The same team plans to open 'the funkiest bar-cum-club-cum-restaurant' in town in the 15th century Gothic cellars beneath the old town hall on Rotušės aikštė, entrance from Didžioji.)

Naktinis Vilkas
Lukiškių aikštė 3 – Vilnius' first purpose-built Soviet club capturing the whole Soviet experience down to newspaper squares for toilet paper (as a compromise it offers real toilet paper too)
Nasa
Laisvės 58 – western-style nightclub in a large, grey Soviet block out of town; open until 6 am at weekends
Ritos Sleptuvė
Goštauto 8 – small (always packed) dance floor and bar adjoining the restaurant, open until 4 am at weekends

Getting the Last Laugh

Five years ago the Balts' top priority was to shed their Soviet past as quickly as possible. Streets were renamed, hammer and sickle emblems unscrewed; and the hated Lenins, Stalins and other Red Army monuments axed with a vengeance and dumped on the scrapheap of history.

Today it is becoming one big joke – at least for Machine Gun Anna's punters and the other bright young sparks cashing in on the late-90s wave of Soviet nostalgia. If this resurgence had been predicted 10 years ago no one would have believed it, and indeed, for many Balts, it is all still a little too close for comfort. But the fact remains, those once detested symbols of Soviet power are making something of a mock comeback in the Baltic states.

It is not only foreign clients that are captivated. In fact, Vilnius' Naktinis Vilkas nightclub, where Machine Gun Anna struts her stuff, draws a predominantly local crowd. Kitted out in full Red Army attire, the Machine Gun gets stuck into her cabaret floor show while punters at the bar down vodka in those horrible old tumblers salvaged from Soviet canteens. Soldiers' sandwiches made from dry black bread with a variety of uninspiring Soviet fillings, are one of the not-so-hot items on the menu, served by waitresses casually dressed in Soviet paratroopers' undershirts.

The decor of Lithuania's first retro-Soviet club is equally incredible. Red is the key colour. There's a model MiG fighter plane on the dance floor, and in the toilets Leonid Brezhnev's interminable Party Congress speeches play when you pull the chain. Oh ... and there are even squares of newspaper instead of soft 'n' smelly toilet paper for those determined to get to the bottom of the authentic Soviet experience.

Communism is likewise dead and buried for those who frequent Rīga's Mārrutku Maizītes café (literally Horseradish Sandwiches), but here too, the Party is far from flagging. Lenin's portrait, a bust of Marx, open sandwiches and vodka sold at rock-bottom prices are all part of the show. Soviet classics crackle out of a cranky old turntable and an abacus sits on the side for bills to be totted up. The Groks Stacija nightclub in Rīga's Old Town is decked out like a Soviet train; and in Tallinn, the wooden benches in the Wagon Lits café opposite the train station recreate the uncomfortable atmosphere of local commuter trains.

And then of course, there is the question of coming up with some new idols to replace those fallen heroes. Lithuania has already found a few. In Vilnius, at a bar called NATO, homage is paid to the defensive alliance its country is so keen to join. Indeed, when NATO Secretary-General Javier Solana visited Vilnius in spring 1996, it was here that he met the Lithuanian defence minister and held a press conference. In the sports world, the American rock band Grateful Dead has topped the charts ever since it sponsored T-shirts for the Lithuanian basketball team, which won a bronze medal at the Barcelona Olympics in 1992.

Finally, there is Frank Zappa. The statue of the American rock 'n' roll legend, said to be the first of its kind in the world, was created by a Lithuanian sculptor prized for his Soviet realist statues. It was unveiled in Vilnius outside a medical clinic by the Lithuanian Frank Zappa fan club in 1995. Unlike the stony-faced Soviet times though, even the authorities seem to have a sense of humour these days. At the inauguration ceremony of the statue dedicated to a man famed for his anti-establishment songs, the Vilnius Municipality sent along the local police orchestra to play.

It seems the Baltic people might be getting the last laugh after all. ■

LITHUANIA

Tobira
Mykolo 4 – Japanese karaoke bar

Cinema

The Lietuva cinema (☎ 623 422) at Pylimo 17, the Vilnius cinema (☎ 612 676) at Gedimino 5a, and the Skalvija (☎ 610 505) at Goštauto 2, screen films in English daily. The British Council (☎ 616 607), at Vilniaus 39, arranges British film weeks. The week-long French film festival, organised by the French embassy, is held every autumn.

Classical Music, Opera, Ballet & Theatre

The Lithuania Chamber Orchestra, the Kaunas State Choir (Kauno Valstybinis Choras) and the Lithuanian State Symphony Orchestra (Lietuvos Valstybinis Simfoninis Orkestras) all have good reputations. Big concerts are usually given at the Opera & Ballet Theatre (☎ 620 636) at Vienuolio 1, whose resident companies perform a wide range of mainly classical opera and ballet.

Tickets for most classical concerts are sold at the National Philharmonic (Nacionalinė Filharmonija, ☎ 627 165) ticket office at Aušros Vartų 5.

Tickets cost between 4 and 15 litų depending on the seat and performance. The ticket office is open Tuesday to Friday from 1 to 6 pm. There are no performances from mid-June to mid-September when it takes a summer break. Concerts are held in a variety of places round town, however, including the Music Academy (☎ 610 144) at Gedimino 42, the Arsenal Museum (☎ 628 080) at Arsenalo 2, and St John's Church in the Old Town.

The main theatres staging a variety of Lithuanian and foreign plays in Lithuanian are the Academic Drama Theatre (Akademinis dramos teatras) at Gedimino 4 and the currently more popular Youth Theatre (Jaunimo teatras) at Arklių 5. There are also one or two smaller experimental theatre groups, plus the Russian Drama Theatre at Basanavičiaus 13.

THINGS TO BUY

For general information of what types of things you can buy, see the introductory Facts for the Visitor chapter.

At weekends, Pilies gatvė is transformed into a bustling arts and crafts market. A small number of traders also sell their wares during the week; the painters always hang out at the southern end of Pilies.

Vilnius' top souvenir shop is Sauluva in a courtyard at Pilies 22. It sells an amazing selection of Verbos (traditional woven dried flowers crafted to celebrate Palm Sunday) all year round, as well as some fine wooden toys, amber jewellery, handmade puppets and glassware.

For amber, try the Amber Gallery at Aušros Vartų 11 or Sage at Aušros Vartų 15. The Astrominerologijos Centras at Basanavičiaus 4 has a good collection of rocks and minerals.

Vilnius' former Soviet department stores are at Ukmergės 16, in the precinct by the Lietuva hotel, and at Gediminas 18. Putting them both to shame is Vilniaus Centrine Gastronomas, a contemporary, flashy three-storey department store at Gedimino 24 (open daily from 8 am to 10 pm).

GETTING THERE & AWAY

See the introductory Getting There & Away chapter for detail on links with countries outside the Baltic states, which includes flights to/from several western and CIS cities, and trains and buses to/from France, Germany, Poland, Russia and Belarus.

Air

Air Baltic flies five times weekly to/from Rīga. A return ticket to Rīga costs 580 litų but you have to stay in Rīga for a weekend. A return ticket with no restrictions is 900 litų and a one-way fare is 440 litų.

Estonian Air flies daily to/from Tallinn. The return fare from Vilnius to Tallinn is 760 litų if you buy the ticket seven days in advance and stay in Tallinn for a weekend. A return ticket midweek with a minimum two-day stay is 1509 litų. Estonian Air also does a one-way/return youth fare (valid if you're between 13 and 24) costing 379/759 litų.

LITHUANIA

Air Baltic plans a future stopover in Vilnius on its current Rīga-Minsk flights.

If you're buying an international air ticket in Vilnius, it is worth trying one or two other travel agents to see if they can do anything cheaper than the airlines themselves. If you are 26 or under, try the Lithuanian Student and Youth Travel (see Information – Travel Agencies).

The airport *(oro uostas)* is five km south of the centre in the suburb of Kirtimai. For information call ☎ 669 481 (international) or ☎ 630 201, 635 560.

Airline offices in Vilnius include:

Aeroflot
    Tauro 8/30 (☎ 621 834)
Air Baltic
    Airport (☎ 236 000, 233 202)
Air Kiev
    Pylimo 6 (☎ 227 208)
Air Lithuania
    Tilto 2a (☎ 227 013)
Austrian Airlines, SAS
    Airport (☎ 236 000, 233 202)
Finnair
    Rūdininkų 18/2 (☎ 619 339)
Hamburg Airlines
    Airport (☎ 262 251)
Lithuanian Airlines (LAL)
    Ukmergės 12 (☎ 752 588, 753 212); Airport
    (☎ 233 345)
LOT
    Room 104, Hotel Skrydis at the airport
    (☎ 260 819, 632 772)
Lufthansa
    Airport (☎ 636 049, 262 222)
SAS
    Airport (☎ 236 000)

Bus

The bus station *(autobusų stotis*, ☎ 262 482, 262 483) is south of the Old Town at Sodų 22, next to the train station. The ticket hall for buses within Lithuania faces you as you enter; the one on your right is for tickets for international destinations including Poland, Belarus, Estonia, Latvia and to the west. Schedules are clearly displayed both here (where white letters on a red background indicate a coach, green letters a microbus), and on the platform. Confirm the times at the

helpful *Informacija* (window No 1) in the booking hall.

Out on the platform, the left-hand side is for buses to nearby destinations (including Trakai). On these, you pay on board. For the long-distance red buses on the right-hand side, you need a ticket unless the bus is in transit, in which case you may have to scrum for a seat when it pulls in. When you buy a ticket at the station, your seat number is marked on the ticket under *Vieta*, and the bus stop number under *Aikštele*.

Tickets for some buses to Poland and the west are also sold by the Varita bus company (☎ 730 219, 733 793; fax 723 884), next to the Lietuva hotel at Ukmergės 12a (open weekdays from 9 am to 6 pm).

A comprehensive bus timetable *(Autobusų Eismo Tvarkaraščiai)* can be bought for 4 litų at the Vilnius bus station ticket windows.

Buses to destinations within the Baltic states and the Kaliningrad Region include:

Bauska
    225 km, 4¼ hours, five buses daily, 19.70 litų
Druskininkai
    125 km, 2 hours, five direct buses daily, 11.80 litų
Ignalina
    110 km, 2½ hours, one bus daily, 13 litų
Kaliningrad
    350 km; 8¼ hours; two buses nightly via Chernyakhovsk and Marijampolė, or Sovietsk and Jurbarkas; 33.90 litų
Kaunas
    100 km, two hours, about 30 buses daily, 9.40 litų (also 12 microbuses daily, 1¾ hours)
Klaipėda
    310 km, five hours, nine buses daily, 23.10 litų
Lazdijai
    150 km, three hours, nine buses daily, 11.20 litų
Molėtai
    75 km, 1½ hours, four buses daily, 8.60 litų
Palanga
    340 km, six hours, more than 15 buses daily, 28 litų
Panevėžys
    140 km, 2¼ hours, about 30 buses daily, 12.60 litų
Rīga
    290 km, six hours, five buses daily, 27 litų
Šiauliai
    220 km, 4½ hours, about four buses daily by various routes, 19.10 litų

Tallinn
    600 km, 12 hours, one bus nightly, 67.40 litų
Trakai
    30 km, 45 minutes, more than 30 buses daily, 3 litų

Train

The train station (*geležinkelio stotis*, ☎ 630 088, 630 086) is next to the bus station at Geležinkelio 16. There is a left-luggage room here too.

Tickets for domestic trains and long-distance trains to Latvia, Russia, Kaliningrad and Belarus are sold in the main station ticket hall as you enter the main station building. You can also buy a ticket for your return journey here, which is particularly recommended if, for example, you are travelling to St Petersburg (where you still have to queue for hours at a ticket booth reserved specially for foreigners). Timetables are clearly displayed here in English. There is an English-speaking information booth (open daily from 8 am to midnight) to the right of the ticket windows in the main hall.

Tickets for departures to Poland and the west are sold at the international desk in the ticket hall to the right of the main ticket hall. Next to the international desk, there is a small tourist information office (open weekdays from 10 am to 5 pm). This office does not actually provide regular tourist information but rather dishes out tickets and information on discounted ScanRail travel passes (see Getting There & Away at the front of the book). If the office is closed, go to the Lithuanian Student & Youth Travel, or the West Express travel agency.

Services Train services between the Baltics have been cut in recent years. There is no longer any rail link between Vilnius and Tallinn, and there is just one train nightly from Vilnius to Rīga (eight hours, 71 litų).

Other direct services from Vilnius within the Baltic states and the Kaliningrad Region include:

Daugavpils
    175 km, three to 3½ hours, four trains (some terminating at St Petersburg) daily, 29 litų
Druskininkai
    125 km, 2½ to 3½ hours, two trains daily, 10.20 litų
Ignalina
    110 km, two hours, nine trains (some terminating at St Petersburg) daily, 9 litų
Kaliningrad
    350 km, 5¼ to 6¼ hours, one train daily, 25 litų
Kaunas
    100 km, 1¼ to 2¼ hours, 18 trains (some terminating at Šeštokai, Klaipėda, Rīga or Kaliningrad) daily, 9 litų

LITHUANIA

Flower Power

There's an old saying from the Soviet days that goes something like: 'It's impossible, but if you really want it...' Traveller **Derek Emson** from the UK was treated to a classic example of the ingenuity that this implies (and of the Baltic peoples' frequent willingness to help foreigners) when he went down to Vilnius bus station to get a ticket to Warsaw.

I got into a conversation with a young Lithuanian medical student whose name, Šinšinaitis, sounded like it had come out of a medical book itself. The queue at the ticket office was long and hardly moving, so he said he would help me.

The door into the ticket office was unlocked so he entered and closed it behind him. Some minutes later he emerged saying we had to buy a rose. 'A rose, what for?' I asked myself as we went outside the bus station to a flower stall. Šinšinaitis explained that we had to buy one for the woman in the ticket office because then she would sell me a ticket straight away. 'I'll get her two,' I said, thinking it might make the deal an absolute certainty. 'No, you must buy one, three or five,' he said. 'Oh, OK, get three.'

There was an uneasy silence as we waited outside the door, which had been locked during our absence. But soon two women came along with a key to let themselves in and Šinšinaitis slipped in with them. He emerged once again, only this time accompanied by a middle-aged woman, who was smiling radiantly and clutching three roses in one hand and a ticket in the other. ■

Klaipėda
    350 km, 6¾ or 9¾ hours, four trains daily, 55 litų
Šiauliai
    200 km, 4½ hours, one train daily, 21 litų
Trakai
    30 km, 40 minutes, seven trains daily, 2 litų

Car & Motorcycle

Numerous 24 hour petrol stations run by the western oil companies Neste, Shell, Statoil and Texaco selling western-grade fuel, including unleaded petrol and diesel, are dotted at strategic points all over the city and across the country. In town, Statoil runs stations at Goštauto 13 and Geležinio vilko 2a. Most western car manufacturers are represented in Vilnius and sport showrooms and repair services.

Here is a list of car rental companies in Vilnius:

Avis
    Inside the Hotel Naujasis Vilnius, Ukmergės 14 (☎ 733 226, 733 005)
Europcar
    Vilnius Airport & Vilniaus 2/15 (☎ 222 739)
Hertz
    Ukmergės 2 (☎ 726 940)
Litinterp
    Bernardinų 7-2 (☎ 223 850, 223 291; email litinterp@post.omnitel.net)
Rimas
    (☎ 77 62 13, 8-298-21662)

GETTING AROUND
The Airport

Vilnius airport is five km south of the centre, off Dariaus ir Girėno gatvė in the suburb of Kirtimai at Rodūnė skelias 2. Bus No 1 runs between the airport and train station about 35 times a day between 5.50 am and 11.50 pm. Bus No 2 runs between the airport and the north-western suburb of Šeškinė via the Žaliasis (Green) bridge over the Neris, just north of the city centre, and past the Lietuva hotel. A taxi from the airport to the city centre should be about 15 litų but you'll probably be asked to pay exceedingly more. Bargain!

Bus & Trolleybus

Most routes run from about 5.30 or 6 am to around midnight. Bus and trolleybus tickets cost 0.75 litų and are sold in most news kiosks. Unpunched tickets warrant a hefty 20 litų on-the-spot fine.

Taxi

Taxis officially charge 1.20 litų a km but it is rare that you'll get that. Former state taxis (all pale blue or yellow Volgas) are the best as they have meters which the drivers can be persuaded to use. A five minute journey across town should cost no more than 10 litų.

There are taxi ranks located outside the train station, and in front of the old Town Hall on Didžioji gatvė. The cheapest type of taxis are those that you call by telephone (☎ 228 888).

Around Vilnius

There are four obvious day trips from Vilnius – three pleasant, the other appalling.

PANERIAI

The WWII Nazi 'death camp' of Paneriai is 10 km south-west of central Vilnius. Over 100,000 people were murdered in this forest between July 1941 and July 1944, and some 70,000 of them were Jews from Vilnius and around. About half the city's Jewish population – about 35,000 people – had already been massacred here by the end of the first three months of the German occupation (June to September 1941). Lithuanian accomplices are reported to have done at least as much of the killing as their German masters.

The entrance to the forest – now more of a wooded site – is marked by a memorial, the **Panerių Memorialas**, with text in Hebrew, Lithuanian and Russian, states that 70,000 of the victims here were Jews. In the Soviet period the victims were all referred to simply as 'Soviet citizens'.

A path leads down to the small but terrible **Paneriai Museum** (Panerių muziejus), open daily, except Tuesday, from 11 am to 6 pm, and two monuments – one Jewish, one Soviet. From here other paths lead to a number of grassed-over pits among the trees where, from December 1943, the Nazis burnt the exhumed bodies of their victims in order to hide the evidence of their crimes. One of the deeper pits, according to its sign, was where they kept those who were forced to dig up the corpses and pulverise the bones.

Getting There & Away

Bus No 8 from Vilnius train station runs to Aukštieji Paneriai about every 15 minutes throughout the day. It follows Savanorių prospektas then climbs a hill; the bus turns left on to Galvės gatvė, then left again along Vilijos gatvė and stops at the end, near a footbridge. Get off the bus, cross the footbridge, and turn right along the street on the far side of the rail tracks, Agrastų gatvė, which leads straight to the site, about 900m away.

Some suburban trains also run from Vilnius to Paneriai station, which is on Agrastų gatvė, a couple of hundred metres east of the footbridge already mentioned.

TRAKAI
• ☎ (238)

The old Lithuanian capital, Trakai, with its two lakeside castles, is 28 km west of Vilnius. Gediminas may have made it his capital in the 1320s while Kęstutis certainly made it his base later in the 14th century. The castles were built to fend off the German knights. Today Trakai – the centre of the Trakai National Park spanning 8200 hectares – is a small, quiet town in an attractive country area of lakes and islands.

Orientation & Information

Most of the town stands on a two-km-long, north-pointing tongue of land between Lake Luka to its east and Lake Totoriškių to its west. A third lake, Lake Galvė, opens out from the north end of the peninsula. From the train station at the south end of town, Vytauto gatvė leads 400m north to a square where you'll find the bus station, then continues north up the peninsula for about 1.25 km until it becomes Karaimų gatvė.

The national park runs an information centre (☎ 52 833) close to the peninsula castle at Kęstučio 1. It sells maps of Trakai, arranges guided tours of the park and issues fishing and camping permits. There is also a tourist information office (☎ & fax 51 934) at Vytauto 69. Both are open weekdays from 9 am to 6 pm. The central bookstore is at Vytauto 46.

Peninsula Castle

The ruins of Trakai's peninsula castle, destroyed in the 17th century, are towards the north end of town, in a park close to the eastern shore of the peninsula. It's thought to have been built in 1362-82 by Grand Duke Vytautas' father, Kęstutis. Turn down Kęstučio gatvė, off Karaimų gatvė, to reach it.

Karaites

The peninsula is dotted with old wooden cottages, many of them built by the Karaites (Karaimai) – a Judaist sect originating in Baghdad, which adheres to the Law of Moses. Their descendants were brought to Trakai from the Crimea by Vytautas (around 1400) to serve as bodyguards. Some 150 Karaites still live in Trakai although their numbers are dwindling rapidly and there are fears that Lithuania's smallest ethnic minority could die out. At Karaimų 22, on the west side, is a small Karaites museum which is currently being renovated. A few doors down at No 30 there's an early 19th century Kenessa (Karaite prayer house), also being restored. Both should be open again by mid-1997.

Island Castle

The painstakingly restored, red-brick, Gothic castle, which stands on an island in Lake Galvė, probably dates from around 1400 when Vytautas found he needed stronger defences than the peninsula castle afforded. Off the north end of Karaimų gatvė it is linked to the shore by footbridges. The triangular outer courtyard is separated by a moat from the main tower, which has a cavernous central court and a range of galleries, halls and rooms, some housing the Trakai History Museum, which is open from 10 am to 7 pm daily (admission 4 litų). Concerts and plays are held in the castle in summer.

Island Castle

Activities

It is possible to take a yacht trip on Lake Galvė or rent your own paddle or rowing boat. Simply bargain with one of the boat-owners by the lake. Don't pay more than 12 litų an hour for a boat or around 50 litų an hour for a trip in a yacht.

The Žalgiris yacht club (☎ 52 824) at Žemaitės 3 has yachts to rent. For waterbikes, jet skis and speedboats try the Trakų Sporto Bazė (see Places to Stay & Eat). It also rents out bicycles.

Places to Stay & Eat

The privately run *Slėnje* hostel (☎ 51 387), on the north side of Lake Galvė off the road to Vievis, four km out of Trakai, is one of the most efficiently run hostels in Lithuania. It has double/triple rooms for 60/65 litų, a four-bed room for 70 litų and a room with five beds for 16 litų per person. If you stay more than three nights you get a 10% discount. And you can pitch your tent by the lake for 7 litų a night. The hostel also has a laundry, rents boats and fishing equipment, sports an excellent library with lots of information on the area, and can even arrange trips over Trakai in a hot-air balloon.

Trakų Sporto Bazė (☎ 51 266; fax 52 387) has run-down single/double rooms for 120/160 litų a night. The former training camp for Lithuania's sporting heroes has all the facilities including a gym, sauna, pool and more, but that is about its only appeal. *Žalgiris Yacht Club* (see Activities) also has a couple of multi-person rooms overlooking the lake to rent. There's no running water but it's great in summer, and definitely the cheapest in town at 25 litų per person.

Top of the range is the fairly new *Trakų* hotel (☎ & fax 51 574), alongside Lake Totoriškių at Ežero 7. Double/luxury rooms costing 260/320 litų are comfortably furnished and have all the mod cons. The hotel has a pleasant lakeside restaurant with a fantastic summer terrace serving main dishes for about 10 litų. It is open to non-guests too.

A few cafés and a couple of restaurants are dotted along the Vytauto gatvė-Karaimų gatvė axis. The only one worth mentioning is the unique *Kibininė*, in a small black wooden house (no sign outside) at Karaimų 65. The menu is limited and the house speciality is traditional Karaite pies (kibinai) served with a bread-based drink, similar to gira. *Zidinys* on the road from the bus station to the peninsula castle at Vytauto 91, is a pretty bland restaurant, but with pretty views over Lake Totoriškių and an outside terrace.

Getting There & Away

More than 30 buses daily, between 6.55 am and 10 pm, run from Vilnius bus station to Trakai and back (45 minutes, 3 litų). There are also seven trains daily between 5 am and 8 pm (40 minutes, 2 litų).

CENTRE OF EUROPE

On the road to Moletai, 25 km north of Vilnius, lies the centre of Europe – that is, according to the French National Geographical Institute. Since 1989, when the French made this grand decision, this little-known spot lying at a latitude of 54° 54' and longitude of 25° 19', has attracted thousands of tourists. The small granite sculpture marking the centre is now vandalised and a new sculpture – a 1.5m-tall pyramid with all the European capitals and their distances from the centre of Europe marked on it – is planned for the site. To get to the centre of

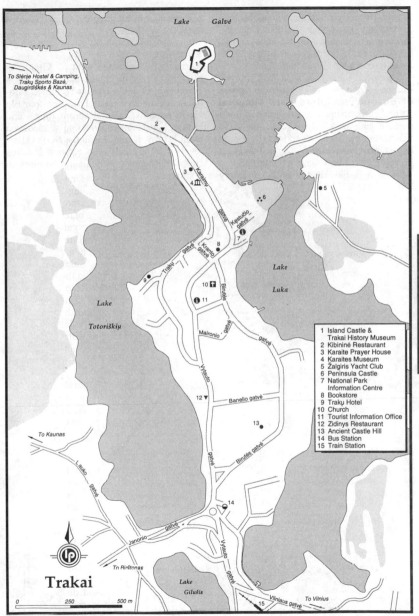

Lake Galvė

To Slėnje Hostel & Camping,
Trakų Sporto Bazė,
Daugirdiškės & Kaunas

Lake Luka

Lake Totoriškių

Maironio gatvė

Banelio gatvė

To Kaunas

Birutės gatvė

To Birštonas

Janonio gatvė

Lake Gilušis

Vilniaus gatvė

To Vilnius

LITHUANIA

1 Island Castle &
    Trakai History Museum
2 Kibininė Restaurant
3 Karaite Prayer House
4 Karaites Museum
5 Žalgiris Yacht Club
6 Peninsula Castle
7 National Park
    Information Centre
8 Bookstore
9 Trakų Hotel
10 Church
11 Tourist Information Office
12 Zidinys Restaurant
13 Ancient Castle Hill
14 Bus Station
15 Train Station

Trakai

0   250   500 m

Europe, turn right off the Vilnius-Moletai road at the sign saying 'Europas Centras'. The centre of Europe is on the side of a small hill opposite a red cross put up by the Lithuanian temperance movement.

Seventeen kilometres from the centre of Europe off the road to Utena is the **Centre of Europe Sculpture Park Museum** (☎ 652 368), an open-air exhibition of postmodern sculptures and wild creations set in five hectares of wooden parkland (be sure to bring mosquito repellent with you if you visit in summer). Every year an international workshop is held in the park, attracting sculptors from all over the world. Guided tours are available.

KERNAVĖ

Kernavė, 35 km north-west of Vilnius, is thought to have been the site of the 1253 coronation of Mindaugas, who united Lithuania for the first time. There are four old castle mounds, in rural surroundings, and archaeologists are uncovering a medieval town nearby. Kernavė is in the Neris valley, reached by a minor road through Dūkštos from Maišiagala on the main road north to Ukmergė.

LITHUANIA

Eastern & Southern Lithuania

HIGHLIGHTS

- Keep an eye out for white-tailed and golden eagles in Aukštaitija National Park
- Step back in time when you visit the preserved farmsteads at Šuminai, Salos and Strazdai
- Follow the wooden sculpture trail round Lake Lūšiai
- Discover a town built round a nuclear power plant when you visit Visaginas
- See stars in the night sky from the Molėtai Astronomical Observatory
- Learn about Čiurlionis' childhood and listen to his music in Druskininkai

Locator & Map Index

Aukštaitija National Park p361

Druskininkai p366

The eastern and southern corners of Lithuania boast some of the most spectacular scenery in all the Baltic states. The area is home to a lakes district that continues east into Belarus and north into Latvia, and two of the country's most favoured national parks. Lithuania's oldest is the Aukštaitija National Park, which extends beyond its southern and western boundaries with the 900 sq km Labanoras-Pabradė forest. The country's biggest park is Dzūkija, in the far south, which incorporates the largest forest, the 1500 sq km Druskininkai-Varėna forest. Also in the far south, on the Nemunas river, is the resort city of Druskininkai – one of the area's few big cities. Predominantly rural, this area of Lithuania is also home to a nuclear power plant which has come under close scrutiny from the west in recent years.

AUKŠTAITIJA NATIONAL PARK
• ☎ *(229)*

The Aukštaitija National Park (Aukštaitijos Nacionalinis Parkas) was founded in 1974 and covers an area of 300 sq km. Around 70% of the park comprises pine, spruce and deciduous forests, inhabited by elk, deer and wild boar. The highlight of Aukštaitija (Lithuanian for highlands) is the labyrinth of lakes

scattered across the park. Good panoramas of them can be enjoyed from the hilltops (up to 200m) around Lake Tauragnas, on the northeastern outskirts of the park. One of the prettiest is Lake Baluošas, which is surrounded by woods on all sides and has seven islands (one of which has its own small lake). The park is home to some 190 bird and 50 animal species – including eight different types of bat. The spectacular whitetailed and golden eagles are known to hunt in the park.

The Trainiškis Wildlife Sanctuary (including Lake Baltys and Lake Gruodiškės) and Ažvinčiai Forest (home to many 150-200 year old pine trees) are both protected zones which can only be visited with park guides. Canoeing and camping along the lakes and the many connecting rivers is a popular activity, as is walking the parks many trails. Mushroom and berry picking is permitted in designated forest areas.

Many of the villages within the park – some dating back to the 18th century – are

359

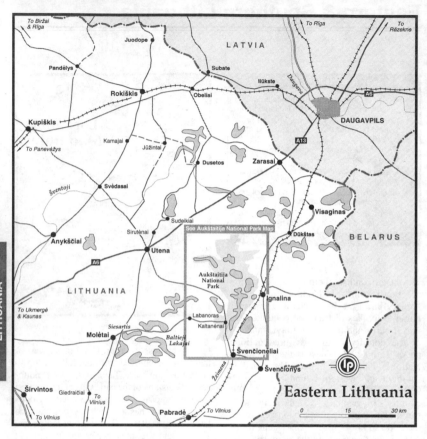

Eastern Lithuania

protected as cultural reserves. The villages of **Šuminai**, **Salos** and **Strazdai** are all preserved farmsteads, while Ginučiai boasts a 19th century **watermill**. North-west of Ginučiai lies the village of Stripeikiai, which is popular with visitors for its **Apiculture museum**. The park also boasts several ancient **fortification mounds** *(piliakalnis)*, such as the Taurapilio mound on the south shore of Lake Tauragnas, and some quaint old wooden architecture, including a fine wooden **church** and **bell tower** (1757) at Palūšė. Around Lake Lūšiai is a **wooden sculpture trail** depicting motifs from tradi-

tional Lithuanian folklore which is worth following.

Detailed maps of the park are available from the tourist and recreation centre (☎ 52 891, 47 430; fax 53 135) at Palūšė, five km west of Ignalina. The centre arranges two to seven-day walking treks and a variety of water tours, including two and three-day trips with overnight stays in specially prepared campsites. It also rents four-person boats (for 2/9 litų an hour/day), as well as tents, sleeping bags, backpacks and other hiking equipment. In winter it rents skiing equipment, sleds and ice fishing gear.

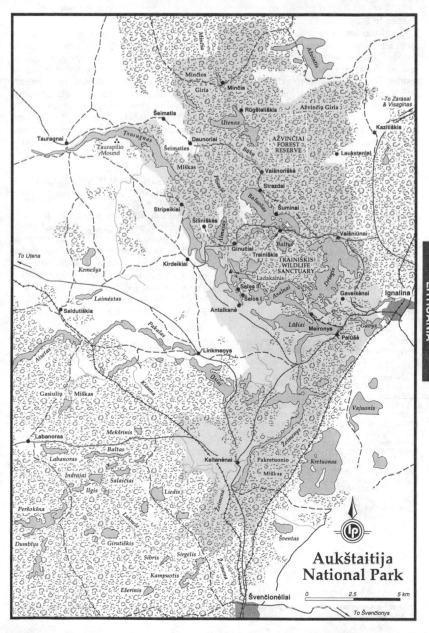

Aukštaitija
National Park

0   2.5   5 km

To Švenčionys

To Zarasai & Visaginas

LITHUANIA

Places to Stay

The park tourism and recreation centre offers summer lodging in one/two/three person wooden cabins with shared facilities for around 7 litų a night. It also features 50 rooms, available all year round, in its main building. The centre provides information on a number of campsites it runs within the park.

The Lithuanian Hostels Association runs the *Ignalina Hostel* (☎ 52 118, 53 476) at Mokyklos 4. It charges a bargain 16 litų a night for a bed in a shared room with communal showers. The *Lithuanian Winter Sports Centre* (☎ 37 029, 54 193), at Sporto gatvė 6 in Ignalina, has a handful of basic two/three room apartments to rent for 40/54 litų a night. The centre operates a ski lift nearby and has sleds for hire. In summer you can hire boats here. To get here from the centre of Ignalina, cross the railway line and follow Budrių gatvė for two kilometres until you reach the 'Lietuvos Žemios Sportos Centras' sign (on the right). The sports centre *café* is only open in summer.

Getting There & Away

If you don't have your own transport the best way to get to the park is to catch a train to Ignalina and then a local bus or taxi from there. Nine trains (some terminating at Daugavpils in Latvia and one in St Petersburg) connect Ignalina with Vilnius daily. It's a two hour trip. There is just one bus daily to/from Vilnius (via Molėtai, Panevėžys and Marijampolė), four buses daily to/from Kaunas, two daily to/from Klaipėda (via Utena), and three to/from Utena.

VISAGINAS & IGNALINA NUCLEAR POWER PLANT
• *pop 32,500* • ☎ *(266)*

The lakeside town of Visaginas (formerly named Šniečkus, after the head of the Lithuanian Communist Party), 50 km north of Ignalina, is an interesting – if somewhat surreal – place which is fascinating to explore for its brief but very unique history. The town was founded in 1975 to house a handful of energy specialists seconded from Russia to oversee the construction of the

---

Ignalina

The Ignalina nuclear power plant, 120 km north-east of Vilnius, is the largest of the RMBK Chernobyl-style plants in the world. Since the Chernobyl disaster in 1986, millions of US dollars in western aid have been spent upgrading Ignalina's safety features to prevent a second Chernobyl disaster.

When one of the RMBK reactors at the Chernobyl nuclear power plant in Ukraine exploded in April 1986, more than 90 times the radioactive fallout of the Hiroshima atomic bomb was produced.

Ignalina has two RMBK reactors, which have been on-line since 1984 and 1987. Unlike reactors in the west, they are graphite-cooled and have no containment system; if an accident occurs, radiation is immediately released into the open-air. Four RMBK reactors were planned for the site but work on the third was stopped in 1988 following large-scale public protests.

Despite increasing international pressure for the closure of the plant – particularly from Sweden who sees it as uncomfortably close to home – the Lithuanian government says it will not shut Ignalina down until the reactor channels burn out and need replacing. This will happen around 2010.

More than US$60 million in total has been set aside by the G7's Nuclear Safety Account and Sweden to bring Ignalina up to western safety standards. Experts from the International Atomic Energy Agency monitor the plant, which produces around 80% of Lithuania's electricity.

In recent years some small accidents at the plant have been reported, none of which have been dangerous according to the Ignalina authorities, who have slammed international press reports as alarmist. In late 1994 Ignalina was shut down for three days following warnings from Germany that the plant was a target for terrorists. In August 1995 two cranes tangled while replacing fuel rods. Days later, a fuel rod broke while spent radioactive fuel was being stored away. In November 1995, there was a fire in one of the turbine rooms and an engineer, who was carrying out routine duties, had to be hospitalised after being exposed to more than 350 times the permitted daily radiation dosage.

The Ignalina nuclear power plant was the last of five Chernobyl-style RMBK plants to be built in the former Soviet Union. Lithuania is the most nuclear power-dependent country in the world. ∎

Ignalina nuclear power plant (so-called because of its location within the Ignalina Region, rather than in the town of Ignalina itself).

The nuclear power plant – which has two Chernobyl-type RBMK reactors generating around 80% of Lithuania's electricity – gained international notoriety in the wake of the 1986 Chernobyl nuclear accident. Original plans to build two more reactors to supply power to the Baltic states and Kaliningrad and Belarus were scrapped following massive public protests.

Since the early 1990s western governments have contributed millions in financial aid to help raise Ignalina's safety standards to western levels. Numerous buses shuttle Ignalina's 5000 shift workers between Visaginas and the plant, two km east of the town centre. In the centre of Visaginas a Geiger counter records the day's radiation level.

Following a massive influx of workers from many other parts of the former Soviet Union, Lithuanians now only make up 14% of the (mainly Russian) population of Visaginas. Street signs are bilingual and Russian is the predominant language spoken on the streets.

A handy A5-sized information booklet with details about the town and power plant is sold at the Aukštaitija hotel – see Places to Stay. Guided tours of the plant can be arranged (in advance) by contacting the plant's press and information centre (☎ 29 111, 29 719).

Places to Stay

The *Aukštaitija* (☎ 31 956; fax 31 346); in the centre of Visaginas at Veteranų 9, offers little to get excited about. Its dimly-lit rooms, in line with the Soviet way of doing things, have inflated prices for foreigners. Luxury singles/doubles with private bath cost 232 litų per person. A room with a private shower is 192 litų per person, and a room with shared facilities is 82 litų per person. The hotel decided not to reveal its room rates for non-foreigners.

MOLĖTAI
• ☎ (230)
The small town of Molėtai, 75 km north of Vilnius and 30 km west of Aukštaitija National Park, is the centre of another lake region. It has one hotel, the *Pastovėlis* (☎ 51 345) at Inturkės 6, with beds in a shared room for 21 litų a night. There's a handful of *campsites* on Siesartis and Baltieji Lakajai lakes, about six to nine km east of Molėtai.

Spectacular views of Moletai's lake-studded landscape and the stars above Lithuania can be gained from the **Molėtai Astronomical Observatory** (☎ 51 728, 45 447) built on Kaldiniai hill, 193m above sea level, in the **Labanoro Regional Park**. The observatory, which boasts the largest telescope in northern Europe, was ranked among the top five in the Soviet Union. Guided tours in English need to be booked in advance, and night visits can also be arranged upon request.

Next to the observatory stands one of the world's most unique museums, the **Lithuanian Ethnocosmology Museum** (☎ 45 424, 45 423). It arranges expeditions tracing the origins of Lithuanian folklore songs and customs as well as anything else which can be justified under its quest to discover 'man's scientific, cultural and educational relationship with the universe'! With such a wide scope it's no wonder staff claim the museum to be the only centre of its kind in the world. Daily excursions are held at 10 am, 1, 4 and 7 pm and need to be booked in advance. To reach the observatory and museum, follow the Molėtai-Utena road for 10 km, then turn right at the 'Lietuvos Ethnokosmologijos Muziejus' sign and follow the dirt track for four km.

Up to four buses run daily from Vilnius to Molėtai (1½ hours, 8.60 litų). One local bus runs daily between the museum and Molėtai.

UTENA
• ☎ (239)
Utena, 34 km north of Molėtai on the road to Rokiškis, is known chiefly for the Utenos beer it brews. The *Sodra* hotel (☎ 51 345) offers comfortable singles/doubles with

LITHUANIA

private shower for 80/60 litų per person, and singles with shared showers for 50 litų. The flash looking (from the outside) *Smelio* restaurant next door is a disappointment.

In the village of Sirutėnai, five km north of Utena on the road to Sudeikiai, there is a wonderful **Bell Museum**. The museum was set up by a local sculptor in defiance of Krushchev's orders to destroy all wayside shrines, crosses and churches in the 1970s. Today the round, red-brick tower overlooking a little lake houses some 300 bells of all shapes and sizes. Every Saturday in summer, Atlanka (as the tower is known locally) is flooded with newlyweds desperate to have their photo taken in front of the fairy-tale tower. While you're here look out for the fascinating pile of Soviet propaganda heaped up high outside the sculptor's workshed, opposite the brick tower. Also note the miniature paintings and sculptures of Lenin on the door.

Some 34 km north-east of Utena is the village of Dusetos, which is famous for its annual **horse race** held on the frozen surface of Lake Sartai. The race dates back to 1865 and attracts horse enthusiasts, musicians and folk artists from all over the region. It is held on the first Saturday of February.

DRUSKININKAI
• *pop 22,000* • ☎ *(233)*

Nestled on the Nemunas river, not far from the border with Belarus in Lithuania's south, is the resort city of Druskininkai. Its resort status stems from its mineral springs which have been in demand for their curative purposes since the 19th century. During the Soviet era Druskininkai was a major holiday resort and several of the vast, purpose built sanatoriums are still operational today. Druskininkai is also well known as the birthplace of the modern Jewish sculptor Jacques Lipchitz, and the home town of the outstanding romantic painter and composer Mikalojus Konstantinas Čiurlionis (1875-1911).

Southern Lithuania

Orientation

The focal point of the city centres around the intersection overlooking Lake Druskonis, where Kudirkos gatvė, coming into town from the south-east, crosses Čiurlionio gatvė. These streets and the pedestrianised Vilniaus alėja, parallel to Kudirkos gatvė a block to its south-west, make up the central area of the city. The bus and train stations are 450 and 600m away, respectively, on the south-east continuation of Kudirkos gatvė (called Gardino gatvė). Coming out of either station, turn left along the road to reach the city centre. The Nemunas river loops round the north side of town.

A large scale tourist map of the town indicating Druskininkai's main hotel, sanatoriums, restaurants and museums is posted up outside the bus station. Pocket-size maps are sold for 3 litų in the porch of the church on Kudirkos gatvė.

Information

You can change money at a number of banks in the city centre – at Kudirkos 33, Vilniaus 16 or at Čiurlionio 4a. The post office is on Kudirkos gatvė. Next door, in the old telephone and telegraph office (open daily from 7 am to 11 pm), at Kudrikos 39, are public card phones. There are more at the train station and inside the Druskininkai hotel. The market is at Čiurlionio 133a, and there are shops scattered along Čiurlionio gatvė and Vilniaus alėja.

Druskininkų gelmė tourist agency (☎ 53 393), inside the Druskininkai hotel at Kudirkos 43, arranges city tours, boat tours along the Nemunas and trips to the Dzūkija National Park.

Things to See & Do

A large stylised **statue** of Čiurlionis stands at the north end of Kudirkos gatvė. The world renowned painter lived for most of his childhood at Čiurlionio 35, about 400m west of Kudirkos gatvė, in what is now the **M K Čiurlionis Memorial Museum** (☎ 52 755). It's open daily, except Monday, from 11 am to 6 pm. Piano and chamber concerts are held here daily in summer and at weekends in winter. Entrance is 0.50/1 litų for students/adults.

There are a couple of **fine art galleries** in Druskininkai, the Vaikų Dailės Galerija (☎ 53 825) opposite the Druskininkai hotel at Kudirkos 7, and the Sofa Art Galerija (☎ 51 865) at Taikos 9.

The **Jewish Museum** (☎ 56 077) at Šv Jokūbo 17 is a branch of the Lithuanian State Jewish Museum in Vilnius. This small yellow wooden cottage houses a variety of temporary exhibitions in commemoration of the sculptor Jacques Lipchitz, who was born in Druskininkai. Prior to WWII, a third of Druskininkai's residents were Jewish. The museum is open daily, except Monday, from 11 am to 5 pm. Entrance is free.

Girios Aidas (Echo of the Forest) at Čiurlionio 102, about two km east of the Kudirkos gatvė corner, is an unusually carved two storey wooden house – supported by a single pedestal – which contains a **forest museum**. It has exhibits on forest fauna and forestry and is open daily, except Monday, from 11 am to 6 pm.

Places to Stay & Eat

The only hotel is the *Druskininkai* (☎ 52 566; fax 52 217) at Kudirkos 43. Sporting little more than a bed, the bottom of the range double rooms are 36 litų. Singles/doubles with B&W TV, telephone and private shower are 35/46 litų, and the best (two-room) doubles come with colour TV, telephone and private bath for 60 litų.

Another option is the *Sanatorium Lietuva* (☎ 52 414; fax 55 490) at the north end of Kudirkos gatvė. Ranked among the top health resorts in the former USSR, this towering block has seen some extensive renovations in recent years and today boasts the most pleasant decor in town.

Eating options are extremely limited. Strolling down Vilniaus alėja you'll find a handful of uninspiring cafés and bars. Places which do stand out include the cowboy-style *Café Galia* in a cellar at Dabintos 3; the *Aguona Billiards Café* at Vilniaus 22, which has two billiard tables and a red and green check ceiling; and *Širdelė*, a cosy home style

LITHUANIA

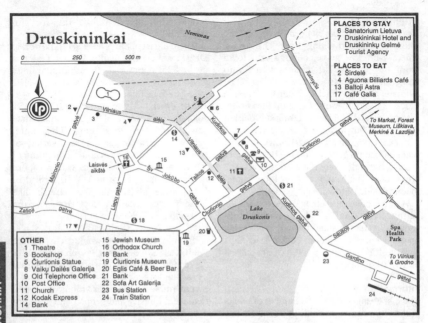

Druskininkai

0   250   500 m

Nemunas

To Market, Forest
Museum, Liškiava,
Merkinė & Lazdijai

Lake
Druskonis

Spa
Health
Park

To Vilnius
& Grodno

LITHUANIA

restaurant tucked inside a yellow wooden house at Maironio 16.

If you're really strapped for cash, you can't go past a mug of bouillon and a greasy *kibinai* (meat pasty) for the bargain price of 2.32 litų from *Baltoji Astra* at Vilniaus 10. And if you fancy a beer at night (overlooking Lake Druskonis), try *Eglis Café & Beer Bar* on Šv Jokūbo gatvė. It is only open in summer.

Getting There & Away

There are five direct buses (two hours, 11.80 litų) and two trains (2½ to 3½ hours, 10.20 litų) daily to/from Vilnius. There are about nine buses daily to/from Kaunas taking two to three hours (most via Alytus), 10 to/from Lazdijai, five to/from Varena, and one each to/from Klaipėda (via Kaunas), Šiauliai (via Kaunas) and Kaliningrad.

For buses to/from Grodno (Lithuanian: Gardinas) in Belarus see the Getting There & Away chapter.

DZŪKIJA NATIONAL PARK

Covering an area of 550 sq km, the Dzūkija National Park is Lithuania's largest park. Four-fifths of its area is dense pine forest, much of which is protected under the park's 20 different nature reserves. Between Marcinkonys and the Belarus border (to the south of the park) is the **Čepkeliai Nature Reserve**, protecting Lithuania's biggest marsh and wildlife sanctuary. A number of villages within the park are cultural reserves. **Liškiava**, 10 km north-east of Druskininkai, on the left bank of the Nemunas, has remnants of a 14th century hilltop castle which figures in several Lithuanian folk tales. The village church is famous for its seven rococo-style altars. The small town of **Merkinė**, a further 10 km down the Nemunas (at its confluence with the Merkys river), also dates back to the 14th century.

The national park headquarters (☎ 260-44 735; ☎ & fax 260-53 637) at Marcinkonys arranges accommodation in villages around the park and provides information on various walking, cycling and water-based trails in the park. It also runs an information centre (☎ 260-57 245) in Merkinė. Druskininkų gelmė tourist agency (see Druskininkai – Information) arranges trips in the park.

Falling just outside the boundaries of the national park, 58 km north-east of Druskininkai, is **Varėna**. Founded in the 15th century when Grand Duke Vytautas built a hunting lodge here, it is also the birthplace of Mikalojus Konstantinas Čiurlionis. The

A Day on Mars

I travelled from Vilnius to Warsaw by the Šeštokai-Suwałki route with an Aussie companion, met on Vilnius station while awaiting the train for the first leg to Šeštokai. Julian rapidly became a firm friend, not least because he had a small supply of Mars bars. I had misguidedly relied on Vilnius market being open early enough to provide food for the trip, and had ended up with nothing. Julian had bought a ticket to Šeštokai at Vilnius station, but I was following what turned out to be outdated advice that a dollar here and a dollar there, handed to the conductor, would do instead of tickets.

I wasn't too upset by the fine – equivalent to US$1.20 – for travelling from Vilnius to Šeštokai without a ticket. Julian and I agreed that at Šeštokai I would run for the ticket office while he would take both our packs and grab seats on the train to Suwałki. I found a throng of about 20 people around the ticket office. No one moved an inch for the next hour and a half. Whether the clerk was ignoring us altogether, or one of the customers was buying all the tickets then reselling them for a 'commission', I never fathomed.

With 10 minutes left before departure, I gave up and wandered through another door of the station building to find half a dozen Central Asians huddled around a wad of passports. *'Bilety?'* ('Tickets?') I chanced. No one even bothered to look up. Outside, I found Julian struggling towards me with both our packs. The conductors wouldn't let him on the train without tickets. Reviewing the alternatives (wait here till tomorrow; go back to Vilnius; try to find a bus), we decided to try to wangle our way on to the train, somehow. Back we went, this time to find no conductors in sight and no one else remotely interested in who was getting on or off the train. We settled into a corner of the corridor and shared half the last Mars bar.

Even standing room was at a premium on this cross-border sector. Every seat was stacked with baggage and the passengers were stuffed into the corridors. After another small fine for the sector from Šeštokai to the border, and several long halts in the middle of nowhere, we entered Poland. That meant Polish ticket inspectors too. Unimpressed by western passports, the English language or feigned incomprehension, they made it clear to us, with the aid of gestures and numbers written in their notebooks, that we had to pay 28,000 złoty (about US$2) each for the fare from the border to Suwałki, plus fines of 300,000 złoty (US$22) each, or else they would impound our passports or something else equally unhelpful. Now I understood why several other passengers had locked themselves in the toilet when these officials appeared.

With hunger and the morning's early start now taking their effect, I protested loudly in an aggrieved mixture of English and pidgin Russian that I had queued 1½ hours for a ticket and the queue hadn't moved; it certainly wasn't my fault that I hadn't got a ticket. The inspectors briefly moved on in pursuit of other quarry, but soon returned to us with the hieroglyphic '$10' in a notebook and the whispered words *'bez kvitantsia'* ('without receipt'). A fair compromise, we reckoned, and paid up, then celebrated with the final half Mars.

Our train pulled into Suwałki just as our 'connection' to Warsaw was pulling out. We ran to the ticket office anyway and found ourselves second in the queue. Soon we were joyfully clutching tickets to the Polish capital. We deciphered from a conductor that the train leaving any minute for somewhere called Sokołka would take us in the Warsaw direction, and boarded it. I noticed many of the Central Asians from the previous train boarding a bus outside the station.

The rest of the trip went something like this: departed Suwałki 3.39 pm; arrived Sokołka 5.39 pm; departed Sokołka 6.14 pm; arrived Białystok 6.55 pm; departed Białystok 7.35 pm, along with all the Central Asians, who now reappeared, still struggling with the same gigantic baggage; arrived Warsaw Central 10.07 pm after a long, tortuous conversation with a Belarusian who wanted us to help him export essence of bee-sting, allegedly an aphrodisiac, to the west; arrived Warsaw youth hostel 10.55 pm, five minutes before closing, to be told 'house full'. We gasped '... But we've come from Vilnius ... by Šeštokai and Suwałki ...', to which they responded 'Ah ... have a seat ...', and found us a room. ■

John Noble

main road leading from Varėna to Druskininkai is lined with traditional wooden 'totem' poles and sculptures, erected in 1975 in commemoration of the 100th anniversary of Čiurlionis' birth.

Getting There & Away
In summer a boat runs along the Nemunas between Druskininkai and Liškiava. Otherwise there are four or five buses daily between the two places. There are also a few buses a day from Druskininkai to Merkinė and vice versa. A whole lot more buses – including all those between Druskininkai and Vilnius, and most of those between Druskininkai and Alytus (or Kaunas) – stop at the Merkinė intersection (Merkinės kryžkelė), two km east of Merkinė town centre.

THE SOUTH-WEST
The nearest town to the infamous Polish border is **Lazdijai**, which is 43 km northwest of Druskininkai, and on the road to Suwałki (Poland). It has a basic hotel, the *Žibintas* (☎ 268-51 983), at Nepriklausomybės aikštė 6.

The town of **Šeštokai**, 18 km north of Lazdijai, is one end of another Lithuania-Poland border crossing, this time for the Šeštokai-Suwałki railway. The main approach to the Kalvarija-Budzisko border crossing with Poland is through **Marijampolė**, where there's the *Sūduva* hotel (☎ 243-50 345), at Basanavičiaus 8. In Marijampolė there is also an Ethnographic Museum (☎ 243-50 754) at Vytauto 31, and just near Sūduva hotel, at Basanavičiaus 18, is the Museum of Urban Architecture (☎ 243-56 288) which is a lot of fun.

Žuvintas Lake, 30 km north of Lazdijai and 20 km south-east of Marijampolė, and its extensive surrounding marshes form the **Žuvintas Nature Reserve**, an important breeding ground for birds.

Getting There & Away
Buses run to Marijampolė and Kalvarija from Kaunas, and to Lazdijai from Druskininkai, Kaunas and Vilnius. One train runs to Šeštokai from Kaunas and Vilnius. For details on crossing into Poland see the Getting There & Away chapter.

Central Lithuania

HIGHLIGHTS

- Wander the streets of Kaunas' Old Town and trek up Laisvés aléja to St Michael the Archangel Church and Mykolas Žilinskas Art Museum on Nepriklausomybés aikšté
- Discover Hitler's and Stalin's satanic natures at Kaunas' Devil Museum
- Ride on one of Europe's few remaining funiculars in Kaunas
- Pay tribute to Kaunas' Jewish population which was wiped out at the Nazi death camp in the Ninth Fort
- Pretend you're on an 18th century Lithuanian farmstead at Rumšiškés
- Plant your own cross next to the many thousands of others at the Hill of Crosses near Šiauliai

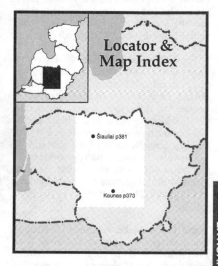

Locator & Map Index

● Šiauliai p381

● Kaunas p373

LITHUANIA

Three of Lithuania's five largest cities lie in a triangle in the centre of the country – Kaunas and Panevėžys, in the Nemunas and Nevėžis valleys, and Šiauliai, on the eastern side of the Žemaitija Upland. Kaunas is the biggest non-capital city in the Baltic states, and is best known for its bohemian arts scene. The central Lithuanian region also has one of the strangest monuments in all the Baltic states – the Hill of Crosses, near Šiauliai, is also a Christian and Lithuanian national pilgrimage site.

KAUNAS
- *pop 423,900* • ☎ *(27)*

Lithuania's second largest city is 100 km west of Vilnius at the confluence of the Nemunas and Neris rivers. About 90% of Kaunas' population is ethnic Lithuanian, and it's often said to be more 'Lithuanian' than the capital itself. Kaunas has a reputation as a bastion of the entrepreneurial spirit and a hotbed of the post-Soviet mafia and other wheeler-dealers.

During Lithuania's period of independence between WWI and WWII, when

Vilnius had been taken over by Poland, Kaunas actually was the national capital.

Founded in the 11th century, it grew up around its castle on the point of land between the two rivers, and from the 13th to 15th centuries was in the battle front against the Teutonic Order on Lithuania's western frontier. After the Order was decisively defeated by the Lithuanians and Poles at Grünwald, in 1410, Kaunas became a successful river trading town in the 15th and 16th centuries. German merchants were influential here, and there was a Hanseatic League office, but Kaunas was never controlled by the Germans, as Estonian and Latvian cities were. Its strategic position is, no doubt, the main reason why it was reduced to ashes 13 times before WWII – when it once again received a battering. Today, it is still a river port as well as Lithuania's chief industrial city and major cultural centre. It has a sizeable student population, some fine architecture, museums and galleries all in an attractive setting.

Orientation

Kaunas' historic heart, Rotušės aikštė (Town Hall square), is on the point of land between the two rivers. Pedestrianised Vilniaus gatvė runs 900m east from Rotušės aikštė to meet the city's main axis, Laisvės alėja, also pedestrianised, which then heads two km east.

The life of modern Kaunas, including most of the shops, galleries, museums, places to eat, and the main hotels, revolves around Laisvės alėja (public smoking is banned on this avenue) and Donelaičio gatvė, which is parallel to it a block north. The bus and train stations are 900m and 1.25 km, respectively, south of the east end of Laisvės alėja, down Vytauto prospektas.

The most central market is the Geležinkelio Turgavietė (Railway Market) at Čiurlionio 29, almost opposite the train station.

Maps

For a pocket-size map of Kaunas centre and environs, pick up *Kaunas In Your Pocket*, an annual city guide available from most hotels, art galleries and news kiosks for 4 litų. Briedis (see Vilnius – Maps) publishes the excellent *Kaunas Centre, Environs and Panorama* map (1:15,000) sold in bookshops for 8.40 litų. The Delta Travel Agency (see Information below) sells road maps for the Baltic states and Europe.

Information

Tourist Office & Travel Agencies Delta travel agency (☎ 204 911; fax 200 621), at Laisvės 88, doubles as Kaunas' official tourist information office as well. The Pentacom-Expo Travel and Business Centre (☎ 209 136) at Laisvės 58 is also a good information source for tourists and business travellers, as is Baltic Clipper (☎ 206 957) at Laisvės 61/1. Lithuanian Student and Youth Travel (☎ 229 905), at Maironio 14/6, and STS travel agency (☎ 220 552), at Kęstučio gatvė 7/4, both offer discount fares.

Money There is a currency exchange at the bus station and numerous others along Laisvės alėja and Vilniaus gatvė, as well as 24 hour exchanges inside the Dali supermarket, at Partizanų 22a, and inside Elivija, at Savanorių 170. Vilniaus Bankas at Donelaičio 62 gives cash advances on Visa and changes travellers' cheques. For cash advances on MasterCard/Eurocard go to Taupomasis Bankas at Donelaičio 76.

Post & Communications The central post office is at Laisvės 102. Faxes and telegrams can also be sent from here. For express mail try UPS (☎ 201 994; fax 204 908), at Laisvės 99-3, or DHL Worldwide Express (☎ 223 129; fax 200 698), at Donelaičio 46.

Phone calls can be made 24 hours a day from the public card phones inside the lobby of the central post office or at public card phones in town. Mobile telephones can be rented from Omnitel at Donelaičio 27, Comliet at Donelaičio 73 or Bitė GSM at Laisvės 12.

Non-commercial email messages can be transmitted free of charge from the Open Society Fund, at Laisvės 53, room 201. The Internet can be accessed at Kaunas Public Library, which is at Radastų 4, and opens on weekdays from 10 am to 9 pm and Saturday from 10 am to 5 pm.

Bookshops Kaunas' central bookshop, at Laisvės 81, stocks the best range of English and German-language newspapers and magazines. For books in foreign languages try the Vytautas University bookshop at Donelaičio 52. The bookshop inside the Mykolas Žilinskas Art Museum, at Nepriklausomybės aikštė 12, is the best for guidebooks on Lithuania, postcards and maps of the area.

Medical Services There is a 24 hour pharmacy *(vaistinė)* opposite the train station on the corner of Vytauto gatvė and Čiurlionio 76. Homeopathic medicines are dispensed at the Homeopatinė vaistinė at Rotušės aikštė 3. Kaunas Medical Centre (☎ 704 440, 259 801), at Savanorių 284, and the Red Cross Hospital (☎ 733 377, 733 360), which is at Januševičiaus 4, both respond to emergency calls. The Cordelectro Medical Centre

LITHUANIA

(☎ 225 031) at Kęstučio 24 offers a 10% discount to Euro<26 holders.

Left Luggage There is a left-luggage hall at the bus station.

✓ Old Town

Vilniaus gatvė is lined with some attractive old buildings. Vilniaus 33 was the president's residence when Kaunas was the interim capital and in its garden stand memorial statues to Lithuania's former presidents. Just off Vilniaus gatvė, at Kurpių 12, is the **Folk Music & Instruments Museum** which is a lot of fun, especially for children. Kaunas' main Old Town sights are on and around Rotušės aikštė.

Rotušės aikštė The old **central square** is a pretty sight with the many (recently restored) 15th and 16th century German merchants' houses around it. The fine, white, baroque former **town hall** in the middle of the square, dating from the 17th century, is now a Palace of Weddings – a function it was given in the Soviet period. Inside, there is a **Ceramics Museum**.

In the square's south-west corner stands a **statue** of Maironis (alias Jonas Mačiulis; 1862-1932), the Kaunas priest who was the poet of Lithuania's late 19th and early 20th century nationalist revival. His works were banned by Stalin. The **Lithuanian Literary Museum** is in the house behind, where Maironis lived from 1910 to 1932. The south side of the square is dominated by a twin-towered **Jesuit church**, college and monastery complex from the 17th and 18th centuries, now back in (church) use after years as a school. The 17th century building at Rotušės aikštė 28 houses a gruesome **Medicine & Pharmaceutical Museum**. In the former post office stables at Rotušės aikštė 19 there is a **Post Office Museum** displaying lots of old telephones.

Kaunas Cathedral Kaunas' single-towered cathedral, on Vilniaus gatvė just off the north-east corner of Rotušės aikštė, owes much to baroque reconstruction, especially inside, but the original 15th century Gothic shape of its windows remains. It is believed to have been founded by Vytautas around 1410. The **tomb** of Maironis stands outside the south wall.

Kaunas Castle A reconstructed tower and sections of wall, and part of a moat are all that remain of Kaunas Castle (Kauno pilis), the hub around which the town originally grew. Founded in the 11th century, it was an important bastion of Lithuania's western borders until the threat from the German knights was eliminated at the Battle of Grünwald in 1410. The castle is a short walk north of Rotušės aikštė.

House of Perkūnas & Vytautas Church At Aleksoto 6, off the south-east corner of Rotušės aikštė, is the curious House of Perkūnas (Perkūno namas) which was built in the 16th century as trade offices, apparently on the site of a former temple to the Lithuanian thunder god, Perkūnas. There's a small museum inside. Just beyond, on the river bank, is the Gothic Vytautas Church (Vytauto bažnyčia).

Lookout Point The hill across the Nemunas from the Vytautas Church offers a good panorama of both old and new Kaunas. Cross the bridge and mount the hill either by the funicular railway (*funikulierius*) or by the steps beside it. A ride on the funicular costs one trolleybus ticket (you can buy this from the conductor). A right turn from the top of the funicular leads to the lookout point a short distance away.

New Town

Kaunas expanded east from the Old Town in the 19th century, and the new town fairly soon became the real city centre.

Laisvės alėja This two-km-long, entirely vehicle-free artery (appropriately its name means Freedom Avenue) is lined with trees and a good number of Kaunas' shops. Towards its western end stands a **statue of Vytautas**. In 1972 a student, Romas Kalanta,

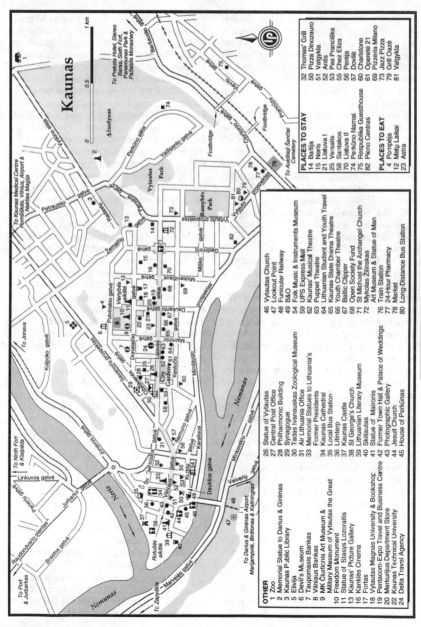

Kaunas

PLACES TO STAY

14 Baltija
15 Neris
21 Lietuva I
25 Versalis
58 Santakos
70 Lietuva II
74 Perkūno Namai
75 Respublika Guesthouse
82 Pieno Centras

PLACES TO EAT

4 Pompėja
12 Metų Laikai
23 Astra
32 Thomas' Grill
50 Pizza Dinozauro
51 Valgykla
52 Antis
53 Pas Pranciška
55 Chez Eliza
56 Perėja
57 Dovilė
60 Charlstone
61 Operetė 21
69 Pizzeria Milano
73 Jazz Pizza
79 Grill Oazė
81 Valgykla

OTHER

1 Zoo
2 Memorial Statue to Darius & Girėnas
3 Kaunas Public Library
5 Elkvija
6 Devil's Museum
7 Taupomasis Bankas
8 Vilniaus Bankas
9 MK Čiurlionis Art Museum &
   Military Museum of Vytautas the Great
10 Freedom Monument
11 Statue of Stasys Lozoraitis
13 Kaunas' Picture Gallery
16 Kanklės Cinema
17 Fortas
18 Vytautas Magnus University & Bookshop
19 Pentacom-Expo Travel and Business Centre
20 Merkurijus Department Store
22 Kaunas Technical University
24 Delta Travel Agency
26 Statue of Vytautas
27 Central Post Office
28 Philharmonic Building
29 Synagogue
30 Tadas Ivanauskas Zoological Museum
31 Air Lithuania Office
33 Memorial Statues to Lithuania's
   Former Presidents
34 Kaunas Cathedral
35 Local Bus Station
36 Litinterp
37 Kaunas Castle
38 St George's Church
39 Lithuanian Literary Museum
41 Statue of Maironis
42 Former Town Hall & Palace of Weddings
43 Photographic Gallery
44 Jesuit Church
45 House of Perkūnas
46 Vytautas Church
47 Lookout Point
48 Funicular Railway
49 B&O
54 Folk Music & Instruments Museum
59 UPS Express Mail
62 Kaunas' Musical Theatre
63 Puppet Theatre
64 Lithuanian Student and Youth Travel
65 Kaunas State Drama Theatre
66 Youth Chamber Theatre
67 Baltic Clipper
68 Open Society Fund
71 St Michael the Archangel Church
72 Art Museum & Statue of Man
   Mykolas Žilinskas
76 Train Station
77 24-Hour Pharmacy
78 Market
80 Long-Distance Bus Station

burnt himself to death in City Garden (Miesto Sodas) – the park facing the statue – as a protest against Soviet occupation, sparking riots which were probably the earliest major public protests against Soviet rule. A memorial comprising 19 stones – one for each year of Kalanta's life – has been planned for the park.

There are remnants of an old defensive wall and tower on the west side of the City Garden. The Philharmonic building, a block north of the Vytautas statue at Sapiegos 5, was Lithuania's Parliament when Kaunas was the interim capital. Lithuanian independence was declared in 1918 inside Kaunas' Musical Theatre at Laisvės 91. At Laisvės 106 the **Tadas Ivanauskas Zoological Museum** has a wide range of exhibits (stuffed animals).

The Merkurijus department store, at Laisvės 60, was occasionally used as a film set in the Soviet period because it had some of the best-stocked shelves in the USSR. The blue neo-Byzantine **St Michael the Archangel church**, on Nepriklausomybės aikštė (Independence Square), is the dominant feature at the east end of Laisvės alėja. It was built in 1895 as a Russian Orthodox church, but was (for many years) used to house a stained glass museum. Now it is again open to worshippers, this time of the Catholic faith.

Directly to the right as you face the cathedral, in front of the **Mykolas Žilinskas Art Museum** at Nepriklausomybės aikštė 12, stands Man, a glorious **statue** of a man revealing his manhood, intended to symbolise Nike, the Greek god of victory.

At Vytauto 46, off the east end of Laisvės alėja, there is a small **Museum of Political Prisoners** recapturing the partisans' forest fight against the Soviet army.

Vienybės aikštė This square (which means Unity Square) straddles Donelaičio gatvė, a street north of Laisvės alėja. On its south side, flanking the north end of Daukanto gatvė, are the main buildings of Kaunas Technological University (Kauno technologijos universitetas), which has 14,000 students, and the smaller Vytautas Magnus University (Vytauto Didžiojo universitetas), refounded in 1989 by an emigré Lithuanian, Lucija Baškauskaitė. On the north side of Donelaičio gatvė are a cluster of monuments to Lithuanian independence heroes, epitomised by an eternal flame which is flanked by some fine carved crosses, and the **Freedom Monument** (Laisvės paminklas), which is dated 16 February, 1918 (the day Lithuania declared independence) – during the Stalin era it was hidden and finally replaced on 16 February, 1989.

The north side of the square, at Donelaičio 64, is occupied by a building housing the **Military Museum of Vytautas the Great** (Vytauto Didžiojo karo muziejus), which isn't a military museum at all but a museum about the history of Lithuania, from prehistoric times to the present day. Of particular interest is the wreckage of the aircraft in which two of Lithuania's unfortunate heroes, Steponas Darius and Stasys Girėnas (pictured on the 10 litas note), died while attempting to fly non-stop from New York to Kaunas in 1933. The pair are buried in the **Aukštieji Šančiai Cemetery**, at Ašmenos 1, and there is a **memorial statue** to them at Sporto, east of the centre.

Also in the same buildings, but with an entrance on Putvinskio gatvė, is the Čiurlionis Art Museum (Čiurlionio dailės muziejus). It is Kaunas' leading museum and has good collections of the romantic paintings of Mikalojus Konstantinas Čiurlionis (1875-1911), one of Lithuania's greatest artists and composers, as well as 17th to 20th century Lithuanian folk art and 16th to 20th century European applied art. Kaunas' Picture Gallery (Paveikslių galerija), at Donelaičio 16, three blocks east of Vienybės aikštė, has mainly western European art including work by Rubens, Cézanne, Goya, Picasso and Matisse.

A statue honoring the exiled Lithuanian politician Stasys Lozoraitis (1924-94) stands at Donelaičio 60. Lozoraitis lost out against Algirdas Brazauskas in the 1993 presidential elections. During the Soviet era he was the Lithuanian ambassador to the US.

Flying Heroes

On 15 July, 1933, the Kaunas-bound *Lituanica* took off from New York. In their little orange plane, which they had bought for US$3200, Lithuanian pilots Steponas Darius and Stanislovas (Stasys) Girėnas were just 7186 km away from setting a world record for the longest non-stop, transatlantic flight.

Two days after takeoff, 25,000 people gathered at Kaunas airport to await the arrival of Lithuania's flying heroes. The crowds waited in vain. After flying 6411 km in 37 hours, the *Lituanica* crashed into tree tops over Germany. Both pilots died.

Darius and Girėnas' deaths were announced over a loud speaker to the waiting crowds. Flags across the country were lowered to half-mast as an entire nation went into mourning. On 19 July, 50,000 people gathered at Kaunas airport to meet the German plane that brought the bodies of the two men home. Even more attended the funeral the following day.

Following orders of the Lithuanian government, the pilots' bodies were embalmed – a nine month procedure – and laid in a chapel of rest in Vytautas the Great University in Kaunas. In the 1940s, with the advance of the Red Army, Darius and Girėnas were taken from the chapel and hidden in a wall within the medical faculty of the university, where they remained for 20 years.

In 1963 the embalmed bodies were uncovered and a year later were moved to the Aukštieji Šančiai military cemetery in Kaunas to rest in peace. Monuments to Lithuania's flying heroes, who are pictured on the 10 litų banknote, have since been unveiled in Kaunas, Chicago, New York, Indiana and Germany.

Why the *Lituanica* crashed remains a mystery. Why Darius and Girėnas did not survive is not so difficult to fathom. They carried no parachutes on board, no radio, and no modern navigation equipment. The six-seater plane, which flew at an average speed of 180 to 200 km, was also overladen with excess fuel.

Darius and Girėnas were the first pilots to officially fly mail from America to Europe. They remain Lithuania's most beloved heroes. ■

At Putvinskio 64, is the very popular **Devil's Museum** (Velnių muziejus) with its bizarre collection of more than 1700 devil statuettes collected by landscape artist Antanas Žmuidzinavičius (1876-1966). Worth looking out for are the satanic figures of Hitler and Stalin, formed from tree roots, dancing over Lithuania.

Parks

Wooded parkland covers much of the hilly area just east of the city centre. Vytautas Park (Vytauto parkas) occupies the slope up from the end of Laisvės alėja. The Ažuolynas is a lovely park stretching more than a km further east from the stadium. South of Vytautas Park is Ramybės Park, which is mainly frequented by worshippers of the Orthodox Cathedral and the mosque which are both within the park. In 1995, a statue commemorating those who fought for Lithuanian independence (1919-22) was unveiled in the park. Ramybės Park was home to the Old City Cemetery until the Soviets tore up all

the graves, including the grave of the unknown soldier, in the 1960s. Panemunas Park (Panemunės parkas), on the south side of the river about 1.5 km further east, is mostly pine woods. You can reach it by catching bus No 29, which goes south down Vytauto prospektas and takes a (roundabout) southern route.

Other Sights

Zoo Far from being an enjoyable experience, a visit to Kaunas Zoo, at the east end of Ažuolynas park at Radvilėnų 21, will probably leave you in tears. Not recommended for the faint-hearted.

Ninth Fort, Jewish Ghetto & Synagogue

The Ninth Fort (written 'IX Fortas' in Lithuanian), at Žemaičių plentas 73 on Kaunas' north western outskirts, was built in the late 19th century to fortify the western frontier of the tsarist empire. In WWII, the Nazis turned it into a death camp. An estimated 80,000 people, including most of Kaunas' Jewish population, were murdered here. Only one of the prison buildings remains and stark, monumental sculptures mark the site of the mass grave. The museum not only has exhibits on the Nazi horrors against Jews, but also includes material on Soviet atrocities against Lithuanians. It is open daily (except Tuesday) from 10 am to 6 pm. You can reach the fort by taking bus No 35 or 23 (from the bus station just north of Rotušės aikštė) to the IX Fortas bus stop seven km out of town.

Kaunas' WWII Jewish ghetto is on the west bank of the Neris, within the area bounded by Jurbarko, Panerių and Demokratų streets. Much of it is derelict today. Close to Laisvės alėja, at Ožeškienės 17, is Kaunas' only operational synagogue. Beside it stands a memorial to some 1600 children who were killed at the Ninth Fort. The remains of two other synagogues can still be seen nearby at Zamenhofo 7 and 9.

Sixth Fort East of the town centre on Baršausko street (where it crosses Kovo 11-osios and Riomerio) stands a mini 'hill of crosses'. Since independence in 1991, and the removal of a Soviet tank monument, the crosses have continued to multiply on this spot.

Pažaislis Monastery This fine example of 17th century baroque architecture stands about nine km east of the city centre, near the shores of the Kaunas Sea (Kauno marios) – the large artificial lake created by damming (for hydro-electricity) the Nemunas on the east side of Kaunas. The highlight is the monastery church with its 50m high cupola and sumptuous interior modelled on a Venetian design, with pink and black marble, brought from Kraków in Poland, and frescoes on the walls and ceilings. There are also some pleasant gardens. The monastery has had a chequered history, passing from Catholic to Orthodox control, then back to Catholic, before being used as a psychiatric hospital for part of the Soviet era. It has been under restoration since the 1960s. To get there, take trolleybus No 5 from the train station (or from Donelaičio gatvė in the city

centre) to its terminus on Masiulio gatvė, a few hundred metres before the monastery. Guided tours (☎ 745 485) need to be booked in advance.

Galleries Kaunas has some of the finest art galleries in the country. Particularly noteworthy venues include the Photographic Gallery, in the Old Town at Rotušės aikštė 1; and Kauno Langas, at Vilnaus 22.

Activities
See the introductory Facts for the Visitor chapter for information on general activities in Lithuania. If you're stuck for something to do in Kaunas, why not fly, glide, parachute or go ballooning at Kaunas' Darius and Girėnas Airport (☎ 295 522), two km from the centre at Veiverių 132.

Special Events
Kaunas' four day jazz festival, which takes place in a variety of venues every year in April, is the largest festival of its kind in the Baltics and attracts top jazz musicians from all over the world.

Places to Stay – bottom end & middle
The Lithuanian Hostels Association has three-bed rooms for 40 litų per person at the *Respublika Guesthouse* (also known as Svečių Namai; ☎ 748 972), at Prancūzų 59, about a 1.25 km walk east of the train station. When you reach Prancūzų gatvė, No 59 is the second nine-storey building on the left and its entrance is at the back.

For B&B get in touch with *Litinterp* (☎ 228 718) at Kumelių 15/4. Singles/doubles cost 60/100 litų. Bookings can be made in advance through its Vilnius office (see Vilnius – Places to Stay). It rents bicycles too. Baltic Clipper (see Information – Travel Agencies) has *self-contained apartments* to rent in the Old Town from 160 litų per person.

There are two cheap central hotels. The *Baltija* (☎ 223 639), at Vytauto 71, charges around 35/50 litų for pretty grotty singles/doubles with equally grotty private shower and toilet. The older *Nemunas* hotel

(☎ 223 102), at Laisvės 88, has largish rooms with TV, toilet and basin for around 100/180 litų. Showers are shared.

Pieno Centras (☎ 202 763), at Kaunakiemo 1, has doubles and rooms with four beds. Rooms for one person/shared rooms cost 40/30 litų per person. The reception is open from 9 am to 6 pm. Equally acceptable is the *Preksta* at Pramonės 16 – which is one of the few remaining hotels to still have a three-tier pricing system for Lithuanians, CIS residents and foreigners. Doubles for foreigners cost from 150 litų a night.

Former Intourist options include the *Neris* (☎ 203 863), at Donelaičio 27, which offers singles/doubles for 100/160 litų; the *Lietuva II* (☎ 221 791), at Laisvės 35, with rooms for 80/120 litų; and the slightly more upmarket *Lietuva I* (☎ 205 992), situated at Daukanto 21, which is as Soviet as the rest of them but has made some attempts at refurbishment. Singles/doubles/triples cost 160/240/300 litų.

Places to Stay – top end

A number of small, family run hotels have sprung up in recent years, offering few rooms (compared to the Soviet ghettos) but boasting top quality service which is hard to fault.

The first to spring up was *Perkūno Namai* (☎ 209 386; fax 223 050), overlooking the city at Perkūno 61. It has singles/ doubles for 260/320 litų. Similar in both size and attitude is *Nakties Magija* (Magical Night; ☎ 797 923; fax 795 832), overlooking a green park at Skroblių 3. Singles/doubles cost 320/480 litų.

More central is *Santakos* (☎ 221 162; fax 229 393), which is down a cobbled street at Gruodžio 21. It was recently awarded a four-star rating by the Best Western hotel chain. Spacious double rooms with luxury en suite bathrooms for one/two people start at 320/400 litų a night. Another favourite for its 'cobbled street' location and impeccable in-house restaurant is the *Minotel* (☎ 229 981; fax 220 355), at Kuzmos 8. Singles/doubles cost 380/ 400 litų and are well worth it.

Places to Eat

Most of the city's restaurants and cafés are located along Laisvės alėja, Vilniaus gatvė, and near Rotušės aikštė – where new places pop up practically every month. Top of the list is the French-inspired *Chez Eliza*, at Vilniaus 30, where the cane furnished interior and wonderful glass conservatory provide a welcome relief whatever the season. The walls are strung with old photographs taken at the Kaunas musical theatre. Equally chic is the offbeat cellar bar and bistro *Antis*, a few doors down at Vilniaus 21. The menu is more European than Lithuanian but the crowd that gathers here is strictly local and worth mingling with. Both places are open daily from noon to midnight. At Vilniaus 56 is the ultra-trendy *Dovilė*; its thick homemade soups and (strictly no fried food) main dishes, starting at around 15 litų, make this the perfect place for vegetarians or those counting the calories.

Along Laisvės alėja, bang in the centre at No 76, is the *Astra*. This restaurant offers a constantly changing range of lunch and evening specials catering for families with kids. Astra also serves the best coffee in town.

Close by, on Kęstučio gatvė, there are a couple of good – if not expensive – options. The *Charlstone*, at No 93, claims to be Spanish, despite having a French chef, but the menu is a sheer delight and features such exotic things as jellied eels and brains. Expect to pay at least 100 litų per head though. Not quite so expensive but still in the great-for-a-special-treat price range is the classy Italian restaurant *Operetė 21*, at Kęstučio 58. Its low-back, cushioned chairs really are very comfortable after a hard day's walk.

Better value is the Greek-inspired *Pompėja*, at Putvinskio 38. The baked trout in Polish sauce and the house speciality – roast boar – are both excellent, and not over-priced at 29 litų. Lighter eaters can choose between a 'natural', 'fascinating' or 'refreshing' salad. It is also one of the few places in town to have a breakfast menu (served daily from 8.30 to 11 am), featuring

LITHUANIA

a 'big sandwich with hot baked egg' and hot apple cake with chocolate. The bohemian *Perėja* (open daily from 8 am to midnight), at Birštono 20, is another must for anyone wanting an early breakfast, a laid-back lunch or a glimpse at the cream of Kaunas' art scene.

Lithuanian fare is pretty widespread. *Pas Pranciška*, at Zamenhofo 11, serves good cheap dishes for 2 to 10 litų. *Metų Laikai*, at Mickevičiaus 40b, serves all the old favourites and some more unique dishes – spicy Chinese chicken, tea with honey, and pint-sized ice-cream floats. Note, smoking inside is not allowed until after 4 pm. Both places are open daily from 11 am to midnight.

For a complete blast back into Kaunas' Soviet past look no further than *Versalis*, just off Laisvės alėja at Vasario 16-osios. Nothing has been touched in this place for at least 20 years and while the food is nothing to write home about, the interior most definitely is!

Another great Soviet institution worth a try is the old *valgykla* (canteen). There is one in the Old Town, at Vilniaus 26, and another at Vytauto 12, a two minute walk from the train station. Koldūnai (Lithuanian-style ravioli) is a mere 2.63 litų, while a mysterious beef concoction is the most expensive item on the handwritten menu at 3.23 litų.

Fast food fanatics have a number of choices. *Thomas' Grill*, in the Old Town at Mapų 2, serves great gyros. Kaunas' first pizza chain, *Jazz Pizza*, has outlets at Kęstučio 6, Gričiupio 9 and Perkūno 3, offering a colourful choice of pizza for around 14 litų. The Italian run *Pizzeria Milano*, at Mickevičiaus 10, serves the best pizza in town for 7 to 12 litų, while *Pizza Dinozauro*, at Daukšos 29, is the place to go if you're into dinosaurs. *Grill Oazė*, close to the train station at Vytauto 20, serves cheap junk food for less than 1.50 litų. *Hamburgerių Baras*, on Laisvės alėja, slaps out every type of burger imaginable, as does the cleaner and slightly more appealing *Hamburgerių Baras*, at Kęstučio 66. McDonald's is expected to hit Kaunas by the end of 1997.

Entertainment
For a complete listing of what's on at the latest 'in' places see the local daily newspaper *Kauno Diena*, *Kaunas In Your Pocket*, and the *Baltic Times*.

Pubs & Clubs Cool hang-outs worth a beer – or two – include the hard-rock *B&O*, at Muitinės 9, and *Skiliautas*, in a tiny courtyard at Rotušės aikštė 26, where local artists meet to play chess. Both places are open daily from 11 am to 11 pm. However, nothing can compete with *Fortas*, Kaunas' first Irish bar, with a definite Lithuanian accent, at Donelačio 65. It offers an unbeatable cocktail of cheap bar food, Guinness, live music at weekends, and an indestructible wooden interior. It stays open until 4 am at weekends.

Classical Music, Opera & Theatre The main classical concert hall is the Kaunas Philharmonic (Kauno Filharmonija, ☎ 200 478) at Sapiegos 5. The booking office is open from 2 to 7 pm. Performances start at 7 pm. Operas are generally staged at Kaunas' Musical Theatre (☎ 227 113) at Laisvės 91. Performances start daily at 7 pm, except on Sunday when they start at 6 pm.

The Kaunas State Drama Theatre (Valstybinis dramos teatras, ☎ 223 185, 224 064), at Laisvės 71, has one of Lithuania's most original theatre companies. They also hold performances at the theatre's smaller hall at Kęstučio 64. The Youth Chamber Theatre (Jaunimo kamerinis teatras, ☎ 228 226), at Kęstučio 74a, is known for its alternative theatre. More light-hearted plays can be seen at the Pantomime Theatre (Pantomimos teatras, ☎ 225 668) at Ožeškienės 12, and the Puppet Theatre (Lėlių teatras, ☎ 209 893) at Laisvės 87a.

Cinema The Kanklės cinema at Laisvės 36, the Laisvė cinema at Laisvės 46d and the Kino Klubas at Nepriklausomybės aikštė 12, all show films in English with Lithuanian subtitles.

Getting There & Away

This section deals with transport within the Baltic states and the Kaliningrad Region. Bus and train connections to/from other countries are covered in the Getting There & Away chapter.

Air Kaunas airport (☎ 541 309) is 10 km north of the Old Town, along Savanorių at Karmėlava. The privately owned Air Lithuania (Aviakompanija Lietuva; ☎ 229 706), at Šv Gertrūdos 7, flies to/from Palanga five times a week, as well as to Budapest, Hamburg, Helsinki, Kristianstad, Prague and Zürich.

Bus Kaunas bus station (☎ 224 192) is at Vytauto 24. There's a useful *Informacija* window in the booking hall, directly opposite the main entrance. Services from Kaunas include:

Druskininkai
    130 km, two to three hours, about nine daily buses (most via Alytus), 12.10 litų
Ignalina
    200 km, four hours, four daily buses, 16.70 litų
Kaliningrad
    250 km, six hours, one daily bus via Sovietsk, 26 litų
Kalvarija
    75 km, 1½ hours, one daily bus, 7 litų
Klaipėda
    210 km, three to 3½ hours, about 15 direct daily buses, 24 litų
Lazdijai
    100 km, two hours, nine daily buses, 10.90 litų
Marijampolė
    55 km, one to 1½ hours, about seven daily buses, 5.30 litų
Palanga
    230 km, 3½ hours, about eight daily buses, 26 litų
Panevėžys
    110 km, two hours, about 20 daily buses, 10.90 litų
Pärnu
    445 km, 9½ hours, two daily buses, 42.50 litų
Rīga
    280 km, 5½ hours, four daily buses, 26 litų
Šiauliai
    140 km, three hours, 14 daily buses, 14.20 litų
Tallinn
    575 km, 12 hours, one daily bus, 54 litų

Vilnius
    100 km, two hours, about 30 daily buses (also 12 daily microbuses, 1¾ hours), 9.40 litų

Train Kaunas train station (☎ 221 093, 292 260) is at Čiurlionio 16, at the south end of Vytauto prospektas. Window Nos 1 and 2 sell tickets for any train – look out for the fantastic Soviet mural depicting the national costumes of the 15 former Soviet republics above the windows.

About 18 trains make the trip to/from Vilnius daily (1¼ to two hours, 9 litų). The *Baltic Express*, travelling between Warsaw and Tallinn (via Rīga and Tartu), also passes through Kaunas (see the introductory Getting There & Away chapter). As does the Vilnius-Šeštokai train, which connects with the daily Šeštokai-Suwałki train into Poland.

To/from Klaipėda there are three daily trains (eight hours, 41 litų); to/from Rīga there is one nightly train (5½ hours, 60.80 litų); to/from Kaliningrad there is one daily train (3½ to 4½ hours, 56.60 litų); and to/from Šiauliai there are three daily trains (four hours, 13.20 litų).

Car & Motorcycle Litinterp (see Places to Stay – Bottom End) has cars to rent, as does Neca (☎ 200 258), at Donelaičio 26. The Pentacom-Expo Travel and Business Centre (see Information – Travel Agencies) is the agent for Hertz car rental.

Hydrofoil Between June and August you can travel daily by Raketa hydrofoil along the Nemunas to Nida (four hours), and at weekends to Klaipėda (4½ hours).

The terminal (☎ 261 348, 227 218) is at Raudondvario plentas 107, on the north side of the Nemunas, about half a km west of the mouth of the Neris. Take bus No 11 from the Kaunas Castle terminal on Jonavos gatvė. Trolleybus No 7 will also get you there. Catch it at the train station or (westbound) on Kęstučio gatvė, in the city centre, or from the roundabout on the east side of the Neris bridge.

LITHUANIA

LITHUANIA

Getting Around

Trolleybus Nos 1, 3, 5 and 7 all go north from the train station along Vytauto prospektas, west along Kęstučio gatvė and Nemuno gatvė, then north on Birštono gatvė. In returning they head east along Šv Gertrūdos gatvė, Ožeškienės gatvė and Donelaičio gatvė, then south down Vytauto prospektas to the train station. You can call a taxi on ☎ 237 777 or 236 666.

AROUND KAUNAS
Rumšiškės

The **Open-Air Lithuanian Country Life Museum** (☎ 256-51 589) in Rumšiškės (formerly Pievelės) is well worth a visit for its large and interesting collection of 18th and 19th century Lithuanian country buildings and artefacts. Some 70 original buildings (several entire farmsteads) from the different regions in Lithuania have been transferred to the site, including a chapel, a roadside inn and a barn theatre, which hosts folklore performances in summer. In the museum workshop, potters, weavers and joiners demonstrate their crafts. There are also Samogitian horses (bred on site) in the museum stud. Cart rides and horseback rides around the musuem are available in summer. The museum is open daily, except Monday and Tuesday, from 10 am to 6 pm. It is closed between November and Easter. Guided tours in English are available.

Rumšiškės is 20 km east of Kaunas, about two km off the Vilnius road. To get there take a Vilnius bound bus from Kaunas (or a Kaunas bound bus from Vilnius), and get off at the Rumšiškės stop. You can walk to the museum from there.

Birštonas
• *pop 4000*

Forty km south of Kaunas on the Nemunas is the small spa town of Birštonas. It is largely unremarkable except for the very popular jazz festival it holds (over about three days) in spring, in even-numbered years, which brings out Lithuania's top jazz musicians and many of their fans. There's also an historical museum at Vytauto 9.

ŠIAULIAI
• *pop 147,000* • ☎ *(21)*

Šiauliai, 140 km north of Kaunas and 80 km west of Panevėžys, is Lithuania's fourth biggest city and the main centre of the north-western region of Žemaitija – known throughout much of history as Samogitia. The real magnet of the Šiauliai area is the bizarre **Hill of Crosses**, which is 10 km north of the town off the Rīga road. By car, it can be visited in a day from any of the main Lithuanian cities (or Rīga), but if you're going there by bus you'll probably need to spend a night in Šiauliai.

History

The Šiauliai region played an important role in the fortunes of medieval Lithuania and its enemies. It was here (or not too far from the modern city) in 1236 that the Knights of the Sword, returning north from a raid in Samogitia, were decisively defeated at the Battle of Saulė. The victors were the Samogitians together with – depending on whose account you read – either the Semigallians, from what's now part of Latvia, to their north, or other allies from what's now Lithuania.

The Knights of the Sword grand master, Volquin, was killed the following year, and the knights were forced to reorganise as a branch of the Teutonic Order. The Teutonic Order finally occupied Samogitia in 1398, but a Samogitian rebellion in 1408 led to a joint Lithuanian and Polish campaign against the knights and their decisive defeat at Grünwald in 1410.

Šiauliai was a relatively big town by the mid-15th century. Much of it was consumed by a fire in 1872 and today's town dates mostly from after that. In recent years various proposals have been made to boost the town's dwindling economy, and one idea mooted was to transform the former Žokniai military airport, abandoned by the Soviet army in 1993, into a free economic zone.

Orientation

Central Šiauliai is quite walkable. The main north-south street is Tilžės gatvė, with the bus station towards its southern (lower) end and the tall SS Peter & Paul's Church, on Pergalės aikštė, towards its northern end, almost a km away. To the south, Tilžės gatvė becomes the road to Sovietsk and Kaliningrad, and to the north it becomes the Rīga road. The main east-west axis is Vilniaus gatvė, which crosses Tilžės gatvė 300m south of the church and is pedestrianised for over half a km either side. A small clock tower in the little square where the two streets meet is a good orientation point and a favourite local meeting place.

Information
There is a small tourist information centre (☎ 430 795) at Vilniaus 88. *Šiauliai At Your Fingertips*, a city guide with maps compiled in 1995 by American Peace Corps volunteers, is available from the reception of the Šiauliai hotel (see Places to Stay & Eat). There is a currency exchange (open 10 am to 7 pm) at the bus station. Cash advances can be made on Visa at Šiaulių Bankas, on the corner of Tilžės gatvė and Vilniaus gatvė, and there is an ATM, which accepts MasterCard and Eurocard, outside the Taupomasis Bankas at Tilžės 229. Snoras Bankas, on the corner of Vasario 16-osios and Pergalės aikštė, cashes travellers' cheques.

The post office is at Aušros 42, two blocks west of SS Peter & Paul's Church. Lithuanian Student and Youth Travel (☎ 430 946), at Višinskio 11, can arrange cheap bus, train and plane tickets and is a handy information source.

Town Centre
The chief landmark is the white **SS Peter & Paul's Church** (Šv Petro ir Povilo bažnyčia) overlooking Pergalės aikštė at the north end of the town centre. The church was constructed between 1595 and 1625, from the proceeds of a sale of four-year-old bulls donated by local farmers. It has a 75m spire – claimed to be Lithuania's highest. **St George's Church** on Dubijos gatvė was, as its appearance indicates, originally Russian Orthodox (it was built for the local Russian

PLACES TO STAY
19 Šiauliai Hotel

PLACES TO EAT
3 Vizija Café & Etninės Kultūros Centras
11 Pinguin Bistri
14 Kaukas
15 Little Johnnys
17 Babilonas
18 Bell Italia Picerija

OTHER
1 Žiburys Bookshop
2 Philharmonic
4 Lietuvos Bankas
5 Post Office
6 Delta Knygos
7 Šiauliai Drama Theatre & Saulė Kino
8 SS Peter & Paul's Church
9 Snoras Bankas
10 Dailė Shop
12 Clock Tower
13 Šiaulių Bankas
16 Bus Station
20 Bicycle Museum
21 Tourist Information Centre
22 St George's Church

LITHUANIA

garrison in 1909) but is now Catholic. Another distinctive landmark of the city is the mammoth **sundial**, topped by a bronze statue of an archer. It is at the intersection of Šalkausko gatvė and Ežero gatvė in what has become known as 'Sundial Square'. It was built in 1986 to commemorate the 750th anniversary of the Battle of Saulė. On Vilniaus gatvė, opposite the central market, a monument marks the spot where participants of the 1893 uprising were hung.

Šiauliai has a fun collection of offbeat museums, like the Aušra muziejus, at Aušros 47, which covers history and ethnography;

as well as one specialising in radio and television, at Vilniaus 174; bicycles are covered at Vilniaus 139, cats at Žuvininkų 18 and photography at Vilniaus 140. The first four are open Wednesday to Sunday from 11 am to 5 (or 6), and the last is open Thursday to Monday from noon to 7 pm. There's also an art gallery at Vilniaus 245.

Hill of Crosses

The Hill of Crosses (Kryžių kalnas) is 10 km north of Šiauliai, two km east off the road to Joniškis and Rīga. This two-humped hillock is covered in a forest of (thousands upon thousands of) crosses – large and tiny, expensive and cheap, wood and metal. There are some crosses which are festooned with literally dozens of smaller crosses, and then there are crosses with heaps of little crosses piled at their feet. Some are devotional, to accompany prayers, others are memorials. Some are finely carved folk-art masterpieces.

The hillock is said to have been originally a fortification, and it's thought that the tradition of planting crosses on it may have begun in the 14th century. A great number were placed here in the 19th century to commemorate people killed (or deported to Siberia) in the 1831 and 1863 anti-Russian uprisings. In the Soviet era the crosses, symbols not only of Christianity but, perhaps more importantly, of Lithuanian nationalism, were bulldozed at least three times, always to spring up again.

The Hill of Crosses is an eerie place, especially when the wind blows and the silence is broken by the rattling of crosses and rosaries. Narrow footpaths cut through the forest of crosses. Souvenir sellers sell crosses and rosaries in the car park, if you want to add your mark. Easter brings the biggest flocks of pilgrims.

You can get there from Šiauliai by taxi (around 18 litų one way) or bus. Buses to Meškučius, Joniškis and Rīga pass the beginning of the two km tree-lined road to the hill. Look for the sign 'Kryžių kalnas 2' to indicate where this road is. There are around eight daily buses just to Meškučius, eight to Joniškis, and 12 to Rīga. If you're

coming from the north (say from Rīga or Jelgava, in Latvia), get off on the way past, to avoid going into Šiauliai then coming back out again. If you want to head north after visiting the Hill of Crosses, it may be better to wait for a bus on the main road here and not bother going back into Šiauliai (try to check the schedules before you leave Šiauliai).

Places to Stay & Eat

The Lithuanian Hostels Association operates a *hostel* (☎ 427 845, 421 607) at Rygos 36. A bed in a shared room costs 16 litų a night. The 14 storey *Šiauliai* hotel (☎ 437 333), at Draugystės 25, is quite well run despite its lack of heating and hot water. A three-tier pricing system is still in place. Singles with TV and private bathroom for Lithuanians/Baltic residents/foreigners cost 75/85/140 litų, and doubles are 110/130/200 litų – given the price difference, it is worth trying to persuade the staff that you do, in fact, 'live' in one of the Baltic states.

Unlike hotels, restaurants seem to have mushroomed in recent years, leaving diners with ample choice of places to eat.

A few of the more noteworthy establishments include the authentically Italian *Bella Italia Picerija*, inside a state-of-the-art business complex at Vilniaus 167; the pleasantly plush *Babilonas* next door at Vilniaus 169; and the funky *Vizija*, next to the Etninės Kultūros Centras, at Aušros 15. You can also play billiards here. *Little Johnnys*, close to the bus station at Tilžės 139, does pizza and fried chicken. *Kaukas*, at Tilžės 144, has great conservatory-style windows overlooking the street and is good for an evening drink.

Entertainment

Šiauliai Drama Theatre (☎ 432 940) is at Tilžės 155. The Etninės Kultūros Centras at Aušros 15 hosts a variety of performances. Next door is the Philharmonic. Saulė kino (cinema), at Tilžės 155, occasionally has films in English with Lithuanian subtitles.

Getting There & Away

Šiauliai has quite good connections by bus and train with Rīga, as well as with other places in Lithuania.

Bus The bus station is at Tilžės 109. Services include:

Kaliningrad
    245 km, five hours, one daily bus via Sovietsk
Kaunas
    140 km, three hours, 14 daily buses
Klaipėda
    155 km, 2½ hours or more, six daily buses
Mažeikiai
    80 km, 1½ hours, about 12 daily buses
Palanga
    150 km, 2½ hours, four daily buses
Panevėžys
    80 km, 1¼ to 1½ hours, 12 daily buses
Rīga
    130 km, 2½ to three hours, eight daily buses
Tallinn
    440 km, 8½ hours, two daily buses
Vilnius
    220 km, four hours or more, about 14 daily buses
    (the quickest route is via Panevėžys)

Train The station is at Dubijos 44, about 700m east of the bus station and 700m south of the Šiauliai hotel. Services to/from Šiauliai include:

Daugavpils
    4½ to 5½ hours, two daily trains
Kaunas
    four hours, three daily trains
Klaipėda
    three to four hours, four daily trains
Rīga
    two to 2½ hours, one daily train
Tallinn
    10 hours, one daily train
Vilnius
    4½ hours, one daily train

RADVILIŠKIS & ŠEDUVA
• *pop 21,000 & 3600* • ☎ *(292)*

The railway town of Radviliškis, 22 km south-east of Šiauliai, and its neighbouring village, Šeduva, a few km further south-east on the road to Panevėžys, are both worth making a brief stop at. Dating back to the 16th century, Šeduva is an official architectural monument. The village's highlights include a fine **baroque church,** an **Ethnographic Museum** in an old tannery at Veriškių 7, and the **Daugyvenė Cultural History Museum,** on Aušros aikštė. In Kleboniškiai there is another **Open-Air Museum** (☎ 44 292) stretching for 18 hectares and open daily, except Sunday and Monday, from 10 am to 5 pm. Near Šeduva, at the Radviliškis-Kaunas intersection, stands a windmill, known as the 'windmill of devils' and housing the pre-independence restaurant *Užuovėja,* which serves traditional Lithuanian fare.

Getting There & Away

From Radviliškis, there are two daily trains to Klaipėda via Šiauliai (five hours). There is one daily bus to/from Ignalina (4¾ hours), 10 daily buses to/from Kaunas (1¾ hours), three daily buses to/from Klaipėda, 13 daily buses to/from Panevėžys (55 minutes), five daily buses to/from Vilnius (three hours), and a bus every half-hour to/from Šeduva.

PANEVĖŽYS
• *pop 132,000* • ☎ *(254)*

Panevėžys, 140 km north of Vilnius on the Nevėžis river and on the main road to Rīga, is Lithuania's fifth largest city. The road from Vilnius crosses the western edge of the Aukštaitija Upland, which is largely unremarkable except for some long vistas. Panevėžys is a drab, industrial place full of Soviet era buildings. There's an **Ethnographic Museum** at Vasario 16-osios 23, a **Folk-Art Museum** at Respublikos 56, and an **art gallery** at Respublikos 3. There is also a Lithuanian Student and Youth Travel office (☎ 439 635) at Daukanto 12/106.

Places to Stay

The *Nevėžis* hotel (☎ 35 117) at Laisvės 26 is fairly reasonable. Cheaper options include the *Rambynas* hotel (☎ 61 007), at Respublikos 34, and the *Upytė* hotel (☎ 66 747), at Respublikos 38. Top of the range with all the facilities to match, including a fitness suite, swimming pool and solarium, is the *Ekranas* hotel (☎ 36 821, 69 632), at Elektronikos 1.

Getting There & Away

From Panevėžys, there are buses to/from Vilnius (about 30 daily, taking 2¼ hours), Kaunas (18 to 20 daily, two hours), Šiauliai (12 daily, one to 1½ hours), Bauska (eight daily, two to 2½ hours), Rīga via Bauska (six daily, about four hours), Tallinn via Rīga (one daily, about eight hours) and other destinations. The bus station is at Savanorių aikštė 5.

Left: Antanas Žmuidzinavičius House/Devil's Museum, Kaunas, Lithuania
Right: Folk Festival in Teatro aikste, Klaipėda, Western Lithuania
Bottom: Palanga resort architecture, Lithuania

LIVIJUS GRIGALIUNAS

JONATHAN SMITH

Top: Canoeing in Aukštaitija National Park, Lithuania
Bottom: The Nemunas river in winter, Lithuania

Western Lithuania

HIGHLIGHTS

- Witness one family's persecution under the Soviet regime at the Orvydas rock and sculpture garden
- Trace the region's history at the Kretinga History Museum
- Stroll the streets of Klaipėda's Old Town; go north of the river to visit the post office
- Scale the sand dunes in Nida in the Kuršių Nerija National Park
- Hunt for amber washed up on the beach after spring and autumn storms
- Rub shoulders with the vodka-warmed ice-fishers on the Curonian Lagoon

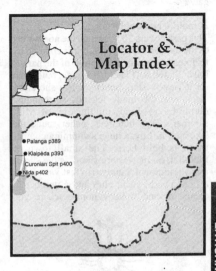

Locator & Map Index

LITHUANIA

Lithuania has a short but attractive coastline. Palanga is the country's main seaside resort and the hottest party spot in summer, while historic Klaipėda, at the mouth of the 100-km-long Curonian Lagoon, is Lithuania's third largest city and a major port.

South of Klaipėda stretches the Baltic states' most unusual natural feature – the Curonian Spit. The cluster of four villages on the spit are known collectively as Neringa. The anorexically thin finger of sand, 98 km long, but nowhere more than four km wide, divides the Curonian Lagoon from the Baltic Sea. It is a place with a touch of magic, the landscape being a heady mix of pine forest and sand dunes up to 66m high. Its northern half is Lithuanian territory, but its southern half Russian – part of the Kaliningrad Region. A paved road runs its entire length, from Smiltynė, the northern tip opposite Klaipėda, to Zelenogradsk, in the Kaliningrad Region. In the Lithuanian half there is accommodation at Smiltynė and at two small fishing villages, Juodkrantė and Nida, which double as holiday resorts.

ŽEMAITIJA UPLAND

North-west Lithuania, historically called Samogitia, is today known as Žemaitija, or Lower Lithuania – in contrast to the northeast of the country which is Aukštaitija (Upper Lithuania). This distinction can hardly be one of altitude since Žemaitija is only slightly lower than Aukštaitija. Samogitians, as west Lithuanians are still called today, are known for their strong sense of ethnic identity.

The Kaunas-Klaipėda highway crosses the southern edge of this upland, passing within 13 km of its highest point, Medvėgalis (234m).

Plungė

Plungė is one of the main towns of the area. It's on the Klaipėda-Kretinga-Šiauliai railway and just off the Palanga-Kretinga-Šiauliai road. A major attraction is the vast neo-classical manor house and estate, which was home to the Oginski family in the 19th century, and today, is home to the **Žemaitija Art Museum** (☎ 218-54 731). The beautiful

385

grounds, covering 50 hectares, are well worth wandering around. Plungė has a hotel, the *Gandinga* (☎ 218-52 345), at Minijos gatvė 4.

Žemaitija National Park

This park covers 200 sq km in the north-west of the upland. Nearly half of it is covered by fir forests. A major focal point of the park is Lake Plateliai (Platelių ežeras), renowned for its seven islets, seven ancient shore terraces, and the many legends surrounding them. Every June, on the eve of Midsummer's Day, hundreds gather round the lake and, in July, a huge swimming competition is held here. The small town of **Plateliai**, on its western shore, is the site of many traditional Samogitian festivals. It has a fine church, yacht club and a number of campsites and holiday homes where you

A traditional Lithuanian roadside cross, typically found in the Žemaitija National Park and Orvydas Garden area.

might find a room. Twenty km to the north-east, just off the Plungė-Mažeikiai road, is **Žemaičių Kalvarija** (Samogitian Calvary). This small town, built on the site of 9th to 13th century burial grounds, is a popular centre of Catholic worship. There are 20 chapels here, forming a seven km 'Stations of the Cross' route, which commemorates Christ's life, death and resurrection. During the first week of July, thousands of pilgrims flock here (for western Lithuania's biggest church festival) commemorating Mary's visit to Elizabeth, mother of John the Baptist.

The park headquarters (☎ 218-49 231, 49 337; fax 218-51 281), at Didžioji gatvė 10 in Plateliai, arranges accommodation and guided tours, issues permits for fishing and camping, and can provide you with information on horse riding and renting yachts, windsurfers, water bikes and other boats.

Getting There & Away

See the Klaipėda, Palanga and Šiauliai sections for information on transport from those places to Plungė.

SALANTAI & MOSĖDIS

The main reason people visit Salantai in the Salantas river valley, 25 km north-west of Plungė, on the road to Skuodas, is to see the **Orvydas Garden** (Orvydų sodyba). This is a large garden decorated with grottos, arches, huts and many fantastic and imaginative wood and stone carvings, often on Christian themes. All the work is by the Orvydas family, who were persecuted in the Soviet years. Most of the bizarre collection dates back to the 1980s, although there are some – with a blue ink mark – that survived Khrushchev's wrath in the 1960s. More recent additions to the collection include the graves of Kazys and Vilius Orvydas (the founder of the garden and his oldest son), and a memorial to AIDS victims. The garden is visible as a grove of trees, to the east of the road just south of Salantai. A traditional Samogitian roadside cross marks the entrance.

Twelve km north of Salantai, on the Skuodas road, is the small town of Mosėdis.

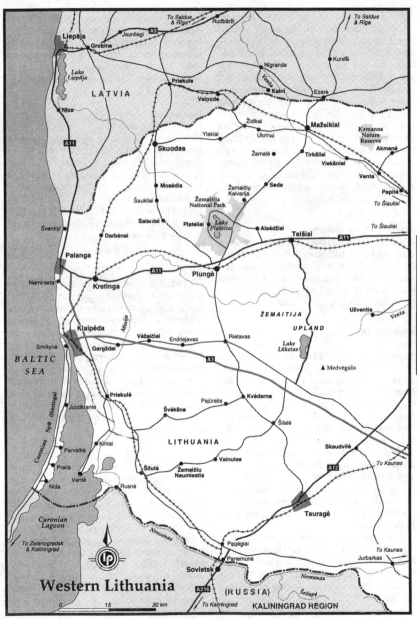

LITHUANIA

Western Lithuania

The goal here is the **Rock Museum** (Akmenų muziejus) on the north side of town. Its main focus is the pit with an obelisk in the middle, which is regarded as a monument to the Lithuanian partisans who resisted Soviet rule – and often died doing it – in the 1940s and 50s. In the village square, three rocks – one of which is carved with writing in the local dialect – pay tribute to the Samogitians born in Mosėdis and its environs. Off the square, close to the village church, is the home of the museum's founder. Peacocks strut through the garden which is filled with traditional Samogitian folk carvings, crosses and shrines of all different shapes and sizes.

Getting There & Away
There are four daily buses each way between Klaipėda and Skuodas (via Salantai and Mosėdis). Buses also run to Salantai and Mosėdis from Plungė. For the Orvydas Garden get off at the last stop before Salantai town and walk about one km.

KRETINGA
• ☎ (258)
Kretinga lies some 10 km east of Palanga, on the Vilnius-Klaipėda railway. Its chief landmark is the classical **Palace & Winter Garden**, built in the 1800s and one of the many homes of the Tyszkiewicz family, Polish nobles. The palace today houses the **Kretinga History Museum** (☎ 51 366) and the exotic glasshouse boasts one of the most appealing cafés and restaurants in the Baltics. Both are open daily, except Sunday and Monday, from 10 am to 6 pm. The remains of a **Franciscan Monastery**, damaged in WWII and never restored, and the **Church of the Annunciation**, are close to the palace.

The *Vienkiemis* guesthouse (☎ 46 425), overlooking a small lake on the north edge of Kretinga at Padvariai, has double rooms with private bath, fridge and TV for 160 litų a night. It also arranges fishing and sailing on the lake. In Žibininkai, there is a small guesthouse with eight rooms attached to the

Pajūrio egzotika brewery (☎ 44 423, 44 413). Guests are invited to sample its freshly-brewed Juozas beer, allegedly made according to the recipe of a 16th century duke. In town, the *Gintaras* restaurant, at Rotušės aikštė 1, is said to be the best.

PALANGA
• *pop 20,000* • ☎ *(236)*
Palanga is 30 km north of Klaipėda and 18 km south of the Latvian border, on a 10 km sandy beach backed by dunes and pine woods. A small and quiet city in winter, it becomes Lithuania's premier seaside resort in summer – a busy place with a bustling happy atmosphere and far too few hotels to cater for the hundreds of Baltic and overseas holiday-makers.

History
Although it appears there are no ancient remains now, Palanga apparently dates back to the 12th century. Lying on what was for centuries a very short stretch of Lithuanian coast, between German (or Prussian) territory to the south and German or Polish-dominated territory to the north, Palanga has often been Lithuania's only port – or potential port, for it was completely destroyed by the Swedish army in 1710. It began to develop as a resort in the 19th century and during the Soviet era the city was one of its leading hot spots.

Orientation
Vytauto gatvė, the main street, runs parallel to the coast about one km inland. The Catholic church at Vytauto 51, on the west side of the street, is roughly the middle of town. The bus station is a few steps east of it at Kretingos 1. Most other places of importance are to the south. Basanavičiaus gatvė, 150m south of the church, is the main avenue to the beach. Klaipėdos plentas, the main road between Klaipėda and the Latvian border, skirts the town to the east, never more than 750m from Vytauto gatvė.

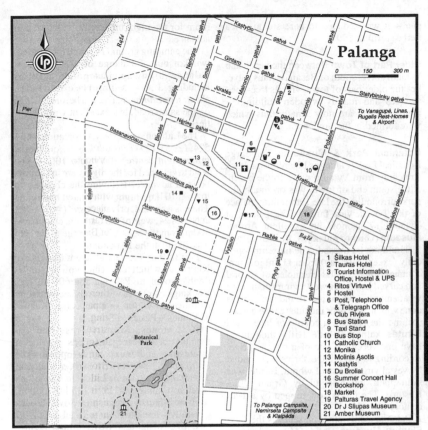

Palanga

0   150   300 m

To Vanagupé, Linas,
Rugelis Rest-Homes
& Airport

To Palanga Campsite,
Nemirseta Campsite
& Klaipéda

Botanical
Park

LITHUANIA

1 Šilkas Hotel
2 Tauras Hotel
3 Tourist Information
   Office, Hostel & UPS
4 Ritos Virtuvé
5 Hostel
6 Post, Telephone
   & Telegraph Office
7 Club Riviera
8 Bus Station
9 Taxi Stand
10 Bus Stop
11 Catholic Church
12 Monika
13 Molinis Ąsotis
14 Kastytis
15 Du Broliai
16 Summer Concert Hall
17 Bookshop
18 Market
19 Palturas Travel Agency
20 Dr J Sliupas Museum
21 Amber Museum

Information

The tourist information office (☎ 53 927), at Vytauto 106, arranges cheap accommodation and guided tours. It's open weekdays from 9 am to 8 pm, and on weekends from 9 am to 4 pm.

Palturas travel agency (☎ & fax 53 598), at Daukanto 33, can arrange day trips to Kretinga and Klaipéda and also organises city tours. The main post office is at Vytauto 53. For express mail, you should try UPS (☎ 53 927) which has a desk inside the tourist information office. Phonecards are also sold here for the public phones in the post office and dotted at strategic locations around town.

Things to See & Do

There are only a couple of 'sights' in Palanga, but the city has plenty of pleasant places to stroll.

Beach Palanga's beach is long, sandy, and backed by pine covered dunes. Despite talk that the sea is not safe to swim in, plenty of people do. From the end of Basanavičiaus gatvé, a wide boardwalk leads over the dunes to what remains of Palanga's long wooden pier – it was reduced to bare stumps by a fierce storm in 1993.

Older Part of Town Between the beach and Vytauto gatvė, south of Basanavičiaus gatvė, lies the older part of town with its tree-lined avenues and mainly wooden buildings – many of them are now sanatoriums which were formed in the Soviet era.

Botanical Park & Museums The large Botanical Park (Palangos botanikos parkas), stretching from Vytauto gatvė to the beach, at the south end of town, was originally the park surrounding the late 19th century palace of the Tyszkiewicz family. The palace, at Vytauto 17, is now an excellent **Amber Museum** (Gintaro muziejus, ☎ 53 501), and it should not be missed. The museum, open daily (except Monday) from 11 am to 7 pm, contains some 20,000 examples of natural and carved amber, as well as information on what amber is, where it is found and what is done with it. The park includes a rose garden (behind the palace), a couple of lakes, and **Birutės kalnas** (Birutė Hill), thought to have once been the site of a pagan shrine. According to legend, the shrine was tended by vestal virgins, one of whom, Birutė, was kidnapped and married by Grand Duke Kęstutis. The hill is now topped by a 19th century chapel.

Palanga's only other museum is the **Dr J Sliupas Museum** (☎ 54 559), at Vytauto 23a. It features local history.

Special Events

Palanga hosts its grand opening of the (summer) season every year on the first Saturday of June. The closing of the season, held the last Saturday in August, is likewise marked by a massive street carnival, song festival, market and pop concert.

Places to Stay

Prices in Palanga change like the wind, dependent not so much on the product offered but the demand. At the height of the season it is practically impossible to get a

room for the night unless you've booked in advance.

The camping ground *Palanga* (☎ 51 676), two km out of Palanga on the Klaipėda-Palanga highway, has good facilities including a shop selling basic provisions. *Nemirseta Campsite*, five km before Palanga on the same road, has excellent wash facilities.

The Lithuanian Hostels Association (☎ 51 524; fax 57 125) runs a *hostel* adjoining the information centre, at Vytauto 106. If you want to get a bed for the night here in summer book in advance! Beds are the cheapest in town at 10 litų a night with shared bathroom. There is a second, private *hostel* (☎ 57 076), at Nėries 24, west of the Catholic church and 300m from the sea. A bed for the night here was 20 litų at the last count.

For B&B try the very efficient *Litinterp* in Klaipėda, which can find you a single/double room in Palanga for 60/100 litų. Bookings can be made in advance through its offices in Vilnius or Kaunas (see Kaunas & Vilnius – Places to Stay).

Rest-homes, formerly reserved for members of Soviet organisations, provide an interesting and inexpensive option. The *Baltija* (☎ 53 841; fax 52 686), at Ganyklų 39, arranges accommodation in any of its seven rest-homes for 25 to 135 litų a night. All its rest-homes – large, grey Soviet blocks generally – are kitted out with all the facilities, like swimming pool, fitness centre, conference hall, bar and restaurant. The *Linas* rest-home (☎ 51 137), at Vytauto 155, offers singles/doubles for 100/150 litų.

The former Jūratė holiday home at Mickevičiaus 8 has been converted into the small, privately run *Kastytis* hotel (☎ 53 504), with comfortable rooms. North of the centre is the *Vanagupė* (☎ 56 102), at Vytauto 171, with over 100 rooms on six floors. It belongs to the Lithuanian Shipping Company and ranks as one of the best holiday homes in Palanga, complete with saltwater swimming pools.

Popular for its more personal and friendly service is the *Du Broliai* (Two Brothers) hotel (☎ 54 028), at Daukanto 15. But prices have soared since it first opened its doors. Expect to pay at least 300 litų for one of its nine double rooms. The *Šilkas* hotel (☎ 575 19), at Gintaro 25, is a more reasonable bet. Singles/doubles cost 80/140 litų. The *Tauras* hotel (☎ 54 437), close by at Vytauto 116, is kitted out with new modern wood furnishings and is another good option. Singles/doubles start at 80/150 litų.

Places to Eat

Practically every other building along Vytauto and Basanavičiaus gatvė is some sort of café, bar or restaurant – each one with blaring music, which makes dining out in Palanga a far from calm experience.

Some of the more distinctive places include *Monika*, in a wooden cabin at Basanavičiaus 12; *Molinis Ąsotis* at Basanavičiaus 8; and *Du Broliai*, less central at Daukanto 15. All three serve traditional Lithuanian dishes and ales.

Beatles fans should try *Ritos Virtuvė*, a fantastically coloured café at Vytauto 106, serving huge plates of pasta, giant 'sub' sandwiches and pizza for around 15 litų.

Ida Basar, out of town at Kretingo 57, is well worth the trek. Be prepared to pay dearly for it though. Main meals at Palanga's most stylish restaurant and exclusive beer bar start at around 40 litų. It is open daily from 11 to 1 am.

Villa Ramybė, at Vytauto 54, is said to be about the coolest bar-cum-café in town. Also recommended is the more mainstream *Club Rivjera*, at Vytauto 98a, where you can bop (or eat) until you drop. It's open daily from 10 am to 2 am. *Metaxa*, close to the beach, is another must.

Entertainment

The tourist information office (see Information) always knows what's on where. Alternatively, watch for posters on the corner of Basanavičiaus and Birutės gatvė. Palanga holds many summer music festivals, covering everything from hard rock to light classical or chamber music. The main venue is the Summer Concert Hall (Vasaros koncertų salė) at Vytauto 43.

Getting There & Away

You can reach Palanga by road or air. Services tend to be more frequent in summer. Kretinga is the nearest train station and it is served by at least four daily trains to/from Klaipėda, and two each to/from Vilnius and Šiauliai.

Motorists are required to pay a small entrance fee to drive into Palanga.

Air Air Lithuania flies five times a week to/from Kaunas, and twice a week to Kristianstad in Sweden. Its nearest ticket office (☎ 26-210 665) is in Klaipėda at Janonio 5/1. Lithuanian Airlines flies to Hamburg daily. It has an office in Klaipėda (see Klaipėda – Getting There & Away) and in Palanga (☎ 53 541), at Kretingos 1. The airport is six km from the town centre on the main road north.

Bus The bus station is on Kretingos gatvė, just east of Vytauto gatvė, in the centre of town. Services include:

Kaliningrad
    six hours, two daily buses
Kaunas
    3½ hours, eight daily buses
Klaipėda
    45 minutes, more than 30 daily buses
Kretinga
    20 minutes, up to 30 daily buses
Liepāja
    1¾ hours, two daily buses
Rīga
    5½ hours, one daily bus
Šiauliai
    2½ hours, four daily buses
Vilnius
    six hours, 15 daily buses

Getting Around

Bus No 2 runs to/from the airport, roughly every hour from 6 am to 10 pm. Timetables are posted at its town centre stop, on Poželos gatvė behind the bus station. Bus No 1 runs the length of the town (via the same stop on Poželos gatvė), but is erratic and infrequent. The main taxi stand is also on Poželos gatvė behind the bus station.

You can also rent bikes from the hostel or tourist information centre.

KLAIPĖDA
• *pop 204,600* • ☎ *(26)*

The port of Klaipėda, the third biggest city in Lithuania, is 315 km west of Vilnius, beside the narrow strait where the Curonian Lagoon opens into the Baltic Sea. Though most of the city now dates from after WWII (when much of it was wrecked) it's an interesting and attractive place. It has a long, curious, and mostly German history which still draws thousands of German tourists every year. Its other drawcard is the Curonian Spit, which is just a five minute ferry ride away.

History
There was probably a fishing village here – settled by ancient Balts at the mouth of the Danė river – before the German crusaders arrived in the region, but Klaipėda has been a predominantly German town, called Memel, for nearly all its history. A castle was founded here in 1252 by the Livonian Order and transferred, along with its surrounding settlement, to the Teutonic Order in 1328.

Memel was the northernmost town of the territory ruled by, firstly, the Teutonic Order (until its demise in the 16th century), then the Duchy of Prussia, the order's successor state. From 1871 to WWI, it was part of a united Germany that stretched as far west as the borders of France and Switzerland.

The town has been destroyed several times by war, beginning in the 13th and 14th centuries when the Teutonic Order and Lithuania were at war. In 1678 it was reduced to ashes by Sweden. Up to the 17th century, brick and stone houses were forbidden, because, it was reasoned, they would likely survive the city's fall and provide cover for an enemy.

By WWI, Memel had about 30,000 inhabitants – and an even ratio of Germans and Lithuanians – after economic development, through timber trade and shipbuilding, in the 18th and 19th centuries.

Under the Treaty of Versailles at the end of WWI, the town, the northern half of the Curonian Spit, and a strip of land (about 150 km long and 20 km wide) along the east side of the Curonian Lagoon and the north side of the Nemunas river, were separated from Germany as an 'international territory'. An autonomous government was established and a French garrison stationed there. This 'Memel Territory' remained in a kind of stateless limbo until January 1923, when Lithuanian troops marched in, drove the French out, and annexed it. In 1925 Memel officially became Klaipėda for the first time.

Hitler annexed the territory in March 1939 – his last land grab before WWII began. In January 1945, whole sections of the town were flattened in the bombardment leading to its capture by the Red Army. Most of the population had already been evacuated. Only a handful of Germans live in or around Klaipėda today.

After WWII, Klaipėda was rebuilt, repopulated (mainly by Lithuanians and Russians) and developed into an important Soviet city on the back of shipbuilding and fishing.

Orientation
The Danė river flows westward across the city centre and enters the Curonian Lagoon four km from the Baltic Sea. The key street axis is the single, long, north-south main street called, variously, Manto gatvė (north of the river), Tiltų gatvė (for its first 600m south of the river), and then Taikos prospektas.

The heart of the old part of town lies within the 400m south of the river, mostly west of Tiltų gatvė. Most hotels, the train and bus stations, and many other services are north of the river.

Smiltynė, the northern tip of the Curonian Spit, lies about 500m off the mouth of the Danė, across the narrow channel which forms the north end of the Curonian Lagoon.

Maps Briedis (see Vilnius – Maps) publishes a useful Klaipėda and Palanga map (1:15,000), which is available from most news kiosks for 8.40 litų. For a detailed city

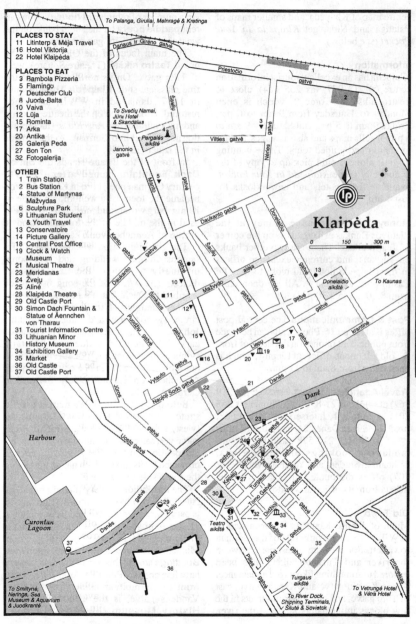

To Palanga, Girulai, Melnragé & Kretinga

PLACES TO STAY
11 Litinterp & Méja Travel
16 Hotel Viktorija
22 Hotel Klaipėda

PLACES TO EAT
3   Rambola Pizzeria
5   Flamingo
7   Deutscher Club
8   Juoda-Balta
10 Vaiva
12 Lūja
15 Rominta
17 Arka
20 Antika
26 Galerija Peda
27 Bon Ton
32 Fotogalerija

OTHER
1   Train Station
2   Bus Station
4   Statue of Martynas Mažvydas
6   Sculpture Park
9   Lithuanian Student & Youth Travel
13 Conservatoire
14 Picture Gallery
18 Central Post Office
19 Clock & Watch Museum
21 Musical Theatre
23 Meridianas
24 Žvejų
25 Aliné
28 Klaipėda Theatre
29 Old Castle Port
30 Simon Dach Fountain & Statue of Äennchen von Tharau
31 Tourist Information Centre
33 Lithuanian Minor History Museum
34 Exhibition Gallery
35 Market
36 Old Castle
37 Old Castle Port

Dariaus ir Giréno gatvé

Priestočio gatvé

To Svečių Namai, Jūra Hotel & Skandalas

Pergalés aikšté

Vilties gatvé

Janonio gatvé

Šaulių

Néries gatvé

Daukanto gatvé

Donelaičio

Mantu

Šaulių aléja

Kanto gatvé

Daukanto

Simkaus

Puodžių gatvé

Mažvydo

Karoso

Jūros

Vytauto

Vytauto

Naujoji Sodo gatvé

Danés

Klaipėda

0   150   300 m

Donelaičio aikšté

To Kaunas

Kranté

Liepų

Dané

To Palanga, Girulai, Melnragé & Kretinga

Harbour

Uosto gatvé

Danés

Curonian Lagoon

Žvejų

Kurpių gatvé

Turgaus

Tono gatvé

Vandens gatvé

Teatro aikšté

Aukštoji gatvé

Pilies gatvé

Daržų gatvé

Turgaus aikšté

To Smiltyné, Neringa, Sea Museum & Aquarium & Juodkranté

To River Dock, Shipping Terminals, Šilute & Sovietsk

To Vetrungé Hotel & Vétra Hotel

Talkos prospektas

LITHUANIA

centre map of Klaipėda, and smaller maps of Palanga and Nida, get *Klaipėda In Your Pocket* (see below).

Information

Klaipėda has an excellent tourist information centre (☎ 213 977; fax 255 124), close to Teatro aikštė at Tomo 2, which is open Monday to Thursday from 9 am to 6 pm, Friday 9 am to 5 pm, and Saturday 9 am to 4 pm. It sells maps and also arranges accommodation and guided tours. Those wanting to go it alone should pick up a copy of the annual city guide *Klaipėda In Your Pocket*, available from hotels and news kiosks for just 4 litų.

Money You can change money at the Lietuvos Bankas at Turgaus 1, on the corner of Teatro aikštė. There are two other banks on Turgaus, and currency exchange offices in the Klaipėda hotel and close to the Old Castle port, at Žvejų 8. All are open daily from 8.30 am to 5.30 pm.

Post & Communications The central post office is at Liepų 16. Phone calls can be made from public card phones on the street or from the old telephone office, at Liepų 1, which is open daily from 8 am to 11 pm.

Travel Agencies Mėja (☎ 216 962; fax 219 862) at Šimkaus 21-8, Baltic Clipper (☎ 255 801) at Kurpių 1, Interservice (☎ 210 663; fax 212 389) at Danės 21, and Eurikos turas (☎ 253 375; fax 218 578), all offer accommodation bookings and excursions. Lithuanian Student and Youth Travel (☎ 212 707) offers discounted air, plane and bus tickets from its office at Manto 14.

Old Town

Much of central Klaipėda was wrecked in WWII, so there are only bits of the German town left. Some of the oldest part, between the river and Turgaus aikštė, has been restored to something like its old appearance. Along Kurpių gatvė and Kepėjų gatvė, east of Tiltų gatvė, and other narrow streets in the few blocks immediately south of the river,

are a number of rebuilt **old houses**. You can rent **paddle boats** on the south bank, on the west side of the Tiltų gatvė bridge.

The main focus of the Old Town is the broad **Teatro aikštė** (Theatre Square), west of Tiltų gatvė. On its north side stands the fine classical-style **Klaipėda Theatre** built in 1857, damaged in WWII, and since restored. Hitler stood on the theatre balcony and proclaimed the *Anschluss* (incorporation) of Memel into Germany to the crowds in the square in 1939.

In front of the theatre stands the **Simon Dach Fountain**, named after the 17th century German poet, born in Klaipėda, who became the focus of a well known circle of Königsberg writers and musicians. On a pedestal in the middle of the fountain stands a **statue** of Äennchen von Tharau.

The girl in question was the subject of a famous German wedding and love song, originally written in the East Prussian dialect. The words of the song used to be ascribed to Dach, but it's now thought that another member of the same Königsberg circle, the composer and cathedral organist Johann Albert, wrote them. The original early 20th century statue and fountain, symbols of Memel, did not survive WWII, but replicas were put in place in 1989 by the Äennchen von Tharau Society, founded in Germany for the purpose.

Before WWII, Klaipėda's market used to stretch west from Teatro aikštė to the far (west) side of Pilies gatvė. West of Pilies gatvė you can make out the site of Klaipėda's old **castle**, south of Žvejų gatvė, and still protected by its moat which has an outlet into the south side of the Danė.

The **Exhibition Gallery** (Parodų rumai), at Aukštoji 3, two blocks south of Teatro aikštė, is partly housed in a converted fish warehouse in the exposed timbers style known as *Fachwerk*, which was typical of German Memel. There are a few more **Fachwerk Buildings** around this part of town – a particularly fine one is at Pilies 19. Around the corner from the Exhibition Gallery, on Didžioji Vandens gatvė, is the **Lithuanian Minor History Museum** (Mažosios Lietuvos

Istorijos muziejus), open Wednesday to Sunday from 11 am to 7 pm.

North of the River

There's a **riverside park** along the north bank of the Danė, immediately east of the Tiltų/Manto gatvė bridge. Klaipėda's **Picture Gallery** (Paveikslų galerija) and sculpture garden (which was formerly the German cemetery) is at Liepų 33. It's open Wednesday to Sunday from noon to 6 pm. There's a **Clock & Watch Museum** (Laikrodžių muziejus) at Liepų 12, open daily, except Monday, from noon to 5.30 pm. Liepų gatvė was once, for an inglorious brief spell, called Adolf-Hitler-Strasse. Manto gatvė was Hermann-Göring-Strasse. The nearby **Post Office** is worth a visit for its beautiful painted wooden interior.

A monument to the Red Army used to stand on the square between Manto gatvė and Vilties gatvė. A three metre tall, granite **statue** of Martynas Mažvydas – the author of *Catechisms*, the first book to be published in Lithuanian in 1547 – was unveiled here on the book's 450th anniversary in September 1997. During the late 19th century, when printing books in the Lithuanian alphabet was banned (the official language was Russian), writers followed Mažvydas' example by printing their books in Königsberg (Kaliningrad) and smuggling them into Lithuania.

Smiltynė

Smiltynė, at the narrow north end of the 98 km Curonian Spit, is Klaipėda's playground. There are beaches, high dunes, pine forests, and a collection of exhibitions and museums. Smiltynė is easy to reach, with regular ferries making the five minute crossing from the Old Castle port in Klaipėda to the ferry landing on the east side of Smiltynė, two km from the tip of the peninsula. On hot summer weekends people pour across in their thousands, and the beaches become absolutely packed.

The office of the Kuršių Nerija National Park, which covers most of the Lithuanian part of the Curonian Spit, is also at Smiltynė (see Neringa section).

Exhibitions On the east side of Smiltynė, heading north along the path to the Sea Museum & Aquarium, there are three exhibitions with a particular local flavour. The Kuršių Nerija Nature Museum (Kuršių nerijos gamtos muziejus ekspozicija), 200m from the ferry landing, gives an introduction to the flora, fauna and landscape of the spit. About 700m further along is a 'garden of veteran fishing boats' ('žvejybos laivai-veteranai'). Next along is an Ethnographic Coastal Fishing Settlement (Etnografinė pajūrio žvejo sodyba) with a small collection of traditional 19th century, wooden, fishing houses. Those reluctant to make the 20 minute walk along this path can always take a horse and cart or catch a little train from the ferry landing to the Sea Museum & Aquarium, for around 25 litų.

Sea Museum & Aquarium Smiltynė's main showpiece is 1.5 km north of the ferry landing. It's set in a large 19th century fort, built by the Prussian army betweeen 1865 and 1871. Sea lion performances are at 1 and 3 pm, and the dolphin shows are at noon, 2 and 4 pm. The aquarium has tropical fish as well as 'local' fish from the Curonian Lagoon and the Baltic Sea, a coral and shell display, and a section tracing the history of ship design. It is open daily between May and September, except Monday, from 11 am to 7 pm. From October to April it is open daily, except Monday and Tuesday, from 11 am to 6 pm. Admission is 10 litų.

The fortress itself was intended to protect Klaipėda from naval attack, but, by the end of the 19th century, advances in military technology had rendered it obsolete. In WWII the Germans used it as an ammunition store, then blew it up in 1945 as the Red Army was moving in to take Klaipėda. It was reconstructed for its present purpose in the 1970s.

Within the museum, the **Wrecked Rowing Boat** of Gintaras Paulionis (1945 – 1994), the first Lithuanian to cross the Baltic

LITHUANIA

Sea in a rowing boat, is on display. The Klaipėda fisherman set off on 28 June, 1994, and arrived in Sweden some three weeks later. During the return journey, his boat capsized and he is thought to have drowned in the storm that also brought the *Estonia* ferry down in September 1994.

Beaches A sandy beach fronts the Baltic Sea all the way down the west side of Smiltynė. Intertwined branches have been placed on the dunes to help prevent the sand from shifting. For this very reason, it is forbidden to stray off the marked tracks.

Sections of beach signposted *'Moterų pliažas'* are meant for women only; sections marked *'Vyrų pliažas'* are for men. A *'bendras pliažas'* is a mixed beach. Tracks lead through the forest from the east side of the peninsula to the west. If you follow the track straight ahead from the ferry landing, or the one veering off the road 300m further south, after about one km you'll come out on a general beach.

Places to Stay

Don't be deceived by the seemingly new sign advertising the Smiltynė hotel which greets you when you step off the ferry. At the time of writing, Smiltynė's only place to stay, 300m down the coast from the ferry landing, was boarded up – but watch out for future renovations!

The bed and breakfast agency *Litinterp* (☎ 216 962; fax 219 862; email litinterp@ klaipeda.omnitel.net), at Šimkaus 21/8, offers single/double rooms in Klaipėda for 60/100 litų a night. It also rents bicycles.

The central *Viktorija* hotel (☎ 213 670), at Šimkaus 28, is not particularly luxurious but its spartan rooms are incredibly clean and brilliant value. Singles/doubles/triples with shared bathrooms cost 35/55/65 litų. If there are five of you, go for the spacious five-bed rooms costing 100 litų a night.

A bottom end place worth trying if you're really desperate is the *Vetrungė* hotel (☎ 254 801, 254 808), south of the city centre at Taikos 28. Singles/doubles with grotty private bathrooms are 80/130 litų. The

service must be among the most unfriendly in town.

The hotel *Vėtra* (☎ 275 002; fax 278 622), at Taikos 80a, offers 10% discount to Euro<26 card holders.

Pretty ordinary, but improving all the time, is the former Intourist hotel, *Klaipėda* (☎ 217 324; fax 253 911). A modern brick building with a 12 storey central tower, it is just north of the Dané river, beside Manto gatvė, at Naujoji Sodo 1. The hotel sells a wide range of maps and guidebooks at the reception, has a currency exchange, bar and restaurant, and is the only place in town to serve an early, all you can eat breakfast buffet (20 litų, 7 to 11 am). Singles/doubles with private bathroom cost 160/240 litų. In summer it is often fully booked with German tour groups.

There are more modern hotels, which have sprung up in recent years, offering a more western service, including the *Jūra* (☎ 299 857), close to the port at Malūnininkų 3, which has singles/doubles for 100/110 litų. The luxurious *Mabre* (☎ 210 638; fax 219 197) is tucked away in the Old Town at Skerdėjų 12 and has doubles for one/two people for 200/225 litų, while the friendly *Fortūna* (☎ 275 242; fax 360 174), at Poilsio 64, has singles/doubles for around 170/210 litų.

Outstripping them all in price and prestige is *Svečių Namai* (☎ & fax 310 900), at Janonio 11, which has luxurious apartments for 200 to 400 litų. One of Klaipėda's few remaining Soviet hammer & sickle symbols is carved on the top of the building opposite.

Overlooking the beach amid some pretty pine forests, eight km north of Klaipėda centre in the suburb of Giruliai, at Slaito 18a, is the *Pajūris* (☎ 290 154; fax 290 137). A few doors down, at Slaito 12, is the privately run *Youth Travellers Station* (☎ 296 106) which charges around 40 litų a night for a bed in shared accommodation. Euro<26 card holders get a 20% discount. The large, former sanatorium has singles/doubles for 160/180 litų. At Melnragė, near the coast four km north of the centre, is the smaller, family run *Morena* (☎ 298 456), at Audros

8a, which offers wood panelled rooms in the attic for 100/220 litų.

Places to Eat

The top place to eat in Klaipėda is also one of the best bars in the Baltics. Decked out with swing chairs suspended from the ceiling and a public phone installed in an old black car parked inside, *Skandalas* (The Scandal), at Kanto 44, is a place you cannot miss. One trip here and you'll be dreaming of its giant-sized American steaks, served in a variety of sauces with creamed, fried, jacket or boiled potatoes, every time you eat somewhere else. It's open daily from noon to 3 am. Take note, prices – about 25 litų for a main course – rise by 40% after 7 pm, so get there early!

The other eatery Klaipėda is famed for (in Lithuania at least) is *Bambola Pizzeria*, a two minute walk from the train station, at Nėries 10, which serves over 40 different types of pizza for around 13 litų. It is open daily from 11 am to 10 pm.

Inside an art gallery, the stylish *Galerija Peda*, at Turgaus 10, is the best place for light evening snacks, especially at weekends when it has live jazz.

Fotogalerija, in the heart of the Old Town at Tomo 7, is a touch more offbeat with traditional soups and karbonadas for 4 to 8 litų. The popular *Bon Ton*, close by on Mėsininkų gatvė, serves many a cheap fill in a cheerful setting. Its outside courtyard is one of Klaipėda's hottest spots in summer – along with the outside seating at *Raytės'* at Tiltų 6.

The *Deutscher Club*, at Daukanto 24, is a little enclave of German food and beer, and local bands often play here in the evening. *Antika*, next to the clock and watch museum at Liepų 12, serves good food with good service in elegant surroundings. As does *Emilija*, at Turgaus 23, which specialises in traditional karbonadas served with a variety of fruits. *Arka*, at Liepų 20, is the place to go for central Asian dishes.

On Manto gatvė there are numerous choices. The bright and breezy *Flamingo* at No 38 is the best spot for people-watching. No 20 is home to *Lūja*, Klaipėda's most expensive restaurant – which demands formal dress and offers a cabaret show most nights. Opposite, in a former cinema at No 11, is *Vaiva*, which specialises in seafood. No 13 houses the Soviet era *Juoda-Balta*, where lunch can still be had for less than 5 litų! *Rominta*, with its big window overlooking the street at No 5, was also around during the Soviet era but is still equally popular for its cheap light snacks and extensive breakfast menu, which kicks off daily at 8 am.

The *Nesė* canteen-cum-bar, in the Old Castle port at Žvejų 8, serves cheap salads for 4 litų, coffee for 1 litų and is open daily from 8 to 6 am. McDonald's is expected to hit Klaipėda by the end of 1997.

Entertainment

The Drama Theatre (Dramos teatros) is at Teatro aikštė 2. Klaipėda's Music Academy has a concert hall at Donelaičio 4, and the city's Musical Theatre (Muzikinis teatras), home to the Klaipėda Philharmonic, is at Danės krantinė 19, on the corner of Manto gatvė, just north of the river.

Beer Bars Klaipėda's Old Town seems to boast more traditional Lithuanian beer bars than any other place in Lithuania. The most popular include *Žvejų* (open daily from 10 am to 10 pm), overlooking the river at Žvejų 3, and *Alinė*, at Jono 5, which is open daily from 11 am to 11 pm. The *Meridianas*, an old sailing ship moored on the river by the Manto gatvė bridge, now operates as a bar.

Getting There & Away

This section concentrates on services within the Baltic states and the Kaliningrad Region. Information on buses to/from Poland, Belarus, and more on the ships to/from Germany, is given in the Getting There & Away chapter.

Klaipėda's train and bus stations are 150m apart on Priestočio gatvė, about 1.5 km north of the river and 750m east of Manto gatvė. The train station has an unusual tall, helmeted clock tower. Both stations have *Informacija* windows.

LITHUANIA

Air The nearest airport is north of Palanga (see the Palanga section – Getting There & Away). Lithuanian Airlines (☎ 230 409) has a booking office at Taikos 107 in Klaipėda. Air Lithuania (☎ 210 665) is at Janonio 5/1.

Bus The Klaipėda-Kaunas-Vilnius highway is one the best in the Baltics, and the (roughly) nine daily buses to/from Vilnius take about five hours, while the 15 or so daily buses to/from Kaunas take three to 3½ hours.

Most buses to Juodkrantė, Nida and Kaliningrad do not depart from the main bus station, but from the ferry landing on the Curonian Spit at Smiltynė. Their (theoretical) schedules are posted up at the stop at Smiltynė, but it is better to ask at the Informacija window at the bus station. In summer, microbuses to Nida (via Juodkrantė) run every half-hour from the ferry landing.

Services to/from Klaipėda include:

Druskininkai
  5½ hours, one daily bus
Jurbarkas
  2½ hours, eight daily buses
Kaliningrad
  3½ to four hours, four daily from Smiltynė (via Nida)
Kretinga
  one hour and 10 minutes, 11 daily buses
Liepāja
  2¾ hours, two daily buses
Mažeikiai
  2½ to three hours, six daily buses
Nida
  1½ to two hours, two daily buses from the bus station; 1¼ hours, microbuses every half-hour from Smiltynė
Palanga
  45 minutes, 13 daily buses; plus local microbuses every half-hour in summer
Rīga
  six or seven hours, two daily buses
Šiauliai
  2½ hours or more, six daily buses
Sovietsk
  two hours, two daily buses

Train There are one night and three day trains each way to/from Vilnius, via Kaunas. The night train also goes via Šiauliai. Trav-

elling times are: Vilnius five hours (afternoon) or 9¾ hours (overnight), Kaunas eight hours. There are two daily trains to/from Šiauliai (3¾ hours) originating in Radviliškis, and others to/from Tauragė, Pagėgiai, Kretinga and Mažeikiai.

Hydrofoil & Ship Between June and August there's a hydrofoil service along the Nemunas river between Nida and Kaunas (four hours). The Raketa speedboat sails at 3 pm daily (except Monday) from Nida. Upon special request, it is also possible to arrive/depart from Klaipėda (☎ 212 224, 227 218). Ask hotels and travel agents for information on schedules, tickets and departure points.

See the Getting There & Away chapter for schedules and fares on the ferries to/from Kiel and Mukran in Germany, Århus in Sweden, and Fredericia and Copenhagen in Denmark. For information and bookings on the Kiel and Århus ferries in Klaipėda, contact Krantas Shipping (☎ 365 444, 399 420; fax 365 443; email krantaspass@ klaipeda.omnitel.net; www.omnitel. net/krantas). For the Mukran ferry, contact Ost-Reise Service (☎ 255 052; fax 257 377) inside the Klaipėda hotel, at Naujoji Sodo 1. And for the Fredericia and Copenhagen services, contact DFDS Transport (☎ 310 598; fax 310 596) in Klaipėda, at Kareivinių 2/7.

Getting Around

Bus Bus Nos 1 and 8, from the Geležinkelio Stotis stop outside the train station, run south to Pergalės aikštė then down Manto through the city centre to the Turgus stop, on Taikos prospektas just past the market.

Ferry The main Smiltynė ferry leaves from the Old Castle port, on the south bank of the Danė river on Žvejų gatvė, 100m west of the Naujoji Uosto/Pilies gatvė bridge. It docks on the east side of Smiltynė, the start of the road to Nida, and 1.5 km south of the Sea Museum & Aquarium.

Timetables are posted at the ticket office. Ferries sail to/from Smiltynė daily, every hour between 6 and 9 am, half-hourly between 10 am and 10 pm, and hourly again between 9 pm and 1.30 am. The crossing takes five minutes and a return journey (only return tickets are sold) is 1 litų for foot passengers, 1.5/three litų for bicycles/motorcycles, and 11 litų for a car and driver.

Another ferry service – recommended for motorists – sails half-hourly from 7.30 am to 9.30 pm from the New River port (upių prieplauka), three km south of the mouth of the Danė. On the Curonian Spit this ferry docks 2.5 km south of the ferry landing at Smiltynė. Bus No 1 continues down to the New River port from its stops in Klaipėda city centre. Get off at the New River port stop.

Curonian Spit (Neringa)

• *pop 2700* • ☎ *(259)*

The typical Baltic coastal scent of mingled ozone and pine is at its headiest on the northern Lithuanian half of the Curonian Spit. This area is made up of four settlements – Juodkrantė, Pervalka, Preila and Nida – which form the Neringa township. Never more than a couple of km from a coast, and usually much closer than you think, there's a magical air to this isolated 98 km thread of sand between the Curonian Lagoon and the Baltic Sea which is held together by wondrous sand dunes and lush pine forests inhabited by elk, deer and wild boar. The only industry on the spit is fishing, and savouring the fish freshly smoked (to an old Curonian recipe) is a must.

There is a universal affection for this place, not only by Lithuanians and Russians, but also by the many Germans who once lived on the spit and now enjoy holidays here instead.

The entire Curonian Spit was Prussian or German territory until WWI. The northern half was annexed by Lithuania, along with the rest of the 'Memel Territory', in 1923, but remained a retreat for Germans until WWII. It has probably changed less since then than anywhere else in the northern half

of the (old) East Prussian area, giving it a magnetic attraction for returning German exiles. During the Soviet era the holiday accommodation was more or less reserved for communist *apparatchiks* and their families.

The southern half of the spit is Russian, and a road runs the whole length to Kaliningrad. The main settlement on the Lithuanian side is Nida (former German name: Nidden), a popular summer resort just north of the Russian border where amber is washed up on the shores after spring and autumn storms. Like the handful of other settlements, Nida is on the sheltered lagoon coast and began life as a fishing village. Nida and Juodkrantė, further north, now also function as laid-back resorts. The good, sandy beaches are all on the west coast of the spit, where the waters can get quite rough as it faces the widest part of the Baltic Sea. Don't bathe in the lagoon – it's badly polluted – and check locally on the cleanliness of the waters on the Baltic coast.

The Curonian Spit is called the Kuršių nerija in Lithuanian, and is known to Germans as the Kurische Nehrung. According to Lithuanian folklore, it was the motherly sea giantess Neringa who lovingly carried armfuls of sand in her apron to form the spit and so build a protected harbour for the local fishing folk. The truth is almost as enchanting, the spit being formed 5000 or 6000 years ago as the waves and winds let sand accumulate in shallow waters near the coast.

Its trees were originally a mixture of deciduous and coniferous, but heavy felling in the 16th and 17th centuries removed most of the deciduous forests, leading to severe sand shift – the result, tragically, saw 14 villages buried beneath the golden sands. Reforestation to stabilise the sands began in the 19th century and since 1991, the Lithuanian part of the spit has been protected under the **Kuršių Nerija National Park**. The dunes are delicate and their continual steady erosion is of great concern to environmentalists. It's for this reason you should only walk along the marked tracks and don't pick the flowers, they help to stabilise the sands.

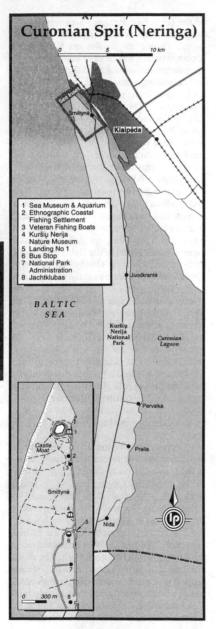

Curonian Spit (Neringa)

1 Sea Museum & Aquarium
2 Ethnographic Coastal
   Fishing Settlement
3 Veteran Fishing Boats
4 Kuršių Nerija
   Nature Museum
5 Landing No 1
6 Bus Stop
7 National Park
   Administration
8 Jachtklubas

BALTIC
SEA

Smiltynė
Klaipėda
Juodkrantė
Kuršių
Nerija
National
Park
Curonian
Lagoon
Pervalka
Preila
Castle
Moat
Smiltynė
Nida

Information on the park is available at the park office eight km down the road from Smiltynė. Entrance to the park is 2/10 litų per person/car and driver. ISC holders enter for free. If you are travelling into the park by bus, the fee is automatically included in the bus fare. The speed limit for cars is 40 km/h and cars need to be parked in specially designated parking areas. Beware of the occasional elk crossing the road too!

JUODKRANTĖ

The small, quiet village of Juodkrantė (former German name: Schwarzort) is 20 km south of Smiltynė on the east (lagoon) coast of the spit, and is the first settlement you come to travelling south from there. Between 1854 and 1855, and again in 1860, amber was excavated in the village in three separate little clusters. At the north end there's an area around a pretty little fishing harbour known as the Amber Bay. The central part, a km south, focuses on a bunch of holiday homes, and here you'll also find a couple of shops, a post office, a canteen-and-bar called the *Kavinė Naglis*, and the main bus stop and pier. A km further south there's a little village area with an old German Protestant church. Juodkrantė has quite a number of prettily painted, old wooden cottages – with colourful gardens in summer.

The spit is about 1.5 km wide here and the fine stretch forest (inhabited by elk) is among the loveliest on the peninsula, with some fine walks. There are good views from the hill Raganos kalnas, 500m inland from the northern part of the village. A track called the *promenada* leads north to it from the central area. The forests around Juodkrantė are also among the better places on the peninsula for spotting elk, which tend to emerge from cover in early morning and evening.

A short way up a side road, between the central and southern parts of the village, is the **Witches' Hill Museum** (Raganų kalno muziejus). The fairy-tale path weaving through the forest to the top of the Hill of Witches is lined with fantastical, and in places, quite grotesque wooden carvings of favourite Lithuanian folk art.

Places to Stay & Eat

There are few cheap options in Juodkrantė itself and it might be worth continuing to Nida where slightly cheaper accommodation can be found. Ask in the shops or at the post office to see if anyone knows of cheap rooms available – local people are often prepared to let you stay in their home for around 40 litų a night.

Rooms are moderately priced at *Smilga* (☎ 53 283) in the centre of the village, at Kalno 18. It has 20 rooms. Doubles/triples and rooms for four cost about 100 litų per person but, as with everywhere on the spit, prices can drop or soar in a day depending on how many guests a place does or doesn't have.

In a rather different price bracket is *Ąžuolynas* (☎ 53 316, 53 310; fax 25 838), next to the church in the southern part of the village at Liudviko Rėzos 54. It is the most modern rest-home in Juodkrantė with singles/doubles costing 300/400 litų but, again, prices fluctuate. The similarly priced *Santauta* (☎ 53 167, 53 348), at Kalno 26, has billiard and bowling facilities. To get there, take the first turn to the right, south of the bus stop.

Eating options are limited and you might prefer to stock up on provisions in Klaipėda before arriving. The in-house restaurant *Kopos*, at Ąžuolynas, serves fairly decent meals for around 15 litų. It also rents boats. Close by, at Liudviko Rėzos 34, is the family run *Kavinė*, where simple but more than satisfactory Lithuanian home cooking can be sampled. If you are staying at the Smilga, try *Meškos Galva* down the road at Kalno 3.

Getting There & Away

From Juodkrantė it is half an hour to Smiltynė or 50 minutes to Nida, by bus. In summer microbuses run about every half-hour in each direction between Smiltynė and Nida, passing through Juodkrantė. A one-way fare depends on how full the bus is. Don't pay more than 5 to 7 litų, even in the height of the season. The daily Smiltynė-Kaliningrad bus also stops at Juodkrantė.

Off season, buses run less regularly –

about every two hours if you're lucky. Your best bet is to hitch a ride from Smiltynė or, alternatively, team up with other Juodkrantė/Nida bound travellers and share a taxi. Be sure to negotiate the fare with the driver before you set off. With a bit of haggling, taxi drivers can be persuaded to take you to Juodkrantė for around 8 litų per person (not including the 2 litų entrance fee for the national park).

JUODKRANTĖ TO NIDA

Shortly south of Juodkrantė the road switches from the east side of the peninsula to the west. Between the two main settlements are two smaller villages, **Pervalka** and **Preila**, both on the east coast and reached by side roads from the main road. These tiny fishing villages are comparatively new, formed in the 19th century by the peoples of the once neighbouring villages, Karaičiai and Naujieji Nagliai, after shifting sands forced them to flee. Records show that Naujieji Nagliai became nothing more than a mountain of sand in 1843. The highest dune on the whole peninsula (66m) is near Preila.

NIDA

With its unique natural environment, Nida's combination of old-fashioned fishing village and fashionable resort makes it one of the most attractive places on the Baltic coast. Nida (former German name: Nidden) is the largest settlement on the Lithuanian half of the Curonian Spit, lying on the lagoon side of the peninsula, 48 km from Klaipėda and just three km from the Russian border. It also has a sizeable harbour. Just to the south stand some of the most impressive dunes on the peninsula, while a fine Baltic beach is less than a two km walk across the peninsula through the woods.

Originally a fishing village, Nida attracted a colony of mainly East Prussian artists from the late 19th century. It developed as a tourist resort and there were five hotels by the 1930s, when the writer Thomas Mann had a summer home built here. During the Soviet period, Nida enjoyed elite status among seaside resorts. In 1968, French philosopher

LITHUANIA

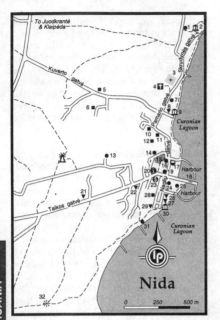

Jean Paul Sartre was granted special permission by Khrushchev to spend some time on the dunes.

Orientation

The settlement is very spread out by former Soviet standards and stretches nearly two km along the coast, but the hub, where Nida's few shops and other services are concentrated, is at the south end, behind the harbour. Three roads link the village to the main road. The southernmost of these, which you'll probably take if you're coming from Kaliningrad, is Taikos gatvė, which leads straight to the village heart. Coming from the north you'll probably enter Nida along Kuverto gatvė. Turn right onto Pamario gatvė to reach the centre.

Information

The tourist information centre (☎ 52 345; fax 52 344) is inside the Agila Cultural Centre at Taikos 4. It is open daily from May to September, except Saturday and Sunday, from 9 am to 6 pm.

You can change money in the post office, at Taikos 13, or at Lietuvos Taupomasis Bankas, next to the police station in the centre on Taikos gatvė. There are public card telephones next to the taxi rank, at Naglių 18, and outside the Prekšta Bar, at Kuverto 2. Phonecards are sold at the kiosk in the centre of the village.

Things to See & Do

The main things to do here are go for walks, relax and enjoy yourself. During the spring and autumn storms, amber is washed up on the shores. In the depths of winter the frozen lagoon is dotted with people, warmed by vodka, ice fishing. In summer you can hire jet skis or paddle boats from a small wooden hut at the south end of Lotmiškio gatvė. From the harbour you can sail around the lagoon in a replica of a traditional 19th century wooden fishing boat. Helicopter rides (☎ 8-298 216 10) over the spit are also available. Book in advance or pick up the free shuttle bus to the airstrip at Naglių 16. A 15 minute ride costs 30 litų per person.

On land you can travel in three directions from the harbour – north, west or south.

North of the Harbour There's a pleasant waterfront promenade stretching for over a km to stroll down, and then a road leads a couple of km further on. A bit over a km from the harbour, the street Skrudzdynės gatvė comes down close to the waterfront. A flight of steps leads up the bank beside it to the **Thomas Mann House** (Tomo Mano namelis; ☎ 52 260), which the German writer spent summers in from 1930-32. It is now a museum which is open daily between May and September, except Monday, from 10 am to 5 pm. Back towards the town centre, on the inland side of the road, 200m from the corner of Kuverto gatvė, a path leads up to a little red-brick church with a peaceful woodland cemetery. Beautiful pre-Christian crosses carved from wood – and called **krikštai** – dominate the cemetery and are particular to the Curonian Spit. On the opposite side of the road at Pamario gatvė, is a small privately run **Amber Gallery** (☎ 52 712) which explains how amber is formed. It is open daily from mid-April to September from 9 am to 9 pm. The gallery also has outlets selling amber at Naglių 14 and Skruzdynės 17a. Heading back towards the harbour, at Kuverto 2, there is a **Fisherman's Museum** which traces the development of Nida through an exhibition of local crafts and trades. It is open daily from May to September, except Monday and Tuesday, from 11 am to 5 pm.

West of the Harbour All westward routes lead ultimately to the beach on the far side of the peninsula. One good one is to turn right

(north) off Taikos gatvė, opposite the post office. The street you're now on bends sharply left after 150m and climbs. Just over 400m later on this road, a path leads up the hill to a lighthouse on the right, which is the highest point in the area. If you continue a further 700m along the path, behind the lighthouse, you'll come out on a good, straight path leading back down to the main road and, 400m beyond that, to the beach.

South of the Harbour Heading south from the harbour are two or three streets of old-fashioned fishing cottages with pretty gardens. At Naglių 4 there is a second **Fisherman's Museum**, inside an old fishing cottage. The rooms have been arranged as they were in the 19th century. It is open daily from May to September, except Monday and Tuesday, from 11 am to 5 pm. Beyond Naglių gatvė there's a path that leads through a wooded area and starts to climb up the spectacularly high and bare dunes that you can see from the village. A flight of steps enables people to climb without destroying the dune. From the top of the steps a track leads directly to the highest point, where there are great views to both coasts, the forests to the north, and a mixture of sand and forests to the south. You can explore in any direction from here, but bear in mind that the Kaliningrad border is only about two km south – it's made pretty obvious by the signs and Lithuanian border guards there to stop you straying into Russian territory.

Places to Stay

Nida is rapidly becoming a year-round destination. Unlike a few years ago, many hotels and rest-homes now stay open in the winter. Between winter and summer, prices fluctuate wildly.

The tourist information centre (☎ 52 345; fax 52 344), at Taikos 4, can find you a room in a private home (without wash facilities or linen) for 25 litų a night. Rooms in a private home or wooden summerhouse with a bath or shower and linen start at 35 litų. Clean, modern public showers are in the town centre at Taikos 29, and are open daily from

8 am until midnight. If these are full (which they often are) try Nida Yacht Club (☎ 52 828), at the harbour end of Taikos gatvė.

A stone's throw away from the magnificent dunes, at Lotmiškio 11, is *Rasytė* (☎ 52 592), a traditional wooden cottage offering cosy little rooms with a bath and a second TV room for around 40 litų a night. The landlady is one of the few remaining German Lithuanians still living on the spit. Book ahead as it is often booked out by German tour groups. Rasytė runs a second rest-home at Pamario 7.

The best of Nida's huge, grey and rather ugly rest-homes is the *Jūratė* (☎ 52 618), at Pamario 3. It is open year-round and has good, quite big, slightly old-fashioned single/double rooms with private bath for around 120/180 litų. It also rents bicycles. Other rest-homes are dotted around the village centre, and back along Taikos gatvė and Kuverto gatvė. They include the former rest-home of the Communist Party, *Rūta* (☎ 52 367), at Kuverto 15, a favoured summer spot of the Lithuanian president. It's a grey building with a flat, reddish-brown roof, about 600m back from Pamario gatvė. Another is the sprawling *Auksinės Kopos* (☎ 52 212), close by at Kuverto 17. Singles/doubles at the Rūta start at 150/200 litų, and at the Auksinės Kopos at 60/95 litų.

Lineja (☎ 52 390), at Taikos 18, is the only new hotel to be built in recent years in Nida and features all the mod cons, including luxury sauna, real double beds (all the others just have two singles pushed together) and a two lane tenpin bowling alley. Singles/doubles cost 180/360 litų.

Places to Eat

For fresh smoked fish try the wonderfully authentic *Seklyčia*, at Lotmiškio 1. Located in a wooden house, this family run restaurant overlooks the dunes by the beach. Another house, at Naglių 8, also sells smoked fish. One fish costs 6 to 8 litų, depending on the size.

Traditional Lithuanian home cooking can be sampled at the *Rasytė Kavinė*, inside the Rasytė guesthouse at Lotmiškio 11.

Blyneliai su uogiene (pancakes with jam) cost 4.50 litų, and an omelette with cheese is 4.20 litų. It is open daily from 10 am to midnight. *Užeiga Sena Syba*, at Naglių 6 (next to the Fisherman's Museum), serves more than adequate fare but is always packed with German tourists. There are also a number of café-cum-bars in the town centre and along the promenade leading from the harbour.

For a touch of upmarket cuisine try *Antis*, tucked behind the Jūratė rest-home, at Pamario 7. Veal with plums and raisins costs 17.90 litų, eel šašlykas (eel kebab) is 35 litų, and Jūratė pike perch is 19.90 litų. *Peteris*, at Taikos 13, is equally upmarket, but tacky as well. In winter many restaurants and cafés are closed.

Entertainment

Discos are held every Friday from dusk until 4 am at the *Agila Cultural Centre* in the centre of Nida. Films, plays and other theatrical events are also held here in the summer. Look for posters outside. The annual Nida Music Festival takes place in June.

Getting There & Away

You can reach Nida by bus or private vehicle from Klaipėda, or Smiltynė, at the northern tip of the Curonian Spit, or Kaliningrad (via Zelenogradsk). The Lithuanian border post is on the main road, immediately south of the petrol station (open 24 hours) at the corner of Taikos gatvė. The Russian post is 2.5 km further south.

Bus All Juodkrantė-bound buses continue to Nida. From Nida there are microbuses every half-hour to/from Smiltynė (1¼ hours), two daily buses from Klaipėda bus station (1½ to two hours), and one daily to/from Zelenogradsk (1½ hours) and Kaliningrad (2½ hours). Last departures from Smiltynė to Nida (and vice versa) are normally about 7 pm, however, there may be one or two later buses between May and mid-September.

Hydrofoil Between June and August you can travel daily by Raketa hydrofoil from

Kaunas to Nida (and back) along the Nemunas river, and across the Curonian Lagoon. The hydrofoil departs daily from Nida (except Monday) at 3 pm, and arrives in Kaunas four hours later.

CURONIAN LAGOON (EAST COAST)

The low lying, marsh-dotted east side of the Curonian Lagoon was, like Klaipėda and the Curonian Spit, historically Prussian/German territory. There are views of the high white dunes of the spit across the lagoon. The Nemunas river splits into a delta to enter the lagoon, with the town of **Rusnė** lying at the point where the main stream divides into three – the Atmata, the Pakalnė and the Skirvytė. The main town of the region, with 22,000 people, is **Šilutė** (former German name: Heydekrug), which is on the Klaipėda-Sovietsk road and railway. It has a hotel, the *Nemunas* (☎ 241-52 345), at Lietuvininkų 70.

Probably the most intriguing point to head for is **Ventė**, on the tip of the south-pointing promontory west of Šilutė. It was here, known locally as Ventės Ragas (World's Edge), that a Teutonic Order castle was built in the 1360s to protect shipping in the area. However, the castle and its church collapsed within a couple of hundred years. In the church's case at least, this was due to the severity of the storms on this isolated point – as indicated by Ventė's German name, Windenburg (Windy Castle). The church was rebuilt but wrecked again by storms in 1702. Its stones were used a few years later to build the church at **Kintai** – a town 10 km further north, also on the edge of the Curonian Lagoon – which is today linked to Ventė

by road. In 1837, a wooden tower (lit by an oil lamp) was built at Ventė, which was replaced (in 1862) by the lighthouse that still stands today. The old German cemetery can still be seen on the shore of the lagoon at Ventė.

Ventės Ragas is a sparsely inhabited area – there are just a few fishers' houses and a lighthouse at the tip – which can be either beautifully tranquil or beautifully wild. The main attraction of Ventė today, besides its dramatically wild nature and uplifting isolation, is an **Ornithological preserve, station** and **museum**. Here 2000-3000 birds are banded every day during the migration season. Some 200 different species have been observed at the centre, including the white stork which favours Ventė as its prime breeding ground. Quail are also raised here.

For information on visiting the 'edge of the world' contact the privately run Ventė Tourist Centre (☎ 241-445 10, 445 34, 44 510; fax 241-472 94) on the preserve. It also has five rooms with private shower, costing 150 to 200 litų, depending on the view – the rooms overlooking the Curonian Lagoon are the more expensive. In winter, prices drop to 80 to 100 litų. The in-house restaurant serves quail for about 10 litų. The centre also rents boats, and in the summer of 1997 it operated a small tourist boat, with a restaurant on-board, between Ventė and Nida.

Another fine place to stay, ideal for exploring this area, is *Vilkėnų Malūnas* (☎ 241-48 371; fax 241-52 082) in the village of Šėkšna, 24 km north of Šilutė. The family run guesthouse inside an old water mill (that still functions!) has single/double rooms for 100/120 litų.

Kaliningrad Region

Kaliningrad Region
Калининградская область

HIGHLIGHTS

- Discover the amber story at Kaliningrad's Amber Museum
- Visit the red-brick cathedral and the tomb of Immanuel Kant
- See one of the ugliest Soviet architectural creations – the House of Soviets
- View the Bunker Museum and see what the German command post looked like during the Red Army's assault on Kaliningrad
- Tour the remaining defensive bastions dating to 17th century Königsberg
- Follow the amber trail: train it to Yantarny to see the world's only opencast amber mine, visit the museum there and rub shoulders with amber fishers on the beach

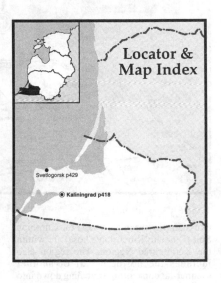

Locator & Map Index

Svetlogorsk p429

Kaliningrad p418

• *pop 1,000,000*

A disconnected wedge of Russia too strategic to have been left in anyone else's hands, the 21,000 sq km of the Kaliningrad Region lie between Lithuania, Poland and the Baltic Sea. From the 13th century until 1945, the Kaliningrad Region was German, part of the core territory of the Teutonic knights and their successors, the dukes and kings of Prussia. Its capital, named Kaliningrad after an early Soviet leader, was the famous German city, Königsberg.

After WWI, East Prussia (the northern half of which the Kaliningrad Region approximates) was separated from the rest of Germany. Hitler's desire to reunite it was one of the sparks that lit WWII. The three month campaign by which the Red Army took it in 1945 was one of the fiercest of the war, with hundreds of thousands of casualties on both sides.

Until 1991 the Kaliningrad Region was closed to western tourists. Today it is home to the Russian naval base at Baltiysk (Russia's only ice-free port since the loss of the Baltic states and their respective sea ports) and as such, is still a strongly

militarised area. The number of military personnel remains a state secret and estimates range from 40,000 to 200,000. The region is also home to the only opencast amber mine in the world, from which almost 90% of the world's amber is mined.

The Kaliningrad Region is one former Soviet region where the street names remain firmly intact – unlike elsewhere in Russia where street names are being changed back to their pre-communism names.

This chapter contains information specific to the Kaliningrad Region. For more detail see Facts about the Region and Facts for the Visitor chapters at the front of this book.

GEOGRAPHY

The city of Kaliningrad stands on the Pregolya river, which collects most of the waters of the Kaliningrad Region and enters the Kaliningrad Lagoon just west of the city. The southern half of the Curonian Lagoon

KALININGRAD REGION

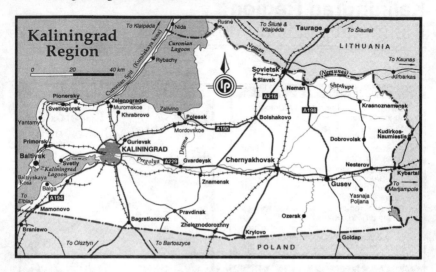

(Russian: Kurshsky zaliv) and the Curonian Spit (Russian: Kurshskaya kosa) are within the Kaliningrad Region. The region also includes the northern half of another sandbar-lagoon pairing stretching down into Poland, with the lagoon mouth at Baltiysk.

The Kaliningrad Region is mostly low and gently rolling terrain, rising only in the south-east (to just over 200m), near the Polish and Lithuanian borders.

GOVERNMENT

The Kaliningrad Region is one of several dozen *oblasty* (regions) into which Russia is divided. Like other oblasty, it has its own *soviet* (local assembly), headed by a governor, with powers over some of its affairs, but also answerable to Moscow.

In October 1996, elections were held for a number of key positions in the assembly, including – for the first time – governor. Yuri Matutchkin, an ex-sailor and qualified economist who had been appointed governor of the region by Russian president Boris Yeltsin in 1993, was beaten at the polls by Communist Party candidate, Leonid Gorbienko, director of Kaliningrad's fishing port. Only 43% of the electorate turned out to vote.

ECONOMY

For the past few years local authorities have attempted to set up economic incentives for local companies to boost Kaliningrad's bankrupt economy. And after a lot of bungling in Moscow, Kaliningrad was made a free economic zone in 1992. This was then abrogated by mistake in March 1995 (by another law passed in Moscow), leading to massive compensation payouts for local companies. The region finally became a free economic zone in January 1996, meaning that local companies are exempt from import and export duty.

So far the effects of this are barely evident and the economy remains reliant on heavy federal subsidies from Moscow. Inflation stood at 110% in 1995 and foreign investment is minimal (US$5 million in 1995). At the time of writing there was talk of South Korean car manufacturer, KIA, implementing a US$1 billion five year investment programme in the region. In Moscow, however, the fear of Kaliningrad becoming economically self-sufficient and becoming the fourth Baltic state, still lurks.

The region's traditional mainstay industries are fishing and fish processing, engineering, and paper and pulp production. Major export partners are Switzerland, Germany and Namibia. The region relies heavily on Lithuania, Poland and Belarus for imported goods.

In 1994, the European Union declared the Kaliningrad Region a priority region for receiving technical assistance (totalling ECU 8.1 million). Two of six projects are currently underway in the energy and fishing sectors.

POPULATION & PEOPLE

The Kaliningrad Region has seen even bigger ethnic changes than the Baltic states since WWII. Virtually its entire pre-WWII German population was evacuated or fled to Germany during the war, or was shot or deported to Siberia afterwards. They were replaced with people from the USSR, mainly Russia. In the last few years some ethnic Germans from Russia (mainly from the Volga region and Kazakstan) have made their way there, too.

People living in the Kaliningrad Region today generally think of themselves as Kaliningraders first and Russians second. The population of the Kaliningrad Region is 78% Russian, 10% Belarusian, 6% Ukrainian, 4% Lithuanian and 0.8% of German origin. Just over 42% of the total population live in the city of Kaliningrad.

Facts for the Visitor

VISAS & DOCUMENTS

Because the Kaliningrad Region is part of Russia, you need a Russian visa to visit.

Invitations & Registration

To obtain a Russian visa, you need an invitation or proof of accommodation from a company or organisation in the place you are visiting (see Facts for the Visitor at the front of the book for full details on obtaining Russian visas). For visa support in Kaliningrad try the Ministry of Foreign Affairs (☎ 0112-211 668) at ulitsa Kirova 17

or Baltma Tours (see Kaliningrad – Information) which can arrange tourist visas. The Alvis Travel Agency (☎ 0112-434 240, fax 0112-431 247, email postmaster@alvis. koenig.su) at Leninsky prospekt 14, also issues invitations for visas.

All Russian visas must be registered with OVIR (see Facts for the Visitor – Russian Visas at the front of the book) within three working days of your arrival in Russia. The main OVIR office in Kaliningrad (☎ 0112-22 82 74) is at Sovietsky prospekt 13, room 9. If you are staying in a hotel, the hotel administration will do this for you.

EMBASSIES
Russian Embassies Abroad

Australia
 78 Canberra Ave, Griffith, ACT 2603 (☎ 02-6295 9033, 6295 9474)
Canada
 285 Charlotte Street, Ottawa, Ontario K1N 8L5 (☎ 613-235 4341, 235 5376)
Denmark
 Kristianiagade 5, DK-2100 Copenhagen (☎ 31 38 23 70, 31 42 55 85)
Estonia
 Hobusepea 3, EE0200 Tallinn (☎ 2-443 014)
Finland
 Tehtaankatu 1b, FIN-00140 Helsinki (☎ 09-66 14 49, 66 18 76/77)
France
 40-50 Boulevard Lannes, 75116 Paris (☎ 01 45 04 71 71, 01 45 04 05 50)
Germany
 Waldstrasse 42, D-53177 Bonn (☎ 0228-31 85/6/7)
Latvia
 Atonijas iela 2, Rīga (☎ 7220 693, 7332 151)
Lithuania
 Latvių 53/54, Vilnius (☎ 22-721 763, 723 893)
Netherlands
 Andries Bickerweg 2, NL-2517 JP, The Hague (☎ 070-345 13 00)
Norway
 Drammensveen 74, 0271 Oslo (☎ 22 55 32 78)
Poland
 Ulitsa Belwederska 49, PL-00761 Warsaw (☎ 022-213 453)
 Consulate. ulica Batorego 15, PL-80251 Gdańsk (☎ 058-414 200)
Sweden
 Gjoerwellsgatan 31, S-11260 Stockholm (☎ 08-130 441, 533 732)

KALININGRAD REGION

UK
> 5 Kensington Palace Gardens, London W8 4QS
> (☎ 0171-229 8027)

USA
> 1825 Phelps Place NW, Washington, DC 20008
> (☎ 202-939 8907)

Foreign Embassies in Kaliningrad

There are two foreign consulates in Kaliningrad:

Lithuania
> Consulate: Sovietsky prospekt 39 (☎ 0112-273 217; fax 0112-216 651)

Poland
> Consulate: Kutuzova 43-45 (☎ 0112-274 282; fax 0112-274 035)

CUSTOMS

Entering Russia, you can take in a litre of hard liquor or wine and up to 250 cigarettes. When leaving, all art works including antiquarian books (those published before 1975), coins, jewellery, musical instruments etc have to be assessed by the Ministry of Culture which will issue a receipt for tax paid (usually 100% of the purchase price so be sure to always carry your sales receipt). In Kaliningrad take the object to the Customs office (☎ 0112-499 245, 443 450) at Prichalnaja 4a, building 1.

Exporting works of art dating back to before the Russian Revolution (1917) is prohibited.

MONEY

As part of Russia, the Kaliningrad Region uses the Russian rouble, which is the only legal tender. Transactions in other currencies are forbidden – some hotels may give their rates in Deutschmarks, but you have to pay in roubles. The best currencies to take are Deutschmarks or US dollars. Credit cards and travellers' cheques are useless in Kaliningrad; even major hotels and restaurants do not accept them. At the time of writing only one bank gave cash advances on Visa/Eurocard – and that is Investbank (see Kaliningrad – Information).

Costs

Living standards are slightly higher than the rest of Russia and, with lower prices than most other cities in Russia, Kaliningrad is an attractive option for travellers who want to 'do' something of Russia quickly and on the cheap.

Currency Exchange

Australia	A$1	=	R4467
Canada	C$1	=	R4135
France	1FF	=	R1011
Germany	DM1	=	R3416
New Zealand	NZ$1	=	R3993
United Kingdom	UK£1	=	R9333
United States	US$1	=	R5754

PUBLIC HOLIDAYS

Russian national holidays include:

New Year's Day, 1 January
Russian Orthodox Christmas Day, 7 January
International Women's Day, 8 March
Labour Day Holiday, 1 & 2 May
October Revolution Anniversary – Day of Unity, 7 November
Victory Day, 9 May, (WWII)

Kaliningrad
Калининград

• *pop 419,000* • ☎ *(22)*

Kaliningrad is an absorbing city. Today the capital and main city of the Kaliningrad Region of Russia, it was an almost entirely German city from 1255 to 1945. For much of that time it was the chief metropolis of Prussia – the state which grew from its southeast Baltic origins to become the crux of a united Germany in the 19th century.

The fascination of the place is the contrast between the Soviet-style city that's here today and the utterly different German city which was here just half a century ago. Huge areas of Königsberg (the city of Kaliningrad's former German name), including most of the centre, were totally wrecked by British bombing in 1944 and the Red Army's successful assault in 1945. After WWII the new Soviet authorities levelled most of the ruins and built a completely new city. They also brought in a whole new population of Russians to replace the Germans who had all been evacuated, killed or deported. The city was renamed after Mikhail Kalinin, a Stalin loyalist who survived the purges and was the formal head of the Soviet state from 1919 almost until his death in 1946.

Soviet-built Kaliningrad is a city of very drab architecture, semi-desolate open spaces where nothing has been rebuilt, and awful pollution – the traffic fumes are thick, and the Pregolya river, flowing through the city's heart, is black as pitch and usually stinks. Kaliningrad's people, however, are surprisingly jolly and friendly.

Königsberg must have been, if nothing else, far more pleasing to the eye than Kaliningrad. What makes Kaliningrad such a poignant place is that just enough of Königsberg's 700 year history survives to give a taste of the old city. The restored Gothic cathedral, the ornately turreted, red-brick city gates and the dilapidated Luisen wall woodland park, in their bizarre contrast with the Soviet apartment blocks or seas of semi-desolate space around them, tell the story of the city's unique and dreadful transformation better than any number of history books could.

Group travel is favoured here because of the huge numbers of German 'nostalgia tourists' (here to trace their ancestry) who flooded into Kaliningrad when the area opened up. With the rapid decline of this niche market however – the estimated 50,000 tourists in 1991 plummeted to less than 5000 in 1995 – the tourism industry has yet to adapt to the demands set by

---

Where is Prussia?

The original Prussians were a Baltic people, related to the Lithuanians and Latvians, who inhabited the south-east hinterland of the Baltic Sea roughly from the Vistula river in modern Poland to the Nemunas river along today's Lithuania/Kaliningrad Region border (see map on next page). They were wiped out and/or assimilated by the German crusading knights of the Teutonic Order, who took over their territory in the 13th century. The knights also took over Pomerelia, an adjoining area stretching about 100 km west of the lower reaches of the Vistula, in the 14th century. Poland then drove the Teutonic Order out of Pomerelia and some western parts of its earlier territory in the 15th century, leaving Prussia in control of what was basically the territory the order had taken from the Prussians in the 13th century, minus a few bites in its southern half.

This knightly territory was transformed into the Duchy of Prussia, ruled by the successors of the knights' last leader in the 16th century. It amounted more or less to what are now the Kaliningrad Region and a similar-sized chunk of Poland immediately to the south (minus the aforesaid bites, but including a strip along the north bank of the Nemunas and the east side of the Curonian Lagoon). Its capital was Königsberg.

In the 17th century, the Duchy of Prussia became linked through royal marriage to the extensive north German state of Brandenburg, centred on Berlin, and at the start of the 18th century Brandenburg's ruler was crowned the Prussian king. In the late 18th century, Prussia-Brandenburg took over large sections of a disintegrating Poland including Pomerelia, which became known as West Prussia. The former Duchy of Prussia, with its lost bites restored, correspondingly came to be called East Prussia.

By the early 19th century, the whole Prussia-Brandenburg bloc was going by the single name of Prussia, and after further territorial gains later that century, Prussia stretched all the way from Memel (now Klaipėda, Lithuania) to the borders of Belgium and Luxembourg. This Prussia pulled in a variety of lesser states to create a united Germany in the late 19th century.

With Germany's defeat in WWI, most of the old West Prussia was handed to a reborn Poland, while Danzig (now Gdańsk) and its surrounds around the mouth of the Vistula, became a free port. This meant that East Prussia was separated from the rest of Germany. Hitler temporarily reunited them in 1941, but after the Red Army swept through in 1945, East Prussia was divided between the USSR, which got its northern half (the modern Kaliningrad Region), and Poland, which got the southern half.

Germans refer to the Kaliningrad Region as *Das nördliche Ostpreussen* (Northern East Prussia). ■

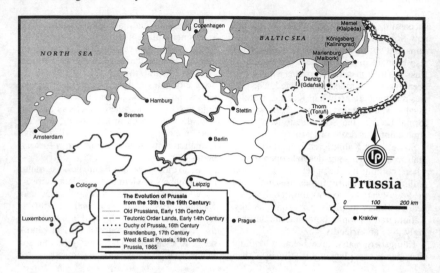

The Evolution of Prussia
from the 13th to the 19th Century:
- Old Prussians, Early 13th Century
- Teutonic Order Lands, Early 14th Century
- Duchy of Prussia, 16th Century
- Brandenburg, 17th Century
- West & East Prussia, 19th Century
- Prussia, 1865

Prussia

0   100   200 km

the few independent travellers who make their way here.

Although some still refer to the city as 'König', any talk of restoring its German name has long since died away.

HISTORY

Founded as a fort of the Teutonic Order in 1255, on the site of a fortress of the displaced Prussians, Königsberg became a leading city of the Teutonic Order state, joining the Hanseatic League in 1340 and becoming the residence of the order's grand masters after they abandoned Marienburg (now Malbork, Poland) in 1457. In 1525 the last grand master of the Teutonic Order, Albrecht, who had converted to Protestantism, dissolved the order and converted its territory into the secular Duchy of Prussia, under Polish suzerainty. Albrecht became the Duke of Prussia, with his capital at Königsberg, where he is credited with founding the city's university in 1544 – named Albertina in honour of him. The duchy was united by royal marriage to the powerful German state of Brandenburg in 1618 and transferred from Polish to Brandenburg control in 1660 (partly as a consequence of Poland's unsuc-

cessful wars with Sweden). In the first half of the 17th century Königsberg gained a ring of strong fortifications and became the centre of an artistic and musical circle focused on the writer Simon Dach.

Friedrich III of Brandenburg was crowned Friedrich I, King of Prussia, in Königsberg castle in 1701. Through the 18th century, particularly under Friedrich II (Frederick the Great, who ruled from 1740 to 1786), Prussia-Brandenburg steadily increased in power, and Königsberg enjoyed its golden age. A Russian occupation from 1758 to 1763, during the Seven Years' War, saved the city from being fought over by numerous European powers involved in that conflict. Cultural life flourished; this was the age of the great philosopher Immanuel Kant (1724-1804), author of the *Critique of Pure Reason*, who was born, studied, taught and died in Königsberg.

Napoleon marched into Königsberg in 1807, causing (the popular) Prussian Queen Luise to flee along the Curonian Spit to Memel (now Klaipėda). By the Treaty of Tilsit (now Sovietsk) that year, Prussia had to cede much of its territory to France. However, after Napoleon's defeat in 1815, Königsberg's economy developed through the 19th century along with Prussia's steady territorial gains.

After WWI, East Prussia's isolation from the rest of Germany hit Königsberg's economy, but this was to some extent countered by holding a huge trade fair, the Deutsche Ostmesse, on a specially built site in Königsberg. The city's population was somewhere over 250,000.

Königsberg was wrecked by British air raids in August 1944, which killed about 4200 people, and by the final assault of the Red Army from 6 to 9 April, 1945, after an extremely fierce three month battle – with huge losses on both sides – for the rest of East Prussia. Of the roughly 110,000 Germans who were captured, many were deported to Siberia. The rest were sent to Germany between 1946 and 1948.

ORIENTATION

Leninsky prospekt, a broad north-south avenue, is the main artery of Kaliningrad, running three km from the bus station and the main train station, the Yuzhny Vokzal (Southern Station), to the suburban Severny Vokzal (Northern Station) on ploshchad Pobedy (Victory Square). About halfway it crosses the Pregolya river and the island on which Kaliningrad's cathedral – a major landmark – stands. Just north of the river, Leninsky prospekt passes through Tsentralnaya ploshchad, with the Kaliningrad hotel and the unmistakable House of Soviets.

Other important arteries include Moskovsky prospekt, the main east-west thoroughfare, which passes beneath Leninsky prospekt between the Pregolya and Tsentralnaya ploshchad; ulitsa Chernyakhovskogo, heading east from ploshchad Pobedy, past the central market to the Amber Museum in the Dohna Tower on ploshchad Vasilevskogo; and prospekt Mira, winding west from ploshchad Pobedy to Kalinin Park.

Maps *Kaliningrad City Plan*, published by Kaliningrad-based company UAB Argument in 1996, is clear (if you can read Russian), up-to-date and available at hotels and kiosks for US$3. For a pocket-sized city map with a very handy English/Russian street register look no further than *Kaliningrad In Your Pocket*.

The Kaliningrad-based Koskartographya company publishes an excellent map of the Kaliningrad region (*Kaliningrad Oblast 1:200,000*, 1995). It costs US$5 and is sold at the Kaliningrad hotel (see Places to Stay). The German publisher, Verlag Gerhaud Rautenberg, produces historical maps of Kaliningrad indicating the old German street names (see the introductory Facts for the Visitor chapter).

INFORMATION
Tourist Offices

There is no official tourist office so your only hope is the International Information Centre inside the Kaliningrad hotel. The staff speak Russian, German and a little English, and, if they feel in the mood, can be quite helpful.

Baltma Tours travel agency (☎ 211 880, 228 419; fax 211 840) at Mira 49-50, apartment 30, has staff who speak English and is the most customer-orientated establishment in town.

Money

It is impossible to cash travellers' cheques in Kaliningrad. Cash advances on Visa and Eurocard are available from three Investbank branches: opposite the Kaliningrad hotel at Leninsky prospekt 28, a few doors down at Shevchenko 11, and the branch on ulitsa Ivannikova. They are open weekdays from 9 am to 6 pm, except for a one hour break from noon.

Most hotels can change money. The exchange bureau at the Kaliningrad hotel is particularly useful, although the banks and non-hotel exchange bureaus offer better rates – the best rate is at the bureau next to the Sailor's Hostel and Flagman Restaurant. There is a 24 hour currency exchange inside the Skan hotel (see Places to Stay). If you plan to go elsewhere in Russia change extra money here as the rates are likely to be better.

SAS (☎ 459 451, 459 452), at the international airport, offers cash advances on Diners

Club. Its office is open weekdays from 9 am to 5.30 pm. The company will also offer this service at its new offices, in the centre at ploshchad Pobedy, scheduled to open by the end of 1997.

Post & Communications

The central post office *(pochtamt)* is at Kosmonavta Leonova 22, about 600m north of prospekt Mira. It's open weekdays from 9 am to 9 pm, and weekends from 10 am to 6 pm. Trolleybus Nos 1 and 3 come up here from the Yuzhny Vokzal via Leninsky prospekt, ulitsa Teatralnaya and prospekt Mira. The telephone section, from which international calls can be made, is open 24 hours. A central telephone office, also open 24 hours, is at ulitsa Teatralnaya 13/19. For express mail try UPS (☎ 434 684, 474 354) at Chernyakhovskogo 66.

The Soviet public telephones can only be used for local calls. They accept tokens, costing US$0.10 from kiosks. Public card telephones from which international calls can be made are at the Kaliningrad hotel, Skan Hotel, Valencia restaurant and other strategic locations in town. Telephone cards are sold at some kiosks and at the Kaliningrad hotel where there is also a handy international telephone, fax, telex and email office (☎ 451 515; fax 469 590; email konig@sovam.com), open daily from 7.30 am to 11 pm. Faxes and emails can also be received here for a small fee.

Kaliningrad's city telephone code (22) becomes 8-0112 if you are dialling from the CIS, Lithuania or Estonia, and 7-0112 if you are dialling from Latvia or the west.

Media

For a complete guide to the region pick up a copy of *Kaliningrad In Your Pocket* (http://www.inyourpocket.com), published annually in English and German and available from major hotels for the equivalent of US$1.

The German-language *Königsberger Express* is a monthly news magazine costing US$0.80 and available at most kiosks. You may find a German newspaper in hotels, but not much else unless you can read Russian. The Russian-language *Kaliningradskaya Pravda* comes out daily.

English-language news reports and music can be picked up on Voice of America (VOA), transmitted by local radio station *Baltic Plus* on 105.2 and 72.11 FM daily from 2 to 6 am.

Medical Services

Seek help in your hotel in the first instance, if you're in one. There's an emergency service at the hospital (☎ 434 556) at Nevsky 90. You can phone ☎ 03 for emergency medical help. For western medicines try the pharmacy in the Kaliningrad hotel.

Left Luggage

There's a left-luggage room *(kamera khranenia)* at the Yuzhny Vokzal (Southern train station), open daily from 6.30 am to 11 pm. It is immediately on the left as you walk through the gates to the platform area.

WALKING TOUR

Kaliningrad's sights are fairly spread out but the following 4.5 km route takes you around the heart of the city and some of its most interesting spots in half a day or so.

Starting from the **cathedral** on its island in the Pregolya, head north past the **House of Soviets** on Tsentralnaya ploshchad, along the bank of the **Prud Nizhny** (Lower Pond), perhaps calling in at the **History & Art Museum**, to the **Amber Museum** in the Dohna Tower. Then go west along ulitsa Chernyakhovskogo to the **market** and ploshchad Pobedy (trams can help you along this bit).

Head back south down Leninsky prospekt, by trolleybus if you like. You can stop in at the **Bunker Museum** on ulitsa Universitetskaya just before you get back to Tsentralnaya ploshchad. An extension for the energetic is to head out west along prospekt Mira from ploshchad Pobedy.

CATHEDRAL

The recently rebuilt red-brick cathedral, founded in 1333, stands at the heart of the

Left: Kaliningrad neo-Gothic architecture, Kaliningrad Region
Right: 19th century houses on Komsomolskaya, Kaliningrad
Bottom: Hammer & sickle emblem on bridge with cathedral in background, Kaliningrad

JOHN NOBLE

JOHN NOBLE

JOHN NOBLE

Top: Street market, Kaliningrad
Left: Water tower & bathhouse, Svetlogorsk, Kaliningrad Region
Right: Silver-painted Lenin, Zelenogradsk Sanatorium, Kaliningrad Region

city, on the island at the meeting of the two arms of the Pregolya. You can walk on to the island from Oktyabrskaya ulitsa at its east end or by steps down from the Leninsky prospekt bridge over the river. The cathedral is very much a symbol of the city, representing both its German past and serving as a permanent reminder of the Soviet conquest in 1945.

It was built in the 14th century in the Gothic style. Several bishops, grand masters of the Teutonic Order and other leading figures from Königsberg's history were buried inside. Originally, there were two towers at the west end but they burnt down in 1544 and only the southern one was initially rebuilt. Before the cathedral's destruction in 1944, the tower was topped by a pointed spire rather like a taller version of the one on the Vytautas Church in Kaunas (Lithuania).

The **tomb of Immanuel Kant**, the great 18th century philosopher who was born, studied and taught in Königsberg, remains on the outer north side of the cathedral. The cathedral ruin was partially restored after WWII, but it wasn't until 1995 that sufficient funds were finally found to complete the restoration work, including rebuilding the roof and the tower on the northern side of the west end.

There's a small **sculpture park** with statues of Russian and Soviet cultural figures on the south bank of the island, to the west of the cathedral.

STOCK EXCHANGE

The fine, blue, Italian Renaissance style building on the south bank of the Pregolya, is the old Stock Exchange (Torgovaya birzha). Built in the 1870s, it became the Sailors' Culture Palace (Dvorets Kultury Moryakov) under Soviet rule.

TSENTRALNAYA PLOSHCHAD

Tsentralnaya ploshchad (Central Square), on the mound above the north bank of the Pregolya, is an apt centrepiece for post-WWII Kaliningrad – a typical wide Soviet city square surrounded by drab buildings, among

them the Kaliningrad hotel and the brighter, more modern 'kiosk shopping village'. However, the entire area is dominated by the H-shaped **House of Soviets** (Dom Sovietov), which has been described as the ugliest creation of Soviet architecture – which is some achievement.

The House of Soviets was originally meant as a kind of city hall, but funds to complete the building works dried up in 1971, leaving Russia's ugliest building standing empty and unused for more than 25 years. Many people reckon dynamite is what it most needs. Its construction began after **Königsberg Castle** was blown up in the 1960s. The castle had stood for over 700 years just west of the site of the House of Soviets, covering much of what is now Tsentralnaya ploshchad.

The castle was really where Königsberg began, founded by the Teutonic Order as a redoubt against the rebelling Prussians. (It replaced a temporary wooden fort built in 1255 on the site of Prussian fortifications which were probably on the site of the House of Soviets.) The grand master of the Teutonic Order resided in the castle after abandoning Marienburg to the Poles in 1457. The order's successors from 1525, the dukes of Prussia, greatly expanded the castle. It was wrecked in the 1944 bombing and 1945 shelling, but its remains stood for another 20 years.

The buildings behind the east side of the House of Soviets include Kaliningrad's **Palace of Weddings** (Dvorets brakoso-chetaniy).

BUNKER MUSEUM

The first opening on the right as you go north up Leninsky prospekt from Tsentralnaya ploshchad leads into a square that was called Paradeplatz in German times but doesn't seem to have its own name today. However, the street along its north side is named ulitsa Universitetskaya, after the building of Kaliningrad University which stands on its northern aspect.

Down a flight of steps at the west end of the square is the **Bunker Museum** (Muzey-Blindazh, ☎ 430 593), the German command

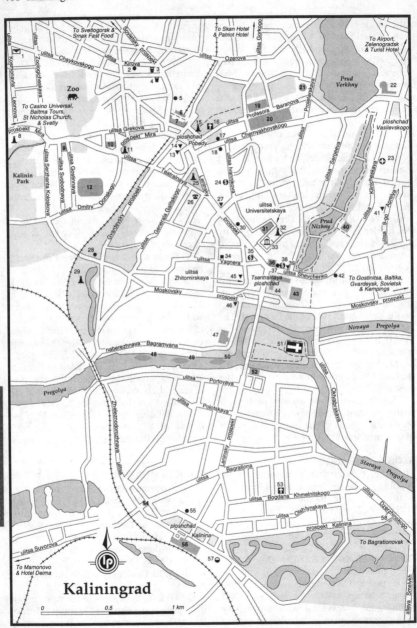

Kaliningrad

PLACES TO STAY
7 Sailors' Hostel & Flagman Restaurant
9 Moskva Hotel
34 Ekspress-Kvartira
36 Kaliningrad Hotel
48 Hotelschiff Baltcompany A
50 Hotelschiff Hansa

PLACES TO EAT
13 Bingo
14 Valencia Spanish Restaurant
27 Italian Café
39 Mini-Café & Shopping Centre
41 Chorny Tiulpan (Black Tulip)
44 Kiosk Village, Oleg's Restaurant, Karolina's Bar & Coffee Shop
45 Belarus
46 Smak Fast Food
47 Dvorets Sporta Yunost (Youth Sports Palace)

OTHER
1 Central Telephone & Post Office
2 Branch of Ministry of Foreign Affairs
3 Charm Nightclub
4 Francis Drake
5 Central OVIR Office
6 Severny Vokzal (Northern Train Station)
8 Cosmonaut Monument
10 Kaliningrad Drama Theatre
11 Friedrich Schiller Statue
12 Baltika Stadium
15 Lenin Statue
16 Russian Orthodox Church
17 Ocean Grocery Store
18 UPS Express Mail
19 Former Technology House
20 Central Market
21 Wrangel Tower
22 Amber Museum, Dohna Tower & Rossgarten Gate
23 Hospital
24 Investbank

25 Mother Russia Statue
26 Central Telephone Office
28 Astonomers' Bastion
29 11th Guards Army Monument
30 Europa Food Store
31 University
32 Kant Statue
33 Bunker Museum
35 Investbank
37 Delicacies Grocery Store
38 Investbank
40 History & Art Museum
42 Palace of Weddings
43 House of Soviets
49 Museum of the World Ocean
51 Cathedral
52 Former Stock Exchange
53 St Katherine's Church & Philharmonic Organ Hall
54 Brandenburg Gate
55 Aeroflot's Main Office
56 Yuzhny Vokzal (Southern Train Station)
57 Bus Station
58 Friedland Gate

post during the Red Army's assault on Kaliningrad. This now strangely quiet set of rooms lining an underground passage contains models, maps, photos and other material recounting the four-day Soviet storming of the city in April 1945. Room 13 is left as it was at 9 pm on 9 April when the German commander, General Otto Lasch, and Soviet officers, Janovsky and Kruglov, signed the surrender document in it. It's open daily from 10 am to 5 pm. Entrance is US$2/0.80 for adults/students.

At the north end of the square stands a **statue of Immanuel Kant**. There's a small museum and library (on Kant and his epoch) in the university building at ulitsa Universitetskaya 2 – visits by appointment only.

PRUD NIZHNY

Stretching north from the House of Soviets is the Prud Nizhny (Lower Pond). Over one km long this former mill pond became the city's favourite relaxation and recreation place during the German era (then known as the Schlossteich) when its banks were home to many restaurants and dance spots. During summer evenings, concerts were held in the surrounding gardens and lanterned boats conducted cruises on the waters. Today the Prud Nizhny is much less festive, but still a very pleasant place for a stroll. Three bridges or causeways cross from one bank to the other.

Backing on to the east bank of the Prud Nizhny and close to its south end, is Kaliningrad's **History & Art Museum** (Istoriko-Khudozhestvenny Muzey). The museum has permanent displays on the natural and human history of the Kaliningrad Region and a collection of Soviet era art. The building was originally constructed before WWI as Königsberg's main concert hall, the Stadthalle, and rebuilt in the 1980s. It's open daily, except Monday, from 11 am to 6 pm.

KALININGRAD REGION

PRUD VERKHNY & AMBER MUSEUM

The north end of the Prud Nizhny is separated from the wider Prud Verkhny (Upper Pond), stretching over a km further north, by ulitsa Chernyakhovskogo. About 100m to the east along ulitsa Chernyakhovskogo, in the fat red-brick **Dohna Tower** (Russian: Bashnya Dona; German: Dohnaturm), is Kaliningrad's Amber Museum (Muzey Yantarya, ☎ 460 613), which is open daily, except Monday, from 10 am to 5.30 pm. Adjoining the Dohna Tower and facing ploshchad Vasilevskogo is the turreted **Rossgarten Gate** (Russian: Gorodskie vorota Rosgartenskie; German: Rossgärter Tor), one of the old German city gates, built in the 19th century. Litovsky val, heading east from ploshchad Vasilevskogo, is lined with a series of pre-WWI fortifications – see Other Sights.

Another rotund German bastion, the 19th century **Wrangel Tower** (Russian: Bashnya Vrangelya; German: Wrangel-Turm), stands near the south-west corner of the Prud Verkhny on the corner of ulitsa Proletarskaya and ulitsa Profesora Baranova. Parkland lines most of the west side of the Prud Verkhny.

AROUND PLOSHCHAD POBEDY

Ulitsa Chernyakhovskogo leads about 1.5 km west from the Dohna Tower to ploshchad Pobedy, at the north end of Leninsky prospekt. Halfway along, on the north side, is the large **central market** *(tsentralny rynok)*, open daily, except Monday. Its northern section is housed in the shell of the former Technology House (German: Haus der Technik), built for the Deutsche Ostmesse, a big east-west trade fair held in Königsberg to counter East Prussia's isolation between world wars. The site of the Deutsche Ostmesse stretched all the way along the park strip, west of the Technology House, to where the **Lenin statue** now stands on ploshchad Pobedy.

Lenin apart, the dominant feature of ploshchad Pobedy (Victory Square) is the grand **Severny Vokzal** building built in 1930, which is now used, in part, as a sailors'

hostel. The present Severny Vokzal (Northern train station) is a rather paltry affair behind it. The pink building opposite the station's western exit on Sovietsky prospekt was the local KGB headquarters. Kaliningrad's city hall is on the south side of ploshchad Pobedy, with the Restoran Valencia on its ground floor. Behind Lenin stands a beautiful wooden **Russian Orthodox church**, strung with six exterior bells which call the faithful to worship daily. The church was miraculously built in the space of two months in 1996.

A large heroic **statue of Mother Russia** dominates the park just south of here, between Leninsky prospekt and ulitsa Teatralnaya.

ALONG PROSPEKT MIRA

Prospekt Mira winds west from ploshchad Pobedy. The fine building overlooking the west end of the little park, on the north side of its first stretch, houses the General Staff of the Russian Baltic Fleet. About 400m from ploshchad Pobedy, west along prospekt Mira, is the **Kaliningrad Drama Theatre**, first built in 1927 and restored in 1980. Opposite is a **statue** of the German playwright Friedrich Schiller, which has stood hereabouts since 1936. By the theatre, prospekt Mira turns right, passing the Baltika Stadium on the site of a former park, Walter-Simon-Platz, and a little later (on the right) is the absolutely heartbreaking **Kaliningrad Zoo**. Dating back to the 1890s it was, in its heyday, considered one of the world's top zoos, along with London and Berlin, but is now at the bottom of the pile. (The crocodile is rumoured to have barely seen daylight since 1952, when it was first caged in the bathtub in which it spends its days).

About 400m beyond the zoo, on the south side of prospekt Mira, opposite the corner of ulitsa Kosmonavta Leonova, is the tall **Cosmonaut Monument**. A further 400m along is the main entrance to the **Kalinin Park of Culture & Rest** (PKiO im Kalinina), formerly the Luisen wall, a favourite Königsberg park. The park now has a funfair, café and domino and card pavilion, as well as the

Luise Church (tserkov Luizy), built in 1901, and now used as a puppet theatre – and a shabby-looking treed section with a stream running through it. Though originally named after the wife of a teacher who owned the land in the 18th century, the park was long associated with Queen Luise of Prussia whose statue stood here until 1945.

The **Museum of the World Ocean**, opened with much ceremony to mark the 300th anniversary of the Russian naval fleet in 1996, is moored along the Pregolya between the two floating hotels. It is open daily, except Monday and Tuesday, from 11 am to 6 pm.

OTHER SIGHTS

Kaliningrad is dotted with a couple of dozen more old bastions and remnants of the fortifications built up from the 17th century on. Königsberg had an imposing defensive ring about two km out from its castle.

Perhaps most interesting are the old gates in this ring, which are red brick and quite picturesque. One is the Rossgarten Gate on ploshchad Vasilevskogo (see Prud Verkhny & Amber Museum). From ploshchad Vasilevskogo, Litovsky val curves to the south, just inside the line of the pre-WWI defensive works, to the **King's Gate** (Russian: Gorodskie vorota Korolevskie; German: Königstor) at the east end of ulitsa Frunze. The **Sackheim Gate** (Russian: Gorodskie vorota Zakkhaymskie; German: Sackheimer Tor), on Moskovsky prospekt, is a further 1.5 km along.

South of the river are the **Brandenburg Gate** (Russian: Gorodskie vorota Brandenburgskie; German: Brandenburger Tor), on ulitsa Bagrationa, just west of the Yuzhny Vokzal, and the **Friedland Gate** (Russian: Gorodskie vorota Fridlyandskie; German: Friedländer Tor) at the east end of prospekt Kalinina, 1.5 km from the station. The park along the south side of prospekt Kalinina was itself a section of the old fortifications.

One particularly large bastion, which is not open to visitors, is the **Astronomers' Bastion** (Russian: Bastion Astronomichesky; German: Astronomische Bastion) on Gvardeysky prospekt. In the park south of the Astronomers' Bastion is an **obelisk monument** at the mass grave of 1200 Soviet soldiers of the 11th Guards Army who died in the 1945 assault. This is the best known of the city's many monuments and graveyards for Soviet troops.

There's a fine 20th century red-brick **neo-Gothic church**, modelled on some of the old churches from the Teutonic Order period, at ulitsa Bogdana Khmelnitskogo 63A, east off the southern part of Leninsky prospekt.

ORGANISED TOURS

Baltma Tours (see Information – Tourist Offices) arranges 3½ hour city tours, day trips to Svetlogorsk and Baltiysk, one to three-day tours of the 'fortresses of northeastern Prussia', and botanical tours. It also arranges wild boar hunting, fishing and other specialist tours – a big hit with some tourists.

The Alvis Travel Agency (☎ 434 240; fax 431 247; email postmaster@alvis.koenig.su), Leninsky prospekt 14, also organises tours.

SPECIAL EVENTS

The Amber Necklace Music Festival is an annual event held in June or July. Another annual summer festival is the week-long Days of Kaliningrad celebrations, which usually coincides with the Day of the Fleet on the last Sunday in July. This is the only day of the year when the closed naval port of Baltiysk is open to the public (see Other Destinations – Baltiysk).

PLACES TO STAY – BOTTOM END

There are no hostels, although at the time of writing there was talk of transforming the extremely seedy *Moskva Hotel* (☎ 272 089), at Mira 19, into a youth hostel. Singles/doubles cost US$4/6 although these prices are known to fluctuate depending on the day/staff/your face. It is owned by the same team that runs the town's principal hotel, the Kaliningrad.

Another cheap option is the *Patriot Hotel* (☎ 275 017), three km north of the city at

Ozernaya 25A. Take tram No 6 or 10 north up ulitsa Gorkogo from the central market. Ozernaya ulitsa is the first street on the right after ulitsa Gorkogo crosses a bridge over the railway (the nearest tram stop is a bit past the Gorkogo/Ozernaya corner). Walk 200 or 300m along Ozernaya ulitsa then turn into the side road (beside house No 25) on the north side. Keep going through a couple of yards until you see the nine-storey slab of the Patriot ahead. Singles/doubles are US$14/23.

Another good value option is the *Turist Hotel* (☎ 460 801) at ulitsa Alexandra Nevskogo 53, about 2.5 km north-east of the centre. It was renovated in 1991 and takes quite a few German groups. Rooms with private bath for independent travellers are US$26/36. You can get there by tram No 8 from ploshchad Vasilevskogo; or bus No 11 from any stop on Leninsky prospekt, ulitsa Chernyakhovskogo or ploshchad Vasilevskogo; or bus No 2, 17 or 32 from ulitsa Chernyakhovskogo or ploshchad Vasilevskogo. The hotel is about one km along ulitsa Alexandra Nevskogo from ploshchad Vasilevskogo.

PLACES TO STAY – MIDDLE & TOP END
Kaliningrad (☎ 432 591; fax 469 590), handily placed on Tsentralnaya ploshchad at Leninsky prospekt 81, is said to be the city's top hotel despite the fact that it is filled with staff who apparently work 24 hour shifts (which explains their surly manner). Singles/doubles are expensive at US$40/72.

The *Baltika* (☎ 453 543, 437 977) is seven km east of the centre on Moskovsky prospekt at Zaozerie. This 10 storey block has doubles with private bathroom for US$30. There's also a *Kemping*, with cabins, next door. Bus No 25 goes to the hotel – its stops in the city centre include the southbound Kinoteatr Rossia stop on Gvardeysky prospekt, just off ploshchad Pobedy, and the eastbound Grazhdanproekt stop on Moskovsky prospekt, east of the Oktyabrskaya ulitsa corner.

More expensive – and not even exotic – options include the two cruise ships moored to the north bank of the Pregolya, just west of the Leninsky prospekt bridge. The *Hotelschiff Hansa* (☎ 433 737; fax 433 806) is fairly shabby from the outside and smells somewhat damp and stuffy inside. Singles/doubles cost US$49/91. Second in line is the *Hotelschiff Baltcompany A* (☎ & fax 46 16 04), definitely more swanky (to the point of being tacky) with singles/doubles for US$33/56. On the top deck is an even tackier casino.

Intourist (☎ 228 482), the Russian government's foreign tourism company, in room 111 of the Dom Ofizerov (Officers' House) on ulitsa Kirova, has a small hotel for groups of up to 30 tourists called the *Hotel Der Dohna*. Get to it through the Ama shop at ploshchad Vasilevskogo 2.

One of the few hotels prepared to let guests stay without an advance reservation is the more expensive *Skan Hotel* (☎ 465 461; fax 451 823), at ulitsa Alexandra Nevskovo 53, which claims to be a 'Königsberg hotel with a European accent'. Singles/doubles are US$40/60.

Also veering towards the European way of things is the *Hotel Deima* (☎ 44 92 14; fax 44 92 00) at Tolstikova 15-2. All its rooms have been tastefully renovated and equipped with private bathrooms. Singles/doubles are around US$46/66. The management has grand plans to further modernise what promises to be Kaliningrad's most westernised hotel.

Often booked out but a pleasant place to stay is the *Gostevoi Dom* (☎ 21 57 08; fax 27 95 40) north-east of the centre at Chapaeva 22. Set among a pretty garden of trees, it is one of the few places where you can almost convince yourself that you are not in Kaliningrad. During the mushroom and berry season, you can pick enough mushrooms for breakfast (in the grounds) and the hotel chef will fry them for you. Singles/doubles start at US$80/100.

PLACES TO EAT
Cheap, cheerful and one of the busiest places in town is the *Italiun Café* at Leninsky prospekt 27, serving veal in red wine sauce, or crepes with black caviar, for around US$5.

Pizza is served after 6 pm and it closes daily at 2 am. Take note: the Italian Café also has the fastest service in town – expect to wait at least 45 minutes for a simple bowl of soup anywhere else.

A more old-time Soviet experience can be had at the *Belarus* at Zhitomirskaya 14. It serves quite palatable dishes (to the blare of German MTV) for around US$5, and it's open daily from noon to 11 pm.

Along Sovietsky prospekt is Kaliningrad's first British pub, the *Francis Drake*. It serves toasted sandwiches, soups (including 'Golden Hinde', which is actually the traditional Russian broth seljanka), Welsh-style baked fish and other dishes purporting to be typically British are around US$6. British lagers and bitters are on tap for US$2 a pint.

The *Chorny tiulpan* (Black Tulip), at 9-go Aprelya 60a, specialises in Armenian food. The menu is a book of photographs, which is extremely handy if you can't speak Russian.

Within the kiosk shopping village opposite the Kaliningrad hotel, there are a couple of great little places. *Oleg's* at Kiosk No 52 is glam and glitzy but serves reasonable Uzbek cuisine at a fair price. *Karolina's Bar* is at Kiosk No 2 and is the best place for cocktails. Nothing can beat the smell of the freshly-ground coffee beans in the western-style coffee shop inside Kiosk No 63 (maybe that is why the management banned smoking inside). It's open daily from 11 am to 10 pm and serves the best coffee and cakes in town.

The *Mini-Café* inside the shopping centre opposite the kiosk village, next to Investbank at Shevchenko 13, also serves palatable light snacks in a clean and pleasant atmosphere. Caviar on toast is around the US$3 mark. It is open daily from 11 am to 11 pm.

If you're after recognisable western fare, you'll have to go to a more expensive restaurant. Try *Valencia* (open daily 1 pm to midnight), at ploshchad Pobedy 1, for exotic and delicious Spanish dishes, or *Casino Universal* at Mira prospekt 43. Valencia must have the slowest service in town and the food is far from piping hot when it finally arrives,

but the fish soup, tortillas and paella are pretty tasty. The complimentary almonds and olives served to nibble on beforehand and the free glass of champagne after are welcome touches. Casino Universal's extensive menu includes 40 starters, 33 desserts and tantalising main dishes such as fried frogs paws for US$12. It is open daily from noon to 6 am.

The completely over-priced *Flagman* restaurant beneath the Sailors' Hostel is open from noon to 2 am and also gets good reports food-wise.

Bingo, next door to Valencia, is popular with Kaliningrad's young trendy folk. It sports a huge neon Coke sign outside and the management imposes a US$10 fine if clients bring their own alcohol. Another popular hang-out is the large *Dvorets Sporta Yunosti* (Youth Sports Palace), in front of the Hotelschiff Hansa. Its *bufet* – no signs, just enter and walk along the passage to the left – attracts quite a variety of customers, because of its rock videos (not too loud), good service, and food (which is nothing spectacular but at least it corresponds to what the Russian menu says).

Smak fast food outlets, doling out rubberised burgers from mobile kiosks, are dotted all over, including at Sovietsky 12, close to ploshchad Pobedy; at Moskovsky 127, within walking distance of the Kaliningrad hotel; at the central market and at the Southern and Northern train stations.

The gigantic *Ocean* grocery store, east of ploshchad Pobedy on ulitsa Chernyakhovskogo, is the best place for fresh fish as well as other food products. Two handy food shops selling both local and imported products include the *Delicacies* grocery store (open daily from 11 to 2 am), next to the Kaliningrad hotel, and the *Europa* food store (open daily from 10 to 1 am), 300m north on Leninsky prospekt. The *Central Market* is situated east of the Ocean store on ulitsa Chernyakhovskogo.

ENTERTAINMENT

You could always try a play in Russian at the Kaliningrad Drama Theatre (☎ 212 422), or a film in Russian at one of the cinemas *(kinoteatry)*. The former Luise Church, in Kalinin Park, houses the Puppet Theatre (☎ 212 969).

Occasional organ recitals and classical music concerts are held in St Nicholas Church (☎ 274 743), at Tenistaya 39, and St Katherine's Church, at ulitsa Bogdana Khmelnitskogo 61a, which houses the Philharmonic Organ Hall (☎ 448 890).

The *Charm Nightclub* (☎ 228 151), at ulitsa Kirova 7, is open daily from 8 pm to 6 am. Be careful, for it is full of over obliging women and big boys playing tough.

GETTING THERE & AWAY

Kaliningrad's long-distance transport hub is at ploshchad Kalinina, at the south end of Leninsky prospekt, where the Yuzhny Vokzal (Southern train station), the bus station *(avtovokzal)*, and the main Aeroflot office are all located.

Air

SAS has four weekly flights from Kaliningrad to Copenhagen. Its office (☎ 459 451, 459 452) is at Kaliningrad International Airport. It also plans to open a city centre office on ploshchad Pobedy.

Aeroflot has scheduled flights to Hamburg once a week and to Kiev twice weekly, as well as numerous flights to a whole host of other cities in Russia, including a daily flight to Moscow and a flight five times weekly to St Petersburg. Aeroflot's main office (☎ 44 46 66, 44 66 57) is opposite the Southern train station, on the north side of ploshchad Kalinina. Window Nos 1 to 9 are for Russians while the window to the right inside the main entrance is for foreigners.

The airport (☎ 459 426, 441 396) is at Khrabrovo, about 24 km north of the city, east off the Zelenogradsk road. You must check in at least 40 minutes before departure. See Getting Around for information on getting to the airport. The international terminal is three km from the domestic terminal.

Bus

The bus station (☎ 44 36 35) is towards the east end of ploshchad Kalinina, next to the Southern train station. Buses run to/from main points in Lithuania, Latvia and Estonia as well as within the Kaliningrad Region. They include:

Baltiysk
50 km, 1½ hours, two buses daily, US$1.50
Chernyakhovsk
90 km, two to 2½ hours, one bus daily, US$3
Druskininkai
330 km, seven hours, one bus daily, US$8
Gusev
115 km, three hours, five buses daily, US$4
Kaunas
250 km, six hours, one bus daily, US$6.50
Klaipėda (via Zelenogradsk and Nida)
130 km, 3½ hours, four buses daily (terminating at Smiltynė), US$3.50
Liepāja
305 km, 7½ to 9½ hours, two buses daily via Sovietsk, Klaipėda and Palanga, US$7.50
Mamonovo
55 km, 1½ hours, eight buses daily, US$1.50
Nida
80 km, 2½ hours, four buses daily, US$2.50
Palanga (via Sovietsk and Klaipėda)
235 km, six hours, two buses daily, US$6
Pärnu
560 km, 11 hours, one bus nightly, US$14
Rīga
370 km, nine hours, one bus daily via Sovietsk and Šiauliai, US$8.50
Šiauliai
245 km, five hours, one bus daily via Sovietsk, US$6.50
Sovietsk
115 km, three to 3½ hours, eight or more buses daily, US$4
Tallinn (via Pärnu)
690 km, 13½ hours, one bus nightly, US$17.50
Vilnius
350 km, 8¼ hours, two buses nightly via Chernyakhovsk and Marijampolė, or Sovietsk and Jurbarkas, US$9
Yantarny
45 km, 1½ hours, two buses daily, US$1.50
Zelenogradsk
30 km, 50 minutes, six buses daily, US$1.50

Bus fares fluctuate by about US$2. For information on bus routes and frequencies to/from Poland, the rest of Russia, and Belarus, see the introductory Getting There

& Away chapter. For Poland, tickets are sold at window No 11 in the bus station from 9 to 10 am, 11 am to 1.50 pm and 2.20 to 4.30 pm. The company operating the buses to Poland is König Auto (☎ 430 480).

Train

Kaliningrad's two important stations are the Yuzhny Vokzal (Southern Station) on ploshchad Kalinina, and the Severny Vokzal (Northern Station) just off ploshchad Pobedy.

Only local trains use the Severny Vokzal, most of which continue to the Yuzhny Vokzal, arriving there nine minutes later. International and long distance trains only use the Yuzhny Vokzal.

International Trains Tickets for trains to Poland and Germany are sold at the international ticket office (mezhdunarodnih kassovih zal), at Yuzhny Vokzal. The office – the second door on the left inside the main entrance – is open daily from 10 am to 6 pm with a break between 2 and 3 pm. To guarantee a seat, buy your tickets as far in advance as you can.

Long-Distance Trains There's an advance-booking hall (kassy predvaritelnoy prodazhi) for long distance tickets, bought 24 hours or more before departure, at Yuzhny Vokzal. It is the first door to the left inside the main entrance.

The advance-booking hall also has a chart showing what types of seats are available for which trains on which dates. Trains are listed by their numbers (which are given on timetables): '**R**' means kupeynyy (compartment class), platskartnyy (reserved class) and obshchiy (general class) seats are all available; '**G**' means only platskartnyy and obshchiy are available; '**J**' means only obshchiy is available; a – means the train's booked out. Ticket windows for same-day trips are round to the right once you have entered the station.

Fares from Kaliningrad are comparatively low – US$26 to Vilnius and US$40 to Rīga in compartment class. Soft class is available

on some 'fast' trains to Kaunas, Vilnius, Minsk, Moscow and St Petersburg. Prices fluctuate month by month.

Long distance trains from Kaliningrad to other places within the Kaliningrad Region and the Baltic states include:

Chernyakhovsk
  90 km, 1½ to two hours, five trains daily, terminating at Vilnius, Moscow, St Petersburg, Kharkov or Gomel (also see Local Trains)
Gusev
  115 km, two to 2½ hours, five trains daily, terminating at Vilnius, Moscow, St Petersburg, Kharkov or Gomel (also see Local Trains)
Kaunas
  240 km, 3½ to 4½ hours, one train daily, terminating at Vilnius
Vilnius
  350 km, 5¼ to 6¼ hours, one train daily, terminating at Vilnius

Services to 'mainland' Russia and other countries including Belarus, Ukraine, Poland and Germany are covered in the introductory Getting There & Away chapter.

Local Trains There's a fairly good 'suburban' (prigorodnyy) train service between Kaliningrad and several towns in the Kaliningrad Region including Zelenogradsk, Svetlogorsk, Gvardeysk, Chernyakhovsk, Gusev, Nesterov, Mamonovo, Bagrationovsk, Gurievsk, Polessk, Sovietsk, Primorsk, Yantarny and Baltiysk (which is a restricted zone – see Other Destinations). Gvardeysk, Chernyakhovsk, Gusev, Nesterov and Sovietsk are also served by some long distance trains.

From Severny Vokzal (Northern Station) trains go to Svetlogorsk, Zelenogradsk, Yantarny, Sovietsk and Primorsk. However, all trains to Svetlogorsk, Zelenogradsk and Yantarny continue to the Yuzhny Vokzal (Southern Station). Trains to all other destinations within the Kaliningrad Region originate and terminate at the Yuzhny Vokzal.

You can buy tickets at the station a few minutes before departure. Fares are low – US$1 for a one way ticket to Svetlogorsk (55 minutes) and US$0.80 to Zelenogradsk (45 minutes).

KALININGRAD REGION

Car & Motorcycle

The main road entry points into the Kaliningrad Region from Lithuania are at Sovietsk (from Panemunė, Lithuania), and between Kybartai (Lithuania) and Nesterov. The road down the Curonian Spit (Kursh-skaya kosa), from Klaipėda to Zelenogradsk, is an attractive alternative.

Entry points from Kaliningrad into Poland include the Mamonovo-Braniewo crossing in the Elblag direction, the Bagrationovsk crossing heading towards Olsztyn, and the entry point at Krylovo, just south of Ozersk and Gusev.

Boat

See the introductory Getting There & Away chapter for information on ferry services between the Kaliningrad Region, Poland and Germany. All ferry services use the city port, 1.5 km east of the centre, referred to locally as 'Pravaya naberezhnaya' (the right bank). Tickets are sold by Inflot (☎ 471 442; fax 471 146) at the port office, on the opposite side of the river, at Portovaya 24. The port administration (☎ 472 217) is in the same building. Alvis Travel Agency (see Organised Tours) also sells ferry tickets, as does Baltma Tours (see Kaliningrad – Information). Tickets have to be bought 24 hours before departure.

GETTING AROUND
The Airport

A bus runs from Kaliningrad to the domestic terminal one or two times an hour between 6.30 am and 9.30 pm. The trip takes about 50 minutes and tickets are sold on the bus. The first return bus leaves the airport's domestic terminal at 7.20 am.

Getting to/from the international terminal is trickier. An airport bus runs between Kaliningrad bus station and the international terminal three times daily on Monday, Saturday and Sunday; once daily on Tuesday; five times daily on Wednesday; and four times daily on Friday. The SAS office at the international airport can arrange private transport to the centre upon request as can Baltma Tours (see Information) which

charges US$33 for a taxi (up to three people) and US$46 for a minibus (three to seven people).

City Transport

Kaliningrad is compact enough to cover on foot. Trams, trolleybuses and buses use the usual ticket-punching system. Tickets are sold in strips of 10 for US$1 from kiosks around town. The fine for not having a punched ticket is the equivalent of the minimum monthly salary (US$13 in late 1996).

A real life-saver is the tram and trolleybus section (in English and indicating all the city routes) included in *Kaliningrad In Your Pocket*. Bus routes are mapped out in *Kaliningrad – Plan of the City and Transport*, a small booklet published by the Yantarny Skaiz publishing house in 1995 and sold at kiosks for US$5.

Some bus services stop on the Yuzhny Vokzal forecourt, but the best place to get transport north to the city proper (if you've just arrived at the bus station or Yuzhny Vokzal) is the prospekt Kalinina stop – at the far north-east corner of ploshchad Kalinina, just north of the corner of prospekt Kalinina itself.

Car & Motorcycle

The wide and well kept roads (a rare beneficial spin-off of the region's heavy military presence) make private transport an ideal way to get around, especially as most previously restricted areas can now be entered by tourists. On some roads you may encounter trilingual signs (in Russian, German and English) indicating you need special permission to enter that territory. Although this is the official story, you're unlikely to be stopped. Be aware that some of these areas are still under military control. If you *are* stopped you will not be fined or arrested, unless you have been stupid enough to climb over a barbed wire fence into an obviously closed-off area. Generally, you will just be told to go back to where you came from. Gaining special permission is all but impossible for mere tourists. In border areas you will come across blue signs (in Russian only) stating that you need documents to proceed further. Your passport, visa, vehicle registration and driving licence should be sufficient.

Car Rental Car rental companies do not exist in the Kaliningrad Region – the law requires cars to be owned by individuals. Taxis are prepared to embark on longer trips out of town for US$10 an hour. Baltma Tours (see Kaliningrad – Information) can arrange a car with interpreter for US$12 an hour or mini-bus for US$18 an hour.

Taxi
Taxis are cheap but difficult to find. Private drivers are prepared to use their cars as makeshift taxis. A trip across the centre (about one or two km) should cost no more than US$3. Taxis can be picked up outside the Kaliningrad hotel, bus station and Yuzhny Vokzal.

The Nocturne Travel Agency (☎ 453 216; fax 469 578), inside the Kaliningrad hotel, claims to be the official taxi dispatcher and can call a cab or hire you a car (with driver) for US$10 an hour.

Other Destinations

The Kaliningrad Region is mostly farmland, with about 20% woodland and some marshes. Many of the roads are lined with avenues of trees, which were (mostly) planted during the German period. There's also some attractive coastline, like the two seaside resorts of Svetlogorsk and Zelenogradsk, and the southern half of the 98 km Curonian Spit – the northern half of the spit is in Lithuania. During spring and autumn storms, amber pieces are washed up on the shores all along this coastline.

Inland are a number of former German towns, all now with Russian names, Russian populations and, for the most part, Russian architecture. Many of them were fought over at least as fiercely as Kaliningrad itself in 1945.

SVETLOGORSK
Светлогорск
• ☎ (2533)

Svetlogorsk (former German name: Rauschen) is a pleasantly treed coastal town, 35 km north-west of Kaliningrad city. The town began to develop as a resort with the building of the railway from Kaliningrad at the beginning of the 20th century. Svetlogorsk retains quite a lot of the appearance of old Rauschen, with its tree-lined streets and numbers of small, wooden houses, some of which were used in the Soviet era for sanatoriums or holiday homes for Soviet workers and officials. The number of visitors has dropped since the collapse of the USSR, and Svetlogorsk is now a pleasantly relaxed town to wander round.

Orientation
Svetlogorsk is a slightly confusing place because it has two train stations – Svetlogorsk I and Svetlogorsk II – and in between the two the track does a 180° loop. The first station you reach coming from Kaliningrad is Svetlogorsk I. It's about 1.5 km inland, on the main line from Kaliningrad through to Yantarny and Primorsk. You'll have to really look out for the small sign on top of one of the station buildings (on the right-hand side, from Kaliningrad) which proclaims it 'Svetlogorsk I'. There's a taxi stand beside Svetlogorsk I.

Much more convenient is Svetlogorsk II, on ulitsa Lenina, which is at the end of its own branch line and much nearer the beach and the centre of town.

Information
The post office is on ulitsa Ostrovskogo off ulitsa Oktyabrskaya. There's a telephone office nearby on ulitsa Gagarina. There's a small market just off ulitsa Oktyabrskaya, opposite the water tower.

To call Svetlogorsk from abroad dial 7-011533.

Things to See & Do

A walk along the sandy **beach** itself, particularly westwards from Svetlogorsk, is one of the best things to do. A **chair lift** *(funikuler)* runs down to the beach, from the north side of Svetlogorsk II station, and a ride costs about US$0.10.

Ulitsa Lenina, on the south side of Svetlogorsk II station, runs roughly parallel to the coast. If you follow it 450m eastwards you reach its corner with ulitsa Oktyabrskaya, the main boulevard of the resort. About 150m along ulitsa Oktyabrskaya (inland from the corner) are the 25m **water tower** and, adjoining it, the domed (in red tile) *Jugendstil* **bathhouse**. Both structures are symbols of the town and even appeared on a Soviet postage stamp in the 1960s. In a wooded park near here are four **sculptures**

The *Water Carrier* by Hermann Brachert (Svetlogorsk)

by the renowned German artist Hermann Brachert (1890-1972), including the *Water Carrier* (Wasserträgerin) – a marble figure of a bare breasted woman carrying a pitcher of water on her head. Brachert had a house at Otradnoe (then called Georgenswalde), a couple of km west along the coast from Svetlogorsk, where he retreated to when the Nazis came to power.

At ulitsa Lenina 5 there is a **Commemorative Chapel**. Opened in 1994 it is a memorial to the 34 people (23 of whom were children aged between three and seven) who were killed in a kindergarten (on the site) when a Soviet A-26 military transport plane, on a low flying training mission above the Baltic Sea, crashed into the building. The tragedy was hushed up for almost 20 years and only came to light when the Russian Orthodox Church decided to build the chapel in 1991.

Some 200m north from the ulitsa Lenina corner, ulitsa Oktyabrskaya reaches the top of a zig-zag path down to the beach. Not far from the foot of this path is an ugly landmark – the tower of the lift that used to carry people up and down from Svetlogorsk's military sanatorium.

About 200m east along ulitsa Lenina (from the ulitsa Oktyabrskaya corner), is an intersection where a left (north) turn takes you to the main steps down to the beach. On the beach promenade, near the bottom of these steps, is a very large and colourful **sundial**. Further along ulitsa Lenina is a sports stadium and a **park of culture & rest** (PKiO).

A long **lake**, Ozero Tikhoe, stretches beside Kaliningradsky prospekt in the lower part of the town between the two train stations. In summer you can hire rowing boats at its west end. One of Svetlogorsk's most striking pre-war houses – a turreted, blue and white painted edifice on Kaliningradsky prospekt, just beyond the eastern end of the lake – is now occupied by the GAI traffic police.

Places to Stay

Don't be deceived by the fact that Svetlogorsk boasts the finest hotel (the Hotel

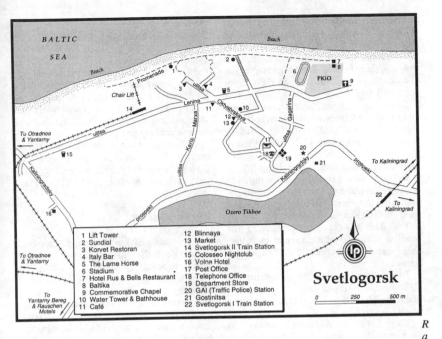

1 Lift Tower	12 Blinnaya
2 Sundial	13 Market
3 Korvet Restoran	14 Svetlogorsk II Train Station
4 Italy Bar	15 Colosseo Nightclub
5 The Lame Horse	16 Volna Hotel
6 Stadium	17 Post Office
7 Hotel Rus & Bells Restaurant	18 Telephone Office
8 Baltika	19 Department Store
9 Commemorative Chapel	20 GAI (Traffic Police) Station
10 Water Tower & Bathhouse	21 Gostinitsa
11 Café	22 Svetlogorsk I Train Station

Svetlogorsk

0   250   500 m

Rus) in the entire Kaliningrad Region. Unfortunately, there are few really good places to stay in the town.

The *Volna* (☎ 3733), at Kaliningradsky prospekt 68A, has reasonable singles/doubles with private bathroom for around US$20/28. It's set back from the west side of the road, about 300m south of the ulitsa Lenina corner.

There's also a small, very basic looking *Gostinitsa* (hotel) at the other end of Kaliningradsky prospekt, just past the eastern end of the lake.

Another grey option is the *Yantarny bereg* (☎ 3469; fax 3040) at Kaliningradsky prospekt 79a. The twin concrete blocks which make up this supposedly delightful hotel are indicative of its Soviet service and style. Single/double rooms with shared bathrooms cost about US$16/24, although prices do fluctuate.

Opposite the Yantarny bereg, at Novaja 2, is one of Svetlogorsk's better hotels. The

uschen (☎ 3729) is definitely the most customer-orientated place in town. And its rooms have even been renovated in recent years. Singles/doubles with private bathroom are US$30/50.

Close to the beach, at Vershlagina 8, is the even greyer and uglier *Baltika* (☎ 3082; fax 3082). A former rest-home for ministry employees, the hotel offers full board (which includes three meals a day) for US$30.

Next door to the dreary Baltika is the region's top hotel. Simply walking into the marble floored, exquisitely furnished lobby of the *Hotel Rus* (☎ 0112-43 64 08, 0112-22 25 10) is enough to make you want to check in immediately. Plush singles/doubles with balcony cost US$65/125. Make sure you ask for a room with a sea view – unless of course you fancy staring out at the Baltika hotel.

Places to Eat

Svetlogorsk also boasts one of the finest bar-cum-restaurants in the region.

The *Lame Horse* is the best place to eat, drink and be merry for miles around. The spicy Mexican-style food here is far from lame and the bar stools with real saddles are truly a sight to behold. The Lame Horse is at Oktyabrskaya 23, and is open daily from noon to 3 am.

Second in line is the *Italy Bar*, at the beach end of ulitsa Oktyabrskaya, which is run by the same team as the Italian Café in Kaliningrad. Prices are higher here than in the city and pizza is not on the menu. It's open daily from 10 am to midnight

Beyond that the story is uninspiring. The *Blinnaya* on ulitsa Oktyabrskaya, across the road from the water tower, serves pancakes, fried chicken and small salads.

The *Korvet Restoran*, overlooking the beach at ulitsa Oktyabrskaya, can do a tolerable meal if you can tolerate the blaring pop music.

Top of the range – in price and quality – is *Bells Restaurant* (open daily from 7 to 4 am) inside the Hotel Rus. It also features a disco when the sun shines.

The *Colosseo Nightclub*, next to Svetlogorsk II station on Kaliningradsky prospekt, gets fairly decent reports. As does the *Volna (Hotel) Casino*, where you'll find roulette, blackjack and over a hundred types of cocktail, if you really need it.

Getting There & Away

There are around 20 to 25 trains a day from Kaliningrad to Svetlogorsk (55 minutes to 1½ hours, US$1).

About one-third of the trains start from the Severny Vokzal in Kaliningrad and don't go through the Yuzhny Vokzal. The others start from the Yuzhny Vokzal but also stop at the Severny Vokzal. All go to Svetlogorsk I station and most – but not the last couple of trains at night – go on to Svetlogorsk II.

Around 10 trains a day go from Svetlogorsk to Zelenogradsk. Most start at Svetlogorsk II and also stop at Svetlogorsk I, but a few run only from Svetlogorsk I. Most are going on to Kaliningrad but some terminate at Zelenogradsk.

Getting Around

The town is small enough to walk around, especially if you arrive at Svetlogorsk II station. Taxis are fairly easy to find, although only a few are allowed into the central part of the resort area. One taxi stand is by Svetlogorsk I station. Taxis – or private cars willing to act as taxis – also wait by the bus stop on the corner of ulitsa Lenina and Kaliningradsky prospekt.

Only residents are allowed to drive private cars into the resort area. There is a car park (*avtostoyanky*) by the Kaliningradsky prospekt railway crossing, near Svetlogorsk I station.

ZELENOGRADSK
Зеленоградск

Zelenogradsk, 30 km north of Kaliningrad, used to be (in the mid-19th century) the most popular beach spot of the Kaliningrad Region.

Today it is just another dead resort, struggling to revive some of the charm it lost after the German era (when its name was Cranz). There are still a number of old German-style houses in Zelenogradsk, but the seafront promenade (*naberezhnaya*) is dotted with semi-derelict buildings which offer little hope of a revival for the town.

Orientation & Information

The train and bus stations are side by side on the south side of ulitsa Lenina, the main east-west street running through the town. To reach the beach, cross ulitsa Lenina and take any street heading north. The beach is about 200m ahead.

There's a busy little market immediately east of the train station. The post office faces the market on the street at its far end. The telephone office is on the corner of ulitsa Lenina, 80m north of the post office.

Things to See & Do

If you walk east along ulitsa Lenina from the stations, after 200m you'll reach a small square with a statue of Lenin (the telephone office is on the south side of this square). Further along ulitsa Lenina there's another, silver-painted Lenin in the grounds of the Zelenogradsk Sanatorium, which occupy much of the area between here and the seafront promenade.

The beach stretches a long way, particularly to the east, and you can have a good stretch of the legs and lungs along here.

Getting There & Away

About 20 trains a day, plus a few extra in summer on Saturday and Sunday, run from Kaliningrad to Zelenogradsk (45 minutes, US$1.50). Slightly more than half of them start from Kaliningrad's Yuzhny Vokzal and also call at the Severny Vokzal on the way out of the city. The others only run from the Severny Vokzal.

About 10 trains a day run from Zelenogradsk to Svetlogorsk I, most continuing on to Svetlogorsk II.

There are about 12 buses a day to/from Kaliningrad, plus four daily each way to/from the Lithuanian town of Smiltynė, at the northern tip of the Curonian Spit, opposite Klaipėda. The Smiltynė buses stop at places along the Curonian Spit such as Lesnoy, Rybachy, Morskoe and, over the Lithuanian border, Nida and Juodkrantė.

SOVIETSK
Советск
• ☎ (261)

Sovietsk is the Kaliningrad Region's second largest city. It lies on the Neman (Lithuanian: Nemunas), which is the border with Lithuania, and on the main Kaliningrad-Rīga road, connecting it with Kaunas, Vilnius and Klaipėda.

Sovietsk is famous as the scene of the 1807 Treaty of Tilsit (the city's former German name) during the Napoleonic Wars, when Napoleon, having defeated Prussia at the battles of Jena and Auerstädt, dictated severe peace terms to the Prussian king, Friedrich Wilhelm III, on a barge anchored in the Neman. Prussia had to pay large sums to France, cede half of its territory and accept an occupation of much of what was left. The tables were turned eight years later, however, when Prussian forces took part in Napoleon's final defeat at Waterloo.

The symbolic landmark of the town today is the **Queen Luise Bridge** over the Neman River – the stone portal is all that survived WWII, the bridge itself was rebuilt in 1948 after being blown up in 1944 by the retreating German army. The bridge is named after the wife of Friedrich Wilhelm III, who made

Queen Luise Bridge, which straddles the Neman River, Sovietsk

an unsuccessful appeal to Napoleon, at Tilsit (in 1807), for clemency for Prussia.

The town centre is a mix of old German buildings, including some in the Jugendstil style, and newer Soviet designs. The main street, ulitsa Pobedy, runs from the bridge to the town's biggest square. Off the square is a lake which was once the mill pond of Tilsit Castle. The castle was burnt down in 1876 and some of its remains can still be seen by the lake. A Soviet tank monument has replaced the statue of an elk which, before WWII, stood opposite the **Sovietsk Drama Theatre**, which was built in the 1890s.

Getting There & Away

Sovietsk's train and bus stations are on ulitsa Gorkogo, where a big Russian military barracks also stands. Eight or more buses run daily between Kaliningrad and Sovietsk (3½ hours, US$4), many of them on their way to/from places across the border including Šiauliai, Vilnius, Liepāja and Rīga. Two or three long distance trains also stop here daily, en route between Kaliningrad (Yuzhny Vokzal) and Moscow.

BALTIYSK
Балтийск
• ☎ (2533)

On the north side of the Kaliningrad Lagoon's narrow opening to the sea is the naval port of Baltiysk (former German name: Pillau). It is a restricted military area and entry requires special permission – impossible for travellers to obtain independently. Baltma Tours arranges tours to Baltiysk by bus or by military cutter along the Kaliningrad Lagoon. Every year on the last Sunday in July, on the Day of the Fleet celebrations, the port is freely open to the public. Baltiysk is connected to Kaliningrad by two daily buses and one daily train (from Yuzhny Vokzal).

YANTARNY
Янтарный
• ☎ (2533)

West of Kaliningrad, on the Baltic coast, is the little-known (and once closed) village of Yantarny. Formerly known as Palmicken, Yantarny (which means made of amber) is the site of the world's largest amber mine and a place not to missed in your travels through the Kaliningrad Region.

The Russky Yantar amber mine produces almost 90% of the world's amber, its annual yield of the fossilised resin estimated to total 750 tonnes. Access to the mine is limited to organised tours, but if you are travelling independently it is possible (if you call in advance) to arrange a visit to the small **amber museum** (☎ 450 458; fax 466 729) inside the mine. Exhibits include an impressive amber rock weighing 2.86 kg and a portrait of Lenin made from amber beads. At the northern end of the main street, ulitsa Sovietskaya, next to the museum, there is also a **factory outlet**, unfortunately selling the least interesting pieces of amber jewellery. It is open Monday to Friday from 8 am to 12.30 pm, and from 1.30 to 5 pm.

On the beach, several hundred metres west of ulitsa Sovietskaya, there is a waste water pipe originating from the mine (three km inland). Here, men and women by the dozens (dressed in full fishing gear) 'fish' for amber in the black water that shoots from the pipe. The day we were there some caught up to half a kilo in just four hours, which they were happy to sell. The going rate was US$140 for 200g of small pieces, or US$1 a gram for larger ones.

Baltma Tours arranges tours of the amber mine and factory. Alternatively you can call the amber mine's official guide, Alfred Schlosser (☎ 7353), who worked at the mine for 30 years. He can gain official permission for you to enter the mine, factory and museum, and then guide you, for about US$15 per group. With a little persuasion he will even take you to visit the amber fishers. He only speaks Russian and German.

Getting There & Away

Trains to Pokrovskoe, Primorsk and Baltiysk, from Svetlogorsk I station, stop at Yantarny six times a day – many of these services start in Kaliningrad. Two buses run

The Amber Trail

Amber was formed in the Baltic region 40 to 60 million years ago. Yet it was not until the 1860s that the amber trail really began.

An organic substance rather than a mineral, the golden 'stone' that sparkles in sunlight is in fact nothing more than fossilised resin. During the sub-tropical climes of the early Cenozoic era, the vast pine forests of Fennoscandia (later to be engulfed by the Baltic Sea) secreted rivers of resin, entombing and preserving insects along the way – much to the delight of modern-day scientists. Fifteen years later, this sticky resin became buried by ice – kilometres thick – and it was not until the warming of the earth's atmosphere millions of years later that the region's 'Baltic gold' came to light once more.

Early man used amber as heating fuel (it burns extremely well). In the middle ages it was used as cash. For the tribal Prussians inhabiting the south-east shores of the Baltic Sea around 12,000 BC, rubbing amber was the best known way of generating static electricity (hence its ancient Greek name *elektron*). During the 12th century, this sunny stone was said to contain mystical qualities – amber worn next to the skin helped a person become closer to the spirits. Perhaps not surprisingly, the German crusading knights of the Teutonic Order, who took over this Baltic region in the 13th century, claimed the region's amber as their own; yet they too failed to understand just where and how more of this Baltic gold could be found.

A bizarre tale surrounds the dramatic discovery of amber in the Kaliningrad Region. In 1869 the King of Prussia ordered a coastal shipping channel to be dug between Baltiysk and Primorsk and, quite by accident, workers found the 10 to 12m-thick layer of blue amber-bearing material lying five metres below sea level. Two sea-mines – the *Anne* and *Maria* – were opened off the coast of Yantarny in 1905, but seven years later they were both shut down because too many miners had been buried alive.

Efforts to mine inland proved substantially more successful. A German mine, built in 1912 immediately following the collapse of the two sea mines, employed 10% of Yantarny's population and yielded sufficient amber to warrant the establishment of a processing factory in Berlin as well as Königsberg (Kaliningrad). The entire mining complex was destroyed in 1945 during the Red Army's assault on Königsberg, but by 1947 the Soviet authorities had opened, on the same site, the Russky Yantar mine, today recognised as the world's only opencast amber mine.

For many years the USSR's treasure-seeking fortunes followed a similar trend to that of its German predecessors. Between 1947 and 1981, the mine's annual amber yield quintupled, totalling 715 tonnes in 1981. Just over a kilo of amber was being extracted from every cubic metre mined. At its peak, up to 20% of Yantarny's total population was employed to follow the amber trail.

After the collapse of the Soviet Union, Russky Yantar's fortunes paled. A declining world market in Russia's 'Baltic gold' forced production levels to be severely controlled – so much so that 1996 production levels matched those of 15 years previous. The effects of the recent privatisation of the complex – the mine, museum and two processing factories – are far from evident (walking round the factories is a bit like walking into a Charles Dickens novel). Horror stories surrounding the mine field are rife – ranging from talk of an amber stockpile worth US$120 million, which remains unsold, to armed gangs raiding the factories at night for amber to sell on a thriving black market. Top grade amber fetches an estimated US$1000 a kilo.

While the Russky Yantar complex is ailing, outside its confines the amber trail continues with a vengeance. Three km west of the mine on the beach, weather-beaten men – faces carved from wrinkles – fish for amber in the muddy slop that shoots out of a waste pipe originating from Russky Yantar. The small pieces of unpolished sunlight they catch are only bottom-grade amber (77% of all amber mined in Yantarny is), but the monthly income of these men is higher than the average.

Regardless of the future of Russky Yantar, however, it is doubtful whether the intrigue surrounding this amber-bearing region will ever really die – that is, providing the treasures of the legendary 'amber room', believed to be somewhere in the Kaliningrad Region, remain lost. Treasure seekers worldwide still come to the Russian enclave on the trail of the amber room, which was given to Peter the Great by the King of Prussia in 1716 and later assembled in the Catherine Palace in Pushkin. In 1942 the room – made up of over 10,000 panels of polished, worked amber – was plundered by the invading Germans and it is believed that they shipped it from the St Petersburg region to the castle of the Teutonic Order in Königsberg.

It's unclear whether the amber room really did burn to the ground during British bombing raids on Königsberg in 1944, or if the Germans did in fact manage to move it to safety. Hence the intrigue surrounding its fate. ∎

daily from Kaliningrad, taking 1½ hours and costing about US$1.50.

MUROMSKOE
• ☎ (22)

This small village 30 km north of Kaliningrad has been dubbed the 'Klondike of Kaliningrad' since 1993, when a tractor driver uncovered a huge piece of amber in a nearby field. The lucrative find sparked off a massive amber rush in the area, although not always with happy results. In the summer of 1995, a 12 year old boy died after the hole he was digging collapsed around him. Despite stiff fines being imposed (in early 1996), for anyone caught digging for amber, the rush continues. The field is covered with countless holes, some up to five metres deep, and still attracts hundreds of amber seekers every year.

To reach the amber field from the centre of town, take the first right turn off the Muromskoe-Zelenogradsk road and continue for 2.5 km (through a wooded area) to a cluster of trees, where the road veers left.

Muromskoe is between Kaliningrad and the jaded seaside resort of Zelenogradsk. One train daily to Svetlogorsk (via Zelenogradsk) stops at Muromskoe, which is the fifth stop on the line after Kaliningrad's Severny Vokzal.

KURSHSKAYA KOSA
Куршская коса

The Kurshskaya kosa is the Russian half of the 98 km long, two to four km wide Curonian Spit, which divides the Curonian Lagoon from the Baltic Sea. The Kurshskaya kosa shares the same dramatic landscape as the northern, Lithuanian half – high sand dunes, pine forests, an exposed western coast and a calmer lagoon coast.

A few fishing-cum-holiday villages dot the eastern coast. The main ones, from south to north, are Lesnoy (former German name: Sarkau), Rybachy (former German name: Rossitten) and Morskoe (former German

name: Pillkoppen) which is just six km short of the Lithuanian border.

Four buses a day from Kaliningrad (via Zelenogradsk) take the road up the peninsula to Smiltynė at its northern tip, opposite Klaipėda. It's about 1¾ hours from Kaliningrad to Rybachy, the biggest settlement in the Russian half.

YASNAJA POLJANA

Not far from the Lithuanian border, in the Kaliningrad Region's far east, is the town of Yasnaja Poljana. Formerly known by its German name of Trakehnen, this area once boasted the German state's most famous **horse stud**. Founded in 1732 by King Frederick Wilhelm I, the stud was best known for breeding the Trakehner horse. The advance of the Red Army in 1944 forced the stud to close and the staff and horses to flee, many of whom died of exhaustion en route. The survivors made it as far as Rostov on Don in southern Russia. Today, Trakehner horses are once more being bred (with horses from Rostov) near the vast stud. When you visit take note of the distinctive 'elchschaufel' royal stud emblem on the farm gate.

Baltma Tours arranges day trips to the horse stud. Gusev, 12 km west of Yasnaja Poljana, is served by buses and trains from Kaliningrad.

GURIEVSK, MORDOVSKOE & POLESSK
Гурьевск, Мордовское и Полесск

At Gurievsk (former German name: Neuhausen), 10 km from central Kaliningrad, are the ruins of a 14th century **Teutonic church**. At Mordovskoe (its former German name was Gross Legitten, but it is also called Turgenevo on some maps) there is another old church dating back to around 1400. At Polessk (former German name: Labiau), there are the scant remains of a 13th century **Teutonic Order castle** by the Deyma river.

Language Guide

Knowing a few words and phrases in the local languages will help you find your way around and will also help you break the ice with the local people. This guide introduces you to the alphabet and pronunciation of each of the Baltic languages and Russian and includes some words and phrases you will find useful on your travels.

Estonian

Like Finnish, Estonian is a Finno-Ugric language, which sets it apart from Latvian, Lithuanian and Russian, which are all in the Indo-European language family. It's a very Nordic-sounding language with lots of deep 'oo's and 'uu's. The south, particularly the south-east, of the country has some dialect differences from the north. You're unlikely to get far with learning Estonian in a short visit – its nouns decline through no less than 14 cases – but the odd word goes down well.

Alphabet & Pronunciation

Estonian lacks a few letters of the English alphabet but has some extra ones of its own. Its alphabet is as follows:

a b d e f g h i j k l m n o p r s š z ž t u v õ
ä ö ü

Note that **š** is counted as a separate letter from **s**, **ž** from **z**, **õ** and **ö** from **o**, **ä** from **a**, and **ü** from **u**. The alphabetical order becomes important if you're using a dictionary or any other alphabetical list, for instance words beginning **ä** are listed near the end, not after **a**. The letters are generally pronounced as in English except:

a	is pronounced like the 'u' in 'cut'
b	like 'p'
g	like 'k'

j	like the 'y' in 'yes'
š	is pronounced 'sh'
ž	like the 's' in 'pleasure'
õ	somewhere between the 'e' in 'bed' and the 'u' in 'fur'
ä	like the 'a' in 'cat'
ö	like the 'u' in 'fur' but with rounded lips
ü	like a short 'yoo'
ai	like the 'i' in 'bite'
ei	like the 'ay' in 'day'
oo	like the 'a' in 'water'
uu	like the 'oo' in 'boot'
öö	like the 'u' in 'fur'

Latvian

Latvian is one of only two surviving languages of the Baltic branch of the Indo-European language family (the other is Lithuanian). Even more than Estonians, the speakers of Latvian regard their language as an endangered species – only just over half the people in the country, and just over a third of the inhabitants of the capital, Rīga, speak it as their first language. The east and west of the country have some dialect differences from standard central Latvian.

Latvian and Lithuanian share quite a lot of words but are not quite close enough to each other to be mutually intelligible. They separated from each other round about the 7th century AD.

Alphabet & Pronunciation

The Latvian alphabet is as follows:

a b c č d e f g ģ (Ģ) h i j k ķ l ļ m n ņ o p r
s š t u v z

Note that **č**, **ģ**, **ķ**, **ļ**, **ņ**, **š** and **ž** are counted as separate letters from **c**, **g**, **k**, **l**, **n**, **s** and **z**. The

435

letters are generally pronounced as in English except:

c	is pronounced 'ts'
č	as 'ch'
ǵ	like the 'j' in 'jet'
j	like the 'y' in 'yes'
ķ	like 'ty' in 'tune'
ļ	like the 'lli' in 'billiards'
ņ	like the 'ni' in 'onion'
o	like the 'a' in 'water'
š	as 'sh'
ž	like the 's' in 'pleasure'
ai	like the the 'i' in 'pine'
ei	like the 'ai' in 'pain'
ie	like the 'ea' in 'ear'

The sign has the effect of lengthening the vowel it is placed over:

ā	is pronounced like the 'a' in 'barn'
ē	like the 'a' in 'bare'
ī	like the 'e' in 'he'
ū	like the 'oo' in 'boot'

Lithuanian

Lithuanian is one of only two surviving languages of the Baltic branch of the Indo-European language family (the other is Latvian). Because many of its forms have remained unchanged longer than those of other Indo-European languages (which cover most of Europe and a fair bit of Asia) Lithuanian is very important to linguistic scholars. It's certainly a subtle and refined language, as a look through a Lithuanian dictionary will show.

Nor is it averse to hurried borrowings from other tongues where necessary, as Lithuanian phrases like *ping pong klubas* and *marketingo departamento direktorius* demonstrate. Žemaičiai or Low Lithuanian, spoken in the west, is a separate dialect from Aukštaičiai or High Lithuanian, spoken in the rest of the country.

Alphabet & Pronunciation

The Lithuanian alphabet is as follows:

a b c č d e f g h i/y j k l m n o p r s š t u v z ž

The **i** and **y** are partly interchangeable and **y** comes straight after **i** in alphabetical lists. Note that **č**, **š** and **ž** are separate letters from **c**, **s** and **z**. The letters are generally pronounced as in English except:

c	is pronounced as 'ts'
č	as 'ch'
y	between the 'i' in 'tin' and the 'ee' in 'feet'
j	as the 'y' in 'yes'
o	like the 'oa' in 'boat'
š	as 'sh'
ž	as the 's' in 'pleasure'
ei	like the 'a' in 'hay'
ie	like the 'ye' in 'yet'
ui	like the 'wi' in 'win'

The signs ‾, ·, and ¸ all have the general effect of lengthening the vowel they go with:

ą	is pronounced like the 'a' in 'father'
ę	like the 'ai' in 'air'
į	like the 'ee' in 'feet'
ų	like the 'oo' in 'boot'
ū	like the 'oo' in 'boot'
ė	like the 'a' in 'late'

Russian

Russian belongs to the Slavic branch of the Indo-European language family. The Slavic languages are the closest relatives to the Baltic languages: Lithuanian and Latvian. Russian uses the Cyrillic alphabet (see chart opposite).

Lonely Planet's *Russian Phrasebook* by James Jenkin is a good introduction to the Russian language, detailing many useful words and phrases.

Cyrillic Alphabet

Letter	Transliteration	Pronunciation
А, а	*A, a*	if stressed, like the 'a' in 'father'
		if unstressed, like the 'a' in 'about'
Б, б	*B, b*	like the 'b' in 'but'
В, в	*V, v*	like the 'v' in 'van'
Г, г	*G, g*	like the 'g' in 'god'
Д, д	*D, d*	like the 'd' in 'dog'
Е, е	*Ye, e*	if stressed, like the 'ye' in 'yet'
		if unstressed, like the 'ye' in 'yeast'
Ё, ё	*Yo, yo*	like the 'yo' in 'yore'
Ж, ж	*Zh, zh*	like the 's' in 'measure'
З, з	*Z, z*	like the 'z' in 'zoo'
И, и	*I, i*	like the 'ee' in 'meet'
Й, й	*Y, y*	like the 'y' in 'boy'
К, к	*K, k*	like the 'k' in 'kind'
Л, л	*L, l*	like the 'l' in 'lamp'
М, м	*M, m*	like the 'm' in 'mad'
Н, н	*N, n*	like the 'n' in 'not'
О, о	*O, o*	if stressed, like the 'o' in 'more'
		if unstressed, between the 'a' in hang
		and the 'u' in hung
П, п	*P, p*	like the 'p' in 'pig'
Р, р	*R, r*	like the 'r' in 'rub' (but rolled)
С, с	*S, s*	like the 's' in 'sing'
Т, т	*T, t*	like the 't' in 'ten'
У, у	*U, u*	like the 'oo' in 'fool'
Ф, ф	*F, f*	like the 'f' in 'fan'
Х, х	*Kh, kh*	like the 'ch' in 'Bach'
Ц, ц	*Ts, ts*	like the 'ts' in 'bits'
Ч, ч	*Ch, ch*	like the 'ch' in 'chin'
Ш, ш	*Sh, sh*	like the 'sh' in 'shop'
Щ, щ	*Shch, shch*	like the 'shch' in 'fresh chips'
ъ		('hard sign')
Ы, ы	*Y, y*	like the 'i' in 'ill'
ь		('soft sign')
Э, э	*E, e*	like the 'e' in 'end'
Ю, ю	*Yu, yu*	like the 'u' in 'use'
Я, я	*Ya, ya*	if stressed, like the 'ya' in 'yard'
		if unstressed, like the 'ye' in 'yearn'

ENGLISH	ESTONIAN	LATVIAN
Greetings & Civilities		
Hello.	Tere.	Labdien or Sveiki.
Good morning.	Tere hommikust.	Labrīt.
Good day/Good afternoon.	Tere päevast.	Labdien.
Good evening.	Tere õhtust.	Labvakar.
Good night.	Head ööd.	Ar labu nakti.
Goodbye.	Head aega (HEY-ahd EI-gah) or Nägemiseni.	Uz redzēšanos or atā.
Excuse me.	Vabandage.	Atvainojiet.
Useful Words & Phrases		
Yes.	Jah.	Jā.
No.	Ei.	Nē.
Please.	Palun.	Lūdzu.
Thank you.	Tänan or Aitäh ('thanks').	Paldies.
There is/are...	Ole...	Ir...
There isn't/aren't...	Ei Ole..	Nav..
Where?	Kus?	Kur?
Do you speak English?	Kas teie räägite Inglise keelt?	Vai jūs runājat Angliski?
I don't speak Estonian/ Latvian/Lithuanian/Russian.	Mina ei räägi Eesti keelt.	Es Nerunāju Latviski.
I don't understand.	Mina ei saa aru.	Es nesaprotu.
Do you speak Russian?	—	—
How much?	Kui palju?	Cik?
cheap	odav	lēts
expensive	kallis	dārgs
Getting Around		
airport	lennujaam	lidosta
railway station	raudteejaam	dzelzceļa stacija
train	rong	vilciens
bus station	bussijaam	autoosta
bus	buss	autobuss
port	sadam	osta
taxi	takso	taksometrs
tram	tramm	tramvajs
trolleybus	trollibuss	trolejbuss
stop (eg bus stop)	peatus	pietura
petrol	bensiin	benzīns or degviela

LITHUANIAN	RUSSIAN	RUSSIAN PRONUNCIATION
Labas *or* Sveikas.	Здравствуйте.	ZDRAST-vooy-tye
Labas rytas.	Доброе утро.	DOH-bra-yuh OO-tra
Laba diena.	Добрый день.	DOH-bry dyehn
Labas vakaras.	Добрый вечер.	DOH-bry VYECH-er
Labanakt.	Спокойной ночи.	spa-KOY-nay NOCH-i
Sudie *or* Viso gero.	До свидания.	das-fi-DA-nya
Atsiprašau.	Извините.	iz-vi-NEE-ti-yeh
Taip.	Да.	da
Ne.	Нет.	nyet
Prašau.	Пожалуйста.	a-ZHAHL-stuh
Ačiū.	Спасибо.	spuh-SEE-ba
Yra...	Есть...	yist
Nėra...	Нет...	nyet
Kur?	Где?	gdyeh?
Ar kalbate angliškai?	Вы говорите по-анг лийски?	vih ga-var-EE-tye pa-an-GLEE-ski?
Aš nekalbu lietuviškai.	Я не говорю по-русски.	ya nye ga-var-YOO pa-ROOSS-ki
Aš nesuprantu.	Я не понимаю.	ya nye pa-ni-MA-yu
—	Вы говорите по-русски?	vih ga-var-EE-tye pa-ROOSS-ki?
Kiek?	Сколько?	SKOL-kah?
pigus	дешёвый	desh-YOV-y
brangus	дорогой	da-ra-GOY
oro uostas	аэропорт	ah-EH-ra-port
geležinkelio stotis	вокзал	vahk-ZAHL
traukinys	поезд	PO-yezd
autobusų stotis	автовокзал	af-tah-vahk-ZAHL
autobusas	автобус	uf-TOH-boos
uostas	порт	port
taksi	такси	tak-SI
tramvajus	трамвай	tram-VAY
troleibusas	троллейбус	trahl-YEY-buss
stotelė	остановка	asta-NOHV-kuh
benzinas	бензин	ben-ZIN

ENGLISH	ESTONIAN	LATVIAN
Where & When?		
departure/departure time	väljub or väljumine	atiet or atiešanas laiks
arrival/arrival time	saabub or saabumine	pienāk or pienākšanas laiks
every day	iga päev	katru dienu
even dates	—	pāra datums
odd dates	—	nepāra datums
except	välja arvatud	izņemot
not running/cancelled	ei sõida	nekursē or atcelts
through/via	läbi or kaudu	caur
Train & Bus Types		
express	ekspress	ekspresis
fast	kiir	ātrs
fast train	kiirrong	ātrvilciens
passenger train	reisirong	pasažieru vilciens
diesel train	diiselrong	dīzeļvilciens
suburban or local (train or bus)	linnalähedane	piepilsētu
electric train	elektrirong	elektrovilciens
transit (bus)	transiit	tranzīts
Tickets		
ticket	pilet	biļete
ticket office	piletikassa or kassa	kase
advance-booking office	eelmüügikassa	iepriekšpārdošanas kases
Train Classes		
soft class/deluxe	luksus	mīksts or grezns or luksus
sleeping carriage (soft class)	magamisvagun	guļamvagons
compartment (class)	kupee	kupeja
Signs		
open	avatud or lahti	atvērts
closed	suletud or kinni	slēgts
break (eg for lunch)	vaheaeg	pārtraukums
street	tänav	iela
square	väljak or plats	laukums
avenue or boulevard	puiestee	prospekts or bulvāris
road	tee	ceļš
highway	maantee	lielceļš or šoseja

LITHUANIAN	RUSSIAN	RUSSIAN PRONUNCIATION
išvyksta *or* išvykimo laikas	отправление	at-prav-LIN-ia
atvyksta *or* atvykimo laikas	прибытие	pri-BEET-i-ye
kasdien	ежедневно	yezh-ed-NYEV-nay
dienomis porinėm	чётным	CHOT-nim
dienomis neporinėm	нечётным	nye-CHOT-nım
išskyrus	кроме	KRO-my
nekursuoja	отменён	at-min-YON
sper	xthtp	CHYER-ez
ekspresas	экспресс	ex-PRYESS
greitas	скорый	SKOH-ri
greitasis traukinys	скорый поезд	SKOH-ri PO-yezd
keleivinis traukinys	пассажирский поезд	passa-ZHIR-ski PO-yezd
dizelinis traukinys	дизельный поезд	DEEZ-el-ny PO-yezd •
priemiestinis *or* vietinis	местный*or* пригородный	MYEST-ny *or* PREE gor-ad-ny
elektrinis traukinys	электричка	el-ek-TREECH-ka
pravažiuojantis	транзитный	tran-ZEET-ny
bilietas	билет	bil-YET
kasa	касса	KASS-ah
išankstinio bilietų pardavimo kasa	кассы предварителбной продажи билетов	KASS-y prid-vah-REET-il-noy pra-DAZH-y bil-YET-ahv
minkštas *or* liuksas	мягкий *or* люкс	MYAG-ky *or* li-OOKS
miegamasis	спальный вагон	SPAHL-ny va-GOHN
kupė	купейный	kup-EY-ny
atidarytas	открыт	aht-KRIT
uždarytas	закрыт	zuh-KRIT
pertrauka	перерыв	pi-ri-REEV
gatvė	улица	OOL-it-suh
aikštė	площадь	PLOSH-id
prospektas *or* bulvaras	проспект *or* бульвар	prahs-PYEKT *or* BOOL-vahr
kelias	дорога	da-ROHG-ah
plentas	шоссе	sha-SEH

ENGLISH	ESTONIAN	LATVIAN
Around Town		
city centre	kesklinn	centrs
hotel	hotell	viesnīca
room	tuba	istaba
currency exchange	valuutavahetus	valūtas apmaiņa
bank	pank	banka
post office	postkontor	pasts
stamp	mark	pastmarka
telephone	telefon	telefons
shop	kauplus *or* pood	veikals
market	turg	tirgus
department store	kaubamaja	universālveikals
castle	loss	pils
church	kirik	baznīca
Food		
restaurant	restoran	restorāns
café	kohvik	kafejnīca
canteen/cafeteria	söökla	ēdnīca
snack bar	einelaud	bufete
bread	leib	maize
butter	või	sviests
starters	eelroad	uzkoda
caviar	kalamari	kaviārs *or* ikri
salad	salat	salāti
sausage	vorst	desa
cheese	juust	siers
soup	supp	zupa
pancake	pannkook	pankūka
fish	kala	zivs
meat (red)	liha	gaļa
meat or main dishes	liharoad	gaļas ēdieni *or* otrie ēdieni
national dishes	rahvusroad	nacionālie ēdieni
kebab	šašlõkk	šašliks
grilled 'chop'	karbonaad	karbonāde
'beefsteak'	biifsteek	bifšteks
beef stroganoff	biifstrogonoff *or* böfstrooganov	stroganovs

LANGUAGE GUIDE

LITHUANIAN	RUSSIAN	RUSSIAN PRONUNCIATION
centras	центр города	tsyentr ga-ROHD-uh
viešbutis	гостиница	guh-STEE-nit-suh
kambarys	комната	KOHM-na-tuh
valiutos keitimas	обмен валюты	ab-MYEN val-YOOT-uh
bankas	банк	bank
paštas	почта	POCH-ta
pašto ženklas	почтовая марка	pach-TOHV-aya MARK-a
telefonas	телефон	ti-li-FON
parduotuvė	магазин	ma-ga-ZIN
turgus	рынок	REE-nak
universalinė parduotuvė	универсальный магазин	u-ni-vyer-SAL-ny ma-ga-ZIN
pilis	замок	ZAHM-ak
bažnyčia	церков	TSYER-kav
restoranas	ресторан	ryest-ah-RAHN
kavinė	кафе	ka-FEH
valgykla	столовая	sta-LOH-vuh-yuh
bufetas	буфет	bu-FYET
duona	хлеб	khlyep
sviestas	масло	MAHS-luh
užkanda	закуски	za-KOOSS-ki
ikrai	икра	i-KRA
salotos or mišrainė	салат	suh-LAHT
dešra	колбаса	kal-bass-AH
sūris	сыр	seer
sriuba	суп	soop
blynas	блин	blin
žuvis	рыба	RIH-buh
mesa	мясо	MYASS-uh
mėsos patiekalai	горячие блюда	gah-ri-ACH-i-yeh BLYOOD-ah
nacionaliniai patiekalai	национальные блюда	nahts-ya-NAHL-ni-yeh BLYOOD-ah
šašlykas	iашлык	shash-LUYK
karbonadas	—	—
bifšteksas	бифштекс	bif-SHTEKS
befstrogenas	бефстроганов	byef-STROH-guh-nof

ENGLISH	ESTONIAN	LATVIAN
chicken	kana	vista
vegetables	köögivili	saknes *or* dārzeņi
potato	kartul	kartupelis
mushroom	seen	sēne *or* šampinjons
desserts	magusroad	saldie ēdieni
ice cream	jäätis	saldējums
fruit	puuvili	augļi
bill	arve	rēķins

Drinks

bar	baar	bārs
water	vesi	ūdens
mineral water	mineralveesi	minerālūdens
juice	mahl	sula
tea	tee	tēja
coffee	kohv	kafija
milk	piim	piens
sugar	suhkur	cukurs
beer	õlu	alus
vodka	valge viin	degvīns
brandy	konjak	konjaks
champagne	šampus	šampanietis
wine	vein	vīns

Days & Months

today	täna	šodien
yesterday	eile	vakar
tomorrow	homme	rīt
Sunday	pühapäev	svētdiena
Monday	esmaspäev	pirmdiena
Tuesday	teisipäev	otrdiena
Wednesday	kolmapäev	trešdiena
Thursday	neljapäev	ceturtdiena
Friday	reede	piektdiena
Saturday	laupäev	sestdiena

The days of the week are often abbreviated to their first one or two letters in timetables etc. In Latvian and Lithuanian note the difference between PR (Monday) and P (Friday); in Latvian, between SV (Sunday) and S (Saturday); and in Lithuanian, between S (Sunday) and Š (Saturday).

LITHUANIAN	RUSSIAN	RUSSIAN PRONUNCIATION
vištiena	курица	KOO-rit-suh
daržovės	овощи	OH-va-shchi
bulvė	картофель	karr-TOFF-el
grybas	гриб	greeb
saldumynai	сладкиеблюда	SLAT-kye BLYOO-dah
ledai	мороженое	mah-ROZH-in-ay
vaisiai	фрукты	FROOK-ti
sąskaita	счёт	shyot
baras	буфет	buf-YET
vanduo	вода	va-DAH
mineralinis vanduo	минеральная вода	mi-ni-RAL-nuh-yuh va-DAH
sultys	сок	sohk
arbata	чай	chay
kava	кофе	KOF-yeh
pienas	молоко	ma-la-KOH
cukrus	сахар	SAKH-arr
alus	пиво	PEE-vah
degtinė	водка	VOHT-kuh
konjakas	коняк	kahn-YAHK
šampanas	шампанское	sham-PAN-ska-yuh
vynas	вино	vi-NOH
šiandien	сегодня	sye-VOHD-nya
vakar	вчера	fchi-RAH
rytoj	завтра	ZAHV-tra
sekmadienis	воскресенье	vas-kri-SYEN-yuh
pirmadienis	понедельник	pa-nyi-DYEL-nik
antradienis	вторник	FTOR-nik
trečiadienis	среда	sri-DA
ketvirtadienis	четверг	chit-VERK
penktadienis	пятница	PYAT-nit-suh
šeštadienis	суббота	su-BOHT-uh

ENGLISH	ESTONIAN	LATVIAN
January	januar	janvāris
February	veebruar	februāris
March	märts	marts
April	aprill	aprīlis
May	mai	maijs
June	juuni	jūnijs
July	juuli	jūlijs
August	august	augusts
September	september	septembris
October	oktoober	oktobris
November	november	novembris
December	detsember	decembris

Numbers

one	üks ('yooks')	viens
two	kaks	divi
three	kolm	trīs
four	neli	četri
five	viis	pieci
six	kuus	seši
seven	sitse	septiņi
eight	kaheksa	astoņi
nine	üheksa	deviņi
ten	kümme	desmit
eleven	üsteist	vienpadsmit
twelve	kaksteist	divpadsmit
thirteen	kolmteist	trīspadsmit
fourteen	neliteist	četrpadsmit
fifteen	viisteist	piecpadsmit
sixteen	kuusteist	sešpadsmit
seventeen	seitseteist	septiņpadsmit
eighteen	kaheksateist	astoņpadsmit
nineteen	üheksateist	deviņpadsmit
twenty	kakskümmend	divdesmit
twenty-five	kakskümmendviis	divdesmit pieci
thirty	kolmkümmend	trīsdesmit
forty	nelikümmend	četrdesmit
fifty	viiskümmend	piecdesmit
sixty	kuuskümmend	sešdesmit

LITHUANIAN	RUSSIAN	RUSSIAN PRONUNCIATION
sausis	январь	YAN-var
vasaris	февраль	FIV-ral
kovas	март	marrt
balandis	апрель	ap-RIL
gegužė	май	my
birželis	июнь	i-YUN
liepa	июль	i-YUL
rugpjūtis	август	AV-gust
rugsėjis	сентябрь	sin-TYA-br
spalis	октябрь	ahk-TYA-br
lapkritis	ноябрь	na-YA-br
gruodis	декабрь	di-KA-br
vienas	один	ah-DYIN
du	два	dva
trys	три	tree
keturi	четыре	chi-TIR-yeh
penki	пять	pyats
šeši	шесть	shehst
septyni	семь	syem
aštuoni	восемь	VOSS-yem
devyni	девять	di-YEY-vits
dešimt	десять	di-YEY-sits
vienuolika	одинадцать	ad-YEEN-at-sats
dvylika	двенадцать	dvi-NAHT-sats
trylika	тринадцать	tri-NAHT-sats
keturiolika	четырнадцать	chi-tir-NAHT-sats
penkiolika	пятнадцать	pit-NAHT-sats
šešiolika	шестнадцать	shess-NAHT-sats
septyniolika	семнадцать	sim-NAHT-sats
aštuoniolika	восемнадцать	voss-im-NAHT-sats
devyniolika	девятнадцать	di-yey-vit-NAHT-sats
dvidešimt	двадцать	DVAHT-sats
dvidešimt penki	двадцать пять	DVAHT-sats pyats
trisdešimt	тридцать	TREET-sats
keturiasdešimt	сорок	SOR-ak
penkiasdešimt	пятьдесят	pi-di-SYAHT
šešiasdešimt	шестьдесят	shess-di-SYAHT

ENGLISH	ESTONIAN	LATVIAN
seventy	seitsekümmend	septiņdesmit
eighty	kaheksakümmend	astoņdesmit
ninety	üheksakümmend	deviņdesmit
one hundred	sada	simts

Emergency & Medical

toilet	tualett	tualete
chemist's	apteek	aptieka
doctor	arst	ārsts
hospital	haigla	slimnīca
ambulance	esmaabi	ātrā palīdzība
police	politsei	policija

LITHUANIAN	RUSSIAN	RUSSIAN PRONUNCIATION
septyniasdešimt	семьдесят	sim-di-SYAHT
aštuoniasdešimt	восемьдесят	VOSS-im-di-syaht
devyniasdešimt	девяносто	di-vi-NOSS-tah
šimtas	сто	stoh
tualetas	туалет	twal-YET
vaistinė	аптека	ap-TYEK-a
gydytojas	врач	vrach
ligoninė	больница	bahl-NIHT-sa
greitoji pagalba	амбулатория	am-bu-la-TOR-i-ya
policija	милиция	mi-LIT-sia

Appendix – Alternative Place Names

The following abbreviations are used:

(Eng)	English
(Est)	Estonian
(Finn)	Finnish
(Ger)	German
(Lat)	Latvian
(Lith)	Lithuanian
(Pol)	Polish
(Russ)	Russian
(Sov)	Soviet name
(Swed)	Swedish
(Uk)	Ukrainian

Aizkraukle – Stučka (Sov)
Augustów – Augustavas (Lith)
Aukštaitija – Upper Lithuania (Eng)

Bagrationovsk – Preussisch Eylau (Ger)
Baltic Sea – Baltijas jūra (Lat), Baltijos jūra (Lith), Baltiyskoe More (Russ), Itämeri (Finn), Läänemeri (Est), Morze Bałtyckie (Pol), Östersjön (Swed), Ostsee (Ger)
Baltiysk – Pillau (Ger)
Bartoszyce – Bartoshitse (Russ)
Belarus – Baltarusija (Lith), Baltkrievija (Lat), Belorussia (Eng)
Białystok – Belostok (Russ)
Braniewo – Branevo (Russ), Braunsberg (Ger)

Cēsis – Võnnu (Est), Wenden (Ger)
Chernovtsy – Černovcai (Lith), Chernivtsy (Uk)
Chernyakhovsk – Insterburg (Ger)
CIS – SNG (Russ)
Curonian Lagoon – Kurisches Haff (Ger), Kurshsky zaliv (Russ), Kuršių marios (Lith)
Curonian Spit – Kurische Nehrung (Ger), Kurshskaya kosa (Russ), Kuršių nerija or Neringa (Lith)

Daugava – Düna (Ger), Zapadnaya Dvina (Russ)
Daugavpils – Borisoglebsk (Russ), Daugpilis (Lith), Dünaburg (Ger), Dvinsk (Pol)
Denmark – Dania (Russ), Danija (Lith), Dānija (Lat), Taani (Est)

Elblag – Elbing (Ger), Elblong (Russ)
England – Anglia (Russ), Anglija (Lat, Lith), Inglismaa (Est)
Estonia – Eesti (Est), Estija (Lith), Estland (Ger), Estonia (Russ), Igaunija (Lat), Viro (Fin)

Finland – Finlyandia (Russ), Somija (Lat), Soome (Est), Suomija (Lith)

Gauja – Koiva (Est)
Germany – Germania (Russ), Saksamaa (Est), Vācija (Lat), Vokietija (Lith)
Great Britain – Didžioji Britanija (Lith), Lielbritānija (Lat), Suurbritannia (Est), Velikobritania (Russ)
Grodno – Gardinas (Lith)
Gurievsk – Neuhausen (Ger)
Gusev – Gumbinnen (Ger)
Gvardeysk – Tapiau (Ger)

Helsinki – Helsingfors (Ger, Swed)
Hiiumaa – Dagö (Ger, Swed)

Ivangorod – Jaanilinn (Est)

Jelgava – Mitau (Ger)
Juodkrantė – Schwarzort (Ger)

Kaliningrad – Kaliningradas or Karaliaučius (Lith), Königsberg (Ger)
Kaliningrad Lagoon – Frisches Haff (Ger), Kaliningradsky zaliv or Vislinsky zaliv (Russ), Vistula Lagoon (Eng), Zalev Wiślany (Pol)
Kaunas – Kowno (Ger)
Kharkov – Charkovas (Lith), Kharkiv (Uk)
Kiel – Kylis (Lith)
Kiev – Kiiv (Uk), Kijeva (Lat), Kijevas (Lith)
Klaipėda – Memel (Ger)
Kuldīga – Goldingen (Ger)
Kuressaare – Arensburg (Ger), Kingissepa (Sov)
Kurzeme – Courland (Eng), Kurland (Ger), Kuršas or Kuržemė (Lith)

Lake Peipus – Chudskoe Ozero (Russ), Peipaus ežeras (Lith), Peipsi järv (Est)
Lake Pskov – Pihkva järv (Est), Pskovskoe Ozero (Russ)
Latvia – Läti (Est), Latvia (Russ), Latvija (Lat, Lith), Lettland (Ger)
Lazdijai – Łazdijaj (Pol)
Lesnoy – Sarkau (Ger)
Liepāja – Libau (Ger), Liepoja (Lith)
Lithuania – Leedu (Est), Lietuva (Lat, Lith), Litauen (Ger), Litva (Russ), Litwa (Pol)

Marijampolė – Kapsukas (Sov)
Mamonovo – Heiligenbeil (Ger)
Mordovskoe – Gross Legitten (Ger), Turgenevo (Russ)
Morskoe – Pillkoppen (Ger)
Moscow – Maskava (Lat), Maskva (Lith), Moskva (Est, Russ)

450

Nemunas – Memel or Njemen (Ger), Neman (Russ)
Nida – Nidden (Ger)

Olsztyn – Allenstein (Ger), Olshtyn (Russ), Olštynas (Lith)
Otradnoe – Georgenswalde (Ger)

Palanga – Polangen (Ger)
Pärnu – Pernau (Ger), Pērnava (Lat), Piarnu (Lith)
Pechory – Petseri (Est)
Poland – Lenkija (Lith), Polija (Lat), Polsha (Russ)
Polessk – Labiau (Ger)
Pregolya – Pregel (Ger)
Pskov – Pihkva (Est), Pleskau (Ger), Pleskava (Lat), Pskovas (Lith)

Rēzekne – Rossitten (Ger)
Rīga – Riia (Est), Riika (Fin), Ryga (Lith, Pol)
Rūjiena – Ruhja (Est)
Russia – Krievija (Lat), Rossia (Russ), Rusija (Lith), Venemaa (Est)
Rybachy – Rossitten (Ger)

Saaremaa – Ösel (Ger, Swed)
St Petersburg – Leningrad (Sov), Pietari (Fin), Sankt-Peterburg (Russ), Sanktpeterburga (Lat), St Peterburg (Est)
Salacgriva – Salatsi (Est)
Šeštokai – Szestokai (Ger)
Šiauliai – Šauļi (Lat), Shaulyay (Russ)
Sigulda – Segewold (Ger)
Šilutė – Heydekrug (Ger)
Sovietsk – Tilsit (Ger)
Suwałki – Suvalkai (Lith), Suvalki (Russ)

Svetlogorsk – Rauschen (Ger)
Svetly (Kal) – Svetlyj (Lith), Świetly (Pol), Zimmerbude (Ger)
Sweden – Rootsi (Est), Shvetsia (Russ), Švedija (Lith), Zviedrija (Lat)

Tallinn – Talinas (Lith), Tallina (Lat), Tallinna (Fin), Reval (Ger)
Tartu – Dorpat (Ger), Tartto (Fin), Tērbata (Lat)

USA – ASV (Amerikas Savienotās Valstis – Lat), JAVD(Jungtinės Amerikos Valstijos – Lith), SShA (Soedinyonnye Shtaty Ameriki – Russ)

Valga – Walk (Ger)
Valmiera – Volmari (Est), Wolmar (Ger)
Ventė – Windenburg (Ger)
Ventspils – Windau (Ger)
Vienna – Vīne (Lat), Viena (Lith)
Viljandi – Fellin (Ger)
Vilnius – Vilna (Fin, Ger), Viļņa (Lat), Wilno (Pol)
Voronezh – Voroneža (Lat)

Warsaw – Varšava (Lat), Varshava (Russ), Varssavi (Est), Varšuva (Lith), Warschau (Ger)

Yantarny – Palmnicken (Ger)

Zalivino – Rinderort (Ger)
Zelenogradsk – Cranz (Ger)
Žemaitija – Lower Lithuania or Samogitia (Eng)
Zemgale – Semigallia (Eng)

Index

ABBREVIATIONS

Est – Estonia
Kal – Kaliningrad

Lat – Latvia
Lith – Lithuania

MAPS

TEXT

454 Index

LONELY PLANET PHRASEBOOKS

**Building bridges,
Breaking barriers,
Beyond babble-on**

Listen for the gems

Speak your own words

Ask your own
questions

Master of
your
own
image

- handy pocket-sized books
- easy to understand Pronunciation chapter
- clear and comprehensive Grammar chapter
- romanisation alongside script to allow ease of pronunciation
- script throughout so users can point to phrases
- extensive vocabulary sections, words and phrases for every situations
- full of cultural information and tips for the traveller

'...vital for a real DIY spirit and attitude in language learning' – Backpacker

'the phrasebooks have good cultural backgrounders and offer solid advice for challenging situations in remote locations' – San Francisco Examiner

'...they are unbeatable for their coverage of the world's more obscure languages' – The Geographical Magazine

---

Arabic (Egyptian)
Arabic (Moroccan)
Australia
  Australian English, Aboriginal and Torres Strait languages
Baltic States
  Estonian, Latvian, Lithuanian
Bengali
Burmese
Brazilian
Cantonese
Central Europe
  Czech, French, German, Hungarian, Italian and Slovak
Eastern Europe
  Bulgarian, Czech, Hungarian, Polish, Romanian and Slovak
Egyptian Arabic
Ethiopian (Amharic)
Fijian
Greek
Hindi/Urdu

Indonesian
Japanese
Korean
Lao
Latin American Spanish
Malay
Mandarin
Mediterranean Europe
  Albanian, Croatian, Greek, Italian, Macedonian, Maltese, Serbian, Slovene
Mongolian
Moroccan Arabic
Nepali
Papua New Guinea
Pilipino (Tagalog)
Quechua
Russian
Scandinavian Europe
  Danish, Finnish, Icelandic, Norwegian and Swedish

South-East Asia
  Burmese, Indonesian, Khmer, Lao, Malay, Tagalog (Pilipino), Thai and Vietnamese
Sri Lanka
Swahili
Thai
Thai Hill Tribes
Tibetan
Turkish
Ukrainian
USA
  US English, Vernacular Talk, Native American languages and Hawaiian
Vietnamese
Western Europe
  Basque, Catalan, Dutch, French, German, Irish, Italian, Portuguese, Scottish Gaelic, Spanish (Castilian) and Welsh

---

LONELY PLANET JOURNEYS

JOURNEYS is a unique collection of travel writing – published by the company that understands travel better than anyone else. It is a series for anyone who has ever experienced – or dreamed of – the magical moment when they encountered a strange culture or saw a place for the first time. They are tales to read while you're planning a trip, while you're on the road or while you're in an armchair, in front of a fire.

JOURNEYS books catch the spirit of a place, illuminate a culture, recount a crazy adventure, or introduce a fascinating way of life. They always entertain, and always enrich the experience of travel.

THE GATES OF DAMASCUS
Lieve Joris
Translated by Sam Garrett

This best-selling book is a beautifully drawn portrait of day-to-day life in modern Syria. Through her intimate contact with local people, Lieve Joris draws us into the fascinating world that lies behind the gates of Damascus. Hala's husband is a political prisoner, jailed for his opposition to the Assad regime; through the author's friendship with Hala we see how Syrian politics impacts on the lives of ordinary people.

Lieve Joris, who was born in Belgium, is one of Europe's leading travel writers. In addition to an award-winning book on Hungary, she has published widely acclaimed accounts of her journeys to the Middle East and Africa. *The Gates of Damascus* is her fifth book.

'*Expands the boundaries of travel writing*' – Times Literary Supplement

---

KINGDOM OF THE FILM STARS
Journey into Jordan
Annie Caulfield

Kingdom of the Film Stars is a travel book and a love story. With honesty and humour, Annie Caulfield writes of travelling in Jordan and falling in love with a Bedouin. Her book offers fascinating insights into the country – from the traditional tent life of nomadic tribes to the first woman MP's battle with fundamentalist colleagues. *Kingdom of the Film Stars* unpicks some of the tight-woven Western myths about the Arab world, presenting cultural and political issues within the intimate framework of a compelling love story.

Annie Caulfield, who was born in Ireland and currently lives in London, is an award-winning playwright and journalist. She has travelled widely in the Middle East.

'*Annie Caulfield is a remarkable traveller. Her story is fresh, courageous, moving, witty and sexy!*' – Dawn French

LONELY PLANET TRAVEL ATLASES

Lonely Planet has long been famous for the number and quality of its guidebook maps. Now we've gone one step further and in conjunction with Steinhart Katzir Publishers produced a handy companion series: Lonely Planet travel atlases – maps of a country produced in book form.

Unlike other maps, which look good but lead travellers astray, our travel atlases have been researched on the road by Lonely Planet's experienced team of writers. All details are carefully checked to ensure the atlas corresponds with the equivalent Lonely Planet guidebook.

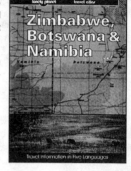

The handy atlas format means no holes, wrinkles, torn sections or constant folding and unfolding. These atlases can survive long periods on the road, unlike cumbersome fold-out maps. The comprehensive index ensures easy reference.

- full-colour throughout
- maps researched and checked by Lonely Planet authors
- place names correspond with Lonely Planet guidebooks
  – no confusing spelling differences
- legend and travelling information in English, French, German, Japanese and Spanish
- size: 230 x 160 mm

Available now:
Chile & Easter Island • Egypt • India & Bangladesh • Israel & the Palestinian Territories •Jordan, Syria & Lebanon • Kenya • Laos • Portugal • South Africa, Lesotho & Swaziland • Thailand • Turkey • Vietnam • Zimbabwe, Botswana & Namibia

---

LONELY PLANET TV SERIES & VIDEOS

Lonely Planet travel guides have been brought to life on television screens around the world. Like our guides, the programmes are based on the joy of independent travel, and look honestly at some of the most exciting, picturesque and frustrating places in the world. Each show is presented by one of three travellers from Australia, England or the USA and combines an innovative mixture of video, Super-8 film, atmospheric soundscapes and original music.

Videos of each episode – containing additional footage not shown on television – are available from good book and video shops, but the availability of individual videos varies with regional screening schedules.

Video destinations include: Alaska • American Rockies • Australia – The South-East • Baja California & the Copper Canyon • Brazil • Central Asia • Chile & Easter Island • Corsica, Sicily & Sardinia – The Mediterranean Islands • East Africa (Tanzania & Zanzibar) • Ecuador & the Galapagos Islands • Greenland & Iceland • Indonesia • Israel & the Sinai Desert • Jamaica • Japan • La Ruta Maya • Morocco • New York • North India • Pacific Islands (Fiji, Solomon Islands & Vanuatu) • South India • South West China • Turkey • Vietnam • West Africa • Zimbabwe, Botswana & Namibia

The Lonely Planet TV series is produced by:
Pilot Productions
The Old Studio
18 Middle Row
London W10 5AT UK

For video availability and ordering information contact your nearest Lonely Planet office.

Music from the TV series is available on CD & cassette.

PLANET TALK

Lonely Planet's FREE quarterly newsletter

We love hearing from you and think you'd like to hear from us.

*When...*is the right time to see reindeer in Finland?
*Where...*can you hear the best palm-wine music in Ghana?
*How...*do you get from Asunción to Areguá by steam train?
*What...*is the best way to see India?

For the answer to these and many other questions read PLANET TALK.

Every issue is packed with up-to-date travel news and advice including:

- a letter from Lonely Planet co-founders Tony and Maureen Wheeler
- go behind the scenes on the road with a Lonely Planet author
- feature article on an important and topical travel issue
- a selection of recent letters from travellers
- details on forthcoming Lonely Planet promotions
- complete list of Lonely Planet products

To join our mailing list contact any Lonely Planet office.

Also available: Lonely Planet T-shirts. 100% heavyweight cotton.

LONELY PLANET ONLINE

Get the latest travel information before you leave or while you're on the road

Whether you've just begun planning your next trip, or you're chasing down specific info on currency regulations or visa requirements, check out Lonely Planet Online for up-to-the minute travel information.

As well as travel profiles of your favourite destinations (including maps and photos), you'll find current reports from our researchers and other travellers, updates on health and visas, travel advisories, and discussion of the ecological and political issues you need to be aware of as you travel.

There's also an online travellers' forum where you can share your experience of life on the road, meet travel companions and ask other travellers for their recommendations and advice. We also have plenty of links to other online sites useful to independent travellers.

And of course we have a complete and up-to-date list of all Lonely Planet travel products including guides, phrasebooks, atlases, Journeys and videos and a simple online ordering facility if you can't find the book you want elsewhere.

www.lonelyplanet.com
or
AOL keyword: lp

LONELY PLANET PRODUCTS

Lonely Planet is known worldwide for publishing practical, reliable and no-nonsense travel information in our guides and on our web site. The Lonely Planet list covers just about every accessible part of the world. Currently there are eight series: *travel guides, shoestring guides, walking guides, city guides, phrasebooks, audio packs, travel atlases* and *Journeys* – a unique collection of travel writing.

EUROPE

Amsterdam • Austria • Baltic States phrasebook • Britain • Central Europe on a shoestring • Central Europe phrasebook • Czech & Slovak Republics • Denmark • Dublin • Eastern Europe on a shoestring • Eastern Europe phrasebook • Estonia, Latvia & Lithuania • Finland • France • Greece • Greek phrasebook • Hungary • Iceland, Greenland & the Faroe Islands • Ireland • Italy • Mediterranean Europe on a shoestring • Mediterranean Europe phrasebook • Paris • Poland • Portugal • Portugal travel atlas • Prague • Russia, Ukraine & Belarus • Russian phrasebook • Scandinavian & Baltic Europe on a shoestring • Scandinavian Europe phrasebook • Slovenia • Spain • Spanish phrasebook • St Petersburg • Switzerland • Trekking in Greece • Trekking in Spain • Ukrainian phrasebook • Vienna • Walking in Britain • Walking in Switzerland • Western Europe on a shoestring • Western Europe phrasebook

NORTH AMERICA

Alaska • Backpacking in Alaska • Baja California • California & Nevada • Canada • Florida • Hawaii • Honolulu • Los Angeles • Mexico • Miami • New England • New Orleans • New York, New Jersey & Pennsylvania • Pacific Northwest USA • Rocky Mountain States • San Francisco • Southwest USA • USA phrasebook • Washington, DC & the Capital Region

CENTRAL AMERICA & THE CARIBBEAN

Bermuda • Central America on a shoestring • Costa Rica • Cuba • Eastern Caribbean • Guatemala, Belize & Yucatán: La Ruta Maya • Jamaica

SOUTH AMERICA

Argentina, Uruguay & Paraguay • Bolivia • Brazil • Brazilian phrasebook • Buenos Aires • Chile & Easter Island • Chile & Easter Island travel atlas • Colombia • Ecuador & the Galápagos Islands • Latin American Spanish phrasebook • Peru • Quechua phrasebook • Rio de Janeiro • South America on a shoestring • Trekking in the Patagonian Andes • Venezuela

Travel Literature: Full Circle: A South American Journey

ANTARCTICA

Antarctica

ISLANDS OF THE INDIAN OCEAN

Madagascar & Comoros • Maldives• Mauritius, Réunion & Seychelles

AFRICA

Africa on a shoestring • Arabic (Moroccan) phrasebook • • Cape Town • Central Africa • East Africa • Egypt • Egypt travel atlas• Ethiopian (Amharic) phrasebook • Kenya • Kenya travel atlas • Malawi, Mozambique & Zambia • Morocco • North Africa • South Africa, Lesotho & Swaziland • South Africa, Lesotho & Swaziland travel atlas • Swahili phrasebook • Trekking in East Africa • West Africa • Zimbabwe, Botswana & Namibia • Zimbabwe, Botswana & Namibia travel atlas

Travel Literature: The Rainbird: A Central African Journey • Songs to an African Sunset: A Zimbabwean Story

MAIL ORDER

Lonely Planet products are distributed worldwide. They are also available by mail order from Lonely Planet, so if you have difficulty finding a title please write to us. North American and South American residents should write to Embarcadero West, 155 Filbert St, Suite 251, Oakland CA 94607, USA; European and African residents should write to 10 Barley Mow Passage, Chiswick, London W4 4PH; and residents of other countries to PO Box 617, Hawthorn, Victoria 3122, Australia.

NORTH-EAST ASIA

Beijing • Cantonese phrasebook • China • Hong Kong • Hong Kong, Macau & Guangzhou • Japan • Japanese phrasebook • Japanese audio pack • Korea • Korean phrasebook • Mandarin phrasebook • Mongolia • Mongolian phrasebook • North-East Asia on a shoestring • Seoul • Taiwan • Tibet • Tibet phrasebook • Tokyo

Travel Literature: Lost Japan

MIDDLE EAST & CENTRAL ASIA

Arab Gulf States • Arabic (Egyptian) phrasebook • Central Asia • Iran • Israel & the Palestinian Territories • Israel & the Palestinian Territories travel atlas • Istanbul • Jerusalem • Jordan & Syria • Jordan, Syria & Lebanon travel atlas • Middle East • Turkey • Turkish phrasebook • Turkey travel atlas • Yemen

Travel Literature: The Gates of Damascus • Kingdom of the Film Stars: Journey into Jordan

ALSO AVAILABLE:

Travel with Children • Traveller's Tales

INDIAN SUBCONTINENT

Bangladesh • Bengali phrasebook • Delhi • Hindi/Urdu phrasebook • India • India & Bangladesh travel atlas • Indian Himalaya • Karakoram Highway • Nepal • Nepali phrasebook • Pakistan • Rajasthan • Sri Lanka • Sri Lanka phrasebook • Trekking in the Indian Himalaya • Trekking in the Karakoram & Hindukush • Trekking in the Nepal Himalaya

Travel Literature: In Rajasthan • Shopping for Buddhas

SOUTH-EAST ASIA

Bali & Lombok • Bangkok • Burmese phrasebook • Cambodia • Ho Chi Minh City • Indonesia • Indonesian phrasebook • Indonesian audio pack • Jakarta • Java • Laos • Lao phrasebook • Laos travel atlas • Malay phrasebook • Malaysia, Singapore & Brunei • Myanmar (Burma) • Philippines • Pilipino phrasebook • Singapore • South-East Asia on a shoestring • South-East Asia phrasebook • Thailand • Thailand travel atlas • Thai phrasebook • Thai audio pack • Thai Hill Tribes phrasebook • Vietnam • Vietnamese phrasebook • Vietnam travel atlas

AUSTRALIA & THE PACIFIC

Australia • Australian phrasebook • Bushwalking in Australia • Bushwalking in Papua New Guinea • Fiji • Fijian phrasebook • Islands of Australia's Great Barrier Reef • Melbourne • Micronesia • New Caledonia • New South Wales & the ACT • New Zealand • Northern Territory • Outback Australia • Papua New Guinea • Papua New Guinea phrasebook • Queensland • Rarotonga & the Cook Islands • Samoa • Solomon Islands • South Australia • Sydney • Tahiti & French Polynesia • Tasmania • Tonga • Tramping in New Zealand • Vanuatu • Victoria • Western Australia

Travel Literature: Islands in the Clouds • Sean & David's Long Drive

THE LONELY PLANET STORY

Lonely Planet published its first book in 1973 in response to the numerous 'How did you do it?' questions Maureen and Tony Wheeler were asked after driving, bussing, hitching, sailing and railing their way from England to Australia.

Written at a kitchen table and hand collated, trimmed and stapled, *Across Asia on the Cheap* became an instant local bestseller, inspiring thoughts of another book.

Eighteen months in South-East Asia resulted in their second guide, *South-East Asia on a shoestring*, which they put together in a backstreet Chinese hotel in Singapore in 1975. The 'yellow bible', as it quickly became known to backpackers around the world, soon became *the* guide to the region. It has sold well over half a million copies and is now in its 9th edition, still retaining its familiar yellow cover.

Today there are over 240 titles, including travel guides, walking guides, language kits & phrasebooks, travel atlases and travel literature. The company is the largest independent travel publisher in the world. Although Lonely Planet initially specialised in guides to Asia, today there are few corners of the globe that have not been covered.

The emphasis continues to be on travel for independent travellers. Tony and Maureen still travel for several months of each year and play an active part in the writing, updating and quality control of Lonely Planet's guides.

They have been joined by over 70 authors and 170 staff at our offices in Melbourne (Australia), Oakland (USA), London (UK) and Paris (France). Travellers themselves also make a valuable contribution to the guides through the feedback we receive in thousands of letters each year and on our web site.

The people at Lonely Planet strongly believe that travellers can make a positive contribution to the countries they visit, both through their appreciation of the countries' culture, wildlife and natural features, and through the money they spend. In addition, the company makes a direct contribution to the countries and regions it covers. Since 1986 a percentage of the income from each book has been donated to ventures such as famine relief in Africa; aid projects in India; agricultural projects in Central America; Greenpeace's efforts to halt French nuclear testing in the Pacific; and Amnesty International.

'I hope we send people out with the right attitude about travel. You realise when you travel that there are so many different perspectives about the world, so we hope these books will make people more interested in what they see. Guidebooks can't really guide people. All you can do is point them in the right direction.'

– Tony Wheeler

LONELY PLANET PUBLICATIONS

Australia
PO Box 617, Hawthorn 3122, Victoria
tel: (03) 9819 1877 fax: (03) 9819 6459
e-mail: talk2us@lonelyplanet.com.au

USA
Embarcadero West, 155 Filbert St, Suite 251,
Oakland, CA 94607
tel: (510) 893 8555 TOLL FREE: 800 275-8555
fax: (510) 893 8563
e-mail: info@lonelyplanet.com

UK
10 Barley Mow Passage, Chiswick,
London W4 4PH
tel: (0181) 742 3161 fax: (0181) 742 2772
e-mail: 100413.3551@compuserve.com

France:
71 bis rue du Cardinal Lemoine, 75005 Paris
tel: 1 44 32 06 20 fax: 1 46 34 72 55
e-mail: 100560.415@compuserve.com

World Wide Web: http://www.lonelyplanet.com